INTERNATIONAL
HANDBOOK
OF WOMEN'S
EDUCATION

INTERNATIONAL HANDBOOK OF WOMEN'S EDUCATION

Edited by
GAIL P. KELLY

Greenwood Press
New York • Westport, Connecticut • London

Library of Congress Cataloging-in-Publication Data

International handbook of women's education.

   Bibliography: p.
   Includes index.
   1. Women—Education—Handbooks, manuals, etc.
2. Comparative education—Handbooks, manuals, etc.
I. Kelly, Gail Paradise.
LC1411.I47   1989   376   88–34730
ISBN 0–313–25638–1 (alk. paper)

British Library Cataloguing in Publication Data is available.

Library of Congress Catalog Card Number: 88–34730
ISBN: 0–313–25638–1

First published in 1989

Greenwood Press, Inc.
88 Post Road West, Westport, Connecticut 06881

Printed in the United States of America

(∞)

The paper used in this book complies with the
Permanent Paper Standard issued by the National
Information Standards Organization (Z39.48–1984).

10 9 8 7 6 5 4 3 2 1

CONTENTS

INTRODUCTION

Gail P. Kelly

The *International Handbook of Women's Education* is a source book for students and scholars. Its focus is on women's schooling—its history, current status, and outcomes—and its intent is to provide comparable information about women's education across a broad spectrum of countries. Each chapter in this volume considers the history of women's education, ideological and religious beliefs, as well as cultural and political traditions which account for the pace of development of women's education and particular forms education has taken. The historical context of each chapter serves as a basis for understanding the extent of sex inequality in school and society which has characterized the world in the past and persists in most places in the present. The focus of the work is women's education today. A central concern is to chart enrollment patterns—how many women relative to men attend what kinds of schools for how long—and to examine how educational, social, and economic policies affect these patterns. Each chapter also considers the content of women's education as well as the outcomes of education for women in the labor force, in the political system, and in the family. Finally, the handbook considers contemporary government policies which seek to redress inequalities in education or the outcomes of education, and the role of the women's movement in seeking change.

This book is both descriptive and analytic. It does not seek to provide a theory of women's education, its determinants, or its outcomes. Perhaps such theory-construction will become possible as data, such as are reported in this volume, become more widely available for each and every country in the world. Although the chapters in this volume are not explicitly theoretical, they are guided by implicit feminist theory. They all look at education in the context of women's oppression. None presumes that women's subordination is determined solely by the economy and easily remedied by "quick fixes" like a socialist revolution or a mass entry of women into paid labor. None presumes that society or the schools are gender-neutral; rather, they look at schools in the context of patriarchal institutions that have served to oppress women. The work asks whether, how, and under what conditions education can become a force for liberating women rather than oppressing them. Description and analysis are the first step in developing theories about schooling, patriarchy, and liberation, and it is this first step to which this volume is devoted.

That this book provides detailed enrollment data and charts women's educational patterns is a major contribution in and of itself. Unesco and the World Bank—two of the major agencies that report enrollment statistics internationally—have been hard pressed to provide gender-based enrollment statistics for many countries. When such statistics are reported, they are fragmentary and are sometimes confined to the primary level of education. When secondary enrollments are reported, attrition rates and the types of programs in which women are enrolled tend to be missing. Statistics on these questions tend to be more available for Western industrialized nations such as the United States, Great Britain, and the Soviet Union. They are rarely available for Third World nations like Nigeria, Vietnam, Botswana, Iran, or China. Even in Western industrialized nations, where gender breakdowns for school enrollment, by type of school and field of study, are generally available, data on racial, ethnic, and regional variations among female enrollments are rare. The statistics on women's educational patterns contained in this book, while not always comprehensive, constitute a major contribution that we hope will facilitate further research.

Although this handbook provides as comprehensive a picture as possible of women's educational enrollment patterns, it also seeks to explain why the pattern is as it is. Such explanations not only involve analysis of the cultural and historical context in which the schools operate, but they also look to public policies regarding women and the nature of educational provision. Why women attend school is not simply a question of women's choice or long-standing cultural prejudice or parental preference. Rather, the reasons relate to contemporary policies that seek to encourage or discourage women's participation in public life and equalize women's life chances with those of men. Governments that have set gender equality as a priority have tended to enroll women in schools and have kept them there. Different types of educational provision have different results. Coeducation versus single-sex education, differentiated versus common schools, nonformal versus formalized programs, free versus fee-paying schooling—all affect whether women are educated and how long they are educated. History and culture notwithstanding, educational provision is the key to understanding women's educational patterns and that provision is often a function of state policy. The chapters presented examine the policies responsible for contemporary patterns as well as newly adopted policies that have the potential to change women's educational attainment patterns.

The concern with schooling and with education in this volume derives from a belief that educational patterns profoundly affect social status. Much of the literature on women's subordination views women's undereducation—or lack of education—relative to men as a reason why gender-based inequalities persist in income and in political power as well as in the family. Whether changing women's education changes gender-based asymmetrical economic and political relations or relations in the family is a complex set of issues which each chapter seeks to address, with varying degrees of success. For the most part, research on women is a relatively new phenomenon. Before the mid-1960s, few governments were interested in whether women entered the workforce or earned money or whether women gained access to political power. Little or no gender-based workforce statistics were available. This has been more the case in the Third World nations of Africa, Asia, Latin America, and the Middle East than in Europe and North America. Data are usually available on women's entry into the workforce; what are not available are comprehensive sets of data on the types of occupations women pursue, women's access to managerial and executive employment, and women's income. In addition, data are not always available on the age, educational, and familial characteristics of women who do work over time. However, even with the fragmentary data that exist, each chapter explores the relation between changes in women's educational patterns and their entry into and status in the labor force.

For a long time the literature on women's education focused exclusively on the workforce, assuming that the workforce outcomes of education were the only ones that counted. For feminists, particularly those working from a Marxist perspective, entry into the paid workforce signaled women's liberation. Gaining an income was seen as the way in which women would gain freedom and autonomy and power. Those working from the perspective of economic development theories, particularly in Third World contexts, saw women's entry into paid labor as crucial to the process of enhancing national production and leading to economic development. Thus, a great deal of data has been generated on the workforce outcomes of women's education. Until recently, few asked about the relation between women's schooling and access to power and authority in society. This handbook asks whether women's participation in politics and their access to government posts has changed as a result of their widened access to schooling. Some of the chapters ask whether schooling has anything to do with the increased mobilization of women into autonomous women's movements designed to bring women's issues to the fore. Although these issues are explored here, they are only tentatively examined because so little research has been conducted on these questions in most countries beyond a simple enumeration of women who hold political office.

The relationship between changes in women's education and public life—

economy and politics—is not the only issue raised in this volume. As important are questions that relate to education and women's lives in the private, domestic sphere. Does education change women's marriage patterns? The relation between husband and wife? The work women do in the household? Childbearing and childrearing patterns? In short, what effect does women's education have on the family? Does it change patriarchal relations within the family and in what way? These issues are not easily addressed. Research traditions in education and the social sciences have long ignored women, or when they have studied women, they have done so either by assuming women are no different than men (and therefore ignored the domestic sphere) or that women are by nature confined to the domestic sphere (and that sphere was by no means worthy of study except to elaborate on the preordained sex-role divisions of labor). Thus, our research on the domestic sphere has tended to ask about control of reproduction only— leading to the literature on fertility—but not about power relations in the family. This volume tried to pull together information on these issues, but found the data base particularly wanting except in most instances on fertility control.

In sum, this handbook looks at the historical context of women's education, patterns, and outcomes. It attempts to show how educational reform can help correct gender-based inequalities in the economy, the family, and the political system and how government policy and women themselves can bring about sexual equality. These studies of individual countries are limited to the extent that the data on specific issues outlined above are available. However, each chapter addresses the issues raised here as fully as possible, given the state of the current data and research base.

THE COUNTRIES

No single volume can consider, in depth, women's education in every country in the world. Consequently, the handbook has chosen to cover twenty-three nations representing a range of political, social, and economic systems; levels of industrialization and wealth; historical contexts; and dominant ideologies about women's proper place. They also represent countries with a diversity of policies toward women and their education. Included here are highly industrialized nations like the United States, Japan, Canada, Sweden, Great Britain, the German Democratic Republic, and the Soviet Union. Third World nations are also represented. There are chapters on India, Botswana, Peru, Nigeria, Iran, Egypt, and other African, Asian, and Latin American nations struggling with the problems of underdevelopment. Socialist as well as nonsocialist countries are considered. In addition to the Soviet Union, there are chapters on Poland, China, and Vietnam.

This handbook also includes nations that have recently emerged from colonialism like Senegal, Zaire, and India as well as countries that have recently experienced far-reaching revolutionary change. Both Vietnam and China underwent communist revolutions with a strong commitment to liberating women after World War II. In contrast, within the past decade, Iran has instituted a revolutionary Islamic fundamentalist state guided by a very different set of ideologies.

The countries considered in the handbook are diverse in their economic, political, and educational histories as well as their traditional ideologies about women and women's proper roles. Included here are Islamic societies which practice seclusion of women and countries like Egypt which have sought to change them in the past. Israel, a Jewish state with quite different sex-role ideologies, is also a part of this volume. Also considered are Japan, Vietnam, and China which share Confucian ideologies which "valued 100 women less than a man's testicle" and Latin American countries with strong traditions of Marianism and machismo. Western Christian patriarchal traditions characterize other countries studied here—the United States, France, Britain, and Australia.

A range of cultural traditions and sex-role ideologies and religious traditions are represented in the countries studied in the handbook. Countries with diverse sex-role divisions of labor are also included. In some of the countries, women traditionally were confined to the domestic sphere and did not engage in production outside the household as in Sweden, Egypt, and Chile; in others—as in Nigeria and Vietnam—there has been a strong tradition of female labor force participation. The countries also represent a range of family structures. The United States, Canada, and France are among the nations with established traditions of nuclear family structures. Several countries considered here have long practiced polygamy—namely, Egypt, Vietnam, Nigeria, and Botswana—and others have a strong tradition of joint families as in India.

The countries examined in this work represent societies with very different contemporary policies toward women and with varying commitments to sexual equality in school and in society. Countries like the United States, the Soviet Union, Sweden, Canada, and, to a lesser extent, India have attempted to bring about gender-based equality via affirmative action, and they view education as an enabling condition of that equality. Accordingly, Sweden, the United States, Australia, and Canada have initiated curriculum revision and have sought to incorporate women's knowledge into educational processes as well as to open women's access to the schools. Other nations, like Vietnam and China, Egypt and Israel, do not look to the schools to provide gender-based equality. Instead, priorities have been placed on educational efficiency and economic development which are often seen as being in opposition to sexual equality. Countries like Japan do not have any policies specifically designed to bring about sexual equality through the schools or otherwise.

The countries in this handbook also have a range of school systems. Some, like Nigeria, Vietnam, Botswana, Chile, Israel, and the Soviet Union, have highly centralized educational systems, whereas others, like the United States, Canada, England, and Australia, are decentralized systems controlled locally. In some of the countries, a large private sector serves elite children—as in Chile and Britain—in others, as in Poland, China, and East Germany, there are no private schools. Some of the countries examined have highly stratified school systems; others provide a common schooling and have tended away from diversification on the secondary level.

Yet another point of diversity among the countries is the distribution of education among the general population. In Western industrialized countries as well as in Australia and a handful of Third World nations like Chile, primary education is universal. In most of the Third World, however, primary education reaches 33 to 80 percent of the age cohort. The countries covered in this volume represent nations with a range of educational enrollment ratios. Some have universal primary education; others do not. Some, like the United States, which provides nearly 50 percent of the age cohort with higher education, approach universal secondary education. Others enroll under 25 percent of the age cohort in secondary school and 10 to 15 percent in higher education.

Finally, gender-based disparities in educational enrollments vary considerably among nations and are not always related to the percentage of the age cohort enrolled in schools at each level. In some countries, females make up a small proportion of the school population, and their percentage declines with each succeeding grade level. However, in other countries, there are more females than males in secondary school and in higher education. (This is the case in Chile, Poland, and East Germany and is becoming the case in France.) The countries surveyed here include those in which women form a small portion of the school population as well as those in which women are the majority of students in secondary and higher education.

In sum, the countries examined in this work are diverse. They were chosen for their diversity in both the political system and the level of industrialization. The countries also have diverse cultural traditions and long-standing ideologies about women's proper place which have profoundly affected women's status in society, women's role in the family, women's participation in productive labor in and outside the household, and women's access to political power. The countries represent a range of traditions of female education as well as of policies that focus on providing women education in the contemporary world. Finally, the countries have different kinds of school systems and reach varying proportions of the schoolaged children. The disparity between male and female enrollments also differs across nations. In some countries today, more females than males are enrolled in school, and these differences are represented in the countries selected for inclusion in this volume.

The range and diversity included here provide us with a basis not only for obtaining a realistic view of women's educational pattern worldwide, but also for posing questions about how political, social, cultural, and educational systems affect the persistent patterns of gender-based inequalities throughout the world, as well as the variety of options that might change such patterns. From such a consideration, theories as well as policies may emerge which may lead to a more equal and just society.

ORGANIZATION

The chapters are arranged according to geographical divisions and within each division by country (listed alphabetically). We begin with the African nations of Botswana, Kenya, Nigeria, Senegal, and Zaire and then move to Asia: China, India, Japan, and Vietnam. Australia, Europe, the Latin American countries, and the Middle East follow. The individual country chapters end with a consideration of North America. The handbook concludes with an essay on worldwide trends in women's education, which puts the individual chapters in perspective and suggests avenues for future research. This is followed by a bibliography of published book, journal, and monograph research conducted over the past two decades on women's schooling worldwide.

INTERNATIONAL
HANDBOOK
OF WOMEN'S
EDUCATION

AFRICA

1

BOTSWANA

Wendy A. Duncan

One other factor which strikes an observer's eye . . . is the great disparity
between the numbers of the boys and those of the girls. Throughout the first
five years of the Primary Course the girls outnumber the boys by 2:1 . . .

. . . the numbers of boys attending school are disturbingly low, and an improvement in that respect is one of the most pressing educational needs of
the Bechuanaland Protectorate.[1]

In the heart of the rich mining and agricultural region of southern Africa lies
the country of Botswana, the home of the Tswana people. Proclaimed a British
protectorate in 1885, the country was known as the Bechuanaland Protectorate
until it achieved independence in 1966 when the name was changed to Botswana.
Much of the country is arid, but cattle-herding, the traditional activity of the
Tswana, is carried out on a large scale. Since independence, a lucrative mining
sector has also developed, making Botswana's economy one of the most successful capitalist economies in Africa. Along with other countries in the region,
however, Botswana has developed in the shadow of South Africa. Although
much of its colonial and contemporary history is marked by the struggle to
maintain political independence, Botswana remains significantly dependent on
South Africa economically and, being a land-locked country, needs the right of
transit for its imports and exports.

One of the major causes and consequences of its dependency on South Africa
was Botswana's development during the early part of this century. Large numbers

of young Botswana men were recruited to work in the South African mines, with smaller numbers of women working on farms and in domestic employment. Mine wage labor reached a peak in 1976. Since then, numbers have been declining owing largely to changes in South Africa's recruitment policy. The system of mine labor migration has particularly affected the roles of women as wives and mothers. The prolonged absences of men from the village brought about significant changes in gender relations. Women took over many of the traditionally male tasks and participated more actively in tribal politics and rituals.[2] Most significantly, the reduction in the marriage rate led to a dramatic rise in the number of female-headed households. Today, female-headed households constitute 45 percent of all households in Botswana.[3]

The pattern and nature of educational provision for women in Botswana can be seen as a product of traditional, missionary, tribal-controlled, colonial, and nationally administered education. Although the nature of the education provided under these systems has varied according to the gender ideology of those in control, the interest and participation of women in Botswana in formal schooling has always been unusually high.

TRADITIONAL EDUCATION

Traditional Tswana society was marked by rigid segregation and hierarchical stratification by sex.[4] The segregation permeated all aspects of life, extending even to physical separation for much of the year. Women were responsible primarily for food production, whereas men had sole responsibility for pastoral agriculture, the basis of the traditional Tswana economy.

Although women functioned as independent economic producers, they were socially, legally, and politically subordinate to men. Laws concerning the inheritance of cattle and land strongly favored sons, and men remained the guardians of women throughout their lives. Women could not participate in political or legal matters on their own account and were not permitted to head a household by themselves.[5] These restrictions applied to all women, whether of the aristocratic or commoner class.

In accordance with their roles as both independent producers and subordinate citizens, girls were taught from an early age to accept heavy manual labor and the authority of men. Skill training began early, with young girls (primarily those of the commoner classes) learning how to perform agricultural work and domestic chores.

Initiation schools formed a central part of this education process. Girls between the ages of ten and thirteen attended the *bojale,* which constituted "conscious, intensive sex role training." According to contemporary sources, the tuition had two main aims: to prepare girls for the process of childbirth; and to "inculcate in them the appropriate social stance of 'passive obedience'."[6] The preparation for childbirth involved learning about sexual behavior as well as how to endure pain. Unfortunately, since the demise of the bojale, no other institution has taken over the important task of sex education. One way in which this failure is evidenced today is in the high rate of teenage pregnancies.

The sexual segregation and female subordination practiced by the Tswana meant that men had the opportunity to accumulate property (cattle) over time, while women did not. This placed men in an entirely different position from women and gave them greater chance to exploit the opportunities afforded by the coming of the cash economy.[7] The independent economic role of women in arable agriculture was gradually eroded, making many peasant women increasingly dependent on men.

MISSIONARY EDUCATION

The cash economy and the Christian religion arrived hand in hand in Botswana during the nineteenth century in the form of itinerant traders and missionaries. As Britain had scant interest in the area and made little attempt to develop it, even after the declaration of the protectorate, educational development during the late nineteenth and early twentieth centuries was left largely to the missions. But progress was slow, and, by 1904, only 2 to 3 percent of the population was enrolled in school. The low enrollment levels and poor attendance were thought to be due partly to the migratory life of the Botswana and partly to the poor quality of the schooling. Botswana life revolved around three dwelling places which were often located at considerable distance from each other: the main compound in the village, a more temporary shelter at the agricultural plots where the women and girls stayed for the planting and growing seasons, and the "cattle-post" where the men and boys took care of the cattle. The continual movement between these three areas made it difficult for children to attend school in the village, where schools were generally located.[8]

The missionaries pressed for changes in the situation of women in line with Christian views and campaigned against many of the traditional customs such as polygamy, *bogadi* (bridewealth), and initiation. The particular form of Christianity developed by missionaries in Africa formed the basis for their views concerning the proper role for African women, views that had little to do with the reality of most women's lives. These values were in turn reflected in the gender ideology of the education provided in mission schools. Mission schooling stressed practical education and the adaptation of education to the local community, but the aims and thus the content were different for girls and boys. In 1920, one of the school principals described these different aims: "We seek to raise the native boys and girls to their true place—the boys to become skilled artisans and teachers in their own sphere of work, the girls to become examples of clear and healthy living in their own houses—the two together to become the forebearers of an industrious, capable and Christian community."[9]

"Industrial work" formed an important part of the mission school curriculum but was strictly segregated by sex. The subjects provided for girls and boys were closely tied to the gender role ideology of the missionaries: "For the girls, provision was made for sewing, knitting, machining, and washing and ironing, while at some of the centers a little cookery was included (breadmaking). The boys invariably did carpentry."[10] Significantly, the girls were often taught by the missionaries' wives on a voluntary basis, while qualified teachers were recruited for the boys.

From 1910, most of the protectorate's schools were placed under the control of tribal committees because of local discontent with the evangelical and practical nature of mission schooling. Although the system of local control had many positive features, the placing of education in the hands of the chiefs meant that education became predominantly a privilege of the aristocratic families and their supporters.[11] The content of education became increasingly academic in orientation, emphasizing the learning of English. The effects of these developments on the education of girls have not been documented. However, given the tradition of male rule among the Tswana, it is unlikely that girls received the same encouragement as boys to succeed in schooling which was aimed primarily toward employment in the tribal or colonial administrations.

THE COLONIAL ERA

Colonial interest in the educational affairs of the protectorate began around 1930. Considerable improvement was made in the provision and quality of primary education, including the introduction of the first school syllabus in 1931. It was adapted to local conditions and advocated practical education for girls and boys in an attempt to reorient education to the local environment.

The imbalance of girls over boys in primary schooling reached a peak in the 1930s, with girls accounting for almost 75 percent of total enrollment. The greater enrollment of girls caused much disquiet among missionaries and colonial officials, leading the Director of Education to refer to the situation in dire terms in 1935, as one that "can but lead to disaster."[12] In fact, girls dominated only in the lower grades. In the upper grades, the number of girls and boys was equal, albeit very small.

In an attempt to overcome the problem of low male enrollment, several innovative measures relating specifically to the education of boys were instituted. The Director of Education considered that the chief reason for the nonenrollment of boys in school was that "the boys as soon as they are of a suitable age, have to be sent to herd cattle and other stock at distant grazing grounds far removed from any existing school facilities."[13] A special cadre of itinerant teachers was thus established to teach the boys at the cattle posts.

No such measures were ever instituted to ease the poor attendance of girls. The preoccupation with the greater number of girls than boys in school seems to have resulted in an almost complete neglect of the special problems faced by girls whose enrollment, while higher than that of boys, was still very low. The rearrangement of the school schedule in accordance with the annual cycle of agricultural activities, for example, was advocated at different times but never implemented. The officials regarded the dominance of girls as a shortcoming of the educational system rather than as an achievement.

The gender ideology held by colonial authorities can be inferred from the concern which the Director of Education expressed over the serious shortage of female teachers. The new curriculum introduced by the colonial authorities in 1931 had stressed the teaching of such work as is "necessary for and meaningful to African girls." However, the lack of female teachers meant that the subjects thought most "meaningful" to girls, such as needlework, homecraft, hygiene, and health care, could not be offered in most schools. Where there were women teachers, girls in the higher classes were taught "Housewifery" and simple laundry work instead of other subjects "of less immediate importance" ! The content of "Female Education" was thus firmly embedded in domestic subjects and bore little relation to other aspects of women's lives.

Why more girls than boys attended school has given rise to much speculation. Were parents more concerned for the future of their daughters than their sons? Or did they feel that girls were more likely to benefit from schooling than boys? Perhaps boys had other options that could guarantee them a sound future? Or perhaps their labor was more indispensable? In fact, the answer seems to lie in a combination of all these factors.

That parents placed equal value on the education and economic success of their daughters and sons is apparent from the comments of older people in Botswana today. The women in Hoyt Alverson's study, however, agreed that they regarded education as being more important than did men: "For women fulfillment is children and education, for men it is cattle and fields."[14] Women and men also saw the role of education differently. Whereas women saw it primarily in terms of "the light" needed to understand modern life, men evaluated it mainly in terms of its possible economic benefits. It is this difference which provides the major explanation for the low enrollment of boys. Economic success for boys, unlike that for girls, was intimately linked with the family's cattle herd. The importance of cattle in the Tswana economy cannot be overstated. Despite the transition of Bechuanaland from a subsistence to a cash economy, cattle remained the key to wealth and social status. The economic benefits of schooling for boys, at least for elder sons, were probably perceived as being considerably less than the benefits that could be accrued, both economically and socially, from cattle-herding. In addition, the task of tending cattle was traditionally carried out by young boys at the cattle-posts, which were often located at a considerable distance from the village. The agricultural lands where young girls worked, on the other hand, were generally located closer to the village, making it easier for girls than for boys to combine schooling with their domestic labor.

This pattern was reinforced by a further development. The introduction of taxes and the education levy meant that families needed a cash income. To avoid having to sell cattle to raise this money, thereby reducing their herds, many Botswana turned to the option of cash employment. At this time, the major opportunity available to uneducated Botswana males for wage employment was the mines in South Africa. Migration surged in the 1930s, and, from that time until the early 1970s, approximately one-quarter of all working-age Botswana men worked as mine labor.[15]

The precise effects of mine labor recruitment on the development of school enrollment patterns remain a matter of debate. Whether mine labor migration directly contributed to the sexual imbalances in school enrollment is not clear, but it did reinforce those tendencies already established. In households where most of the men were absent, for example, boys had to substitute for the absent male labor and perform traditionally male tasks. Conversely, as there was abundant female labor and girls were able to combine schooling with traditionally female chores such as housework, girls could both attend school and be of economic benefit to the household.[16] So, while mine labor may have provided the cash necessary to cover the direct costs of schooling, it benefited girls more than boys. The important job of looking after the cattle, in which much of the cash was invested, was the responsibility of younger sons. In two villages studied in 1978, for example, it was found that 43 percent of the primary schoolaged boys who came from cattle-owning households with absentee male members were tending cattle.[17]

Another effect of mine labor migration, more difficult to investigate directly, is the way it affected the perceived benefits of education in relation to employment opportunities. As long as men without education had no difficulty in finding profitable employment, one could expect schooling for boys to be seen as having less value. Furthermore, families established a tradition of mine labor migration which was essential for the maintenance and expansion of the cattle herd. Consequently, the new tradition of mine labor migration coupled with the ancient tradition of cattle-herding resulted, for many boys, in a tradition of no formal education.[18] Sometimes all boys in the family would be involved, with the younger sons taking over cattle-herding responsibilities after their elder brothers were recruited for the mines. In other families, some sons were sent to school while others were integrated into the cattle-herding–mine labor migration cycle.

Secondary education in the protectorate did not begin until 1944, once again as a result of missionary and tribal efforts. The British government was content to rely on secondary institutions in South Africa, whereas the tribal chiefs recognized the importance of developing their own system of secondary schooling.

The enrollment patterns at the secondary level were markedly different from those in primary schools. Although equal numbers of girls and boys attended the final grades of primary schooling, many more boys than girls studied in secondary schools. The dominance of boys at the secondary level formed part of a deliberate policy by the British administration and Botswana chiefs for the education of a future ruling elite. Girls were deemed unimportant, since they were not expected to join the elite. Of the 117 students following the "scholastic" program at one prominent secondary school in 1920, for example, only 15 were girls. Although girls were encouraged to attend primary schools, entrance into the education leading ultimately to the assumption of power was strongly directed toward boys. The 1955 Annual Report of the Bechuanaland Protectorate points with satisfaction to the "growing proportion of boys" in schools, "the increase in numbers being particularly evident in secondary education."[19]

INDEPENDENCE AND BEYOND

During the twenty years preceding the attainment of independence in 1966, the pace of educational development slowed down considerably. At the time of independence, there were around 240 primary schools serving approximately 55,000 pupils. Girls formed a slight majority. At the secondary level, eight schools had been established, only two of which covered the entire secondary course. All in all, there were fewer than 1,500 secondary school students, around 45 percent of whom were girls. Limited vocational training was available in homecrafts, commerce, and trades. For university education, students generally attended the jointly run University of Botswana, Lesotho, and Swaziland, located in Lesotho.[20]

The rapid economic growth after independence led to a demand for skilled personnel which far exceeded the supply. To overcome this critical shortage, the new government instituted a strict personnel-planning approach to educational planning. Top priority was initially given to the development of secondary education. From the eight secondary schools which existed at independence, Botswana boasted 65 by 1985, all coeducational. Despite the expansion, the demand for secondary school places still far outstrips the number available, and fewer than 15 percent of those entering primary school manage to enter senior secondary school. Boys are considerably more successful in this attempt than girls.

After the initial concentration on secondary education, attention turned to primary education. Since then, the provision and quality of primary schooling have increased substantially. In 1981, 83 percent of the primary schoolage population (seven to thirteen years) was enrolled in primary schooling.[21] The current aim is to provide nine years of basic education for all.

This expansion has naturally benefited some groups more than others. School participation is higher in urban than in rural areas, higher among the upper and middle classes than among poor peasants, and higher among male-headed than female-headed households. It does not appear, however, that any of these factors affect the enrollment of girls and boys differently. The proportions of girls and boys in junior secondary school from rural areas, lower socioeconomic groups and female-headed households are almost identical.[22]

Few initiatives within the formal education sector since independence relate specifically to girls. The influential National Commission on Education,[23] whose recommendations form the basis for present-day educational developments, was composed entirely of men and made no special mention of girls apart from the problem of schoolgirl pregnancy. Until recently, the fact that girls always formed the majority of the school population led policy-makers and administrators to

Table 1.1
Female Enrollment in Primary School, 1965–1985

Year	F	N	%F
1965	37 169	66 061	56.3
1970	44 053	83 002	53.1
1975	63 949	116 293	55.0
1980	93 803	171 914	54.6
1985	117 185	223 608	52.4

Sources: Report of the Education Department for the Years 1965 and 1966;
Education Statistics, selected years.

neglect the situation of girls in school. Girls today suffer from systematic disadvantage within secondary education, higher education, and vocational training. As in other countries, the position of girls is particularly poor within technical and scientific fields.

PRIMARY AND SECONDARY SCHOOLING

The development of primary and secondary education has constituted one of the most important goals of Botswana's development strategy since independence, and the number of girls enrolled has increased dramatically.

The growth in overall primary enrollment, as well as the growth in girls' enrollment and girls' percentage share of enrollment, is presented in Table 1.1. As can be seen, total enrollment has increased almost fourfold since 1965, the last year of colonial rule. In contrast to colonial times, girls now predominate even at the upper levels of the primary system. Overall, however, the gap between girls and boys has narrowed, and it can be assumed that parity in primary enrollment will soon be reached.

Table 1.2 shows the enrollment trends for secondary schools during the period 1965 to 1985. Despite the expansion that has occurred in this sector, it can be seen that the number of students completing secondary school is still very small. Nevertheless, there has been a steady increase in the proportion of girls passing through the secondary system. The right-hand column of Table 1.2 shows that in 1965 girls comprised only 43 percent of total secondary enrollment and that this figure had increased to 53 percent by 1985. So, even at his level, girls now constitute the majority of enrollments, a unique situation for Africa.

A closer look at Table 1.2 reveals a less rosy picture. At the junior secondary level (Form 1–3), the enrollment of girls has improved considerably. Prior to

Table 1.2
Female Enrollment in Secondary School, 1965–1985

Year		Form 1	Form 2	Form 3	Sub Total	Form 4	Form 5	Sub Total	TOTAL SECONDARY
1965	N	601	364	213	1 178	84	45	129	1 307
	F	292	155	78	525	28	14	42	567
	%F	48.6	42.6	36.6	44.6	33.3	31.1	32.6	43.4
1970	N	1 336	1 199	826	3 361	292	252	544	3 905
	F	692	1 199	440	1 618	116	97	213	1 831
	%F	48.2	49.0	46.7	48.1	39.7	38.5	39.2	46.9
1975	N	4 295	3 672	2 511	10 478	917	706	1 623	12 101
	F	2 411	2 085	1 270	5 766	348	278	626	6 392
	%F	56.1	56.8	50.6	55.0	37.9	39.4	38.6	52.8
1980	N	6 081	5 160	4 194	15 435	1 602	1 288	2 890	18 325
	F	3 665	2 992	2 433	9 090	692	501	1 193	10 283
	%F	60.3	58.0	58.0	58.9	43.2	38.9	41.3	56.1
1985	N	10 577	10 455	6 772	27 804	2 277	2 091	4 368	32 172
	F	5 706	5 912	3 765	15 383	913	879	1 792	17 175
	%F	53.9	56.5	55.6	55.3	40.1	42.0	41.0	53.4

Sources: Republic of Botswana, Report of the Education Department for the years 1965 and 1966; Republic of Botswana, Education Statistics, selected years.

N = Total number of Students; F = Number of Female Students; %F - Percent Female Students

1975, boys were in the majority at this level, but, from 1975 onward, there were more girls than boys. In 1985, 55 percent of enrollments in junior secondary school consisted of girls. However, girls have tended to concentrate in the community-run schools, which generally have poorer facilities, fewer trained teachers, and lower rates of achievement than the government schools.

At the senior secondary level (Form 4–5), the position of girls changes dramatically. From being the majority at the junior level, girls are suddenly in the minority. In 1985, girls made up only 40 percent of enrollment at this level. However, there has been some improvement since 1965, when under one-third of the final year enrollment was made up of girls.

It cannot be denied that, in terms of overall access to the educational system, girls in Botswana are favorably placed in comparison with girls in most other African countries. The government has expanded opportunities considerably since independence, and girls and their families have been quick to exploit the opportunities offered. The interest shown by women in education remains as high today as in colonial times. Nevertheless, there are many indications that, in the final analysis, it is boys who now benefit most from the educational system. The most telling indicator is the predominance of boys at the senior secondary level. Access to the university, to several of the technical and vocational training courses, and, increasingly, to white-collar jobs is based on the examination taken at the end of this stage. Of course, only a small minority of students manage to proceed this far, but, as they constitute a future elite, their importance is quite disproportionate to their numbers.

The first question we should ask, then, is what causes the sudden decrease in girls' enrollment as they pass through secondary school? A recent study of two high school cohorts found that, at the junior secondary level in government schools, the dropout rates for girls ranged from 16 to 18 percent, whereas rates for boys ranged from 6 to 8 percent. Dropout rates in community-run schools were much higher (around 45 percent for girls and 30 percent for boys at the junior level), but the lack of reliable statistics for these schools makes reliable estimates difficult.[24]

The outstanding cause of dropout among girls was pregnancy, which results in immediate expulsion. Pregnancy accounted for around 75 percent of all female "dropouts" at the junior level and around 85 percent at the senior level. Hence, in government secondary schools, almost 15 percent of the female entrants left school pregnant before completing the junior cycle. During the senior cycle, 10 percent of the entrants were forced to leave because of pregnancy.[25] Although no figures are available, it is likely that the pregnancy rates in community-run schools are even higher.

Dropout, or wastage, occurs not only during the junior and senior cycles, but also between the cycles. At this point, around 50 percent of the girls and 38 percent of the boys in a cohort are "pushed out." So, there are also large disparities in the number of girls and boys leaving the system between the junior and senior secondary cycles.

Selection for the limited number of senior secondary school places is dependent on the results of a national examination taken at the end of junior secondary school. A higher number of girls drop out at this stage because they perform much more poorly than boys on this exam.[26] This is in stark contrast to the results obtained in the national primary school-leaving examination taken just three years earlier, in which girls do slightly better than boys.[27] Thus, although the problem of schoolgirl pregnancy deserves immediate attention, an equally serious obstacle to the educational progress of girls at present is their poor academic performance. In comparison with boys, girls perform particularly badly in history, geography, science, and agricultural science. In other words, girls do more poorly than boys in both science and arts subjects, unlike the situation in Western countries. Only in Setswana, the local language, do they do better.[28]

UNIVERSITY EDUCATION

The disparities in the senior secondary school are also evident at the university. Nevertheless, women's access to university education has improved dramatically since independence. Although only 7 of the 62 students in 1966 were women, in 1985 women constituted around 40 percent of total enrollment. This figure would be somewhat reduced, however, if those students studying abroad were also taken into account.

A breakdown of the courses taken by men and women at the university level reveals the gender-linked patterns of subject achievement seen in the secondary school. Girls are overrepresented in commerce and primary education, equally represented in the social sciences, and greatly underrepresented in the law and science faculties. In nursing, 100 percent of the enrollment is female. The high interest in education among women, as well as their desire to better themselves, is reflected in the fact that the correspondence and evening courses offered in accountancy are heavily dominated by women.

TEACHER TRAINING

At the time of independence, Botswana had two teacher training colleges, both for primary school teachers. Together these colleges enrolled fewer than 300 students in 1965, half of whom were women. The fourfold increase in teacher training capacity which has taken place since that time has been accompanied by an equally dramatic change in the "gender" of primary teacher training. By 1975, more than 75 percent of primary teacher trainees were women, and by 1985 almost 85 percent. The proportion of women among secondary school teachers is also increasing, although the majority are men. By 1983, around 40 percent of trainees were women, but most elected to train as humanities rather than science teachers.

VOCATIONAL TRAINING

One of the main objectives of educational policy during the last decade has been to provide skilled personnel in technical fields. To this end, access to vocational training facilities is being increased as rapidly as possible. Despite the importance of these crucial fields, however, it is here that the most serious disparities in access between men and women are found.

Women have consistently been a minority in vocational education, constituting only 35 percent of the enrollment in 1985. Once again, however, closer examination of the situation reveals much deeper disparities. In 1985, students doing vocational training were enrolled in three major fields: trades, agriculture, and health. Of the women classified as undergoing vocational training, 65 percent were training for health-related occupations such as nurse, pharmacist, and laboratory assistant. Fewer than 30 percent of the women were involved in trades training, which in many cases still involved textiles and handicrafts. Men, on the other hand, were concentrated almost exclusively in the trades areas, particularly bricklaying, carpentry, and auto mechanics. A similar pattern can be seen in the brigades, which carry out vocational training for primary and mid-secondary school leavers. Of the 1,000-odd brigades trainees in 1985, only 167 were women. Of these 167, many were working with textiles and homecrafts.

From these examples, it is evident that boys have greater vocational training opportunities than do girls. This situation is in part due to institutional practices. The Polytechnic, for example, provides hostel accommodation only for boys. The heavy male bias among the teaching staff and student body discourages girls from applying for courses and makes it difficult for girls to compete equally with men even if they do gain entry.[29] The lack of technical training opportunities for girls in a country where women have traditionally been the builders, thatchers, and agriculturalists deserves immediate attention.

That there is a great demand among girls for vocational training, particularly among secondary school dropouts, is evidenced by the large number of private typing and secretarial schools that have sprung up around the country. In 1984, more than 10 such institutions were operating in Botswana with around 1,200 students, in addition to a number of other institutions teaching sewing, cookery, and other homecrafts. All of these institutions charge quite high fees, which means that large numbers of girls and their families are being forced to make considerable financial sacrifice in order to receive vocational training which boys receive without charge or at subsidized rates.

NONFORMAL EDUCATION

The major nonformal educational program in Botswana to date is the literacy program. In contrast to the general experience of literacy campaigns, but in accordance with school enrollment trends in Botswana, women have dominated the program since its inception in 1980. For most of these years, women have formed around 60 percent of all literacy group participants.[30] The imbalance in enrollments is particularly marked in rural areas, probably because many of the young men are absent in the towns, and older men have shown a lack of interest in learning.[31]

Generally, substantial improvements have been made in women's access to education and training opportunities since independence. Nonetheless, it can be argued that gender disparities have widened in some fields, leading to a narrowing of women's roles and a narrowing of the opportunities available to women. Women have been channeled into primary teacher training, health, clerical, and craft fields, with a few receiving training in agriculture and the operation of small businesses. Few women have been trained in scientific and technical fields, or in senior management (apart from the health sector). A strict sexual segregation has developed in education, based not on traditional gender-role divisions or even on those now current in most Western societies. Instead, it has its origins in the unique gender ideology which the missionaries developed for the African context and which the colonial authorities later propagated.

EDUCATIONAL OUTCOMES

The benefits accruing to women as a result of their high levels of interest and participation in the educational system will be assessed here within three spheres: the labor market, the family, and political life.

Despite the fact that women in Botswana are on the average more well educated than men, both their participation and status in the workforce are considerably below those of men. The "cash-earning" sector (formal employment and self-employment) of the Botswana economy incorporates less than 25 percent of the total adult population. Of this group, only around 30 percent are women.[32]

In 1981, a mere 40 percent of the female population was classified as economically active (housewives were regarded as economically inactive), compared with almost 75 percent of the men. Among the women regarded as economically active, half were involved in family agriculture, 30 percent were cash-earning, and 15 percent were looking for jobs. Around half of the economically active men were involved in cash-earning activities, 40 percent were involved in family agriculture, and 10 percent were seeking work. Hence, the women are concentrated in subsistence family agriculture, whereas the men are concentrated in cash-earning activities.

The proportion of each educational group engaged in cash-earning activities is illustrated in Figure 1.1. There is a clear relationship between level of education and participation in the labor market, indicating that education does "pay off" in terms of employment, albeit much more so for men. For both women and men there is an almost linear relationship between educational attainment and labor force participation, ranging from 6 percent for women with no education to 55 percent for those with postsecondary schooling, and from 29 percent for men without education to 84 percent for those who attended beyond the secondary

Figure 1.1
The Participation of Different Educational Groups in the Cash-Earning Sector, by Sex

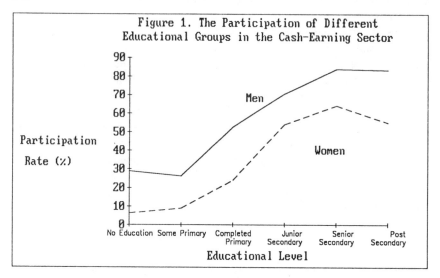

Figure 1. The Participation of Different Educational Groups in the Cash-Earning Sector

level. The only exception occurs among highly educated women, whose participation drops somewhat in comparison with those with only secondary education.
This may be due to the fact that such women, if they marry, tend to choose men
with high salaries in high positions and are expected to devote themselves to
other duties.

Although the relationship between educational attainment and labor force
participation is virtually the same for women and men, there are significant
gender differences in participation rates. Overall, only 13 percent of all women
participate in the cash-earning sector compared with 35 percent of the men.
Furthermore, these differences occur regardless of educational attainment. At
every educational level, the proportion of males involved in cash-earning activities is greater than that of females. The discrepancies are greatest at the lower
educational levels and smallest at the higher levels. Again, however, there is a
slight decline in the percentages at the highest level due to the lower participation
rates of women with postsecondary education.

Labor market absorption rates are particularly low for women with no education or with only some primary schooling. Even among those women who
have completed primary schooling, fewer than one-quarter are involved in cash-
earning activities compared with more than half of the men, which reflects the
lack of labor market opportunities for unskilled and semiskilled female labor.
However, even at higher educational levels, marked disparities are apparent.
Only 55 percent of women with junior secondary qualifications or higher have
been absorbed by the labor market compared with around 75 percent of the men.

Why does the labor force participation of women fall below that of men at all educational levels? Is it because girls have been channeled into a relatively narrow range of courses and have been excluded from almost all areas of vocational training? This question can be considered by examining the occupational distribution of women in the cash-earning sector.

The occupational characteristics for each educational group are given in Table 1.3. For women with only primary schooling, service work, consisting primarily of domestic service, is by far the largest source of employment. Smaller numbers of women are employed as sales assistants and primary school teachers. Men with little education, on the other hand, find employment in almost all occupational categories. The major sources of employment for such men are agriculture, unskilled production work, construction work, and services. Marked gender differences are also evident among those with junior secondary schooling. Girls at this level are heavily concentrated in the professional category, including teaching, nursing, and clerical work. At this level, these areas constitute almost the sole source of employment for girls. Again, men have a much wider choice— in professional jobs, skilled service jobs, clerical work, and production work. Finally, among both girls and boys with senior secondary schooling or higher education, professional and clerical jobs are clearly dominant. This dominance is nevertheless greater among girls, for while professional and clerical jobs are held by more than 80 percent of well-educated girls, this is true for only 55 percent of the boys. The service and production sectors account for a further 25 percent of male employment, revealing yet again the greater degree of labor market choice open to boys.

Further indication of the status of women in the labor market can be gained by examining their position within specific employment areas. The education sector, for example, employs about 15 percent of the female workforce.[33] Nevertheless, in both the primary and secondary teaching forces, the proportion of untrained teachers among women is greater than among men, and women are underrepresented as principals. A similar situation exists in the civil service, another major employer of women. In 1984, only five women occupied senior administrative posts out of a total of thirty-eight such posts.[34]

The overall population figures for Botswana show that women have higher levels of educational attainment than men at all levels except senior secondary and higher education. Nevertheless, fewer than 15 percent of women have been absorbed by the formal labor market compared with 35 percent of the men. Furthermore, their status within the cash-earning sector is clearly inferior to that of men. The majority of women are restricted to the service and professional categories, with limited opportunities available in the clerical and sales areas. Particularly noticeable is the absence of women from all occupations in the productive and technological sectors. In terms of occupational outcomes, the educational system benefits boys more than girls.

We might conclude that much of women's striving for education has been wasted. The economic benefits from education have been much greater for men.

Table 1.3

Occupational Characteristics and Educational Attainment of Formal Sector Employees, by Sex, 1981

		No Educ		Primary		Junior Sec		Higher Ed		TOTAL Formal Sector[a]	
		M	F	M	F	M	F	M	F	M	F
Professional	N	444	153	1 218	2 963	1 386	3 472	3 212	1 887	6 311	8 508
	%	1.3	1.9	3.1	13.2	16.7	47.9	40.4	51.7	6.9	20.5
Administrative	N	68	1	195	45	127	109	316	80	716	236
	%	0.2	0.0	0.5	0.2	1.5	1.5	4.0	2.2	1.3	0.6
Clerical	N	340	55	2 425	1 574	1 542	2 259	1 198	1 133	5 580	5 058
	%	1.0	0.7	6.2	7.0	18.7	31.2	15.1	31.0	6.1	12.2
Sales	N	810	732	2 215	4 007	454	543	516	169	4 053	5 479
	%	2.3	9.3	5.7	17.9	5.5	7.5	6.5	4.6	4.4	13.2
Services	N	3 163	4 942	5 587	11 598	1 651	620	817	234	11 358	17 492
	%	9.0	62.6	14.3	51.7	20.0	9.0	10.3	6.4	12.5	42.2
Agriculture	N	9 597	675	1 996	195	276	33	274	21	12 218	927
	%	27.4	8.6	13.9	0.9	3.3	0.5	3.4	0.6	13.4	2.2
Production	N	3 243	674	5 443	1 267	1 245	112	1 058	88	11 131	2 152
	%	9.3	8.6	13.9	5.6	15.1	1.5	13.3	2.4	12.2	5.2
Construction	N	3 305	59	5 891	109	341	6	72	4	9 736	179
	%	9.4	0.7	15.1	0.5	4.1	0.1	0.9	0.1	10.7	0.4

Transport	N	2 605	27	4 533	91	310	35	239	8	7 820	164
	%	7.4	0.3	11.6	0.4	3.7	0.5	3.0	0.2	8.6	0.4
Other	N	11 233	557	7 834	517	171	22	42	8	19 526	1 123
	%	32.1	7.1	20.0	2.3	2.1	0.3	0.5	0.2	21.4	2.7
TOTAL Formal Sector[b]	N	34 979	7 894	39 075	22 447	8 268	7 250	7 944	3 649	91 140	41 483
	%	100.0	100.0	100.0	100.0	100.0	100.0	100.0	100.0	100.0	100.0

Source: Adapted from Republic of Botswana, Census Administrative/Technical Report, Table 21.

a) Includes those whose education was unknown.
b) Includes those whose occupation was unknown.

19

Perhaps, however, education has helped women to improve their lives in other spheres, for example, in the family and in public life. Fertility rates, for example, are lower among educated women,[35] but it is not clear that education has brought about concomitant changes in attitudes regarding gender roles in the family. Although many well-educated women competently manage demanding and important jobs in the formal economic sector, their family lives are often run along much more traditional lines. In a national survey carried out among sixteen-to-eighteen-year-old secondary school students in 1983, for example, the great majority of girls and boys endorsed the notions that wives should always obey their husbands and that men should never do housework.[36]

That there is a complex intermixing of traditional and Western attitudes toward family life among well-educated students is also apparent from the fact that both girls and boys felt strongly that it was the man's duty to provide for his wife and children. In addition, when asked to describe their future lives many of the girls envisioned themselves as housewives, being married to wealthy men, living in large houses, and not working. These attitudes suggest a tendency among educated girls toward the Western model of dependent nonwage-earning housewife. However, the high proportion of female-headed households is just one indication that this type of marriage is far from the norm. Furthermore, most unmarried mothers receive no financial help from the fathers of their children.[37] Although female-headed households seem to be most common among lower social classes (particularly domestic workers), they are by no means restricted to these groups. Some awareness of this situation is revealed by the fact that nearly 60 percent of the girls expected to be solely responsible for the upkeep of any children they would have. The attitudes of these girls toward the form of their future family lives reveal many contradictions. Although the Western model of the ideal family type (husband, dependent wife, and dependent children) transmitted by the school has permeated girls' attitudes, they are themselves aware that their future may be somewhat different.

Politics in Botswana has traditionally been a male sphere, and this tradition has been maintained in some important respects. Women take an active interest in political questions, participate in voting to the same extent as men, and are important grass-roots activists in the major political parties.[38] However, women are generally absent from leadership positions and high office. Men represent the great majority of political candidates and hold most of the official positions within the political parties. As a result of this pattern, in 1984, there were no women in the upper house of Parliament, only two in the lower house, and only one female minister. Apart from the rather obvious fact that women achieving such positions are well educated (the minister has a doctorate), there is no information yet available on the relationship between education, political awareness, and political participation.

CONCLUSIONS

The picture revealed by this overview of the position of women in the labor market, in the family, and in political life is not what one could have hoped for given the high interest and investments in education which women in Botswana have consistently shown. The parents of those girls presently in the educational system had high hopes that education would guarantee their daughters good jobs and a sound future. Mothers especially have been favorably disposed toward education and have invested heavily in the education of their daughters. As Alverson indicates: "Few of the young men mentioned education as a hope for themselves or their children. . . . The women, however, both young and old, waxed eloquent of the topic of education whenever I inquired of their hopes for the future."[39]

It is sad that their faith has not been completely fulfilled. Selolwane argues that "History has reduced Botswana's peasant women from the position of economic productivity to that of unproductive housekeeping for men, children, the aged and the rich."[40] This is revealed most starkly in the labor market, where men have a great advantage over women. Girls are required to have higher educational levels than boys to enter the labor market, are absorbed at much lower rates regardless of their educational level, and are restricted to a narrow choice of occupations. The educational system has played an important part in bringing about this situation. From the beginnings of formal schooling, girls were presented with a very narrow definition of their potential and possibilities. This situation was reinforced by the provision of only limited training opportunities for girls, especially in the trades and technical fields. Even for many of the "female" occupations such as clerical and secretarial work, however, state-run training facilities are negligible.

What the future will bring to the women of Botswana is difficult to predict. Since colonial times, the enrollment of girls has been steadily increasing at all levels of the educational system. From being the majority, until independence, in only the lower primary grades, girls now predominate not only in senior primary but also lower secondary levels. Whether this trend will continue into higher levels, as well as in the strategic fields of science and technology, remains to be seen. The government is at present embarking on a comprehensive new vocational training policy in which it has been promised that the needs of girls will be given higher priority. It is therefore possible that girls' opportunities will expand in this area. Nevertheless, as in all African countries, the government of Botswana is coming under increased pressure to reduce educational expenditures. Lower economic growth rates have been forecast;[41] in addition, the future development of the entire region is uncertain owing to the unstable situation in South Africa. All of these factors indicate that there will be an economic slowdown in Botswana in the coming decades, and it is likely that the effects of this change will be felt most severely by women. Such pressures do not augur well for policies and strategies designed specifically to improve the situation of girls in school, which many male policy-makers tend to regard as luxuries. In a country in which almost half of all households are headed by women, however, this is hardly the case.

NOTES

1. B. C. Thema, "The Development of Native Education in the Protectorate 1840–1946" (Master's Thesis, University of South Africa, 1947). Thema was a colonial school inspector and later became Botswana's first minister of education.

2. Wendy Izzard, "The Impact of Migration on the Roles of Women," in *Migration in Botswana: Patterns, Causes and Consequences,* Vol. 3 (Gaborone: Central Statistics Office, 1982).

3. Republic of Botswana, *1981 Population and Housing Census, Administrative/Technical Report* (Gaborone: Central Statistics Office, 1983).

4. Hoyt Alverson, *Mind in the Heart of Darkness. Value and Self-Identity Among the Tswana of Southern Africa* (London: Yale University Press Ltd., 1978).

5. Wendy Izzard, "The Impact of Migration on the Roles of Women," Paper No. 9, National Migration Study, 1981; Bonnake Tsimako, "The Socio-Economic Status of Women in Botswana," in Frank Youngman, ed., "Women and Productive Activities—The Role of Adult Education" (Gaborone: Institute of Adult Education, 1980).

6. Margaret Kinsman, " 'Beasts of Burden': The Subordination of Southern Tswana Women, ca. 1800–1840," *Journal of Southern African Studies* 10 (1983): 39–54, 49.

7. Ibid.

8. Thema, "The Development of Native Education."

9. Reverend Haile, "Tigerkloof, Native Institution," 1920, cited in Ingemar Gustafsson, *Schools and the Transformation of Work: A Study of Four Productive Work Programmes in Southern Africa* (Stockholm: University of Stockholm, 1987).

10. Report to the District Committee of the London Missionary Society, 1906, from Reverend Lewis, Molepolole, cited in B. C. Thema, "The Development of Native Education."

11. Jack Berningham, "Perspectives on Colonial Education in Botswana," in Agrippah T. Mugomba and Mougo Nyaggah, eds., *Independence Without Freedom. The Political Economy of Colonial Education in Southern Africa* (Santa Barbara: ABC-Clio, 1980).

12. Bechuanaland Protectorate, *Education Department Annual Report 1935* (Mafeking, 1935).

13. Ibid.

14. Alverson, *Mind in The Heart of Darkness,* p. 184.

15. Ralph Field, "Botswana Labour in South Africa: Migration to the Mines," in *Migration in Botswana: Patterns, Causes and Consequences,* Vol. 3 (Gaborone: Central Statistics Office, 1982).

16. Christine Allison, "The Determinants of Participation in Primary Schools in Kweneng with Special Reference to Cattle and Mine Labour Migration." National Migration Study, November 1978. See also John Case, "The Effects of Migration on Primary Education," in *Migration in Botswana,* Vol. 2, 1982, and Dov Chernichovsky and Christine Smith, "Primary School Enrollment and Attendance in Rural Botswana" (Population and Human Resources Division, World Bank, 1979).

17. Allison, "The Determinants of Participancy."

18. Christine Allison, "Constraints to UPE: More Than a Question of Supply?" mimeo, n.d.

19. Commonwealth Relations Office, *Report for the Year 1950* (London: Her Majesty's Stationery Office, 1955), p. 40.

20. Edwin K. Townsend Coles, *The Story of Education in Botswana* (Gaborone: Macmillan, 1985).

21. Republic of Botswana, *National Development Plan 1985–91* (Gaborone: Ministry of Finance and Development Planning, 1985).

22. Wendy A. Duncan, *Gender Stereotypes and School Achievement. A Study of Science Among Adolescents in Botswana* (Ph.D. diss., University of Stockholm, 1989).

23. Republic of Botswana, *Education for Kagisano*. Report of the National Commission on Education (Gaborone, 1977).

24. Wendy A. Duncan, *School Dropout in Botswana. Gender Differences at Secondary Level*, Report No. 81 (Stockholm: Institute of International Education, 1988).

25. Ibid. The effects of pregnancy on school attainment are also discussed in Julia Majaha-Järtby, ''Women and Educational Opportunities in Botswana,'' in Michael Crowder, ed., *Education for Development in Botswana* (Gaborone: The Botswana Society, 1984); and in Barbara Brown, ''Women's Role in Development in Botswana'' (Gaborone: Ministry of Agriculture, 1980).

26. Wendy A. Duncan, *Schooling for Girls in Botswana: Education or Domestication?* Working Paper No. 49 (Gaborone: National Institute of Research, 1985).

27. Republic of Botswana, ''Primary Education Survey 1982'' (Gaborone: Ministry of Education, 1983).

28. Wendy A. Duncan, ''Schooling for Girls in Botswana: Patterns of Enrollment and Performance,'' *BOLESWA Educational Research Journal* 4 (1986): 52–61.

29. Kathy M. Higgins, ''Women and Education in Botswana. Facts and Fantasies'' (Gaborone: Institute of Adult Education, 1984).

30. Ulla Kann, ''Problems of Equity in the Education System: The Provision of Basic Education'' in Michael Crowder, ed., *Education for Development in Botswana* (Gaborone: Botswana Society, 1984); Samora Gaborone, Johannes Mutanyatta, and Frank Youngman, ''An Evaluation of the Botswana National Literacy Programme'' (Gaborone: Institute of Adult Education, 1987).

31. Republic of Botswana, ''How Can We Succeed? Evaluation of the National Literacy Programme. A Progress Report'' (Gaborone: Department of Non-Formal Education, 1982).

32. Nessim Tumkaya, ''Economic Activity and the Labour Force,'' in *1981 Population and Housing Census. Analytical Report* (Gaborone: Central Statistics Office, 1987).

33. Republic of Botswana *1981 Population and Housing Census. Administrative/Technical Report*.

34. Higgins, ''Women and Education in Botswana.''

35. Gwen Lesetedi, ''Fertility Differentials in Botswana,'' in *1981 Population and Housing Census. Analytical Report*.

36. Duncan, ''Gender and Schooling in Botswana.''

37. Barbara Brown, ''Women, Migrant Labor and Social Change in Botswana,'' *African Studies Center Working Papers*, No. 41 (Boston: Boston University, 1980).

38. Athaliah Molokomme and Judy Kimble, ''Gender and Politics in Botswana: Some Thoughts on the 1984 Elections,'' Paper presented to the Election Study Workshop (Gaborone, 1984).

39. Alverson, *Mind in the Heart of Darkness*, 184.

40. O. Selolwane, ''The Proletarianization of Women: A Case for Adult Education,'' Paper presented to the Department of History, University of Botswana (November 1981).

41. Republic of Botswana, *National Development Plan 1985–91*.

2
KENYA

George S. Eshiwani

Women constitute slightly over 50 percent of Kenya's population, accounting for over 10 million of a total population of 20 million people according to 1985 statistics. Women in rural areas bear major responsibility for small-scale agricultural productivity and farm management. In both rural and urban areas, women are engaging in an increasing number and variety of economic and development activities. In addition, women are chiefly responsible for home management and child care and therefore play a major role in the quality of family life and the training given to future generations.

It is important to examine women's participation in education because to the extent that Kenya's educational system fails to reach, or inadequately develops, women's abilities and skills, it is inadequately serving national, and especially rural, development. It is generally agreed that the surest way of minimizing the gap between women and men, both in and between nations, is through education. To this end, enormous resources have been and continue to be poured into education, and Kenya has made enormous efforts to advance its educational system.

This chapter analyzes the participation of women and girls in the schools of Kenya. First, it outlines enrollment patterns in primary, secondary, and higher education, and then it considers the workforce outcomes of women's schooling.

KENYA'S EDUCATION SYSTEM

Kenya's education system consists of eight years of primary school, four years of secondary school, and four years of university education leading to a basic bachelor's degree. Figures 2.1 and 2.2, respectively, depict the structure of the system. Figure 2.1 shows that there are two national examinations at the end of the primary cycle (the Kenya Certificate of Primary Examination) and at the end of the secondary cycle (the Kenya Certificate of Secondary Examination). These examinations are important hurdles in determining who proceeds to the next level of education or who goes into what training or employment. Figure 2.2 underscores the fact that Kenya's educational system is a sharp pyramid. Only a small proportion of those who enroll in Grade 1 can survive to the university. This is an important point to keep in mind as one discusses the participation of girls in the education system.

GIRLS' PARTICIPATION IN PRIMARY EDUCATION

The enrollment of girls in primary school has been increasing steadily since Kenya attained independence in 1963. Enrollment rose from 304,829 to 2,108,352 in 1984. During the decade 1975 to 1984, the number of girls attending primary school rose from 1,340,429 to 2 million. This represents a rise of 50 percent. Figure 2.3 shows that since 1963 girls' primary school attendance has increased at a faster rate than boys', enabling girls to approach equality in enrollment. In 1963, girls accounted for 34 percent of primary enrollment. By 1975, female enrollment constituted 45 percent of total registration at this level. By 1979, the proportion had risen to 47.2 percent. This proportion has been maintained nationally and has been surpassed in many districts. It shows the parents' increased willingness to invest in the education of their daughters, at least at the primary level.

Among the major factors that may have caused low educational enrollment among girls at the primary school level in the 1960s and early 1970s were the domestic work girls were called on to perform, traditional views toward the proper role of women, and their premature exit from school owing to pregnancies. These factors seem to be disappearing with time.

Female underenrollment in primary schools between 1963 and 1975 also resulted from parental choice. When confronted with constraints of limited opportunities or resources for primary schooling, parents have generally favored the education of male children. The preference given males in schooling is related to the patrilineal descent system in which inheritance passes through the male line. Sons retain responsibility for their parents as they grow older, whereas daughters are incorporated into their husbands' families. The perceived link between education and employment in an economic system in which males have had better prospects for wage jobs in the formal sector has also given additional economic incentive to educate sons before daughters. Family chores like looking after young children or cooking for the family are delegated to girls. Girls are often taken out of school to perform these duties.

The second important observation regarding female enrollment in primary school is the high correlation between opportunities for female primary education

Figure 2.1
Structure of Education

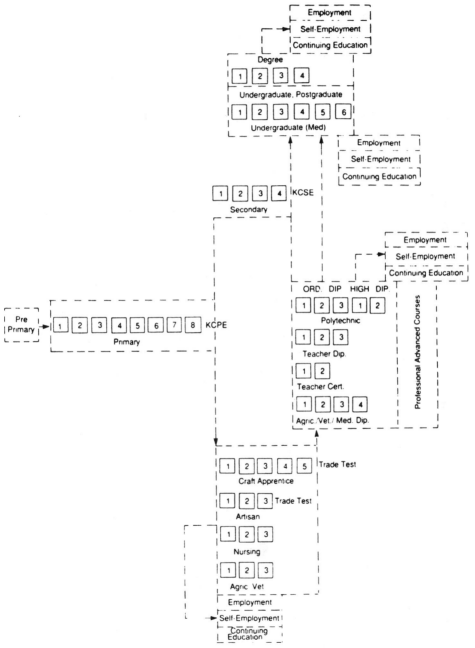

Figure 2.2
The Structure of Formal Education, 1985

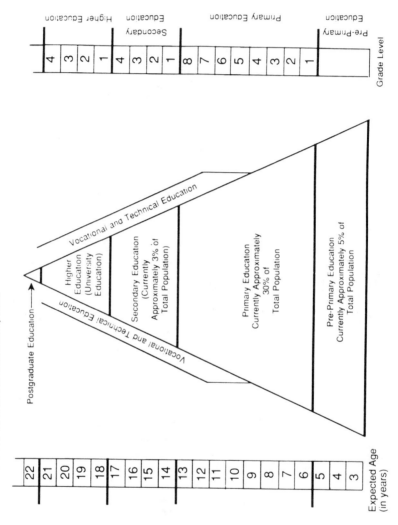

Figure 2.3
Enrollment of Boys and Girls in Primary School, 1963–1979 (in Percentages)

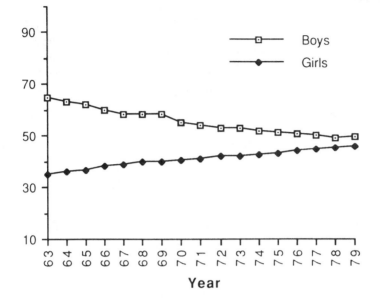

and regional economic development. The regions with most employment opportunities and greater agricultural activity, especially of cash crops, are also the regions of greatest educational progress and proportionately greater participation of women in primary education.

Districts that have relatively low female enrollments in the primary school are generally located in the arid and semiarid parts of Kenya and in poorer agriculture regions where the populations are predominantly pastoral farmers. Some of these districts have strong contravailing cultural or religious norms and traditions that depress female enrollment in the primary school. The Central Bureau of Statistics and UNICEF have observed that ''Economic realities and traditions combine to reinforce the perception that there is no benefit—and often some potential threat— in girls' acquisition of formal education. Girls' educational opportunities are further constrained by comparative inaccessibility of educational facilities.''[1]

During the two decades after independence, both the people and the government of Kenya have emphasized the expansion of education, especially at the primary level. This expansion has taken the form of self-help efforts (Harambee Schools); government provision of teachers and schools; and the construction of boarding primary schools for pastoral populations. As a result, girls have made great gains in enrollment in primary school.

These gains are perhaps better understood by considering Grade 1 enrollment, which generally provides a good indication of the status of girls' education at a

Table 2.1
New Entrants, Population of Admission Age, and Apparent Intake Rates, by Sex, 1970–1981

Year	New Entrants		Population		Apparent Intake Rate	
	Boys	Girls	Boys	Girls	Boys	Girls
1970	160,329	127,122	184,100	185,100	0.871	0.687
1971	165,616	130,973	192,500	193,600	0.860	0.677
1972	191,568	154,745	200,500	197,200	0.956	0.785
1973	200,314	166,458	207,600	205,800	0.965	0.909
1974	...	...	215,400	215,300	...	...
1975	...	...	224,100	225,700	...	...
1976	...	...	235,100	136,700	...	...
1977	299,992	268,259	247,400	245,400	1.213	1.093
1978	297,489	264,266	258,300	257,600	1.152	1.026
1979	...	...	270,200	270,600	...	...
1980	330,616	318,940	283,100	284,500	1.168	1.121
1981	371,336	350,097	297,700	298,900	1.247	1.171

Source: New Entrants: Calculated from data on enrollment and repeaters by grade supplied by the statistics unit, Ministry of Education, Science and Technology.

given point in time. Unlike total enrollment which reflects the past as well as the present, Grade 1 enrollment is uncontaminated by factors such as dropouts and, to a lesser extent, repetition. Table 2.1 shows Standard One enrollment, population of admission age, and apparent intake rates by sex for 1970–1981. The data presented in this table show that the chances of girls entering primary school have improved significantly from 1975 to the present.

GIRLS' PARTICIPATION IN SECONDARY EDUCATION

The number of girls attending secondary school has risen steadily during the past two decades. The enrollment of girls at this level rose from 9,567 (32 percent) in 1963 to over 160,000 (40 percent) in 1980. Several observations can be made regarding these figures. First, although the rise in the number of girls attending secondary school is impressive, it is not as significant as the rise in the number of girls attending primary school. Second, the proportion of girls in

Table 2.2
Gross Enrollment Ratios for Primary Education, by Sex, 1970–1982

Year	MF	M	F
1970	64.4	75.7	53.2
1975	104.9	114.1	95.7
1976	101.0	108.9	93.1
1977	99.4	106.4	92.4
1978	95.8	102.3	89.3
1979	113.2	119.9	106.4
1980	114.8	121.2	108.3
1981	111.0	116.3	105.6

Source: Enrollment data - Ministry of Education, Science and Technology.

secondary school in Forms 1-IV actually declined from 32 percent in 1963 to a record low of 25 percent in 1967 and to 31 percent in 1970. It has not been possible to determine the reasons for this decline.

Enrollment ratios are the most commonly used indicators for assessing a country's coverage of enrollment at a particular level or of a particular social group. Table 2.2 shows the gross enrollment ratios for secondary education by sex for the period 1970 to 1982. The enrollment ratios for the two secondary school stages, Forms I-IV and Forms V-VI, show a very modest increase for girls between 1975 and 1984.

The disparity between boys and girls in secondary school education may be explained by several factors. The main one relates to the provision of school places. Unlike primary education, secondary school education in Kenya is not coeducational. Kenya has traditionally maintained separate schools for boys and girls, and the number of boys' schools far exceeds the number of girls' schools.

In 1975, there were almost three times the number of government secondary schools for boys than for girls: boys' schools, 235; girls' schools, 82; mixed, 47. In that year, the Kenya government decided to "freeze" the expansion of the maintained schools in order to upgrade the rapidly growing numbers of unaided schools (mainly Harambee). This resulted in a slight increase in the proportion of girls' schools maintained and a significant rise in female secondary school enrollment. Thus, the growth of female secondary school enrollment that occurred during the period 1975 to 1984 was primarily a growth in Harambee school enrollment. In 1975, government-maintained secondary schools absorbed

45 percent of the male school intake compared to less than one-third of the female intake.

Government-maintained secondary schools provide a higher quality of education at lower cost than unaided secondary schools (mainly Harambee and private schools). The fact that parents have continued to send their daughters to the less endowed schools demonstrates the attitudinal change that has taken place during the past decade toward women's education. Parental attitude change has been confirmed through interviews by a cross-section of women leaders. However, in some areas of Kenya parental attitudes toward the education of women are still very negative. Some of these areas are among the districts where the enrollment of girls in primary school is very low.

In recent years, the Kenya government has emphasized science education, especially in the second cycle of the secondary school (Forms V-VI) and at the university. (Forms V-VI was the upper segment of the secondary school in the education system that was in operation up to 1984. The system then was 7:4:2:3. It is being phased out. The last year of Form IV will be 1989.) A study of the curriculum options in the Sixth Form schools reveals that most of the places available to girls are in arts subjects like history, geography, and religious studies. Boys have proportionately greater access to schools offering courses in the sciences and mathematics. Whereas the number of boys and girls enrolled in arts courses has been nearly equal over the past few years, in the sciences boys overwhelmingly dominate. About five boys to every girl are enrolled in science.

This situation demonstrates that there are no strong science programs in most girls' secondary schools, and in most unaided schools, where enrollment of girls is quite high, no science programs are offered. (This situation has changed in the new educational structure where all students in the secondary school are expected to take science subjects.) Because few girls take science subjects up to the end of the fourth year of the secondary school, the few science places that are available to girls in Forms V and VI are not fully utilized. Where these places are filled, it is usually with weak candidates, especially in physics and mathematics.

As was noted earlier, initial enrollment in any educational cycle may be used as an indicator of a group's access to that cycle. Table 2.3 shows the proportion of Forms I and V entrants by sex for the years 1974 to 1984. Two conclusions can be drawn from this table. First, although the access of girls to secondary education has improved with time, boys seem to have a major advantage, especially in Form V. Second, the Ministry of Education has attempted to hold down the proportion of boys entering Forms I and V while raising the proportion of girls. In order to increase the enrollment of girls in secondary school significantly, the government should increase the number of girls' maintained schools.

There is regional variation in the distribution of secondary education. Girls from less economically developed regions and less affluent families have little chance of receiving secondary education. In 1984, the Central Bureau of Statistics and UNICEF observed that, unlike maintained schools which have national or

Table 2.3
Form 1 and Form 5 Enrollment, by Sex, 1974–1984

	1974	1975	1976	1977	1978	1979	1980	1981	1982	1983	1984
FORM 1 Percent	62.2	60.8	59.2	58.2	56.5	56.5	57.3	56.9	59	59.5	—
MALES Number	40,243	44,806	56,444	61,943	59,160	60,618	67,037	10,196	76,467	83,090	—
Percent	37.8	39.2	40.5	41.8	43.5	43.5	42.7	43.1	41	40.5	—
FEMALES Number	24,463	28,884	38,390	44,553	45,573	46,709	49,863	53,264	53,137	56,524	—
FORM 5 Percent	73.7	73.7	70.8	72.6	71.4	68.6	70.02	69.1	65	59.5	—
MALES Number	3,046	3,534	3,689	3,803	5,027	5,877	7,860	7,733	6,878	6,876	—
Percent	26.3	26.3	29.2	27.4	28.6	31.4	29.98	30.9	35	40.5	—
FEMALES Number	1,089	1,258	1,519	1,437	2,012	2,691	3,366	3,453	3,705	4,678	—

Source: Ministry of Education, Science, and Technology.

provincial intakes, the catchment area of Harambee (community) secondary schools is usually confined to the district or subdistrict units. Because of the limited availability of places in maintained schools, a majority of girls who have completed primary school and passed their end-of-primary examination credibly must therefore depend on the initiative, resources, and self-help priorities of their local communities to have even a possibility of continuing their education. It is not surprising therefore that districts with comparatively high levels of educational and economic development maintain an advantage in the access of girls to secondary education.

FEMALE PARTICIPATION IN UNIVERSITY EDUCATION

The proportion of women students at university and other tertiary institutions in Kenya is less than 20 percent. The distribution of women within the university reflects the narrow range of their secondary school options. (See Table 2.4.) Women are underrepresented in the Faculties of Architecture and Design, Building Economics/Land Economics, Engineering, Science, and Veterinary Medicine.

The underrepresentation in science may be explained in part by the fact that these combinations are available at three-quarters of the boys' schools with Forms V and VI, but at only 40 percent of the girls' schools. The increased provision of mixed schools at Forms V and VI seems to be one of the ways of increasing science opportunities for women. However, this strategy cannot guarantee quality science education for girls. For this reason other intervention strategies should be proposed. There seems to be a need for compensatory enrollments for women in science fields at both university and other postsecondary training institutions. One year of remedial instruction at university for women science students who are low achievers at the end of the secondary school level would go a long way in closing the gap between the number of men and women studying science and related fields. The fact that relatively few women attain higher levels of education and training in science-related fields contributes to the lack of science opportunities for girls at lower educational levels and to girls' tendency to avoid science subjects. One way to break this cycle is through special programs designed to assist women to receive advanced training in science. In this connection, it may be prudent to establish several centers of excellence for girls specializing in science and mathematics. Such centers could be run like junior colleges with a high concentration of well-qualified teachers and facilities. International agencies as well as women's organizations could be approached for financial assistance in establishing such centers.

Perhaps one area in which there has been a significant rise in the number of women in university education is the Faculty of Education. Kenyatta University is the only institution charged with responsibility of offering the Bachelor of Education degree and the postgraduate diploma for secondary school teaching. During the past decade, the number of women at this institution has been rising

Table 2.4
Students at the University of Nairobi, by Discipline and Sex, 1980–1981

Undergraduate Courses:	1980–81		
	Males	Females	Total
Agriculture	286	77	363
Architecture & Design	191	30	221
Building Eng., Land Econo.	115	25	140
Art	891	520	1,411
Commerce	379	160	539
Engineering	520	8	528
Law	149	85	234
Education (B.Ed. & Dip. Ed.)	1,250	888	2,138
Medicine	453	118	571
Science	817	96	913
Veterinary Medicine	288	37	325
Dental Surgery	45	37	82
Pharmacy	70	41	111
TOTAL	5,454	2,122	7,576

Post Graduate Courses:			
Agriculture	115	24	139
Architecture & Design	45	6	51
Arts	119	51	170
Commerce	39	6	45
Education	111	58	169
Engineering	45	--	45
Law	18	5	23
Medicine	143	32	175
Science	193	26	219
Veterinary Medicine	68	7	75
School of Journalism	9	--	9
TOTAL	905	215	1,120

Source: Economic Survey 1981, p. 206.

steadily. In 1984, women constituted 44 percent of the total student enrollment at Kenyatta University. Almost as many women were enrolled at Kenyatta University in 1981–1982 (1,104) as in all undergraduate programs at the University of Nairobi (1,202).

EDUCATION AND THE WOMEN'S WORKFORCE

Defining Women's Work

The usual economic definition of work in the national accounts does not measure a large proportion of the work done by women. The statistics therefore

Table 2.5
Patterns of Employment, by Sex, 1979

Sector	Men		Women	
Formal/Informal Urban Areas	Regular Casual	629,000 123,799	Regular Casual	120,942 37,778
Self-Employment in Informal Urban Areas		125,833		47,671
Informal in Rural Areas		79,450		34,671

Source: Employment and Earnings in Modern Sector, Central Bureau of
         Statistics, 1979.

understate women's contribution in the economy. The services of housewives, such as domestic chores and childrearing, are not counted. In the long run it will be necessary to reexamine basic socioeconomic theories and statistical methods in order to include more of the work contributed by women.

In the following pages, an attempt is made to examine the distribution of men and women in different types of work and particular skills and occupations and in various income and remuneration levels. It also includes the agricultural, informal (self-employment), public, and industrial sectors. Table 2.5 shows the patterns of female and male employment in the modern formal (paid employment) and informal (self-employment) sectors in a typical year.

Roughly one woman is employed for every five men employed in the modern sector and one woman for every two to three men working in the formal sector. Women are therefore largely underrepresented in the modern sector. Hence, despite the significant progress that has been made in the enrollment of women in education at all levels, extension of education to women has had little impact on workforce participation.

The vast majority of Kenyan women (88 percent of the total) reside in rural areas where they contribute most of the labor required for the cultivation of food crops on family farms. They also contribute most of the labor used in production of cash crops in small and medium-sized farms. When women are not occupied on farm work, they concentrate on household activities that contribute to the general welfare of the households. Therefore, the education of women, at both formal and informal levels, is critical to the economic development of Kenya.

When earnings are examined on the basis of the nature of employment and by sex, women are no better off; indeed, they may be worse. Table 2.6 summarizes the earnings of women in 1978. Although men earned over 85 percent of the total earnings, women earned the other 14 percent in the modern sector.

Table 2.6
Earnings, by Sex and Nature of Employment, 1978 (in Thousands of Pounds)

Employment	Men	Women
Regular	388,223.3	63,478.1
Casual	26,475.2	64,645.5
Percentage Earnings	85.89	14.11

Clearly, female representation in modern sector wage employment has remained low, although the trends indicate that it is increasing, albeit slowly. The percentage of women in total modern sector wage employment was 12.2 in 1964, rising to 14.8 in 1972 and to 18.0 in 1981. Table 2.7 shows the trends in employment by sex.

In both the private and public sector, women constitute less than 20 percent of total employment. Even in the self-employed category women constitute only 30 percent of total employment.

Within the wage labor force, women's representation is relatively high in agriculture and forestry, finance, insurance, real estate, business services, and community, social, and personal services (teaching, nursing). Secretarial services is the only sector in which the majority of workers are women. (The 1984–1988 plan states that the percentage of unemployment among job-seekers in the modern sector is higher among women than men.)

Women's representation is also substantial and rising in a broader occupational group of professional, executive, and managerial personnel. Table 2.8 illustrates the case of doctors.

Generally, women are underrepresented in science and then technical fields because the educational gap between men and women is widest in the technical fields. The increasing participation of women in the education system can be expected to help bridge part of this gap. However, it will take more than formal education. The obstacles are not necessarily formal education but also the entrenched traditional attitudes of both men and women. These factors make it difficult for girls to avail themselves of any forms of technical education even where legal barriers have been removed.

Employment in Industry

Table 2.9 summarizes employment in Kenya by broad industrial categories and by sex. Again, women are shown to be underrepresented in specific industries.

The underrepresentation of women in industry could be explained by their

Table 2.7
Modern Sector Employment, by Type and Sex, 1971–1982

Year	Private Sector Women	Totals	%	Public Sector Women	Totals	%	Self-Employed Women	Totals	%
1971	63,560	423,730	15	37,373	267,456	14	2,073	58,208	2
1972	66,976	432,819	15	39,492	286,958	14	15,214	83,912	1
1973	69,366	452,443	15	44,561	298,932	15	16,467	95,418	1
1974	80,984	496,218	16	65,408	330,045	20	35,443	132,091	2
1975	69,865	476,677	15	59,996	342,409	18	30,355	130,953	2
1976	75,570	501,136	15	63,587	356,394	18	40,233	152,268	2
1977	83,607	526,54˙	16	71,137	378,354	19	45,889	160,904	2
1978	86,504	521,586	16	72,225	389,975	19	46,272	173,504	2
1979	90,407	546,551	16	74,824	424,756	18	50,302	184,598	2
1980	90,827	534,277	17	74,824	471,456	18	54,0˙7	185,041	
1981		540,192	18		484,117	19		219,433	
1982		540,424	18		505,607	19		234,906	

Percent growth rate 4.3

Table 2.8
Distribution of Doctors, by Institution and Sex, 1979 and 1980

Institution	Males		Females	
	1979	1980	1979	1980
Ministry of Health	641	749	81	99
Ministry of Defense	12	15	--	--
University of Nairobi	112	127	8	9
Mission Hospitals	41	71	4	7
Local Authorities	53	59	18	19
Private Practice	15	23	0	2
Private Hospitals & Nursing Homes	39	41	12	16

underrepresentation in secondary and tertiary levels, especially in the science and science-related fields.

CONCLUDING REMARKS

The issue of female enrollment in any educational system in Africa is currently important for policy-makers. Since 1961, following the now historic Addis Ababa Conference, most African countries have officially been committed to a policy of universal primary education. In many cases, this goal has not been achieved owing to disparities between female and male enrollments. In such situations, one of the central policy questions is whether female participation rates can be increased by manipulating the supply of schools and facilities, or whether the nonschool factors associated with demand is so overwhelming as to outweigh such measures.

In this chapter, it has been noted that Kenya has made gigantic progress toward making the enrollment of girls at par with boys at the primary school level; at the secondary school level, the enrollment of girls is slightly over 40 percent that of boys; and at the tertiary level the enrollment of women stands at about 30 percent in relation to men students.

In Kenya, the initial rapid expansion of enrollment apparently occurred largely in those regions where the demand for schooling was already high and where there was a high economic growth owing to cash crops. In those areas where female enrollment is still low, measures required to get girls into schools may be more expensive. These measures include building more girls' schools in these areas. But the supply-side change will not by itself guarantee increased enrollment

Table 2.9
Wage Employment, by Industry and Sex, 1980

Industry	Males		Females		Total
	Regular	Casual	Regular	Casual	
Agriculture & Forestry	147,448(64)	38,998(17)	22,311(10)	22,604(10)	231,361(101)
Mining & Quarrying	1,189(52)	1,037(45)	29(1)	34(2)	2,289
Manufacturing	106,254(75)	21,959(16)	8,789(6)	4,278(3)	141,280
Electricity & Water	7,496(74)	2,132(21)	445(4)	98(1)	10,171
Construction	32,105(51)	28,618(45)	1,747(3)	686(1)	63,156
Wholesale and Retail Trade, Restaurant & Hotels	52,371(74)	10,811(15)	6,728(10)	594(1)	70,504
Transport & Communication	43,141(78)	5,728(10)	4,116(7)	2,146(4)	55,131(99)
Finance, Insurance, Real Estate and Business Services	27,009(68)	6,381(16)	5,906(15)	442(1)	39,738
Community Social & Personnel Services	293,036(75)	3,251(1)	94,661(24)	1,175(0.03)	392,123
Totals	710,049	118,915	144,732	32,057	1,005,753

Note: Figures in brackets are percentages.

among female students. Specific causes of the nonparticipation of girls in the schooling process should be established and remedied.

Although this chapter has not dealt with the question of the quality of female education, this issue is very important. It is not enough for women to have access to education. How they survive in the educational system and what happens to them when they exit from it are equally critical issues.

There seems to be evidence that, because of the increased enrollment of women in the educational system in Kenya, their participation in the workforce has improved, albeit not significantly. A more worrying concern is their underrepresentation in industry and in technical fields. This situation is directly due to the underrepresentation of girls in science and science-related subjects at the secondary and tertiary school levels.

NOTE

1. CBS and UNICEF, *Situation Analysis of Children and Women Kenya*, Section 3 (Nairobi, 1984), p. 55.

REFERENCES

Central Bureau of Statistics (Kenya). *Women in Kenya, Nairobi.* 1978.
Eshiwani, G. S. "Sex Differences in the Learning of Mathematics." *The Kenya Educational Review* (1975).
———. *A Study of Women's Access to Higher Education in Kenya with Special Reference to Mathematics and Science Education.* Mimeo. Bureau of Educational Research, 1983.
———. *The Education of Women in Kenya 1975–1985.* Mimeo. Bureau of Educational Research, 1986.
Smock, A. C. *Women's Education and Roles in Kenya.* Mimeo. Institute of Development Studies, University of Nairobi. Working Paper No. 316, July 1977.
UNICEF and CBS. *Situation Analysis of Children and Women in Kenya.* Nairobi, Republic of Kenya, 1984.

3
NIGERIA

Eunice A. C. Okeke

Nigeria, a developing nation on the west coast of Africa, is densely populated (about 100 million). Women account for over 50 percent of the total population. Despite their greater proportion of the population, few women occupy notable positions in the social, political, and economic life of the nation. Instead, the men are in full control of the nation's politics. In the economy, women in Nigeria engage in small-scale farming and petty trade, whereas men work in large-scale farming and industrial production, the locus of economic power. Accordingly, men control and even direct the affairs and lives of women, often using mores, cultural values, and sanctions. In sum, the social, political, and economic status of Nigerian women is low.

Women's lack of formal education helps explain their inferior position in Nigeria's social, political, and economic affairs. The latest available literacy data on Nigeria reveal that only about 52 percent of the population is literate. The statistics also show that 65 percent of men but only 38.5 percent of women are literate.[1] This lower rate of literacy has meant a lower status for women.

This chapter seeks to answer the following questions with regard to the education of women in Nigeria:

1. What type of education did women have prior to the introduction of formal schooling under colonial rule?

2. To what extent did women have access to formal schooling when it was introduced?

3. What factors affect women's formal education and women's use of that education?

4. How have women fared in contemporary Nigeria, in the area of educational opportunities and achievements?

5. What factors have encouraged or discouraged women acquiring education even in the present time?

6. What work plan/actions have been undertaken or proposed, intended to increase women's participation in education, and what chances are there to bridge the gap between men and women in education?

THE TRADITIONAL EDUCATION OF WOMEN

In Nigeria, prior to the introduction of formal, Western-type schooling, the education of the young, male or female, was nonformal and consisted of socialization into adult roles. Male children were socialized to the father role of providing protection, shelter, and food for the family, whereas female children were socialized to the mother role of housekeeper or homemaker. The girl followed in the footsteps of her mother, helping her in household chores, caring for the younger siblings, and accompanying her to the market or farm. In short, girls understudied their mothers' roles, and the boys understudied their fathers during farming or hunting expeditions. Each child not only acquired skills required for economic survival, but also adopted the values and norms of the society, which in Nigeria clearly differentiated sex roles.

Both males and females received *equal* education in that each person was prepared for gender-specific functions in the society. There was no discrimination in educational opportunities. What existed was the relative value and importance that was placed on the functions fulfilled by each sex in the society which, as will be shown later, had profound implications for women's access to Western education. Although women engaged in farming good crops and in petty trading, their earnings or contribution to the family income or national income remained unrecognized for a long time. For example, while each woman was responsible for feeding her husband and children from the proceeds of her farm and trade, the husband was still regarded as the breadwinner because he raised crops that were readily translated into cash. However, sociologists have concluded that in traditional economies women possessed some confidence in their ability to cater for their children. In most polygamous homes, women have continued to provide for their own biological children without the husband's help. In short, traditional education bestowed on each sex experiences that promoted equal economic growth. Marriage led women to leave their homes and live in the man's home. This connotation of male superiority embedded in the culture existed in traditional education. The extent to which the introduction of formal education has affected these values is discussed in the following section.

WOMEN'S ACCESS TO FORMAL EDUCATION

Formal education was introduced into Nigeria in 1842 when Christian missionaries established mission schools in Badagry and Abeokuta. Through missionary work, Western educational opportunities spread to other areas, notably Lagos, Calabar, Onitsha, Warri, and Benin. The missionaries, together with the colonial masters, set up a type of education that would serve their mutual interests, namely, to inculcate Christian ideals and values in the Nigerians and teach them to read and write English. Products of this educational system became catechists for the churches, teachers for schools, and clerks, messengers, and administrative assistants for the trading companies and public services.[2] These salaried jobs were attractive and suited men more than women since the jobs were outside the home. To receive the Western education which was the passport to salaried posts, the recipient had to leave home for outside established centers called schools. Schooling therefore favored the already outgoing males and discriminated against females whose traditional roles lay in home care. This situation gave men a head start in education and ultimately created a fertile ground for the subordinate position women occupy today in the sociopolitical–economic life of Nigeria.

While missionary/Western education was taking firm root in the southern part of Nigeria, the contrary was the case in northern Nigeria where the commitment to Islam made Africans reject Western education. The northerner's resistance to this education marked the beginning of educational disparities between northern and southern Nigeria. A. Babs Fafunwa reports that in 1912 there were a total of 142 primary schools and over 35,000 pupils in the south, but fewer than 50 primary schools with under 1,000 pupils in the north.[3] This disparity, though narrowing today, has created two different pictures of educational opportunities within the same country. Indeed, the disparity is greater in women's education because Islamic tradition restricts women to the home.

Whether Western education as it was presented then discriminated against women is a matter for debate. Some people believe that the education did not discriminate against participants on the basis of sex, since the doors of the school were open to all. Others believe that certain practices directly or indirectly worked against women's enrollment and educational advancement. Victorian England relegated women to the domestic sphere, viewing them as inferior to men in every way. These attitudes are reflected in the type of education given to Nigerian women. The orientation was heavily biased in favor of cookery, laundry work, housewifery, and mothercraft. This curriculum handicapped women in obtaining well-paying jobs in the western sector of the economy and pinned them to British-defined roles as wives and mothers. Their husbands, however, through formal schooling acquired new economic status and formed a new male elite. The educational, political, and economic future of women came to be in the hands of this new elite. This background easily explains the very low proportion of women in schools several decades after the introduction of formal education. O. Taiwo notes that in 1912, out of a school population of 21,153 schoolchildren, only 3,151 were girls.[4]

Later years witnessed a rapid expansion of Western education in Nigeria following greater government involvement in education. The recommendations of various commissions—notably, the Phelps-Stokes Commission (1920–1922), the Elliot Commission (1945), and the Ashby Commission (1960); the 1969 curriculum conference; and the introduction of the Universal Free Primary Education Programme (UPE) in 1976 gave momentum and direction to the growth and development of formal education in Nigeria. The extent to which the recommendations of these various commissions or educational innovations has affected women's education can be drawn from school enrollment figures or the number of girls' schools in Nigeria. Table 3.1 shows the percentage of girls in schools in Nigeria just before independence to thirteen years after independence. A gap has long existed between the enrollment of boys and girls. There was a slow increase in the girls' share of school enrollment—from 36.7 percent in 1959 to 39 percent in 1966. The figures dropped steadily to 1973, perhaps as a result of the effects of the Nigerian civil war of 1966–1970.

When we consider that the population of males equals or is less than that of females in Nigeria, it is evident that a greater proportion of men receive primary education than women. The disparity is greater in the northern states where the Muslim religion does not encourage women's education.

With regards to secondary education, Table 3.2 shows the proportion of women who were enrolled in secondary schools. In the period under study, girls in the southern states on the average made up about 30 percent of all students, whereas in the northern states girls averaged 3 percent of enrollment. Indeed, in 1959 girls represented 0.4 percent of the total school population of 64,209 pupils. An interesting feature of the educational imbalance is that the total percentage of girls from the southern states enrolled in both primary and secondary schools is greater than the total percentage of boys enrolled in northern states. Further insight into the education of women in terms of institutions built for girls during 1859–1978 is shown in Table 3.3. Between 1939 and 1948, while twelve boys' schools existed in the south, only three were established for girls. In the same period in the north, there were three boys' schools and no girls' schools. The first girls' schools were built between 1949 and 1958. On the whole, by 1978 there were fifty-three boys' schools in the north, while girls' schools numbered twenty-three. In the same period in the south, there were ninety-three boys' schools and sixty-two girls' schools. There were 394 coeducational schools. At the university level, by 1959, when Nigeria had just a university college (an affiliate of the University of London), women accounted for 4 percent of the total student population. These figures serve to show the wide gap between men and women in the field of education. The following conclusions can be drawn from the statistics.

- Men had a head start over women in education.

- A smaller number of schools was built for girls.

- A smaller proportion of girls attended schools.

Table 3.1
Primary School Enrollment, by Sex and States, 1959–1973 (in Percentages)[a]

	SOUTHERN STATES			NORTHERN STATES			TOTAL % BY SEX	
	Boys	Girls	TOTAL	Boys	Girls	TOTAL	Boys	Girls
1959[b]	56.6	34.3	90.9	6.7	2.4	9.1	63.3	36.7
1965	49.5	33.5	83.0	12.0	5.0	17.0	61.5	38.5
1966	48.8	34.0	82.8	12.2	5.0	17.2	61.0	39.0
1967[c]	41.73	29.77	71.5	20.44	8.06	28.5	62.17	37.83
1968[d]	36.45	26.39	62.84	26.87	10.29	37.16	63.32	36.68
1969[c]	40.18	28.57	68.75	22.44	8.81	31.25	62.62	37.38
1970	59.1	23.0	82.1	13.9	4.0	17.9	73.0	27.0
1971	58.0	23.6	81.6	14.2	4.2	18.4	72.2	27.8
1972	57.9	24.0	81.9	14.0	4.1	81.1	71.9	28.1
1973	57.2	24.2	81.4	14.3	4.3	18.6	71.5	28.5

[a]Source: Compiled from statistics in the Annual Abstract of Statistics, Federal Office of Statistics, Lagos, 1966, and 1974.

[b]Source: Compiled from Digest of Statistics, Federal Ministry of Information, 1959.

[c]Numbers do not include enrollment in the Eastern States.

[d]Numbers do not include enrollment in the Eastern and Mid-Western States

Table 3.2

Secondary School Enrollment, by Sex and States, 1959–1972 (in Percentages)[a]

	SOUTHERN STATES			NORTHERN STATES			TOTAL & BY SEX	
	Boys	Girls	TOTAL	Boys	Girls	TOTAL	Boys	Girls
1959[b]	75.7	20.1	79.5	3.8	0.4	4.2	79.5	20.5
1965	63.8	28.8	92.6	6.1	1.3	7.4	69.9	30.1
1966	62.2	29.4	91.6	6.9	1.5	8.4	69.1	30.9
1967[c]	55.9	29.9	85.8	11.7	2.5	14.2	67.6	32.4
1968[d]	—	—	83.3	13.4	3.3	16.7	—	—
1969[c]	44.3	33.2	77.5	17.7	4.8	22.5	62.0	38.0
1970	56.7	30.9	87.6	9.7	2.7	12.4	66.4	33.6
1971	54.6	30.4	75.0	11.8	3.2	15.0	66.4	33.6
1972	62.9	22.6	85.5	11.9	2.6	14.5	74.8	25.2

[a]Source: Compiled from statistics in the Annual Abstract of Statistics, Federal Office of Statistics, Lagos, 1966, and 1974.

[b]Source: Compiled from Digest of Statistics, Federal Ministry of Information, 1959.

[c]Numbers do not include enrollment in the Eastern States.

[d]Numbers do not include enrollment in the Eastern and Mid-Western States

Table 3.3
Distribution of Secondary Institutions, by Sex and Year Founded, 1859–1978[a]

	NORTH			SOUTH			ALL NIGERIA		
	MALE	FEMALE	MIXED	MALE	FEMALE	MIXED	MALE	FEMALE	MIXED
1859–68				1			1		
1869–78				1			1		
1879–88					1			1	
1889				1			1		
1899–1908	1			1		1	2		1
1909–1918	1			2		3	3		3
1919–1928	2			4		2	6		2
1929–1938	2			9	3	4	11	3	4
1939–1948	3		3	12	3	17	15	3	20
1949–1958	11	5	1	54	27	86	65	32	87
1959–1968	22	13	41	95	88	196	117	101	237
1969–1978	53	23	138	93	62	394	146	85	479
DATE UNKNOWN	13	6	2	16	12	31	29	18	33
TOTAL	108	47	185	289	196	734	397	243	866

aFoundation dates not specified

Source: Compiled from Federal Republic of Nigeria: _Directory of Post Primary Educational Institutions in Nigeria 1980–81 Edition._ Lagos: Federal Government Press, 1983, pp. 9–52.

49

• The disparity in education between north and south was greatly evident in the case of girls.

• There was a slow but steady increase in the total enrollment of girls.

The reasons for women's low educational opportunities is the focus of the next section.

MAJOR CONSTRAINTS ON WOMEN'S EDUCATION IN THE PAST

D. G. Burns summarized the prevalent views on the education of women in Nigeria in his Memorandum on Educational Policy in Nigeria in 1947. He wrote:

It is claimed that schooling makes girls discontented and immoral, that girls who have been to school are less willing to undertake heavy labour in the fields, that there are no women teachers in the schools; and that there is a real moral danger to adolescent girls in mixed schools with male teachers; and where custom of bride wealth is strong, parents commonly prefer marriage rather than schooling for their daughters.[5]

Schooling was seen as an attempt to change cultural behaviors associated with women. Clearly, Nigerian culture dictated innumerable ''dos'' and ''don'ts'' for women which were initiated and sustained by men to ensure female submission and male supremacy. Although males could know concubines and the wives were expected to accept this situation as normal, the wives could not have any form of association, no matter how Platonic, with other men. Hence, the fear arose that if women received the same education given to men, they would be discontented with their lot. Again, much as the acquisition of formal education raised the status of men from farmers and hunters to salaried workers, the status of women who acquired formal education also went up. Indeed, a number of myths about educated women arose. G. Alele-Williams identified some of them as follows:

Educated women do not make good (submissive) wives.

Educated women are morally corrupt or promiscuous.

Educated women are barren.

Educated women find it difficult to get husbands.[6]

These myths worked to dissuade parents from sending their daughters to schools. Only parents who defied societal pressures managed to send their daughters to schools. Nevertheless, every parent had a permanent and genuine fear of the moral danger that would ensue from letting the girls out of their parents' sight, especially when the girls attended coeducational schools. Because many parents believed that the girl's place was in the home and that her traditional role was homemaking and childbearing, functions requiring no formal education, in fact there appeared to be no need to risk social disapproval by enrolling girls in school.

The view that formal education was irrelevant to women is stronger in the Muslim culture, where *Purdah* or female seclusion is practiced. In Muslim culture, young girls of ten or eleven are married off to much older men, who then restrict their movements to the family compound. Women can leave the compound at night, if they are accompanied by small boys. Formal education which kept girls in schools beyond the marrying age was not acceptable to Muslim parents in northern Nigeria. This explains the gap in women's education between northern and southern states today.

Brideprice helped limit the number of girls who received formal education when it was introduced. Among many communities in Nigeria, as part of a marriage contract the bridegroom is required to make some sort of payment to his prospective parents-in-law. The coming of Europeans introduced cash payment for goods instead of payment in kind. Educated men, now salaried, had ready cash to pay in fulfillment of marriage contracts. This came to be known as brideprice. Marrying daughters off to men with ready cash became a source of income for parents. Allowing a girl to go to school or remain in school would therefore delay the income or cause the parents to miss a chance of having a wealthy son-in-law. When parents did not have enough money to pay the school fees of all their children, it was always the girls who were withdrawn from school to get married. The brideprice money realized was used to pay school fees for sons. Consequently, the dropout rate of girls was excessively higher than that of boys. Theoretically, the school doors were open to both boys and girls, but the nation's societal/cultural values and practices interfered greatly with women's education. Today, many of the beliefs held about women's education are rapidly dying. Women in Nigeria today have increased opportunities to benefit from formal education. The extent to which they have fared in education and the factors promoting or inhibiting their participation today are discussed in the following section.

WOMEN'S EDUCATION IN PRESENT-DAY NIGERIA

Present-day Nigeria has witnessed a large increase in the number of females acquiring formal education at all levels. Wide opportunities are open to them, and the educational climate has changed for the better. There are an appreciable number of women lawyers and judges, women economists and bankers, women educators and researchers, women engineers and technologists, women scientists and doctors, women politicians and activists, women entrepreneurs, and so on. These achievements are due to the increased opportunities women have had in formal education since the mid-1970s.

Table 3.4 provides data on the growth of female primary school enrollment since mid-1970. By 1983–1984, girls accounted for 44 percent of the total primary school enrollment. When enrollment in various states is considered,

Table 3.4
Primary School Enrollment, by Sex and Ratio of Female to Total Enrollment,
1975/1976–1983/1984

YEAR	NUMBER OF FEMALES	NUMBER OF MALES & FEMALES COMBINED	PERCENTAGE OF FEMALE
1975–76	2,625,061	6,165,547	42.6
1976–77	3,511,785	8,100,324	43.4
1977–78	4,257,815	9,867,961	43.1
1978–79	4,696,862	10,798,550	43.5
1979–80	5,295,363	12,117,483	43.7
1980–81	5,970,244	13,777,973	43.3
1981–82	6,150,810	14,311,608	43.0
1982–83	6,321,715	14,676,608	43.1
1983–84	6,331,658	14,383,487	44.0

some states have had greater growth than the national average reported in Table 3.4. While enrollment figures in the northern states of Sokoto, Niger, and Bauchi in 1980–1981 stood at 190,837 females versus 373,492 males, 136,018 females to 282,058 males, 144,114 females to 250,598 males, respectively, the story is different in the southern states. In the same year Anambra, Imo, and Oyo recorded the following figures: 487,674 females to 495,600 males; 599,080 females to 584,220 males; and 703,114 females to 760,102 males, respectively. Female enrollment in Imo State is higher than male enrollment. The other states have almost equal proportions of males and females.

In secondary schools, the proportion of girls to boys is not as high as in primary schools. The girls' share of academic and commercial track enrollments has risen since 1975, but not consistently. They reached their peak in the 1980–1981 school year and experienced a proportional (but not a numerical decline) thereafter. The same is the case for female enrollment in vocational/technical secondary schools (see Table 3.5). While in 1980–1981 females made up 35.5 percent of total enrollment, the situation varies again from state to state. Latest figures from Anambra State indicate that there are more girls in secondary schools than boys. Some of the boys' schools are being converted to girls' schools or mixed schools. The commissioner of education of Anambra State recently pleaded with parents to encourage their boys to attend secondary schools. While in some states, girls are marching side by side with boys, it is not in all courses as the figures in Table 3.5 show. The enrollment of girls in technical subjects

Table 3.5

Secondary School Enrollment, by School Type, Sex, and Ratio of Female to Total Enrollment, 1975/1976–1983/1984

YEAR	GRAM/COMM			TECHN/VO		
	FEMALE	MALE-FEMALE COMBINED	PERCENT OF FEMALE	FEMALE	MALE-FEMALE COMBINED	PERCENT FEMALE
1975–76	20,763	601,652	3.5	3,212	27,843	11.5
1976–77	80,768	730,899	11.1	3,968	29,858	13.3
1977–78	61,090	913,648	6.7	5,029	40,538	12.4
1978–79	397,902	1,194,479	33.3	5,849	46,712	12.5
1979–80	543,564	1,553,345	35.0	8,381	61,856	13.5
1980–81	708,832	1,995,417	35.5	11,562	67,943	17.0
1981–82	732,466	2,503,952	29.3	8,682	83,899	10.3
1982–83	798,447	2,899,215(+)	27.5	7,722(+)	75,392(+)	10.2
1983–84	N/A	3,059,088(+)	N/A	N/A	76,242(+)	N/A

Table 3.6
**Level of Female Students and Academic Female Staffing Growth in Universities,
1981–1985**

YEAR	FEMALE STUDENT	TOTAL ENROLLMENT	PERCENT OF FEMALES	TOTAL ACADEMIC STAFF	PERCENT OF FEMALES
1981	17,099	77,791	21.9	589	.75
1982	20,386	90,751	22.5	716	.79
1983	25,219	104,774	24.1	964	.92
1984	26,587	116,822	22.7	1163	1.0
1985	28,739	126,285	22.7	1142	.90
TOTAL	118,030	516,423	22.8	4574	.89

Source: National Universities Commission Annual Report, December 1984

is still quite low. The factors that have hindered girls from obtaining education in general may be operating strongly in technical fields.

The gap in enrollment widens with educational levels. In polytechnics where most of the courses are technical, there are far fewer girls. The distribution of male/female students in all but three federal and state polytechnics in Nigeria in 1983–1984 shows that there were 9,906 girls to 41,268 boys, giving the females 24 percent of total enrollment.[7] Indeed, if the figures of the other three polytechnics were obtained, the percentage would be still lower, since the three other polytechnics are in the northern states, where women's education lags far behind men's.

In universities, the story is the same. The enrollment figures of females in federal universities and academic staff strength as shown below speak for themselves (see Table 3.6).

Women are underrepresented in higher education. They also tend to be segregated into a limited number of fields: education, pharmacy, and medicine, where in the 1983–84 academic year they represented 31.5 percent, 35.4 percent and 26.5 percent of all graduates, respectively. In 1983–1984, women accounted for 24.4 percent of all arts graduates and 23.1 percent of all law graduates. However, they made up 7.0 percent of all veterinary medicine, 13.9 percent of social science, 4.3 percent of engineering/technology, and 10.1 percent of all environmental design graduates (see Table 3.7). Women's choice of fields of study in higher education can be explained by two factors. First is the culture which through socialization paints a picture to a growing girl of what she should be aspiring to. The Nigerian girl is usually made to see herself as a prospective wife, mother and homemaker rather than as a professional. She therefore shuns any career that might interfere with her wifely and motherhood functions. Careers

Table 3.7
Female University (Federal) Graduates, by Faculty and Sex, 1980–1984 (in Percentages)*

Faculty	1980–81	1981–82	1982–83	1983–84	PERCENT INCREASE 1980–1984
Business Administration	9.9	9.6	10.5	17.2	7.3
Agriculture	13.4	13.6	8.2	12.4	-1.0
Arts	17.7	20.9	20.5	24.4	3.7
Education	26.6	32.1	31.7	31.5	4.9
Engineering/Technology	4.5	3.0	4.2	4.3	-0.2
Environmental Design	8.0	8.2	6.4	10.1	1.2
Law	21.1	24.1	20.5	23.1	2.0
Medicine	17.1	21.6	26.7	26.5	9.4
Pharmacy	22.3	27.0	26.0	35.4	13.1
Sciences	16.6	17.0	18.0	21.6	5.0
Social Sciences	11.6	17.1	13.0	13.9	2.3
Veterinary Medicine	8.5	4.9	8.6	7.0	-1.5

*This includes about 2 percent who enrolled in diploma and other non-degree courses.

Source: Federal Ministry of Education, Lagos.

in engineering, environmental studies, and business administration tend to take the worker away from home, touring sites or business establishments, and the like. But, if the girl goes into nursing, pharmacy, education, social welfare, or nutrition, these jobs can accommodate housewifery duties. In addition, these courses resemble functions associated with women's family role.

Another factor that keeps girls away from certain fields of study in higher education is the lack of qualifications to enter such fields. The performance of girls in physics and mathematics, as shown by a 1987 study by S. O. Adeyegba and S. O. Olamousi, is depressingly poor.[8] Entry to university-level courses in engineering, environmental studies, and technology require basic education in these subjects. Since there is no evidence that Nigerian males are more intellectually able than Nigerian females, the culture which socializes persons into prospective roles may account for girls' low motivation to study physical science. E. A. C. Okeke discusses the factors that affect girls' attainments in science, technology, and mathematics.[9] Although women now pursue higher education, they are still limited to the traditional fields of arts, education, and social science. Many more women are entering legal studies, which do not require proficiency in science.

In summary, there has been a slow but steady increase in female enrollment at all levels of formal education. This increased access to education has greatly enhanced the opportunity of Nigerian women to seek employment outside their homes and to participate in the paid workforce. Today women are employed in both public and private sector employment and are paid according to their educational qualifications. Women work as nurses, teachers, secretaries, technicians, engineers, pilots, doctors, lawyers, administrators, and so on. There is virtually no area of paid work where women have not entered, even if women contribute a small minority in that occupation. While in some professions there is a relatively large number of women—namely, in nursing, teaching, secretarial jobs, and social work—in others, such as engineering and other science technology and math-based careers, the number of women is relatively low.

Table 3.8 reports women's employment in the Nigerian Federal Civil Service (one of the country's major employers in the paid labor market). The table reports the number of women and men the government employs; it does not report the level at which they are employed. However, relatively few women hold managerial positions. Many women work as receptionists, typists, confidential secretaries, cleaners, clerks, technicians, and the like. They hold such jobs as a result of their education.

Paid work has become increasingly important to Nigerian women. Work for a wage, even if the work is not at a status equal to that of men's work, enhances a women's prestige and provides her with economic independence from both her parents and her husband. Today men prefer marrying women who are in the paid labor force. Women's income supplements the men's income and enhances male prestige. It is now common in Nigeria to find married women returning to school after years of absence. She does so at the urging of her husband so that

Table 3.8

Federal Civil-Service-Established Staff, by Ministry/Department and Sex, as of December 31, 1985

Ministry/Department	1981 M	1981 F	1982 M	1982 F	1983 M	1983 F
General Staff Headquarters/ State House	281	83	304	82	430	119
Cabinet Office	806	313	749	268	645	292
Office of the Head of Civil Service	1,913	949	2,179	1,010	2,400	1,180
Police	86,372	1,145	91,537	1,437	101,915	1,615
Agric. & Water Resources	8,256	1,116	8,376	1,177	8,019	1,114
Commerce and Industries	4,028	1,347	3,094	1,056	3,854	1,333
Communications	25,950	5,459	27,644	6,100	27,783	6,092
Defence	9,424	2,966	9,499	2,917	15,938	6,476
National Planning	4,005	1,362	4,045	1,913	4,073	1,952
Education Science & Technology	5,936	1,896	6,099	2,268	6,213	2,345
External Affairs	2,075	346	2,489	704	2,489	704
Finance	21,732	6,368	17,503	4,367	15,855	3,492

Table **3.8** (continued)

Ministry/Department	1981 M	1981 F	1982 M	1982 F	1983 M	1983 F
Health	2,228	1,152	2,464	1,333	1,969	898
Information, Soc. Dev., Youth, Sports, & Culture	6,118	1,411	6,030	1,377	6,321	1,556
Internal Affairs	13,850	1,090	16,256	1,283	16,548	2,552
Justice	350	206	359	246	398	281
Employment, Labor and Prod.	1,858	344	2,183	368	2,340	573
Mines, Power and Steel	1,398	239	1,326	346	1,753	390
Transport and Aviation	7,570	1,215	8,281	1,603	8,905	2,069
Works and Housing	12,876	1,461	16,019	2,090	17,938	2,242
Audit	758	142	677	157	1,176	190
Civil Service Commission	363	209	327	202	327	202
Police Service Commission	--	--	117	40	127	50
Public Complaints Commission	643	184	792	251	792	251
National Population Bureau	407	253	383	231	722	347
Advisory Judicial Committee	--	--	--	--	10	3

Judiciary	998	281	1,072	288	1,559	377
Federal Capital Territory	80	29	149	56	149	56
Federal Electoral Commission	--	--	707	148	1,034	185
National Assembly	188	74	1,714	653	1,714	653
Rivers Basin	3,878	353	--	--	--	--
Total	224,341	31,993	232,374	33,971	253,396	39,589

Source: Establishments Department, Office of the Head of the Civil Service of the Federation.

she can have a better chance of obtaining higher status work and a greater income. Entry into the paid workforce has an effect on marriage and the family, as the following section shows.

WOMEN AND THE FAMILY

The fact that educated Nigerian women gain high-paying jobs, which make them economically independent of their men, has influenced family patterns. Substantial changes have taken place in marriage patterns, family finance, family size, education of children, and property ownership. Some explanation would be useful here.

Marriage patterns have changed significantly as a result of women becoming educated. Although the average age for girls to marry was eighteen years in the 1950s, today the average age is twenty-four years. This is because many girls pursue higher education before marriage. Those who married before completing their education convince their husbands to allow them to return to formal education. Some institutions of higher learning even make provision for nursing mothers. Combining formal education with family life is a common feature among women in Nigeria today. The educated girl has a lot of say in the choice of life partner. In fulfilling marriage rites, her views and suggestions are seriously considered.

Most married women keep their jobs to ensure economic independence. They control their income while contributing to the family upkeep. In family matters, women do not remain passive. For instance, women's views on family size have begun to be recognized. Family planning/birth control is common among educated women. The more educated a woman, the smaller her family size is likely to be. In addition, women are contributing more than ever before to the financing of their children's education. Today mother's education is a stronger predictor of children's educational levels than is father's education.

The increasing educational levels of women have affected the stability of the family. Divorce is on the rise among educated women who have refused to put up with a number of abuses women have traditionally suffered in Nigeria.

While there has been considerable change for women in Nigeria, inequalities still persist, many of which are supported by the legal system. Although the principle of equal pay for equal work is in force, there is discrimination against women in employment and in the awarding of fringe benefits in public sector employment. These fringe benefits are considerable and include rent subsidies, leave transport grants, children's tax relief, and leave pay. Women still lack equal access to landownership and to inheritance. Many have argued that increased access to education will provide women with greater equality. However, a number of factors militate against women's education.

BARRIERS TO OBTAINING EDUCATIONAL EQUALITY

Despite the improvement in women's educational access since the 1950s, several factors still impede educational equality. As summarized by Alele-Williams, the major obstacles are availability of facilities for girls to be schooled, accessibility of facilities to girls, and the achievement level of girls.[10] There are presently more schools for boys than for girls, despite the nearly equal or greater proportion of girls in the total population. In several communities, boys' schools are normally established first; much later a girls' school may be built. In equipping the schools, there is discrimination in favor of boys' schools, especially in the provision of science laboratory equipment. Even in present Nigeria, the idea that women's education is not as important as that of men still holds, especially in educationally backward states.

That the facilities have been made available does not mean that education is now accessible to girls. Still, several factors—cultural/religious, economic, job opportunities/work experiences, marriage considerations, career information/misinformation—keep girls from school. These will be discussed briefly.

Women's access to schools depends on the extent to which culture and religious beliefs accord them a role outside the home. As was previously discussed, female seclusion, early marriage, inferior status, fear of "excessive" emancipation—all combine to militate against education.

In Nigeria, no school fees are charged, but all forms of levies are imposed in some states. These levies, together with textbook, school uniform, boarding, and other costs, are borne by parents. Where parents are unable to bear the cost of educating all their children, they are forced to choose which are to go to school and which are to be withdrawn. Usually, girls are withdrawn. Parents still believe that investing in a boy's education is an investment whose returns will remain with the family, whereas the girl will marry after her education and her husband and his family will reap the rewards of her schooling. Even at young ages, girls are more useful in the home than boys; for this reason, they are withdrawn whenever the family income is insufficient. The young girl of ten can take over family and domestic responsibilities and free her parents to pursue their economic ventures. Girls are also able to help parents farm or trade. Street trading, a common feature in Nigeria, is carried out primarily by young girls and women. In short, the high economic cost of education reduces girls' access to education, especially higher education.

Formal education, which in Nigeria starts at the age of six years and ends after four or more years of university education, is considered by some parents as being too long and wasteful of a woman's "productive" age. Under normal circumstances, a girl is about twenty-two years of age at the time of graduation. Because the circumstances are seldom normal, however, many females graduate at the age of twenty-five or twenty-six years. Before she finds a suitable husband, a woman university graduate will be nearly thirty years old, an age considered too old for childbearing. For fear of getting too old to bear children (children are highly treasured in Nigeria), many girls stop their education at some point to get married and bear their children at the "right time."[11] Today in Nigeria, even in those states where formal education is valued, girls have tended to get married after secondary education, especially when they experience difficulty gaining admission to higher education.

Another factor that inhibits girls from gaining educational parity with boys is low self-concept. Girls are socialized into believing themselves inferior to boys, and they have little faith that they can achieve well in school, especially in science and technology. Girls opt for secretarial studies, nursing, and the like and avoid computer sciences, engineering, and physics which they perceive as "male subjects."

The fear of not getting a job upon graduation also contributes to the girls' lower educational pattern. Understanding that employers prefer to hire men, girls tend to stop their education at lower levels where there is still less competition with men in the labor market.[12] Women tend to chose jobs that are heavily female—primary and secondary teaching, secretarial work, and nursing, where they know they can find employment. This limits them to a particular level and type of education.

The Nigerian school system does not have services that might counter girls' low educational and career aspirations. As a result, the home is the only source of guidance for students. When boys experience difficulty in school, the family usually offers support; but when girls have the same problems, families usually advise their daughters to drop out of school.

Although a number of barriers inhibit the attainment of educational equality, a number of factors have helped open women's access to schooling.

FACTORS FACILITATING WOMEN'S ACCESS TO EDUCATION IN CONTEMPORARY NIGERIA

Three factors have helped open women's access to formal education: changing social values and attitudes toward women; economic necessity; and government policies.

In Nigeria attitudes toward women have changed over the past thirty years. In large part these have been a result of worldwide trends and influences. Nigerians have been affected by the ascendancy of women to political power in other countries. Political figures like Golda Meir, Indira Ghandi, and Margaret Thatcher have shown that women can be competent, and in some cases, outstanding national leaders.

Also instrumental in changing attitudes toward women have been women's organizations which have advanced the status and rights of Nigerian women. Women in Nigeria (WIN) is one such association which has worked long to reduce inequalities in education, economy, commerce, and health. These associations have been successful in the northern states in promoting women's education. A number of professional women's associations have formed, particularly among female lawyers, engineers, and doctors. These organizations have agitated for changes in social norms and in attitudes toward women.

Economic considerations have also led to changes in women's educational patterns. Paradoxically, the brideprice, which in the past inhibited women's schooling, today serves to encourage it. Brideprice has recently come to be related to a woman's educational level: the more education a woman receives, the higher the brideprice. This has occurred because an educated woman earns more money than the less educated woman and thus can add to her husband's family income in the long run.

Government policies have also been responsible for increasing women's education. The Nigerian government has built a number of special schools for girls. It has also provided liberal scholarships to females who have managed to gain admission to university. In the 1950s, all the women attending the University of Ibadan were on full scholarship. The introduction of Universal Primary Education (UPE) in 1975, while directed at all children, did much to promote female education. After UPE was adopted, an astronomic increase in school enrollment occurred. The increase in female enrollment outstripped that of males. Despite the collapse of UPE in the 1980s because of economic recession, many parents have kept their daughters in school and have paid the school fees that have been imposed. By the 1980s, the principle of female education had become entrenched.

The 1985 Nairobi Conference celebrating the United Nations' International Decade for Women, with its well-publicized programs promoting women's education, has stimulated the Nigerian federal government's interest in providing greater educational opportunities for women. In 1986, for example, the federal government organized a national workshop to develop a Blueprint on Women's Education. The Blueprint identified several objectives:

1. To awaken the awareness of all citizens to the fact that equal opportunity is the right of all citizens, regardless of sex, age, locality, creed, or social status, and should therefore be made available to all.

2. To educate parents and the general public so as to bring about a change in attitude toward women's educational programs so developed.

3. To reorient the attitude of all females, regardless of age, toward education.

4. To awaken the consciousness of all women to the need to develop a positive self-image. [13]

To implement the Blueprint, the government established a Women's Education Unit in the federal Ministry of Education. In addition, it has funded similar units in each of the twenty-one states of the country. The government has launched a program entitled Educate Women for Development. Much of this program has been directed toward encouraging female education in the Muslim-dominated states of northern Nigerian where female enrollment lags substantially behind that of males.

The Women's Education Unit of the federal Ministry of Education has actively promoted its work through a number of seminars, lectures, and workshops. In December 1987, it sponsored a seminar on Gender Stereotyping in Science, Technology, and Mathematics. The Women's Education Units at the state level have also been active and have sponsored adult education programs.

The effects of these recent initiatives to encourage educational parity in Nigeria have not yet been fully evaluated. However, the fact that the government has taken the initiative in promoting female education bodes well for the future.

NOTES

1. G. Alele-Williams, "Science, Technology and Mathematics for All, Including Women and Girls in Africa," Keynote Address at the Commonwealth Workshop on Gender Stereotyping in STM (Accra, Ghana, 1987).

2. O. Nduka, *Western Education and the Nigerian Cultural Background* (Ibadan: Oxford University Press, 1965).

3. A. Babs Fafunwa, *History of Education in Nigeria* (London: George Allen and Unwin, 1974), p. 110.

4. O. Taiwo, *Agencies of Education* (Lagos: Macmillan Publishers, 1966).

5. D. G. Burns, "The Education of Women and Girls," *Memorandum on Educational Policy in Nigeria,* Chapter 11 (1947), pp. 30–35.

6. Alele-Williams, "Science, Technology and Mathematics for All."

7. Extract from "Digest of Statistics on Technical Education in Nigeria 1983–1984" (Kaduna: National Board of Technical Education, 1984).

8. S. O. Adeyegba and S. O. Olamousi, "Pattern of Enrollment and Achievement in WAEC Examinations in Science, Technology and Math 1980–85," Paper presented at the Commonwealth Regional Workshop on Gender Stereotyping in STM Education (Ghana, 1987).

9. E. A. C. Okeke, "An Evaluation of Efforts Made in Nigeria to Increase the Participation of Girls and Women in Science and Technology," Contributions to the Fourth GASAT Conference, Ann Arbor, Michigan, 1987.

10. G. Alele-Williams, "Blue Print on Women's Education in Nigeria," Keynote Address at the National Workshop on Women's Education in Nigeria (Lagos: Federal Government Printer, 1986), pp. 21–27.

11. J. Nevadomsky, "Motivations of Married Women in Higher Education in Nigerian Settings," in F. I. Omu et al., eds., *Proceedings of the National Conference on Integrated Rural Development and Women in Development,* Vol. 2 (Benin: University of Benin, 1980), pp. 840–854.

12. E. E. Amechi. "Constraints on Women's Labour Force Participation in Nigerian Society," in F. I. Omu et al., eds., *Proceedings of the National Conference on Integrated Rural Development and Women in Development,* Vol. 2. (Benin: University of Benin, 1980), pp. 671–691.

13. "A Blue Print on Women's Education in Nigeria," *Proceedings of the National Workshop on the Production of a Blue Print on Women's Education in Nigeria* (Lagos: Federal Government Printer, 1986).

4

SENEGAL

Diane Barthel

Senegal, part of the African Sahel, was the capital of former French West Africa. Signs of this colonial legacy are still perceptible within its educational system. A small elite of highly educated women are found working in education, government, social work, librarianship, and medicine, especially as nurses and midwives. Others are in pharmacy and law. These elite women are recognized for their sophistication and *savoir faire:* their ability to take advantage of all the benefits of modern society without losing the traditional supports provided by family, extended kin, and religious observance.

The mass of women, however, remains scarcely touched by educational efforts. Senegal is a primarily agricultural society with some 75 percent of its labor force engaged in agriculture and another 5 percent in fishing. In 1980, women constituted 38 percent of the overall labor force, although their participation in agriculture is estimated at 60 percent.[1]

The monoculture of peanuts dominates the economy, much to its detriment and that of any independent position for women. In many areas, peanut cropping occurs under the authority of the dominant male in an extended kin network, with women thereby having no control over their own production. In areas to the south, rice takes over as the major crop. Among one ethnic group, the Diola, the women are recognized as having some rights over their own produce. According to the traditional division of labor, the husbands prepared and maintained the fields and the women sowed and harvested the crops. As Paul Pelissier writes, "The Diola household is first of all a work association, at the heart of which the tasks of the man and the woman are complementary and solidary."[2]

A second rice-producing group, the Mandingues, are, by contrast, characterized by a highly conservative Islamic observance, with the status of the woman considerably depressed. "Nowhere else in Senegal are the respective positions of men and women more neatly drawn, the tasks attributed to each more categorically defined, the domination of men over women as brutally affirmed."[3]

To the far north, the Toucouleur are also conservative Muslims, and the Toucouleur woman has been seen by some as little more than a slave to her husband. "The general social condition of the Toucouleur woman, writes Y. Wane, "thus appears as congenital inferiority and as definitive imperfection. Naivete, even stupidity, but especially deceit and double dealing. . . . such are, according to the men, the principal specific traits of femininity."[4]

While the Toucouleur are strongly patrilineal, the Serer of the Sine-Saloum region are among the most matrilineal of groups. Serer women are traditionally accorded a certain amount of respect, although authority in most important decisions remains with the male. Serer custom follows given names with the mother's name, though this is changing. A Serer proverb states, "It was a maternal baton which traced the Sine." Along with participating in the collective production of meal and peanuts, Serer women increasingly cultivate and sell their own cash crops.[5]

Other ethnic groups in Senegal include the Fulani, the Niominka, the Lebu, and the Wolof, the largest group comprising approximately 30 percent of the population. Wolof women are not as subservient as the Toucouleur to the north, although they are still very much under the authority of the extended kin network and the local Muslim leaders. Wolof has emerged as the language of commerce in Senegal, and French is widely used in the coastal cities and among the educated population.

Senegal has been fortunate in having no major ethnic schisms on a scale found elsewhere throughout Africa. There is, however, a small independence movement among the Diola in the Casamance region. Its recent political history has included trade union and student rioting, and reports of attempted coups, but no major upheavals. Like most other former French West African colonies, excluding Guinea, Senegal voted to assume authority over its own affairs under a French federation in 1958. A brief federated union of Senegal and Mali in early 1960 was followed by full independence later the same year. The man who led Senegal to independence, Leopold Sedar Senghor, held the office of president until he retired in June 1981, when he was succeeded by his then prime minister, Abdou Diouf. The one-party system that brought Senegal to independence has gradually been opened to allow the legitimate operation of competing political parties. A woman's wing of the still dominant socialist party is meant to channel and serve the needs of women, although it has been criticized by some as serving primarily to further the political mobilization of the masses.

To understand the challenges facing Senegal in its efforts to expand education and to make it serve development purposes, we need first to examine the colonial legacy from its origins in the nineteenth century through to government formulations in the twentieth. Then we can observe Senegal's efforts at expansion in the decades following independence and consider to what extent it is serving the needs of Senegalese women and their promotion in a country where "women's liberation" is still more than slightly suspect.

TENTATIVE BEGINNINGS

French interest in Senegal revived only around 1815–1817, but already in 1821–1822 the first school for girls was being founded at St. Louis. Its early establishment was due to the interest of missionaries, who had already gained experience opening similar schools in the Maghreb and southeast Africa, and also to the support of the colony's administrators. These administrators, as it turned out, would prove more supportive of the missionaries' endeavors than would their counterparts at a later and equally critical stage in the mission schools' development.

During her visit to Senegal in 1822–1824, the Mother Superior (Mère Javouhey) of the Sisters of St. Joseph de Cluny obtained permission from Governor Jean Roger to establish schools for girls at the old city of St. Louis and on the island of Gorée, off the coast of Dakar. Roger approved of such schools, believing they could play a definite role in the conversion of the Goreens and St. Louisiens to both Christianity and European cultural norms. "The population of Goree is gentle and docile," he explained, "but it is entirely deprived of light and activity. The inhabitants' customs, in certain respects, have nothing of the Christian, nothing even of the European: marriage is unknown and polygamy is established by universal usage." He added, "We must hope that a school for girls will contribute to make better morals be adopted." Roger also sounded a note that was to be repeated a century later when he suggested that, "If the young *signares* leaving the school take up the resolution to speak French to their children, the experienced difficulties in teaching will disappear and instruction, starting from this more advanced point, will of necessity progress."[6]

Initially, however, the schools had difficulty attracting pupils, and the separate school for African black girls in St. Louis had to be merged with that for the *signares,* the daughters of Senegalese mothers and French fathers. The feeling among the populace was that French education was not appropriate for girls. The indigenous population also found little of practical value in the instruction provided by the Catholic Sisters. Up through 1848, their schools provided an "aristocratic" form of education intended to cultivate a certain sensibility among the girl students. The subjects taught included history, geography, and French grammar. In mathematics the Sisters were admittedly weak, and such practical subjects as sewing were not deemed appropriate to the school's purpose, which was "to move as well as instruct, to form at the same time the heart and the spirit, to elevate curiosity at the same time as the taste for the good."[7]

Change was soon to come, however, for the repercussions of 1848 in France were felt as far away as Senegal and in as unlikely a place as the Sisters' schools for girls. Their curriculum took on a definitely more plebeian slant: sewing and embroidery were introduced in 1852. Both French and Senegalese welcomed the change for it rendered service to the French by preparing seamstresses, while providing a source of revenue for the Senegalese. The number of pupils slowly began to rise. From their shaky first decades when the schools had approximately a dozen students each, the school at St. Louis registered an average of 150 students during the years 1852–1854, and Gorée registered an enrollment of 178 students in 1853. Most of the students in the schools were Catholics and mulatto, but for the first time there was a significant minority classified as African blacks, including a number of Muslims. The Senegalese, while remaining suspicious of the religious motives of the Sisters, appeared somewhat reassured when the education their daughters received began showing some relationship to the adult roles their daughters might play within the colonial order. Later enrollment figures, from 1878, indicate a total of 300 students at the St. Louis and Gorée schools.[8] Throughout the nineteenth century, such girls' education as there was rested totally in the hands of the Sisters.

Boys' education, on the other hand, was available both through the schools of the Catholic Fathers, the first of which was established in 1840, and also, importantly, through the elite School for the Sons of Chiefs established in 1853. Initiated by the great colonizer of Senegal, Louis Faidherbe, the school was originally called the School of Hostages. The name belies the purpose, for the school was designed to serve the dual functions of training an administrative elite and of assuring the loyalty of traditional authorities by caring for their sons. Sometimes, however, a suspicious chief would send a young slave in his son's place; the slave, of course, would then stand to fill a high position within the colonial order insofar as it was out of this school that the new Senegalese elite emerged. Needless to say, the administrators did not consider a similar elite training school for girls.

In 1904, the long-running tension in the French polity and society between church and state came to a head and was resolved in laicization, a rejection of clerical control over schools. Catholic schools in Senegal, which had been funded by the colonial administration, now found themselves without support and were forbidden to continue operation. The Sisters did manage to keep the schools going in a minimal fashion by transforming them into "workshops," with students learning such practical skills as ironing and sewing, but the academic effort was totally undermined.

The administrators had argued that Muslim families would be more eager to send their daughters to public schools than to those run by the Sisters. As one inspector of education wrote in 1906,

Confidence in our European female teachers, especially when they are married, has grown considerably among the Moslem Africans. After having held both the Sister and the lay teacher in the same distrust, they have become aware of the clear impartiality of our official education, which respects the doctrines of Islam and which in no way aims, for the moment at least, to emancipate the woman or to modify the fundamental bases of the Moslem family.[9]

This statement reveals an underlying tension among the three major forces determining social policy in Senegal: namely, the indigenous elite, the French administrators, and the Catholic missionaries. It was not simply the indigenous elite that viewed the missionaries with distrust: it was also many of the administrators, among whom there was a long tradition of anticlericalism. In Senegal, it was in their interest *not* to side with the missionaries in pressing for social reforms related to elevating the status of women, as defined by European cultural norms. The practice of polygamy, for example, was clearly viewed by the missionaries as an outrage: to the administrators, it was an indigenous custom to be tolerated in order to maintain the cooperation of the Muslim leaders in more serious, political matters. These included the supply of Senegalese soldiers to fight the French cause in World War I.

While some public primary schools for girls were founded in the early twentieth century, enrollments remained low, at between 200 and 500 pupils. Comparative enrollments at schools for boys climbed into the 2,500 to 5,000 range.[10] The Catholic schools did recover to some extent in the 1910s and 1920s but never made impressive gains, and girls' education remained stagnant for the first thirty years of the twentieth century.

COLONIAL FORMULATIONS

Compared to the miserable record of girls' education in the 1920s and early 1930s, as the 1930s progressed administrators expressed increased interest in the general question. A report by the Superior Council on Education (1931) reviewed the existing education for girls in all the colonies of French West Africa. It found that the proportion of females enrolled in primary school seldom rose above one-tenth of the total population and depended in large measure on how extensive mission schools were. The Council similarly noted that both public and private schools were concentrated in the major cities, with rural education for girls being nearly nonexistent.

The Council went on to list the obstacles facing female education. Chief among those obstacles was the force of Islam, followed by women's conservative role as the guardians of tradition, and the domestic work expected of even young girls. Although they themselves did not see it as an obstacle per se, the Council members conceded that the French had been in no hurry to establish schools for girls. Their main concerns up to this time, as the Council saw it, had been to pacify the indigenous opposition and to establish the basic infrastructure. "Under these conditions it was completely natural that education for girls, which has a character more social than utilitarian and which prepares for the future rather than corresponding to immediate and visible necessities, appeared as a problem of second importance about which one spoke in theoretical terms, but of which the realization was tabled."[11]

The typical girls' school which the Council proposed was to be a "school for the native household." The emphasis was on promoting European notions of hygiene and child care. A logical extension was the suggestion that the girls might also be trained in health care and teaching. The School for Midwives had already been operating to a limited degree since 1922; now the administration began to explore the possibility of establishing a girls' teacher training institute.

By 1935, the thinking on female education had become formalized into two levels. For the first level, the Council called for the development of primary schools in regional centers that would offer training in the household arts, hygiene, and child care. The second level would involve the selection and training of "indigenous female cadres" as midwives, nurses, and teachers. Their education was to be above all practical, "tied tightly to the double role that the native woman functionary will have to fill later, a social role and a domestic role."[12] It was suggested that a school be established in Dakar to train girls not yet old enough for the division of midwives at the medical school. Such a school could also take on the training of teaching assistants for broadening instruction in the household arts.

In 1937, the governor general of French West Africa, M. de Coppet, issued a circular to his lieutenant governors of the different colonies on "The Instruction of Native Girls." In underlining the need for female education, de Coppet summarized the arguments already made and included both the necessity of training suitable wives for the French-trained male elite and the socialization of the children in French norms and customs. "The education of the native woman permits the evolution of an indigenous elite in the equilibrium of the family, assures the evolution of the group and of the family, and does not limit to the individual the action of the education; it will consolidate in successive generations the new habits acquired by the education and will permanently install our action in the indigenous society."[13]

De Coppet criticized the few existing girls' schools for having followed too closely the curriculum taught to boys, questioning the use of "all this theoretical instruction." He preferred to make of the West African girl "an excellent housekeeper." On the primary level, girls would be taught only enough French to be able to communicate and enough arithmetic to make out a budget. Other than that and some "moral discussions," the curriculum would focus, as suggested above, on hygiene, child care, and household arts.

As for the second level, de Coppet proposed it be reserved for daughters of chiefs, notables, and functionaries. Girls with these family backgrounds would, presumably, make appropriate wives for the male elite being drawn from the same social level. Along with further refinement of their household skills, these girls would also be drilled in French, taught arithmetic, and instructed in drawing and singing: all in order that they might perform their roles as "the future spouses of chiefs, notables, and functionaries."[14]

An even more selective third level was envisioned that would involve the formation of a cadre of teachers. The curriculum again combined the theoretical with the practical.

The administrators' interest in preparing a small female elite was at least in part a response to demands being made by the Senegalese male elite, which was becoming increasingly active in the 1930s. As one M. Berthet, then director of Political and Administrative Affairs, wrote in a letter to the inspector general of education, "Certain native groups, more or less concerned with playing openly or not, their role in public affairs, have not failed to write (girls' education) into their program of action, thus responding to one of the principal aspirations justly manifested at the present, by the evolved elements of the local population."[15]

The year 1938 saw the culmination of these lines of discussion and planning in the formation of the girls' normal school at Rufisque outside of Dakar. It was to be a federal establishment, open to candidates throughout French West Africa who wished to prepare either for teaching or for the Section for Midwives in the Medical School. Students were to be recruited from those age thirteen to twenty who had already attended either public or private schools and who had obtained both the elementary school diploma and attended an advanced course for at least one year. Along with passing an examination that tested such diverse subjects as French composition, mathematics, drawing, and needlework, applicants were required to submit birth and health certificates, their school records, and a statement engaging them to enter into primary school teaching for at least ten years after the termination of their studies. Discussion following the proposal reinforced the idea that the primary function of the new normal school was to train homemakers. What is particularly interesting, then, is how the school's function became redefined by its directress and the girls who attended it.

Among the girls admitted in the first entering class (1938–1939), ten came from Dakar, another seven from the rest of Senegal, nine from Dahomey, eight from Togo, seven from Guinea, four from the Ivory Coast, and one from the Sudan. Twenty-eight were Catholic, eleven Muslim, and five Protestant. The largest number came from families of functionaries (twenty-four, eleven were from commercial families, seven were daughters of artisans employed by the public works, and one was the daughter of a navigator). A comparison of these figures to the administrator's statements reveals that none of the girls were daughters of chiefs or of other traditional authorities. This may be attributed to the great reluctance of traditional authorities to send their daughters to a school far away, as far as Rufisque was from Togo or the Sudan, where their daughters would learn such exotic subjects as embroidery and where they might be corrupted through a lack of adequate supervision.

By January, a group of more advanced students had been separated to form a second-year class. These eleven students all came from Dahomey and Togo (eight) and Senegal (three). In fact, the students from Togo and Dahomey tended to be superior to others, both in entrance scores and during their course of study. This superiority was attributed to the quality of missionary school preparation in their respective colonies.

Similar distributions in terms of colony, religious background, and father's occupation continued in following years. A large number of mulattoes attended (27 out of 115 students in 1943, for example), and, according to the directress, tended to be classed among the social elite of the school. Students were recruited from such schools as the Sister's School of Dakar, the Urban School of Binderville (Ivory Coast), the Higher Primary Course of Lomé (Togo), and the Mulatto Hall of the Sudan.[16]

In a school day that started at 6:00, the morning classes were dedicated to French, writing, arithmetic, and the basic sciences, while afternoons were usually devoted to hygiene, child care, sewing, cooking, and drawing. In the evening, following dinner, there might be dancing, games, or singing schedules.

Under the direction of Madame Le Goff, the school enjoyed a successful first decade. The only two major problems were, first, the repeated event of girls either arriving for the first time or returning from their vacations pregnant. This led to their expulsion and even to the suggestion that a more complete physical examination be required for admission.[17] The second, more serious, problem lay in the fact that many students were being tempted away from teaching by the comparative advantages to be found in becoming midwives. As early as 1939, Madame Le Goff asked for more pay for teachers, a plea she repeated in years following, arguing that parents were requesting to have their daughters transferred to the Section for Midwives as soon as they qualified. The advantages of being a midwife, in terms of both money *and* status, were well known to that proportion of the population that allowed its daughters to continue their studies.

The issue came to a head in 1945, when of the then graduating class of thirty-two, eight wanted to be midwives. These eight, wrote Madame Le Goff, represented the best of the class. The director of public instruction seconded her request that henceforth the normal school prepare only teachers, writing, "There is here a very serious threat to the development of female instruction."[18] Following an unsuccessful compromise that limited the number of midwife recruits to six, in 1947 the normal school finally began training girls only for teaching—and, of course, to be suitable wives for the male elite.

In 1945, the directorship changed hands to a Madame Weiss and again in 1946 to Mlle. Yvonne Paquet. In 1957 with the breakdown of the federation, the Girls' normal school moved to Thies and became restricted to Senegalese students.

While educating only a relatively small number of girls, the Normal School was significant. It enabled the selection and preparation of a female professional elite, while it served as a model for what female education could do and be in the colonies. From their school letters and later comments, it is evident that the students took seriously their role as models in the spread of female education. Their dedication, as well as that of their Madame Le Goff, who had their confidence and affection, has borne fruit. A considerable number of female normal school graduates are now to be found in commanding positions in education, government, and private business in Senegal as throughout former French West Africa. The school thus served for more than its founders originally

Table 4.1
School Attendance, by Sex, 1951, 1954, and 1958

	1951		1954		1958	
	Number	Percent	Number	Percent	Number	Percent
Males	34631	85	42316	75	69552	72
Female	6345	15	13880	25	26023	28
Total	40976	100	56196	100	95575	100

Source: Bureau Universitaire de la Statistique, unpublished document, 1965, p. 2.

planned: it prepared not only homemakers, but congressional representatives as well.

EDUCATIONAL EXPANSION

The 1950s were years of great expansion in education in Senegal. Many of the schools in the capital city were built during this period. Primary school attendance more than doubled from 1951 to 1958, with the level of attendance increasing from less than 5 percent to 25.5 percent of all children in Senegal.

As Table 4.1 indicates, along with the general increases, female enrollment increased from 15 percent in 1951 to 28 percent of all students enrolled in 1958. Looking at figures from 1954 in more detail, one sees evidence of other trends in education: first, the higher percentages of females in private as opposed to public schools and, second, the declining percentages of girls, compared to boys, in secondary as opposed to primary levels (Table 4.2).

Senegal achieved independence in 1960. The new government developed ambitious plans to expand education. While up to 1966 it was successful in opening new schools and expanding enrollment, the process slowed after 1966, owing largely to budgetary constraints. In 1981, Senegal dedicated approximately 23.5 percent of all government expenditures to education, compared to 32.8 percent for Nigeria and 39.8 percent for the Ivory Coast. Figured as a percentage of gross national product (GNP), Senegal's educational expenditures totaled 4.4 percent, compared to 2.5 percent in Nigeria and 5.9 percent in the Ivory Coast.[19]

The government's early hopes to achieve universal primary education have

Table 4.2
Education, by Sex, Level, and Sector, 1954

	Boys		Girls		Total	
	Number	Percent	Number	Percent	Number	Percent
Primary:						
Public	35,700	77	10,700	23	46,400	100
Private	5,400	59	3,800	41	9,200	100
Secondary:						
Public	2,726	75	902	25	3,628	100
Private	434	54	369	46	803	100

Source: Annuaire Statistique de l'AOF (Paris: Imprimerie Nationale, 1955),
        p. 73.

Table 4.3
Primary School Enrollment, 1975, 1980, and 1981

Year	Number of Pupils Enrolled	Number of Female Pupils Enrolled	
1975	311,913	131,315	(42.09%)
1980	419,748	166,913	(39.77%)
1981	452,679	179,594	(39.67%)

Source: United Nations, Statistical Yearbook, 1983-84 (New York: United
        Nations, 1986), p. 350.

had to be postponed. In 1985–1986, total enrollment at primary schools for children ages seven to twelve was 53.6 percent, with 80 percent enrolled in urban areas and only 30 percent in rural areas.[20] Comparative figures from 1975, 1980, and 1981 show that some progress has been made (Table 4.3).

The educational reforms of 1973 shortened primary school from six to five years, but these reforms have not gained universal acceptance. Part of the problem lies in the fact that much time is still spent in the teaching of French during these early school years. Other parts of the curriculum at both the primary and secondary school level have, however, undergone a ''Senegalization.'' Senegalese history has gained a place in a curriculum formerly dominated by French history and the colonial view of African history; African flora and flauna are now the subject of biology and botany classes.[21]

Based on examinations held at the end of primary school and secondary school entrance examinations, the student will either undertake a final year aimed at providing low-level vocational skills or will enter a secondary school program. Secondary-level education is divided into an initial four-year program, after which students receive their *brêvet d'études du premier cycle de l'enseignement secondaire* (BEPC), or lower school-leaving certificate. They then may enter either a three-year *lycée* or a *lycée technique*, followed by a two-year baccalaureate or baccalaureate technician program.[22]

Overall secondary enrollment for 1984 was only 13 percent of all school age children, or 17 percent of secondary school age boys and 8 percent of girls.[23] Figures for 1980–1981 show a secondary academic total enrollment of 83,431, of which 28,133, or 34 percent, were female. These figures are up from the 1970–1971 enrollment of 53,298, of which 14,942, or 28 percent, were female. For secondary technical and vocational schooling, the enrollment figures for 1980–1981 were 95,604, of which 31,307, or 33 percent, were female, up from 59,401, of which 16,925, or 28 percent were female in 1970–1971.[24] In both primary and secondary levels, the curriculum has increasingly emphasized science and technical courses that will serve development needs.

Thus, traces of the colonial legacy in education are still evident. There remains evident a higher percentage of boys than girls enrolled and higher percentages of girls in private as compared to public schools (comparing girls' rates to total school rates). Regional differences compound the problem, with education more readily accessible in the cities and along the coast than in the rural interior.

UNIVERSITY EDUCATION

Reflecting its former centrality as administrative center for French West Africa, as early as 1916 Dakar became home to an institute for the training of auxiliary doctors and pharmacists. In 1922 the Section for Midwives was opened. The Institute of Higher Studies, founded in 1950 and incorporating the School of Medicine, became the University of Dakar in 1957. Originally designed to serve all of French West Africa, the University of Dakar has experienced a gradual decrease in the proportion of non-Senegalese students. This is due both to Senegalization of staff and curriculum, and to the subsequent relative decline of the French population. Contributing also is competition from other former French colonies, notably the Ivory Coast, which have opened their own university centers. In 1959–1960 a total of 67 percent of University of Dakar students were French; the 1974–1975 figures reveal 70 percent Senegalese, with another 20 percent from other West African societies, only 5 percent French, and 5 percent classified as "other."[25]

The University of Dakar is, nonetheless, a cosmopolitan university, host both to numerous foreign students and staff (50 percent of staff are non-Senegalese) and to a number of important institutes. Besides the four faculties (Letters and Humanities, Law and Economic Sciences, Medicine and Pharmacy, and Sciences), the university is home to the *Higher Normal School Supérieure,* the *School of Librarians and Archivists Documentalists,* the *University Institute of Technology,* the *Center for the Study of the Information Sciences and Technology,* the *Interstate School of Veterinary Sciences and Medicine,* the *Institute of Applied Tropical Medicine,* and the *Course in French Language and Civilization.*[26]

To encourage study of practical subjects at an advanced level, the Polytechnic School at Thies, a smaller city slightly inland from Dakar, was opened in 1973. In 1979, a second university, Gaston Berger University, was founded in the old coastal city of St. Louis. It is designed as a center for the human sciences, with Dakar assuming more responsibility for scientific and technical education. In 1987, the University of Dakar was renamed Cheikh Anta Diop University after the Senegalese politician and writer.

What proportion of university students are female? Table 4.4 provides enrollment figures for the first ten years, by sex but not by nationality.

For the years in which data by sex are available, we see that, while women never constituted much more than 10 percent of the university population, their increasing attendance demonstrates an improvement over their representation in the early 1960s. More recent data from 1980–1981 show 13,560 students enrolled, of which 2,507, or 18 percent, were women. When we subtract the foreign student population (3,065 total; 752 female), we see that the relative percentages of female Senegalese students enrolled were approximately the same, namely, 17 percent.[27]

In what fields do women concentrate? In looking at statistics regarding women's fields of specialization, one should note that all kinds of diplomas are included, ranging from certificates to yearly diplomas in the schools of medicine or law, or diplomas at the end of a course of study, including the *license,* the *maîtrise,* and the *doctorate.* One can still, however, gain a sense of area of specialization by sex (see Table 4.5).

Women are concentrated largely in letters, the social sciences, and librarianship. Those in the School of Medicine and Pharmacy are heavily clustered in pharmacy. Although there are relatively few female physicians in Senegal, pharmacy is generally considered a rather glamorous profession for women with the required diploma and enough financial support to run their own establishment. Law is increasingly popular among women who desire further education but are attracted neither to teaching (the logical outcome of a diploma in letters) nor to medicine or science.

Once again, more recent data do not suggest radical alteration in these early patterns. Drawing on 1978 figures, Asa S. Knowles finds that nearly 50 percent of the female Senegalese students enrolled in the University of Dakar were concentrated in the Faculty of Letters and Humanities. Contrasted to these 374 women, only 35 were enrolled in the Institute of Technology.[28]

Table 4.4
Students at the University of Dakar, by Sex, 1958–1968

	Total
1958–59	276
1959	395
1960–61	434

	Males		Females		Total	
	Number	Percent	Number	Percent	Number	Percent
1961–62	566	95	27	5	593	100
1961–63	699	96	30	4	729	100
1963–64	702	94	44	6	746	100
1964–65	820	93	60	7	880	100
1965–66	849	92	73	8	922	100
1966–67	1062	93	82	7	1144	100
1967–68	1350	90	145	10	1495	100

Source: Fatou Sow, "Les diplomes senegalais," unpublished manuscript, 1972, p. 2.

ADULT EDUCATION AND LITERACY PROGRAMS

Senegal has always been recognized for its elite education as provided by the above institutions of higher learning. Now it is also being recognized for its efforts in adult education and literacy. With illiteracy estimated at 71.9 percent, the figure higher still for women (80.9 percent), Senegal has embarked on a multifaceted program. Several different agencies are involved, including government ministries, religious organizations, and philanthropic groups. Literacy programs are run by the Secretariat for Human Development in the Ministry of National Education. These include remedial programs aimed at bringing low-level civil servants up to full language competency.

In rural areas, there is considerable recognition of the importance of the "peanut peasants" to the economy and of the necessity of providing the education

Table 4.5
Total Number of Diplomas Received, by Sex

	Male		Female		Total	
	Number	Percent	Number	Percent	Number	Percent
Law / Economics	274	94	18	6	292	100
Letters / Social Sciences	196	86	33	14	229	100
Sciences	71	95	4	5	75	100
Medicine / Pharmacy	65	89	8	11	73	100
Librarian	10	56	8	44	18	100
Technology	23	100	0	0	23	100
Total	639		71		710	

Source: Fatou Sow, "Les diplomes senegalais," unpublished manuscript, 1972, p. 7.

that will allow them to participate in the development process. Programs aimed at serving this rural population emanate from *Centres d'animation rurale* and *Centres d'expansions rurale*. These include an extension service provided by SATEC/SODEVA. (SATEC is a French semipublic consulting firm, and SODEVA, a Senegalese private enterprise.) An experimental radio network, called Dissou and established by Unesco, also serves to further adult education in the rural areas.[29]

MARRIAGE AND FAMILY STATUS

The variety of family forms in Senegal is remarkable. Under its 1971 Family Code, Senegal recognizes both monogamous and polygamous unions. At mar-

Table 4.6
Attitude toward Polygamy, by Religion and Marital Status

Opinion toward polygamy	Catholic union	Moslem monogamous union	Moslem polygamous union	Moslem single	Total
Pro	0	6	2	5	13
Ambivalent	2	4	2	5	13
Con	15	39	7	5	66
Total	17	49	11	15	92

Source: Diane Barthel, "The Impact of Development on Women's Status in Senegal" (Ph.D. diss., Harvard University, 1976), p. 160.

riage, men can record their intentions not to enter into other marriages, that is, not to become polygamous. Repudiation is not tolerated, but divorce is. In most cases, the divorced woman has far more to lose than the man. The preferred traditional marriage is one between cross cousins: in some polygamous unions this is the form of the first marriage, with the husband later adding a second, younger wife of his own choosing. Catholics view polygamy as either a custom of the land (which, of course, does not apply to them) or as an abomination. Muslims point to the usefulness of polygamy in the rural areas, where many wives mean many arms to share the hard work of subsistence farming, cash cropping, and childrearing. Polygamy loses much of its *raison d'être* in the move to the city. Co-wives and their children must coexist in small quarters, unless they are part of the elite and each is supplied with a separate villa in one of the fashionable quarters. The functions of polygamy in the city are to provide the man with higher status and to insure that as many women as possible are "on the right path." This leaves a population of younger, poorer men, who find it hard to marry.

In a 1976 study of professional women in Dakar, when asked "What do you think of polygamy?" the women divided as shown in Table 4.6, according to religion and marital status.

The table offers some support, though hardly conclusive, for the often proposed suggestion that single women would be more likely to temper their comments on polygamy compared to those already in Muslim monogamous marriages, who might hope to remain the only wife. Indeed, a number of highly educated, single

Muslim women in their mid-to late twenties stated, as regards polygamy, "One must not try to be too intellectual about that."

Among those women in the sample who favored polygamy, the most common reason was that it was a way of assuring that all women would have a husband. As one lawyer said, "It's a question of choice. When you love a man, in Europe you become his mistress—here you have the possibility of becoming his legitimate wife."

The theme sounded most often, however, was that polygamy was bad for both women and children. Respondents spoke of what they saw as men's inability to follow the Muslim prescription to share their affection and favors equally among wives. Quarreling among children and wives, even wives resorting to magic to gain preference for their children and cause ill to the children of co-wives, were commonly mentioned as problems endemic in polygamous unions. One woman summed up many of the answers provided by others when she said, "Well, I'm against it, largely because of the education of the children, but really on all levels. For all women, even women in the bush, it's something that you undergo, and you submit to, but which certainly doesn't make you happy. I see *female intellectuals* who accept it in order not to break up their homes. Women submit, but don't accept it in general. If it happened to me I would not divorce because of the children, but it would be as if he were dead."[30]

Besides variety established by differences between Catholics and Muslims, and between monogamous and polygamous households, women's family status also depends on the closeness and breadth of the extended kin network. The multigenerational family is not uncommon, even in Dakar, nor does a relative from the bush stay for an unspecified period. In a few cases, a woman who has many children may allow one of them to be raised by a female relative who is childless. Weddings, baptisms, and funerals are great occasions for kin gathering, and considerable expense is involved, for both hosts and guests. Many Muslim couples hold their finances separately, allowing each member to respond to separate kin demands as well as personal needs. Increasing numbers, however, are reported as following the Western habit of pooling resources to underline the solidity of the couple. This may represent a daring step backward as regards the woman's autonomy and control over her own finances.

While there is much concern in Senegalese society about women being "on the right path," large numbers of women are not. Prostitutes are officially tolerated and periodically inspected by health officials, yet subject to abuse by clients and pimps. Uneducated girls who flee rural areas for the cities, especially Dakar, often fall into prostitution. Other opportunities for them are severely limited. The urban markets are controlled by local ethnic groups, with stalls passed down within market families. Factory work is limited and often seasonal. The market for servants is crowded with other rural migrants and women from the Dakar slums and outlying villages.

Given this ready availability of servants, elite women find it easier to combine career with family than do their Western counterparts. Many women in this class have three servants: one for the cooking, one for cleaning, and one to look after the children. Pay for servants is low—$25 to $50 a month in 1975—and hours are long. Many professional women have four to six children, which suggests that motherhood is still the most certain route to esteem for a woman of any class.

Both in evaluating their own lives and in anticipating what they would want for the children, well-educated women in Diane Barthel's 1976 study converged on the description of what they termed *une bonne situation*. This results when a woman succeeds in first gaining a solid education, with several degrees, then professional work, and then a happy marriage blessed with children. These are the elements of *une bonne situation,* and this is the preferred order.

The importance of education and profession was stressed precisely because of polygamy and divorce, because, in today's world, "you never know." As one woman said regarding her hopes for her daughter, "That she continue her studies and have as many diplomas as possible to take care of her own needs herself. That she then won't have to depend on anybody—not her mother, not her father, not her husband, not anybody!"[31]

This is a remarkable statement, having been made in a society where, of all family forms, the most suspect is the woman without a family: the single woman living alone. It suggests some of the contradictions facing women in a developing society: a society that both wants to raise the status of women through education and job training and wonders whether it can afford to do it. A 1965 report from the Ministry of Education put the case as follows:

Certain people believe that the equality of the sexes cannot exclude equality in the right to work, and that this principle is more important than any other consideration. However, how can we help but fear that the bitter chase after the few jobs available will bring a competition which will sow discord and even more widespread social problems? Does not equality in work mean rather the right to an equal salary for equal work instead of the right for women to have the same training facilities in order to penetrate into jobs usually given to men? If you add that, often, women's salaries today are only partially given over to the support of their family, should one not wish that, in the broader social interest, the few salaried positions be reserved for that element of the human couple which is usually charged with the support of the family, that is to say, the husband?[32]

Those who argue for separate, and frequently, unequal, education for women, might do well to recall a warning sounded earlier by the first inspector general for education in French West Africa. In 1921, Georges Hardy expressed his fears that, by being concerned solely with boys' education, the French administration was creating two separate groups. In one group were the African men, increasingly allied with the French in their acculturating efforts. In the other were the women, deprived of the benefits of French culture and antagonistic to colonial purposes. Hardy concluded that the African woman so left in ignorance could become a dangerous, rebellious force: a "Lysistrata under the coconut trees."[33]

French colonialism officially ended in Senegal almost thirty years ago, but the potential for social dislocation remains. That all people must be involved in development and that education is central to the process are facts of which the Senegalese are well aware. How to proceed in accomplishing these goals is a more difficult matter altogether.

NOTES

1. Robin Morgan, ed., *Sisterhood Is Global* (Garden City, N.Y.: Doubleday, 1984), p. 589.

2. Paul Pelissier, *Les Paysans du Sénégal* (Saint Yrieux, Haute Vienne: Imprimerie Fabregue, 1966), p. 685.

3. Ibid., p. 553.

4. Y. Wane, *Les toucouleurs du fouta-toro: stratification sociale et structure familiale* (Dakar: IFAN, 1969), p. 179.

5. Marie-Angelique Savane, "Senegal: Elegance Amid the Phallocracy," in Robin Morgan, ed., *Sisterhood Is Global,* p. 595.

6. Georges Hardy, *L'Enseignement au Sénégal 1817–1854* (Paris: Emile Larose, 1920), p. 111.

7. Ibid., p. 119.

8. M. Recoing, "L'Instruction publique et privé au Senegal, 1878," Series O, Archives nationales, Dakar, p. 8.

9. "L'Enseignement en afrique occidentale francaise," 1906, Series O, Archives nationales, Dakar.

10. These figures come from a series of government reports in Series O, Archives nationales, Dakar.

11. Superior Council on Education, "Report on the Education of Girls in the AOF," 1931, in Series G moderne, Archives nationales, Dakar.

12. Superior Council on Education, "The Instruction of Native Girls," 1935, in Series G moderne, Archives nationales, Dakar.

13. Governor General Jules de Coppet, "The Instruction of Native Girls," 1937, in Series G moderne, Archives nationales, Dakar.

14. Ibid.

15. Letter from M. S. Berthet, Director of Political and Administrative Affairs, to the Inspector General of Education for the AOF, February 7, 1938, in Series G moderne, Archives nationales, Dakar.

16. Diane Barthel, "The Impact of Development on Women's Status in Senegal" (Ph.D. diss., Harvard University, 1976), p. 110–111.

17. Ibid., p. 112.

18. Ibid., p. 113.

19. United Nations, *Statistical Yearbook,* p. 401–403.

20. *The European Yearbook 1987,* Vol. 2 (London: Europa Publications Ltd., 1987), p. 2371.

21. See Gail P. Kelly, "Interwar Schools and the Development of African History in French West Africa," *History in Africa* 10 (1983), pp. 163–185.

22. Asa S. Knowles, ed., *International Encyclopedia of Higher Education,* Vol. 8 (San Francisco: Jossey-Bass Publishers, 1977), p. 3813.

23. *The European Yearbook 1987*, p. 2371.

24. United Nations, *Statistical Yearbook*, p. 363.

25. Knowles, ed., *International Encyclopedia of Higher Education*, Vol. 8, p. 3812.

26. Torsten Husen and T. Neville Postlethwaite, eds., *The International Encyclopedia of Education*, Vol. 8 (Oxford: Pergamon Press, 1985), p. 4528.

27. Ibid., p. 4528.

28. Knowles, *International Encyclopedia of Higher Education*, p. 3817.

29. J. Cameron, R. Cowan, et al., eds., *International Handbook of Education Systems*, Vol. 2 (New York: John Wiley & Sons, 1983), p. 312.

30. Barthel, ''The Impact of Development,'' p. 166.

31. Ibid., p. 50.

32. Ibid., p. 61–62.

33. Hardy, *L'enseignement au Sénégal*, p. 111.

5
ZAIRE

Barbara A. Yates
and Mary Ellen Seaver-Taylor

Zaire, the former Belgian Congo, is a clear-cut example of the impact of a church-dominated, imported, Western education system on the schooling, socialization, and subsequent economic opportunities of Third World women.[1] When Henry Morton Stanley completed his historic exploration of the vast Congo basin in 1877, there were no known Westerners in the interior and no Western-style schools in what would become one of the dozen largest countries in the world. Zaire was described by early missionary educators as a *tabula rasa,* a blank slate on which they could transfer their own set of values and ideas of proper schooling without the annoyance of competing Western notions, such as the "immoral" behavior models of Western traders or secular schools or extensive, established traditional African kingdoms. Missionary educators found this an exciting opportunity to shape and mold the minds of a then estimated population of 14 million Africans.

Christian missionaries, especially conservative Catholics, came to dominate education in Zaire from the founding of the first Western-style schools in the late 1870s to the present. At independence in 1960, 97 percent of schoolchildren attended Catholic-run (77 percent) or Protestant-run (20 percent) primary, "post-primary" and secondary schools. One of the two fledgling universities and half of the six postsecondary institutions were managed by Catholics. Catholic domination of the school system continued after political independence. Indeed, other than Burundi (also a former Belgian-administered United Nations Trust Territory) and Lesotho, Zaire has one of the highest percentages of private (i.e., church-related) schools in Africa.[2]

Historically, the presence of Christian missionaries has affected educational development throughout Africa. However, in Zaire, because of various factors the Roman Catholic Church, both in the colonial era and in the present independence period, has attempted, with considerable success, not only to dominate spiritual and educational matters, but also, in varying degrees, to assume temporal power. Secular governments in Zaire, both colonial and independent, have given over the educational system to the church in order to discourage the seeking of further authority in other spheres of life. The church's powerful position in education has not been altered either through the ascendancy to power of non-Catholic party Belgian colonial administrations or independent Zairian governments.

Political independence brought neither change in the basic ideological views of Catholicism on the role of women nor domination of the educational system by the church. Although girls' enrollments in school increased at all levels and Zairian leaders speak and write of "women's emancipation," by and large, the nature of women's schooling has not changed. The colonial legacy survives.

This chapter attempts to describe how the school system was and still is used to create and perpetuate gender differences in educational opportunity and consequently in socioeconomic and political participation in modern life; (2) to analyze the reasons behind the hold of the Roman Catholic Church and the colonial legacy on contemporary Zairian education; and (3) to discuss possible future trends in the provision of education for women and the potential social outcomes of that education.

EDUCATIONAL OPPORTUNITIES FOR WOMEN

Educational opportunities for girls and women depend on two separate but related factors: (1) the availability of various educational programs and (2) the degree to which these programs are utilized. That is, educational programs may or may not be provided for females. Conversely, various curricular options may be open to women, but available places are not filled. It is important to make this distinction in order to analyze the varied reasons for gender differences in education, that is, one cannot participate in something that does not exist. But taking advantage of available formal and nonformal education programs is only part of how schools create and perpetuate gender differences. Once admitted to schools, boys and girls were and are offered quite different learning experiences in Zairian schools.

The Provision of Schools

Based on the Education Acts promulgated in 1890 and 1892, and a Concordat with the Vatican in 1906, the educational system for Zairians took shape during the first three decades of colonialism. Females were not mentioned in these early documents, which were designed to provide state subsidies to Catholic missions for the preparatory training of males as soldiers, artisans, and agriculturists for the colonial administration or as catechists for the missions. Beginning in 1897, owing to Catholic lethargy in training subalterns, the government also established a handful of secular state vocational schools in order to train males as noncommissioned servicemen, artisans, clerks, nurses, and plantation workers/foremen. This move was the beginning of "parallelism" in education, which replicated the practice in Belgium whereby government-subsidized parochial and state-run secular schools coexisted and competed for pupils.[3]

Although the formal decrees of the late nineteenth and early twentieth centuries did not mention females, at Catholic instigation separate church-run and state-subsidized Catholic parochial schools for girls were established beginning in the 1890s. These single-sex schools taught domestic skills and Christian virtues in a local language. Girls' schools did not provide the French-language literacy and vocational programs offered boys. Catholic missionaries saw these schools as "nurseries of virtuous young girls," hardworking and well-brought-up, "where our boys can find faithful and devoted wives."[4] In addition, in the late 1890s the White Fathers opened a seminary to train the first Zairian priests and in 1912 began the training of Zairian nuns. Protestant missions, which were not part of the government-subsidized system until 1948, also concentrated on the preparation of male teacher-evangelists.

The gap between opportunities for boys and girls increased in the years between world wars I and II as opportunities widened for young men and those for women remained relatively stagnant. Girls were now mentioned specifically in educational decrees rather than omitted. An Education Code of 1929, codifying the educational practices of the past four decades, recognized three levels of schooling: two-year village primary schools (Grades 1 and 2), three-year upper primary schools (Grades 3,4,5), and three-year "postprimary" vocational schools (Grades 6,7,8).[5] These postprimary programs provided job-oriented schools for boys: (1) clerk schools (écoles des candidats-commis, subsequently called écoles moyennes), (2) normal schools (later called écoles de moniteurs) and (3) vocational schools (écoles professionnelles).[6] In contrast, "postprimary" vocational schools for girls remained limited by the 1929 Code to (1) elementary school teaching (écoles de monitrices) and (2) home economics–agricultural programs (écoles ménagères-agricoles). The normal schools prepared elementary teachers for mission primary schools and later aides to European social workers in the new foyers sociaux (government-subsidized Catholic adult education centers for married women). The home economics–agricultural "vocational" schools led only to the hearth, and not to employment in commercial agriculture or to marketable domestic science skills. Males served as domestics in European households and as workers and foremen in modern export agriculture.

The stipulation in the 1929 Education Code that after Grade 2 boys and girls were to be separated in class allowed educators easily to manipulate learning experiences by gender, especially teacher expectations, role models, curricula, and the language of instruction. Since most girls' schools were taught by women, role models were European or Zairian nuns or African women trained in Catholic teacher-training programs. Consequently, teacher behavior expectations reinforced notions of Christian patriarchy. Zairian women were expected to have the character traits of industriousness, docility, obedience, gentleness, and passivity and to exhibit these traits both to Europeans (men and women) and to African males.[7] Moreover, single-sex schools also enabled colonial educators to restrict girls to instruction in a local language, rather than French, the key to participation in the modern sector.

Single-sex schools also facilitated gender-differentiated curricula. Girls' schools were dominated by the ubiquitous presence of home economics and the almost complete absence of agricultural education (as distinct from manual labor in school gardens). Beginning with Grade 3, when segregation by gender was required by law in government-subsidized schools, time devoted to the three R's was reduced in girls' schools in order to add more character education and needlework, sewing, and child care. For girls, "agriculture" focused on practical exercises in vegetable gardening and medicinal plants and in the care of small barnyard animals, whereas the schools for boys emphasized technical training in animal husbandry, soils, irrigation, horticulture, and agricultural machinery.[8] Indeed, most Catholic primary education for girls prior to World War II could best be described as resocialization rather than as instruction in literacy.

Following shifts in Vatican policy in the 1920s toward more Africanization of the religious establishment, Catholic missions in the Congo expanded their nongovernment-subsidized seminaries and convent schools to train more Zairian priests, brothers, and nuns. In addition, work in hospitals as midwives and nurses' aides now became acceptable for a few young women. These new "postprimary" schools of nursing, however, were well below the academic level of the more prestigious *assistants médicaux* schools, also opened in the interwar years, to train male medical assistants. Nor were girls admitted to the new *assistants agricoles* schools. Indeed, Belgian commentators conceded that these postprimary programs for girls were not really secondary education, but mainly filled the time between primary school and marriage age (usually fourteen to sixteen years of age). This further schooling would keep girls out of sexually oriented "mischief" until they could find suitable husbands.[9]

New educational programs were initiated after World War II in two phases: the 1948 Education Code[10] and the 1954 educational reforms.[11] Indeed, the 1948 reorganization widened the gender gap in educational opportunities. Based on Catholic policy to create a secular male "elite" as well as priests, the 1948 Code provided for the establishment of the first full six-year academic secondary schools for Zairian males, using French as the language of instruction. In 1954, the Catholic-run Lovanium University opened in Kinshasa with a solely male Congolese student contingent. The 1948 Education Code, however, embodied no new aims for girls' education; they still remained the preparation of "good wives and mothers." The medium of instruction in all girls' schools remained a vernacular.

Primary education was further differentiated by gender. Beginning with Grade 3, primary schools for boys were now to be of two types: a three-year "ordinary" program and a four-year "select" program leading to the new six-year general academic secondary schools. Girls' upper primary schools were to be only of the "ordinary" type. The 1948 Education Code also continued to stipulate that some academic courses for girls be replaced in the timetable by sewing and housecleaning under the rubric *travaux féminins*.

Although no new aims were set forth for the education of girls in the 1948 Code, the reorganized educational system nonetheless embodied a commitment to improve the schooling of girls as much as was "possible and opportune." The major "change" was to differentiate further programs in home economics, teaching, and nursing. This reorganization meant a new three-year secondary (as distinct from postprimary) home economics program (*écoles moyennes ménagères*) for daughters of *évolués* (e.g., government clerks, medical assistants, teachers) who would hopefully marry the new secular male elite. The aim was "to create a class of young girls capable of making a good appearance [*de faire bonne figure*] in the world of native *évolués*, as much from the standpoint of upbringing (e.g., *savoir-vivre*, care of the home) as from that of instruction." To prepare this new feminine elite a transitional *classe de 6ème préparatoire* made up for the lack of girls' "select" primary programs and thereby rounded off their sixth primary year and qualified them to enter these new secondary schools of home economics.

New two-year postprimary programs in elementary school teaching and in hospital work were also created by the 1948 Code for girls (and boys) who completed the "ordinary" primary cycle. Girls who were at least sixteen years of age might now enroll in new two-year nurses' aides (*écoles d'aides-infirmières*) or midwife aide (*écoles d'aides-accoucheuses*) schools. Two new types of schools at the lower level of the educational ladder (*écoles ménagères peripri-maires* and *écoles ménagères du 2è degré*) were created to draw into the missionary orbit girls who had not attended primary school at the usual age. Many of these girls were directly from the "bush" and illiterate. Moreover, the postprimary *écoles ménagères-agricoles* of the 1929 Code, which had prepared the female "elite" of the interwar years, dropped the agricultural label and became what they were—postprimary schools of domestic science (*écoles ménagères postprimaires*) catering to rural girls who had completed the "ordinary" five-year primary program and were of normal school age. As before, such schooling kept them "properly" occupied until marriage.

In the early 1950s, vocational postprimary and secondary schools (*écoles d'auxilliaries* and *écoles professionnelles*) were opened to prepare girls for jobs in commerce and industry. The few schools created, however, specialized in *metiers féminins* (e.g., clothing and textiles).[12]

The election in 1954 of a Liberal-Socialist, generally anti-Catholic, coalition government in Belgium to replace the Catholic party brought some changes for education in the Congo. The new Liberal minister of colonies established the first secular primary and full academic secondary schools for Congolese—on a coeducational basis—and inaugurated a secular university at Elisabethville with an all-male African student body, but theoretically open to both men and women (European women did attend).

The expansion of "parallelism" to general as well as vocational education increased competition between church and state to attract pupils. Consequently, "select" upper primary sections were now provided for girls as preparation for academic secondary education, and sections for girls finally were added to Catholic six-year programs of general academic secondary education and to the senior academic technical high schools. The sections were for teacher training or nursing. The original "postprimary" midwife schools were replaced by a higher standard three-year upper secondary school for maternity nurses (*écoles d'accoucheuses*) requiring at least four years of general academic secondary education for admission.

Thus, it was only beginning in 1954 that girls could receive an education as preparation for university study in which French was both a subject and the medium of instruction. But the essence of the educational system remained the same for women—an emphasis on Christian morals for all and on home economics, nursing, and teaching for upper-class, mainly urban, women, and homecrafts, but little agricultural training, for rural women.

After independence in 1960, priority was given to the reform of secondary education. School enrollments were expanded, more state secular schools were established, the curriculum was to be "Africanized," and more technical options were offered. Religious education was made voluntary, not compulsory. French became the language of instruction in theory, if not in practice. The nonelitist, terminal "postprimary" programs, which led nowhere, were phased out so that most secondary education became preparatory to some form of tertiary education. But single-sex schools continued to characterize the system. Therefore, women continued to be concentrated in the technical fields of education, home economics, and social work.

Although statements were made about changing curricula after independence, apparently little was changed. A Swedish study published in 1981 reported that "although many disciplines had been added to the old curriculum together with the emphasis on the inclusion of local elements and local experiences in some subjects, still all the teachers were following the curriculum and syllabi of the 1950s." Many teachers never received the new syllabi, nor were the new teaching materials and texts "available in the majority of the schools."[13]

Foyers sociaux continue to be the major form of nonformal education for women. The *foyers* today consist of two main educational activities: (1) nursery and kindergarten schools and (2) "Circles of Youth" for illiterate girls between the ages of ten and eighteen. The Circles of Youth are meant to morally inspire young women as they are taught a smattering of French and "useful skills," such as weaving, sewing, knitting, cooking, and table manners.[14] With the

exception of French, much the same programs as before independence continue
to be taught.

Women's Educational Participation

In 1920, fewer than 10,000 girls were receiving any sort of formal education,
a participation rate of less than 1 percent of girls of school age. During the
interwar years, most of the expansion in enrollment for girls (as well as for boys)
took place in village primary schools (Grades 1 and 2). Despite legislative
provision for the postprimary education of girls, few opportunities actually were
provided. On the eve of World War II, no more than 20,000 girls attended
primary school, and fewer than 2,000 were in postprimary schools, whereas
over 50 percent of the boys of school age reportedly attended formal classes.
Catholic missions had only twenty-four postprimary schools for girls in all the
Congo; nine *écoles de monitrices,* twelve *écoles ménagères-agricoles,* and three
écoles médicales as well as several dozen convent schools for training nuns
scattered over an area the size of the United States east of the Mississippi. In
addition, there were several dozen Protestant postprimary home economics and
teacher-training schools. The few programs for nurses' aides, conducted by the
colonial Medical Service and the missions, probably enrolled no more than 100
young women.[15]

In the post-World War II decade, enrollment rates in schools continued to be
sharply differentiated by gender. Unesco data indicate that in the early 1960s
girls made up approximately one-third of the primary and secondary enrollment
in most African countries.[16] At independence in the Congo, however, fewer than
9 percent of Congolese schoolaged girls (aged five to nineteen) were attending
formal schools, compared with over 70 percent of boys. Of the 1.6 million
primary pupils in 1959–1960 (the last school year before independence), only
about 20 percent were female, and of the 29,000 students in secondary schools
under 4 percent (fewer than 1,000) were girls.[17] Probably no more than 10,000
girls attended any postprimary school representing in total about 1.5 percent of
girls of secondary school age (fifteen to nineteen years). Over half of this postprimary and secondary enrollment was in teacher-training programs. There were
only seven industrial vocational schools (*metiers féminins*) with an enrollment
of 430 girls and sixteen hospital schools with about 350 young women. Only
200 girls were taking general academic secondary programs, mainly in the urban
centers of Leopoldville (Kinshasa) and Elisabethville (Lubumbashi). Data are
sparse, but on the basis of the number of Congolese nuns in 1960 it can be
estimated that there were probably almost as many girls enrolled in convents
preparing for religious vocations as in all these government-subsidized postprimary and secondary programs. There were, as yet, no female high school graduates and no Zairian women attending the two universities or the half-dozen
two-year postsecondary institutes. The most advanced female student (the daugh-

ter of the then mayor of the capital, Kinshasa) was in her final year in an academic high school.[18]

Although political independence brought little change in the nature of educational opportunities, many more girls were encouraged to take advantage of them. A new emphasis on "freedom of education," the parental right to choose between church and state schools, led to the expansion of "parallelism" and thereby an increase in the number of coeducational, secular, academic secondary schools, principally in urban areas. There was also an expansion of Protestant schools and the state funding of Kibanguist schools.[19] The first Zairian women entered the university system in the 1960s.

After a half decade of political chaos and economic collapse, General Joseph Mobutu (later known as Mobutu Sese Seku) took over the government in November 1965 in a military coup d'état. "When Mobutu came to power his intention was to continue to reinforce the power of the State while curtailing that of the Church, but paradoxically, his rule led to the strengthening of the power of the latter." Although the number of state schools and their enrollments increased, Catholic and Protestant schools "expanded more rapidly after 1965 than during colonialism."[20] Consequently, female participation in the educational system and enrollment rates increased significantly after 1960, but in the same kinds of school programs as during the colonial era.

During the late 1960s and the 1970s and 1980s, a time of political disturbance, the figures available on school enrollment resemble the makings of a patchwork quilt, particularly enrollment figures disaggregated by gender. As one author has noted, access to education "ebbs and flows with the political-economic tide of the times."[21] In 1985, 100 percent of Zairian schoolaged boys and 75 percent of Zairian girls purportedly attended primary school. In addition, 33 percent of boys and 13 percent of girls attended a secondary school.[22]

The increase in secondary and university enrollment after independence, as in the interwar years, when primary enrollment soared, has probably again widened the gender gap. Zairian males replaced many Belgians and other expatriates in the civil service and in the professions. Since independence, more women have been enrolled in school, especially in academic secondary education and now in the universities. That is, frequently things expand but do not change. However, women continue to participate mainly in those areas in the curricula and in the economy associated with the home, religion, and related social services, not with agriculture or with the professions of medicine, law, agronomy, or engineering.

THE SOCIAL OUTCOMES OF EDUCATION

The nature of women's education—the availability of educational opportunities and the process of schooling—substantially reinforced the policy intent and attitudes of the colonial establishment toward the limitation of economic and political participation of women in the modern sector of colonial society. Eighty years of Belgian colonial education in a Catholic-dominated system reinforced the social relations of a conservative Christian patriarchy. The access to schools and the educational attainment of girls were affected greatly by the legal requirement for differentiation into single-sex schools and by the restriction on the use of the French language for instruction or as a subject for study. Most importantly, the objectives of Belgian colonial education were firmly fixed; men belonged in the fields, the shop, the pulpit, and the marketplace, whereas women belonged in the home as good Christian wives and mothers. Limited numbers of men were schooled to enter the army, the colonial administration, trading firms, the railway, and the missionary enterprise; women who ventured outside the home were limited to the elementary school, the hospital, and the convent.[23]

In the Westernized towns, the differences between the economic and social opportunities of Zairian men and women were found to be more acute than those in other African urban areas. Typical of the minority of women, those in urban areas, was a description in the 1950s of Stanleyville (Kisangani), a major city. "Most women had little or no involvement in either wage-earning or trading and were largely confined to work in and around their homes." Moreover, Congolese women in Stanleyville also had little contact with Western education or culture, as compared with Congolese men. "Only two or three" Congolese women could conduct even the "most ordinary conversation" in French, fewer than 5 percent worked for wages, only about 15 percent had ever attended school compared with 50 percent of the men, and only about 35 percent of girls under sixteen years of age in the city were then attending school, as compared with nearly 80 percent of the boys. Few Congolese women ever visited the center of the "European town." In addition, the *évolués'* wives made virtually no attempt to emulate the dress and public behavior of the European women.[24]

After independence, female labor participation in the modern sector continued to be low and in the same fields. For example, in a study of Lubumbashi (Elisabethville) in 1977, almost two decades after independence, out of a total adult female population of 66,000, it is estimated that only 3.2 percent were considered "working" and only 73 of these working women were in a professional job. These professional women were engaged primarily as teachers, nurses, directors of health clinics or home economics schools, and university assistants in these fields (the university assistantship being the only "new" occupation).[25] Reportedly, these professional women were discriminated against both socially and economically.

Throughout the history of modern schooling in Zaire, there has been a significant congruence between the actual socioeconomic roles and tasks of women and the nature of their formal and nonformal educational opportunities. The most relentless and economically detrimental assault by the colonial establishment and later independent governments was on gender roles in agriculture and consequently agricultural education. Most Zairian women (80 percent) reside in rural areas and occupy themselves with subsistence agriculture.[26] Childbearing, child-caring, and home management frequently occupy a minority of their daily schedule or are combined with agricultural tasks. However, colonial education would take women out of the fields or at best ignore their role in food production. Women were thought to be overworked, whereas men were said to be lazy. Mission school teachers reported that boys refused to work in school gardens, saying it was women's work. Yet the colonial establishment provided little agricultural education for girls. Few efforts have been made to provide agricultural education for girls since political independence.[27] The emphasis at the secondary and university level in agricultural education is still directed overwhelmingly at boys and young men.

Before independence, the Belgian Congo was self-sufficient in food production, but in recent years, Zaire, like many agriculturally based Third World countries, has become a food importer—60 percent in 1985.[28] This unfortunate economic situation necessitates the reallocation of scarce foreign exchange earnings from the purchase of capital goods for development to the purchase of food for immediate domestic consumption. Although deterioration in roads and pricing policies are major obstacles to profitable agricultural production and marketing, the lack of formal and nonformal agricultural education (e.g., extension services) of women has also played an important role in fostering this food deficit in Zaire, as elsewhere in the Third World.

The attempted transfer of alien values in business and industry, like those in agriculture, presented paradoxes regarding women's expected roles and the education provided women. Certain occupations were found to be more suitable for women than for men, such as "domestic service and shorthand typists." However, few Congolese women were capable of holding these jobs "best suited to their abilities" because of their lack of vocational training. Moral concerns, however, were more paramount to colonial industrialists. The Congolese woman's place was in the home, either that of her father or that of her husband. Working in factories meant that a woman's "moral standards" were "bound to suffer." It was believed that men and women should be separated in factories; it was preferable that supervisors be European women. Although the shop foreman could be male, he should not have African women working directly under his supervision.[29] Given these patriarchal attitudes toward women's education and women's work, there was little motivation for the church to supply more formal vocational education for women.

As for political activity during the colonial period, the guide to Congolese elites, published just after independence, listed no Zairian women.[30] In 1966, Madame Marcel Lihau was appointed the first minister of state, the minister of social affairs. At the age of twenty-seven, she was one of the first Zairian women to earn a university degree. However, she reportedly spent much of her time listening to complaints by matrons of the *foyers sociaux*, who operated nursery schools and kindergartens on a volunteer basis. Much later, in 1975, President Mobutu appointed three female ministers, among them the commissioner for the environment, a zoologist, and the commissioner of culture and the arts, a jurist and magistrate.[31]

Other social outcomes of women's schooling, such as its effect on fertility, maternal behavior, or choice of spouse, have received little systematic analysis. Apparently, the acquisition of schooling, at least for some women, was a double-edged sword. In the study of Stanleyville referred to earlier, it was found that the few women who had received schooling were in great demand as wives for educated male *évolués*, but that their supply was so scant that the "overwhelming majority" of men, even those with secondary education, married illiterate women. Even the few women with schooling were in a double bind. *Evolué* males complained that such women were not sufficiently educated, while uneducated men usually regarded women with some education "as less trustworthy than others."[32]

FACTORS AFFECTING WOMEN'S PARTICIPATION IN EDUCATION AND SOCIETY

Various supply and demand factors account for the inadequate provision of schools for girls, the low participation rates of Zairian females in education, and subsequently the modern sector, and gender differences in the process of schooling. Colonialists blamed the African; Africans blamed colonialism. Both views are too simplistic. There was and continues to be much more of an overt as well as a subtle interaction between Westerner and Zairian and among Zairians, both before and after political independence, concerning the education of girls in relation to the roles of women.

Colonialism and Christian Patriarchy

Missionaries and colonial officials controlled the supply of education. They claimed that Zairians made little demand for the education of girls; Congolese women were reluctant to attend or to participate in the emerging colonial society. Therefore, the provision of school places was low. Typical of Belgian attitudes was a statement in the 1948 Education Code which noted that, although government would have preferred that the education of boys and girls proceed at the same pace, education for girls lagged because of (1) the "social organization" of native communities, (2) the attitude of "atavistic servitude" which burdened the Congolese female, (3) the generally lower "intellectual receptivity" of girls, and (4) the "prejudices" and "opposition" of Congolese families to the education of girls. Consequently, "we cannot think of developing the instruction of girls at the same rate nor on a plan as widespread nor according to a curriculum as complete as that for boys."[33]

True, many Zairian families did object to girls' attendance at colonial schools. This reluctance centered principally around missionary attempts to disrupt local marriage customs and to alter the division of labor in agriculture. True also, the educational opportunities available to women were and are affected by economic constraints on attendance. Schoolaged girls are needed for childcaring and to assist their mothers in agricultural work. Others are kept home from school because of family inability to provide for school uniforms, texts, or lunch fees. Cultural factors represent other constraints: lack of encouragement, early marriage, criticism from ignorant parents, and health factors, such as illness and undernourishment.[34]

Much more pertinent to opportunities for women, however, were the colonial establishment's excessively conservative patriarchal attitudes regarding the purpose of girls' education and the subsequent social roles of women. Although church and state frequently fought over educational priorities for males, both agents of Western colonialism viewed women almost exclusively in the roles of Christian wives and mothers. The foundation of a Christian nation was based on the establishment of the monogamous Christian family.

Those customs that flouted establishment of the Christian family—polygamy, fetishism, and premarital sexual relations—were especially abhorred by Christian churchmen. Missionaries viewed the taking of a pagan wife by male converts as a major cause of spiritual and moral backsliding; the unschooled country girl led males back to paganism, whereas the unsupervised, but more sophisticated, town girls led males into debauchery. Thus, central to the goal of Christian patriarchy was the desire to undermine polygamy and to establish instead the monogamous Christian family and to have Christian values and behaviors permeate the home. Consequently, the aim of education for girls was centered on implanting Christian morality, an awareness of "proper" family relationships between the sexes, and a favorable disposition toward children learning their prayers and catechism.[35]

The roles of catechist and evangelist or of soldier, clerk, artisan, and agriculturalist were not thought suitable for women by either missionary or colonial administrator either in the home countries of the colonizer or in colonial society. Accordingly, apart from the "sacramental" duties of wifehood, African girls needed to prepare for few new roles through attendance at schools. Indeed, some Catholic educators regarded reading and writing as dangerous for girls. A Jesuit missionary's comment from the early twentieth century is illustrative: "To learn to read and write is usual for all our boys. But the majority of our female savages have none of it and it is reported even that certain ones, who have learned to read, neglect the care of their homes."[36]

Although the purpose of the education of males would shift after World War II from concentration on the preparation of priests and pastors to new attention to secular elites, the primary objective of girls' education at all levels would remain unaltered—the training of Christian wives and mothers. The election of a non-Catholic coalition government in Belgium (1954–1958) and the appointment of a colonial minister from the Liberal party did not equalize opportunities for schooling between boys and girls, either in Belgium or in the Congo. Even the joint Liberal-Socialist Education Commission, which visited the Congo in 1954, criticized education for girls, not so much because of sparse academic opportunities as because it did not teach home economics efficiently.[37] A provincial director of education, serving under the coalition government, maintained even in 1957 that the "atavism of servitude" imposed on the Congolese female by her own culture could best be overcome by educating her "to occupy in a dignified manner her place in the true [i.e., Christian] home."[38]

The colonial administration was by and large content with the church's monopoly of education. The church could provide at less cost the necessary dedicated teaching force and the needed organizational supervision of an educational system. Moreover, the church shared with the administration common attitudes toward the need for corporal punishment and authoritarian control of colonial subjects.

Mobutuism and the Church

Political independence has not effected much change either in Catholic views on the proper roles of women, and consequently women's education, or in the church's control of the educational system. One of the primary goals of the Mobutu regime has been to decrease the power of the church in secular affairs. In April 1967, President Mobutu founded the *Mouvement populaire de La Révolution* (MPR), which replaced all existing political parties. Its ideology, Mobutuism, is based on three concepts: radicalization, revolution, and *authenticité*. The first two concepts have never been explained fully. The third, *authenticité*, involves a turning away from Western ideas toward traditional cultural values, a sort of mental decolonization, as a basis for national identity and as a political effort to break the power of the Catholic Church. Through the "secular theology" of *authenticité*, the MPR prescribes various aspects of social conduct.

In 1972, when all Zairians were requested to adopt names derived from their ancestors, the church objected to this de-Christianizing and a new period of crisis began in the ongoing church-state conflict.[39] For example, the government banned religious radio and television programs and publications as well as Catholic youth group activities. Charging that Catholic priests never ceased interfering in politics, President Mobutu later threatened to close down Catholic churches if the priests continued to use them to make political comments on Zaire. Later, the Papal Nuncio was dismissed as dean of the Diplomatic Corps, and the only Zairian cardinal was banished for four months to the Vatican, primarily because he publicly proclaimed that the mental decolonization or *authenticité* campaign was merely an attempt to divert attention away from the nation's economic problems.

In 1973, the Zairian National University (UNAZA) was created, combining the already existing three universities—Lovanium University in Kinshasa (Catholic), Kisangani University (Protestant), and the secular State University at Lubumbashi. In 1974, all primary and secondary schools were nationalized. The teaching of religion was forbidden and replaced by civics and morals based on Mobutuism and the philosophy of *authenticité*. This nationalization move, however, was presumptive and mainly on paper. The state did not have the personnel, financial resources, or administrative experience to operate the vast parochial school system. In 1976, after failure to break the hegemony of the church, Mobutu adopted a policy of "dialogue rather than confrontation" with the church.[40] In 1977, schools were denationalized and returned to their original owners. A compromise agreement in 1977 provided that the Ministry of National Education would be the highest educational authority and coordinate educational programs but would not interfere in daily management of church schools. Religion was again a subject in the curriculum together with civics based on Mobutuism.

Despite President Mobutu's destruction of the outward symbols of Catholic temporal power (e.g., dismissal of the papal nuncio as dean of the Diplomatic Corps, temporary expulsion of the only Zairian cardinal, curtailment of Catholic meetings and retreats), the hold of Rome on the secular fate of Zairian schoolgirls and women continues. First, Catholic goals for female education have not changed appreciably. Second, as in the colonial period, the secular state is willing to trade off control of the school system for Catholic withdrawal from overt political meddling. Third, the government has no money to pay the civil servants it hired to administer the schools. Fourth, parochial schools are said to be successful because the teaching personnel and administrators possess a sense of obligation not to be found among lay teachers, which gives them more motivation to overcome difficulties. Finally, parents have continued to send their children to Catholic schools. In sum, the churches were clearly more efficient at dispensing education. Indeed, it has been suggested that the "demise—albeit temporary— of the nation's religious educational networks did not result in any basic educational changes. The system was taken over at the summit, not reformed at the base."[41]

Social Class and the Failure of Mental Decolonization

On the demand side, social class has been the major factor in expanding educational opportunities for women, especially those at the upper end of the educational ladder. Initially, Catholic missionaries concentrated on refugee children, ransomed domestic slaves, and alleged "orphans." By the beginning of the twentieth century, however, Western observers noted that many former refugees, now the schooled male "elite" (e.g., artisans, noncommissioned officers, clerks, catechists) were increasingly establishing their families in urbanized areas. During the interwar years, the offspring of these Christianized families were sent to the local mission school, usually Catholic. Thus, the source of female pupils, especially those few in the higher grades, slowly shifted from refugees and orphans to daughters of the emerging urban, Westernized male elite. As colonial Zaire became more urbanized, this new African male elite would pressure the colonial establishment, especially after World War II, to expand educational opportunities for their daughters and thereby to challenge the availability, if not the nature, of female "elite" education. For example, Catholic educators reported that it was only in 1952, after being partly empty for years, that girls' postprimary schools were finally filled. The better postprimary and secondary schools for girls in towns began to have waiting lists.[42] *Evolué* families were reported to be dissatisfied with the amount and quality of education available for girls. In 1952, the council of the African Quarter in Leopoldville (*Conseil de la Cité Indigène*) had unanimously asked that Congolese girls be given the same educational opportunities as boys. There was little response from the colonial educational establishment. Consequently, in the early 1950s, several hundred daughters from Zairian *evolué* families attended school across the Congo River in Brazzaville, the capital of French Equatorial Africa, where it was reported they would at least learn French.[43]

After independence, social class continued to be a principal factor in the expansion of opportunities for the education of women. Much of the impetus for expanding school access for women came from elite men "who discovered after independence that most Congolese women were ignorant when moving in Western business, diplomatic and government circles and that only a few women were socially acceptable."[44] Thus, the right to "equal education" became a central theme in concerns regarding the emancipation of women.

But while each prime minister and each minister of national education from independence onward has included among national goals "the promotion of the Zairian woman," little action has been taken to operationalize these statements. Indeed, such statements were only a minor part of the rhetoric accompanying the introduction of Mobutuism. Mental decolonization and cultural *authenticité*, however, do not seem to have greatly changed the views of Zairian elite men regarding the appropriate place for professional women in the modern sector and therefore the *nature* of their education.

Although the independent government has taken stringent steps to reduce ethnic imbalance in the civil service and professions through ethnic quotas for entry into the universities, for university assistantships, and for study abroad,[45] little attention has been given to gender as an element of equal opportunity. Rather, colonial patterns persist in the education of women. For example, at independence there were no Zairian physicians, male or female. Through scholarships offered by Western nations, several hundred Zairian practicing male medical assistants (as well as younger men) were sent to Europe for medical training. Consequently, by the early 1970s, there were almost 300 Zairian physicians—all male. Despite the fact that, in order to graduate, Zairian female maternity nurses were required to deliver twenty-five babies alone, no maternity nurses were included in the contingent sent abroad for training as physicians.

LINKS BETWEEN PAST, PRESENT, AND FUTURE

Present-day Zairian women do not seem to have succeeded in escaping from colonial influences, which have also been adopted and sanctioned by their own men. After more than 100 years of experience with Western-style schooling and a Western-oriented modern political and economic arena, women continue to lag far behind men in access to schooling and in participation in the modern labor force. Even in subsistence agriculture, where women predominate as food producers, their skill levels have changed little, even after almost forty years of political independence.

The colonial legacy has also produced conflicts between modern and traditional values for Zairian women regarding work, marriage, motherhood, and the extended family. As a result, professional women engage in self-development through the use of sacred or descriptive folk society values rather than secular or achievement-oriented, urban-society values. As Terri Gould showed, urban marriage does not offer a woman the same security as marriage did in the village because women lose the security of the communal group and the strong bonds among women therein.[46] It also shows that, despite the emulated role of motherhood, urban working women try to maintain professions, be good mothers, and live as wives of individual men who do not ordinarily take responsibility for day-to-day childrearing.

Future trends concerning women's education in Zaire are difficult to predict because of the paucity of research on certain aspects of the education system and its relationship to various social outcomes. For example, little, if any, research has been done on the relationship of changes in women's education to changes in their participation in the labor force and polity or changes in their domestic lives now or in the past. Few data are yet available about the effect of educational and occupational stratification by gender on the self-concept and motivation of young Zairian women.

Some generalizations, however, can be made with regard to the future of women's education in Zaire. Unfortunately, gender differentiation in schooling during the colonial epoch continues to affect the lives of women in contemporary Zaire. First, the gap between male and female participation in education and the modern economy may widen as stringent budgets require cutbacks in educational investment and government employment. "Last hired and first fired" could well be applied not only to minority workers but also to the admission of girls, particularly to secondary schools and universities in Zaire. As the rate of expansion of places in these institutions declines, providing aspirations hold constant, the competition for them will become more intense. The apparent percentage gains in enrollment ratios made by women since independence could level out or decline. Such reductions in opportunities for women could probably be justified on the "colonial" basis that they belong in the home and therefore investment in their further schooling in a period of stringent budgets is of low priority.

Second, 100 years of gender stereotyping of the curriculum (e.g., home economics for girls and artisan training for boys) and of occupations (e.g., trades for men and elementary school teaching for women) have culturally retarded efforts to broaden gender roles. Whatever the existing Congolese traditions about gender roles, Belgian colonial practices reinforced the legitimacy of gender as an appropriate basis for differential treatment. Gender-segregated schooling and the related gender-segregated structure of the labor force made overtly clear to Zairians that there was something profoundly different in what males and females could and should learn and do. Research in Western societies indicates that women continue to congregate in "female" occupations because they receive more social approval and fewer negative social sanctions. Only with the political pressure of the recent feminist movement and subsequent shifts in public opinion have women in the West officially been accorded broader educational and occupational opportunities (e.g., access to U.S. military academies). The risk Zairian women must take to advance economically and politically in new fields means they must compete in an educational system that has not welcomed their participation. The Zairian woman must also risk isolating herself socially from the very support systems that validate her accepted role in society—family and church. The Zairian woman who struggles as a rational being for upward mobility in her own right has no alternative support system to leave a suppressive subculture.

Third, colonial education superimposed on traditional African views Western concepts of appropriate roles for men and women. Particularly unfortunate was the assault on women in agriculture. Although female pupils were required to garden, they were not trained for modern farming. This worldwide "colonial" blunder especially handicaps contemporary schemes of rural development in many Third World countries. Heretofore, development planners and researchers have devoted disproportionate resources and attention to the rural male. "This oversight can be attributed most readily to a tendency among some project planners and authorities to see African women in Western terms—i.e., essentially as domestic workers whose primary responsibility should be in the home and not in the fields."[47] Agriculture remains a basic "industry" in Zaire as in most developing countries. Most food production is still a female responsibility. The continued stereotyping of agricultural education as a male domain raises serious questions for the improvement of agricultural productivity in Zaire in the future.

Fourth, as the experience of racial and ethnic minorities illustrates, generally it is difficult to redistribute opportunity once some groups obtain an initial lead. Even if quotas for women were established—for example, in medical programs at Zairian universities—it would be decades before there could be appreciable representation of women in the medical profession. Such difficulties of "catch up" apply to most occupations dominated by one group.

During eighty years of Belgian colonial rule in Central Africa, schools were used to socialize men and women to European norms of conservative Christian patriarchy. Christian patriarchy was firmly planted by colonial administrators and missionaries, but paradoxically, only now are developers beginning to recognize the economic—and human—costs. As Judith Van Allen has noted: "African women have paid dearly for carrying the white man's burden."[48]

Today Zairian women carry an additional burden. "Mental decolonization" has been a failure for women's concerns. In terms of the stated goals of Zairian officials to emancipate women and to improve their opportunities to contribute to Zairian development, little change has occurred. Psychologically, colonialism is an absentee patron of the mind—and has a certain ideological base. Zaire is an outstanding example of an educational system that was imported from abroad and has been able to withstand internal revolution and major political change. Validated from without by a respected and powerful international organization, the Vatican, the system has survived internal political chaos. Wherever the Roman Catholic Church predominates, rarely is an environment created that is conducive for large numbers of women as a group to experience upward mobility via the educational system. The Roman Catholic Church is a double-edged sword. With one hand it gives the stability of a centuries-old organizational framework, a tradition of learning, and a dedication to the upbringing and socialization of children. On the other hand, that very tradition binds the church and those who accept or follow its philosophy to an excessively gender-segregated society, imposed from without.

The Zairian man continues to allow his vision to be clouded by this ideology of the past. Whatever the local traditions, Belgian colonialism introduced the Western-type school and the modern economic sector and gave preeminence to conservative Western concepts about gender roles—even in agriculture, where Zairian women had clearly defined managerial responsibilities. European educators sponsored a deliberate pattern of gender-differentiated roles whose norms were embodied in the life of schools. As would be expected, strongly emphasized patriarchal traditions led to stereotyped linkages between gender differences in access to education, on the one hand, and involvement in the modern sector, on the other. Until Zairians can take back their own family traditions or create new ways of life, all Zairians, male as well as female, will continue to bear the white man's burden.

NOTES

1. Belgium also administered the neighboring United Nations Trust Territories of Rwanda and Burundi, which achieved independence separately in the early 1960s. Their school systems before independence were regulated along the same lines as the Belgian Congo.

2. World Bank, *Education Sector Paper*, Annex 16, 1980, as cited in Vinayagum Chinapah and Holger Daun, *Swedish Missions and Education in the Republic of Zaire* (Stockholm: Institute of International Education, University of Stockholm, Report No. 53, 1981), p. 52.

3. Barbara A. Yates, "Church, State and Education in Belgian Africa: Implications for Third World Women," in Gail P. Kelly and Carolyn M. Elliott, eds., *Women's Education in the Third World: Comparative Perspectives* (Albany: State University of New York Press, 1982). Belgian Africa also had one of the highest Third World educational participation rates for males and one of the lowest rates for females.

4. *Missions d'Afrique des Pères blancs*, December 1898, p. 360.

5. Congo belge, *Organisation de l'Enseignement Libre au Congo belge et au Ruanda-*

Burundi, avec le Concours des Sociétés de Missions Nationales (Bruxelles: Dison-Ver-viers, 1929).

6. The clerk schools prepared young men to be office workers, customs agents, tax collector aides, or railway conductors. The normal schools prepared primary teachers for mission schools. The vocational schools provided four options for boys: (1) woodworking (carpenter, cabinetmaker, joiner), (2) general mechanics (blacksmith, locksmith, found-ryman), (3) metalworking (plumber, metalworker), and (4) agriculture.

7. Barbara A. Yates, "White Views of Black Minds: Schooling in King Leopold's Congo," *History of Education Quarterly* 20, No. 2 (Spring 1960).

8. Though unsubsidized, most Protestant schools also followed these government-approved curricula. See *Report of the First Education Conference,* 2nd ed., December 18–23, 1931 (Kimpese, Belgian Congo, 1934), mimeographed; and *Report of Second Education Conference 25 July–22 August, 1933* (Kimpese, Belgian Congo: 1934), mim-eographed.

9. Oswald Liesenborghs, "L'instruction publique des indigènes du Congo belge," *Congo* 21, No. 3 (March 1940): 263.

10. Congo belge, Service de l'Enseignement, *Organisation de l'Enseignement Libre Subsidié pour indigènes avec le concours des sociétés de missions chrétiennes. Dispo-sitions Générales* (Brussels, 1948).

11. Congo belge, Ministère des Colonies, *La Réforme l'Enseignement au Congo belge* (Mission Pédagogique Coulon-Deheyn-Renson) (Brussels, 1954) (hereafter Coulon Re-port).

12. M. Moffarts, "Enseignement secondaire," *Problèmes d'Afrique Centrale,* No. 36 (2ème trimestre 1957): 120.

13. Chinapah and Daun, *Swedish Missions and Education,* p. 62.

14. James C. Ching, "Public Education Trends in the Democratic Republic of the Congo: 1960–1967," *Comparative Education Review* 12 (October 1968): 336–337.

15. E. P. Goetschalckx, *Situation des Ecoles Postprimaires pour autochtones 1952–1953* (Leopoldville: Bureau de l'Education Catholique, 1953), pp. 6–73.

16. See figures quoted in David R. Evans, "Image and Reality: Career Goals of Educated Ugandan Women," *Canadian Journal of African Studies,* 6, No. 2 (1972): 213 N. 1.

17. M. Crawford Young, William M. Rideout, Jr., and David N. Wilson, *Educational Survey in the Democratic Republic of the Congo* (Washington, D.C.: American Council on Education, 1969), p. 13.

18. Yates, "Church, State and Education in Belgian Africa."

19. Kimbanguism was a local messianic religious movement founded in the Lower Congo in the early 1920s by a former Protestant pupil, Simon Kimbangu, who claimed to be a Christian prophet, a black Jesus. Kimbanguism is an amalgamation of Christianity and local-tradition religious beliefs. Members accept monogamy and ban the wearing of fetishes. There are about 3 million professed Kimbanguists. The religion was recognized by the government after independence, and its schools were subsidized on the same basis as Catholicism and Protestantism.

20. Chinapah and Daun, *Swedish Missions and Education,* p. 23. See also pp. 53–56.

21. Ching, "Public Education Trends," p. 325. For example, secondary school en-rollment rose from 35,000 students in 1961 to 101,800 students by 1966 and 218,400 by 1970 (see Chinapah and Daun, *Swedish Missions and Education,* pp. 53–56). In 1968, it is reported that just under half of primary school pupils were female, a significant rise.

Although the absolute number of girls in secondary programs increased, apparently their proportion of enrollment declined to 2.7 percent. (See Terri F. Gould, "The Educated Woman in a Developing Country, Professional Women in Lubumbashi, Zaire" (Ph.D. diss., Union Graduate School, 1976), pp. 21–22. In 1970, however, only 37 percent of the 3.1 million pupils enrolled in primary schools were reportedly female, a decline over the past two years. Of the 248,318 pupils enrolled in secondary schools (38,615 in general secondary programs, 5,041 in vocational and 9,694 in teacher training) reportedly 21 percent now were female, an amazing increase in two years. At the tertiary level, 350 or 3 percent of the total 10,447 university students were female. Another 12 percent (280 women out of a total of 2,261 students) were enrolled in nonuniversity postsecondary teacher-training programs, and 45 females (about 2 percent) of the total 2,537 students were enrolled in other nonuniversity post secondary institutes. See Unesco, *Unesco Statistical Yearbook* (Belgium: Unesco, 1986), pp. 146–147, 168–169, and 288–289).

22. Jane Martin, ed., *Global Studies, Africa* (Guilford, Conn.: Duskin Publishing Group, 1985), p. 107.

23. For example, by 1960, males could enter several score occupations which required postprimary, secondary, or higher education. In religion alone there were 600 Congolese priests, 500 Protestant pastors, and 400 Congolese brothers. All 136 of the prestigious *assistants médicaux* were male as were the agricultural (250) and veterinary (15) assistants. There is no evidence that any of the more than 11,000 Africans in the administrative services were female nor were many, if any, of the thousands of skilled and semiskilled artisans employed in industry, commerce, and transportation. Zairian women were employed mainly as mission elementary school teachers (several thousand) and as Catholic sisters (745). There were only 15 Congolese maternity nurses and 485 assistant midwives. For documentation, see Yates, "Church, State and Education in Belgian Africa."

24. Valdo Pons, *Stanleyville: An African Urban Community Under Belgian Administration* (London: Oxford University Press, 1969), pp. 214–215.

25. In 1974–1975, fifteen years after independence, there were no female doctors, lawyers, or engineers in Lubumbashi. See Gould, "The Educated Woman in a Developed Country" p. 238.

26. Ester Boserup, *Women's Role in Economic Development* (New York: St. Martin's Press, 1970), p. 60. Boserup indicates that 60 percent of subsistence farmwork in the Congo was performed by females. Swedish missionaries reported in the late nineteenth century that women exclusively cultivated the ground and produced food in the Lower Congo. See Sigbert Axelson, *Culture Confrontation in the Lower Congo* (Falkoping, Sweden: Gummessons, 1970). More recent studies of rural labor in the Kivu region found that women provided two to three times as much food by weight as men. This work included soil preparation, planting, weeding, transport of produce to home and/or market, as well as the selling of produce. Although young boys might look after grazing cattle, young schoolaged girls (ages five to fourteen) assist their mothers with agricultural cultivation. Women are also responsible for the time-consuming and heavy tasks of carrying water and the gathering of firewood. See African Training and Research Center for Women, Human Resources Development Division, "The Role of Women in African Development," *Economic Bulletin for Africa* II (New York: United Nations, 1975), pp. 57–78.

27. Chinapah and Daun, *Swedish Missions and Education,* pp. 7–9. For a general statement of Belgian policy, see Jean-Jacques Deheyn, "Réalisation et objectifs de la Belgique en matière d'enseignement agricole au Congo Belge," *Bulletin Agricole du*

Congo Belge 68, No. 1 (1957): 1–22. Also see T. Turner, "Mobutu's Zaire: Permanently on the Verge of Collapse?" *Current History* 80 (March 1981): 127.

28. Henry Kestin, "God and Man in Zaire," *Forbes* 136 (November 18, 1985): 101.

29. Gerard Capelle, "Emploi de personnel féminin dans les entreprises du Congo belge," *Bulletin of the Inter-African Labour Institute* 2 (1959): 56–59.

30. Pierre Artigue, *Qui sont les leaders congolais?* (Brussels: Editions Europe-Afrique, 1961).

31. Ching, "Public Education Trends," p. 332 and "Women Named Ministers," *African Recorder* (June 18-July 1, 1975), p. 4008.

32. Pons, *Stanleyville*, p. 217.

33. 1948 Code, p. 26.

34. Washington Bongeye, "Accession de la Fille Congolaise à la Culture Moderne," *Congo-Magazine* (January-February 1961), p. 30, as quoted in Ching, "Public Education Trends," p. 327.

35. Yates, "White Views of Black Minds."

36. *Missions belges de la Compagnie de Jésus,* September 1907, p. 328.

37. Coulon Report, p. 100.

38. Moffarts, "Enseignement secondaire," p. 120.

39. For discussions of the church-state conflict, see Kenneth Adelman, "Recourse to Authenticity and Negritude in Zaire," *Journal of Modern African Studies* 13 (March 1975): 138; Michael G. Schatzberg, "Fidelité au Guide: The J.M.P.R. in Zairian Schools," *Journal of Modern African Studies* 16 (September 1978); Kenneth Adelman, "Church-State Conflict in Zaire; 1969–1974," *African Studies Review* 18 (April 1975): 103–109; and Robert L. Nicklaus, "Reversal in Zaire: Returning Administration of Public Primary and Secondary Schools to the Churches," *Christianity Today* 21 (January 7, 1977): 43.

40. Chinapah and Daun, *Swedish Missions and Education,* p. 13.

41. Schatzberg, "Fidelité au Guide," p. 431.

42. Goetschalckx, *Situation des Ecoles Postprimaires,* p. 2.

43. Coulon Report, p. 235.

44. Ching, "Public Education Trends," p. 336.

45. James S. Coleman and Ndolamb Ngokwey, "Zaire; The State and the University," in R. Murray Thomas, ed., *Politics and Education: Cases from Eleven Nations* (New York: Pergamon Press, 1983), p. 68. An ethnic factor probably also plays a part in women's access to education. Since males in certain ethnic groups (e.g., the Bakongo and the Baluba) have for decades been more involved in the modern sector, it is likely that their daughters receive more education than those from other ethnic groups, although no studies have been found on this topic.

46. Terri F. Gould, "The Educated Woman in a Developing Country . . . "

47. Uma Lele, *The Design of Rural Development: Lessons from Africa* (Baltimore and London: Johns Hopkins University Press for the World Bank, 1975), p. 77.

48. Judith Van Allen, "African Women, 'Modernization,' and National Liberation," in Lynne B. Iglizin and Ruth Ross, eds., *Women in the World* (Santa Barbara, Calif.: ABC-Clio Books, 1976).

ASIA

6
PEOPLE'S REPUBLIC OF CHINA

Grace C. L. Mak

Chinese women have for centuries been assigned an inferior social status. Any significant attempt to change their conditions on a national scale was realized only with the communist liberation of China in 1949. It is generally believed that since then Chinese men and women have enjoyed equality on almost all fronts, at least on paper. How has constitutional equality between the two sexes been interpreted? What kind of equality and how much do Chinese women enjoy? If full equality is not yet a reality, what else needs to be done? In this chapter we will first look at how culture and ideology shaped Chinese women's fates traditionally. We will then present a picture of women's participation in schooling in today's China and examine the causes behind it. In the second half of the chapter we trace how education has changed women's roles in the private sphere of the household and the public spheres of the economy and politics. It will be argued that, in spite of increased opportunities, Chinese women still experience discrimination in education, and that while education has brought women unprecedented participation and status in the workforce, it alone has not been able to bring about women's equality with men. Even four decades after a major political transformation in the country, traditional attitudes are still omnipresent, though less blatant. Honest effort toward gender equality has to be made not only in policy formulation, but also in implementation.

HISTORICAL AND CULTURAL BACKGROUND

In China, knowledge performed opposite functions depending on one's gender. It could elevate a man's social status, but the same knowledge would only demean a woman even further. In the Ming Dynasty (1368–1644), Xu Xuemo stated that "literacy only makes women loose in morals."[1] To keep women servile, men told them that "women without knowledge are virtuous."

The Chinese respect for education, which many point out as a general phenomenon, was true of male China only. Traditionally, Chinese women were deprived of education. The very few exceptions were some women from aristocratic families; even so, their education differed from that for men. Women were taught feminine virtues and literacy skills, but the classics were men's business. Daughters of well-to-do families were taught literacy at home, and those of poor families had no education whatsoever. Regardless of social class, education for women, if any, was to train them to be good wives and mothers.[2]

The late Qing Dynasty (1644–1911) saw a weakening China. In 1842, five treaty ports were opened to the West for trading as a result of China's defeat by Britain in the first Opium War (1840–1842). Western missionaries also gained access to these ports and later the interior of China. One of the means they used to spread evangelism was the setting up of schools. The first girls' school was founded in 1844 by Miss Aldersey, a member of the Church of England, in Ningbo, a town near Shanghai.[3] Not only did missionary effort mark the beginning of modern schooling in China, but it also admitted girls to educational institutions outside of their homes for the first time in Chinese history. The social background of female students was also reversed. Because traditional Confucian education remained prestigious and the Chinese despised and distrusted Western missionaries, only poor parents sent their children to mission schools. However, with the growing recognition of these schools and the rise of the new merchant and professional classes, more and more students in mission schools came from families of well-to-do backgrounds. A survey conducted by Ida Belle Lewis across China toward the end of the 1910s found that almost 50 percent of female students in mission schools came from merchant families and almost 40 percent from scholar families (i.e., educators, nurses, officials, physicians, and religious workers). Only 7.7 percent came from farmer families, 2.7 percent from servant families, and a mere 1.4 percent from artisan families.[4] Education, even that provided by Westerners, had again become the preserve of the wealthy.

At the end of the nineteenth century, Chinese intellectuals began to advocate women's rights. Associations against footbinding and for promoting girls' schooling were set up. One of the most influential of these intellectuals was Liang Chichao (1873–1929), an ardent supporter of reform.[5] Amidst the call for widespread reforms was the recognition of the importance of educating girls in their roles as wives and mothers in a modern China. The first Chinese-sponsored girls' school was founded in 1898.[6] More private girls' schools opened thereafter.

The inclusion of girls in government schools came later. To strengthen China, the Qing government developed a modern education system in 1902. Schools were provided for girls only after 1907 when the government issued an edict opening teacher training schools and primary schools for girls. Lower primary schools were to be founded for girls aged seven to ten and higher primary schools for those aged eleven to fourteen. Those who finished higher primary school could enter teacher training schools for four years.[7] The revolution of 1911 saw the end of dynastic rule in China and the beginning of the Republican era. The next year a new education system was established. In theory gender equality was granted, but in practice far fewer girls than boys had access to schools. For example, in the school year 1918–1919, there were 4,177,519 boys in Chinese lower primary schools but only 190,882 girls (or 4.4 percent of the total), and 421,893 boys in higher primary school but only 24,744 girls (or 5.54 percent of the total).[8] The absolute number of girls in school grew at an impressive rate—from 468 pupils in 1904 to 170,789 in 1917.[9] However, in relative terms, probably fewer than 1 percent of the schoolaged girls were attending school in the 1910s.[10]

In the 1910s and 1920s, waves of patriotism swept across China, culminating in the May Fourth Movement of 1919. During this era new thought and knowledge were introduced into China from the West and Japan. Large numbers of female students became aware of their role in the movement to save the country. Many enrolled in colleges in China as well as abroad. In 1919, Chinese national and private universities also began to admit female students.[11] (Before then, there had already been four mission colleges for women.[12]) The next three decades were also marked by turmoil: the civil war between the Guomindang and the communists from the 1920s on, and the Japanese invasion (1937–1945), only to be followed by another civil war until the Communist party gained power in 1949. Data on education in the 1930s and 1940s are scattered. According to the Chinese Ministry of Education, in 1935 the total enrollment in secondary schools across China was 547,207, of which 103,055 (or 18.83 percent of the total) were girls.[13] In 1936, of some 800 Chinese students who went abroad to study, about 10 percent were female.[14] The extremely low literacy rates of women relative to men before 1949 leads us to assume that far fewer women than men benefited from education in pre-1949 China.[15]

WOMEN AND EDUCATION IN CHINA TODAY

Reforms Affecting Women's Education

Even before the Chinese communists established firm political power, in the 1930s and 1940s their leader Mao Zedong had pointed out that women and men alike were oppressed by three systems, namely, the state system (political authority), the clan system (clan authority), and the supernatural system (religious authority), but that women were also oppressed by the husband's authority.[16] One of the goals of the communist government was to liberate women from the centuries-old oppression by men. Major government efforts aiming at raising women's status were manifested in the Marriage Law,[17] the land reform,[18] and the Constitution. In September 1949, the Common Program of the Chinese People's Political Consultative Conference was adopted. It would serve as the precedent of the official constitution adopted in 1954. Article 6, Chapter 1, of the Common Program stated that "The People's Republic of China abolishes the feudal system which holds women in bondage. Women shall enjoy equal rights with men in political, economic, cultural and educational and social life. Freedom of marriage for men and women shall be enforced."[19] Other than that no specific policy was issued on educating girls.

Four decades have passed since 1949. During this period, the country has experienced dramatic political, economic,and social changes in the course of its pursuit of effective government. This chapter cannot examine these changes in detail. However, in order to provide a context for understanding women's education in contemporary China, the major reforms in education from 1949 to the present are considered briefly.

From 1949 to 1957, the Chinese education system was in transition. It inherited the academic model from the Guomindang government. At first, mission and private schools were allowed to exist, but they were gradually nationalized. The aim of education was to train personnel for national reconstruction and modernization. Literacy classes for the large number of illiterates and basic education for all schoolaged children were also emphasized. The period was marked by heavy Soviet influence. The Great Leap Forward campaign in 1958–1959 called for rapid modernization of both agricultural and industrial production. The aim of education was to contribute to this process. Widespread efforts were made to attack illiteracy. Priority in education was given to children from peasant and worker backgrounds.

The failure of the Great Leap Forward resulted in the polarization in the early 1960s between the Maoists who saw adhering to political principle as the paramount task and the "rightists" who believed that a hierarchical structure from top down would be more efficient. In education there was a dual emphasis on both training highly skilled personnel to meet the needs of economic development and providing popular education to the masses which emphasized political ideology. The struggle between the two political camps was a major cause leading to the Great Proletarian Cultural Revolution (1966–1976) during which the whole country went through massive disruptions. From 1966 to 1968, the schools were closed. When they were reopened, politics ruled over academic quality. Since 1976, China has been moving toward the more pragmatic approach of developing the country's economy and deemphasizing politics. Great emphasis is placed on the contribution of education to the country's modernization. Quality again reigns. This policy has been further intensified as China is experimenting with a series of economic reforms to bring the country closer to the industrialized world.[20]

Women's Participation in Education and Obstacles to It

The changes in education after the revolution did not directly address inequality in women's access to education, although they did affect it. Before looking at enrollment trends and how women fared in them, we will briefly discuss the structure of the Chinese education system. As in other countries, the Chinese education system has three levels: primary, secondary, and tertiary. Secondary education is differentiated as secondary specialized schools (including secondary technical schools and teacher-training schools), general secondary schools (which are divided into lower and higher secondary levels), and agricultural and vocational schools. In general, there has been remarkable expansion in education since the early 1950s. In 1952, 49.2 percent of the primary schoolaged children were in school. In 1965, the figure went up to 84.7 percent, and by 1975, it reached 95 percent. Thereafter the percentage has been more or less stable.[21] Other statistics illustrate the postrevolutionary expansion. In 1952, total enrollment at all levels of education made up 9.47 percent of the total Chinese population. By 1965, it had doubled to 18.09 percent. Although the percentages have fluctuated since then, they have generally remained in the neighborhood of 18 percent.[22]

Women benefited from this expansion. Table 6.1 shows that the percentages of females versus males at all levels of education have been increasing. In the primary school, females made up only 28 percent of total enrollment in 1951; this figure rose to 44.8 percent by 1985. In secondary education, female enrollment also rose from 26 percent to around 40 percent. In tertiary education, the growth is less impressive, from slightly over 20 percent in the beginning of the 1950s to nearly 30 percent in 1985. The higher the level, the less represented females are. Clearly, equalization of education for girls is less elusive at the lower end of the educational hierarchy. Educational provision becomes scarcer at the higher end, and more men than women attend.

Great gains have been achieved for women in recent history. Table 6.2 shows that by 1982 the ratios of males and females who had received at least primary education ranged from some 117:100 to 127:100 among those aged ten to twenty-nine. This is the generation born after 1949. The contrast with those born and raised before 1949 is astounding. In the age forty-five to sixty and above groups, the ratios range from about 300:100 to 754:100.

In spite of this improvement bias against women remains. Chinese newspapers and periodicals have reported such incidents in recent years. About 80 percent of China's population is rural, and only about 20 percent is urban. Policies issued by the central government do not always reach all rural areas. The discrepancies between central government policy and local practice are best demonstrated by the violation against the one-child policy and the existence in some rural areas of teenage marriage. (Teenage marriage is illegal; the minimum legal marriage age as stated in the Marriage Law is twenty-two for men and twenty for women.) In education a similar problem exists. Although the state government has declared the equal rights of the two sexes to education, many peasant families send sons to school and keep daughters at home. Many rural parents still believe, as their ancestors did, that "daughters will be married out of the family, just like water poured out." Sending daughters to school may mean foregone earnings for rural

Table 6.1
Enrollment Trends of Female Students, by Level of Education, 1947–1985 (in 10,000)

Year	Graduate School	Reg. Inst. of Higher Educ. No.	% Total	Secondary Schools			
				Sec. Techni- cal Schools No.	% Total	Teacher Training No.	% Total
1947	...	2.76	17.8	...	...	...	...
1949	...	2.32	19.8	...	...	...	...
1950	...	2.91	21.2	...	...	...	...
1951	...	3.51	22.5	5.19	31.9	5.72	26.0
1952	...	4.54	23.4	7.56	26.0	8.29	24.0
1953	...	5.47	25.3	7.80	26.0	9.53	25.8
1954	...	6.77	26.3	7.61	25.4	8.18	26.6
1955	...	7.58	25.9	7.87	24.7	5.93	27.1
1956	...	10.04	24.6	13.55	23.2	7.97	29.1
1957	...	10.33	23.3	12.23	25.4	8.40	28.4
1958	...	15.37	23.3	27.51	25.4	12.17	31.5
1959	...	18.33	22.6	26.00	27.3	19.80	36.7
1960	...	23.56	24.5	43.11	31.3	26.24	31.3
1961	...	23.35	24.7	23.88	35.8	17.13	43.7
1962	...	21.03	25.3	13.83	39.7	8.75	48.8
1963	...	19.38	25.8	12.71	39.5	6.10	47.2
1964	...	17.63	25.7	13.01	32.7	6.39	47.6
1965	...	18.13	26.9	15.40	37.9	7.36	48.6
1973	...	9.65	30.8	No.		% Total	
1974	...	14.52	33.8	24.29		38.3	
1975	...	16.33	32.6	24.35		34.4	
1976	...	18.65	33.0	24.51		35.5	
1977	...	18.16	29.0	24.15		35.0	

Table 6.1 (continued)

Year	Secondary Schools				Primary Schools	
	General Sec. Schools No.	% Total	Agric. & Voc. Schools No.	% Total	Primary Schools No.	% Total
1947	..	..	..	..	..	..
1949	..	..	..	..	..	..
1950	34.61	26.5	..	..	..	..
1951	40.12	25.6	..	..	1,206.3	28.0
1952	58.58	23.5	..	..	1,679.7	32.9
1953	71.44	24.4	..	..	1,782.2	34.5
1954	89.60	25.0	..	..	1,707.1	33.3
1955	104.94	26.9	..	..	1,775.8	33.4
1956	151.43	29.3	..	..	2,231.5	35.2
1957	193.53	30.8	..	..	2,215.9	34.5
1958	266.33	31.3	..	..	3,325.7	38.5
1959	286.08	31.2	..	..	3,566.9	39.1
1960	320.10	31.2	..	..	3,665.6	39.1
1961	274.54	32.2	..	..	2,082.5	27.5
1962	256.43	34.1	..	..	2,406.7	34.8
1963	258.63	34.0	7.68	25.0	..	..
1964	291.51	34.1	27.36	24.4	3,250.5	35.0
1965	300.67	32.2	104.58	23.6	4,560.0	39.3
1973	1,136.91	33.0	..	..	5,527.2	40.7
1974	1,392.14	38.1	..	..	6,330.8	43.7
1975	1,753.71	39.3	..	..	6,824.3	45.2
1976	2,357.10	40.4	..	..	6,823.3	45.5
1977	2,825.39	41.7	..	..	6,632.1	45.4

Table **6.1** (continued)

Year	Graduate School		Reg. Inst. of Higher Educ.		Secondary Schools			
					Sec. Techni-cal Schools		Teacher Training	
	No.	% Total	No.	% Total	No.	% Total	No.	% Total
1978	...	...	20.65	24.1	18.69	35.3	10.71	29.8
1979	...	...	24.57	24.1	24.84	34.8	12.33	25.4
1980	0.26	11.8	26.81	23.4	26.65	37.2	12.52	26.0
1981	0.27	14.3	31.24	24.4	22.78	36.0	12.59	28.8
1982	0.36	13.7	30.54	26.5	22.08	35.2	13.94	33.9
1983	0.53	14.3	32.49	26.9	24.07	35.0	16.94	37.2
1984	0.92	16.0	39.98	28.7	30.15	37.2	20.88	40.8
1985	1.62	18.6	51.06	29.9	38.77	38.3	21.93	39.3

Source: Compiled from Department of Planning, Ministry of education of the PRC, Achievement of Education in China. Statistics 1949–1983 (Beijing: People's Education Press, 1984), pp. 39–40; and Achievement of Education in China. Statistics 1980–1985 (Beijing: People's Education Press, 1986), pp. 39, 47, 59, 74, 77, 84.

Table 6.1 (continued)

Year	Secondary Schools				Primary Schools	
	General Sec. Schools No.	% Total	Agric. & Voc. Schools No.	% Total	Primary Schools No.	% Total
1978	2,715.48	41.5	...	...	6,570.4	44.9
1979	2,410.52	40.8	...	...	6,577.4	44.9
1980	2,180.08	39.6	14.83	32.7	6,517.4	44.6
1981	1,895.37	39.0	19.33	40.2	6,301.2	44.0
1982	1,777.44	39.3	27.22	38.7	6,099.9	43.7
1983	1,735.12	39.5	47.63	39.0	5,937.2	43.7
1984	1,821.87	40.0	71.12	40.8	5,937.7	43.8
1985	1,893.13	40.2	95.43	41.6	5,986.2	44.8

Source: Compiled from Department of Planning, Ministry of education of the PRC, Achievement of Education in China. Statistics 1949–1983 (Beijing: People's Education Press, 1984), pp. 39–40; and Achievement of Education in China. Statistics 1980–1985 (Beijing: People's Education Press, 1986), pp. 39, 47, 59, 74, 77, 84.

Table 6.2
Proportion of Males to Females with Primary Education Attainment or Above, by Age Group, 1982

Age Group	Male:Female
6-9	120.3:100
10-14	117.6:100
15-19	117.5:100
20-24	116.3:100
25-29	127.6:100
30-34	157.4:100
34-39	168.8:100
40-44	208.3:100
45-49	297.7:100
50-54	448.1:100
55-59	547.2:100
60 and above	754.9:100

Source: Zhu'Chuzhu and Jiang Zhenghua, "Social and Economic Situation of China's Female Population," Renkou xuekan (Journal of Population Studies) 3 (1985): 5.

parents as girls who stay at home can help with housework, herd domestic animals, and look after younger siblings. In a letter to the editor of *Remin ribao (People's Daily)* in 1985, a New China News Agency reporter pointed out that 3.5 million schoolaged girls across China were still kept out of school, especially those in remote regions with minority groups.[23] Even if girls are enrolled at school, they are more likely to drop out than boys.[24] A commune in Fujian province is an illustration. In 1976, of the 1,000 or so schoolaged girls in that area, about 80 percent went to primary school, but only about 400 got to the end of it by 1981.[25] The attrition rate was as high as 50 percent. In the government's recent attempts to promote modernization, change has been introduced to the economic system. Instead of a high degree of centralization, some autonomy has been granted to local levels. However, economic reform has indirectly had a regressive effect on girls' schooling in parts of China's countryside. In recent years, the rural responsibility system has been introduced to rural areas whereby households sign contracts with the collective to turn over a certain amount of production to the collective but can keep the surplus to sell to state or private markets. Sideline production is encouraged.[26] The new system aims at raising peasants' initiative in agricultural production. Because peasant parents work harder than before, many transfer farmwork to their children, especially daughters. As a result, rural enrollment in some areas has dropped further.[27]

Residence in rural areas further cuts across gender to reduce a girl's access to education at the secondary level. The female enrollment rate in lower secondary schools in villages is 36.5 percent and in higher secondary schools, 31.1 percent.[28] These are aggregated rates; in some cases entire schools have no female students.

Girls in urban areas have greater access to education than girls in rural areas. The urban population has been more receptive to new ideas, including social movements that seek to improve women's situation.[29] However, the problem exists in cities, although its expression and extent vary with geographical setting. Numerous stories in the press point at what must be a common phenomenon of schools setting higher admission scores for female applicants than for males for the same academic program, especially when the program is in great demand. The prestigious keypoint schools, which are allocated more resources and select teachers, provide an example of sex bias in the cities. A letter to the editor of *Guangming ribao* states that, in order to enter a keypoint secondary school in Tianjin, girls have to have a higher score.[30] The reason given is that girls usually perform better than boys at primary and early secondary school. School administrators have decided that if they fail to intervene, more girls will be admitted to keypoint schools.[31] The writer of this letter observed that keypoint school administrators believe that if they admit too many girls, their ability to get students into colleges and universities will be undermined. Behind this thinking is the belief that girls' ability relative to boys' declines with age and that it is due to "biological reasons" rather than a combined result of socialization, great responsibilities for girls in the household, lower parent and teacher expectations, and so on. The Tianjin case is probably not an isolated one. Some secondary technical schools and vocational schools also raise the admission score for girls in order to maintain boys' enrollment.[32] Parent and student protest has not significantly changed the situation.

Although more females are admitted to secondary school relative to males than before, when more prestigious schools are involved females are discouraged in one way or another, as witnessed by the Tianjin case. Women have also been discouraged in the workplace and the Communist party. This problem will be discussed in greater detail later in this chapter; here the focus is on measures taken to enhance the articulation between work and school, given that work units (units of organizations, e.g., administrative departments, factories, hospitals, and schools) have been unwilling to recruit female school leavers. The All-China Women's Federation, a national umbrella organization that promotes women's rights, has established special vocational schools for girls.[33] Thirteen such women's vocational schools and three women's vocational universities had been established as of 1986.[34] Specifically set up to tap female human resources, these schools usually offer programs "that are suitable for females" such as clerical and secretarial skills, early childhood care, and tourist services. The response to these schools has been positive, and they are believed to be a partial solution to workplace sex discrimination. However, they do not confront the problem of inequality in female access to technical, vocational, and higher education. They prepare female students for the type of work believed to suit their aptitudes and abilities. The emergence of such girls' vocational programs perpetuates the assumption that sexual segregation in the workplace makes sense. New vocational schools for girls also reverse a trend to provide coeducation. By 1970, the last girls-only schools were phased out.[35] In the 1980s, under the guise of safeguarding women's employment, single-sex schools are on the rise.

At the tertiary level, many institutes recruit few female students. Although the data in Table 6.1 show that the percentage of female relative to male students is increasing, many Chinese publications see a regressive trend. *Zhongguo funubao* (Women of China Newspaper), for example, has reported on this matter. In some colleges and universities there has been a proportional drop in female enrollment.[36] In the case of graduate students, the percentage of females has been rising but remains low.

What are the variables that cut across gender to determine women's educational opportunity? The Marxist notion of class difference whereby the ruling class controls the means of production is no longer an effective explanation in a country where social class stratification has officially been denounced. In China, as in other developing nations, geographical location is a major determinant of life chances. Urban women are more likely than their rural counterparts to be educated, but even within cities there is a hierarchy. Children of cadres and intellectuals have greater educational opportunity than do children of workers. This also holds for children from more affluent peasant families or for those who reside in villages near urban settlements. While there are exceptions, most Chinese parents are more willing to invest in their sons' than daughters' education. Families that cannot afford education for all their children often give priority to sons. More prosperous families can and may be more willing to send daughters to school as well. More female than male students tend to come from wealthier or educated families, especially at the secondary and tertiary levels.

China is a multiethnic country. Apart from the Han who comprise 93.4 percent of the population, there are fifty-six named minority groups (called the nationalities) which comprise 6.6 percent of the population.[37] These nationalities are scattered in pastoral areas, and mountainous or remote regions along the land border. All nationalities in China have equal constitutional rights and duties.[38] The expansion of their educational opportunities since the communist revolution has been impressive. In 1951, the total enrollment of nationalities was 0.99 million; by 1978, it had soared to 10.24 million, a more than ninefold increase.[39] Nonetheless, primary education is far from universal. In some regions only 20 to 30 percent of schoolaged children are in school.[40] The enrollment of girls is lower than that of boys. For example, most Muslim girls in Ningxia region are kept at home.[41] Reports focusing on the Salar[42] and other nationalities paint a similar picture.[43]

Women in Nonformal Education

As elsewhere, nonformal education in China is a loose term that includes all types of education outside formal schooling. The major types of nonformal education are literacy classes, agricultural or technical skill training courses for peasants and workers, evening schools, correspondence programs, radio and television universities, and spare-time universities. In the 1950s, great emphasis was placed on literacy classes. These classes taught about the new people's government, family hygiene, and basic reading skills. They were directed primarily at women since before 1949 about 90 percent of all illiterates were female.[44] In the countryside, literacy classes were held in the winter months when agricultural work was slow. These were called ''winter studies.'' In the cities classes were organized for housewives, factory workers, and other poor female laborers. Although literacy classes reached large numbers of women denied formal schooling, today about 70 percent of illiterates in China are women.[45] Among rural women aged twenty or so, about a third are illiterate or semi-literate.[46] Data on participation by sex in other nonformal education programs are difficult to obtain. The female participation rate in in-service training programs for workers is estimated at about 30 percent of the total.[47]

WOMEN'S EDUCATION AND THEIR PARTICIPATION AND STATUS IN THE WORKFORCE

In China, economic policy is probably a stronger determinant of women's entry into the workforce than education. Some scholars argue that women have served as a reserve labor force. When the economic policy demands more labor than can be supplied by men, women enter the labor market. The Great Leap Forward mobilized women to work in the field and factories.[48] In times of surplus labor, women have been thrown out of work first. A second-class status has been attached to the female labor force. Attitudes of work unit administrators against recruiting women workers do not always translate into practice, thanks to government-imposed fixed ratios of women employed in state industries. This section focuses on how this policy works and how sex discrimination remains in spite of government regulations and women's educational attainment.

Distribution of Women in the Workforce

Table 6.3 provides statistics on the sexual composition of the workforce. In 1982, the workforce participation rate was 81.7 percent for women and 91 percent for men.[49] Of those gainfully employed, 56.31 percent were male and 43.69 percent female. A total of 73.6 percent of the labor force worked in agriculture, stock farming, forestry, and fishing; 11.83 percent in manufacturing; 2.97 percent in wholesale/retail trade, restaurants, hotels, and storage; and 2.37 percent in educational and cultural services. The women's employment pattern is roughly the same as that of the labor force as a whole: 77.97 percent worked in agriculture, stock farming, forestry, and fishing; 11.94 percent in manufacturing; 2.94 percent in wholesale/retail trade, restaurants, hotels, and storage; and 1.92 percent in educational and cultural services. Approximately 80 percent of those employed

Table 6.3
Composition of Sex-Specific Labor Force, by Industry, 1982

Industry	Labor Force		% Composition		% Distribution	
	Number	% of Total	Male	Female	Male	Female
Total	521,505,618	100	56.31	43.69	100	100
Agriculture, stock farm-ing, forestry and fishing	384,155,030	73.66	53.75	46.25	70.32	77.97
Mining and lumbering	8,401,845	1.61	80.64	19.36	2.31	0.71
Electricity, gas and water supply	1,500,343	0.29	74.06	25.94	0.38	0.17
Manufacturing	61,668,204	11.83	55.90	44.10	11.74	11.94
Geological exploration	824,043	0.16	77.93	22.07	0.22	0.08
Construction	11,009,419	2.11	81.13	18.87	3.04	0.91
Transport and Communications	8,980,972	1.72	77.12	22.88	2.36	0.90
Wholesale/retail trade, restaurants, hotels and storage	15,507,928	2.97	56.76	43.24	3.00	2.94
Housing management, public amenities, and community services	2,441,405	0.47	55.13	44.87	0.46	0.48
Public health services, sports and social services	4,101,355	0.79	51.87	48.13	0.72	0.87

Education and cultural services	12,382,079	2.37	64.62	35.38	2.72	1.92
Natural and social sciences and general technical services	1,202,272	0.23	63.36	36.64	0.26	0.19
Finance and insurance	1,022,975	0.20	68.06	31.94	0.24	0.14
National organizations, communist party and political groups	8,018,546	1.54	79.55	20.45	2.17	0.72
Others	289,202	0.05	63.25	36.75	0.06	0.05

Source: Compiled from Guojia tongjiju, Zhongguo tongji nianjian 1986 (China Statistical Yearbook 1986) (Beijing: Zhongguo tongji chubanshe, 1986), p. 109; and Women's Economic Participation in Asia and the Pacific, ed. United Nations, Economic and Social Commission for Asia and the Pacific (Bangkok: United Nations, 1987), p. 73.

in national organizations, the Communist party, and political groups were men and about 20 percent were women.

Although women may participate almost equally with men in manufacturing, their participation is a direct outgrowth of government regulations which mandate that the workforce in heavy industries be 60 percent male and 40 percent female and that in light industries the labor force be 60 percent female and 40 percent male.[50]

Women's Education and Entry into the Workforce

In recent years, a phenomenon has emerged which may discourage women's entry into the workforce. Even if they possess the same educational qualifications as men do, female job applicants are often turned down by employers. The reason employers provide is that female workers may require maternity leave and are not usually available for overtime work since they have household obligations. Although educational provision has equipped more women for work, employers who are predominantly male assume that reproductive and domestic roles prevent women from being competitive with men who do not face the same dilemma of family and work obligations. Another reason employers give for not recruiting women is related to the bonus given the working one-child mother. In order to check population growth, the government rewards the working woman who follows the one-child policy by paying her a bonus through her work unit which operates under a system of ownership by the state government. The government does not issue such a bonus through work units that operate under collective ownership, that is, those at regional levels. Work units of this kind may or may not issue bonuses to the one-child mother. Many work units that operate under collective ownership are reluctant to hire women because they fear that more female workers will cost more.

While educational qualifications alone are not enough to enable women to compete in the urban labor force on an equal footing with men, lack of education has made rural women lag further behind men. Even when women and men do the same work, women are paid only about 70 percent of what men earn.[51] Although complete data on how recent emphases on modernization and west-ernization interact with education to change the pattern of women's participation in agricultural production is lacking, a report by a journalist in the *Renmin ribao* suggests an emerging phenomenon that may hold true for other Chinese villages. In visits to villages in recent years, the journalist has observed that fewer and fewer men work in the fields while the ratio of women is rising.[52] Production brigades draw men from villages to help develop village industries and sideline undertakings. With less education women appear to be left behind to do simple manual work.

Education may or may not facilitate women's entry into the professions. Women are already underrepresented in higher education. But possession of educational qualifications does not always guarantee access to relevant jobs.

Some colleges and universities acknowledge that female students do as well as males, yet the males always fare better in getting jobs. The prestigious Beijing Institute of Foreign Languages had a 1:1 ratio between male and female students in 1984, but none of its female graduates had been accepted by work units when the male graduates' job allocation was settled.[53] A considerable number of work units in Shanghai had rejected a number of graduates from Fudan University in 1984 simply because they were female. Although some institutes of higher education sign contracts with work units to secure jobs for female graduates, these contracts are not always respected. The work units cite a number of reasons for not hiring women, in spite of educational qualifications. First, the recruiting officers claim that women are not suitable for jobs that require business trips. Second, and more commonly, they complain that women have too much to do at home, which in turn affects their performance at work and their professional growth.[54] The demand for university and college graduates at present is twenty times greater than the supply[55], so that despite their unwillingness, work units end up hiring women. But the distrust in women's ability and suitability for the professions is so deeply rooted that it triumphs over the urgent need for human power. Again, it shows that education alone will not help women enter the workforce.

Women's Education and Occupational Status

The status of women in the professions also reveals that education has not brought them rewards equal to men's. Women are concentrated in the lower ranking positions. In 1984, there were 344 million female teachers across the nation, which accounted for 38 percent of the total teaching force. Women made up 94 percent of the early childhood teachers, 39 percent of teachers in primary school, 27.7 percent in general secondary school, and 26 percent in institutions of higher education.[56] There were 239.6 million female scientific and techno-logical workers in 1984, or 32.1 percent of the total.[57] (Scientific and techno-logical workers are those in the natural sciences, engineering, agricultural technology, health care, and so on.) The average ratio of male and female scientific and technological workers in 1984 was 2.1:1, but the ratio at the rank equivalent to engineer was 4.4:1 and surged to 7.6:1 at the rank equivalent to senior engineer.[58] In the province of Sichuan, although male and female scientific and technological workers started with similar educational attainment, senior and leadership positions are seldom filled by women.[59] In academia across the nation, only 5 percent of the full professors and full researchers are female, compared to 26 percent of females teaching in institutions of higher education.[60] The most frequent explanation given is the family. Since it is impossible for husband and wife to manage work and family equally effectively, a common practice among families in which both husband and wife are professionals is to "guarantee (the success of) one out of the two." That is, one shoulders most of the household responsibilities so that the other can concentrate on his or her job. But it is almost always the husband whose success is guaranteed. Because female professionals are believed to yield less, they are not welcome by work units, which in turn gives a reason for schools and universities not to admit them. The vicious cycle goes on. Not surprisingly, in places such as Shanghai 70 to 80 percent of the waiting-for-employment youth are female.[61]

WOMEN'S EDUCATION, MARRIAGE, AND FAMILY

Education, and Marriage Prospects

Success in education and work which increases a man's worth as a potential husband may work just the opposite way for women. Traditionally, a "suitable" marriage means the husband should be older and better educated than the wife. Now that education has been extended to women, marriages between husband and wife with the same amount of education are accepted. But even today, the Chinese disapprove of a marriage in which the wife is better educated than her husband. Before the 1970s, female university graduates did not seem to have problems marrying.

One explanation for this phenomenon is that in the old days so few women went to college that they were sought after. But today more women attend college, and so some of them cannot find husbands.[62] Another reason provided is that during the Cultural Revolution, many young men and women in the cities were sent to the countryside. Parents tried to arrange for daughters to return to the city first as they were less worried about sons living away from home. Some daughters came back just in time to attend college. The sons returned later, and many missed the opportunity. Consequently, many urban women in the late twenties and thirties age cohort today have received more education than their male counterparts. As a result, "overaged" single women are becoming a social phenomenon in the cities. The same problem does not exist in the countryside because most women there are less educated than men and therefore are not a threat to them. Many of the unmarried urban women are graduate students, university teachers, technological workers, journalists, and cadres.[63] In 1984, of the unmarried women aged twenty-eight to thirty-six registered with a match-making center in Beijing, 34.7 percent had received higher education.[64]

Education and Fertility

In China, education, occupation and geographical location all affect fertility. Here we will only examine education, although the three are interrelated. Women with more education tend to have fewer children than those with less education. Data on women aged fifty by 1982, a generation whose childbearing span co-incides with the communist revolution, show that among this cohort the illiterates had an average of 5.86 children, those with primary education had 4.8, those with lower secondary education 3.74, those with higher secondary education 2.85, and those with tertiary education 2.05 children.[65]

In addition to fertility, education for women may affect the sexual balance of their offspring. In China, female infanticide is not new. Its extent depends on rural-urban differences and the family's economic well-being. In new China, equal rights for men and women still does not always hold true for rural parents. What has not changed especially in the countryside is the preference for sons. This problem has become more acute with the implementation of the one-child policy. Under this policy, each couple is allowed to have only one child, male or female. This policy has been more successful in the cities; in the villages it has met great resistance. Some couples manage to have more than one child by paying a fine for each additional baby. Where the government can enforce this law effectively, some rural parents get rid of their newborn babies if they are female by drowning or abandoning them. Numerous such cases have been uncovered in the press. In addition, the arrival of unwelcome female babies may break up a family. The husband may divorce his wife so as to try his luck at getting a son, whereas the wife may feel ashamed of herself for not having produced a son and commit suicide. This artificial screening of the sex of offspring has offset the natural balance between the number of male and female babies that survive. In some places, the imbalance is startling.[66] In theory, women with more education should be more open to having female babies, but we do not know the weighting of education in determining a rural mother's attitude toward the sex of her baby. For example, how does the attitude of a rural mother with secondary education differ from that of a mother with primary education?

Education and Housework

Education does not seem to have significantly changed the traditional distribution of housework for women. Often female workers and professionals are not promoted at a rate equal to men. Although husbands help out, wives remain chiefly responsible for domestic chores. There are reports of husbands doing significant amounts of housework.[67] Unfortunately, there are more reports on how housework prevents women from climbing up the occupational ladder.

WOMEN'S EDUCATION AND POLITICAL PARTICIPATION

The Chinese political structure is predominantly male. For example, the representation of women in both the state government and the national people's congress has been weak. In the congress, although women's representation rose from 12 percent of the total in the 1950s to 21.2 percent in 1983 (or 632 out of 2,978 representatives), the final figure we have is still disproportionally low.[68] The common explanation for it is women's low level of educational attainment. Articles abound in the press urging women to raise their educational standards. Since traditionally women have benefited less from education than men, education may be a reason for women's weakness in the political structure. However, there have also been voices in the press pointing out sexual discrimination in recruiting and promoting cadres. Numerous articles cited in this chapter in regard to discrimination against women in admission to school and recruitment to work units also mention a similar problem in recruiting cadres. Women's presence in the provincial political structure is dismal. For example, only 4.7 percent of the cadres in provincial bureaus and departments in Hebei are female[69]; the corresponding figure for Guangdong is 4.6 percent.[70] We do not have data on the educational attainment of cadres in general, but it is often criticized for being low. It is not just a female cadres' problem. Therefore, other factors are likely bringing down the number of female cadres in China.

FUTURE TRENDS

In the course of its pursuit of a better and more efficient society, China has been undergoing constant change. Currently, the country has launched the modernization campaign, coupled with reform of the economic structure, which includes opening up Chinese ports and cities for trade and joint ventures with foreign businesspeople. In general, the modernization campaign has had a mixed impact on women and their education, workforce participation, and family responsibilities. In the workforce, there have been expanded opportunities for female workers. The current emphasis is on the development of manufacturing industries with foreign capital. More and more capital is being introduced into China, and a large labor force is needed. It is generally believed that women, with their nimble fingers, are more suitable than men for work in light industries. Expanded opportunities perhaps benefit young women the most. When the cities cannot meet the demand for labor, young women from nearby villages are recruited. In some Chinese towns near Hong Kong, female workers, many from villages, make up high percentages of factory employees. Many of them live in single-women workers' quarters.

Not only are industries becoming more diversified, but also the rise of tertiary industries is particularly favorable to women.[71] Among these industries are restauranteering, tourism, transport and communications, wholesale and retail trade, education, and commerce. Another new channel for women opened when the government began to mobilize the people's initiative to raise economic productivity in the form of self-employment. Individual operations in the form of small business or agricultural production have mushroomed. It is believed that the flexibility in individual operation suits women since they can look after their families while carrying on economic activities at or near their homes.[72]

In farming, an attempt has been made to introduce technology to raise the agricultural yield. Farming is becoming more female-dominated than before as increasing numbers of men have left their villages to become small traders or workers in building construction and transport in the cities. Women with children are left at home. Many of them are involved in food crop growing and stock farming. In Kaiping County, Guangdong Province, the ratio of men to women in farming is 1:6.4, and it is said to be a rather common phenomenon in Guangdong.[73] Unmarried women can be mobile like men, whereas women with children must seek new or improved channels of wage earning near their homes. This situation is likely to continue in the future. In addition, we must remember that such prosperity is still a privilege of the coastal and southern regions. These regions have a good industrial base and a tradition of trade with foreign countries owing to their geographical location. Although farmers and workers in the interior are also given incentives to produce, it will take many years for the interior to reach the level of the more developed areas of China. Women in remote areas, including minority women, are less directly affected by the four modernizations than those in the south and coastal areas. This is because in the remote areas, men have traditionally been in contact with the outside. Their women have yet to catch up in order to be more involved in economic modernization.[74]

In the professions and government service, the impact of the four modernizations on educated women has also been mixed. Measures have been instituted to reform the hiring and promotion system. Although the emphasis is on ability, which appears to be a fair practice leading to the emergence of a number of successful women, women still experience more difficulty than men in applying for jobs and obtaining promotions. A new hiring policy that is likely to affect female employment at the upper middle stratum of the hierarchy will be carried out in two years. University graduates will have to look for jobs themselves instead of being placed by the government. This policy will give employers more autonomy in selecting their staff. However, since many work units already reject women when they recruit, it is likely that they will have all the more excuse and authority to reject female applicants.

It is often pointed out that women must be better educated to meet the demand for more skilled workers, scientific and technological personnel, and middle and upper management personnel. Chinese leaders have stated that women must raise their educational level before they can be equal to men.[75] Parents now tend to invest as much in their daughters' as in their sons' education including sending them to prestigious schools and keeping them in school for more years.[76] However, this is an urban phenomenon. The one-child policy has been more successful in the cities, and since the single-child family is becoming more widespread, urban parents invest in the child regardless of gender. On the one hand, there seems to be more demand from parents to have their daughters educated; on the other, these parents have little say about schools' unfair admission policies which discriminate on the basis of gender. As the educational base is broadened to include more women, competition will be keener at the upper levels of schools for scarce places in higher and technological education. Unless discriminatory practices are ended, women will lag further behind.

Dropping out of primary and secondary schools in rural areas is becoming a serious problem. Children in their early teens leave school to help their parents in agriculture, village industries, or trading. Of these child workers, 85 percent are female.[77] Village farmers and workers tend to be more attracted by short-term monetary gains than long-term prospects from village school education. The high percentage of girls among child workers shows once again that if education has any value to rural parents, sons are more likely than daughters to get it. Rural girls will find themselves in a vicious cycle.

While the four modernizations call for more educated workers, economic opportunities for their parents have disrupted their schooling probably at an earlier point than before. A form of compensation for those deprived of education, especially females, is nonformal education. There has been a great demand for nonformal education in towns and villages and from men and women. Spare-time classes such as evening literacy classes, agricultural technology, and skills courses are extremely popular. In some counties in Guangdong Province, the female participation rates range from 76 to 98 percent.[78] This rage for knowledge is likely to continue.

For working women, an important question to be resolved is housework. There has been much talk about the socialization of housework[79] which means reduction of each woman's time spent on housework due to market supply of, for example, prepared meals, ready-to-wear clothing, and paid child care. Although such services can help women better utilize their energies in economic development, few families can afford them. The socialization of housework may not be realized at a massive level in the near future. In the short run, alternative methods must be sought in order to reduce women's burdens. More men are reported to share household responsibilities with wives, though women continue to shoulder most of the work. The double burden will remain a dilemma for working women.

Currently, the Chinese women's movement does not seem to be in conflict with state policy. Activities are organized at all levels of the All-China Women's Federation to encourage women to participate in work and politics. Some cadres of the Women's Federation define their work as implementing government policies in the women's sphere.[80] It appears that the women's movement will serve government orientations that are strongly economic. Inequalities will be pointed out, as the Women's Federation has always been doing, but the economic priority will take precedence over the challenge to the fundamental unequal gender structure.

NOTES

1. Xu Xuemo, "Worldly Talk at Guiyouyuan," in Feng Keben, ed., *Guangbaichuan xuehai*, Vol. 4 (Taipei: Hsinhsing Book Co., 1970), p. 1872.

2. Yu Qingtang, "Women's Education in China in the Past Thirty-five Years," in Li Youning and Chang Yufa, eds., *Zhongguo funu lunwenji* [Essays on the History of Chinese Women] (reissued in Taipei: Commercial Press, 1981), p. 343.

3. Ida Belle Lewis, *The Education of Girls in China* (New York: Teachers College, Columbia University; reprinted by New York: AMS Press, 1972), p. 18.

4. Ibid., Part 2, Chapter 2.

5. Liang Chichao's essays on the promotion on girls' education can be found in his work *Yinbinshi wenji* [Collected Works of Yinbishi] (Taipei: Zhonghua Book Co., 1960).

6. Yu, "Women's Education in China," p. 344.

7. Ibid., p. 348.

8. Ibid., p. 349.

9. Lewis, *The Education of Girls in China*, p. 84.

10. Ibid., p. 84.

11. Yu, "Women's Education in China," p. 363.

12. They were institutes for teacher training: North China Women's College in Beijing, Ginling College in Nanjing, Fuzhou Women's College and the American Board College in Fuzhou, and Guangzhou Christian College. In 1916, the total attendance at these colleges was sixty-four girls. The data are from the *China Mission Yearbook, 1917*, cited in Lewis, *The Education of Girls in China*, p. 22.

13. Zhongguo Jiaoyubu, *Quanguo zhongdeng jiaoyu tongji* [Ministry of Education, National Statistics on Secondary Education] (Shanghai: Shangwu yinshuguan, 1936), pp. 1–2.

14. *Zuijin quanguo gaodengjiaoyu gaikuang 1936* [Latest General Situation of Higher Education in China, 1936], (Ministry of Education, 1936).

15. Zhu Chuzhu and Jiang Zhenghua, "Social and Economic Situation of China's Female Population," *Renkou xuekan* [Journal of Population Studies] 3 (1985): 5.

16. Cited in Margery Wolf, *Revolution Postponed: Women in Contemporary China* (Stanford Calif.: Stanford University Press, 1985), p. 15.

17. The 1950 Marriage Law was not the first of its kind to appear in Chinese history. In both 1924 and 1926, Chiang Kai-shek's government passed resolutions declaring equal rights and freedom for women in marriage and divorce. These resolutions were not given much substance as many men were opposed to them. During the Kiangsi Soviet Period in 1929–1934, when the communists were based in Jiangsi (Kiangsi) and western Fujian provinces, a provisional constitution was adopted that promised freedom of marriage to women. The Marriage Law of 1950 and after was developed from these two earlier frameworks. See Kay Ann Johnson, *Women, the Family and Peasant Revolution in China* (Chicago and London: University of Chicago Press, 1983), Chapters 3 and 4.

18. For an excellent study of the impact of the Marriage Law and the land reform on rural Chinese women, see Johnson, *Women*.

19. Shi Ming Hu and Eli Seifman, eds., *Toward a New World: A Documentary History of Education in the People's Republic of China, 1949–1976* (New York: AMS Press, 1976), p. 10.

20. An example of studies on education in China is R. F. Price, *Education in Communist China* (London: Routledge & Kegan Paul, 1970).

21. Guojia Tongjiju, *Zhongguo tongji nianjian, 1986* [China Statistical Yearbook] (Beijing: Zhongguo tongji chubanshe, 1986), p. 738.

22. Ibid., p. 739.

23. *Renmin ribao* (September 30, 1985).

24. Hu and Seifman, *Toward a New World*, p. 245.

25. *Renmin ribao* (September 3, 1981).

26. For an account of the impact of the rural responsibility system on education, see Hubert O. Brown, "Primary Schooling and the Rural Responsibility System in the People's Republic of China," *Comparative Education Review* 30 (May 1987): 373–387.

27. *Renmin ribao* (see n. 25 above); *Guangming ribao* (January 23, 1987).

28. Zhu and Jiang "Social and Economic Situation," p. 4.

29. See, for example, Johnson, *Women*.

30. *Guangming ribao* (August 11, 1982).

31. Ibid.

32. *Renmin ribao* (September 4, 1984).

33. See, for example, *Renmin jiaoyu* [People's Education], No. 10 (October 1985): 12–13; *Guangming ribao* (October 8, 1984 and November 5, 1984), and *Renmin ribao* (May 2, 1986).

34. Tan Manni, "Is There Discrimination Against Working Women in China?" *Zhongguo jianshe* [China Reconstructs] No. 3 (1986): 20.

35. "Women in People's China," *China Now* 5 (September-October 1970): 3.

36. *Zhongguo funubao* [Women of China Daily] (September 22, 1986). Suzanne Pepper also points out the declining female enrollment in some Chinese universities in both absolute numbers and percentages of total. See Pepper, *China's Universities* (Ann Arbor: Center for Chinese Studies, University of Michigan, 1984), pp. 112–113, 142.

37. Calculated from Guojia, *Zhongguo tongji nianjian 1986*, pp. 97–98.

38. Hu and Seifman, *Toward a New World*, p. 10.

39. Zhang Chengxian, "Speech at the Fifth Meeting of Presidents of Colleges for the Nationalities," *Jiaoju yanjiu* [Educational Research] No. 4 (1979): 70.

40. Ibid.

41. *Renmin ribao* (January 30, 1986).

42. *Guangming ribao* (February 7, 1982).

43. *Renmin ribao* (September 30, 1985).

44. *Guangming ribao* (October 8, 1984).

45. Xiong Zhennan, "A Look at Chinese Women's Status as Reflected by Some Statistics," *Zhongguo funu* [Women of China] No. 7 (1985): 20.

46. Ibid.

47. *Guangming ribao* (October 8, 1984).

48. Johnson, *Women*.

49. Xiong, "A Look at Chinese Women's Status," p. 19.

50. Fan Fan, "Why Are Enterprises Unwilling to Recruit Female Comrades?" *Zhongguo funu*, No. 11 (1986): 11.

51. Wolf, *Revolution Postponed*, Chapter 3.

52. *Renmin ribao* (March 20, 1980).

53. *Zhongguo funubao* (February 27, 1985).

54. Chenyan, "Trend of Sex Discrimination in Job Allocation for University Graduates Must Be Corrected," *Zhongguo funu*, No. 6 (1983): 15.

55. Tan "Is There Discrimination," p. 18.

56. *Renmin ribao* (September 9, 1985).

57. Guojia kewei rencai ziyuan yanjiusuo, "Voice from Women in the Fields of Science and Technology," *Rencai tiandi* [World of Qualified Personnel] No. 3 (1986): 3.

58. Ibid., p. 4.

59. *Renmin ribao* (November 28, 1986).

60. "The Hiring System: Female Intellectuals' Feedback and Ways to Deal with It," *Zhongguo funu*, No. 9 (1986): 2–3.

61. *Zhongguo funubao* (January 30, 1985).

62. Interview with two retired female secondary school principals in Beijing on April 11, 1988.

63. *Guangming ribao* (April 13, 1985).

64. *Renmin ribao* (overseas edition) (January 8, 1986).

65. Zhu and Jiang, "Social and Economic Situation," p. 2.

66. The proportion is as low as one female to five male babies that survived in a place in Anhui Province as cited in *Renmin ribao* (April 7, 1983).

67. For example, *Wen Wei Po* (Hong Kong) (October 21, 1987).

68. See Guojia, *Zhongguo tongji nianjian,* p. 4.

69. *Hebei ribao* (January 28, 1986).

70. *Renmin ribao* (overseas edition) (December 7, 1985).

71. Guan Xiufang, "A Discussion of Women's Status During the Period of Reform and Opening Up," in All-China Women's Federation, Guangdong, and Guangdong Women's Studies Association, eds., *Gaige kaifang yu funu* [Reform, Opening Up, and Women] (Guangzhou: Zhongguo funu chubanshe, 1986), p. 5.

72. Wu Cuimei, "Views on the Future of Women's Employment from the Reform of the Economic Structure," in *Gaige kaifang yu funu,* p. 68.

73. Zhang Yini, "Women Are an Important Impetus for Economic Development," in *Gaige kaifang yu funu,* p. 29.

74. Li Xiaowen, "Help Minority Women to Move Toward Modernization," in *Gaige kaifang yu funu,* p. 79.

75. Liang Shihong, "Reform and Women's Liberation," in *Gaige kaifang yu funu,* p. 18.

76. Interview with a cadre of an All-China Women's Federation office in southern China on February 3, 1988. The interviewee prefers to be anonymous.

77. Cited in *Wen Wei Po* (March 7, 1987, Hong Kong).

78. See Zhang, "Women Are an Important Impetus."

79. Chen Yu, "Thoughts on the Socialization of Housework" and Zeng Hui, "The Socialization of Housework and Women's Liberation," in *Gaige kaifang yu funu,* pp. 133–156.

80. See n. 76 above.

7
INDIA

Suma B. Chitnis

A SHARED CONCERN

All over the world, the formal education of women has lagged behind the education of men. However, the shape of the gap, the circumstances by which it has been shaped, and the manner in which it is being handled differ from one society to another. Understanding these differences is important, not merely from the point of view of enriching the comparative perspective on education, but also from the point of view of using the experience of others to sharpen strategies to remove the gender gap in education in one's own society. This chapter offers a glimpse of the Indian experience.

THE CONSTITUTIONAL COMMITMENT AND ITS GENESIS

A Global Impulse

The constitution of independent India, adopted in 1950 after the country acquired freedom from British colonial rule, pledges equality of opportunity for education and promises universal, free, and compulsory education to all children up to the age of fourteen. In a somewhat unique gesture, it also names the "scheduled castes" (the former untouchable and some other castes that stand low in the Hindu caste hierarchy), the " scheduled tribes" (the culturally and physically isolated aboriginals of the land), and women as "weaker sections of society" to be "specially protected" and enabled to advance. From the outset, education has been viewed as both an aspect and an instrument of this advance.[1]

The constitution was framed soon after the conclusion of the Second World War, at a point in time at which the commitment to equalize educational opportunity and to universalize schooling was being taken on by several governments. To an extent, the promises made in the constitution are part of a global impulse. But this impulse had its roots deep in the social history and politics of the country. It is necessary to look at these roots, as well as the context which subsequently determines outcomes, in order to understand the current situation regarding the education of women in India.

HISTORICAL ROOTS OF THE COMMITMENT

A Tradition of Exclusiveness

In contrast to the constitutional commitment to equalize opportunity and to universalize schooling, the ancient, highly developed, Vedic tradition of knowledge and learning in India, going back to the second millennium B.C., was highly exclusive. Following on the caste system practiced by the Hindus, it categorically excluded the untouchables and some of the other lower castes. Knowledge was considered sacred and, therefore, inaccessible to those with a low ritual status. Religious reform movements that gave birth to more egalitarian, breakaway religions like Jainism and Buddhism, and to a series of devotional sects from the thirteenth century A.D. onward, did not change the situation substantially— nor did Muslim rule, with the Islamic ideology of the brotherhood of man. In fact, although the minority religions and sects had their own educational institutions, free from the principle of exclusion as practiced by the Hindus, mainstream Hindu education continued to be exclusive on the basis of caste.

The Education of Women

In the early Vedic period (2000 B.C.–1500 B.C.), women from among the castes that had access to learning shared the privilege with men. The "Upanayana" and "Savitravachana" rites for initiation to sacred knowledge were performed for girls as well as for boys. There are ample references to women scholars of the period—Brahmavadini, Gargi, Vachaknavi, Maitreyi, and others—who achieved eminence in philosophy, logic, grammar, and poetry, and participated in learned discourses with men.[2] However, over the centuries, they gradually lost this status. The Code of Manu formulated about 200 B.C. describes women as fickle, untrustworthy, devoid of judgment, impure as falsehood itself. It equates them with Shudras in the matter of learning and declares that they are unfit for knowledge.[3]

Within the limits of this brief chapter, it is not possible to trace this erosion of women's right to education, but it is important to note that it coincided with an overall deterioration in their status, culminating in harsh practices like *suttee*,[4] child marriage, and female infanticide, and in the shrinking of their rights in marriage and in property. Since the religious sanctions against the education of Hindu women were not as categorical as those against the education of the untouchables, women in ruling or priestly families did occasionally acquire education. But these were rare exceptions. Moreover, as custom hardened into superstition, the myth that education would bring widowhood on a woman and evil fate to her family gained firm ground. This was the situation when Europeans first arrived as traders in India in the fourteenth century and when the British established their rule later in the eighteenth century.

Equality of Opportunity and Hierarchical Tradition

From the point of view of understanding the cultural constraints to the establishment of equality of opportunity for education in India, it is important to recognize that traditional Indian education was not only exclusive, but also highly hierarchical. Access to learning was "graded" by caste. Only Brahmins of the highest caste were allowed to study all the Vedas. The number of Vedas allowed declined at successively lower levels of the Brahmin subcaste hierarchy. The education of the other castes was geared to the occupation assigned to them in the caste system. For instance, the education of the Kshatriya castes centered around military operations and statecraft. Similarly, the learning of the Vaishya castes was restricted to knowledge and skills relevant to trade. Although grading was not thus structured in the education provided in Muslim schools or Buddhist schools, there were pronounced social class differences in how much schooling was available.

In most parts of the country, however, all (except the castes), who were categorically denied knowledge had some access to learning in the indigenous system. Schooling was variously organized in regular schools, in temples, and in private homes. It was supported by native rulers, as well as by the community or the local elite who, together with the native rulers, were responsible for education at the village or small town level.[5]

British Displacement of Indigenous Education and Knowledge

As the British gained ascendancy over India and displaced the native elite, this support of schooling was lost. Similarly, native knowledge pertaining to arts and crafts, and native services and skills of different kinds shriveled and shrank, as European tastes, European modes of functioning, and British imports steadily dislocated and destroyed the indigenous.[6] As a consequence, the indigenous system of school, as well as indigenous knowledge both at the level imparted through formal education and at the level imparted informally as children helped adults in the various occupations, decayed and disintegrated.

Only the shrewdest of the upper caste Hindu elite were able to survive this catastrophe. Quick to recognize that mastery over the English language and European culture was the key to position and power under British rule, they shifted to European education. By the beginning of the nineteenth century, in fact even earlier, they were taking lessons from Christian missionaries who were only too willing to help, in the hope that their clout as teachers could be used to bring these influential natives into the Christian fold.

The Apathy of the East India Company

Although the East India Company found the natives educated by missionaries extremely useful in its administration and its trade, it was unwilling to take any responsibility for their education. It was happy to leave it to the missionaries. For that matter, the company was not even willing to take on the schooling of the children of its own European employees. Only in 1813, at the time of the renewal of its Charter and in response to pressure from the British public, did the company concede to move in the matter.

But gradually, Britain's trade and administrative responsibilities grew to be too extensive to be managed by functionaries brought in from England. The company, realizing that it would be advantageous to extend the educational facilities that it had grudgingly established at the time of the renewal of its Charter, used them to develop a cadre of European-educated native administrative aides who were even superior to those produced by the missionaries. It also recognized that the missionaries tended to mix education with religion and that it was politically unwise to continue to leave education in their hands. Therefore, the British government consciously decided to advance its support to European education in the country. This decision was formally taken in 1835.[7]

Downward Filtration Policy

Initially, it was categorically emphasized that education was being supported with the specific purpose of training a small cadre of natives to serve the administration and no more. However, this limited concept expanded when the British government realized that Western-educated Indians constituted an elite supportive of its rule. Official support for education expanded correspondingly. All the same, in principle, it remained restricted. Perhaps the complex thinking that defined British policy in the matter is best summed up in what was described as the "downward filtration policy," or the argument that the benefits of education provided to the elite would eventually "trickle down to the masses."[8]

Voluntary Effort

Regardless of what the British desired, however, European education in India advanced rapidly. The concrete material gains from this education were so massive and so clear that Indians were stimulated to develop it on their own. Religious and caste organizations, eager to advance the prospects of their communities, as well as public-spirited individuals inspired by a spirit of progress, came forward to start and to run schools. It was difficult for the government to curb this initiative. Official support continued to be guarded and restrained, but by 1857, the first three universities, modeled after the University of London, had been established.

The Nationalist Impulse

By the end of the nineteenth century, Indian aspirations for education had mounted phenomenally. With faith in the benevolence of the rulers, or, rather, with a naive conviction that the liberal humanist convictions of the British were strong enough to move them to provide educational facilities in India that were considered "basic" and "minimally essential" at home in England, Indian leaders began to press for the institution of free, compulsory, universal primary school education in India. In 1911, a bill incorporating this demand was formally introduced in the Imperial Legislative Council.

The British response to this demand was sharp, divided, and mixed. A section of the British administration and its advisers considered the demand just and valid. But another section could not forget that what British historians have described as the "mutiny" of 1857, and what Indians regard as the first "national move for independence" had occurred. They underlined that it was through British education that the Indian elite had imbibed the Liberal European philosophy which had generated nationalism, and they warned that extension of education to the masses would only hasten the end of British rule. Thus, the demand for universal, free, and compulsory elementary school education was finally rejected. With its rejection by the British, this demand became a prestige point with the Indian National Congress. It was high among the priorities of the Congress agenda for the postindependence development of the country.[9]

The Dismantling of Caste and Gender Exclusion from Education

During the course of the three decades that intervened between these events and independence, European education in India expanded considerably at both school and university levels. But it never really reached the masses. Moreover, as will be discussed later, it remained elitist and restricted in many ways. Yet, from the points of view of our concern with the education of women, British policy on education proved to be radical in that it quietly put an end to traditional restrictions to their schooling.

In fact, it struck at the very roots of the age-old exclusiveness of Hindu education by admitting "untouchables" to government-supported schools. Concerned about the stability of their rule and, therefore, eager to gain the goodwill of the upper caste elite, the British had initially hesitated to admit them. But their hesitation was shortlived. Emboldened by their success as colonizers, by 1860 they had found the courage to stand up for their liberal and their Christian convictions and to declare that their schools were open to all. Since the castes traditionally denied education did not, in any case, belong to the social strata from which clerks and officers were drawn, they rarely sought admission to school. But it is significant that the right to education, categorically denied to them earlier, was now established in principle.

By the beginning of the nineteenth century, Christian missionaries had been providing schooling for girls from the families of converts. They had tried to extend this facility to non-Christians in the hope that it would help propagate Christianity, but without much success. By about 1830, the Western-educated Indian elite, eager to socialize with the Europeans, were beginning to want to teach English to their families. Their engagement of European women, missionary or otherwise, led to the Zenana schools, which mark the beginning of European education for women in India.[10]

In this context, the education of women served a very limited purpose. Photographs of upper class Indian women of the period suggest a pathetic parallel. The blouses that the women in the photographs wear with their Indian sarees are unexpectedly Victorian in design. Fashioned out of imported European fabric and lace, abundantly trimmed with frills, pin-tucks, and gathers, they emulate garments European women of the period wore. Perhaps the ability to converse in English was likewise no more than a European trimming to their personalities— an accomplishment aimed at making them more "companionable" to their Westernized men and more acceptable in European social circles. Nevertheless, a beginning had been made.

More Substantial Purpose

The transition from a limited motive for the education of women to a more substantial purpose was rapid and firm. Throughout the late eighteenth and the early nineteenth centuries, Christian missionaries had mounted a vitriolic attack on customs such as suttee, child marriage, female infanticide, and the denial of remarriage to widows. The Hindu attitude toward women was being criticized as barbarous and inhuman. Shamed by this criticism and touched by the Liberal European humanism they had imbibed in the course of their European education, the Hindu elite started to reflect critically on the situation of women. The outcome was a wave of religious revisionism and a movement for social reform on behalf of women. The social reform movement provided a powerful impetus to their education.

Basically, the reformers pressed the government for legal restrictions on some of the obnoxious practices. Their efforts resulted in a spate of reform legislation, starting with the act against the practice of suttee in 1829. However, some of the reformers went much further and formed sects such as the Brahmo Samaj, the Arya Samaj, and the Prarthana Samaj to uphold the practice of "pure" Hinduism and to work continuously toward reform.

All these sects believed that the education of women was the cornerstone of reform. Accordingly, they set up their own facilities for the education of women—innovating a trend that was extensively followed by other educated Indians who did not belong to these sects but shared their faith in the education of women.[11] Thus, from the second or third decade of the nineteenth century onward, the education of women acquired a new meaning and support and advanced visibly.

This advance was restricted to a small section of the elite and to certain centers of reform in the country. Nevertheless, wherever it occurred there were spectacular gains, particularly where the efforts to educate women were linked with specific programs for reform, such as work on behalf of widows or unmarried mothers. For instance, as early as 1860, in Pune, in the former province of Bombay (now the state of Maharashtra), Jyotiba Phule, a social reformer who had already done considerable work toward ameliorating the lot of widows and oppressed women, set up a school for women. Since the orthodoxy of the times did not tolerate male teachers for girls, he equipped his own wife to teach. The saga of how he braved all obstacles and succeeded in his venture illustrates one of the most vital phases in the history of women's education in the country.[12]

Following upon the work of Phule, a Poona reformer by the name of Dhondo Keshav Karve sought to promote the remarriage of Hindu widows and to lead widowed women on to economic self-sufficiency and self-reliance. Toward this end, in spite of strong public opposition, he set up a refuge in Poona where widows could not only seek help from oppression and exploitation by their families, but also acquire the three Rs. Before long the refuge was training candidates to be nurses or primary school teachers. By 1916, it had grown into the first women's university in the country.[13] The movement for the advancement of the education of women had caught on.

Nationalism and Reinforcement of Women's Education

Around the second decade of the twentieth century, the education of women acquired further meaning and purpose, as the national movement for freedom took a somewhat unexpected and unique turn under the leadership of Gandhi.

Having decided to use nonviolent protest, or *satyagraha,* as the weapon with which to fight British imperialism in India, Gandhi declared that the tenacity and resilience of women, their capacity to meet aggression with peace, and their tradition of silent self-effacement were the qualities with which volunteers for the country's nonviolent struggle for freedom must be armed. At an immediately practical level, he underlined the importance of coopting women in the national struggle, with the argument that they constitute half the nation. He called on women to step out of their homes, to expand their horizons, and to join the struggle. At the same time, he publicly declared that their education was vital for the advancement of the nation.[14] As part of his armament for the nonviolent movement that he had launched, he put some of his young women volunteers through higher education. These women later made distinguished contributions, both to the movement for freedom and to the task of national reconstruction after independence. One of them, Durgabai Deshmukh, was the first chairperson of the National Committee on Women's Education (1959) set up after independence. Thus, by the time the country acquired independence, the commitment to the education of women had been firmly established.

Education for Women in Independent India

Upon the achievement of independence, this commitment was reaffirmed and reinforced. It was emphasized that as 50 percent of the electorate, they had to be educated to function as responsible voters. It was asserted that the success of the several programs of planned development which the country had outlined for itself hinged precariously on the cooperation of women, and they had to be educated to contribute to these programs effectively. Above all, it was pointed out that in fulfillment of the national commitment to equality, women as a "weaker" section of society had to be educated in order to advance as equals. Thus, the education of women came to be one of the core concerns in the country's blueprints for planned development. The postindependence performance of education for women in India must be evaluated with reference to all these commitments that have matured through a century and a half of the country's history.

THE FAILURE TO UNIVERSALIZE SCHOOLING FOR GIRLS

School Enrollment

Since the constitution promises universal education up to the age of fourteen, it is pertinent first to examine the school enrollment of girls on this count. The latest statistics available for the purpose from the Ministry of Human Resources Development documents are already between four and seven years old. However, they should do inasmuch as the scenario in education has not changed substantially during this period.

The 1981 decennial census reveals that 67 to 79 percent of the girls in the age group five to nine years and 62 to 73 percent in the age group ten to fourteen years are not yet enrolled at school. School enrollment statistics routinely provided by the Ministry of Education and by other official bodies, which suggest that 75.5 percent of the girls in the age group six to eleven years and 34.4 percent in the age group eleven to fourteen years are at school, mask this fact. First, Ministry enrollment figures indicate enrollment without providing any clue to the high attrition (about 60 percent) that occurs. Studies that have probed the issues reveal that fewer than 40 percent of the students who join Standard I reach

Standard V, which is the terminal year of the primary school (six to eleven years). Barely 23 percent survive to finish Standard VIII, which marks the termination of the middle school stage (eleven to fourteen years). The same studies indicate that attrition among girls is consistently 10 percent higher than it is among boys.

Ministry data perhaps inadvertently distort the truth because it is established practice to describe school enrollment in terms of "actual" enrollment at a stage, for example, Standards I-V as a percentage of the total population in the "relevant" age group, in this case six to eleven years. The underlying assumption here is that children in Standards I-V actually belong to the age group six to eleven years. However, many children actually enter school much later than six, or fail and repeat classes, with the result that the actual population of children in Standards I-V consists of several children who are much older than the eleven-year outer limit specifies. This distorts the percentage. The scale of the distortion may be gauged from the fact that the latest available enrollment figures (1983–1984) indicate that the enrollment of boys in Standards I-V constitutes 110 percent of the boys in the relevant age group!

Making allowance for these inadequacies in the data, we find that according to the latest statistics (1983–1984) the enrollment in Standards I-V accounts for only 75.5 percent of the female population in the age group six to eleven years and the enrollment in Standards VI-VIII accounts for only 34.4 percent in the age group eleven to fourteen years. The drop in the percentages from Standards I-V to Standards VI-VIII provides some hint of the scale of attrition after primary school. Table 7.1 offers further details on current school enrollment in the country and on growth since independence.

Literacy

Data on literacy provide another perspective on the situation. According to the census of 1981, 24.88 percent of the female population of the country is literate. However, poor as it is this national average masks serious imbalances. For instance, only 10.93 percent of the scheduled caste women and 8.04 percent of the tribal women, as compared to 24.82 percent of the general population of women are literate. Or again, only 17.96 percent of the general population of rural women, as compared to 47.82 percent of the general population of urban women, are literate. Furthermore, census details reveal severe interstate disparities. For instance, in the educationally advanced state of Kerala in South India, 72.2 percent of urban women and 64.25 percent of rural women are literate. In educationally backward states like Rajasthan and Uttar Pradesh, the level of literacy for women drops to a fraction of what it is in Kerala. For instance, only 34.45 percent of urban women and 5.46 percent of rural women in Rajasthan, and 35.43 percent of urban women and 9.49 percent of rural women in Uttar Pradesh are literate. The states in which the women's literacy level is particularly low (ranging from 11 percent to 21 percent—the combined average for the rural

Table 7.1
Growth of Education, 1950–1951 to 1983–1984

	1950–51	1983–84
A. School Level		
No. of Pre-primary schools	303	10,003
No. of Primary Schools (Std. I-V)	209,671	509,143
Enrollment of Boys in Primary Schools	13,770,000 (60.6)	49,322,000 (110.3)
Enrollment of Girls in Primary Schools	5,385,000 (24.8)	31,775,000
No. of Middle Schools (Stds. VI-VIII)	13,596	140,000
Enrollment of Boys in Middle Schools	2,586,000 (20.6)	16,500,000 (62.7)
Enrollment of Girls in Middle Schools	534,000 (4.6)	8,497,000 (34.4)
No. of High/Higher Secondary Schools Stds. IX-X/II/III	7,288	55,235
Enrollment of Boys in High/Higher Sec.	1,058,000	8,937,000
Enrollment of Girls in High/Higher Sec.	162,000	3,935,000
B. University Level		
No. of Universities	27	133
Pre-University/Intermediate Enrollment of Boys	195,000	1,473,000
Pre-University/Intermediate Enrollment of Girls	26,000	501,000
Graduate Enrollment of Boys	75,000	1,602,000
Graduate Enrollment of Girls	17,000	679,000
Post-graduate Enrollment of Boys	14,000	200,000
Post-graduate Enrollment of Girls	2,000	94,000
Doctoral Enrollment of Boys	1,100	17,800
Doctoral Enrollment of Girls	100	800

Source: Handbook on Social Welfare Statistics, 1986, Government of India, Ministry of Welfare, New Delhi.

and the urban populations) are Orissa, Andhra Pradesh, Madhya Pradesh, Uttar Pradesh, Bihar, and Rajasthan. Together, they account for 52.77 percent of the population of the country. Primary school, middle school, high school, and university enrollment figures differ correspondingly from state to state.

Girls continue to lag behind boys, in spite of the fact that in the four decades since independence their education has advanced more rapidly than that of boys. For instance, official statistics show that the total student population in the country increased from 28 million in 1950–1951 to 114 million by 1982–1983, yielding a growth rate of 4.5 percent per annum. During this period, the enrollment of girls increased at the compound rate of 5.5 percent, while the comparable figure for boys was only 3.9 percent per annum.

Government Support

That the education of girls has grown faster than the education of boys must be credited to the fact that the Indian government has followed up its special commitment to the education of women with special effort. For instance, in 1951, soon after independence the Central Social Welfare Board was appointed to look after the welfare of women. This board's terms of reference include the responsibility for advancing their education. Similarly, soon after independence, a National Committee on the Education of Women was specially appointed to look into the issue of women's education. The report of this committee, submitted in 1959, offered a sensitive and detailed appraisal of the situation and made several recommendations.[15] In 1971, the government appointed a committee with the much larger mandate of examining women's overall status. The report of this committee, submitted in 1975, is a rich document of different aspects of their status. The chapter on education is sharp in its assessment of the situation and sensitive in the recommendations offered.[16] From the First Plan onward the government has taken careful note of, and acted on, the observations and recommendations of these various committees. Nevertheless, the problems of poor school enrollment of girls, their poor retention, and their eventual failure to obtain adequate schooling remain.

The Larger Problem

The failure to universalize education for women is part of a larger failure which must be recognized and understood.

When the commitment to universalize schooling was made, it was believed that the basic task was to establish schools, and it was assumed that full enrollment would occur as soon as this was done. However, experience has belied this faith. Enrollment has remained poor, attrition is high, and attendance, with respect to the mass of the children, remains disturbingly irregular. Studies that have probed into the situation offer some shattering explanations. Basically, the finding is that children from within the mass of the population living below the poverty

line—about 40 percent by conservative estimates and 60 percent by some—
simply cannot afford to go to school. The extent of their poverty is such that
they have to work for their livelihood, either as wage labor or as unpaid family
help. Regardless of whether they belong to rural families living by agriculture,
fishing, forestry, crafts, or services, or to urban families living by urban occupations and services, their contribution is vital to their own survival and to that
of their families. In the metropolitan situations of imbalance created by employment, for instance, children often find paid work when parents cannot.[17]

While the core problem is that both the rural and the urban poor are altogether
unable to spare their children for school, there are other difficulties. For instance,
although the government sees schooling as a fundamental right, the masses have
not yet internalized this norm. Consequently, they lack the drive and the determination required to rise above the constraints of poverty and to send their
children to school.

The situation is further complicated by the fact that both the content and the
structure of schooling are inappropriate to the lives and the needs of the mass
of children. Studies on the issue reveal this vividly. They show that images,
narratives, norms, and the like projected in school primers are not those with
which the mass of children can easily identify. Similarly, they cannot readily
use the substance of primary and middle school instruction.[18]

In this context, it is important to recognize that the content of schooling in
India has not really changed since independence. It continues to be much the
same as it was in the schools established by the British. These schools, it may
be recalled, were established primarily with the purpose of turning out clerks,
administrators, civil servants, and functionaries in the professions of law, medicine, and teaching. Thus, they were strictly white collar and middle class in
orientation. Moreover, since all these functions required a minimum of a high
school education, it never recognized that primary and middle school education
could be terminal for some, as is implied in universalizing school up to the age
of fourteen. Consequently, the school curriculum for these stages was only
designed to lead on to higher learning. It did not meet the needs of those who
would go on to further schooling. Furthermore, because this school system was
modeled on schooling in industrialized Europe, the knowledge it imparted belonged to a society that had long ceased to be a simple agricultural economy.
It was thus distanced from the life of the Indian masses who lived and continued
to live by simple subsistence agriculture, farming, fishing, forestry, and crafts.
It was remote from both their experience and their needs. This problem did not
matter much then, for education was openly elitist and was not meant for the
masses anyway. But stretching the same curriculum to serve the needs of universal schooling in independent India has caused serious problems for the mass
of children, who come from homes that continue to live by occupations in a
world that continues to be preindustrial in character.

The same studies also reveal that the structure of the school system, inherited
from the British era, is, in myriad ways, unsuitable for the masses. The eight-

hour school day runs through hours that overlap with their work. The school terms extend over seasons in which agricultural operations are at their peak. To allow their children to attend school and remain absent from work at these periods is a luxury the poor cannot afford.

Additional Constraints to the Schooling of Girls

While poverty is the primary obstacle to universal education for children in India, the problem has a distinct gender dimension. For instance, in the gender definition of livelihood roles for rural and urban children, both girls and boys have tasks that are directly related to production. But, in addition, girls are expected to help with housework and with the care of younger siblings. Considered to be old enough for these tasks at the age of seven or eight, they are withdrawn from school earlier than their brothers, who may be allowed to continue until a little later, when they, in turn, are considered old enough to earn money or at least to help as family labor. The schooling of the more fortunate, who are allowed to continue with school also suffers, as it is continuously interrupted by the requirement that they stay at home and help when there is sickness or any other emergency in the family.

Apart from domestic obligations, there are several other constraints, one of the most crippling of which is that girls are married or betrothed at a very young age. It is not considered "proper" for a married girl to attend school. Therefore, marriage invariably means termination of schooling. In many cases, this restriction extends to betrothal as well. Furthermore, because the value system places a high premium on the virginity of girls at marriage, parents are unwilling to take the risk of exposing their daughters after puberty by sending them over long distances to school. This restriction operates most sharply in regions where *purdah* or the seclusion of women is practiced.

Another major restriction to the education of daughters is that girls are not seen as breadwinners, or as the "support" of parents in old age, whereas sons are. Consequently, the education of sons is seen as an investment in the future of the family and as old age security for the parents. A daughter's education is seen as an investment only to the extent that it adds to her value in the marriage market. Inevitably, when a family faces an economic crisis, or is forced to be selective in educating its children, boys get priority and girls may be passed over. Parents who can afford to do send their daughters to high school and university, but because of the cultural norm that a wife should be less educated than the husband, this education is carefully limited. This factor surfaces visibly in the data on the higher education of girls. In fact, it is frustrating to observe how it distorts the otherwise impressive advance of women in higher education.

HIGHER EDUCATION

Barely 2 percent of the girls who enter primary school make it to the university. But as a net result of the differentials in the enrollment and dropout of girls and boys at different levels of school education, this 2 percent constitutes roughly 38 percent of the total enrollment at the university level. Intercountry comparisons reveal that this percentage is higher than the percentage of the enrollment of girls at universities, not only in many developing countries, but also in some of the developed countries—notably Great Britain at least until very recently.

This happy situation reflects the spectacular growth of the higher education of women throughout this century. Though restricted to the middle and upper classes, it has been more rapid than at any level of school education.

The Centrality of Marriage

At least two features of this growth suggest that the centrality accorded to marriage and motherhood in the life of women adversely affects the quality of their advance. First, a large number of women enter college for only a short exposure, perhaps without an intent to complete the college course. Second, most of them shy away from professional courses leading to definite careers and crowd into the liberal arts faculty. Tables 7.2 and 7.3 illustrate this point.

As Table 7.2 indicates, the percentage of the enrollment which girls account for from secondary school indicates that their representation increases visibly, from 31.09 percent at the secondary school level to 40.32 percent at the predegree level. It drops sharply to 22.75 percent at the intermediate level, before it stabilizes to around 30 to 31 percent at the graduate and postgraduate levels. This strange phenomenon—a spurt in representation at the predegree level, followed by a sharp drop at the intermediate stage—could be due to existing differences in function which a university education is expected to serve for boys and for girls.

Basically, university education is supposed to equip boys to earn a livelihood. Since anything less than a degree has no more value than completion of secondary school in the job market, boys who cannot afford the full four years of a degree course do not enter college at all. On the other hand, although university is also supposed to equip girls for a livelihood, it performs what some consider the more important function for them: to improve their prospects for marriage. Practically all the studies that have explored why Indian girls go to college indicate that this function is a major consideration in parents' decision to send their daughters to college.[19] Even a year or two of college education is considered adequate for this purpose. The exposure involved and the slight sophistication acquired are all that is needed. Thus, the sharp increase in the representation of girls at the predegree level, followed by the decline in their representation at the intermediate level observed in Table 7.2, could be explained by the fact that a large number of girls enter university only to improve their prospects for marriage by taking a year or two of college education.

In all fairness, it must be conceded that, while most parents value university education as a means of improving their daughters' prospects for marriage, the large majority also consider it valuable because it enables their daughters "to

Table 7.2
Enrollment of Girls as a Percentage of Total Enrollment, by Level of Higher Education, 1982–1983

Educational Levels	No. of Girls Enrolled	Total Enrollment	Girls as a % of the Total
Ph.D/B.Sc/D.Phil	7,536	24,938	30.22
M.A./M.Sc/M.Com.	88,224	2,80,963	31.40
B.Ed/B.T.	34,999	73,521	47.60
B.A/B.Sc/B.Com	6,37,995	21,20,482	30.08
M.B.B.S.	19,021	71,303	26.67
B.E/B.Sc/B.Arch	5,113	1,17,408	4.35
Intermediate/Junior College	4,07,971	17,92,662	22.75
Pre-degree (2 years)	1,66,493	4,12,851	40.32
Stds. IX-XII	36,75,252	1,18,18,365	31.09
Stds. VI-VIII	75,24,306	2,22,13,765	33.87
Stds. I-V	2,97,63,280	7,70,38,922	38.63
Stds. Pre-primary/ Pre-basic	4,58,291	10,21,093	44.88

Source: Selected Educational Statistics - 1982-83, Ministry of Education and Culture (Department of Education), Planning, Monitoring and Statistics Division, Government of India, New Delhi, 1984.

earn and to stand on their own feet."[20] Table 7.3 describes the course-wise distribution of women at Indian universities in the context of these two considerations.

Arts Courses as Neutral Ground

The percentage of girls is largest in the Faculty of Arts (Table 7.3), considerably larger than in any of the other faculties, all of which have better prospects for employment than the arts stream. This suggests that the notion of educating girls to be earners is not yet sufficiently widespread for girls to be enrolled in career-oriented courses in significant numbers. If so, the large percentage of girls in the relatively less career-oriented Arts Faculty can be explained by the fact that it accounts for a population of university girls who are not permitted

Table 7.3
Enrollment of Women in Faculty, 1970–1971 and 1980–1981

Faculty	Women as Percentage of Total in the Faculty	
	1970-71 Enrollment	1980-81 Enrollment
Arts (a)	31.7	37.7
Science	17.8	28.7
Commerce	3.7	15.0
Education	36.5	47.3
Engineering/Technology	1.0	3.8
Medicine	22.8	24.5
Agriculture	0.4	3.3
Veterinary Science	0.7	3.3
Law	3.7	6.8
Others (b)	40.0	39.7
Total	21.9	27.1

Note: (a) Includes students of Library Science, Journalism, Social Work, Theology, etc.

(b) Includes students pursuing courses in Music/Fine Arts/Physical Education, etc.

Source: University Grants Commission, University Development in Basic Facts and Figures, 1970-71, New Delhi, 1974 and 1986. U.G.C. leaflet on last figures.

Highlights

1. At the university level we still find women predominant in 'traditional' faculties like Education, Arts and Medicine.

2. Increasing enrollment in Science, Commerce, Engineering, Agriculture, Veterinary Science is indicative of a shift from traditional faculties to non-traditional ones.

by convention to take up careers, unless compelled by circumstances to earn a living.

Meanwhile, it is important to recognize that the Faculty of Arts probably also holds a small population of girls who have career ambitions but who must keep these ambitions masked and in abeyance until they are married and have ascertained the inclinations of their husbands and their in-laws in the matter. Cultural norms require that married women who wish to pursue careers do so only with the "approval" of husbands and in-laws. That a girl has enrolled in a professional course could be interpreted to mean that she has decided to pursue a career without waiting for the permission required. Not too many parents are bold enough to allow their daughters to take the risk to marriage arrangements which such an interpretation involves. They generally advise their daughters to join arts courses, remain appropriately neutral for outward appearances, and "sweetly" work on their husbands and their in-laws for approval, if their career ambitions persist after marriage.

Career Ambitions toward Equality

Although the university education of women is heavily influenced by the centrality of marriage to their lives, it would be wrong to underestimate the impact of their growing career aspirations. Table 7.3 shows that during the 1970s the percentage of girls enrolled increased in every faculty of university education, and that the increase was most pronounced in career-oriented fields like commerce, agriculture, veterinary science, and engineering which were formerly considered male preserves.(See also Table 7.4.)

The brevity of this chapter makes it impossible to trace the fascinating manner in which tradition, changing values, economic needs, and the burgeoning of new employment opportunities for educated women have combined to shape women's career aspirations. Nor is it possible to prove that, small though it may seem at present, the increase in the representation of women in professional courses is a precursor of further advance. But many indicators suggest that this advance will continue. If it does, the enrollment of women in professional courses at universities will soon catch up with the enrollment of men. However, it is important to recognize that the polarization characteristic of postindependence development in the country is so great that professional education is becoming the exclusive preserve of the middle and upper classes. Therefore, the parity that women are likely to achieve in this sector of university education will be confined to the Indian elite.

OUTCOMES OF EDUCATION

Smug Assumptions

What, one may ask, is the outcome of all these advances in the education of women? How far have the objectives that prompted its postindependence ex-

Table 7.4
Women and Men in Different Professions

Sl. No.	Name of the Profession	Year	Number	
			Men	Women
1.	Regular Employees Ministries and Department of Central Govt.	1976	2,945,416	99,272
2.	Judges in Supreme Court	1978	13	–
3.	Judges in High Court	1978	302	7
4.	Personal in IAS	1977	2338	218
5.	Indian Foreign Service	1977	371	38
6.	Indian Police Service	1977	1907	10
7.	Indian Forest Service	1977	1098	–
8.	Central Information Service	1977	709	33
9.	Indian Economic Service	1977	426	22
10.	Indian Statistical Service	1977	222	6
11.	Central Secretariat	1977	795	9
12.	Chartered Accountants	1976–77	1569	15
13.	Advocates Registered with the Bar Council	1974	140,276	2904
14.	Nurses–Senior or A Grade	1974	5141	86,769
	Nurses–Junior or B Grade	1974	286	6207
	Midwives–Senior or A Grade	1974	–	90,181
	Junior–Asst. of B Grade	1974	–	10,373
	Auxiliary Nurse, Midwives	1974	–	39,790
	Health Visitors	1974	–	5,561
15.	Teachers–Primary or Junior Basic Schools	1976–77	1,029,148	310,717
	Teachers–Middle or Senior Basic Schools	1976–77	513,700	202,263
	Teachers–High or Higher Secondary	1976–77	529,726	206,327
16.	Teachers–Higher Education	1973–74	132,978	28,441

Table 7.4 (continued)

| Sl. No. | Name of the Profession | Year | Number | |
			Men	Women
17.	Scientific and Technica Personnel	1977	315,376	34,147
18.	Doctors	1977	169,789	39,544
19.	Dentist	1976	3,917	451

Source: Women in India, A Statistical Profile
         Govt. of India
         Dept. of Social Welfare 1978, pp. - 277 -2.

pansion been fulfilled? Has education increased the political efficacy of women, enabled them to benefit by and contribute to development, or improved their status in the family?

In trying to answer these questions, we discover that India's faith in education as an instrument of development was so complete that these questions were not even raised. Only with the report of the National Committee on the Status of Women (1974) and the spate of explorations generated in the course of the Women's Decade were serious doubts raised about the efficacy of this instrument.

Education and Political Efficacy

One of the core objectives of postindependence education was to equip women to function as responsible citizens. It is difficult to determine whether this objective has been achieved

Reference to studies on the political status of women since independence reveals that very few women enter the democratic race for power.[21] Even fewer win. Those who enter the fray come from families that are very well off. They are therefore able to read and write, but many of them have no formal education and no degrees. Most of them also come from families that are heavily steeped in politics. Consequently, they have learned to be articulate and have acquired a sharp perspective on political matters.

Although it is difficult to establish the influence of education on the political functioning of women who venture out as representatives, it is even more difficult to do so with reference to the female electorate. On the whole, uneducated voters in the country are more enthusiastic than the educated. They turn out in larger numbers at elections. Moreover, Indian elections have repeatedly proved that lack of formal education, even of literacy, has not stopped voters from exercising appropriate pressures or from choosing their representatives wisely. Studies on the voting behavior of Indians also reveal that the Indian democracy has not yet matured enough that people vote on the basis of carefully considered interests or issues. They are swayed by caste, kin, and regional loyalties. Therefore, education does not seem to make any substantial difference to their political behavior. Indian women conform to this general pattern.

The feminist impulse, generated through the International Women's Decade, has changed the situation somewhat. Increasingly, educated women have been coming forward to organize protests and to influence opinion on issues, ranging from rape and violence against women to their rights in employment. The lead and example provided by these educated women in responsible citizenship marks a new threshold in the maturation of the Indian democracy.

The Participation of Women in Economic Development

In assessing the impact of education on the economic status of women in India, it is important to recognize that 80 percent of the Indian economy is simple, if not primitive, and does not require formal education. Barely 20 percent is technologically and industrially advanced enough to require formal education. The sector that uses the simple traditional technologies also happens to be somewhat loosely and informally organized and is referred to as the "unorganized" sector in contrast to the more formally structured "organized" sector distinguished by the use of more modern technology and organizational practices and procedures characteristic of industrialization.

The Omission of Women

In the mid-1970s, the National Committee on the Status of Women (1974) made the startling revelation that postindependence industrialization and technological development had severely marginalized and, in some cases, even pushed women out of work in both the technological and organizational sector. Using figures from the country's decennial census to illustrate the steady decline in the participation of women in the labor force, they pointed out that, although this process had been in motion from the first decade of the twentieth century onward, it had accelerated enormously after independence.

At about the same time that this committee submitted its report, the National Commission on Agriculture (1976) pointed out that the failure to recognize women's role in agriculture and, therefore, to give them relevant knowledge or to equip them with necessary skills, techniques, and tools was one of the major factors responsible for the slow progress in improving agricultural productivity in the country. The same sentiment was being echoed with respect to other spheres of economic development.

Most of this damage has either occurred in the traditional sector where no formal education is required or in the modern sector at levels of work where no formal education is required either. Therefore, it could be argued that this displacement of female labor has nothing to do with women's education. On the other hand, the fact remains that the education that many of the women received in the course of the massive expansion of schooling in the country did not help to halt their dislocation or elimination from the labor force.

Some of those who have been displaced belong to the clerical or supervisory levels in the organized sector. Their tasks have been taken over by computers, word processors, mechanized packing, and so on. They have been unable to retrain or reeducate themselves fast enough to keep pace with the technological advances that displaced them.

New Opportunities for Educated Women

While working-class women have thus been displaced, a spectacular growth of new employment opportunities for educated women, particularly for highly educated women, has occurred. This growth has coincided with the rapid increase in the higher education of women, with a revolution of rising expectations and standards of life stimulating them to earn money and with a new recognition and social acceptance of women's right to self-fulfillment through work.

The conjunction of all these factors has brought about a virtual explosion in the employment of educated women. One of the most interesting consequences of this phenomenon is that the percentage of secondary school and university educated women (18.85 percent) in the female workforce is almost twice the corresponding percentage for males (9.94 percent), as may be seen from the accompanying data.

	Female	Male
Illiterate	52.59	48.43
Literate up to middle school	28.56	41.63
Secondary school	13.79	7.39
Graduate and above	5.06	2.55
Total	100.00	100.00

Source: NNS 32nd round.

The typical curve for aggregate female labor in the country takes a U-shape with respect to education. At the lowest level, the mass of illiterate women continues with traditional occupations in agriculture, fishing, farming, forestry, the services, and traditional crafts. In the middle, with modest education, women's participation tapers off because the jobs available are low status. At higher levels of education, the employment of women increases.[22]

This growth in the employment of educated women is not only substantial in quantity, but also impressive in quality. One finds women in practically every high position of employment and office. Apart from the fact that the country has had a woman prime minister, there are women ministers, ambassadors, and high court judges. Women function as vice-chancellors of universities and in senior positions in the civil service, the foreign service, and the police force. Women hold senior positions as researchers, managers, and professionals in the private sector.

These achievements are somewhat tempered by the fact that though the absolute number of women in professional employment is quite large, the size of their representation is small. A 1984 census of women employed in the various ministries of the union government showed that women constituted only 2.5 percent of total employment. In the higher administrative cadres, data for 1978, which unfortunately are the latest available, show that there are only two women high court judges, nine Indian Administrative Service officers, five Indian Education Service officers, and barely 0.09 Indian Police Service officers for every 100 men.

Furthermore, studies of educated women in employment continuously reveal that few women make it to the highest position and that the positions they hold are lower than they are qualified for. A study of professionally educated women scientists in the city of Bombay, which shows that the overwhelming majority of the women interviewed are functioning as administrators, teachers, and researchers, indicates that 90 percent of the administrators, 73 percent of the teachers, and 50 percent of the researchers functioned at the bottom of the ladder they were on.[23]

Studies that explore the issue of the underutilization of women do not reveal overt discrimination, but they categorically indicate that women have to curb their career aspirations in order to manage their dual responsibilities as earners and homemakers.

Child Care as a Contribution to Development

By far the most positive return of educated women to development is their contribution as educated mothers. For instance, maternal education plays a major role in reducing the level of infant and child mortality. The inverse relationship between infant mortality and the level of mothers' education has been confirmed in the rural as well as the urban areas of almost all states in India. The most telling illustration is from a 1982 study of villages in the state of Karnataka where observation of differentials in infant mortality, by mothers' education, revealed a rate of 130 per 1,000 where the mother had not been to school, 80 where she had only had primary schooling, and 70 where she had some secondary schooling.[24]

Apart from its intrinsic worth, this reduction in infant mortality is of tremendous value to the country's efforts to control population growth. The shift from a large to a small family norm on which this control eventually hinges is determined by several social and psychological factors. One factor is that couples have a measure of confidence that the children born to them will live. Since infant mortality has always been high in India, this confidence is not easily developed. By reducing infant mortality, the education of women indirectly serves the critical function of generating this confidence.

A review of relevant research and literature reveals that the education of women helps generate attitudes conducive to the small family norm. For instance, higher aspirations of parents for their children's education, and, similarly, parental aspirations for a better standard of life for them are consistently quoted as attitudes that favor the small family norm. Education helps because educated mothers have higher aspirations for their children than uneducated mothers. In addition, the aspirations of educated mothers are more concrete and focused and therefore more conducive to the planned approach to life, which is so important to a conscious and purposive adoption of the small family norm.

Studies reveal that education reduces fertility for several other reasons: (1) On an average, educated women marry much later than uneducated women— generally late enough to have fewer children. (2) Education reduces a woman's unrealistic fears about the use of contraceptive devices, as well as about sterilization and medical termination of pregnancy, and thus enables her to use the birth control facilities provided under the family planning program more effectively. (3) Education helps a woman face and sort out religious and traditional objections to contraception more rationally and successfully. (4) Finally, education equips and stimulates women to take up gainful employment and to develop their own careers, and thus motivates them to keep their families small enough to be accommodated within their career goals.[25]

Apart from these several gains to the population program, another major gain from the education of women has been to the country's effort to universalize school education. Studies on enrollment and school dropouts clearly reveal that a child with an educated mother has a better chance of being enrolled at school and is less likely to drop out. Similarly, educated mothers have been observed to be more careful about the nutrition, immunization, and overall health of their children. As a result, they contribute massively to the country's efforts to provide better health care for the people.[26]

Education and Women's Status within the Family

The impact of education on raising the status of women within the family has been quite mixed. There are some obvious and visible gains, such as a new companionship between husband and wife—in all strata of society; a new partnership in business or in the professions among the more affluent and better educated; and, for upper and middle-class women, a new, earlier unavailable, status as earners. Equally evident in all strata of society is the addition of rich new dimensions to women's traditional roles. As mothers, educated women help their children with school work, and encourage and guide children's career aspirations. As homemakers, they are better able to care for the health and nutrition of the family, and to take an informed interest in the outside activities of family members. As daughters, they have acquired a new capacity to supplement the family income and to support parents.

Serious Inadequacies

On the other hand, feminist research which reveals that few women are allowe to use their support capacity after marriage because tradition does not approve of parents being supported by daughters opens up a pandora's box of distortions about women's education. One of the ugliest distortions is the practice of treating it as a dowry in marriage. A corollary is that educated brides may be compelled to earn for the family, regardless of their own inclinations.

Surprisingly, educated women are not able to fight this oppression. For example, even university-educated women are the victims of dowry death (suicides of women who are harassed by their husbands and/or in-laws for bringing in an inadequate dowry), and few women in white-collar occupations have full autonomy or real control over their earnings. Feminist research reveals that educated women are rarely aware of their legal rights in marriage, motherhood, or property and that many lack the confidence, the sense of self-worth, and the sense of efficacy required to liberate themselves from the bondage of traditional expectations and norms.

The problem is that education does not make a frontal attack on these traditions. It does not equip women to understand, much less to use, the rights available to them. Meanwhile, such is the paradox of Indian life that, although girls are increasingly being educated to "stand on their own feet," they are also socialized to adjust to the needs of the husband and the wishes of the in-laws. They are conditioned to be compliant and yielding. Some educated women are able to live with this paradox, whereas others have broken through to find their freedom. But a large number struggle unsuccessfully to smother their new aspirations. The tranquility of the Indian family is gradually being shaken by the conflicts and contradictions involved.

Meanwhile, an extensive dialogue is taking place on how the education of women and of men can be more purposively geared to serve the national commitment to equality. The official response to the question is most impressive. The new education policy emphasizes the "empowerment" of women through a "conscious transformation" of their values and attitudes. The National Council of Education Research and Training has been commissioned to design ways and means by which school curricula can be geared to this task. The University Grants Commission has requested universities to consider ways of incorporating women's problems and concerns in teaching, research, and extension activities in various disciplines. It offers generous support for the establishment of women's studies.

TOWARD THE EMPOWERMENT OF WOMEN

It is still too early to expect results from these new measures. But from the point of view of understanding how colonial systems of education are being shaped by the forces of development, it is important to look at the public response to the realization that the promise to universalize schooling for girls has failed, and more disturbing yet, that their education does not fully equip them to handle their marginalization. Because this realization came in the mid-1970s and practically coincided with the declaration of the International Women's decade, the response was particularly powerful. It radically altered existing notions about schooling and led to an expanded concept of education and to some revolutionary innovations.

The importance of schooling was basically acknowledged and the commitment to universalization was reiterated and renewed, but it was asserted that quick and efficient strategies have to be worked out to bridge the gaps in the knowledge, skills, and attitudes of women. The spontaneity, enthusiasm, and efficiency with which voluntary bodies have acted in the matter marks a massive breakthrough.

Specifically designed to meet needs as experienced at the grass roots, the strategies used are as variegated as the life of the Indian masses. They range from programs aimed at improving the performance of schoolgirls in science and mathematics, or at enabling girls who have dropped out from school to resume their studies, to programs for young and adult women which may not include numeracy or literacy at all, but concentrate on equipping them to handle specific challenges of life. Among the better known are two that have won the coveted Magasasay Award.

In one of these programs, a husband and wife team of doctors—Dr. and Dr. (Mrs.) Arole, who run a highly successful rural community health center in the state of Maharashtra—have imaginatively combined their development effort for rural health with a program for the advancement of women. Their center trains as health workers, illiterate, low caste, village women who would never routinely have qualified for such jobs. They conduct the training themselves and give the women all the basic medical knowledge and skills required. In addition, they give them a clear understanding of how far their expertise can be used and where it ends. They are instructed on where to take patients for more specialized care, and they are equipped to deal with authorities at different levels.

In the second program chosen for the award, Ila Bhat, a trade union leader who functions in the metropolitan city of Ahmedabad in Gujarat, has helped poor, illiterate women, working as vegetable or fruit vendors, hawkers, or piece-rate workers, to organize the Self-Employed Women's Association (SEWA). This organization helps women to understand their rights. Producers and traders equip them to acquire and use loans and other development facilities available under the several government plans provided in the country; teach them to cooperate for purposes of bulk purchase of new materials and sale of finished goods; and help them to organize themselves for action in matters involving civic or administrative authorities or the producers for whom they work on a piece-rate basis. Over the years, SEWA has empowered women for a range of other functions in life, such as better care of their own health, more effective exercise of their civic and political rights, or more efficient fulfillment of corresponding obligations.

Neither of these two programs gives priority to literacy. Yet both have found that once women are empowered to handle their immediate needs, beneficiaries are enthusiastic about learning to read and write.

Examples of such projects could be multiplied. The important point is that each has developed a distinctive pedagogy—consisting of curricula tailored to the specific needs of the population covered and teaching methods particularly suited to the specific milieu in which the programs are run. The language for instruction and the imagery used are drawn from the lives and experiences of those who are taught.

Wrangling Over Definitions

Purists wrangle over whether these and other such ventures can be labeled education. But policy makers, planners, and even educators, determined to meet the commitments made, are already beginning to draw on the experience of these programs, not only to reorganize the structure and content of education at school and university level, but also to redefine its objectives. The latest National Policy on Education clearly emphasizes the obligation to empower women.[27] The National Council of Educational Research and Training (NCERT) now has a special so-called cell charged with the task of innovating ways and means to use the school curriculum to do so.[28] This concept of the empowerment of women is drawn straight from the heart of the programs we have described. The University Grants Commission has a special Advisory Committee on Women's Studies, and over the last three years it has pursued an active policy of sponsoring women's studies. The Indian Council of Social Science Research, the apex body for social science research in the country, has also appointed a special Advisory Committee for Research on Women. It has also named "women" as one of the priority areas for its research funding. All this is powerful evidence of the government's commitment to the empowerment of women through education. One only hopes that empowerment will not stagnate into bureaucratic rhetoric.

Meanwhile, India's failure to realize its postindependence aspirations for education has triggered a radical questioning of concepts and models of education borrowed from the West and hitherto confidently used in the country. One observes an earnest quest for relevance, leading to a confrontation with the pristine meaning of education as "equipment for life." It is gratifying that this exciting development has come out of the efforts of educated Indian women to make education more meaningful for their less educated sisters.

NOTES

1. Government of India, *Third Five Year Plan*. Government of India, *Report of the Education Commission: Education and National Development* (New Delhi: Manager of Publications, 1964–1966).

2. A. S. Altekar, *Position of Women in Hindu Civilization* (Delhi: Montilal Banarsidas, 1962), pp. 410–414.

3. Ibid.

4. According to the practice of suttee, a Hindu woman, when widowed, immolates herself on her husband's funeral pyre.

5. For a description of indigenous schools in the early nineteenth century, see W. Adam, *Reports on the State of Indigenous Education in Bengal* (1835); R. V. Parulekar, *Survey of Indigenous Education in the Province of Bombay, 1820–1830* (Bombay, 1951); J. P. Naik, and S. Narullah, *A Student's History of Education in India (1800–1973),* 6th revised ed. (New Delhi: Macmillan Co. of India Ltd., 1974).

6. Sen Anupam, *The State, Industrialization and Class Formation in India* (London: Routledge & Kegan Paul, 1982).

7. For a description of British education in India, see Naik and Narullah, *A Student's History of Education in India.*

8. Basu Aparna, *Essays in the History of Indian Education* (New Delhi: Concept Publishing Co., 1982), p. 65.

9. For a discussion of this issue, see Basu Aparna, *Growth of Education and Political Development, 1898–1920* (London: Oxford University Press, 1974).

10. For a description of Zenana schools, see Gulam Murshid, *Reluctant Debutante: Response of Bengali Women to Modernization, 1849–1905* (Rajashahi University, 1983); Meredith Borthwick, *Changing Role of Women in Bengal* (Princeton, N.J.: Princeton University Press, 1984).

11. D. Keer, *Mahatma Jotirao Phule* (Bombay: Popular Prakashan, 1974).

12. M. K. Gandhi, *Women and Social Injustice* (Ahmedabad: Navajivan Publishers, 1942).

13. Government of India, *National Committee on Women's Education* (New Delhi: Ministry of Education, 1959).

14. Gandhi, *Women and Social Injustice;* Gandhi, To the Women of India in Young India, 10th April 1938.

15. Government of India, *National Committee on Women's Education.*

16. Government of India, *Towards Equality,* Report of the Committee on the Status of Women in India (New Delhi: Department of Social Welfare, Ministry of Education and Social Welfare, 1974).

17. Indian Express, August 27, 1985, quotes a figure of 44 million children in India's labor force. Suma Chitnis and C. Suvanathar, in P. J. Richards and A. M. Thomson, eds., *Basic Needs and the Urban Poor;* An ILO-WEP Study (London: Croom Helm, 1984), pp. 184–207.

18. J. P. Naik, *Equality, Quality and Quantity: The Elusive Triangle in Indian Education* (Bombay: Allied Publishers, 1975).

19. John S. August, *The Indian Family in Transition* (New Delhi: Vikas Publishing House, 1982); Rhoda Lois Blumberg, *India's Educated Women—Options and Constraints* (New Delhi: Hindustan Publishing Corp., 1980); Margaret L. Cormak, *She Who Rides*

a Peacock (Bombay: Asia Publishing House, 1961); Promilla Kapur, *Marriage and the Working Woman in India* (New Delhi: Vikas Publishing House, 1970); Aileen D. Ross, *The Hindu Family in an Urban Setting* (Toronto: University of Toronto Press, 1961).

20. John S. August, *The Indian Family in Transition;* Promilla Kapur, *Marriage and the Working Woman in India.*

21. Vina Mazumdar, *Symbols of Power: Studies on the Political Status of Women in India* (Bombay: Allied Publishers, 1979).

22. Neera Desai and Maitreyi Krishnaraj, *Women and Society in India* (Delhi: Ajanta Publications, 1987), p. 81.

23. Maitreyi Krishnaraj, "Women, Work and Science in India," in G. Kelly and C. Elliot, eds., *Women's Education in the Third World: Comparative Perspectives* (Albany, N.Y.: SUNY Press, 1982).

24. John C. Caldwell et al. "The Causes of Demographic Change in Rural South India: A Micro Approach," *Population and Development Review* 8 (1982): 689–728.

25. Anirudh K. Jain and Moni Nag, "Importance of Female Primary Education for Fertility Reduction in India," in Ghosh Ratna and Zachariah Mathew, eds., *Education and the Process of Change* (New Delhi: Sage Publications, 1987), pp. 158–177.

26. U. S. Naidu, and S. Parasuraman, *Health Situation of Youth in India* (Bombay: Tata Institute of Social Sciences, 1982).

27. Government of India, *Programme of Action. National Policy on Education* (New Delhi: Ministry of Human Resources Development, 1986).

28. NCERT has brought out three handbooks on textbook writing, namely, *Status of Women Through Curriculum, Elementary Teachers Handbook* (1982); *Status of Women Through Curriculum, Secondary and Senior Secondary Stages* (1984); and *Status of Women Through Teaching of Mathematics—A Teacher's Handbook* (1984). All three are interesting and informative.

8
JAPAN

Kumiko Fujimura-Fanselow

Following World War II, the participation of Japanese women in education increased markedly at all levels. Even so, gender differences and inequalities continue to persist, particularly as one moves up the educational ladder. Issues relating to women and education have been given little attention by policy makers or, for that matter, by most Japanese. Thus, for example, discussions of educational reform that took place in the early 1970s[1] as well as those undertaken by the National Council on Educational Reform, which was appointed by Prime Minister Yasuhiro Nakasone in 1984, failed to address these issues. This neglect may derive in part from a widely held assumption that since the postwar reforms granted women access to education at all levels and the principle of sex equality in education has been adopted, the problem no longer exists. It may also reflect the fact that, until very recently, most Japanese have not really thought it important or desirable to have women participate in society in the same capacities as men and therefore have not been concerned with the question of how women are educated. Whatever the reasons, little effort has been made either to explore sexual inequalities, to investigate their root causes, or to attempt to redress gender imbalances in educational participation.

This chapter examines enrollment trends within various educational levels by Japanese women over the postwar years. It highlights sexual differences in participation, the factors affecting women's access to education, and the impact of education on the lives of Japanese women in the family, the workplace, and the political system. In order to provide a historical perspective for understanding women and education in contemporary Japan, women's education over the past century will be discussed briefly.

HISTORICAL BACKGROUND

Before World War II education in Japan reflected a concept of female education that came to be referred to as *ryōsai kembō no kyōiku,* or education for the training of good wives and wise mothers.[2] This ideology has strong influence even in contemporary Japan. Despite an overall rise over the postwar years in the levels of education which the Japanese desire for their children, most people continue to exhibit lower aspirations for daughters than for sons and to view university education as less important for daughters on the assumption that they will marry and have children and not take up careers following completion of their education.[3]

The Meiji government, which came to power in 1868, recognized the urgent need for a modern, unified system of education as integral to its goal of promoting military and economic development and creating a unified, national state.[4] Under the newly established Ministry of Education, the Fundamental Code of Education was promulgated in 1872 which called for the establishment of a modern, comprehensive system of elementary schools, secondary schools, and universities throughout Japan. Compulsory education was set at four years for both boys and girls, and while the principle of coeducation was adopted, after third grade boys and girls were educated separately. Attendance rates among females at elementary schools lagged considerably behind those of males (30 versus 68 percent in 1888) largely because most parents continued to feel that it was at best unnecessary for daughters to receive any academic training; at worse, it was unfeminine. Spurred in part by the expanding needs of the rapidly industrializing economy for female workers following the Sino-Japanese War (1894–1895), the female rate of attendance rose. By 1904, 90 percent of all girls went to elementary school.[5] In 1907, compulsory education was extended to six years, and beyond this there were two years of higher elementary school. By the end of the Meiji era in 1912, compulsory school attendance was nearly universal.

Although there was relative equality in access for males and females at the elementary level, education for females beyond the elementary level was slow to develop. The government did begin establishing normal schools for women in 1875. These enrolled students who graduated from higher elementary school (eighth grade) and, later, those who transferred from girls' high school.

Christian mission schools, such as the Ferris Seminary in Yokohama established in 1870 and Kobe Jogakuin established in 1875 in Kobe, were the first to carry education for women beyond the elementary grades. It was not until 1882 that the government formed a system of schools for girls' secondary education with the establishment of a girls' high school in Tokyo. Secondary schools for girls slowly made their appearance in other parts of the country. As late as 1894, there were only thirteen public girls' high schools throughout Japan with a total enrollment of just 2,000.[6] The 1899 Higher Girls' School Law called on local governments to establish at least one such institution in each prefecture, with the length of study prescribed as four years. In 1920, five-year secondary schools for girls opened.

The academic standards at girls' high schools were lower than those at boys' secondary schools, which were called "middle schools," and the curricula stressed women's homemaking skills. This reflected the official view that female education ought to aim at imparting such knowledge as would be helpful to a woman in her role as wife and mother. The percentage of female elementary school graduates who went on to these schools was very small—about 2 percent in 1915 and under 5 percent in 1924.[7] The young women who attended these schools came mostly from middle- and upper class city and town families or wealthier farm families, and their education usually ended upon graduation. There was no equivalent to the three-year higher school that existed for males which prepared students for university. This meant that, although there were no specific regulations excluding females from admission to universities, they were in fact shut out because they lacked access to the means of obtaining the qualifications and training necessary for university admission.

It was not until the turn of the twentieth century that institutions of higher education for women first appeared. The lead was taken by the private sector. The first such institution was the Joshi Eigaku Juku (Women's English College), established in 1900 by Tsuda Umeko, a Christian woman who had studied at Bryn Mawr College in the United States from 1889 to 1892. In the same year a medical school and a school of fine arts for women were opened. The late 1910s and 1920s witnessed the establishment of numerous private women's colleges. By 1937, there were forty-two private women's colleges offering a three-year course.

The national government established national women's higher normal schools: the first opened in Tokyo in 1890 (now called Ochanomizu Women's University), and another appeared in Nara in 1908 (today called Nara Women's University). They provided four-year postsecondary training courses for girls' high school and women's normal school teachers. The first public or prefectural college for women appeared in Fukuoka in 1922; however, only five more such institutions were established in the prewar period. Roughly one-half of all women enrolled in women's colleges majored in home economics; about half of the remainder were in Japanese or foreign languages, and the rest studied medicine, pharmacy, or art.

Although many of the institutions of higher education for women carried the title "university," none was accredited as such. Rather, they stood on a lower level than the universities and had the status of *senmongakkō,* or special schools. As such, they could not award a recognized degree, but merely a certificate of achievement. Some of the men's universities, both national and private, opened their campuses to women on a limited basis, but only as auditors. Women were denied admission, however, to the most prestigious of the imperial universities,

Tokyo and Kyoto Imperial University. It was not until after World War II that university education became available for women on the same basis as men.[8]

The system of education in prewar Japan was very elitist, and in general opportunities for higher education were extremely limited. This was especially true for women. For example, in 1940, less than 1 percent of the relevant age group of women were enrolled in various institutions of postsecondary education, compared to 6.5 percent of males.[9] Women's underenrollment in higher education reflected a general social attitude that intellectual or scholarly training was both inappropriate and unnecessary for women.[10] Nevertheless, by the eve of World War II many upper class families had come to look with favor upon higher education for daughters. They perceived higher education as providing girls with general cultural enrichment, which would enhance their position when it came to marriage. Higher education that had a clear-cut occupational objective, such as training for the teaching profession, continued to be frowned upon. This reflected a general disapproval of women—especially those from well-to-do families—going out into the world and working.

POST-WORLD WAR II REFORMS IN EDUCATION

Following World War II, under the influence of the American Occupation, the entire educational system of Japan was reorganized. Women were granted the legal right to pursue their education as far as their abilities would permit at whatever types of institutions and in whatever fields they might choose. The various sex-segregated streams or tracks that had existed beyond elementary school were consolidated at each level resulting in a single-track structure, each level qualifying students for the next higher level. University status was granted to various existing institutions, including prewar higher schools, *senmongakkō*, technical schools, and normal schools. Compulsory education was extended from six to nine years, and a 6–3–3–4 structure was adopted (six years of elementary school beginning at age six, three years of lower secondary school, three years of upper secondary school, and four years of university). Coeducation, which had formerly been limited to the early years of elementary school, was extended to all levels including university, and a common curriculum was instituted in all schools. These reforms were embodied in the School Education Law and the Fundamental Law of Education of 1947.

Under the reorganized system, Japan initially had only one permanent and legitimate institution of higher education beyond the high school—the four-year university. However, those institutions that did not meet the necessary standards for being upgraded to the status of university were designated *tanki daigaku,* or ''short-term universities'' (the equivalent of junior colleges), with courses of study lasting two or three years. Many of the existing women's colleges and normal schools were in this category. It was expected that all of these would eventually improve their facilities and standards and become full-fledged universities. Following years of negotiations between the Ministry of Education and the junior colleges during which time numerous new junior colleges had been established, it was finally decided in 1964 that these institutions would continue as junior colleges within the framework of the university system.

Other types of postsecondary schools include the *kōtōsenmongakkō* or technical colleges established in 1962, which combine the last three years of high school with two years of college and provide students with intensive vocational and technical training; *senshūgakkō* or special training schools, established in 1976, which offer one- to three-year programs in vocational and technical training to upper secondary school graduates (as well as a general education program for lower secondary school graduates); and *kakushugakkō* or miscellaneous schools, which offer practical or vocational training lasting varying lengths of time at both the secondary and postsecondary levels. In 1985, the Ministry of Education founded the University of the Air, which provides access to university education not only to upper secondary school graduates, but also to working people, housewives, and others on either a degree or nondegree basis using television and radio broadcasting.

ENROLLMENT TRENDS OVER THE POSTWAR YEARS

The intervening years following the post-World War II reforms in the educational system have witnessed a steady rise in the proportions of females, as well as males, completing the nine years of compulsory schooling and entering upper secondary schools. Although pre-elementary education is not part of compulsory education, about 40 percent of all three year olds and 90 percent of four and five year olds attend either *yōchien,* which operate under the auspices of the Ministry of Education and admit children from age three until entry into first grade, or *hoikujo,* which are under the jurisdiction of the Ministry of Health and Welfare and admit children of working mothers from birth until entry into first grade.[11] Both public and private *yōchien* and *hoikujo* exist. There is nearly universal attendance at the elementary and lower secondary school levels for both girls and boys.

The percentage of girls graduating from lower secondary school and continuing their studies in upper secondary school increased from 37 percent in 1950 to 56 percent in 1960 and 83 percent in 1970. Since 1979, 95 percent of female lower secondary school graduates have entered upper secondary school.[12] This rate is higher than it is for boys. Education through Grade 9 is free of charge and is financed jointly by national, prefectural, and municipal governments. However, tuition is charged at both public and private upper secondary schools. About 24 percent of the high schools are private, and they enroll 28 percent of the students.[13] Although most of the public high schools are coeducational, many of the private ones are single-sex schools. There are general academic high schools and vocational high schools, as well as comprehensive schools that offer both types of programs. The vocational schools offer courses in commerce, agriculture, technical/industrial studies, home economics, fisheries, and health.[14]

The expansion in upper secondary school attendance has been reflected in the dramatic growth in enrollment both among females and males at institutions of postsecondary education. The growth has been especially striking, however, in the case of females: there was a fourfold increase in the proportion of girls entering junior colleges and universities between 1960 and 1986 (as compared with about a twofold increase in the case of males). The proportion of female eighteen year olds entering college rose from just 5.5 percent in 1960 to 18 percent in 1970; since the mid-1970s, the figure has exceeded 32 percent.[15] Since their inception in 1981, the postsecondary special training schools have attracted increasing numbers of females graduating from upper secondary school: in 1986, over 100,000 or over 12 percent of all female graduates entered these schools.[16] At the graduate level, the number of women enrolled in master's degree programs has increased more than tenfold since 1960 (from about 700 to 7,400), while the number enrolled in doctor's degree programs has increased eightfold (from less than 400 to almost 3,000).[17]

A variety of social and economic factors have promoted this expansion in women's postsecondary enrollments. One can point, first of all, to the growing prosperity of the Japanese people brought on by the unprecedented economic growth experienced in the 1960s. The general improvement in the Japanese living standard, coupled with a reduction in the number of children per family (from 5.14 in 1940 to 2.30 in 1960 and 1.74 in 1981),[18] has meant that more family resources are available to educate not only sons but also daughters. Second, as higher education in Japan has shifted from an elite to a mass system over the postwar years, college attendance has increasingly come to be viewed as a matter of course for those belonging to certain social strata. Finally, social attitudes have changed in the direction of a growing acceptance of the desirability of providing higher education for women.

WOMEN'S PARTICIPATION IN NONFORMAL EDUCATION

Participation in nonformal types of adult or continuing education, called social education (*shakai kyōiku*) in Japan, has become increasingly common, particularly among women. The 1947 Fundamental Law of Education specifically called for the promotion of social education by national and local public bodies, and the Social Education Law, enacted in 1949, called on the Ministry of Education and local boards of education to promote and assist in such matters as installation of educational facilities, training and placement of social education leaders, development of teaching material, and expansion of learning opportunities.

Today, not only the Ministry of Education and local governments, but also the mass media, women's organizations, and private schools of various kinds carry on social education for women. Facilities and courses designed specifically for women have increased noticeably over the past ten years. In 1984, more than 1.5 million women were enrolled in roughly 34,000 women's classes offered with the support of the national government. These courses not only deal with home and family matters (home management, child care, etc.), but also address a wide range of interests and needs, such as vocational guidance and training, foreign languages, sports, leisure, and discussions of women's issues. Prefectural and local boards of education also offer various classes and courses for both men and women. In 1983, 67 percent of those attending such classes were women.[19] "Cultural centers" established in large cities by various major Japanese business also provide nonformal education for many women. The Asahi Cultural Center, established by one of Japan's major newspapers in 1974, was the first of such centers to be established. In addition, nearly all colleges and universities allow people to audit classes, and many sponsor special lectures and workshops for the community. In a 1984 national poll of women twenty years of age and older, 30 percent reported they were involved in some type of formal or nonformal education.[20]

SEX DIFFERENCES IN EDUCATIONAL OPPORTUNITIES

Despite the postwar expansion in access to education for females at all levels, sex differences have persisted. Nevertheless, only within the last ten years or so, in the wake of the International Women's Year, have issues of various types concerning women, including education, received attention. With pressures being manifested in many countries to provide greater equality for women in all spheres of life, Japanese society and its leaders have been forced to at least recognize and consider these issues, although little has been done in terms of concrete measures aimed specifically at reducing sex inequalities in educational opportunities. More significant, however, has been the interest generated at the non-governmental level. There has been a proliferation of formal and informal groups and organizations, journals as well as scholarly books, concerned with women's education. A number of universities and junior colleges have set up courses in women's studies, and intercollegiate groups have been formed to explore and conduct research on a variety of issues pertaining to female education.[21]

Sex differentiation is not significant in elementary and lower secondary school, where all students pursue a common, uniform curriculum and program of study. There is one exception—in lower secondary school most girls take homemaking and most boys industrial arts, even though they can choose either subject. At the upper secondary school level, sex-linked differences are evident both in the types of schools students enter and the programs and curricula they take. These choices and decisions, in turn, have important consequences in terms of the types of higher educational institutions and fields of study they can apply for.

General academic programs are more likely to prepare students to enter college or university than are vocational programs. More girls than boys are enrolled in the general academic program in high school (74 versus 71 percent in 1986).[22] Yet girls are less likely than boys to apply for admission to the most prestigious and competitive academic high schools which are known for producing large numbers of successful entrants into the top four-year universities. In many cases, girls prefer to enter a private girls' high school. Of those who choose a vocational program in high school, boys are apt to go into technical courses, whereas girls take home economics or enter commercial studies so that they can find clerical jobs after graduation. The proportion of students who go on to four-year universities is much higher among graduates of technical studies than the commercial or home economics curriculum.

Within academic programs there is sex-linked streaming. In the second and third years, students in academic programs have the choice of specializing in either literature or science; literature majors take more courses in English and in Japanese literature, whereas science majors take more math and science courses. Most of those who go into the scientific field are males, whereas most females go into literature. In the third year of high school there is often a further differentiation according to whether a student plans to apply to a national university or to a private one, and within the two types of universities whether he or she plans to apply to a science-related faculty or a literary faculty. Students are given intensive preparation for the entrance examinations in the subject areas required by the institutions and faculties to which they plan to apply. For those who plan to attend a junior college, the preparation is much less rigorous. Most junior colleges require no entrance exams, merely recommendations, and those that do have entrance exams require applicants to sit for exams in just two or three subjects. Young women elect to pursue programs in high school that will prepare them to enter the literature, education, or social science faculties at universities rather than the scientific or technological fields. As an alternative, they may decide to forego the rigorous and competitive preparation for university admission altogether and instead aim for a junior college. Very few female high school students attend *yobikō,* which are privately operated cram schools (numbering more than 200 nationwide) that offer intensive training for the university entrance examinations.

The outcome of different choices made by females and males in high school is clearly reflected at the postsecondary level, where despite the growth in female college enrollment over the past twenty-five years, considerable sex differences in patterns of participation in various types and levels of institutions persist.[23] A large proportion of women pursue postsecondary education through junior colleges rather than through four-year universities. Of the roughly 300,000 young women who entered college in 1986, fewer than four out of ten women went into four-year universities; the remainder entered junior colleges. In contrast, nearly all—95 percent—of the 340,000 males entering college went to four-year universities.[24] Although women overwhelmingly (90 percent) dominate the student population in junior colleges, they constitute a minority at four-year universities (24 percent).[25] Female university enrollment has increased slightly over the last five years; nevertheless, the proportion lags behind that in most industrialized societies. Junior colleges, though they enjoy the title of "university," form the bottom layer of the university pyramid. Although it is possible for graduates from junior colleges to transfer to four-year universities, few in fact do so.

The fact that junior colleges enroll a major proportion of women pursuing higher education is to be explained in part by the fact that in the face of the Japanese government's reluctance under the long-ruling conservative Liberal Democratic party to increase the number of low-cost public (that is, national, prefectural and municipal) universities and junior colleges,[26] it is the private junior colleges that have been by far the most aggressive in establishing facilities catering almost exclusively to female clientele. Thus, in the decade between 1960 and 1970, when expansion in college enrollment was most dramatic, as many as 200 new private junior colleges were established, while the number of private universities increased by 134 and the number of public universities and junior colleges increased by a mere handful. Today, 72 percent of universities and 84 percent of junior colleges are private, and they enroll, respectively, 73 percent and 90 percent of all students.[27] Given the limited access to public institutions and the high tuition costs at private institutions, plus the reluctance of many parents to invest as heavily in their daughters' as their sons' educations, it is not surprising to find many young women opting for junior college, where tuition payments need to be made for just two years instead of four. Data show that women who attend private universities come from families with an average annual income that is considerably higher than that of male counterparts or that of women enrolled in private junior colleges.[28]

Not only do fewer women attend four-year universities than men, but within universities, women tend to be segregated from men. One out of four women is enrolled at institutions with exclusively female student populations (which numbered 85 out of a total of 460 in 1985).[29] Women constitute a very small percentage at the most prestigious coeducational universities such as Tokyo University and Kyoto University, where females comprised only 7 percent and 8 percent, respectively, of all students admitted to the university in 1980.[30] The comparatively low rate of female attendance at four-year universities means that women continue to be a small minority of graduate students, although in terms of both absolute numbers and relative proportions, women's representation has increased over the past twenty-five years. In 1986, women comprised about 14 percent of all students enrolled in master's degree programs and about 12 percent of those in doctor's degree programs (compared to 9 and 5 percent, respectively, in 1960).[31]

Sex segregation in higher education is also evident in the programs of study women pursue, despite the recent entry of women into male-dominated fields. At the university level, women have made greater inroads into the social science faculty, which includes law, politics, economics, and industrial management (up from 7 percent of all women students in 1960 to 16 percent in 1986), as well as into engineering (0.5 to 2.3 percent) and agriculture (0.5 to 2.1 percent). In turn, there has been a decline in the relative proportion enrolled in education (from 28 to 17 percent) and home economics (28 to 8 percent). Nevertheless,

60 percent of all women enrolled in universities were clustered in the traditionally female fields of literature, education, and home economics, in contrast to men, among whom the largest proportion (46 percent) were majoring in the social sciences and another 25 percent in engineering. Relatively few women receive training that equips them to enter professional and specialized occupations, except in fields such as teaching or pharmacy. At the junior colleges, there has been a considerable increase in the proportion of women majoring in teacher education in preparation for teaching in preschools (up from 11 percent in 1960 to 29 percent in 1986), as well as in health-related fields. On the other hand, there has been a decrease in those majoring in home economics, although that is still the most popular major (29 percent), followed by literature (26 percent). Most of the male students, by contrast, are in either engineering or the social sciences.[32]

Similar sex differences show up at the graduate level: one-half of all male students in master's degree programs are in engineering, and the remainder are almost evenly distributed in the fields of science, agriculture, social sciences, and humanities; among females, the largest percentage are in literature, followed by education and then the social sciences. At the doctoral level, medicine and dentistry are the most popular fields among males, followed by engineering, the humanities, science, and the social sciences. In the case of females, the humanities enrolls the highest percentage, followed by medicine and dentistry and the social sciences.[33]

Women's overrepresentation in such fields as literature, home economics, and education and their underrepresentation in science, engineering, law, and economics are reflective of certain cultural norms and attitudes regarding the purposes of higher education for women, but at the same it has a structural underpinning in the educational system. As noted above, the majority of junior colleges and universities in Japan are private. In general, they have placed major emphasis on developing their humanities and social science programs because establishing and maintaining science, engineering, and medical departments is so costly. The range of study options at most private women's universities and junior colleges, where so many women are enrolled, is even more limited. At most women's universities the faculties of literature and home economics are the only ones available. This bias in curriculum offerings is even more pronounced at private junior colleges. What is offered at these institutions reflect sex stereotypes about what are appropriate areas of study for women, and women are not afforded the opportunity to choose nontraditional study options or to prepare for nontraditional careers.

WOMEN'S EDUCATION AND WORKFORCE PARTICIPATION AND STATUS

Attainment of higher levels of education among Japanese women over the last twenty-five years has led to greater participation by women in a wide range of occupations in the modern sector, particularly in clerical and professional-technical jobs. On the whole, educational attainment is associated with higher rates of labor force participation among Japanese women: in 1982, the rate of labor force participation among women was 47 percent among those with elementary education, 55 percent among those with secondary education, and 59 percent for those who had received college education.[34] At the same time, education alone has not enabled women to overcome the various cultural and structural barriers that continue to restrict employment opportunities for women, particularly their advancement into higher managerial and administrative positions. Nor has it been associated thus far with a significant increase in the likelihood of women pursuing work on a continuous, long-term career basis.

As in many countries, one of the most striking developments in Japan over the past thirty years has been the increased employment of women and their redistribution in the occupational structure. Today, more than 50 percent of all women are in the labor force, and unlike the prewar and immediate postwar period when working women were found predominantly on family farms or else in factories, they work primarily in an employed capacity in the nonagricultural sectors of the economy. In addition, there has been a dramatic increase in the number of married women with and without children participating in paid employment. Their proportion (including widowed and divorced women) among all employed women has increased from 40 percent in 1960 to 70 percent today.[35] This, combined with the dramatic decline in labor force participation rates among fifteen-to nineteen-year olds—that is, lower secondary school graduates—(down from 49 percent in 1960 to about 17 percent in 1986),[36] raised the average age of women workers from 26.3 in 1960 to 35.5 in 1986.[37]

The work lives of Japanese women, like those of women in most Western societies, are characterized by discontinuity and follow the "M" curve. That curve has shifted upward over the years, however, with each new cohort of women displaying higher labor force participation rates within each age category or at each life-cycle stage. The dip has become less pronounced as more women have continued to work after marriage and even during the child-raising years. Cultural attitudes pertaining to women's role play an important role in sustaining this pattern. Lack of adequate child daycare facilities is another contributing factor. Another critical factor is that, on the whole, business and industry have tended to regard women as a source of cheap, short-term, rotating labor. Young women straight out of high school or college are hired for jobs based on the assumption that they will work until they get married or, at most, until they have children. Women are generally excluded from the traditional system of lifetime employment and system of promotion and wages based on length of consecutive service within a particular company. Many employers have a policy—either official or unofficial—requiring women to retire at the time of marriage, pregnancy, or childbirth. Women who reenter the workforce after a period of withdrawal are rarely able to go back to their original jobs or even to find another job in the same occupational field. Many of them end up working in low-paying jobs in production or the service industry on a part-time (less than thirty-five hours per week) or temporary basis. As a result, while the average starting pay for women is about 95 percent of that earned by men, the gap in earnings widens with age, particularly after thirty-five.

In regard to college-educated women, in the prewar days it was considered unseemly for women from well-to-do backgrounds to work. Moreover, opportunities were very limited, so that on the average, less than half of all college graduates worked.[38] In recent years, however, it has become a common and socially accepted practice, and today over 80 percent of women graduating from junior colleges and 70 percent of those graduating from four-year universities take up employment following graduation.[39] Not only are today's college graduates more likely to work, but also the range of occupations they enter is much greater. Among prewar graduates who took up employment, about half went into teaching and the remainder went into health medical fields and clerical work; very few took up other types of work.[40] In contrast, among 1986 graduates from four-year universities, 39 percent went into clerical work, 24 percent into teaching, another 12 percent became technical workers, 9 percent went into sales, and 6 percent entered the health and medical fields. Among junior college graduates nearly 60 percent took up clerical jobs, another 11 percent became teachers, 8 percent went into health-related fields, another 9 percent went into other professional-technical fields, and about 7 percent entered sales.[41]

Looking at workforce participation over a lifetime, we find that even among college-educated women, only a minority pursue work on a continuous, long-term career basis. The average length of continuous employment in a single job has been rising over recent years among all women (from 4 years in 1966 to 5.8 years in 1975 and 7.0 years in 1986). Yet, the length of time continues to be shorter among women who have graduated from college than among those with less education.[42] Among women in their twenties, those with higher education are more likely to be working than those with less education, partly because they tend to marry and bear children at a later age. However, among women who are in the childbearing and early childrearing years (thirty to thirty-four), there is little difference in rates of employment according to level of education. College-educated women are just as likely as those with less education—if not slightly more so—to refrain from working during this stage, although of those who do work, more are likely to do so on a full-time basis.

A major reason why they do not work is that, even among highly educated women, the majority subscribe to some of the traditional values and norms regarding women's role. In a 1984 national public opinion survey, only 20 percent of all women and 24 percent of college-educated women expressed support for women continuing to work after they had children. Relatively few women today feel that women should stop working when they get married. A majority, including those with college degrees, think that women should not work while their children are still young. In the same survey, 45 percent of all women and 52 percent of college-educated women endorsed the view that women should stop work when they have children and return after the children are grown.[43]

There is also some indication that the better educated women tend to have higher levels of expectation regarding what they want for their children, and how they should be brought up and educated. Therefore, they may have greater reservations about delegating the task of early childhood socialization to others. In addition, since women college graduates are likely to marry college-educated men who are able to provide for them adequately, most are not in the position of having to work for financial reasons. Instead, they can choose either to work or not to work. Furthermore, the commitment demanded of white-collar workers in terms of hours and periodic transfers in most Japanese companies is often too demanding for married women with children.

The percentage of college-educated women in their late thirties and forties who reenter the workplace after their children have become older is smaller than that of their less educated sisters. Such women are generally unwilling to take the kind of low-paying production or service industry jobs that are most commonly available to women their age; yet employers have negative attitudes toward hiring married, middle-aged women for white-collar work. In the case of women over age fifty, the rate of employment is higher among those with college degrees than less educated female peers because those college-educated women who continue in their careers are usually in professional and technical occupations, where the retirement age is later than in other type of work.

The impact of education on women's occupational attainment has been severely limited by various forms of sex discrimination in employment and the fact that the more highly educated women are more likely to be subjected to such discrimination. In terms of obtaining employment, while high school and junior college graduates are frequently taken on as "OL," or "office ladies" to perform routine clerical work, companies have shied away from hiring graduates from four-year universities for such positions because they are more expensive and presumably have fewer years remaining until they leave their jobs. At the same time, most employers have been reluctant to hire these women to perform tasks comparable to those assigned to male university graduates.

Many companies have made it a policy not to recruit female university graduates. This explains in large part why employment rates among women university graduates have been lower than those for female junior college graduates and male graduates. Even if female university graduates are hired, they are often subject to further differential treatment in terms of on-the-job training, remuneration, and opportunities for promotion to administrative and managerial positions.[44] Until just a few years ago, the differential in starting pay for men and women was greater among university graduates than among high school and junior college graduates.[45] In 1986, women employed in managerial and administrative positions numbered 150,000, representing just 1 percent of all employed women and 7 percent of all persons employed in such positions.[46]

WOMEN'S EDUCATION AND ACCESS TO PROFESSIONAL
AND TECHNICAL CAREERS

The Japanese woman's increased opportunities to pursue higher education has promoted her access to professional and technical occupations, but within these occupations, both horizontal and vertical sex segregation remains.

In prewar Japanese society, teaching at the elementary or secondary level was the most common profession among women. There were very few women professors, except for those who taught women's higher normal schools or at women's colleges. Other professions in which women were found included medicine, nursing, pharmacy, dentistry, journalism, and social welfare work. Certain other professions, such as that of lawyer or politician, however, were closed to them.

Today, nearly 14 percent of all employed women (as compared to under 9 percent of employed males) are engaged in professional and technical occupations, and they comprise 43 percent of all persons in those jobs.[47] Between 1975 and 1985, the total number of female professional and technical workers increased by 60 percent, from 1.4 million to 2.25 million (compared to about a 51-percent increase among males). The most striking increase has been in the number of literary writers, reporters, and editors: from about 9,000 (representing 13 percent of all persons in those occupations) to 20,000 (representing over 21 percent of the total). There has also been a considerable increase in the number of female technicians and engineers (from under 15,000 to over 62,000), but they still represent a very small proportion—4.6 percent—of all technicians and engineers. The number of female scientific researchers, on the other hand, has shown only a modest increase. There are just over 5,200 women so employed, compared to 3,600 in 1975, and they make up 7.5 percent of all scientists.[48] Women constitute a very small minority of individuals working as judges, prosecutors, and other lawyers, certified accountants, and, to a lesser extent, physicians.

Women professionals continue to be concentrated in those occupations where women have long established themselves, namely, teaching, social welfare, pharmacy, and nursing. Sex discrimination is generally less apparent in these fields which tend to be in the public rather than the private sector. Even within teaching, however, the proportion of women is smaller as one moves up the educational ladder, and women are likely to be found teaching subjects traditionally considered feminine. In addition, few women are found in administrative positions.

Kindergartens (*yōchien*) are staffed almost exclusively by women (94 percent); yet women head only 48 percent of all kindergartens.[49] At the elementary schools, women account for 56 percent of the teachers, but just 2.4 percent of the principals.[50] Women comprise 34 percent of the teachers and just 0.4 percent of principals in lower secondary schools,[51] and the corresponding figures at the upper secondary schools are 19 percent and 2.4 percent.[52]

At the college level, more women teach in junior colleges than in universities (60 versus 40 percent). Women account for 39 percent of all faculty members in junior colleges, 8.5 percent of four-year university faculty, and less than 4 percent of graduate-level faculty. The higher the professional rank, the smaller the representation of females: women comprise just 4 percent of full professors at universities and 24 percent of those at junior colleges and 4 percent of university and 14 percent of junior college presidents.[53] Within universities, women's representation is higher at private than at national universities, at all-female than at coeducational universities, and at more recently established universities than at the older, more prestigious universities like Tokyo and Kyoto Universities.[54] In addition, at both the college and high school levels, women are most likely to be found teaching in fields traditionally considered to be feminine, such as home economics, literature, and art; they are almost totally absent from university faculties of law, economics, science, engineering, and agriculture.

The above facts and figures point to the prevalence of discrimination not only in business and industry, but also in higher educational and research institutions.[55] College and university faculty and researchers are recruited primarily through a patronage system, and women are generally excluded from that system except at women's junior colleges and universities, although even those institutions tend to recruit largely males. Positions are rarely announced publicly, so that women do not have an opportunity to compete openly for a university teaching or research position.[56] As a consequence, fewer women than men are able to obtain employment following completion of master's and doctor's degree programs.

The Labor Standards Law of 1947 prohibits sex discrimination only in the area of pay where the type of work performed is the same or of equal value; it does not prohibit discrimination on the basis of sex in hiring, work assignment, promotion, welfare, benefits, and retirement. A major step toward promoting greater sex equality in employment was taken in 1980 when Japan signed the United Nations Convention on the Elimination of All Forms of Discrimination against Women. An equal employment opportunity bill was approved by both houses of the legislature, and the law took effect as of April 1, 1986. One of the major shortcomings of the legislation is that it actually ''forbids'' only certain discriminatory practices; in regard to many other forms of discrimination, such as in recruitment, hiring, job placement, and promotion, it demands only that employers ''make an effort'' to end those practices. Another very serious shortcoming of this legislation is that provisions for enforcing it seem to be inadequate.

WOMEN'S EDUCATION AND THE FAMILY

Evidence pertaining to the impact of educational attainment on women's roles within the family in Japanese society is varied and in many cases inconsistent. College-educated women display as much desire to get married and have children as do other women, although the model of marriage they prefer is more likely to be one in which the wife has greater independence in terms of pursuing her own interests and activities outside the home.[57] The average age at which women get married is somewhat higher among those with college degrees (25.92 among university-educated women, 25.10 among junior college graduates, and 24.59 among high school graduates).[58] College-educated women also have fewer children on the average compared to women as a whole: 1.60 versus 1.92.[59] Surveys conducted among university-educated women have found that those among them with continuous work histories are much more likely to be single, or if married, to have fewer children compared to the average woman.[60]

In recent surveys, a much higher proportion of college-educated women as compared to those with less education have expressed the view that a woman does not necessarily have to marry if she can be independent.[61] It is very possible that as financial independence and occupational mobility becomes a realistic possibility for highly educated women, a career will come to be viewed by at least some as a realistic alternative to marriage. There is already some indication that among professional and businesswomen at least some are postponing marriage beyond the typical "marriageable age" in order to become better established in their careers.

College-educated women are much more likely than less educated women to hold nontraditional views of sex-role divisions of labor in the household. In a 1976 national opinion poll, it was only among the college-educated that the proportion expressing disagreement with the traditional view of sex roles ("men should go out and work while women take care of the home") substantially exceeded that expressing agreement (60 percent versus 33 percent as compared to 40 percent versus 49 percent among all women).[62] At the same time, as indicated earlier, college-educated women, like most women, tend to think that mothers with young children should not work and have negative attitudes about placing children in daycare facilities. Various studies also indicate that, even among those university-educated women who are employed, husbands rarely assume an equal share of housekeeping and child care responsibilities.[63] A higher level of educational attainment on the part of women has been shown to be associated with a greater likelihood of joint participation by wives and husbands in the household decision-making process (with regard to children's schooling, daily household budget, and major household expenditures). The differences are not very significant, however.[64]

The most important effect of women's education on the family seems to be in educational aspirations for daughters. Japanese women (as well as men) are much less likely to have high educational aspirations for their daughters as compared to their sons—21 percent wanted their daughters to receive higher education (versus 54 percent for sons). College-educated women, however, were found to be much more likely to desire a similarly high level of education (i.e., university-level) for daughters as for sons—43 percent.[65] College graduates tend to express more progressive and egalitarian views on some other matters related to education, for example, that "it is necessary for girls (as well as boys) to receive the type of education that will enable them to have an occupation and be independent in the future," "both boys and girls should be required to take home economics in high school or else the requirement should be made optional for both sexes,'' and ''boys (as well as girls) should be trained to take care of themselves by learning to cook, sew on a button, etc.''[66] At the same time, a majority of college-educated women still seem to share the commonly held view that boys should be brought up in a certain way, as should girls.[67]

The evidence indicates that, while education has some influence on women's family roles, it is but one of multiple forces often pulling in opposite directions to shape both attitudes and practices. College-educated women, though they generally profess to hold more liberal attitudes on various issues relating to sex roles, childbearing, and so on, are nonetheless subject to the influence of the more traditional and restrictive elements of family norms.

WOMEN'S EDUCATION AND PARTICIPATION IN THE POLITICAL SYSTEM

Japanese women voted and ran for political office for the very first time in the national election of April 1946. In that election, 67 percent of female (as compared to 74 of male) eligible voters participated in the general election. In 1946, thirty-nine women were elected to the lower house (the House of Representatives). Since the late 1960s, voter turnout among women has exceeded men's in both national and local elections. The impact of education on women's voting behavior can be discerned from the fact that it is the younger women who have been mainly responsible for the increase in the voting rate for women.

Women are significantly underrepresented as elective or appointive office-holders. This undoubtedly reflects the fact that politics continues to be viewed as a male domain in Japanese society. Women have held between twenty and twenty-five seats in the Diet at any time since the war (about 3 percent). Their representation in local level politics has been even lower. Increasing numbers of women serve in appointed or commissioned local and national positions, but they tend to be concentrated in those bureaus and commissions that bear directly on ''women's'' issues. Only two women have served as cabinet ministers—both back in the 1960s.

Although women are generally still excluded from the mainstream of Japanese politics, they have become increasingly active in a variety of cause-oriented groups and organizations (concerned with consumer issues, pollution, quality of life, morality in politics, banning of nuclear testing, etc.) that have, in many cases, been able to exert considerable political influence.[68] The role of political volunteer is attractive to relatively affluent, college-educated women in their mid-thirties or forties. These women find that this role allows them an outlet for their talents and abilities. They can combine political volunteerism quite easily with the wife-mother role.[69]

Women's representation in the national administrative civil service in 1981 was about 14 percent, but women comprised a mere 0.5 percent of those in the position of section chief or higher.[70] To obtain employment in a ministry, a university graduate must pass a government examination, and passing the highest of the three levels is necessary for obtaining a management-level position. Until about ten years ago, many of the highest examinations were closed to women. Most of them are open to women now, and increasing numbers of university graduates are taking and passing these examinations. Even if a woman is successful in the written examination, she may face unofficial discrimination at the point of hiring, and later in promotion.[71] Although discrimination partly explains why so few women are in top positions within the bureaucracy, another critical factor is that success depends on remaining in and moving up the ministry that one has entered. Most women simply have not stayed in their posts long enough to achieve high-level positions.

FUTURE TRENDS

Japanese women's participation in education has expanded considerably over the last twenty-five years. At the same time, as we have seen, sex differences in educational opportunities persist, especially in higher education. In looking at the impact of education on women's roles in the home, the labor market, and the political system, we have found that education alone has not enabled women to overcome the cultural and structural restrictions that still operate to the disadvantage of women.

Nevertheless, many positive developments have occurred since 1980. Important changes have been underway in terms of young women's career orientations and role perceptions. These changes are, in turn, beginning to alter the way some women, at least, view education. Gradual changes in employers' attitudes toward employing women university graduates in permanent positions are taking place, and employment opportunities for these women are growing.

The pattern most widely favored by college women today is to work until they have children and then retire to the home and reenter the workforce either on a full-or part-time basis once their children are older. A growing number, however, are expressing a desire to continue working even after they have children.[72] As career goals become important for young women today, in turn, more of them are looking to college to provide them with specialized, job-related knowledge and training.[73] Simultaneously, among college women as a whole, more are beginning to look beyond occupations traditionally favored by women and to branch out into such diverse areas as advertising, banking and finance, retail sales, architecture, broadcasting, real estate, and computers.[74] These changes have been reflected in turn in a gradual increase at the university level in the proportion of women entering coeducational rather than women's universities and of those choosing nontraditional study options such as law, politics, economics, and engineering. At the junior colleges, too, there has been a considerable decrease in the proportion of women majoring in home economics, accompanied by an increase in those going into teacher-training and health-related fields. Many women's junior colleges and universities have responded to these changes in demand by diversifying their program offerings.

To an important degree, changes in value and attitudes on the part of today's generation of young women should be viewed as a consequence of the rise in the levels of education attained by women over the postwar years. Most of those now reaching college age have been brought up by mothers who attended college under the restructured postwar educational system and represented in most instances the first generation of women in their families to receive higher education. Although most of the mothers have not pursued lifestyles that are radically different from those of other women, they nonetheless tend to hold more liberal attitudes toward sex roles and less traditional aspirations for their own daughters. The impact of expanded educational opportunities for women over the last twenty years or so on women's attitudes and their actual behavior in terms of work paticipation as well as in other realms is being felt among the second generation of college-going women. In addition, as more and more married women, including mothers, reenter the workforce or take up work for the first time in their late thirties and forties, they provide for their daughters (and sons) both a model of a working woman and a foundation for challenging traditional norms and values about the place of women.

The increased interest in pursuing careers and in venturing into less traditional fields of study and work has in turn been stimulated to an important degree by changes in the job market. Opportunities are slowly beginning to widen as more companies, in their eagerness to attract talent, are showing willingness to hire women graduates who possess the desired abilities, talents, and skills for positions formerly reserved exclusively for male graduates and to promote them to positions of leadership and responsibility. This is especially evident among businesses for which women comprise an increasingly important clientele— department stores, supermarkets, retail specialty stores, manufacturers of office and home electrical and electronic equipment, real estate businesses, and financial institutions (banks, securities companies, and consumer credit companies).[75] In the ten-year period between 1975 and 1985, the number of females in officer-level positions in private organizations and corporations increased by 80 percent, from 98,000 to 176,000.[76] Employment rates among female graduates have risen from about 60 percent in the 1970s to more than 70 percent since 1984. The figure was over 73 percent in 1986. The Equal Employment Opportunity Law which went into effect in April 1986 may have further positive impact on women's employment: 80 percent of the more than 600 companies surveyed by the Ministry of Labor in 1986, compared to just 36 percent of those surveyed in 1985, indicated they planned to recruit both male and female university graduates for the following spring.[77] The continuation of these trends should serve as an incentive to women to seek higher education on an equal basis with men and to prepare for a more diversified range of careers.

NOTES

1. Central Council for Education, *Basic Guidelines for the Reform of Education* (Tokyo: Ministry of Education, 1972).

2. *Ryōsai kembō no kyōiku* is discussed in Fukaya Masashi, *Ryōsai kembōshugi no kyōiku* (Toyko: Reimei Shobō); Murakami Nobuhiko, *Meiji joseishi* (Tokyo: Kōdansha, 1977), Vol. 1, pp. 50–55.

3. In a 1984 national public opinion poll conducted by the Office of the Prime Minister, for example, 21 percent of female and 17 percent of male respondents indicated that they felt daughters should receive a university education, in contrast to 54 percent and 48 percent, respectively, in the case of sons. Tanaka Kimiko and Higashi Yoshinobu, *Shin-gendai fujin no ishiki* (Tokyo: Gyōsei, 1985), pp. 40–42, Table 2–3, and pp. 45–47, Table 2–4, compiled from Sōrifu Hōkokushitsu, *Fujin ni kansuru yoron chōsa* (1984).

4. For a discussion of education in Meiji Japan, see Herbert Passin, *Society and Education in Japan* (New York: Columbia University Teachers College Press, 1965); Ronald S. Anderson, *Japan: Three Epochs of Modern Education* (Washington, D.C.: Department of Health, Education and Welfare, Bulletin No. 11, 1959).

5. Shibukawa Hisako, *Kyōiku*, Vol. 1 of *Kindai nihon joseishi* (Tokyo: Kashima Kenkyū Shuppankai, 1970), p. 45, Table 12.

6. Karasawa Tomitarō, *Joshi gakusei no rekishi* (Tokyo: Mokumisha, 1979), p. 163.

7. Chi'iki Shakai Kenkyūjo, *Kōnenrei o ikiru*, No. 7 "Ochanomizu de gojūnen," p. 71, Table 13.

8. For a general discussion of female education in prewar Japan, see Nihon Joshi Daigaku Joshi Kyōiku Kenkyōujo, ed., *Meiji no joshi kyōiku* (Tokyo: Kōdansha, 1967) and *Taishō no joshi kyōiku* (Tokyo: Kōdansha, 1975).

9. Hara Kimi, "Joshi kōtō kyōiku no shakaigakuteki ikkōsatsu," *Kyōiku Shakaigaku Kenkyū* 26 (October 1971), p. 87, Table 3, taken from Mombushō, *Nihon no kyōiku tōkei (Meiji-Shōwa)*, 1971.

10. See the autobiographies of Fujita Taki, *Wage michi—kokoro no de'ai* (Tokyo: Domesu Shuppan, 1979), and Sumie Seo Mishima, *My Narrow Isle: The Story of a Modern Woman in Japan* (New York: Day, 1941).

11. Mombushō (Ministry of Education), *Gakkō kihon chōsa hōkokusho* (1984), pp. 422–423.

12. Mombushō, *Gakkō kihon chōsa hōkousho* for the various years.

13. Mombushō, *Mombu tokei yōran* (1987), p. 52.

14. For a description and analysis of high schools in Japan, see Thomas Rohlen, *Japan's High Schools* (Berkeley: University of California Press, 1983).

15. Mombushō *Gakkō kihon chōsa hōkokusho* for the various years.

16. Mombushō, *Mombu tokei yōran*, pp. 58 and 99.

17. Figures for 1960 taken from Mombushō, *Gakkō kihon chōsa hōkokusho* (1960); figures for 1986 taken from Mombushō, *Mombu tokei yōran*, p. 76.

18. Sōrifu (Office of the Prime Minister), ed., *Fujin no genjō to shisaku* (Tokyo: Gyōsei, 1983), p. 110, Table 1–5–5, taken from Kōseishō, *Nihonjin jinkō no saiseisan ni kansuru shihō*.

19. Ministry of Labor, Social Education Bureau, Japan, *Women and Education in Japan*, 1986, p. 20.

20. Tanaka, *Shin-gendai fujin no ishiki*, p. 118, Table 4–3, compiled from Sōrifu Hōkokushitsu, *Fujin ni kansuru yoron chōsa* (1984). For a discussion of how women today utilize social education, see Kanda Michiko, ed., *Gakushū suru josei no jidai* (Tokyo: Nihon Hōsō Shuppan Kyōkai, 1981).

21. See, for example, Ichibangase Yasuko and Okuyama Emiko, eds., *Fujin kaihō to joshi kyōiku* (Tokyo: Keisō Shobō, 1975); Joseigaku Kenkyūkai, ed., *Onna-no-me de*

miru (Tokyo: Keisō Shobō, 1987); Nihon Kyōikugakkai, ed., *Kyōikugaku kenkyū tokushū: danjo byōdō kyōiku* 49, No. 3 (1982). Satō Yoko, *Onna-no-ko wa tsukurareru* (Tokyo: Hakuseki Shobō, 1977); Rōdō Kyōiku Sentā, *Joshi Kyōiku Mondai* (quarterly).

22. Mombushō, *Mombu tokei yōran*, p. 54.

23. Sex differences in participation in higher education and their causes are discussed in Kumiko Fujimura-Fanselow, "Women's Participation in Higher Education in Japan," *Comparative Education Review* 29, No. 4 (November 1985): 471–489. See also Fujimura-Fanselow, "Women and Higher Education in Japan: Tradition and Change" (Ph.D. diss., Columbia University, 1981), Chapters 3, 7, and 8.

24. Mombushō, *Mombu tokei yōran*, p. 60

25. Ibid., p. 72.

26. See, for example, William K. Cummings, "The Japanese Private University," *Minerva* 11, No. 3 (July 1973): 348–371; "The Problems and Prospects for Japanese Higher Education," in Lewis Austin, ed., *Japan: The Paradox of Progress*, (New Haven Conn.: Yale University Press, 1976), pp. 57–87; Ogata Ken, *Shiritsu daigaku* (Tokyo: Nihon Keizai Shimbun, 1977).

27. Mombushō, *Mombu tokei yōran*, pp. 71 and 73.

28. Mombushō Daigaku Kyoku Gakuseika, "Shōwa gojūichinendo gakusei seikatsu chōsa hōkoku," *IDE* Nos. 134 and 135 (August-September 1977): 6. See also Tomoda Yasumasa, "Educational and Occupational Aspirations of Female Senior High School Students," *Bulletin of the Hiroshima Agricultural College* 4 (December 1972): 247–262.

29. Amano Masako, author and editor, *Joshi kōtō kyōiku no zahyō* (Tokyo: Kakiuchi Shuppan, 1986), p. 141, Table 5–1, taken from Mombushō, *Zenkoku daigaku ichiran* (1985).

30. "Sokuhō '80 daigaku gōkausha shusshin kōkōbetsu ichiran," *Shūkan Asahi* (April 4, 1980), pp. 22–29, 179, 189.

31. Figures for 1960 compiled from Mombushō, *Gakkō Kihon Chōsa hōkōkusho*, 1960; figures for 1986 taken from Mombushō, *Mombu tokei yōran*, p. 76.

32. Figures for 1960 compiled from Mombushō, *Gakkō kihon chōsa hōkusho*, 1960; figures for 1986 taken from Mombushō, *Mombu tokei yōran*, pp. 74–75.

33. Mombushō, *(Mombu tokei yōran)*, pp. 76–77, .

34. Amano, *Joshi kōta kyōiku no zahyō*, p. 207, taken from Sorifu, *Sūgyō kōzkihon chōsa hōkokusho* (1982).

35. Rōdōshō Fujin Shōnen kyoku (Ministry of Labor, Women's and Minors' Bureau), *Fujin rōdō no jitsujō* (1987), App. p. 36, App. Table 28.

36. Ibid., App. p. 3, App. Table 2.

37. Ibid., App. p. 67, App. Table 60.

38. Minshu Kyōiku Kyōkai, *Joshi no kōtō kyōiku to shokugyō oyobi katei no mondai* (Tokyo: Minshu Kyōiku Kyōkai, 1961), p. 198, Table 116.

39. Mombushō, *(Mombu tokei yōran)*, pp. 88–91.

40. Minshu Kyōiku Kyōkai, *Joshi no kōtō kyōiku*, pp. 200–201, Table 118.

41. Mombushō, *Jashi no kōtō kyōiku*, pp. 88–91.

42. Rōdōshō Fujin Shōnen kyoku, *Fujin rōdō no jiksujo*, App. p. 67, App. Table 60.

43. Tanaka, *Shin-gendai fujin no ishiki*, pp. 88–91, Table 3–4, compiled from Sōrifu Hōkokusho, *Fujin ni kansuru yoron chōsa* (1984). The reality is that today 51 percent of all married women are in the labor force. Rōdōshō Fujin Shōnen kyoku, *Fujin rōdō no jitsujō*. App. p. 36, App. Table 29.

44. See, for example, Rōdōdsō Fujin Shōnen kyoku, *Joshi rōdōsha ni kansuru chōsa hōkokusho* (1981).

45. Rōdōshō Fujin Shōnen kyoku, *Fujin rōdō no jitsujō*, App. pp. 14–15, App. Table 12.

46. Ibid., App. p. 66, App. Table 59.

47. Ibid., App. p. 15, App. Table 12, and App. pp. 26–27, App. Table 12.

48. Ibid., App. pp. 26–27, App. Table 21.

49. Mombushō, *Mombu tokei yōran*, p. 41.

50. Ibid., p. 44.

51. Ibid., p. 48.

52. Ibid., p. 56.

53. Mombushō, *Mombu tokei yōran*, pp. 80–81. For a detailed discussion of women academics in Japan, see Michii Takako, "The Chosen Few: Women Academics in Japan" (Ph.D. diss., State University of New York at Buffalo, 1982).

54. See Kano Yoshimasa, "Daigaku kyōin ichiba no hendō," *Kagawa daigaku kyōiku gakubu kenkyū hōkoku*, No. 57 (1983): 171–210.

55. For a discussion of these issues, see Lois Dilatush, "Women in the Professions in Japan," in Joyce Lebra, Joy Paulson, and Elizabeth Powers, eds., (Boulder, Colo.: Westview Press, 1976), and also Saruhashi Katsuko and Shiota Shobei, eds., *Josei kenkyūsha—ayumi to tembō* (Tokyo: Domesu Shuppan, 1985).

56. The Discrimination faced by female professional and technical workers is discussed in Okada Masako et al., *Senmonshoku no joseitachi* (Tokyo: Aki Shobō, 1976).

57. Sugiyama Meiko, "Onna no isshō, onna no kangaekata," in Nihonjin Kenkyūkai, ed., *Nihonjin Kenkyū 3* (Tokyo: Shiseidō, 1975), p. 16, Table 5, taken from Nihon Hōsō Kyōkai, *Nihonjin no ishiki* (1973).

58. Kōseishō (Ministry of Welfare), Jinkō Mondai Kenkyūjo, *Daihachiji shussanryoku chōsa* (Tokyo: Kōseishō, 1982), p. 19, Table 1–1–4.

59. Ibid., p. 137, Table 5–8.

60. Fujii Harue, *Nihon no joshi kōtō kyōiku* (Tokyo: Domesu Shuppan, 1973), p. 139, Fig. 24, and p. 147, Fig. 33; Daigaku Fujin Kyōkai, *Daigaku sotsugyōsei no seikatsu ishiki chōsa—fujin no nōryoku no ikashikata* (Tokyo: Daigaku Fujin Kyōkai, 1969), p. 42, Table 46; Shokugyō Kenkyūjo, *Daigaku sotsugyō joshi no shokugyō keireki to shokugyō ishiki ni kansuru kenkyū* (Tokyo: Koyō Suishin Jigyō Dantai Shokugyō Kenkyūjo, 1976), p. 48, Tables IV–2 and IV–2.

61. Tanaka, *Shin-gendai fujin no ishiki*, pp. 10–15, Table 1–1, compiled from Sōrifu Hōkokusho, *Fujin ni kansuru ishiki chōsa* (1972), *Fujin ni kansuru yoron chōsa* (1979), and *Fujin ni kansuru yoron chōsa* (1984).

62. Sōrifu Hōkokusho, *Fujin ni kansuru yoron chōsa hōkokusho* (1976), pp. 34–35, Table 1.

63. Daigaku Fujin Kyōkai, *Nihon ni okeru fujin no chi'i to fukushi* (Tokyo: Daigaku Fujin Kyōkai, 1976), part 1, p. 55; Fujii, *Nihon no joshi rōtō kyoiku*, pp. 156–159.

64. Tanaka, *Shin-gendai fujin no ishiki*, pp. 49–50, Table 2–5; pp. 52–53, Table 2–6; pp. 56–57, Table 2–7; pp. 59–61, Table 2–8, compiled from Sōrifu Hōkokusho, *Fujin ni kansuru yoron chōsa* (1984).

65. Ibid., pp. 45–47, Table 2–4, compiled from Sōrifu Hōkokusho, *Fujin ni kansuru ishiki chōsa* (1972) and *Fujin ni kansuru yoron chōsa* (1984).

66. Ibid., pp. 219–221, Table 6–3; pp. 224–225, Table 6–4; pp. 227–228, Table 6–5, compiled from Sōrifu Hōkokushitsu, *Fujin ni kansuru yoron chōsa* (1984).

67. Ibid., pp. 28–33, Table 2–1, compiled from Sōrifu Hōkokushitsu, *Fujin ni kansuru ishiki chōsa* (1979) and *Fujin ni kansuru yoron chōsa* (1984).

68. See Dorothy Robins-Mowry, *The Hidden Sun: Women of Modern Japan* (Boulder, Colo.: Westview Press, 1983), Chapters 4 and 5.

69. Susan J. Pharr, *Political Women in Japan* (Berkeley: University of California Press, 1981), pp. 178–179.

70. Sōrifu, *Fujin no genjo to shisaku*, p. 41, Table 1–2–12 and p. 43.

71. Eileen Carlberg, "Women in the Political System," in Lebra, Paulson, and Powers, eds., *Women in Changing Japan*, p. 239.

72. In the 1982 survey by the Japan Recruit Center, more than one-third of the university women sampled said they hoped to continue working even after they had children and until they reached the age of retirement. Nihon Rikurūto Sentā, *Joshigakusei no shūshoku dōki chōsa* (1982), p. 20.

73. In the Japan Recruit Center's 1982 survey of college-bound high school seniors, nearly 56 percent of the female respondents chose "to obtain qualifications or certificates" as one of their top three motives for wanting to attend college, and 29 percent chose this as the single most significant motive. Nihon Rikurūto Sentā, *Shingaku dōki chōsa* (1982), pp. 54–55, appendixes to Tables 9–1 and 9–2.

74. Nihon Seisansei Hombu Rōdōbu, ed., *Korekara no joshi rōdō* (Tokyo: Nihon Seisansei Hombu, Rōdō Shiryō Sentā, 1982), pp. 34–35, Table 2–1, taken from Sōrifu, *Kokusei chōsa*.

75. See Daigaku Fujin Kyōkai, *Daigaku kyōiku o uketa fujin no shakai sanka no kankyō ni kansuru chōsa* (Tokyo: Daigaku Fujin Kyōkai, 1981); Nihon Rikurūto Sentā, *Joshi no saiyō to katsuyō o kangaeru* (1982); Fujitani Atsuko and Uesgugi Takahiro, eds., *Daisotsu josei kyakumannin jidai* (Tokyo: Keisō Shobō, 1982), pp. 109–142.

76. Rōdōshō Fujin Shōnen kyoku, *Fujin rōdō no jitsuiō*, App. pp. 26–27, App. Table 21.

77. "Daisotsu josei 'saiyō no mon' hirogaru," *Yomiuri Shimbun* (December 28, 1986), p. 2.

9
VIETNAM

Gail P. Kelly

Vietnam, a country of over 63 million people, has only recently emerged from centuries of foreign domination and warfare. Standing at the intersection of Southeast Asia and China, this Southeast Asian nation was invaded and ruled by China for over 1,000 years. Chinese influence sustained itself long after the Chinese were driven out. Until the twentieth century the Vietnamese language was written in Chinese characters; Vietnamese traditional architecture is fashioned on the Chinese, and the Citadel in Hue, the Imperial City, mirrors the Forbidden City in Peking.

While Vietnam was set apart from Southeast Asia by China, French colonial rule further deflected the country from other Southeast Asian countries. France dominated the country for nearly 100 years, irrevocably changing the economy and social structure. French rule reoriented Vietnamese intellectual and cultural life away from China toward Western models. France built Western cities, notably Hanoi and Saigon, instituted a plantation agriculture, and introduced capitalism.[1] France also established schools based on Western models. These schools became the basis for the educational system of contemporary Vietnam.

French rule ended only after years of protracted war. The "first" Indochina war left the country divided just north of the city of Hue. The North underwent major social change, becoming a communist state with ties to the Soviet Union and Eastern Europe. The South was initially ruled by Ngo Dinh Diem, a southern intellectual with ties to the Catholic Church and to Vietnam's former monarchy. The South became a state run by the military and bolstered by increasing amounts of U.S. aid and, by the late 1960s, U.S. military forces. In 1975, the government of South Vietnam collapsed after decades of fighting the "second" Indochina war. The North Vietnamese Army occupied Saigon and the South and brought about reunification.

This chapter focuses on the changing roles and status of women in Vietnam through these turbulent times of foreign rule, civil war, and revolution. It will discuss how changes in women's education relate to dramatic changes in women's social, political, and economic roles and status. Over the years women have achieved major advances, gaining access to education, entering economic and political life, and developing basic rights in marriage and the family. Today, more than in Vietnam's feudal past, under French colonialism, or the southern regime, women are better educated, they are in the workforce in unprecedented numbers, and they hold more political power than ever before. However, this does not mean that they have achieved equality. The real commitment of the Vietnamese government to women's liberation has brought about many of these changes, but the problems of poverty—which are very real to Vietnam—and the current economic crisis in which Vietnam finds itself, has created policies which at best will delay further progress for women and at worse will threaten to undermine the progress women have made. The government has made economic development its top priority and, while gender equality remains one of its goals, the government has adopted policies aimed at stimulating economic growth. These policies—privatization, decentralization, and the development of a market-based economy—may put a country long committed to gender-based equality on the road to developing inequalities characteristic of other Third World nations and the industrialized capitalist countries.

Our discussion starts with a consideration of women before and under French colonialism and ends with a look at education in Vietnam during the period of the two Vietnams and after reunification in 1975. It will look at educational policies and enrollment patterns as well as their workforce and political outcomes. The discussion of education in contemporary Vietnam is based largely on interview data collected in January 1988. Other kinds of data on contemporary Vietnam, which are also cited here, are not all that common or comprehensive. The use of interview data may involve some bias since the individuals interviewed were members of Vietnamese governmental and quasigovernmental agencies. Even so, their bias tends to be on the optimistic rather than pessimistic side. Some of the literature on Vietnam is avowedly anticommunist and begrudges any positive changes that may have occurred since 1945.

FROM TRADITION TO THE FRENCH COLONIAL ORDER

Even though Vietnam was ruled by China for over 1,000 years, gender relations in Vietnam did not mirror those of Confucian China. Vietnamese traditions were different. Footbinding, for example, was never practiced, and the Vietnamese family, while patriarchical, did not make the father all powerful. Girls did not take their father's names, and they were free to choose their own husbands.

Females even became folk heroines. The Trung sisters, who led armies to rid the country of foreign invaders, have few parallels in other Asian societies. In the very distant past, Vietnamese women were thought to be the equal of men; some even insist that, before the Chinese invasion, Vietnam was a matriarchy in which women held power and authority.[2] Despite such traditions, in the 1,000 years of Chinese domination (to A.D. 939) and a succession of post-Chinese Vietnamese monarchs, efforts were made to rigidly circumscribe women's roles and reinforce women's subordination to men. From the time of Chinese domination, Confucianism was the official ideology. Confucianism was characterized by an age/gender hierarchy wherein women could gain a modicum of power only through their sons. The dominant ideology held that "One hundred women are not worth a single testicle."[3] Most Vietnamese women were peasant women who toiled in the fields. The ideology that confirmed women's inferiority to men did not preclude a woman's labor in her husband's or her father's fields.

In the fifteenth century, the Le Dynasty Legal Code gave women the right to own property and stated that parents should divide their land equally among sons and daughters. This provision was rescinded by the Gia-Long Code of the early nineteenth century. The Le Dynasty Code also stated that women's property, once hers, remained hers whether she was married or divorced and that she had the right to will her property to whomever she designated. She was entitled not only to her own property, but upon her husband's death, also to half of his.[4]

Despite women's right to hold property and a tradition of contributing to the economy (in the past women formed the bulk of the agricultural labor force, as they do today), they rarely had access to power. In Confucian Vietnam, the route to power was state service, and that was obtained solely through education. Education was for men alone. Vietnam was governed through a highly centralized bureaucracy. Examinations administered every three years were key to obtaining work in the bureaucracy. Throughout the country males attended Confucian schools of characters, memorized the Four Books and Five Classics, and spent their lives taking examinations.[5] Women worked the land to support their sons and husbands who aspired to high office. Women of the landed gentry became traders and the backbone of Vietnam's exchange economy. Many a Vietnamese folk saying warned women against marrying those who aspired to the bureaucracy. One went: "Girls, heed this advice and don't marry a scholar. His back is long. It takes lots of material for his gown. And after he stuffs himself, he goes to sleep."[6]

The Confucian hierarchy depended on women's labor to survive but devalued that labor. The hierarchy accorded merchants and traders the lowest place in social rank and the scholar/bureaucrat the highest. The state could always usurp money. Only males and scholars/bureaucrats had power and status.

The French invasion of Vietnam, which began in the 1850s, profoundly changed Vietnamese society. The advent of French rule meant the alienation of land. Cochinchina (South Vietnam) was the scene of a fruitless "scholars' resistance." Large tracts of land were abandoned as Vietnamese fled to fight against the French further north. This land was redistributed to Frenchmen who often sold it to Vietnamese entrepreneurs, or it was given to Vietnamese collaborators as a reward for their services to the new colonial state.[7] Land-lordism became the rule in Cochinchina through the years of French rule—75 percent of the rural population became landless laborers. In Annam and Tonkin, over half the peasants were landless, and about 90 percent of those who held land had such small holdings that they sold their labor to maintain subsistence.[8]

The alienation of land changed women's economic position. Rural women no longer worked their own land; rather, they became wage labor in the rural economy. By the 1920s, the French abolished the Vietnamese monarchy's civil service, recruited via the triennial examinations, and established their own age-specific educational system which led to salaried employment in the colonial regime. Men who had at one time spent their days studying Chinese classics in the hopes of landing a position in the administration now entered the rural workforce. The impoverishment of the Vietnamese peasantry intensified under French colonialism. With the famines of the 1930s thousands died on the roads of Annam. The Nghe-An-Ha-Tinh uprisings of 1930–1931 took the form of long marches to the cities and towns in search of food and the raiding of local granaries.[9]

Peasants who worked as sharecroppers and tenants were, of course, the most disadvantaged. The sex-role division of labor meant that women not only transplanted rice and weeded it, but also pulled the plow in lieu of water buffalos. Women agricultural workers were given only half the pay males received and were hired solely for planting and harvesting.[10]

Although rural peasants suffered under colonial rule and women's economic position deteriorated along with men's, the impact of colonialism was not the same on elite women from families in which male heads of household had attended French colonial schools or were from the French-created landlord class. These women tended to manage the family's landed wealth whereas the men focused their efforts on business or on work for the French colonial administration. These women were often educated in Catholic or private schools under the French colonial regime.

Colonial rule brought with it a new set of schools. As early as the 1880s, the French established a number of institutions to train administrators and interpreters. By the twentieth century, a new school system controlled from Hanoi by the French was created. It provided the gamut of elementary through higher education and became the basis for the modern schools of Vietnam. They were predominantly schools for boys, for while France may have had a different sex-role division of labor than precolonial Vietnam, France was a patriarchial society. In France gender-based inequality in education and throughout society generally was all pervasive. Perhaps thinking it was upholding local traditions, France reproduced and even exaggerated these traditions in the colonies.

Colonial Schools

Schooling in colonial Vietnam was limited to a very small proportion of the population. Even by the rosiest of French estimates, by 1939 less than 10 percent of the age cohort attended schools.[11] A literacy survey, conducted by P. Chesneau in 1938 and published in the government-sponsored pedagogical journals, the *Bulletin of Public Instruction,* found high illiteracy rates in Thanh Hoa Province (in Northcentral Vietnam) which had 200 schools.[12] In the provincial capital of Phu Quang, 19.5 percent of the men over sixty years of age were literate in Chinese characters whereas no women in that age range could claim any degree of literacy in either Chinese, Vietnamese written in roman script, or French. However, 2 percent of males over sixty years of age were literate in French, and 3 percent could read Vietnamese written in roman script. Among the fifty-one to sixty year olds, the inequality intensified—1.2 percent of the men were literate in French, 12.1 percent in Vietnamese written in the roman script, and 31.7 percent in Chinese. All the women in this age group were illiterate in any language. This held for the forty-one to fifty year olds as well. In the younger age cohorts Chesneau interviewed, literacy rates among males were higher, as were those of females, but gender differences persisted. Among ten to twenty year olds, 26 percent of the males were literate in French, 55.4 percent could read and write Vietnamese written in roman script, whereas 1.2 percent of females ten to twenty years old could read and write French and 5.8 percent, Vietnamese written in the roman script. In short, in thirty years of French school construction Phu Quang City went from total illiteracy, except in Chinese, to a city where half the men were literate in Vietnamese written in roman script and one quarter of the men were literate in French, whereas most of the women remained illiterate in any language. In the rural areas of Thanh Hoa Province, the pattern of male literacy and female illiteracy remained, although men were less likely to be literate than their peers in the provincial capital. Being in the capital made a greater difference for male literacy rates than female literacy rates.

The gap in male and female literacy rates was unquestionably the result of government policies which emphasized the construction of boys' schools. Whether girls attended school was in large part a result of government decisions to build a girls' school or to make a local school coeducational. Public school enrollments, broken down by gender for 1939, are presented in Table 9.1. Girls overall accounted for 16.45 percent of all students. Of the 446,814 who went to any public school, 73,474 were female. Most of the girls in school were in the first three years of schooling where girls comprised 16.55 percent of enrollments. Table 9.1 does not provide dropout rates. In Cochinchina, which enrolled 39,044 girls in official elementary schools, 18,039 girls were in the first year, whereas 7,825 were in the third and last year. The dropout rates were considerable for males as well: there were 36,437 boys in the first grade and 22,535 in the third grade. Girls made up 25.77 percent of the last-year class and 33.11 percent of the first-year class.[13]

Table 9.1
School Enrollment, by Gender and Region, 1939

	Elementary (Govt. Funded)	Elementary (Commune funded)	Educational Level All Elementary	Primary (Govt. funded only)	Primary Superior (includes Normal Courses)	Secondary	Total Enrollment (all levels)
Tonkin							
Males							
Number	70,282	64,438	134,720	18,054	1,849	176	154,799
Percent	88.35	73.07	90.54	88.54	90.06	93.62	90.30
Females							
Number	9,268	4,801	14,069	2,336	204	12	16,621
Percent	11.6	6.93	9.46	11.46	9.94	6.38	9.69
Cochinchina							
Males							
Number	92,460	8,760	101,220	17,673	1,346	152	120,391
Percent	70.3	87.0	71.5	75.95	80.36	87.36	72.22
Females							
Number	39,044	1,306	40,350	5,596	329	22	46,297
Percent	29.7	12.97	28.5	24.05	19.64	12.64	27.8
Annam							
Males							
Number	19,801	62,330	82,131	15,030	892	97	98,150
Percent	83.09	93.05	90.44	89.84	84.23	94.17	90.29
Females							
Number	4,030	4,654	8,684	1,699	167	6	10,556
Percent	16.91	6.95	9.57	10.16	15.77	5.83	9.71

All Vietnam							
Males							
Number	182,543	135,528	318,071	50,757	4,087	425	373,340
Percent	77.72	92.6	83.4	84.05	85.38	91.4	83.5
Females							
Number	52,342	10,761	63,103	9,631	700	40	73,474
Percent	22.28	7.36	16.55	15.95	14.62	8.6	16.45

Source: Government General de l'Indochine française, _Rapports...1939, Deuxieme Partie._ Tableau VI.

In Tonkin (northern Vietnam), half the girls dropped out between first and third grades. In Annam (central Vietnam), girls in government-funded schools tended to remain through the elementary course, whereas boys tended not only to remain but also to repeat grades. In 1939, the third grade class was close to 600 students larger than the first-year class. In Annam, the central provinces which were a protectorate where the Vietnamese monarchy still maintained a presence in governance, the dropout rates were high in the schools funded by local villages—which were the mainstream of education. In 1939, 80 percent of the girls and about 65 percent of the boys dropped out in the first three years of schooling.

Girls' chances of obtaining primary education (Grades 4, 5, and 6) were quite low. Girls accounted for about 16 percent of primary school students in 1939. Again, most were clustered in the fourth grade. In Tonkin, of the 2,336 girls in primary school, 1,042 were in the fourth grade and 562 were in the sixth grade (versus 7,520 males in the fourth grade and 4,897 in the fifth). In Annam, 759 girls were in the fourth grade and 445 in the sixth. In the south, Cochinchina, female enrollment in the primary grades was the highest, but here too of the 5,596 girls, 2,382 were in the fourth grade.

As Table 9.1 shows, very few Vietnamese went beyond the primary grades, and girls remained a minority here as well: 14.62 percent of postprimary students were girls. Again, most were in the first year or two of the course of study. In Annam, 71 were in the first year and 27 in the fourth year; in Cochinchina 118 were in the first year and 47 in the fourth and last year, whereas in Tonkin 69 girls were in the first year and 43 in the last year. Girls did not go to secondary school. In 1939, 40 girls were enrolled (versus 425 boys). The Indochinese University was a male institution. Only the Midwifery School took in girls.

As Table 9.1 shows, there was considerable regional variation in the extent to which government schools were made available to girls. Girls accounted for 27.8 percent of all students in southern Vietnam (Cochinchina), 9.71 percent in central Vietnam (Annam) and 9.69 percent in the north (Tonkin). In the south, the female enrollment share was twice that of the rest of the country.

Girls' access to schooling was a class phenomenon, and it also related to the extent to which Vietnamese traditional structures were replaced by France. The north and the center were French protectorates in which a Vietnamese administration remained in place, albeit directed by Frenchmen who served as advisers. In Annam, the center, the Vietnamese monarchy ruled for the French. It attempted to undermine French efforts to erode the little power it retained, and it sought to prevent the development of new social strata via French-created schools. In Annam, elite girls' schools were opened in the capital, Hue, to serve the daughters of the Vietnamese monarchy and its bureaucrats. The College Dong Khanh was founded in 1922 as the female counterpart to the College Quoc Hoc (literally National Learning), which was an elite all-male *lycée* situated directly across the Perfume River from the Citadel, the Vietnamese equivalent of the Chinese

Forbidden City. In Annam, these girls remained in schools through the primary and postprimary grades. It was in the rural, commune-funded elementary schools where education was offered for the most part to boys only and where the few girls who managed to enter school left quickly. In 1939, a total of 2,833 girls were attending the first grade in rural schools and 393 were in the third grade. The same trend of high female attrition rates among the rural poor held in Tonkin in "unofficial" commune-funded schools. Parental social class was the major factor determining access to schools; for girls it was the only factor, but for boys it was one of several factors.

The public sector formed the major educational route during the French colonial period. However, substantial numbers of children were schooled in private institutions. In 1933, a total of 29,781 students were enrolled in Catholic diocesan elementary schools; another 4,554 attended diocesan primary schools. Most of these Catholic schools were in Cochinchina where over half the elementary Catholic school enrollments were concentrated. The church ran five postprimary schools. On the postprimary level, the private secular schools were far more important than the church-run schools. There were 17 private secular postprimary schools serving 2,429 children in 1933. About 5 percent of the students were girls.[14]

Girls who were educated in the colonial period were rare, and these women constituted an elite. Girls educated in the prestigious private Ecole des Jeunes Filles Indigènes of Saigon, or the government-run Collège Dong Khanh in Hue, or the private Ecole Brieux in Hanoi were taught a curriculum similar to that of their male peers, although they were also instructed in domestic science and in needlework for two to three hours a week in place of the despised manual labor instruction given boys. The school curriculum focused on teaching to males and females alike Vietnamese written in the roman script, French, mathematics, history, geography, moral education, and general science. The moral education curriculum was adapted from what the French thought was Vietnamese traditional moral codes and expurgated of any seemingly anti-French content. This part of the curriculum explicitly emphasized women's subjugation to men. Several moral education texts were developed specifically for girls because Vietnamese neo-traditionalists, in the face of new values and competing social visions, feared that women might abandon their roles long defined in the Confucian texts.[15] The moral education texts approved by the government for school use focused on the cardinal relations and obligations befitting the virtuous. Central was the gender-age hierarchy pointing to the king as the Son of Heaven (and Heaven was male) who was to be obeyed as the son obeys his father and the wife her husband. David Marr, in his study of the women's rights debates in Vietnam in the 1920s, points out that some of the moral education texts put even greater emphasis on the role of woman as docile housewife, loyal and obedient to her husband and ever sensitive to her family's needs, including those of a second wife and servants. Private entrepreneurs produced these texts in large quantities for home study.[16] Like the school texts, they provided a view of women, particularly upper class women who had servants to supervise, which at that point in time was being disputed among Vietnamese intellectuals.

Without doubt, both the informal and formal curriculum of the schools emphasized woman's roles as mother and housewife. In the French-language curriculum, the Ecole Brieux in Hanoi assigned essays on hygiene and health as well as on how mothers should discipline their children and the qualities of a good housewife. In boys' schools, the French composition topics focused on describing objects, on writing letters to the French local administrator, on occupations students might assume after graduation, on the work of the peasant, and on the benefits of France.[17]

Girls did not always easily accept the narrow roles the schools proposed for them. When assigned a composition topic in French, "Describe the Qualities of a Good Housewife," Vu-Thi-Tin, a student in the sixth grade of the Ecole Brieux in Hanoi, wrote of the housewife's work in language befitting a general directing an army or the governor general leading his staff in running Indochina. She wrote: "It is not easy to direct a domestic government with order, economy, and cleanliness. The first method of directing the work well is to have a woman who has all the good qualities [of leadership]."[18] Vu-Thi-Tin continued her essay by describing a division of labor within the household promoted by the school. Her choice of words changed as she repeated the school's teaching, moving from administrative language to domestic language: "The man earns a living, the woman spends, each has his own role. The good housewife does not buy superfluous goods which spendthrift women buy. She knows how to keep to her budget—that is why her money is carefully counted out and allocated for each purchase. But after all [is bought] she puts some of her husband's wages aside to save for days of [his] sickness and unemployment."[19]

While girls may have been asked to write about future roles as housewives, schoolgirls were sometimes embroiled in anticolonial struggles that reemerged in Vietnam in the 1920s. Girls at the Ecole des Jeunes Filles Indigènes in Saigon repeatedly walked out of school in protest over the ways in which they, as Vietnamese elites, were treated by their French teachers. The girls at this particular school went out on strike over racism at least twice in the 1920s. One incident that occurred in the early 1920s involved a dispute over whether Vietnamese girls had to give up seats in front of the classroom to French girls. When Phan Boi Chau, a prominent Vietnamese nationalist, died in 1924, these girls collected money for memorial wreaths, wore arm bands denoting personal as well as national mourning (which was forbidden by the schools), and joined street demonstrations.[20] The girls at the elite Collège Dong Khanh in Hue led the school walkouts in 1926 after a male student, related to the Vietnamese Royal Family, was slapped by a French teacher who accused him of cheating.

Girls educated in colonial Vietnam were schooled in the context of intellectual and social ferment in Vietnamese society. Vietnamese elites of the 1920s and 1930s debated a range of questions, many of which centered on the relevance of Vietnamese traditions and whether those traditions had been responsible for the loss of nationhood and French colonialism. The role of women was one issue hotly debated.[21] Vietnamese traditionalists, like Pham Quynh who wrote a number of tracts on Confucianism and modern moral values, upheld a traditional role for women based on Confucian values. (Pham Quynh later became minister of education in Annam, the central provinces administered by the monarchy under French tutelage.) Pham Quynh argued that Vietnamese culture could be revived if it returned to its Confucian roots—and this included the subordination of women.[22] Not all Vietnamese shared such views. Nationalists like Phan Boi Chau saw women assuming major roles in liberating the country from colonialism as the Trung sisters in the past had led Vietnamese in the struggle against China. A number of women's groups arose like the Women's Labor Study Association which was established in 1926. The association published the journal *Women's Review,* which asserted new roles for women and rejected those embedded in neotraditionalist Confucian ideology. More radical and overtly feminist groups also arose among educated women. The Communist party, and the Vietnam Women's Union both founded in 1930, advocated full equality between men and women and sought to mobilize women, particularly peasant women, in the struggle against colonialism and for a socialist revolution. The Communist party organized women into the Women's Union and into workers' associations. In the 1930s, the party passed a number of resolutions calling for the full emancipation of women from the tyranny of Confucian hierarchy and feudalism.[23] As in China and the USSR, women became an important part of the communist movement, and the liberation of women was an avowedly important goal of that movement.

INDEPENDENCE AND THE PERIOD OF THE TWO VIETNAMS: WAR AND REVOLUTION

Toward the end of World War II, Japan occupied French Indochina, wresting power from the Vichy generals who had cooperated with Japan throughout the war. With Japan's collapse, the Vietnamese Communist party marched into Hanoi and declared itself the legal government of Vietnam. Soon thereafter, Alllied troops dislodged Ho Chi Minh's government and reclaimed Indochina for France, setting off the first Indochina war.

After the defeat of France at Dien-Bien-Phu, the Geneva Accords were signed dividing the country in two. North Vietnam, the Socialist Republic of Vietnam, was a communist state; the South emerged as the Republic of Vietnam, led by Ngo Dinh Diem, a Vietnamese Catholic who had served in the short-lived Japanese puppet government. Elections provided for by the 1954 Geneva Agreements were never held, and Diem established a military government that was backed by the United States. Not until 1975, after years of bloody warfare, was Vietnam reunited as the Saigon government fell, defeated in the battlefield.

The period 1954 to 1975 was a time of separate development for the Two

Vietnams. North Vietman shared the ideology, common to most communist states, of equality between social classes and between the sexes. Commitment to women's liberation was a strong element of government policy. The 1946 constitution granted women the same political, economic, cultural, social, and family rights as men. The constitution openly set forth the principle of equal pay and guaranteed women the right to vote and to hold public office. The marriage laws provided women with the right of free choice in marriage; they outlawed polygamy and legalized divorce. They also established women's right to children, to property, and to the land.[24]

The North set women's liberation, at least on paper, as a national goal. The southern government, dominated as it was by conservative Catholics, many of whom had fled from the North to avoid living under a communist government and many of whom were neotraditionalists, moved to reinforce the family and personal morality, reminiscent of neo-Confucianism but called "personalism."[25] Diem's sister-in-law, Madame Nhu, formed a Women's Solidarity League, which was a paramilitary organization dedicated to supporting personalism as an ideology and fighting against communism. The Solidarity League was an urban organization that reached women of urban, elite families. The southern government did not set forth policies that focused on improving the lives of rural women who formed the vast majority of women in South Vietnam. Madame Nhu's league campaigned against prostitution—an occupation that grew greatly, especially among poor women who had taken refuge in urban areas as the war was waged in the countryside. American soldiers meant big business for bar girls and prostitutes. The women's league also sought to maintain Vietnamese traditional dress codes and inveighed against mini-skirts and Western-style dancing.

The civil war which raged in the South between 1954 and 1975 destroyed much of the fabric of rural life and profoundly affected women's roles. Much of the male population disappeared from the countryside. Men were drafted into the South Vietnamese Army or the National Liberation Front, or were dragged away as suspected Viet Cong. Women became much of the rural population, and they were disproportionately victimized by the bombings, strafings, and search and destroy missions. In many areas women took over the rural economy, and as the war dragged on, large numbers of them joined the Frontline National Liberation Front (NLF) troops.[26] Women also became leaders: the vice-commander-in-chief of the NLF troops in the South was a woman.

EDUCATION, RECONSTRUCTION, AND THE CONTRADICTORY IMPACT OF SOCIALISM AND POVERTY

Literacy campaigns have historically come to be associated with communist revolution. In the USSR, Cuba, and China, literacy campaigns and the spread of mass education were initiated as communist governments came to power.

Vietnam, like these countries, made literacy and the spread of mass education a priority. In 1946, when Ho Chi Minh flew the National Liberation Front flag over the governor general's palace in Hanoi, over 90 percent of all women were illiterate. The NLF, after it was driven from Hanoi by the Allies, initiated literacy campaigns in the zones it controlled. In 1946, the literacy campaigns reached over 2 million adults. By 1948, 4 million women in the liberated zones had moved from illiteracy to being able to read and write in the Vietnamese language. By 1958, all illiteracy was eliminated in North Vietnam.[27]

In 1954, when the first Vietnam War ended, the government in Hanoi set about reforming the school system much in the image of the schools of the Soviet Union. In 1956, private schools were abolished, and public education came to consist of four years of elementary education, three years of junior secondary education, and three years of senior secondary education. University education was also provided. In the South, the school system retained the French colonial form of five years of primary education, four years of junior secondary, and three years of secondary school. Higher education was provided in a number of institutions. Unlike the North where the emphasis in higher education was on specialized technical instruction tied to economic development, in the South the university emphasized the liberal arts. In the early 1970s, 60 percent of all enrollments in the South were in literature and law, and only 10 percent studied medicine, engineering, and agriculture. In the South, over 30 percent of the population was illiterate.[28]

When the country was reunited, the schools underwent reform, harmonizing the northern and southern systems. In January 1979 the Politboro of the Vietnamese Communist party created an educational structure that consisted of nine years of general education, three years of secondary education, specialized secondary-level technical/trade schools, and universities. Although general education in Vietnam is in theory universal, male/female enrollments are not equal at any level. As of 1982, females constituted 42.8 percent of the students in the four years of general education, 45.8 percent of those in secondary education, and 28.4 percent in higher education.[29] This is more unequal than it seems—about 52 percent of the Vietnamese population is female. The sexual imbalance of the population is due to the years of bloody warfare, and it is greatest among those in the age cohorts currently in higher education.[30] The gap in male/female enrollments seems to be lessening somewhat. In 1988, women made up 37 percent of enrollments in higher education. The prospects for educational equality are somewhat dismal since many "key" schools—those schools that are funded out of provincial versus municipal budgets and that recruit from a wide geographical area—tend to have more boys than girls. The Quoc Hoc School in Hue is one such school. It prides itself on being an elite institution, and it was founded by the French early in the twentieth century to serve Annam's male elite. Today it is a coeducational school and accommodates 1,600 students in the three-year secondary course.[31] (Twenty percent of the students go on to higher education; the national average is somewhere under 10 percent of all secondary school graduates.) The students have won prizes in mathematics in international competitions in London and France. In 1988, the Quoc Hoc school enrolled 921 males and 737 females. In Grade 10 there were 275 girls and 333 boys; in Grade 12 there were 213 girls and 257 boys.

Part of the reason for the gender imbalance at Quoc Hoc School has to do with fees, which officially do not exist in Vietnam (except in universities). At Quoc Hoc, parents donate 70 dong a month. They are less willing to invest in girls who ultimately will be paid wages lower than men's and who upon marriage, are thought to join their husbands' family.[32]

The pattern of women's education is quite similar to that of many other countries in that not only are there fewer women than men the higher one goes in education, but also in that the fields of study are segregated by sex. This extends to experimental schools on the primary level like the May the 15th School in Ho-Chi-Minh City which provides working children with basic literacy skills and job training as well as to university-level studies. At the May the 15th School, boys are taught carpentry whereas girls are taught sewing, embroidery, and basket weaving.[33]

In higher education women constitute a minority. Women represent a very small proportion of Vietnamese holding the doctorate, the proportions ranging from 21.2 percent (medicine and pharmacy) to 4 percent (technology).[34] Women tend to concentrate not only in the lower levels of higher education, but also in certain fields—the natural sciences and social sciences in specialized secondary colleges where they earn half the degrees. At the university, women hold 46.4 percent of first degrees in medicine and pharmacy, 35.3 percent of first degrees in the social sciences, and 35.6 percent of first degrees in natural sciences. In contrast, they hold only 16.5 percent of first degrees in science and technology.

Equality in higher education seems a long way off as Table 9.2 indicates. As a percentage of students enrolled in university-level courses, women accounted for 4.8 percent of students in technology, 17.7 percent in agriculture and forestry, and 15.4 percent in social sciences. Women did constitute 32.2 percent of students enrolled in the natural sciences and 24.5 percent of students in medicine and pharmacy at the university level. The pattern only partly approximates that of other socialist countries. In Poland, the USSR, and East Germany, women outnumber men.[35] However the clustering of women in the natural sciences and medicine and pharmacy is reminiscent of other European socialist countries.

The lack of parity in education is partly responsible for the persisting inequalities in the workforce.

The Socialist Workforce in Vietnam

The Vietnamese socialist revolution, like other socialist revolutions, sought to resolve the problem of women's oppression, as well as the problems of underdevelopment, via the workforce.[36] The assumption was, as in Marxist ideology worldwide, that gender-based inequality was due to women's lack of

Table 9.2

Women as a Percentage of Those Possessing Degrees and Enrolled in Higher Education, by Field, 1982

Field	Specialized Secondary (College)	University (First Degree)	Graduate Student (Currently Enrolled)	Ph.D.
Natural Sciences	51.1% (n= 14,711)	35.6% (n= 13,744)	32.2% (n = 287)	7.6% (n= 94)
Technology	30% (n= 1,109)	16.5% (n= 8,284)	4.8% (n= 15)	4% (n= 40)
Medicine and Pharmacy	39.1% (n= 824)	46.4% (n= 7,156)	24.5% (n = 98)	21.2% (n= 35)
Agriculture and Forestry	30.4% (n= 530)	30.7% (n= 5,422)	17.7% (n= 21)	6.6% (n= 9)
Social Science	50.5% (n= 15,833)	35.3% (n= 20,934)	15.4% (n= 176)	10.6% (n= 60)

Source: Hoang Xuan Sinh, "Participation of Women and Their Emancipation Through the Development of Education and Science in Vietnam" in Proceedings of the Southeast Asian Seminar on Women and Science in Developing Countries. Hanoi, Vietnam, 8-10 January 1987, p. 8.

participation in productive labor. Socialist Vietnam focused on getting women into the workforce. By 1988, the government had succeeded in getting women into wage labor where their rate of participation is close to that of men, but their remuneration for their work is quite different from that of men. In 1988, women made up 46 percent of public sector (state) employees and 60 percent of co-operative employees. Women formed 65 percent of the agricultural workforce and 64 percent of the light industry workforce. They accounted for only 29 percent of workers in heavy industry.[37] The segregation of women into agri-cultural employment and work in light industry means that women are paid less than men because their work is different, as are their employers. They, like their sisters elsewhere, earn on an average 60 percent of men's wages, despite leg-islation that on paper guarantees women wages equal to those of men.

The workforce in Vietnam is segregated not only by industry and productive sector, but also within sectors. Teaching, for example, is a feminized profession: 72 percent of all those working as teachers are women. In 1982, in the universities women accounted for 3.4 percent of all professors, 26.6 percent of junior faculty, and 36 percent of the university support staff.[38] Medicine is another "female" field with 68 percent of all workers being women. However, women constitute most of the nurses and few of the hospital administrators.

The entry of women into the workforce did not mean economic equality in the past, nor will it in the future for a number of reasons. Vietnam is an im-poverished nation that has been hard pressed to provide more than rudimentary subsistence, albeit with a modicum of equality not found in other Third World nations. Feeding the growing population has been an easy task, and it is likely to get more difficult as the population continues to grow but food production continues to stagnate.[39] Basic childcare services are lacking, and women work at jobs that can be combined with family and childbearing and rearing. While the old and new marriage laws call for sharing housework and child care re-sponsibilities between spouses, enforcement is not easy.[40] Women will continue to work at jobs where they can juggle home and family in a society that calls for the sharing of and socialization of housework but cannot come up with adequate funding for such programs.

Another reason for the present workforce position of women relates to pro-tective labor legislation introduced in the 1950s and strengthened, in large part, at the instigation of the Vietnam Women's Union. Such legislation has made firms involved with heavy industry reluctant to hire women. Women workers are entitled to six months of paid maternity leave, and there are workplace environment laws relating to having pregnant and nursing women on the job. These laws are typical of other socialist countries, and in Vietnam, like the Soviet Union and many Eastern European countries, industrial firms, pressed to meet production quotas and reinvest profits in new industry, have been reluctant to bring women into their workforce.

Yet another reason for the workforce pattern is the fact that Vietnam is an underdeveloped country strained to provide employment to its growing population. Unemployment has been exacerbated by the demobilization of the army which has flooded the workforce with men seeking employment. This occurred at precisely the time when capital fled the South as the Saigon regime fell and as markets for Vietnamese goods outside the Soviet bloc crumbled. The Vietnamese invasion of Cambodia made a bad situation worse. It is indeed ironic that the invasion of Cambodia has become a way to provide Vietnamese males a job as the Soviet Union has borne the costs of the military outside the country.[41] The government has ended up giving men greater opportunity to find work, although this is not stated policy. The army, heavily female in the war of national liberation against the southern regime and the United States, has become a male army over the past ten years. Policies instituted in the 1960s and 1970s to give priority in industrial and government employment to combat veterans have come to mean preferential hiring of men. Women, who are no longer combat soldiers, have been pushed into agriculture and less desirable forms of work unless they possess educational credentials. The Vietnamese Women's Union, mindful of such trends, has sought to increase female school enrollment, particularly in science and technology. The assumption is that Vietnam will eventually industrialize and that skills will overcome the current policies militating against female employment in industry and government.[42]

The problem with such a strategy is that it neglects the fact that most Vietnamese are employed in agriculture and that the reforms in agriculture over the past decade have served to reinforce gender-based inequalities. Vietnam went through numerous agricultural reforms after the 1954 revolution, including, over time, land redistribution, collectivization, the development of cooperatives, and finally the privatization of production. Under the cooperative system, part of which is still in effect, individuals are allocated points for the work they perform for the cooperative. The model Yen-So Cooperative outside of Hanoi, which is shown to foreign visitors, is involved in brickmaking, rug manufacturing, and embroidery as well as fish culture, hog and poultry raising, and rice and other food crop production. At Yen-So, women's work receives fewer points than men's work—weeding and hoeing simply count for less than plowing; brickmaking more than embroidery or rugmaking (which consists of handlooming and hand-knotting carpets). Until all work receives equal points, women's work will have less value.[43]

Under the economic reforms of the Sixth Congress of the Communist party, the work point system is being abolished. Cooperatives lease land to families. Each family is free to produce and market as well as reinvest its profits as it sees fit. The family is therefore free to exploit female labor. More often than not, land is put under the control of males who are heads of household. The Yen-So Cooperative distributes land to male heads of households. Sons receive land from the cooperative upon marriage. In an interview in 1988, the chief of planning of Yen-So Cooperative explained that women did not need land since they would work on their husbands' land. Most women in the cooperatives worked in crafts and teaching which, she pointed out, was less difficult work than work in brickmaking and plowing and therefore was paid less.[44] Such a policy distorts the intent of Vietnamese marriage and family laws which give women equal right to property. When the chief of the Planning Committee of Yen-So Cooperative was asked about this matter, she thought it was not a problem since after all, all girls marry and, if they do not, they can always work at the cooperative in the rugmaking shop, embroidery factory, the nursery, or, with some education, in the kindergarten or school.

Women and Political Power in Revolutionary Vietnam

Women were an important part of the Vietnamese Revolution. The Vietnam Women's Union was formed in 1930 to fight for women's emancipation and to struggle against French colonialism. Over the years it was an integral part of the war for national liberation, mobilizing women to fight in the National Liberation Front forces as well as in the North in the Vietnamese Army. After 1954, the women's union was instrumental in the literacy campaigns and in the development of night and part-time education.[45] The union has also struggled for and gained protective labor legislation, monogamy, free consent in marriage, equality between husband and wife, obligations of husbands to support children, and the right to inherit and own property. The union through its branches throughout the country has the task of controlling and enforcing implementation of laws concerning women and children. The Vietnamese Women's Union is a quasi-official nongovernmental agency.[46]

Women in Vietnam today have greater access to political power than prior to and after French domination. Progressively, since 1954 in the North, women have risen to positions of national leadership, and women's concerns have been brought to the fore by the Vietnam Women's Union. Despite these very real gains, women's access to political power remains limited and certainly has never been the same as men's. Women are still a small minority in positions of leadership in the government. In 1988, only 17.7 percent of the elected representatives to the Vietnamese National Assembly were women; in 1986, 21.7 percent were.[47] The representation of women may have declined, but the number of women who headed government legislative committees rose from none before 1986 to three (out of seven committee chairs) after 1986. Currently, a woman is vice-president of the government's cultural affairs committee. Clearly, a generation of women did rise to national leadership. They were a small minority, but they were able to gain access to political power through the Communist party and the army. In part, their power in the party was the result of the need to mobilize women to work and sacrifice in wartime—which characterized Vietnam until 1975. The problem, as Duong Thi Duyen of the Vietnam Women's Union pointed out, is that the younger generation of women, coming to adulthood after the war, is less involved in politics and more involved in the day-to-day business of earning a living and raising children. In addition, women have lost some of the traditional pathways to national political leadership. In the past, the army was one such route. After 1975, the Vietnamese Army became a male army. Conscription is restricted to men; women can "volunteer" for the army, but unlike the past, when they served in combat troops and in positions of leadership and authority, today women are assigned support work in communications, logistics, and medical services. Women are trained in local militias where they form half the forces. The militia training comes in addition to work and family.

The Vietnam Women's Union itself has turned some of its concerns away from attempts to gain representation in the national political arena to support of the contemporary Vietnamese government's family planning programs. In the past the Union focused on promoting women's rights; today many of its energies are focused on controlling women's reproduction.

The Future

Without question, over the past 100 years gender relations in Vietnam have changed markedly, and much progress for women has occurred. Before the onset of French colonialism, women were denied the most basic rights, and, while peasant women toiled in the fields alongside men, their economic contribution meant little in terms of giving them power over their lives. Colonialism did not introduce patriarchal relations to Vietnam; it extended them.

French rule did bring lasting changes to Vietnam. With France came the intensification of production for export and the development of a tax system that forced much of the Vietnamese peasantry, male and female, into wage labor. The French built a new bureaucratic and political patriarchal infrastructure. New Vietnamese social classes arose, and the colonial period saw the development of a small urban middle class of entrepreneurs, teachers, medical and technical personnel, and bureaucrats in the service of the French state. A group of intellectuals arose who questioned the political and cultural institutions that had brought Vietnam under Western domination. These intellectuals focused on modernizing the country and searching for new cultural forms that would bring Vietnam into the twentieth century. The intellectual ferment involved the questioning of women's traditional roles and the development of women's organizations among the tiny urban, Westernized elites.

The French did introduce education for women. This education was confined to the urban elites and strove to prepare women to be the wives of urban francophile elites. However much French school authorities may have wanted schools to train women for the role of bourgeois housewife, such roles were not easily assimilated by women who saw education as a route to national renewal in much the same way as did many Vietnamese men caught up in the Vietnam nationalist movement. It is not surprising that a good number of educated women ended up forming the Vietnam Women's Union and its precursors.

In the long run changes for Vietnamese women came less as a result of education, which few women had either before or during the colonial period, and more as a result of protracted armed struggles against foreign domination for nearly three decades. The wars mobilized women for new roles—as producers in wartime economics, as frontline soldiers, and as revolutionaries. As a result, in 1954 and throughout the years to reunification, major changes occurred in the North. The government of socialist Vietnam provided greater access to education, and growing numbers of women have managed to obtain education. Despite the enormous gains women have experienced, equality has remained elusive and is likely to remain so. Although the Vietnamese Women's Union sees education as the means by which women will gain equality, educational enrollments have fallen off in the past five years.[48] In large part, this is due to the economic crisis in which families cannot afford "donations" to keep their children in schools and girls are more frequently withdrawn from school than are boys. Higher education, strapped for funds, has begun admitting fee-paying students. At the University of Dalat, which is a technical university, half of the students in the 1987/1988 school year paid for their own room, board, and tuition; the other half held state scholarships. Not surprisingly, only one-third of the university's students were female.[49]

School fees are new to socialist Vietnam. They were instituted by new party policies that made economic development the top priority in socialist Vietnam and focused on privatization, decentralization, the development of salary differentials and incentive plans in the hopes they would boost productivity, and the opening of the free market. Such programs are not peculiar to Vietnam; they characterize the four modernizations policy in China and Gorbachev's liberalization policies in the Soviet Union. In each, as in Vietnam, the stress on economic development has shifted to the generation of laissez-faire attitudes that put sex and social equality on the backburner. The new policies are also an admission that the government finds the demands of women's liberation and economic development contradictory and has postponed one in the hopes that the other via education or through economic development will resolve itself. Unfortunately, Vietnam has not learned from the experience of other Third World countries or from the industrialized West: namely, that increasing women's education does not resolve persisting gender-based inequalities in income, power, and the family and that economic development does little to change them either.

NOTES

1. For a discussion of changes in intellectual life, see David Marr, *Vietnamese Tradition on Trial* (Berkeley: University of California Press, 1980); Martin J. Murray, *The Development of Capitalism in Colonial Indochina (1870–1940).* (Berkeley: University of California Press, 1980); Milton Osborne, *The French Presence in Cambodia and Cochinchina: Rule and Response (1859–1905)* (Ithaca, N.Y.: Cornell University Press, 1969).

2. Mai Thi Tu and Le Thi Nham Tuyet, *La Femme au Viet Nam*, 10th ed. (Hanoi: Editions en Langues Etrangeres, 1978).

3. Arlene Eisen Bergman, *Women of Viet Nam* (San Francisco: Peoples' Press, 1974), p. 19.

4. For a discussion of the Le Code, see Mai Thi Tu and Le Thi Nham Tuyet, *La*

Femme au Viet Nam, and Ngo Vinh Long, *Vietnamese Women in Society and Revolution. 1. The French Colonial Period* (Cambridge, Mass.: Vietnam Resource Center, 1974), pp. 8–11.

5. For a description of the pre-French examination system, see Alexander Woodside, *Vietnam and the Chinese Model: A Comparative Study of the Vietnamese and Chinese Government in the First Half of the Nineteenth Century* (Cambridge, Mass.: Harvard University Press, 1971); Ngo Vinh Long, *Vietnamese Women in Society and Revolution.* Pierre Pasquier, *L'Annam d'autrefois* (Paris: Challamel, 1907).

6. Cited in Ngo Vinh Long, *Vietnamese Women in Society and Revolution,* p. 12.

7. For a discussion of the land alienation, see Pierre Brocheux, "L'Economie et la société dans l'Ouest de la Cochinchine pendant la période coloniale, 1898–1940" (Université de Paris, Faculté des Lettres, Thèse 3è cycle, 1969); see also Murray, *Development of Capitalism in Colonial Indochina.*

8. Ngo Vinh Long, *Vietnamese Women in Society and Revolution.*

9. See James Scott, *The Moral Economy of the Peasant:Rebellion and Subsistence in Southeast Asia* (New Haven, Conn., and London: Yale University Press, 1976).

10. Ngo Vinh Long, *Vietnamese Women in Society and Revolution.*

11. For school enrollment figures, see Gail P. Kelly, "Schooling and National Integration: The Case of Interwar Vietnam," *Comparative Education* 18 (1982): 175–195.

12. P. Chesneau, "Enquête sur l'analphabetisme en milieu rural dans une province du Nord-Annam," *Bulletin général de l'instruction publique, partie générale,* 17e Année, No. 8 (April 1938): 267–278. Many of the statistics cited here are from page 268.

13. Gouvernement Général de l'Indochine Française, *Rapports au Grand conseil des intérêts economiques et financiers et au Conseil du gouvernement, deuxième partie,* Tableau VI. Effectifs par cours dans l'enseignement public primaire élémentaire et primaire complémentaire Indochinois (Hanoi: Imprimerie d'Extrême Orient, 1939).

14. Gouvernement Général de l'Indochine Française, *Rapports au Grand conseil des intérêts economiques et financiers et au Conseil de gouvernement, deuxième partie: Fonctionnement des divers services Indochinois* (Hanoi: Imprimerie d'Extreme Orient, 1933), Tableau, "Enseignement privé en Indochine" (no page number given).

15. For a discussion of these texts, see David Marr, "The 1920s Women's Rights Debates in Vietnam," *Journal of Asian Studies* 35 (1976): 371–390.

16. Ibid.

17. A number of student composition books and class notebooks (*cahiers de roulement*) are available for the schools of Tonkin for the 1929–1930 and 1930–1931 school year. See Archives de France, Section d'Outre Mer, 46 PA. The differences in student composition topics between girls' schools like the Ecole Brieux and boys' schools like the Lycée of the Protectorate are striking.

18. Cahiers de composition française, Cours superier A, Ecole Brieux, Archives de France, Section d'outre mer, 46 PA, Carton 9, Dossier 89, entry dated October 19, 1929.

19. Ibid.

20. For a discussion of the school strikes of the 1920s, see Gail P. Kelly, "Conflict in the Classroom: Case Study of Colonial Vietnam," *British Journal of Sociology of Education* 8 (1987): 191–212.

21. See David Marr, *Vietnamese Anti-Colonialism, 1885–1925* (Berkeley: University of California Press, 1971); David Marr, *Vietnamese Tradition;* and Marr, "The 1920s Women's Rights Debate."

22. See, for example, Pham Quynh, *L'Evolution intellectuelle et morale des Annamites*

depuis l'etablissement du protectorat Français. Conference faite a l'Ecole coloniale le 31 mai 1922 (Valence: Impr. de Ch. Legrand et M. Granger, 1922); Pham Quynh, *Les Etudes classiques sino-annamites* (Hanoi: Impr. Tonkinoise, 1924); Pham-Quynh, *Nouveaux essais franco-annamites* (Hue: Bui-Huy-Tin, 1938); Pham Quynh, *Un Problème d'education des races. Comment doit être faite l'education des Annamites par la France* (Paris: Alcan, 1923).

23. See Marr, "The 1920s Women's Rights Debate"; on the Communist party, see Mai Thi Tu and Le Thi Nham Tuyet, *La Femme au Viet Nam.*

24. For a full discussion of the marriage laws, see Mai Thi Tu and Le Thi Nham Tuyet, *La Femme au Viet Nam;* and Bergman, *Women of Vietnam.*

25. See also Douglas Warner, *The Last Confucian: Vietnam, Southeast Asia and the West* (Baltimore: Penguin, 1964), especially Chapter 13.

26. Interview with Nguyen Van Luong, President, People's Committee, Binh Tri Thien Province, Hue, January 8, 1988. (Nguyen Van Luong was a colonel in the NLF fighting forces in the Hue District for much of the second Indochina war); Interview with Duong Thi Duyen, Vietnam Women's Union, Hanoi, January 4, 1988. In addition, Tom Mangold and John Penycate's book *The Tunnels of Cu Chi* (New York: Random House, 1985) discusses women fighters in the Vietnamese NLF in the Iron Triangle.

27. For discussions of the literacy campaigns, see *The Struggle Against Illiteracy: Vietnamese Experience* (Hanoi: Foreign Languages Publishing House, 1983); Le Thanh Khoi, *Socialisme et developpement au Viet Nam* (Paris: Presses Universitaires de France, 1978); *Etudes vietnamiennes*, No. 5 (1965), No. 30 (1971), No. 49 (1977), No. 52 (1978) (entire issues); Mai Thi Tu and Le Thi Nham Tuyet, *Vietnamese Women in Society and Revolution*, pp. 137–138.

28. See Le Thanh Khoi, "Vietnam: System of Education," *International Encyclopedia of Education*, Vol. 9, pp. 5449–5451. See also P. W. Naughton, "Some Comparisons of Higher Education in Vietnam, 1954–1976," *Canadian and International Education* 8 (1979): 100–116.

29. Le Thanh Khoi, "Vietnam: System of Education," p. 5450.

30. Interview with Duong Thi Duyen, Vietnam Women's Union, Hanoi, January 4, 1988.

31. Interview with Duong Xuan Trinh, Director, Quoc Hoc School, Hue, January 8, 1988.

32. Interview with Duong Thi Duyen, Vietnam Women's Union, Hanoi, January 4, 1988.

33. Visit to May the 15th School, Ho Chi Minh City, January 16, 1988.

34. Hong Xuan Sinh, "Participation of Women and Their Emancipation Through the Development of Education and Science in Vietnam," *Proceedings of the Southeast Asian Seminar on Women and Science in Developing Countries* (Hanoi, Vietnam: January 8–10, 1987, p. 8.

35. See Chapters 14 and 16 on Poland and the Soviet Union, respectively, in this book.

36. See, for example, Margery Wolf, *Revolution Postponed: Women in Contemporary China* (Stanford, Calif.: Stanford University Press, 1985).

37. Interview with Duong Thi Duyen, Vietnam Women's Union, Hanoi, January 4, 1988. These statistics may be unreliable, but if anything they may present a more optimistic picture of women's workforce participation patterns.

38. See Huang Xuan Sinh, "Participation of Women and Their Emancipation." See

also David Marr, "Tertiary Education, Research, and the Information Sciences in Vietnam," Unpublished manuscript, 1987, pp. 5–6.

39. Interview with Director, Viet-My, Hanoi, January 3, 1988; Interview with Mr. Lindblad, Swedish Ambassador to Vietnam, Hanoi, January 3, 1988.

40. See "La Nouvelle loi sur le marriage et la famille," *Bulletin de Droit,* No. 1 1987 (Numero Special), Association des Juristes de la Republique Socialiste du Vietnam et Union des Femmes de la Republique Socialiste du Vietnam. Interview with Duong Thi Duyen, Vietnam Women's Union, Hanoi, January 4, 1988.

41. Interview with Mr. Lindblad, Swedish Ambassador to Vietnam, Hanoi, January 3, 1988; Interview with Philip Mayhew, Consul for Political Affairs, U.S. Embassy, Bangkok, Thailand, December 29, 1987.

42. Interview with Duong Thi Duyen, Vietnam Women's Union, Hanoi, January 4, 1988.

43. Interview with Chu-Chuc, Chief, Planning Committee, Yen-So Cooperative, Hanoi, January 3, 1988; Interview with Nguyen Van Luong, President, People's Committee, Binh-Tri-Thein Province, Hue, January 8, 1988.

44. Interview with Chu-Chuc, Chief, Planning Committee, Yen-So Cooperative, Hanoi, January 3, 1988.

45. For some of the history of the Vietnamese Women's Union, see Mai Thi Tu and Le Thi Nham Tuyet, *Vietnamese Women in Society and Revolution*.

46. Interview with Duong Thi Duyen, Vietnam Women's Union, Hanoi, January 4, 1988.

47. Interview with Duong Thi Duyen, Vietnam Women's Union, Hanoi, January 4, 1988.

48. See Marr, "Teritiary Education, Research and the Information Sciences in Vietnam."

49. Interview with Chair, Teaching Department, Dalat Technical University, Dalat, January 12, 1988.

AUSTRALIA

10
AUSTRALIA

Lyn Yates

Since the mid-1970s, Australia, a Western, postindustrial country, has devoted considerable attention and funding to women's education. A relatively high sex segregation of the workforce has persisted in this country, where, despite equal pay legislation, women's average earnings are markedly lower than men's and women form a high percentage of those considered to be living in poverty. It is also a country which in the last two decades has witnessed a steady increase in women's participation in education and in employment. At the same time, the socialization of women and men and the differences in their domestic burden have caused marked differentials in the pattern of participation in education and have given women a smaller share of senior positions in employment, even when the women have an equivalent educational background.

Although many formal barriers to women's participation in education and to employment opportunities have been removed, many indirect effects of difference and discrimination remain and they are more difficult to eliminate. While the mid-1970s to mid-1980s was a time of reform in this respect, recent state and federal pronouncements suggest the beginning of a new period. A belief in economic rationalism and a concern about Australia's competitive position in the world are now being seen in new policies which are likely to have a detrimental effect on women's participation in education and access to the workforce.

This chapter will first establish a brief context for our discussion of women's education in Australia and will in turn deal with schooling, postschool education, alternative education, and education and work. The historical background will be cursory; most attention will be given to developments since the mid-1970s, the period of reform directed toward ending sexual inequality in schooling and society.

Neither recounting the facts on women and education in Australia, nor attempting to make sense of them is an easy task. Education in Australia is organized largely on a state rather than a national basis, and there have been some significant differences between states in the forms of provision and in the amount of attention given to girls as an issue. In addition, in recent years the issue of women and education has been one of the liveliest areas of research and government inquiry in Australia. The wealth of material, as well as the range of perspectives now available, makes the task of presenting one brief summary account a daunting enterprise.[1] Finally, even the most solid-looking sets of government statistics are not facts that speak for themselves. In recent years, for example, some controversy has arisen in Australia over whether the extension and development of schooling in the late nineteenth century represented an improved or a worsened provision for girls and women.[2] Questions have been raised about whether school "retention rates" give a falsely rosy picture of the education of girls as compared with boys.[3] Researchers in the area have drawn some quite different conclusions about the educational experience of girls of non-English-speaking background and the strategies appropriate to them.[4]

Much of the context relating to changes in women's education in Australia in this century is common to other Western countries. The gradual lengthening of women's schooling, along with women's increasing participation in the paid labor force, has taken place in a period of markedly decreasing family size (from around six at the turn of the century to under three today). In addition, especially following the Australian Family Law Act of 1975, the divorce rate has risen massively, as a result of which a much larger proportion of women are now sole supporters of their children. Men's participation in domestic labor has increased as married women have entered the workforce in greater numbers (from 4.4 percent in 1921 to over 50 percent today), but women still bear the overwhelming responsibility for both domestic labor and child care. This, too, has shaped the form of their educational and workforce participation, discussed later in this chapter.[5]

Politically, Australia was one of the first countries in the world in which women had the right both to vote and to stand for Parliament, gaining this right for the national legislature in 1902 and in state parliaments as early as 1894.[6] Voting is compulsory for Australian citizens. However, it took several decades in the various parliaments between the granting of the right for women to sit and the first actual election of a woman. In South Australia, where women had been granted the right to vote and to sit in 1894, the first woman was not elected until 1959. Before the impact of second-wave feminism in the 1970s and 1980s, the representation of women in Australian parliaments was minimal. Indeed, "before the 1970s, Australia in most cases lacked even the token representation found in other English-speaking democracies."[7] More recently, younger women with experience in the workforce (frequently as teachers) and often with younger children have been elected. Nevertheless, women's share of political office in the various levels of local, state, and federal politics is only between 6 and 9 percent. In Australia, women's political activity has been more commonly channeled through lobby groups, both of the left and the right. Largely owing to such groups, equal opportunity and the rights of women have been part of the overt political agenda since the early 1970s.[8]

SCHOOLING

The Form of Provision

In the late nineteenth century, all states in Australia developed systems of "free, compulsory and secular" schooling. These systems gradually extinguished a range of small private venture schools for girls.[9] These new schools did not impede the entrenchment of an extensive system of Catholic parish schools or the development of a strong range of fee-charging church schools which have maintained a heavy, largely class-based influence on educational and employment opportunity in Australia. Today such "independent" schools account for between one-fourth and one-third of the total school population in the different states and for well over half of those entering tertiary education. The period of compulsory schooling was initially set (there was and continues to be some variation between states) at around five to six years to thirteen to fourteen years. In the postwar period, the leaving age has been extended to fifteen years in most states and sixteen in Tasmania. At first, compulsory schooling took place largely in elementary schools, perhaps with a higher elementary component. Now the system that exists with some variation in the various states is of a primary school which students attend to around twelve years of age (usually comprising a preparatory grade followed by six other grades) and a secondary school of six year levels. The statutory leaving age usually falls in the fourth year of secondary school. In earlier times, certificates marked the end of each of the final three or four years of schooling. Today in many states the final examination at year twelve (which also serves as the university matriculation examination) is the only form of school certification.

The initial elementary curriculum developed in the late nineteenth century was designed to provide functional skills for girls and boys to enable them to take their place in the developing industrial society, along with an element of social control that could be expected from a compulsory, state-provided moral training. The curriculum was largely common and coeducational. Some differentiation was built into the curriculum: girls were to be taught needlework and to be especially schooled in morality. (European Australia's convict origins had given rise to particular concerns about the moral dangers of women as "damned whores" and their proper role as "God's police."[10]) In the early years, girls' attendance rates were significantly lower than boys' because of their involvement in domestic labor. In the first part of the twentieth century, the efforts of state governments to impose a curriculum that particularly emphasized domestic skills for girls was resisted by women teachers (who were not rewarded for teaching such extras), by parents (who wanted the girls' time in school to be spent learning things they could not learn in the home), and by the girls themselves. State Education Departments continued to promote supposedly useful skills such as needlework when technological developments along with the actual employment patterns of women made such curricula anachronistic.[11]

State-provided secondary education is almost entirely a phenomenon of the twentieth century and did not become universal in Australia until after the Second World War. From an early period there existed a few selective schools designed to prepare the "brightest" students for university. When thought was given to the development of secondary education, it often took the form of establishing some coeducational high schools with a largely academic curriculum, along with some technical schools for boys and domestic high schools for girls. The form of state secondary education now found in Australia consists of largely coeducational, comprehensive high schools, though some selective schools and some single-sex schools continue to exist.

Until very recently, nongovernment schooling in Australia has been almost entirely single sex. In most cases, it is formally provided by church bodies, but the actual ideology and practices of particular schools with regard to the future of the girls they teach is not uniform. A few schools have long been oriented to the preparation of women of high achievement; many others have strongly presumed a domestic destiny for women and have offered a quality and content of curriculum that is highly differentiated from their equivalent "brother" schools.

Participation Patterns

Statistics on the school participation of girls and boys in the prewar period in Australia are not readily available. However, P. Miller's detailed examination of census figures for 1911–1981 for one state[12] gives a good indication of the pattern of changes. In South Australia, in 1911 only about 15 percent of fifteen year olds were at school, and under one-third of this age group were at school in the 1930s. However, in the postwar period there was a rapid increase to well over half of the age group by 1961 and well over 80 percent by 1971. Similar proportions of girls and boys were at school in the period up to the 1920s, but a much smaller number of girls remained at school in the 1930s. This pattern continued until the early 1960s. From the 1960s, the proportions of girls and boys at school begin to equalize, until in the most recent period slightly more girls remain at school than boys. Australia-wide, since 1976 the retention rate for girls to the final year of secondary school has exceeded that of boys.[13] Government policies have tried to increase overall retention in these noncompulsory years, and around half now remain to the final year of school, as compared with under 10 percent in the 1950s.

The fact that girls on average left school earlier than boys in the period up to 1960 no doubt reflected different views on the value of qualifications for them. The growth in the retention rates of girls from the 1960s took place alongside a marked increase in women's labor force participation. The equalizing of general participation rates of girls and boys in school in fact *preceded* the major period of reforms concerned with sexual equity in schools. The equalized school retention has not been translated into equal patterns of higher education participation or workforce rewards for girls.

Until the 1970s a sex-differentiated, vocationally oriented curriculum was commonly offered in addition to the academic core of secondary schooling. Students were divided into "streams" variously designated "technical," "commercial" or "domestic." Since the legislative changes of the 1970s to be discussed shortly, no girl or boy can formally be excluded from any subject.[14] There has also been a tendency for a general program to replace a vocationally differentiated course of study. Nonetheless, there is still a clear sex typing of course choices in the final year of schooling; girls are far more likely to take humanities courses and to avoid mathematics.[15] The difference in participation rates in mathematics and science is significant since mathematics is required for a large range of tertiary courses.[16] It also has an indirect effect in states that statistically standardize students' final examination results to produce one common score which is the basis for tertiary entrance.

The processes involved make it easier for students to achieve a higher score by taking mathematics and science subjects. They may lead to some disadvantage for girls who choose humanities streams in school, even for entry to tertiary courses in nonscience subjects. Women continue to be disadvantaged in relation to further education because of the use of mathematics as a hurdle requirement where this is not required by the nature of the field.[17] Fomin has shown that women's entry into medicine courses in Victoria increased when regulations were changed to allow English to be substituted for one mathematics or science subject in the composite score.[18]

Changing Frameworks for the Education of Girls since the Mid-1970s

Since the mid-1970s in Australia, as in a number of other Western countries, some marked changes have occurred in educational policy, ideology, and processes as they relate to girls. Government reports before 1970 either assumed and promoted a different future for girls and a pattern of unequal provision and outcomes associated with it, or did not mention sex or gender as an issue for schooling. The reports of the 1970s interpreted different experiences and outcomes of girls as a *problem*, which represented "underachievement" and "implicit and explicit discrimination." Commonwealth and state reports recommended that education be designed to help girls "have as many careers and life choices open to them as do boys."[19]

A number of factors contributed to this shift. The development of the women's movement, which in the early 1970s had given rise to such groups as the Women's Electoral Lobby and the Australian Women's Education Coalition, was important. Both groups lobbied the government strongly for more attention to women and their education and for the recognition that women deserved equal rights and opportunities. These demands were also being promoted by the teacher unions. When the United Nations declared 1975 International Women's Year, some government funding was made available in Australia for projects related to women.

The early 1970s was a period of economic boom. It was also a period of reforming optimism which was reflected in the election in 1972, after twenty-three years of conservative rule, of the Whitlam Labor government (under the slogan "It's Time"). The Whitlam government set up a major inquiry into inequality in Australian education,[20] which in turn led to the establishment of the Schools Commission and to Commonwealth funding for special reform projects in schools, of which the work on girls was one example. Pressures to take up issues of sexism and women's rights were widespread. In addition to the national committee of inquiry which produced the report *Girls, School and Society,* all Australian states except Queensland set up committees of inquiry and produced reports in the area.[21]

Girls, School and Society and the various state reports argued that the schools were channeling girls into a narrow range of subjects and outcomes that failed to give them equal opportunity in the workforce. They recommended strategies to overcome this inequality.

Strategies of Reform

Following the publication of *Girls, School and Society,* a good deal of attention was given to educational reforms that would benefit girls. Federal and state-based legislation has been enacted outlawing discrimination on the basis of sex, and most states have developed formal policies on equal opportunity or "The Elimination of Sexism in Schools." Partly as a result of Commonwealth funding, Women's Advisers or Equal Opportunity consultants were appointed to Education Departments in the various states and Equal Opportunity Resource Centers were established. Projects to develop new curriculum materials, school-based action research, and conferences and in-service education for teachers have also been developed. The educational changes emphasized in the late 1970s included reforms in textbooks and readers to increase the inclusion of women; campaigns to persuade girls to take on nontraditional careers, particularly apprenticeships; projects designed to increase girls' self-esteem; and materials for students to examine sex roles in society.

In Australia, much of the attempt to reform schooling for girls has been developed as forms of action research by teachers, supported by Commonwealth funding. The emphasis has been on school-based projects as the site of effective change, in contrast to more formal experimental research or reform projects directed by academics which have been more common in other countries. The Australian approach requires a high degree of teacher involvement and has led to a wide range of initiatives in reforming the curriculum and teaching process. The degree of teacher initiative and involvement in the reforms has been a strength of educational developments in Australia.

The participatory reform encouraged in Australia has also had some drawbacks. Funds are given to those who make submissions, so that those schools whose practices are most in need of reform may be least likely to be changed. The stress on involvement and participation rather than on evaluation of progress has led to much emphasis on changing the dynamics of the classroom and a considerably smaller emphasis on longer term outcomes. At a state policy level, too, although many equal opportunity policies have been produced, the emphasis has been on rhetorical commitments rather than on sanctions. A 1984 report assessing developments of the previous decade concluded that the many initiatives in relation to girls were yet to make a significant general impact on the schooling system.[22] On the matter of outcomes, this report documented greater poverty and more teenage unemployment among females, and continued strong occupational and post-school educational segregation. It also seems that campaigns to persuade women to start nontraditional careers or even to increase retention in mathematics and science to date have had little effect.[23]

Given this experience, strategies for reform in Australia have broadened considerably beyond removal of formal barriers, changing career advice, and adding women to textbooks. Attention has turned to the dynamics and culture of schooling as they affect women's confidence about their abilities in these areas, to the need for support structures in the workplace if women are to enter new areas where they are heavily outnumbered, and to whether the construction and teaching of the subjects themselves are based on male rather than female interests and learning styles. Attention has been given to how the content and process of schooling could be made to reflect equally centrally the interests and learning styles of girls and boys, that is, of how a "sexually inclusive curriculum" might be developed.[24]

TERTIARY AND FURTHER EDUCATION

Women were first admitted to universities in Australia in the 1880s, but consistently far fewer women than men have pursued further education. Those who do have been heavily concentrated in a few areas such as teacher education. At the time of the 1971 census, women constituted only 27.8 percent of students in all types of post-schools and 38.3 percent of those undertaking degrees. The last decade has witnessed a considerable increase in women's participation rate at this level. Between 1969 and 1982, the proportion of women with post-school qualifications tripled, and women now constitute about half of those entering post-school courses.[25] In many respects, these facts do not represent a marked change of women's educational situation and access to employment relative to men. The same period has witnessed increased competition for jobs and higher level of qualification required for entry into many fields. Although women's overall entry into higher education is similar to that of men, the fields in which they study have a different pattern and their participation beyond an initial degree remains markedly lower. Moreover, figures on employment rates and wages indicate that participation in higher education for women is not translated in a simple way into similar access to jobs as men with equivalent qualifications.

In terms of policy, in the last decade women have been encouraged to continue their education and to enter nontraditional areas, particularly areas related to trades and technology. A small number of structural provisions have been made in universities and colleges which have also made participation of women more possible. Specifically, a small proportion of university entrants have been selected via ''mature-age'' criteria that do not require the normal completion of the higher school certificate,[26] and some provision has been made for child care.[27] Under government affirmative action regulations, in recent years institutions of higher education have been required to investigate and report on their procedures with regard to equal opportunity. Most have now appointed an officer with responsibility in this area.

Some policy moves initiated over this period have also worked against the participation of women, especially the greatly reduced financial assistance available to undergraduates; the limited number of places relative to the higher numbers now completing school; the greater emphasis on funding certain technological vocational areas (areas in which women have participated in much smaller numbers, and which reduce funding to areas in which they participate in larger numbers); and, more recently, moves to increase youth participation at the expense of mature-age entrants and the reintroduction of fees.

Women's transition rate from school to higher education (now about 40 percent) is markedly lower than that of males and has been declining at a higher rate over the 1980s.[28] Powles's review of research on this area cites the possible reasons for this decline, all of which draw attention to women's socialization and development, their expectations, and the realities of their life patterns. For example, it may be related to the way they themselves define their abilities (studies show girls have lower self-confidence and need more encouragement if they are to continue their education beyond secondary school) or how others define it (not having taken mathematics and science may deny them access to first-preference courses). Or, given the fact that most girls marry and have children in their mid- to late twenties, research has suggested that they value a period of ''independence'' before marriage, unwilling to accept living at home and having little money, which remaining a student would likely entail. Girls are more likely than boys to defer tertiary places offered to them. Yet again, particularly in periods of economic downturn, parents may be less willing to support daughters in tertiary study. Because of girls' different life patterns and expectations, structural and policy changes such as the abolition of relatively well-paid teaching studentships for tertiary study, the greatly reduced value of undergraduate scholarships, and the imposition of fees are matters that affect them more than boys.

Since 1975, the number of women has increased in all fields of higher and further education other than teacher education, and a proportional increase has taken place in women's participation in "male" fields of study. But, as Tables 10.1 and 10.2 show, women still constitute a tiny proportion of engineering students and less than 30 percent of those in agriculture, building and architecture, and dentistry. (In Australia, engineering has one of the highest job vacancies, whereas dentistry is one of the best paid professions.) Women constitute between 30 and 40 percent of students of applied science, natural science, commerce and economics, just over 40 percent of those now enrolled in medicine, law, and veterinary science but over 60 percent of those in the humanities, arts, fine art, art and design, social science, behavioral science, paramedical studies, and teacher education.

Tables 10.1 and 10.2 also indicate that in some courses women greatly increased their representation in the period between 1975 and 1982. These include agricultural courses in Colleges of Advanced Education (CAEs) (from 17.6 to 29.0 percent), applied science in CAEs (from 19.8 to 36.0 percent), commercial and business studies in CAEs (from 16.5 to 29.5 percent), law in universities (from 24.4 to 40.2 percent), and veterinary science in universities (from 25.1 to 45.5 percent).

TAFE (Technical and Further Education) enrolls over twice as many students as those in universities and CAEs and offers a large number of directly vocational courses. It has been a growing area of government funding and one that seems likely to receive continued support. Table 10.3 shows that, although, overall, women constitute about half of those enrolled in TAFE institutions, they represent a very small proportion of those in apprenticeship-based trades courses (stream 3) and a very large majority of those in the nonvocational and generally non-certificate "adult education" stream 6.

Reports on further education usually do not even list the stream 6 figures. These are often referred to as "hobby" courses, and some funding moves have been made to direct women from these courses to more directly vocational ones. The lack of attention to this popular source of further education for women, both in government reports and in the research literature, reflects ways in which women's access to and participation in education may stray from the traditional, as well as ways in which policy has been slow to look at this situation in its own terms.[29]

Although women now constitute almost half of all students entering higher education, they account for only about 30 percent of higher degree enrollments and an even smaller proportion of tenured staff in these institutions.

Over the last decade changes have been made at a policy level as well as from below, which should affect the situation of women in universities. The policy-

Table 10.1

Enrollment in Undergraduate Courses at Colleges of Advanced Education, by Sex and Field of Study, 1975 and 1982

Field of Study	1975			1982		
	Males	Females (%)	Total	Males	Females (%)	Total
Agriculture[a]	1,392	298 (17.6)	1,690	1,690	690 (29.0)	2,380
Applied Science[a]	5,545	1,368 (19.8)	6,913	8,800	4,950 (36.0)	13,750
Art, Design[b]	2,595	3,035 (54.2)	5,630	3,990	5,930 (59.8)	9,920
Building, Architecture[a]	3,803	430 (10.2)	4,233	3,690	880 (19.2)	4,570
Commercial, Business Studies[a]	18,460	3,646 (16.5)	22,106	23,600	9,890 (29.5)	33,490
Engineering, Technology[a]	10,468	124 (1.2)	10,592	11,210	290 (2.5)	11,500
Liberal Studies[b]	3,730	4,639 (55.4)	8,369	7,290	13,690 (65.3)	20,980
Music[b]	339	704 (67.5)	1,043	640	920 (59.0)	1,560
Para-medical[b]	1,717	3,885 (69.4)	5,602	2,54	7,170 (73.8)	9,710
Teacher Education[b]	14,657	32,978 (69.2)	47,635	10,280	24,760 (70.6)	35,040
Total	62,706	51,107 (44.9)	113,813	73,730	69,170 (48.4)	142,900

	Males			Females		
Total 'Male' Fields-all[a]	39,668	5,866 (12.8)	45,534	48,990	16,700 (25.4)	65,690
Total 'Female' Fields-all[b]	23,038	45,241 (66.0)	68,279	24,740	52,470 (68.0)	77,210

	Males	Females
Enrollment change 'Male' Fields[a] 1975–1982	9,322 (23.5%)	10,834 (184.7%)
Enrollment change 'Female' Fields[b] 1975–1982	1,702 (7.4%)	7,229 (16.0%)

Source: M. Powles, Women's Participation in Tertiary Education, 2nd ed., (Melbourne: University of Melbourne Centre for the Study of Higher Education, 1987), p. 79.

a) Male dominated fields
b) Female dominated fields

Table 10.2
Enrollment in Bachelor Degree Courses at Universities, by Sex and Field of Study, 1975 and 1982

Field of Study	1975			1982		
	Males	Females (%)	Total	Males	Females (%)	Total
Humanities[a]	16,016	22,121 (58.0)	38,137	13,540	24,920 (64.8)	38,460
Fine Arts[b]	240	365 (60.3)	605	340	560 (62.2)	900
Social, Behavioral Sciences[b]	1,986	3,314 (62.3)	5,300	3,020	5,640 (65.2)	8,660
Law[a]	5,988	1,929 (24.4)	7,917	5,340	3,580 (40.2)	8,910
Education[b]	2,933	3,145 (51.7)	6,078	1,830	3,980 (68.6)	5,810
Economics, Commerce[a]	13,063	3,068 (19.0)	16,131	12,970	5,800 (30.9)	18,770
Medicine[a]	6,086	3,534 (36.7)	9,620	6,010	4,190 (41.1)	10,200
Dentistry[a]	1,207	280 (18.8)	1,487	960	370 (27.6)	1,340
Natural Sciences[a]	13,380	6,343 (32.2)	19,723	13,360	8,410 (38.6)	21,770
Engineering, Technology[a]	9,579	197 (2.0)	9,776	10,020	700 (6.5)	10,720
Architecture, Building[a]	2,211	488 (18.1)	2,699	2,310	810 (26.0)	3,120
Agriculture, Forestry[a]	1,680	382 (18.5)	2,062	1,430	600 (29.6)	2,030
Veterinary Science[a]	818	274 (25.1)	1,092	680	560 (45.5)	1,240

Other and not stated	34	33	67	40	50	90
Total	75,221	45,473 (37.7)	120,694	71,850	60,170 (45.6)	132,020
Total 'Male' Fields–all[a]	54,012	16,495 (23.4)	70,507	53,080	25,020 (32.0)	78,100
Total 'Female' Fields–all[b]	21,175	28,945 (57.8)	50,120	18,730	35,100 (65.2)	53,830

	Males	Females
Enrollment change 'Male' Fields[a] 1975–1982	-932 (-1.7%)	8,525 (51.7%)
Enrollment change 'Female' Fields[b] 1975–1982	-2445 (-11.5%)	6,155 (32.9%)

Source: M. Powles, Women's Participation in Tertiary Education, 2nd ed., (Melbourne: University of Melbourne Centre for the Study of Higher Education, 1987), p. 83.

a) Male dominated fields
b) Female dominated fields

Table 10.3
Distribution of Students in TAFE Streams 1–5, by Sex, 1981, 1983, and 1985

Stream	1981		1983		1985	
	No. of Students	Percent Female	No. of Students	Percent Female	No. of Students	Percent Female
1 Professional	3,210	46.1	3,318	40.1	3,546	42.6
2 Para-Professional	191,362	35.2	230,974	44.6	259,279	47.2
3a Basic Trade	131,750	7.1	123,473	8.7	109,259	11.7
3b Post Trade	28,564	4.4	32,245	6.3	32,106	9.1
4 Other Skilled	212,888	55.6	239,544	53.1	282,854	53.3
5 Preparatory	151,466	53.8	200,007	56.2	217,519	58.2
Net Streams 1–5	692,014	39.2	786,222	43.3	859,194	46.3
6 Adult Education	322,945	68.8	359,143	71.6	457,357	72.6

Source: CTEC Technical and Further Education Advisory Committee, Report for the 1988–90 Triennium Vol. 1, Part 5 (Canberra: A.G.P.S., 1987), p. 16.

level equal opportunity investigations and appointments have been mentioned above. From within universities, staff and students have begun to promote courses in women's and feminist studies; and to challenge, critique, and reform the existing disciplines. Gradually, appointments are being made specifically in these areas. But universities strongly resist directives as to their internal appointment and promotion procedures. Despite statements on equal opportunity, progress in increasing the proportion of women on staff has been slow. Although courses with women as their main focus are no longer unusual (and have proved extremely popular), they remain a small minority and are found only in those areas where women form the bulk of the students. In addition, bitterly fought cases have taken place on some campuses as to whether women's studies merely constitutes political propaganda or whether existing courses such as "Man and the Environment" are sexist.

ALTERNATIVE AND NONFORMAL EDUCATION

One issue raised by the women's movement was whether the content and processes of traditional education, in particular competitive, academic, and didactic learning, was appropriate for women. An alternative model of appropriate education was seen as the "consciousness-raising" groups: in ideal type, a group of equals in no formal institutional structure who, by sharing experiences in a nonthreatening setting, would see these in a new light. In Australia, such ideas have had some impact over the last two decades both in experiments within institutionalized education and in the development of educational forms outside this setting.

At the school level, many of the action-research and countersexist strategies funded in Australia in recent years have experimented with ways in which some version of noncompetitive, negotiated, discussion-based approaches can be used. In terms of tangible outcomes of different approaches, some research is now appearing which suggests that girls have done better in and are markedly more favorable toward alternative than traditional forms. At the tertiary level, some initial attempts to develop women's studies courses along lines of consciousness raising have met difficulties given the institutional demands of assessment.

One of the most successful developments of the period in terms of the number of women who have returned to study through them has been the Women's Learning Houses, or Neighorhood Houses. In informal settings, people associated with these projects have developed a range of course offerings, from "hobby" courses to basic literacy and language learning to Higher School Certificate courses and bridging courses for tertiary entry. The houses are now largely incorporated as part of Technical and Further Education (TAFE) stream 6. The Council of Adult Education also provides a large range of noncertificate courses which have been particularly popular with women.

EDUCATION AND EMPLOYMENT

In recent decades an important shift has taken place with regard to women who work in education: from an acceptance of formal inequalities for women to the removal of many of these barriers. In addition, there has been a growing recognition of the many informal differences that work against women's equal opportunity in the workforce.

The pattern of women's participation in the workforce in Australia shows many features common to all Organization for Economic Cooperation and Development countries.[30] Industrialization in the late nineteenth century gradually brought a sharp division of labor between men and women, with women more strongly confined to domestic labor. Women's workforce participation increased in both extent and range during World War II, but the immediate postwar period reversed many of these trends. In the postwar period, with the development of a strong service and information sector of the economy, lowered fertility rates, and an aggressive consumer advertising which has promoted the consumption of goods requiring more than the income of one average wage-earner, women's participation in the paid labor force has more than doubled. Features particular to Australia are the form of wage regulation and its effect on women's wages, and the fact that job segregation by sex has been more marked in Australia than elsewhere.

In Australia, the basis of wage rates is largely set by a national arbitration court. The first national wage judgment, the H. V. McKay Harvester judgment of 1911, enshrined the idea of the determination of a family wage that would be sufficient to support a man, his wife, and children. This principle was used to justify much lower payments to women, on the grounds that theirs was not a family wage. By the 1960s, however, changing demographic patterns were removing much of the justification for this discrimination: large numbers of men were not supporting dependents, and large numbers of women were doing so. Equal pay was gradually introduced in the late 1960s, with teaching being one of the first occupations in which equal pay was instituted. "Comparable worth" for occupations such as nursing or many types of factory work which are almost entirely female has not yet been successfully established.

Despite "equal pay" legislation, the female/male mean income ratio for all full-time workers was only 0.82 in 1985 (up from 0.75 in 1981–1982 and 0.64 in 1973–1974). Many more women than men work part-time, and in 1985 the ratio of female to male wages of all employees' weekly total earnings was 0.65. However, the theory that women form a "reserve army" of labor, the first to lose their job in a recession, has not been borne out.[31] Here both the segregation of jobs by sex and the cheapness of women's labor may have supported their continued (though poorly rewarded) employment in some periods of recession.

In Australia, maternity leave is now a right for those in permanent jobs. Child care provision has been growing, but availability is still far below demand.

The relation between the education and employment patterns of men and women is complex. Statistics suggest that the rate of women's participation in the workforce increases with their level of qualification: in February 1984, 73.4 percent of women with degrees were in the paid labor force; 54.6 percent of those with other post-school qualifications; and 40.5 percent of those with no post-school qualifications. Yet, in terms of those who want to work and are not able to find it, we find that women with post-school qualifications experienced higher rates of unemployment than males with the same qualifications, whereas females who had completed school but had not undertaken further education had lower rates of unemployment than males with the same educational experience. Some similarities can be seen in wage patterns. Whereas women's earnings increase with their educational qualifications, women who have left school at seventeen or over without further education have the highest ratio of wages to male wages (0.80, as compared with 0.74 for those with degrees and 0.70 for those with post-school qualifications other than degrees).[32] Further education gives women an overall opportunity of better employment and pay, but it may also increase their consciousness of discrimination since, on employment, they will be likely to find opportunities and rewards mediated by their sex.[33]

About two-thirds of women in Australia are employed in three occupations: clerical, sales, and service/sport/recreation.[34] C. O'Donnell's analysis of the relation between gender, education, and jobs in Australia suggests that men's and women's participation in the labor market is regulated by length of schooling, type of schooling, and sex preference of employers.[35] O'Donnell argues that in different sectors (partly for historical reasons, including past union activity) different factors may be emphasized and that the potential for change through education needs to be considered accordingly. For example, in recent years the higher echelons of the public service in Australia have given most attention to length of schooling. Here formal bureaucratic procedures of employment, along with the existence of statutory equal opportunity bodies, have made possible considerable growth in women's representation at senior levels. On the other hand, women have made less progress in Technical and Further Education (TAFE) because those in positions of power in this organization have a background that gives considerable preference directly to sex (a belief in sex-based competencies and a mateship ethos) and to type of schooling (technical).

Another report suggests that the higher unemployment of women as compared with men from Colleges of Advanced Education (CAEs), along with the streamed course choices of women, can be explained in terms of the realities of hiring practices.[36] Women are heavily dependent on teaching and paramedical fields because it is more difficult for them to find jobs in more prestigious areas: employers employ men as scientists and researchers. It should be remembered that much of the industrial sector in Australia is multinational, and basic research is done outside the country. As a result, the service and information sectors are the largest areas of employment.[37]

A. Game and R. Pringle's study of work practices in Australia has shown how job segregation which has ostensibly been based on a differentiation of qualities appropriate to women and men (heavy/light; dirty/clean, etc.) has been used to perpetuate advantageous work conditions and rewards for men.[38] Although in many industries new technology has removed the basis of earlier distinctions, new forms of designating "men's" and "women's" work have nevertheless arisen and have perpetuated lower wages and less autonomous work practices for women.

Overall, in recent decades women have made some progress in the range of occupations they enter (following early test cases on such matters as whether a woman could be an airline pilot or a tram-driver) and in their rise to more senior positions. However, the general clustering of women in what are considered traditional occupations has changed little in Australia, and women's entry into senior positions is extremely small relative to their participation at lower levels in given occupations.

Women's employment progress as well as the continuing difficulties they face is illustrated by considering women who work in education. In the early part of the nineteenth century, the private venture "dame" schools provided an occupational identity and opportunity for some women.[39] With the extension of systems of education, schooling continued to provide one employment opportunity for women, but one in which they regularly faced direct discrimination as compared with men in terms of their conditions of employment and career opportunities.[40] In most states, separate female and male teachers' unions developed because men were concerned that a joint union would depress their wages to those seen as appropriate for women.[41] As well as wage discrimination, before the late 1960s and early 1970s female teachers suffered direct discrimination on grounds of marriage (as a result of which they were not allowed to be classified as "permanent" members of the teaching force) and in terms of appointment to senior positions.

Only in the last two decades have all such direct barriers been gradually removed. Committees of inquiry on sexism in education have drawn attention to the need for women to get a higher share of promotions. Yet in this same period in a number of states women's share of senior positions has actually declined. Investigations of the reasons for this decline have drawn attention to continuing structural sources of indirect discrimination (for example, favoring those free to travel widely; or favoring seniority and not giving credit for time spent on maternity leave), as well as to subtle and pervasive cultural assumptions (for example, that women continue to be seen as the partner primarily responsible for children and less able to take on after-school work or to go to conferences; women's own beliefs that they are not confident of their administrative ability; or appointment committees' beliefs which perceive male rather than female personalities as dynamic and appropriately authoritative).[42]

In some states, the recognition of these processes has led to some accrediting of childrearing experience, and workshops have been run to train and support women seeking appointment. However, in general, the attention of state education departments to equal opportunity in making appointments, even where the term *affirmative action* is used, has avoided the use of quotas or even targets. Women continue to account for a high proportion of those in junior positions in schools and the administration and a very small proportion of those in senior positions.

Similar policy changes, strategies, and findings regarding the slowness to change have been found in relation to women working in tertiary and further education.[43] Here the ratio of women's share of senior appointments is even worse than in schools,[44] partly because of the greater difficulty of bureaucratically regulating individual appointments in these institutions. Other factors specific to the development of higher education in Australia have also played a part. The tertiary system expanded when there were relatively fewer qualified women to fill positions. The more recent period, when more women have been qualified, has been one where many fewer academic vacancies occurred.[45] Australian academic institutions give preference in appointments to people with some overseas qualifications (the "colonial cringe," which presumes that qualifications from England in particular are better than Australian qualifications). This favors men who have traditionally been far more likely than women to study abroad.[46]

Academic studies have found that men and women have vastly different experiences of the same marriage, with the majority still assuming the bulk of domestic work and child care to be the woman's responsibility. For example, in one study, even among the small minority of men who reported that responsibility for child care was "mutual," it was found that many had taken "none" or a "minor share" of care for their children until they reached school age![47]

CLASS, RACE, AND ETHNICITY

Girls and women, of course, do not form a homogeneous group, and the patterns of participation as well as the strategies of reform outlined above need further attention in terms of some of the significant differences.

Class

In Australia retention in school is regulated much more strongly by class than by sex. For example, in 1975, when the differences in school retention rates between girls as a group and boys as a group had become negligible, class differences were very large indeed.[48] Notwithstanding many policy and funding moves designed to increase equal opportunity, there has been little change in class-related access to higher education since the early 1970s.[49]

Understanding the dynamics of class and gender in schooling processes and outcomes has been a lively area of research interest in Australia in the last decade.[50] Gradually, both research and practical experience have revealed a recognition of how some of the initial equal opportunity strategies promoted in schools were insensitive to girls of working-class backgrounds. For example, many of the early reforms of textbooks, primary school readers, and careers posters designed to portray new role models for girls featured heavily stereotyped middle-class and Anglo-Celtic figures. Early policies and strategies were based on a sociologically naive conception of the relation between the individual, schooling, and work. It was proposed that schools should present job alternatives, advice about the realities of different careers, and attractive models of women in nontraditional or professional positions, so that girls could "choose" better and so that more girls would go on to higher education or would take on "male" jobs that commanded better pay. But why would working-class kids ever "choose" working-class jobs (or unemployment)?[51] To understand why students leave school early or seek jobs that have glamor rather than good pay, it is necessary to understand the students' own understanding of their future and the messages the processes of schooling give them about their capacities.

A number of recent Australian studies have helped to show why working-class girls have continued to seek the traditional restricted range of jobs (clerical, sales, service).[52] Working-class girls see their future in terms of childbearing, so that it makes sense for them to seek jobs with short-term rewards which can be continued on a part-time basis. Initially, there were concerns about the changing composition of jobs in Australia and the rising unemployment owing to automation and technology in areas such as sales, clerical and secretarial work, and banking. The reality, however, is that there has been an even stronger restriction in job opportunities in some of the traditional apprenticeship areas which were at first promoted and that women's relative share of unemployment has been declining over the period.[53] The reason for this phenomenon (which is partly deceptive owing to the way employment statistics are collected) is a large growth in part-time work and in the advantages for employers in maintaining areas of female work that are low paid. Hence, while the choices of working-class girls may make it possible for them to get jobs of some kind, they also contribute to women's poverty if, as is increasingly common, their marriages break up and they become the sole supporters of their children.[54]

Aborigines

Australia's original inhabitants, Aborigines and the Torres Strait Islanders (in the 1986 census numbering 227,644 out of an Australian population of 16,020,000), continue to be the poorest group in Australia on all social indices. In 1971, only 3 percent of Aborigines had proceeded beyond the tenth grade, and by 1982 the retention rates to years eleven and twelve were still only 25.0 percent and 9.9 percent, respectively.

Traditional Aboriginal culture is fundamentally different from the Western, postindustrial, materialist culture of mainstream Australian society, and it has a different concept of time, spirituality, possessions, and relations between people. This culture is heavily organized around a distinction between "men's business" and "women's business" which permeates authority structures, laws, and ceremonies. Aboriginal women have generally argued that sexism is a problem in

white Australian culture and not in their own.[55] A major recent feminist anthro-
pological study by D. Bell argues similarly that traditional Aboriginal society is
characterized by a division of labor according to sex, but that this division is
not one of patriarchal power.[56] It is one in which both sexes have distinctive
roles and powers in relation to themselves, each other, and the whole community.[57]

Before the postwar period, church missions and the state set up schools designed to replace an Aboriginal cultural identity with a European one and to
prepare Aboriginal students for employment in the lowest rungs of society: in
the case of girls for domestic service. Much coercion was used to have Aboriginal
children attend these schools. There was considerable truancy, and in the case
of one of the earliest state institutions ''10 of the 37 Aboriginal children admitted
by 1820 died.''[58]

By the 1960s and 1970s, some change had taken place in social attitudes,[59]
and the government was providing financial grants to assist Aboriginal children
to continue schooling at the secondary level and beyond school. Nevertheless,
only a small number remain in the final three years of school, and only marginal
differences are apparent between girls and boys. About two-thirds of those taking
up grants for further study have been women, mainly for short courses related
to areas of traditional female work (secretarial, child care, kindergarten and
primary teaching, home management, and dressmaking.)[60] Only a tiny number
of Aborigines have entered higher education.

In recent years, some major funded projects have been started on the needs
of Aboriginal girls, but as yet reforms have made little impact on the extremely
poor situation of this community in terms of employment and further education.

Girls of Non-English-Speaking Background

In the eighteenth and nineteenth centuries, Australia was colonized largely by
people of Anglo-Irish origin. In the early part of the twentieth century, many
of the church schools were staffed with people appointed directly from those
countries, and it was to England in particular that ministers of education looked
when state systems of schooling were being established. However, in the postwar
period large-scale immigration was encouraged to feed the rapid expansion of
Australia's industrial sector, and by 1976, 39 percent of the population was born
overseas or had a parent born overseas.[61] *Girls, School and Society* defined
''migrant girls and women'' as one of its ''groups with special needs'' and cited
figures which suggested that girls of Greek, Italian, and Yugoslavian background
had lower rates of participation in the senior years of school than girls of Australian background and than males of their own background. This report suggested
the lower cultural aspirations of girls; the lower educational levels of their parents;
and cultural conflict in relation to sex roles. The isolation of the mothers who
do not speak English might contribute to such outcomes. In the late 1970s under
the Fraser government, in response to demands from ''ethnic'' groups and from

teachers' unions, a new policy of "multiculturalism" was promoted.[62] Schools were directed to acknowledge and value the diverse backgrounds of students in their curriculum. By 1987, policies were beginning to treat the issue of ethnic differences as an intrinsic part of "nonsexist" and "inclusive" schooling.[63] In the period since 1975, there has been a small but growing body of research on two aspects of schooling with regard to girls of Non-English-Speaking Background (NESB). Statistical data on access and participation have suggested that the aspirations and outcomes for at least some groups of NESB girls are likely to be higher than those of longer Australian heritage.[64] But work on the content of the schooling process has suggested that conflicts and difficulties for these girls nevertheless remain. Statistics on higher education show that most groups whose fathers were born outside Australia had higher proportions of daughters completing degrees than those with fathers born in Australia.[65]

CONCLUSIONS AND CURRENT TRENDS

The changes in education in Australia discussed in this chapter represent some important changes at policy level, along with a great deal of activity "from below" by those concerned about changing the processes of education in the interests of women. Women are active and articulate participants in the development of schooling and post-school education, and in recent times they have been gradually extending their entry to higher positions and to a wider range of studies and jobs, though with clear patterns of difference relating to class, race, and ethnicity. However, the effects of the different cultural assumptions and life patterns of women and men, differences that have often gone unrecognized in the formal provisions for "equality of opportunity," have continued to strongly shape women's educational participation and outcomes.

Overall, in relation to schooling the period from 1975 to 1987 has been one of reform: of many inquiries, policies, research projects, funding, and resource support for this area. These moves culminated with the publication in May 1987 of a new National Policy for the Education of Girls in Australian Schools, whose cited objectives are raising awareness of the educational needs of girls; equal access to and participation in appropriate curriculum for girls; provision of supportive school environments for them; and equitable resource allocation. "Commonwealth" policies have no binding influence on schools, but this policy has been endorsed by all except one of the state ministers of education.

Nevertheless, at the time of writing there were signs that Australia was entering a new period in relation to women and education. A recent Commonwealth government decision has abolished the Schools Commission, the body that has been the main source of funding for reforms as well as the initiator of landmark inquiries and policy commitments. Recent government moves (there are some state-based developments along similar lines) likely signal a new move from social justice and equal opportunity considerations to considerations that are directly focused on education's immediate contribution to the Australian economy. Following the 1987 election, when the Hawke Labor government was returned, the previous minister of education, a woman who had a particular concern for girls and education, was replaced by a male minister who took charge of a newly amalgamated combination of "Education, *Employment* and *Training.*" Under this minister an extensive reorganization of the tertiary sector is underway. One of the initial moves was to reduce the access of adult students, of whom women have been the majority.

In terms of the economy, Australia is no longer seen as a land with plentiful jobs and with scope to reform access to these jobs, but as a land with severe problems in its job structure, and where earning export money for Australia takes priority over concerns about inequality within schooling and post-school education. Yet part of these moves to rationalize the economy have also brought some changes in taxation and welfare provision. These changes no longer encourage a married woman to remain in domestic nonpaid duties. It is likely then that women's increased participation in the paid labor force will continue and grow.

What is not clear is whether the continued reality of participation with a double burden (of domestic labor) and for less reward (in terms of average wages) will lead to ideological changes and new political pressure by women to produce further change. In particular, in the next twenty years, we may see whether girls and women in Australia begin to accept the government's diagnosis of the way to prosperity and take up mathematics and science in much greater numbers; or whether the current educational funding focus on these areas will be exposed as an inadequate solution to the problem of finding rewarding work for the next generation.

NOTES

I would like to thank Robin Burns, Claire Kelly, Julie McLeod, and Sarah Paddle for reading and commenting on the draft of this chapter.

1. This chapter draws in particular on two recent overviews that are of interest in their own right. These are M. Powles, *Women's Participation in Tertiary Education: A Review of Recent Australian Research,* 2nd ed. (Melbourne: University of Melbourne Centre for Research into Higher Education, 1987); and L. Yates, "Australian Research on Gender and Education 1975–1985," in J. Keeves, ed., *Australian Education: Review of Recent Research* (Sydney: Allen & Unwin, 1987). For a historical treatment, see N. Kyle, *Her Natural Destiny: The Education of Women in New South Wales* (Kensington: University of NSW Press, 1986).

2. See, for example, Kyle, *Her Natural Destiny,* M. Theobald, " 'Mere Accomplishments?' 'Melbourne's Early Ladies Schools Reconsidered,' " *History of Education Review* 13, No. 2 (1984): 15–28; P. Porter, "Social Policy, Education and Women in Australia" in C. Baldock and B. Cass, eds. *Women, Social Welfare and the State* (Sydney: Allen & Unwin, 1983); P. Miller, *Long Division: State Schooling in South Australian Society* (South Australia: Wakefield Press, 1986).

3. Although recent figures suggest a higher level of school participation by girls than

by boys, boys who have left school are far more likely than girls to be undertaking continuing education in the form of apprenticeships.

4. See M. Strintzos, "To Be Greek Is to Be 'Good' " in L. Johnson and D. Tyler eds., *Cultural Politics* (Melbourne: Melbourne University Department of Education, 1984); G. Tsolidas, "Girls of Non-English Speaking Background: Implications for an Australian Feminism" in R. Burns and B. Sheehan, eds., *Women and Education* (Bundoora: La Trobe University, 1984); G. Tsolidas, *Educating Voula* (Melbourne: MACMME, 1986); and M. Kalantzis and B. Cope, "Cultural Differences, Gender Differences: Social Literacy and Inclusive Curriculum," *Curriculum Perspectives* 7, No.1 (1987): 64–69.

5. See P. Grimshaw, "The Australian Family: An Historical Interpretation," and A. Game and R. Pringle, "The Making of the Australian Family," both in A. Burns, G. Bottomley, and P. Jools, eds., *The Family in the Modern World* (Sydney: Allen & Unwin, 1983) and Baldock and Cass, *Women, Social Welfare and the State*.

6. See J. Clarke and K. White, *Women in Australian Politics* (Sydney: Fontana, 1983); and M. Sawer and M. Simms, *A Woman's Place: Women and Politics in Australia* (Sydney: Allen & Unwin, 1984).

7. Sawer and Simms, *A Woman's Place*, p. 17.

8. See S. Dowse, "The Women's Movement's Fandango with the State: The Movement's Role in Public Policy Since 1972," in Baldock and Cass, eds., *Women, Social Welfare and the State*.

9. See Kyle, *Her Natural Destiny;* Theobald, "Mere Accomplishments?"

10. A. Summers, *Damned Whores and God's Police* (Ringwood, N.J.: Penguin, 1975).

11. Kyle, *Her Natural Destiny;* J. Matthews, "Education for Femininity: Domestic Arts Education in South Australia," *Labour History* 45 (November 1983): 30–53; P. Porter, "The State, the Family and Education: Ideology, Reproduction and Resistance in W. A. 1900–1929," *Australian Journal of Education* 27, no. 2 (1983): 121–136; and P. Miller, *Long Division,* provide interesting discussions of this period.

12. P. Miller, *Long Division;* see also R. T. Fitzgerald, *The Secondary School at Sixes and Sevens* (Hawthorn: Australian Council for Educational Research, 1970).

13. Powles, *Women's Participation in Tertiary Education,* pp. 40, 42, but also see note 3.

14. A protracted legal challenge in NSW (the Melinda Leves case) extended this right to girls in single-sex government schools to have access to subjects offered boys in the related boys' school.

15. Ibid., 2.25, 2.33. There are significant state differences in participation in these subjects owing to differing requirements concerning the extent of a common compulsory curriculum.

16. G. Leder, "Girls and Mathematics: What of the Future?," in D. Williams, ed., *Learning and Applying Mathematics,* Proceedings of the 7th Annual Conference of the Mathematics Association of Victoria (Melbourne: Mathematics Association of Victoria, 1978).

17. See F. Fomin, "The Best and the Brightest—the Selective Function of Mathematics in the School Curriculum," in *Cultural Politics;* K. Creed, "Gifted Girls, Cultures and Mathematics," in *Theory into Practice,* Proceedings of the 8th Biennial Conference of the Australian Association of Mathematics Teachers (Canberra, 1980); M. Ryan and J. Senyard, *On Their Selection: Participation, Equity and Access in Higher Education,* Report of a Study Initiated by the Victorian Post-Secondary Education Commission, July

1984; and H. Bannister, "Gender and Tertiary Selection," PEP Research Paper No. 2, May 1987.

18. Fomin, "The Best and the Brightest."

19. *Girls, School and Society,* Report of a Study Group to the Australian Schools Commission (Canberra: Schools Commission, 1975), 1.3. Similar changes can be seen in Australian research in this area. Before 1975, very little work had been done which was specifically concerned with gender. Research often failed to distinguish results by sex or used only males in the sample, or took sex differences in results (for example, in mathematics attainment) as self-explanatory, as owing to biology or to taken-for-granted social role allocation. But in the 1970s data of differences between girls and boys begin to be taken as a problem for further investigation, as the possible result of a school effect and as an effect considered undesirable. See, for example, J. P. Keeves, "Differences Between the Sexes in Mathematics and Science Courses," in D. Edgar, ed., *Sociology of Australian Education: A Book of Readings* (Sydney: McGraw-Hill, 1975).

20. *Schools in Australia* (The Karmel Report), Report of the Interim Committee for the Australian Schools Commission (Canberra: Australian Government Printing Service, 1973). See also the discussion of the policies of this period in J. V. D'Cruz and P. Sheehan, *The Renewal of Australian Schools,* 2nd ed. (Hawthorn: Australian Council for Educational Research, 1978).

21. These are listed in Yates, "Review of Australian Research."

22. *Girls and Tomorrow: The Challenge for Schools,* Report of the Commonwealth Schools Commission's Working Party on the Education of Girls (Canberra: Schools Commission, 1984), 1.9.

23. See S. Brown and J. Fitzpatrick, "Girls, Boys and Subject Choice," *Discussion Paper* No. 11 (Perth: Education Department of W.A. Research Branch, 1981) and Powles, *Women's Participation in Tertiary Education,* 2.25.

24. There is a discussion of various perspectives on "inclusive curriculum" in the "Point and Counterpoint" section of the Australian journal, *Curriculum Perspectives* 7 No. 1 (1987): 57–74.

25. *Women in Australian Education* (Research and Statistics Branch of the Commonwealth Department of Education), p. 8; *Quality of Education in Australia* (QERC Report), Report of the Review Committee (Canberra: Australian Government Publishing Service, April 1985), 3.52.

26. Two studies of the characteristics and experiences of mature female students are J. Currie, C. Baldock, M. Murray, and G. Bossinga, *Mature Age Students Report No. 1* (Perth: Murdoch University Schools of Education and Social Inquiry, June 1984); and S. Kelly, *The Prize and the Price: The Changing World of Women Who Return to Study* (North Ryde: Methuen Haynes, 1987).

27. Child care has been established on an ad hoc basis, where women have agitated for it rather than as an automatic provision in universities and colleges.

28. Powles, *Women's Participation in Tertiary Education,* Fig. 2, p. 48.

29. Cf., for example, G. Wesson, ed., *Brian's Wife, Jenny's Mum* (Melbourne: Dove, 1974); *Community Learning: A Public Investment,* TAFE Report, (Melbourne, June 1984); H. Kimberley, *Community Learning: The Outcomes Report,* A Research Report Prepared for the Victorian TAFE Board (Melbourne: TAFE, September 1986); and B. Neville and L. Kennedy, "Learning Centres and Community Houses" in L. Foster and A. Williams, eds., *Personal Fulfillment: Modes, Ideologies and Contradictions* (Bun-

doora: Occasional Paper No. 10, Centre for the Study of Teaching and Human Interaction, La Trobe University).

30. M. Darling, *The Role of Women in the Economy* (Paris: OECD, 1975).

31. M. Power, "Women and Economic Crisis: The 1930s Depression and the Present Crisis," *The Australian Journal of Political Economy*, No. 4 (1979): 3–12.

32. From *Women in Australian Education* statistics, pp. 16, 21, 25.

33. B. Cass, M. Dawson, D. Temple, et al., *Why So Few?*, *Women Academics in Australian Universities* (Sydney: Sydney University Press, 1983) found that consciousness of discrimination was higher in women in the higher academic ranks.

34. C. V. Baldock, "Public Policies and Paid Work," in Baldock and Cass, eds., *Women, Social Welfare and the State*, p. 30.

35. C. O'Donnell, *The Basis of the Bargain: Gender, Schooling and Jobs* (Sydney: Allen & Unwin, 1984).

36. J. Craney and C. O'Donnell, "Women in Advanced Education: Advancement for Whom?" *Higher Education Research and Development* 2, No. 2 (1983): 129–146.

37. B. Jones, *Sleepers Wake! Technology and the Future of Work* (Melbourne: Oxford University Press, 1982).

38. A. Game and R. Pringle, *Gender at Work* (Sydney: Allen & Unwin, 1983).

39. Kyle, *Her Natural Destiny;* Theobald, "Mere Accomplishments?"

40. Kyle, *Her Natural Destiny;* P. Porter, *Gender and Education* (Waurn Ponds: Deakin University, 1986).

41. See, for example, A. D. Spaull, "Equal Pay for Women Teachers and the NSW Teachers' Federation" in A. D. Spaull, ed., *Australian Teachers* (South Melbourne: Macmillan, 1977); N. Williamson, "The Feminization of Teaching in N.S.W.: A Historical Perspective," *Australian Journal of Education* 27, No.1 (1983): 33–44. Western Australia was an exception. In that state there was a combined union with women in the majority which agitated for equal pay for over forty years before the policy was accepted by the government. See Porter, *Gender and Education,* p. 36.

42. See T. Evans, "Being and Becoming: Teachers' Perceptions of Sex-Roles and Actions Toward Their Male and Female Pupils," *British Journal of Sociology of Education* 3, No. 2 (1982): 127–144; S. Sampson, "Teacher Careers and Promotion in Australia," in P. Schmuck, ed., *Women as Educators* (New York: State University of New York Press, 1985); J. Nash and H. Sungaila, "Through the Door Marked 'Men Only': A Report on a Case Study of the Disadvantage Women in Education Face in the Promotion Stakes," in R. Burns and B. Sheehan, eds., *Women and Education.*

43. See Cass et al., *Why So Few?*

44. In 1985, women accounted for only 7.6 percent of those in "senior lecturer and above" positions in universities and 12.3 percent of the equivalent rank in CAEs.

45. R. Over and S. Lancaster, "The Early Career Patterns of Men and Women in Australian Universities," *Australian Journal of Education* (1984); R. Over and B. McKenzie, "Career Prospects for Women in Australian Universities" in R. Burns and B. Sheehan, eds., *Women and Education.*

46. See F. Gale. "Academic Staffing: The Search for Excellence." *Vestes* 23 (1) 1980: 3–8. Cass et al., *Why So Few?*

47. Cass et al., *Why So Few?*, p. 148.

48. *Girls, School and Society,* Table 4.2, p. 33.

49. D. S. Anderson and A. E. Vervoon, *Access to Privilege: Patterns of Participation*

in Post-Secondary Education in Australia (Canberra: Australian National University Press, 1983).

50. See in particular J. Branson and D. B. Miller, *Class, Sex and Education in Capitalist Society* (Melbourne: Sorrett, 1979); R. W. Connell, D. J. Ashenden, S. Kessler, and G. Dowsett, *Making the Difference* (Sydney: Allen & Unwin, 1982); B. Wilson and J. Wyn, *Shaping Futures* (Sydney: Allen & Unwin, 1987); and Yates' review of other research.

51. P. Willis, *Learning to Labour* (Aldershot: Saxon House, 1977).

52. In particular R. W. Connell, *Gender and Power* (Stanford: Stanford University Press 1980); Wilson and Wyn, *Shaping Futures;* and work by P. Moran and by L. Samuel which has been presented as conference papers. See also Yates, "Review of Australian Research" and Powles, *Women's Participation in Tertiary Education.*

53. From data in *Women in Australian Education II: Education Attainment and Labour Force Status,* Report by the Research and Statistics Branch of the Commonwealth Department of Education, June 1985.

54. See M. A. Edwards, *The Income Unit in the Australian Tax and Social Security Systems* (Melbourne: Institute of Family Studies, 1984) and B. Cass, *The Case for Review of Aspects of the Australian Social Security System,* Social Security Review Background/ Discussion Paper No. 1, (Canberra, June 1986), p. 14.

55. In particular, in a much cited address by Lillah Watson to the 1984 Women and Labour Conference.

56. D. Bell, *Daughters of the Dreaming* (Sydney: McPhee Gribble and Allen & Unwin, 1983).

57. Bell argues that the existence of women's law and power was obscured in earlier studies by male anthropologists who did not have access to "women's business." It has also been undermined by many of the interactions of Aboriginal communities with the European bureaucracy, where the Europeans impose their own patriarchal assumptions in presuming that males are the chiefs of the community and in setting up bureaucratic structures which institutionalize this attitude.

58. Kyle, *Her Natural Destiny,* p. 33.

59. Following a referendum of European Australians in 1967, Aborigines for the first time became automatically "Australian citizens" and were counted in the census. This referendum also paved the way for greatly increased Commonwealth funding to Aborigines.

60. From *Girls, School and Society,* 12.17, 12.18. Similar patterns are evident in later data, including the 1986 census which is being released at the time of writing.

61. D. Storer, *Migrant Families in Australia* (Melbourne: Institute of Family Studies, 1981), p. 1.

62. See L. Foster and D. Stockley, *Multiculturalism: The Changing Australian Paradigm* (Clevedon: Multiculingual Matters, 1984); J. J. Smolicz, "Education for a Multicultural Society" in J. Keeves, ed., *Australian Education: Review of Recent Research.*

63. This is reflected in the most recent *National Policy for the Education of Girls in Australian Schools* (Canberra: Commonwealth Schools Commission, May 1987).

64. Powles, *Women's Participation in Tertiary Education,* pp. 91–93.

65. Ibid., Tables 12a, 12b, p. 93.

EUROPE

11
FRANCE

Catherine Raissiguier

Educational equality for women has been on the official agenda of the French government for many decades. Whereas it used to be a controversial topic, today it is assumed that equal access to education should not be denied to the female half of the French population. This chapter will outline the progress that has been made in educational provision for women in France, while underscoring the complex and often subtle mechanisms that have prevented women from enjoying educational equality. While French women have by and large attained educational access, discrepancies in schooling processes and the very nature of the French economic and social structures have prevented women from enjoying equal life chances.

This brief analysis will first explore the historical changes in educational provision for women in France and the factors that have influenced the patterns of women's schooling since the second half of the nineteenth century. The emphasis will be on the most recent reforms within the educational system and the society at large.

AN OVERVIEW OF FRENCH EDUCATION TO THE 1950s

The Fight for Secularization

Until the mid-nineteenth century, the formal education of women in France was extremely limited and under the monopoly of Roman Catholic institutions.

The second half of the century witnessed many attempts by the state to lessen the church's predominance in girls' education. In particular under Victor Duruy, then Minister of Public Instruction, in April 1867 a law was passed which required any commune of 500 inhabitants or more to provide a separate girls' school. The same year, in an administrative memorandum Duruy organized secondary classes for girls. This memo was violently criticized and opposed by the Catholic Church, which did not see the necessity for higher training for girls and which associated women's education with moral and religious instruction only.

In the tradition of republicanism, state representatives began to regard the Catholic Church as a competitor in the moral training of French citizens. Indeed, while public schools were being used as tools of political integration, more than half of the young female population was still being taught to give their primary allegiance to the church.

Since women's role as mother and primary socializer of children was widely accepted in the nineteenth century, it became quite obvious that women would have to be taught within the republican realm in order to ground the roots of secular and national ideals that would bind both male and female citizens together. In this spirit the Ferry laws of 1880–1882 established free and compulsory public schools for all children ages six to thirteen, regardless of sex. Primary schools, normal schools, and state secondary schools for girls were created to inculcate secular and republican values in girls and to restore the ideological equilibrium between the two halves of the French population.

From then on, the fight for control between secular and religious educationists would be waged on the controversial terrain of female education and would create a favorable atmosphere for the development of adequate schooling for growing numbers of French girls.

THE DEVELOPMENT OF THE *ECOLE UNIQUE* AND THE POSTWAR REFORM OF THE SCHOOLS

At the turn of the twentieth century, with changing socioeconomic conditions the emerging middle class wanted to prepare their daughters and give them the means to achieve economic independence and autonomy. In spite of many structural barriers, the first half of the century saw increasing numbers of young women obtaining the baccalaureate and seeking professional training in higher education. This change shattered the age-old tradition of equating women's education with moral instruction.

While the republic's need for genderless national integration had virtually eliminated illiteracy for women under forty after World War I by providing primary education to all children, industrialization and the growing popular demand for universal education was opening the door to secondary schools and universities to rapidly increasing numbers of young women.

The first half of the twentieth century was marked by drastic shifts in the internal mapping of the French economy. Although the number of women employed in the primary sector (agriculture) showed a 50 percent decline between 1901 and 1950, the total number of female workers in the tertiary (service) sector almost doubled during the same period. Indeed, by 1950 while the service sector was becoming the largest one in the French economy and widely opened its doors to cheap female labor, women needed to be adequately educated for lower rank administrative and clerical positions and therefore were fully integrated into the secondary cycle of the French educational system.

Changes in the economy occurred at a time that structural changes in French education were implemented. These included the extension of free schooling through the secondary cycle in 1929 and the raising of the school-leaving age to sixteen in 1959. In the 1960s, with the implementation of the coeducational *école unique* and the rapid expansion of the educational system at all levels, women gained full access to formal education.

As Table 11.1 indicates, while overall primary school enrollment decreased between 1901 and 1950 owing to postwar demographic slumps, the number of students enrolled at the secondary level increased from a mere 2,000 in 1901 to 88,000 in 1950. These figures illustrate the extraordinary educational expansion that marked the first half of the twentieth century in France, and underscore the drastic broadening of the social base of the French educational system during that period. Girls benefited somewhat from that expansion, and their representation rose from 23 percent in 1901 to 39 percent in 1950.

This trend toward a better representation of the female population in secondary schools is also to be found among the students successfully passing the baccalaureate—the competitive exam that marks the end of the long academic secondary cycle. Jacqueline Daubier was the first "Bacheliere" in France; she passed the then prestigious examination in 1861 when she was thirty-seven. More than sixty years later, in 1925, women accounted for only 18.2 percent of the total number of students holding a baccalaureate. In the 1950s, this percentage had reached almost 40 percent.

In a similar way, women slowly gained access to higher education; in the universities in 1955, there were 55,000 young women enrolled out of a total student population of 155,000. In the 1950s, women had come to represent 35 percent of the total enrollment at the university level.[1]

PRESENT STRUCTURE OF THE FRENCH SCHOOL SYSTEM

It might be useful at this point to digress a moment and briefly describe the modern French educational system. The French schooling cycle is divided into three levels: elementary, secondary, and higher education. The elementary level is preceded by preprimary education in the maternal schools. It is not compulsory, and it teaches children of both sexes between ages two and six.

The first level comprises the five grades of elementary education, in which children are taught in comprehensive coeducational primary schools. Only chil-

Table 11.1
Primary and Secondary Education Enrollment and Girls' Participation Rate, 1901–1950

	1901	1906	1911	1922	1925	1930	1935	1938	1945	1950
Primary School:										
Total Enroll-ment in Thousands	5518	5535	5622	4197	3724	4622	5198	5337	4594	4532
Percentage of girls	9.9	49.6	49.6	50.4	49.7	50.2	50.0	50.3	49.7	49.5
Secondary School:										
Total Enroll-ment in Thousands	2	3	11	13	24	32	29	56	61	88
Percentage of girls	22.6	18.9	23.0	20.7	28.6	33.6	30.5	27.6	28.3	38.6

Source: Femmes en Chiffre, CNIDF-INSEE (Paris, 1986) p. 60.

dren who are judged unable to follow the regular curriculum for health or psychological reasons get a different treatment in separate structures providing "special education."

The second level is divided into two cycles of secondary education and presents a differentiated curriculum starting from the third year of secondary studies. At ages thirteen and fourteen, French students are selected for either a short prevocational (CPA, CPPN) or a long academic track. Some students will leave school during or at the end of the first four years of secondary school with no diploma or with the minimal certificate of professional education (CPE). This early selection (as discussed later in the chapter) has long-lasting consequences for students.

The second cycle of secondary education takes place in the French *lycées* which present a highly diversified curriculum. In the long academic and technical tracks, students who pass the final examination marking the end of their secondary education will obtain a baccalaureate, a technical baccalaureate, or a technician's diploma.

The short prevocational tracks offer various programs ranging from one to three years in length, some of which carry over from the first cycle and include apprenticeship contracts. In these programs students are prepared to take vocational exams such as the certificate of professional aptitude (CAP) and the diploma of professional studies (BEP).

The third level encompasses postsecondary education and can be broadly divided between university and nonuniversity training. University training leads to master's, doctoral, and health-related diplomas. Since 1968, Institutes of Technologies (IUT) have been attached to universities and provide high-level technological training which lead to a university diploma of technology (DUT).

In certain *lycées,* sections of high-level technicians (STS) lead to diplomas of high-level technicians (BTS) after a two-year program. Specialized schools offer a variety of diplomas ranging from photography to fashion design. Finally, the *grandes écoles,* which require a preparatory cycle of two years after the baccalaureate (CPGE) and are highly competitive, train, in three to four years, the future scientific, administrative, and political elite of the nation.

In France the state does not hold a monopoly over education, and parents can choose to send their children to private schools.

POST-WORLD WAR II TRENDS IN SCHOOLING

Women's Enrollment Patterns

The trend toward increasing equalization of access for women that marked the first half of the twentieth century was firmly grounded by the establishment of the *école unique* and reached completion in the 1970s.

Secondary Level

The enrollment of female students at the secondary level has increased in the past thirty years. In 1960 the proportion of young women in the French *collèges* and *lycées* reached 48 percent. This proportion rose rapidly in the 1960s and the 1970s, moving to 49.5 percent in 1965, 51.1 percent in 1975 and 51.6 percent in 1980. This slight overrepresentation of girls at the secondary level can be explained by the larger proportion of male students dropping out of full-time academic studies to enter apprenticeship programs and alternative vocational programs. Indeed, in 1980 only 50,000 young women attended out-of-school and apprenticeship programs, which enrolled a total of 215,000 youth. Young women then represented only 23 percent of this specific group of students.[2]

Cycle 1. In the academic first cycle, girls now represent 51 percent of all students. In the short prevocational tracks (CPA, CPPN), however, female participation has been stagnating since the mid-1970s. In spite of a slight increase from 36.7 percent in 1974 to 37.7 percent in 1984, young women are still underrepresented in these low-prestige tracks.[3]

Cycle 2. The proportion of female students in the long academic cycle has been on the rise, reaching 55.6 percent in 1975 and 57.5 percent in 1980. Because of the emergence of technical tracks which directly prepare students for jobs in the service sector of the economy, the proportion of young women in long technical tracks of the *lycées* has now reached 50 percent in public institutions.

The growing proportion of female students in the secondary schools is also illustrated by the increasing number of young women taking and successfully passing the baccalaureate. The proportion of female candidates was 45.5 percent in 1960, 50 percent in 1970, and 57.4 percent in 1980.[4]

Higher Education

At the tertiary level, the increase in women has been striking. In 1955, women constituted only 35 percent of all university students; they now outnumber men on French campuses, representing over 51 percent of the postsecondary student population. Although total university enrollment increased fivefold between 1955 and 1980, female enrollment increased sevenfold.[5]

In France, women now enjoy equal and sometimes better access to all levels of formal education. However, when we look further into women's representation in the various tracks of the French educational system, we can see that the situation is far more complex and far less advantageous to women than it appears at first glance. Indeed, when diversification occurs in secondary education (see Figure 11.1), boys and girls find themselves in different tracks of the French school system.

Educational Differentiation

In this section it is argued that, in spite of a remarkable broadening of the social base in the French educational system, differentiation of schooling has

Figure 11.1
French School Map, 1983/1984

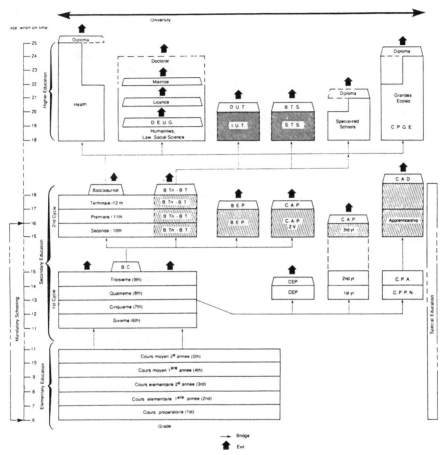

meant an unequal process for different groups in the French schoolage population, resulting in unequal educational outcomes.

The impact of social class on the access to different levels of education has been fully documented. Because of early tracking, pupils from different social backgrounds follow different educational options. The most blatant form of differentiation is between the long and short cycles of secondary education. "The choice between general secondary and technical secondary education is often based on failure, so that those young people likely to experience difficulty with general education are channeled toward technical education."[6]

In 1970, Christian Baudelot and Roger Establet clearly demonstrated that the children of workers and farmers were four to five times more likely to have to repeat the first grade of primary school than the children of professionals and that early repeaters were also more likely to repeat other grades.[7] One can therefore see how social class affects educational progress in France. Not surprisingly then, the majority of the pupils who choose the short cycle come from lower socioeconomic backgrounds because of their lack of cultural capital,[8] the cultural bias in achievement tests and orientation procedures, and economic constraints which might push working-class students into prevocational training, preparing them more rapidly for active life and wage labor.

Other studies have shown that, in spite of the democratizing effects of the educational reforms of the 1960s, the French educational system remains one that sorts out students on ascriptive criteria. Although the implementation of *l'Ecole Unique,* through the sheer increase of educational provision, enabled working-class, rural, female, and minority students to gain greater access to education, a student's background determines his or her place on the school map.

The democratization of the French school system can be documented by the sheer increase of students passing the baccalaureate. In 1959, the *bacheliers* represented only 10 percent of the age cohort, and in 1985, they represented 28 percent of their age group. However, children of professionals have a 50 percent chance of passing, compared to only 11 percent for working-class children. This sorting out mechanism is also illustrated by the internal hierarchy of the French educational system where students from low socioeconomic backgrounds are concentrated in deadend and low-prestige tracks. In 1980–1981, whereas workers represented 40 percent of the active population, working-class children represented 60 percent of the prevocational *Classe Preprofessionnelle de Niveau* (CPPN), 13.6 percent of the university—with a heavy concentration in the less prestigious Institutes Technology (IUTs)—and 9 percent of the *grandes ecoles* enrollments. On the other end of the spectrum, the children of professionals accounted for 0.6 percent of the CPPN, 57.4 percent of the university, and 42.1 percent of the *grandes écoles* enrollments.[9]

Children of migrant workers, if only because they tend to belong to the lower socioeconomic strata, encounter the same obstacles. These difficulties are often further compounded by cultural and linguistic factors which put this particular sub-group at a double disadvantage. "In France, it has been noted that out of 100 foreign children:

—20 leave school at age 16 unable to read or write French.

—60 have experienced irremediable learning problems.

—20 may be regarded as having had a normal schooling."[10]

Children of migrant workers represent 8.9 percent of the total French student population, but they are overrepresented in lower tracks and in special education classes which were developed for students who could not follow the regular curriculum because of mental or physical handicaps. In 1982–1983, 41 percent of the students in these "special" tracks in the Lyon school district were from migrant families.[11]

Similarly, it has been argued that, although male and female enrollment has equalized, differentiation in schooling along gender lines has resulted in an unequal educational process for male and female students.

Secondary Education

Cycle 1. Table 11.2 indicates that girls are significantly underrepresented in the prevocational training of the first cycle of secondary studies. Female students tend to be found in slightly fewer numbers in the short cycle of the secondary schools. These figures can be interpreted in two ways: (1) either girls achieve better, and fewer find themselves in low prestige prevocational tracks, or (2) girls might have been barred from preprofessional training because of sexist counseling, self-exclusion, and internalized socialization. It is probably a combination of both factors.

Young women tend to enroll in the long academic cycles because they believe they will need "better" and longer training than their male peers in order to be competitive in the labor market.

Young women find themselves in tracks that train for jobs that are by and large devalued in the French economy. Young women are heavily concentrated in secretarial, health, and other service vocational training (see Table 11.3). Even women in industrial tracks are enrolled in sectors traditionally dominated by women: the textile, paper, and leather industry. On the other hand, women are almost never found in classes preparing for metal work, or mechanical and electrical engineering. Recent statistics indicate that young girls are not entering male-dominated tracks. There has been a threefold increase of females in the metal-work CAP—from 0.1 percent in 1980 to 0.3 percent in 1983—but the increase is minuscule.[12]

Cycle 2. Gender segregation in the French diversified school system also characterizes the long secondary academic cycles (see Table 11.4).

Although young women are increasingly overrepresented in sections A, B, and to a lesser degree D, and although they have made some progress in the more prestigious math and physics courses since the 1970s, Table 11.4 indicates that in 1983 they still represented only 36.2 percent of the candidates taking the highly valued Baccalaureate C. An even sharper underrepresentation of young women can be found in math and technology, where the proportion of female candidates only slightly improved from 4.2 percent in 1975 to 5.1 percent in 1983.[13]

A similar pattern can be traced in the technical tracks where young women are heavily concentrated in the clerical and paramedical branches and underrepresented in the more lucrative industrial and computer sciences options.

Women also tend to be overrepresented in normal schools which train students

Table 11.2

Girls' Representation in Different Sections of Secondary and Postsecondary Education (Public and Private Schools), 1973–1974 and 1983–1984

Classes	1973–1974	1983–1984
Secondary Education:		
1st Cycle	50.8	50.7
CPPN/CPA (Pre-vocational)	36.7	37.7
2nd Cycle Short BEP (Vocational)	48.0	47.6
2nd Cycle Long (Academic)	54.8	55.9
Total Secondary Education	54.8	51.0
Post Secondary Education:		
Normal Schools	58.9	68.5
High Level Technician Ed BEP	56.8	53.7
Universities of which IUT	46.4 / 30.1	51.2 / 37.7
Grandes Ecoles Prep. programs	28.8	31.7
Engineering Schools	7.9	15.9
Total Post Secondary Education	45.0	50.1

Source: Femmes en Chiffre, p. 61.

252

Table 11.3
Girls' Representation in the Prevocational Tracks, by Type of Training, 1980 and 1983

CAP/BEP	1980	1983
Industrial training		
Secondary sector		
CAP	8.1	9.4
BEP	6.3	9.9
Service training		
Tertiary sector		
CAP	79.7	81.1
BEP	80.6	82.6

Source: <u>Femmes en Chiffre</u>, p. 62.

Table 11.4
Proportion of Girls among Baccalaureate Candidates, by Field, 1975, 1978, and 1983

Field	1975	1978	1983
A Philosophy/Letters	74.3	75.9	79.0
B Economics/Social			
Sciences	59.1	63.8	62.9
C Mathematics/Physics	33.8	36.4	36.2
D Mathematics/Biology	51.6	54.0	54.8
E Mathematics/Technology	4.2	4.2	5.1
Total Academic Tracks	54.4	55.7	58.2
F Industry and Paramedical			
Care[a]	23.3	28.7	31.6
G Secretarial and Clerical			
Work	73.5	75.7	75.3
H Computer Sciences	35.3	40.6	37.2
Total Technical Tracks	52.7	56.1	57.5

[a]Paramedical sections are almost entirely female

Source: <u>Femmes en Chiffre</u>, p. 63.

to become school teachers. The feminization of these schools increased in the 1970s. Women's representation had also increased at the university level in the last ten years. However, this increase is even more remarkable at the lower echelons of the tertiary level, namely, within the less prestigious and more vocationally oriented IUTs.

In spite of their increased participation, women are still a minority in the prestigious preparatory classes which remain the only gateways to the *Grandes Ecoles*. The French *Grandes Ecoles* are still the major routes to elite positions with high levels of prestige, power, and material rewards. As of the 1980s, women in France had yet to completely break through "the golden avenue" to the upper echelons of the social ladder.

Further disaggregation of these figures shows that young women are concentrated in educational tracks that offer little potential for social mobility and participation in the thriving sectors of the French economy. Female students are overrepresented in the service sector and in typically feminine occupations. A good example of this phenomenon can be found in the sections where women outnumber men. However, these high-level technicians are found primarily in low-prestige and low-pay occupations such as clerical work, dietetics, home economics, and tourism.

This tendency can literally be traced at all levels of the French school system. This unequal distribution of students along gender lines parallels the highly sexually segregated French labor force.

Universities

Here again, overall women are better represented at the tertiary level, but they are still lagging behind in medicine, dentistry, and the sciences in general. Women have made particular progress in the economic sciences where their proportion increased from 28.4 percent in 1974 to 42. 4 percent in 1983.

The increased representation of women at the tertiary level must be mediated, as Table 11.5 reminds us, by the fact that the proportion of women is increasing more slowly in the scientific fields than in tracks where there has traditionally been a female presence. This phenomenon is also prevalent in the *Grandes Ecoles* where women have made some inroads in the schools opening up onto occupations in the tertiary sector of the economy, in which their proportion in 1984 almost reached 40 percent. However, in the highly prestigious National School of Administration which has trained many generations of French politicians and top-ranking civil servants, in 1983–1984 women represented only 21.2 percent of total enrollment. Similarly, in the exclusive engineering schools in 1980 young women represented only 14 percent of enrollment. This underscores the extent of the problem in spite of a threefold increase in the past ten years.

This unequal distribution among the disciplines is compounded by unequal representation at different levels within each field. Indeed, women are less and less represented as we move up from the first to the third cycle of postsecondary

Table 11.5
Proportion of Women at the University, by Discipline, 1973–1974 and 1982–1983

Discipline	1973–1974	1982–1983
Humanities	66.0	67.8
Pharmacy	59.7	61.7
Law	42.0	52.4
Medicine	36.5	43.8
Dentistry	36.5	36.4
Economic Sciences	28.4	42.4
IUT	30.1	37.6
Sciences	33.9	32.9
Total	46.4	51.1

Source: Femmes en Chiffre, p. 64.

studies. Interestingly the decrease in women's participation is particularly sharp in the humanities, law, and the economic sciences. Although entry into these fields might be more open to female students as the stakes become higher, more women than men drop out of the educational race. On the whole, women's participation in postsecondary education has been on the rise, except in the scientific preparatory classes and the scientific disciplines within the universities. This overall increase, especially in the third cycle, should eventually facilitate women's representation in teaching and research positions in higher education. However, women's lack of participation in scientific fields bars them from landing jobs in areas that are in high demand and that are still male dominated.[14]

From this brief analysis we can conclude that, although women in France have gained greater access to all levels of education, at the secondary and tertiary levels they tend to be concentrated in certain tracks, fields of study, and disciplines. This unequal representation points in the direction of differences in the educational experience of French students along gender lines.

Educational Wastage

In order to gain a fuller understanding of these differences, we will now look at survival rates for males and females. The data on educational wastage in France show that, unlike girls in many developing countries, in France girls across the board have lower rates of repetition and tend to complete their training more than boys. For instance, in 1983 at the end of the *lycée*, female students who were two years behind schedule represented 15.7 percent of the total number of enrolled students as opposed to 22.8 percent for boys in the same position.

These figures suggest that, overall, women repeat less either because they achieve better or because parents and teachers think it is less important for a girl to repeat a grade in order to fully grasp the material she is supposed to know before moving on.

Girls in France tend to stay longer in school than boys. In 1971, they averaged one more year of schooling than boys.[15] Similarly, fewer girls leave schools without qualification; "whether in general or technical education, only 39.1% of girls have not reached the level of the final lower secondary class, as against 51% of boys."[16] This statistic might be explained by greater job opportunities for boys who have no definite skills and discrimination against women in the French labor market.

Until the mid-1970s, boys could find fairly well-paying jobs in construction and industry, whereas girls could not bank on such opportunities without appropriate training. This situation is likely to change as the job market tightens up, and we may find that in the 1980s boys increasingly tend to finish their training in order to be more competitive in the job market. Although wastage and enrollment data indicate that young women achieve better than young men, especially in general education, female students are at a disadvantage in the labor force.

A brief analysis of the French labor market seems necessary since the state of the French economy in the last thirty years has been of crucial importance in women's representation in the labor force. For the past thirty years, the French economy has stagnated, and since the 1960s unemployment rates have been on the rise. The economic crisis has not hit everybody indiscriminately; white men between the ages of twenty-five and forty have been little hurt by unemployment, whereas youth, immigrants, women, and the elderly have shared the brunt of the economic downturn.[17]

THE WORKFORCE OUTCOMES OF EDUCATION

Women's Participation Rates

In spite of the economic crisis and the tightening of the labor market, women have made tremendous progress. The number of women in salaried occupations increased from 6.5 million in 1962 to 10 million in 1984 (see Table 11.6). During the same period, men's wage labor stagnated, moving from 13 million to 13.8 million. This change has to be viewed against the general deindustrialization of the Western economies and the unprecedented growth and feminization of the tertiary sector.

Recent analyses of women's workforce participation have pointed out that, against all expectations, the female "reserved army" has successfully maintained itself in salaried occupations. This movement toward wage labor has been quite meaningful for women. For women a personal wage marks a definite—and yet insufficient—step toward independence. A personal salary brings about a fun-

Table 11.6
Labor Force Participation, by Sex, 1901–1985

Year	Women N (in thousands)	%	Men N (in thousands)	%
1901	7000	36.0	12600	67.0
1911	7100	35.5	1290ᴧ	67.0
1921	7200	35.5	12900	70.0
1931	7000	33.0	13500	68.0
1946	6700	32.0	12600	66.0
1954	6646	29.8	12848	62.2
1962	6585	27.6	13158	58.3
1975	8132	30.3	13911	54.0
1985	10128	36.8	13867	53.3

Source: Femmes en Chiffres, p. 40.

damental change in women's social status by providing women potential familial and professional autonomy.[18] Women's participation in the labor force has also changed qualitatively in the recent past.

Table 11.7 indicates that female labor force participation for the age group twenty-five to fifty-four has been steadily on the rise since the 1960s, whereas male participation rates have remained stable. On the other hand, because of increasing economic problems, young and older women have had a harder time staying in the labor force.

Interestingly, it is the women who live alone (92 percent) and outside of a traditional family situation—single (87.1 percent) and divorced women (87 percent)—who show the highest activity rates. On the other hand, women who live with a male partner (63.9 percent), women who are married (63.4 percent), and women who have two children (65.5 percent) or more (38 percent) show the lowest activity rates.

Women have also been a special target for unemployment. Although more and more women are entering the labor force, their numbers are swelling the pool of the unemployed. Indeed, women's unemployment rates, regardless of their socioeconomic status, their level of education, and their age, are always higher than those of men. Moreover, women are usually unemployed for longer periods of time.[19]

Table 11.7
Activity Rate, by Age and Sex, 1968–1985

	1968	1975	1982	1984	1985
Age 16–25					
Women	45.9	54.8	42.3	41.1	40.3
Men	69.3	68.0	51.4	49.3	49.0
Age 25–54					
Women	44.5	53.0	66.1	68.2	68.9
Men	95.8	95.6	96.1	96.0	96.0
Age 55–64					
Women	37.3	34.2	35.7	31.0	31.0
Men	74.4	67.0	59.8	50.3	50.1
Age 65 & Up					
Women	8.0	5.0	2.4	2.4	2.2
Men	19.1	10.7	5.9	5.3	5.3

Source: Femmes en Chiffres, p. 40.

Women's work has also been devalued in the recent past through the ghettoization of women in part-time and precarious work, such as limited contract employment and adjunct and auxiliary positions.[20] Such blatant discrepancies between male and female work corroborate the thesis of a sexual "apartheid" of the labor force.

Women's Work

The progress made by women is somewhat tainted by the fragility of their position in the labor force. Although employment has been on the rise for women, work—that is, types of occupations, salaries, promotions, qualifications, and working conditions—has been stagnating at best and, for certain groups of women, worsening in the past thirty years. The sexual segregation of the labor force is clearly illustrated by the fact that women are heavily concentrated in the service sector and are grossly underrepresented in the industry. There, they are found primarily in a few female-dominated sectors such as the textile, leather, and microelectronic industries.

Women are clustered in middle-level and lower-level service occupations. Moreover, as Table 11.8 illustrates, the lower the level of the service sector, the more feminized it tends to be. Indeed, women represent 26 percent of all high-level civil servants and managers, and they comprise 75 percent of all low-level service workers.

Table 11.8
Women's Distribution in the Labor Force, 1985

Socio-Professional Category	Total number of women	Distribution	Percentage women
Agriculture	584.000	6.6	39
Craft/business	613.000	6.9	37
High level management	495.000	5.6	26
Middle level management	1723.000	19.5	40
of which:			
teaching	506.000	5.7	62
health	505.000	5.7	73
technicians	83.000	0.9	10
low level service	4164.000	47.0	75
Industrial & Agricultural			
Wage Labor	1273.000	14.4	20
of which:			
qualified industrial work	176.000	2.0	12
non-qualified industrial work	693.000	7.8	40
Total	8852.000	100.0	42

Source: Femmes en Chiffres, p. 45.

Women's Income

Income differentials between men and women also point in the direction of quite unequal educational outcomes.

Table 11.9 shows that the average professional wage of a man is 1.7 times higher than that of a woman and that this discrepancy increases with age and educational attainment. Not only do women make less than men at their point of entry in the labor force, but their social mobility is much more limited than that of men in general. With the exception of workers with no diplomas, income differentials between men and women increase with age in the same educational level.

Although men start with better wages than women with similar credentials, they also increase their income over time at a faster pace than women, widening in the process the income gap between the sexes as they move along in their professional careers.

This tendency is further compounded by the familial responsibility of women workers. Whereas men's salaries improve with marriage and children, for women the scenario is quite the opposite; the larger the family, the lower the salary, with the exception of women with a university degree (see Figure 11.2).

From School to Work

The sexual segregation of the educational system prefigures and echoes the gender hierarchy and segmentation of the economy. At age nineteen, the edu-

Table 11.9
Income Differentials[a]

Educational Level	Total	26-35	36-55
no diploma	168	173	170
primary school degree	176	154	178
CAP	161	144	164
Baccalaureate	181	148	187
University Degree	208	176	207
U & Technical Degree	232	194	238
Total	171	152	176

a) Index of women's versus men's wages has been calculated as follows:

$$Index = \frac{men's\ wages}{women's\ wages}$$

Source: _Femmes en Chiffres_, p. 52.

cational and vocational attainment of girls appears to be higher than that of boys (see Table 11.10). However, "as soon as they have left school, the advantage slips over to the side of boys."[21]

Overall, young women tend to have a harder time than young men finding a job: "In October 1978, 19.8% of girls under 25 in the active population were looking for a job, as opposed to 11.2% of the boys without work in the same age group."[22] More particularly, we can look at the figures of early school leavers and see the drastic differences in occupational opportunities for boys and girls.

This set of figures illustrates that young women with pre-occupational training, regardless of whether they get a diploma, find themselves at a greater disadvantage when entering the labor force. The gap between potential employment for boys and for girls is more acute at the lower levels of vocational training (CAP). Higher levels of education for women do indeed help them to integrate the labor force on a more equal footing. However, women, because they are heavily segregated in certain tracks of prevocational training, will have a harder time finding employment when they leave school. Women are overrepresented in sectors that are linked to their traditional roles. Needless to say, these sectors are precisely the ones devalued in the French occupational structure.

Figure 11.2
Income Gain, by Familial Status, (26–40 age group)

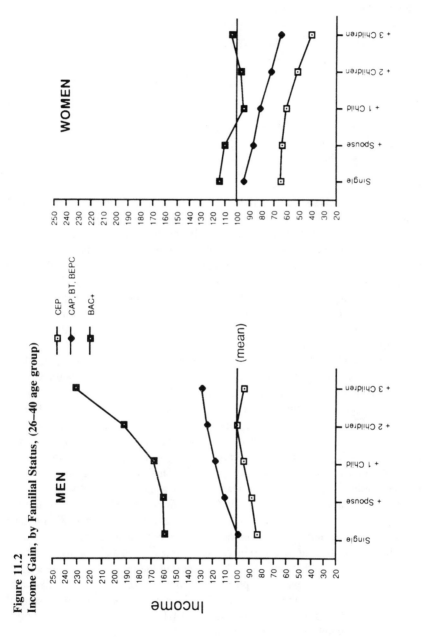

Source: *Femmes en Chiffres*, p. 53.

Table 11.10
Unemployment Rates of 17–19-Year-Old Boys and Girls with and without a Diploma, 1980

	With CAP	Without CAP	With BEP	Without BEP
Boys	17.8	27.7	27.1	37.1
Girls	46.2	56.7	47.1	46.8

Source: Femmes en Chiffres

In this brief analysis we have tried to show that women's increased enrollment at all levels of the French educational system points in the direction of crucial progress in educational equality between the sexes. However, the underrepresentation of women in vocationally oriented training and the more prestigious mathematics and physical sciences fields present serious caveats, especially when we know that the typically female tracks tend to be precisely the ones with less prestige and potential outcomes. These serious disadvantages are further compounded by sexual discrimination in the occupational structure which creates additional barriers for those women who have been able to break through traditionally male-dominated fields.

When we turn to "migrant" women and young girls, it is very difficult to assess their particular situation since no data by gender are available on second-generation migrant children. Several studies on women and migration suggest that girls' expectations vis-à-vis schooling tend to be higher than those of boys. Education for the daughters of migrant workers might have a different meaning and provide "the means for acquiring independence, escape from unwanted aspects of tradition, avoidance of early marriage and relegation to the similar types of employment held by their mothers."[23] This might help them fare better in school than their brothers, but when we look at the highly segmented nature of the labor market, the unequal distribution of resources, and the restrictive immigration policies of the late 1970s, we can see that second-generation female migrants have virtually no chances of achieving vertical mobility.

In the late 1970s, France experienced the feminization of its foreign population. Women of foreign background have been entering the labor force in great numbers; this phenomenon was least pronounced among women from the Maghreb. However, when active, they are clustered in the lowest ranks of the occupational ladder in unskilled, domestic service and industrial positions. Working conditions for migrant women are extremely difficult. They have a greater incidence of night shifts, long periods of unemployment, as well as precarious and clandestine/illegal work.

Table 11.11
Women's Participation in the Political Sphere, 1981–1983

	Total number	Percentage of women
Parliament		
National Assembly	491	6
Senate	317	3
Government		
Ministers and Secretary		
of State	43	14
City Council		
Mayors	1451	4

Source: Femmes en Chiffres, p. 88.

THE POLITICAL OUTCOMES OF EDUCATION

Even though the vast majority of women in France believe that politics is not and should not be a male province—a belief illustrated by an election poll during the presidential election of 1988—women's participation in the traditional political sphere is at best marginal and has worsened since they have been granted the franchise (see Table 11.11). Indeed, while women represented 7 percent of the Parliament in 1946, their proportion has now dropped to 5.5 percent. This blatant underrepresentation is common at all levels of the French power structure but is particularly acute as one moves up the political ladder. This setback has occurred despite the background of increased educational access for women at all levels. It corroborates the fact that women have not yet been able to break through the main avenues to power and prestige that are particularly located in the *Grandes Ecoles*.

RECENT GOVERNMENT POLICIES

In the early 1980s, Yvette Roudy, the minister of women's rights under the socialist government, set up a series of actions with a view to promote better educational outcomes for female students. These actions fall around two major axes: (1) active recruitment of girls and women in professional training where women have been traditionally absent, and (2) a multifaceted ideological campaign combatting sexism within the school.

In order to open up women's occupational training—30 for women as opposed to 300 for men—Ms. Roudy increased post-school/prevocational training programs tailored specifically to women's needs. The plans were to increase the female participation in adult professional training from 19 to 25 percent. Through active recruitment of married women, mothers, and "returning" female students in pilot and regional programs, women were introduced to traditionally male-dominated fields and "new" technologies in particular.

In the same vein, the Ministry of Women's Rights offered competitive prestigious scholarships for female students enrolling at the tertiary level in the sciences and technology. These scholarships were supposed to help young women break certain structural barriers and to increase their proportion among engineers from 17 to 30 percent in a few years.

Roudy also launched a publicity campaign against sexist stereotypes and discrimination within the school and the occupational structure. Specific actions to fight sexist stereotypes in the schools have been put in place. Groups have been delegated to the study of sexism, and education professionals as well as parental associations have been asked to keep track of and report on stereotyping in textbooks and educational practices.

Administrative memoranda were sent to school officials requesting the inclusion of nonsexist teaching guidelines in curriculum outlines. In 1984–1985, for the first time student teachers were officially trained to deal with sexism within the school. Similarly, in a number of large cities, in-service training programs were developed to help teachers combat sexist bias in the formal curriculum and in schooling processes. At the tertiary level, the ministry created four university positions in feminist studies.

These measures are important because it is necessary to keep monitoring and fighting sexist and racist stereotypes in the schools, and to promote female participation in male-dominated fields. However, the liberal, piecemeal quasi-symbolic quality of these actions can do little to challenge the deep-rootedness and complexity of the problems at hand.

In practice, curricular changes in teacher training are still lagging behind in terms of nonsexist teaching strategies, young women are still channeled into "soft" disciplines, and the publishing industry still keeps a tight control over the images and messages conveyed in pedagogical materials. In fact, five years after the beginning of the campaign, little change can be noticed in women's educational outcomes.

Certain critics located the failure of Yvette Roudy's efforts within the French economic and political context. When employment is on the rise, they argue, and when the government reinforces precarious forms of labor and pronatalist policies, we can see the limitations of Roudy's plan.[24] Slick publicity campaigns and symbolic actions have created a certain visibility for Roudy and her ministry. It is unlikely, however, that these actions will move beyond the level of superficial cosmetic changes.

Indeed, they fail to address, as a whole, the complex structural and cultural mechanisms that contribute to the maintenance of gender inequalities within the educational system and French society at large.

NOTES

Most tables in this chapter are excerpted from *Femmes en Chiffres,* CNIDF-INSEE (Paris, 1986).

1. *Notes d'Information* No. 80–42, November 25, 1980, Ministere de l'Education Nationale.

2. Ibid.

3. *Femmes en Chiffres,,* p. 61.

4. *Notes d'Information.*

5. Ibid.

6. Jean-Jacques Paul, "Education and Employment: A Survey of French Research," *European Journal of Education,* 6, No. 1 (1981): 96.

7. Linda Clark, *Schooling the Daughters of Marianne* (Albany: State University of New York Press, 1984), p. 153.

8. P. Bourdieu and J. P. Passeron, *Les Heritiers* (Paris, 1964).

9. Maria Llaumet, "A propos de l'echec scolaire des enfants de travailleurs et immigrés," *Bulletin Bimestriel du Ciemi,* no. 28, September-October 1985.

10. Leslie Limage, "The Situation of Young Migrants of the Second Generation in Europe," UNDP/ILO.

11. Maria Llaumet, "L'Immigration en France côté femmes," *Bulletin Bimestriel de Cimi,* no. 35, November-December 1986.

12. *Femmes en Chiffres,* p. 61.

13. Ibid., p. 63.

14. H. Delavault, "Les Femmes dans les cadres de l'enseignement supérieur et de la recherche," *Diplomées,* no. 138, September 1986.

15. Isabelle Deblé, *The School Education of Girls* (Paris: Unesco, 1980), p. 71.

16. Ibid., p. 62.

17. Odile Benoit-Guilbot, "Acteurs sociaux, politiques de l'emploi et structures du chômage: Le Jeu du mistigri," *Futuribles* (January-February. 1985).

18. Margaret Maruani, "Le Travail inflexible," *Pour,* no. 108, September-October 1986.

19. Benoit-Guilbot, "Acteurs sociaux."

20. Maruani, "Le Travail inflexible"; Benoit-Guilbot, "Acteurs sociaux."

21. Deblé, *The School Education of Girls,* p. 99.

22. Paul, "Education and Employment," p. 99.

23. Llaumet, "Femmes."

24. Claire Bataille, "A l'école ou en stage, le sexe comme critère d'orientation," *Cahiers du Féminisme,* December 1985.

12
THE GERMAN DEMOCRATIC REPUBLIC

Susanne M. Shafer

Tracing the development of women's education in the German Democratic Republic demands an assessment of women's educational status at the end of World War II when the victorious Allies divided Germany into four occupation zones. Unconditional surrender for the Germans in 1945 meant the end of the Third Reich and a total reassessment of the changes National Socialism had brought to German society. Included was the educational system which was now subjected to calls for change from (1) the Allied occupation forces, (2) German traditionalists who wanted a return to the system that had prevailed until 1933, when Hitler had come to power, and (3) German liberals whose efforts to imprint progressive education on the school system during the Weimar Republic had largely failed except in a number of private schools.

As the war drew to an end, Germany's educational system was in serious disarray. Especially in urban areas, schools had been extensively damaged or even destroyed by the Allies' sustained bombing of German cities. To a somewhat lesser extent the same held true for universities. Furthermore, many children had been evacuated to rural areas for safekeeping. Older boys, that is, those aged fifteen and sixteen, had been required for antiaircraft batteries or had been sent to the front. Few males remained to attend universities. Professors, too, had been drafted into the military except for those who (1) had fled the country in the mid-1930s to escape Hitler's wrath against Jews, Freemasons, Social Democrats, and communists, or (2) had been confined to concentration camps. These conditions pertained at least as much for eastern Germany, the later Soviet zone of occupation, as for any other part of Germany.

POSTWAR EDUCATIONAL RECONSTRUCTION

At the Potsdam Conference in 1945, the Allies concurred that the educational system should first and foremost ensure ''denazification, demilitarization, and democratization,'' a statement included in the final Potsdam Agreement of August 2, 1945.[1] Beyond that, the Soviet Military Administration for Germany (SMAD) proceeded to seek changes that would bring the educational system in their zone of occupation into conformity with Marxist-Leninist ideology and hence in general replicate the Soviet system. In pursuing this policy, even if at first indirectly, SMAD rejected the proposals of German traditionalists and liberals for educational reform.

The first efforts of the Soviet occupation authorities to change German education were in the spirit of the Potsdam Agreement. As elsewhere in Germany, the identification of teachers who could be entrusted with the education of the young posed the first major problem. SMAD and those Germans who had been members of the German Communist party prior to the Third Reich or who were prepared at war's end to assist SMAD in the governing of their zone of occupation were recruited to organize the educational system. They dismissed most of the teachers who had been members of the Nazi party, or what amounted to roughly three-quarters of all teachers.[2] They were replaced by new teachers who were given a crash course in education before assuming their classroom duties. The official date for the reopening of schools was October 1, 1945.[3] While before the war only 10 percent of German teachers had been female and most of those were to be found in girls' secondary schools, many more women who had had a complete secondary, if not university, education were now lured into the teaching profession.[4] Some hesitated to become state employees as teachers. Representing the authority of the state evoked a fear of the political commitment implicit in such an act. Others, including women, accepted the job since they needed to feed their families.[5]

SOVIETIZATION OF EDUCATION

For the Soviets, democratization of schools as agreed to at Potsdam meant (1) gender and class equality in regard to access to education and career opportunity and (2) the retention of agricultural and industrial workers' children in the school system beyond age thirteen or fourteen where until 1945 compulsory formal education had ended in Germany.[6]

The sovietization of education in the German Democratic Republic (GDR) found its justification in the same works of communist theoreticians as were used in the Soviet Union. Marx's writings as well as those of Engels which decried educational differentiation based on the prevailing social class structure formed one basis. Another was their insistence on gender equality in educational matters. Lenin echoed their thinking in this regard—not surprisingly since his wife Krupskaya was an educator herself and one of the main proponents of polytechnic education for every student in the schools.

Among the significant structural changes instituted by SMAD and their SED (*Sozialistische Einheitspartei Deutschland*) co-workers was the reorganization of elementary and secondary schools. The Law for the Democratization of German Schools passed in June 1946 established a single-track, unified system of an eight-year compulsory school followed by an optional four-year secondary school or a three-year vocational school. Here females were confronted with exactly the same curriculum as males. SMAD instituted coeducational classes throughout their zone of occupation, even while single-sex schools were being reopened in some parts of West Germany where they were sought mainly for religious reasons.

SMAD's conversion of Germany's traditional three-track educational system after Grade 4 into a single, integrated secondary school conformed with what American educational consultants unhesitatingly recommended in the U.S. zone of occupation. For girls the change meant that their secondary education was no longer considered in any way inferior. Earlier, Germany's intellectual elite generally had thought the education boys received in the classical *Gymnasium* was far superior to that accorded to girls in the *Realgymnasium* or *Oberrealschule*, the secondary schools attended by German girls until Hitler's insistence on a single eight-year *Oberschule*.

In order to equalize rural and urban education, the government in East Germany during these same years made a determined effort to eliminate one-room schools in rural areas as it redistributed and collectivized the land. In time, the quality of education of rural children improved and eventually became equal to that received by children in urban areas. Females benefited along with males.

As universities were slowly reopened in the Soviet zone, the East Germans under SMAD gave preferential access to youth from workers' or farmers' families and to any who readily expressed enthusiasm for communism and belonged to the KPD (Communist party of Germany) or the SED. While at the beginning of the twentieth century German women had finally gained admission to universities after a prolonged struggle to receive a secondary education that would prepare them for higher education, immediately after gaining power Hitler had seriously reduced the number of women at universities.[7] His rejuvenation of the motto first enunciated by Martin Luther of *Kinder, Kirche, Küche* (children, church, kitchen) to describe the desired role of women in Nazi society implied that higher education was unnecessary for a woman. SMAD rejected this Nazi policy.

During the 1950s, with the acquiescence of the Soviet Union, the SED consolidated its power in the newly established German Democratic Republic. Just as Marxist-Leninist ideology was implanted into the legal system, the same principles now guided the GDR's educational system. Traditional German educational practices opposed to socialist theories of education, such as the divided schooling offered to children past Grade 4, were eliminated despite opposition from those German parents who supported the educational differentiation of the past. The curriculum and methodology for history were revised in line with Marxist-Leninist ideology; Soviet textbooks for teacher education were translated into German; the first attempts were made to have a part of polytechnic education take place in factories or on collective farms in cooperation with the workers there; Russian became a required subject for all students; and the subject of religion was dropped from the curriculum. As a supplement to schooling the SED's coeducational youth organizations, the *Freie Deutsche Jugend* (FDJ) for teenagers and young adults and the Pioneers for children, began to provide nonformal education, both political and recreational.[8] Gender equality was ensured not only in the educational system, but also by the new constitution of the GDR (1949) and laws on the protection of mother and child, as well as those dealing with the rights of women such as equal pay for equal work, promulgated in 1950.[9]

LEGAL PROTECTION OF WOMEN

Three articles in the constitution of the GDR deal explicitly with the legal status of women.

Article 20

(2) Men and women shall be equal in rights and enjoy equal legal status in all spheres of social, political and private life. It shall be incumbent upon the community and the state to assist women, especially in gaining higher qualifications.

Article 24

(1) . . . Men and women, adults and young people shall be entitled to equal pay for equal work.

Article 38

(1) Marriage, family and motherhood shall enjoy special protection from the state. All citizens of the GDR shall be entitled to respect, protection and support for their marriage and family.
(3) The socialist state shall show a special concern for the well-being of mothers and children. Pregnancy leave, specialist medical care, material and financial support in the event of childbirth, and family allowances shall be granted.[10]

In addition, the Labor Code, first passed in 1950 and amended in 1961 and 1977, authorizes the development of women's support schemes to tap into their creative potential, "to raise their political and specialist qualifications, to prepare them systematically for managerial positions, and to improve their working and living conditions."[11] In 1972, the government also required workplaces to "lend every possible assistance to women with children under 17 years of age while they undergo vocational and upgrading training."[12] Such training was to take place during normal working hours.

The birthrate dropped below zero population growth in the 1960s, and young women felt pressed to continue in the labor market. At the same time, housing for young families was inadequate, and places in preschools proved inadequate. In 1972, the government initiated specific social measures "to make it easier for women to reconcile motherhood with full participation in working and public life."[13]

"The measures taken included shorter hours for women with children, higher maternity benefits, extended maternity leave before and after birth, construction of more creches and kindergartens, and paid twelve months' leave after the birth of children. A vast housing programme was undertaken simultaneously."[14]

The expansion over the years of creches (nursery schools), kindergartens, and after-school centers offers testimony to the SED leadership's recognition that these facilities are essential if women are to be full and equal participants in the labor force.

In 1950, only 1 percent of all children up to the age of three could be accommodated in creches; in 1970, 29 percent; and by 1985, 73 percent attended creches. The expansion of kindergartens was equally dramatic: in 1950, only 21 percent of the children could attend; by 1970, the figure had risen to 65 percent; and in 1985, 90 percent went to kindergarten. After-school centers have also opened their doors: in 1954, only 10 percent of all children attended them, but by 1985, the figure had risen to 83 percent.[15]

The GDR Family Code (1966) specifies that "both husband and wife play their part in bringing up and caring for the children, and in managing the household."[16] In addition, "husband and wife shall be equal in rights."[17] Abortions are permitted at a woman's request within twelve weeks of conception.[18]

Women have gained rights in the field of education either implicitly or explicitly. Much of the language of the 1965 Act on the Integrated Socialist Educational System of the German Democratic Republic refers to the rights of all citizens to a high standard of general education," including the possibility of proceeding to the next higher stage of education and up to the highest educational institutions, that is, the universities and colleges.[19] The preamble of the same document states that "all citizens of our state have the same rights, irrespective of sex, social position, world outlook, creed, or race. . . . Everybody can unfold his or her abilities. Men and women have every opportunity of performing responsible and managerial work in their vocation and in society."[20] Furthermore, the laws that guide the social development of the GDR "demand an education that corresponds to the modern standard of science and technology and enables men and women . . . to become personalities who are loyal to their socialist mother country, the German Democratic Republic, and who are prepared to strengthen and defend it."[21] One means by which this goal was to be reached was contained in the new constitution of 1968, which stated that "all young people shall have the right and the obligation to learn a trade or profession."[22]

Although the government sought to maximize women's participation in the workplace by legislation that provided equality, zero population growth continued and divorce increased. The divorce rate in the GDR today is 26.7 percent as compared with 13 percent in the Federal Republic.[23] Among younger women, the special provisions the government made to permit women to combine marriage, children, and career advancement were also interpreted as indicators of women's inferior status. Only by means of these provisions were they, the women, really equal to men.

By now, the idea that men help with household duties and with the care of children has been accepted. In order to raise the birthrate, the GDR government has expanded family legislation. Since 1976, women have been entitled to maternity leave on full pay lasting twenty-six weeks. In 1972, maternity grants paid by the state were raised to 1,000 marks per child. Parents now receive a state allowance for all children living in their household up to their tenth year at school. In addition, working mothers may claim paid child care leave after their maternity leave. In the case of their first and second child, this may cover the period up to the twelfth month and from the third child onward, up to eighteen months. Between 65 and 90 percent of average net earnings are payable during this period, depending on the number of children. The women concerned have their jobs guaranteed until they go back to work. Single mothers are entitled to up to thirteen weeks of paid leave to care for sick children. Mothers in full-time employment are given a paid day off each month to attend to domestic duties, and those with two or more children under sixteen work shorter hours (forty hours instead of 43¾).[24]

The GDR's ideological insistence on gender equality was reiterated by Erich Honecker, first party secretary, at the tenth Party Congress of the SED in 1981. He mentioned the real advances that women had made in their occupational and social contribution to the state, their increasing responsibilities in government and the economy, and the continuing rising birthrate.[25] Honecker explained: "And what the women and girls of today actually contribute to the general progress of our country is far more than diligence and clever hands. Rather it is political knowledge and ability, courage and confidence in their own capabilities and strength."[26]

THE EDUCATIONAL SYSTEM

By the 1970s, the German Democratic Republic had arrived at a firm alignment of its educational institutions. A child is first placed in a creche or nursery school until age three. Four to six years olds are in a kindergarten. Having reached the age of six, the child enters a ten-year general polytechnic secondary school. Its middle-level encompasses Grades 4–6, or children aged ten, eleven, and twelve. Its upper level extends to Grade 10, after which students separate according to their achievements, competencies, and interests.

Although some weak students shift to vocational education in Grade 9, most do not face any decision as to their occupational aspirations until Grade 10. The vast majority enter a vocational education program, which, after two years, leads to full entry into the labor market or admission into a professional training program at an institution of higher learning. The best students, or highest achievers, continue in the extended secondary school for an additional two years prior to sitting for the *Abitur,* the traditional German leaving examination for secondary school students who wish to enter a university. In the GDR, the successful takers of the *Abitur* are then admitted to the university. Each year some 10,000 students combine vocational education and preparation for the *Abitur* in a three-year program, after which they then also attend a university.[27] As in other modern industrialized nations, there are special classes and schools for the seriously handicapped.

All educational programs are open to both sexes. The enrollment of girls in the compulsory years of schooling is, of course, equal to that of boys in these years. A slightly higher percentage of girls continue into the *Erweiterte Oberschule,* that is, Grade 11 and 12.[28] Access to postsecondary education is open to young people who seek admission to evening or correspondence programs or who avail themselves of adult education programs to expand their occupational competence.[29]

The curriculum in the coeducational general polytechnic secondary school is identical for boys and girls, be it polytechnic education, civics, and history, that is, political education, or any other subject. Girls may choose an hour of needlework a week as an elective in Grades 4 and 5. Like the boys, they spend 30 percent of the time in school on mathematics and science; 41 percent on German, fine arts, and social science; 10.6 percent on foreign languages, first Russian and later, as an elective, English; 10.6 percent on the components of polytechnic education; and 8 percent on sports.[30]

THE SEARCH FOR GENDER EQUITY IN EDUCATION

Quite clearly, the GDR leadership today has hunted for a formula to ensure, on the one hand, gender equity, and on the other, women's active participation in the workforce, the nation's political life, and marriage, family, and motherhood. In view of the tremendous impact a woman has on her children through the continuous informal education she provides, these governmental goals constitute the means by which the socialist leaders ascertain that Marxism-Leninism remains the ideology of the state. The mother's conviction of its appropriateness and timeliness undoubtedly appears to contribute to that goal.

Political Education

In view of the SED's concern for political continuity, despite the contradictory messages received by East Germans from their "brothers and sisters" residing in the Federal Republic of Germany across the Wall, the educational system places great stress on political education through the subjects of civics (*Staatsbürgerkunde*), history, German, that is, through the literary selections that are read, Russian, and polytechnic education. Teachers of civics may avail themselves of special in-service courses given by SED local party officials.[31] Together, they are to see to it that "in the spirit of the ideology and morality of the working class, all boys and girls are educated for socialist patriotism and proletarian internationalism. With high achievements students should contribute in their social relations to the general strengthening of the GDR and the force of the socialist unity centered on the Soviet Union."[32] As the long-time minister of education, Margot Honecker, the wife of Erich Honecker, SED party general secretary, may serve as a model of the politically committed, activist woman.

Ethics Education

In addition to civics and history, East German male and female students are grounded in Marxism-Leninism. They are taught to be energetic workers and to engage willingly in "socially useful labor." Polytechnic education, which contains a distinct political message, conveys these goals, as do aspects of the subject of Russian.

The displacement of religion may be another factor that has contributed to gender equality. It must be remembered that traditionally German schools taught the subject of religion on a denominational basis to virtually all students. For most this meant either the Protestant or Catholic version of Christianity. One may posit the theory that from this teaching girls inferred that women are to be submissive and carry out their duties as wives and mothers without any attempt to displace the male in his more dominant role in the family. Since the formation of East Germany, religion no longer is a subject in the timetable of schools. Instead, churches offer such instruction, and students attend on a voluntary basis.

In school, moral lessons convey to students the rightness of the working class taking command so as to establish socialism and end class exploitation, as well as each student's obligation to contribute to the socialist society,[33] to work toward the international solidarity of socialist states, and to be prepared to defend the fatherland.[34] Sex education is provided in both schools and the FDJ. Family stability forms the implicit goal. These several elements of the GDR students' lessons in ethics have also been pulled together and designate the socialist personality, that is, the concept that is to guide education.[35]

Defense Education

The emphasis on being willing to defend the country in a search for peace became part of political education, especially once the two Germanies were formed in 1949. Students in the GDR were told that they were to be the defenders of peace now that the West was organizing for the pursuit of "imperialist policies."[36] Thereafter both at school and in the FDJ, boys were encouraged to volunteer for the *Volkspolizei*, also known as the *Vopos*, the only paramilitary organization which SMAD then permitted. Once the Soviets told the GDR to establish an army of its own in 1956, boys were again asked to volunteer for it. Meanwhile, they received premilitary training in the FDJ, and through the East Germans' emphasis on sports were expected to keep fit. Service in the military became compulsory for males in 1962 after the erection of the Wall. Now the school, the FDJ, and the sports organization GST (*Gesellschaft für Sport und Technik*) provided the ideological preparation for military service. By 1978, *Wehrerziehung*, or defense education, became a regular subject in Grades 9 and 10 for male and female students.[37]

Female students learn first aid, fire control, and antiaircraft defense, whereas boys receive an introduction to military training. During the winter vacation in February, Grade 10 students engage in premilitary maneuvers for three days at a camp.[38]

Polytechnic Education

Margot Honecker continues to delineate the GDR's official concept of education. She commented on the central role assigned to polytechnic education at an educational conference at Erfurt in 1985:

Our concept of education derives from the Marxist recognition that instruction should be linked with productive work and physical exercise as the only method for the development of a fully mature person. For that reason we provide for our youth a complete general education in which polytechnic education is solidly integrated. Our polytechnic education includes education in natural science, the teaching of elementary technical knowledge; it includes education on-site in production, and an education which is set so as to generate readiness to go to work on the part of youth, and through recognition in production of those characteristics and moral tendencies and behaviors which correspond to the socialist morality toward work. In the course of education, our youth must be familiarized with the successes of socialism, the tasks and problems, the processes of social development. These are all necessary for those building a socialist society.[39]

The school especially must educate youth to love science and to be interested in technology and production.[40]

Thus girls are never excused or excluded from science, mathematics, or other facets of polytechnic education. Along with the boys, they are introduced nowadays to automation, computer technology, database management, and related topics.[41] They also engage in productive work, that aspect of polytechnic education which takes the students to some specific factory or farm where they participate in one way or another in the production process. For example, boys and girls may assist in the repair of tractors in a rural area; they may learn to do the plowing with a tractor[42] or they may help install a computerized telephone system in an office of a larger enterprise.[43] In the preliminary technical instruction, boys and girls work side by side, and the same is expected of them. They have the opportunity to explore their potential skills in several areas of technology. In grades 9 and 10 ten different fields are supposed to be offered.[44]

Table 12.1

Percentage of Girls among Young People Starting an Apprenticeship in Selected Technical Trades, 1975 and 1977

	1975	1977
Skilled data-processing workers	81.0	83.5
Data-processing and office-machine mechanics	55.7	62.9
Skilled electronics workers	46.4	54.1
Skilled plastics processing workers	81.1	82.6
Skilled chemical workers	77.3	81.2
Mechanical engineering draughtsmen	95.8	96.2
Skilled plant engineering workers	55.8	63.1
Skilled textile engineering workers	92.1	92.5

Throughout polytechnic education, students are given guidance as to their own eventual choice of occupation and therefore the vocational-technical education program for which they wish to apply.[45] They are encouraged to assess their own abilities and interests. In the case of female students, they may still fasten onto the traditionally female occupations such as nursing, sales clerking, or the textile industry.[46] There also often remains a gap between the students' actual experiences in productive work and their comprehension of what is entailed in an occupation generally.

Occupational Preparation

All apprentices, that is, the graduates of the ten-year general polytechnic school vocational education programs, receive a monthly allowance[47] and are taught not only a particular trade or skill, but also some economics, civics, data processing, electronics, and related technologies.[48] "Girls can train in all but thirty occupations, where a health hazard is entailed."[49] Their choice of apprenticeships reveals their opportunities to work in the GDR's major industries as shown in Table 12.1.[50]

The enrollment of female apprentices in the different vocational programs in 1985 reveals both their preferences and their actual opportunities. Females constituted 75 percent of those in chemical occupations, 90 percent of those in textile trades and service occupations, 96 percent of those in sales, half of those in transportation, in food service, and agriculture, but only 10 percent of those learning the mechanical trades and 5 percent of those in construction. Females accounted for 99 percent of those preparing to be secretaries.[51] "Virtually every boy or girl leaves formal education with at least some sort of qualification."[52]

At technical institutes and engineering colleges, women also are represented in significant numbers, as shown in Table 12.2.[53]

Over the past thirty years there has been a continuous increase in the number

Table 12.2
Students at Technical Colleges, by Subject Area, 1982

Subject Area	Students Total	Percentage of Women
Technical sciences	44,061	34.7
Medicine and health sciences	49,239	97.7
Agricultural sciences	9,626	55.9
Economics and related subjects	38,520	84.7
Government, library and documentation studies	2,316	83.3
Culture and sports sciences	724	54.9
Literature, languages and linguistics	109	95.4
Art	1,292	64.8
Education-related subjects	26,153	84.0
Total	172,058	73.4

Table 12.3
Women in Universities and Colleges of Higher Education, 1982

Subject	Total number of students	Women as a Percentage of total
Mathematics/natural sciences	8,391	54.8
Technical sciences	39,513	26.5
Medicine	13,564	55.2
Agriculture	8,116	50.1
Economics	17,305	62.3
Philosophy, history, law, government	8,319	35.1
Culture, art, sports sciences	3,287	35.8
Literature, languages, linguistics	2,228	70.9
Art	3,067	43.5
Education-related studies	26,652	74.5
Total	130,442	49.3

of women admitted to universities. Whereas in 1951 they constituted 21 percent of the student body there, the percentage had risen to 35 percent in 1970 and to 49 percent in 1981. There has also been a shift in the choice of majors selected by women. In 1965, women constituted 6.5 percent and 23.3 percent, respectively, of those studying mathematics and technical sciences. Today their representation in these once all-male fields has expanded measurably, as shown in Table 12.3.[54]

Regardless of their major, all university students during their first two years must take Russian, physical education, a second foreign language, and a course in Marxist-Leninist ideology.[55] In addition, male and female university students receive stipends from the state, and they have access to inexpensive dormitories and meals. Women who have children receive an additional amount and other assistance with placing young children in a nursery school or kindergarten. In that way, too, the state encourages women to engage in university studies.

Educational Contributions of the SED Youth Organizations

The Pioneers and the FDJ are important components of the education received by East German boys and girls. On the one hand, the organizations represent a counterpart to the extracurricular activities offered in most American secondary schools. They feature interest or hobby groups; they offer the opportunity to participate in musical groups and to learn to play an instrument or to sing; they organize sports and athletic activities; and they conduct vacation programs for youth. These activities, organized into 94,300 groups to this date,[56] are available to boys and girls on an equal basis. Those who decide not to join find themselves virtually unable to participate in music, sports or other recreational activities.

Here their second and more critical function may be seen. The Pioneers and FDJ must also convey the political ideology that undergirds the GDR. With a membership of 1.6 million and 2.3 million, respectively, the Pioneers and the FDJ reach most children and youth.[57] The Pioneers has a high membership rate— 86.6 percent—because the Pioneer houses offer a place for children to spend their afternoons while mothers are at work.[58] With 90 percent of mothers working, most East German parents find they have little choice but to become members rather than risk having no supervision of their schoolage children each afternoon when schools are no longer in session.[59]

FEMALE LABOR FORCE PARTICIPATION

If we study women's participation in the GDR labor force, we find that today they are scattered throughout the major occupational fields.

"As things stand now, 91.3 percent of all women of working age hold a job. Half the country's workforce of 8.5 million is female. Just under 82 percent of them have formal qualifications."[60] Women make up 42 percent of those in industry; 30 percent of women are in technical occupations.[61] "Women make up one-third of all university and technical college graduates in the farming world."[62] Of all women in agriculture, 87 percent have acquired formal qualifications.[63] Just as the special provisions for skills improvement in industry, for child care, and for maternity leaves have aided women in the nonfarming sector, so have women in rural areas benefited from the changes introduced into farming by the socialist government of the GDR: "Women on farms have a fixed working schedule, and they are entitled to four weeks' holiday leave each year and earn

Figure 12.1
Qualification Standards of Working People in the Socialist Economy

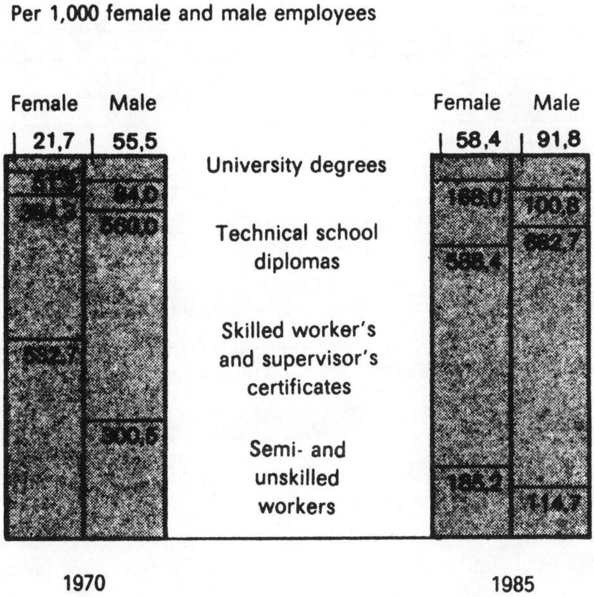

Per 1,000 female and male employees

Female	Male		Female	Male
21,7	55,5	University degrees	58,4	91,8
		Technical school diplomas		
		Skilled worker's and supervisor's certificates		
		Semi- and unskilled workers		

1970   1985

the same income as their male counterparts. On top of this, they benefit from extensive social improvements which apply to all women without distinction.''[64]

Since the inception of the women's movement, the government of the GDR has expressed concern for the underrepresentation of women in positions of greater responsibility in the workplace, as well as for the frequency of women lacking the formal qualifications for the work to which they have been assigned.[65] At the government's urging, industry now operates evening courses, on-the-job training programs, and longer workshops to remedy this condition. Women are given time off their regular work assignments to participate and are financially fully compensated as well.[66] Their enrollment in continuing education programs at universities represents 31.9 percent of the total; at technical institutes and engineering colleges, 46.6 of the total; at program for craftsmen 8.7 percent; and at programs for skilled workers 42.9 percent.[67]

These steps reflect the SED's desire to heighten the efficiency of East German production. The qualifications of workers, male and female, are to be optimized just as productivity is to be increased.[68] At the Eleventh Party Congress Erich Honecker stressed the urgency of these economic goals. In order to attain them, schools are to be more efficient; creativity is to be given a specific place in preschool education; the content of the subjects in the curriculum of the ten-year general polytechnic secondary school is to be updated, as is vocational education; and computer education is to be added. In addition, gifted students are to be

Figure 12.2
Percentage of Women Employees, by Economic Sector, 1985

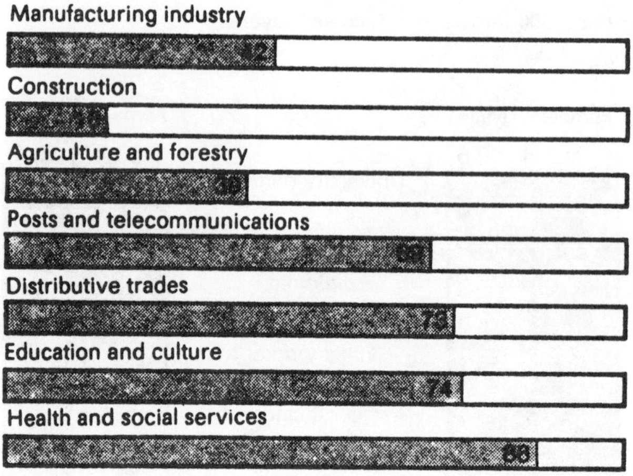

Manufacturing industry

Construction

Agriculture and forestry

Posts and telecommunications

Distributive trades

Education and culture

Health and social services

identified and then encouraged to advance rapidly in their special field of interest.[69] As in other socialist countries, the GDR attempts cohesion among the economic, political, and social goals. Females are expected to participate in all sectors very much as males are.

WOMEN'S EDUCATION: AN OUTGROWTH OF PUBLIC POLICY

Altogether then, women in the GDR receive basically the same education as males. They have opportunities to extend their formal education so as to qualify in one or another occupation (with *very* few exceptions). They may seek to upgrade their skills on a nonformal basis once they have entered the workforce. They are reminded that gender equality also entails equal responsibility to serve their socialist nation.[70]

In recent years, additional accommodations have been made to assist working wives and mothers. Those among them who wish to take courses to advance in their field of work can do so during the normal workday. Moreover, maternity benefits and leaves have been increased, and the number of nursery, kindergarten, and after-school centers has expanded. More and more of the housekeeping conveniences found in other Western countries are available to GDR women.

Still, many women in the GDR experience the double-day, full-time employment outside the home and household chores to be done before and after. The state expects women to be part of the labor force of which today they constitute 48 percent.[71] The state's political education pounds away at the need for production and a high rate of productivity. In addition, women are expected to contribute time and enthusiasm in support of the socialist ideology of the state.

In a different vein, the government has urged husbands to give more time to household needs and to the raising of their children. Although some changes seem to have followed, a woman still has to find a balance between career and family, a balance juxtaposed against the legal equality of women in the workplace but the continued expectation of being the prime homemaker and socializer of the children.[72] The last named responsibilities continue to keep some women from seeking leadership roles at work or in the political sphere. Others forsake family life, as shown by the relatively high divorce rate. That they must share the socialization of their children with the state, that is, the school and the Pioneers, may also trouble some women who view the family as a private domain in life which in many ways should be immune from direct state influence.

Despite equality of access to education, the lives of East German teenagers differ on the basis of gender. Studies of these youth have shown that (1) girls contribute more to household chores than boys; (2) boys handle the more technically demanding tasks when they help; and (3) in school girls continue to prefer the arts, social studies, and languages and boys the technical and science subjects and sports.[73] Furthermore, "parents place higher expectations for achievement on their sons than on daughters who, however, outperform boys in school. Girls have less free time. . . . Despite 30 years of equal influence and sanctioning of equality, girls and boys continue to seek different career goals."[74]

These findings must be seen against others that underline the continued importance of the family in East German society. Young people expect to marry and have children,[75] especially now that the government has initiated a supportive family policy.[76] The family remains a safe haven for a more private life. That many females, therefore, retain certain traditional role expectations is not surprising. What is worth noting is their increased entrance into traditionally male occupations as well as the educational and social policies of the GDR government which are intended to maximize female labor force participation, productivity, and political acquiescence and at the same time raise the birthrate.

NOTES

1. United States, *Foreign Relations of the United States Diplomatic Papers*. The Conference of Berlin (Potsdam Conference), 1954; Vol. 2 (Washington, D.C.: U.S. Government Printing Office, 1960), p. 1482.

2. Hermann Weber, *DDR Grundriss der Geschichte 1945–1981*, 3rd ed. (Hanover: Fackeltrager, 1982), p. 33.

3. Ibid.

4. Gottfried Uhlig, Karl-Marx University, Leipzig; interview, April 24, 1987.

5. Ibid., April 24, 1987.

6. Ibid., April 30, 1987.

7. Gordon A. Craig, *Germany 1866–1945* (New York: Oxford University Press, 1978), p. 628.

8. Karl-Heinz Günther and Gottfried Uhlig, *Geschichte der Schule in der Deutschen*

Demokratischen Republik, 1945–1971 (Berlin: Wolk und Wissen Volkseigener Verlag, 1974), p. 166.

9. Hartmut Zimmerman, ed., *DDR Handbuch,* Bundesministerium fur innerdeutsche Beziehungen, Vol. 1 (Cologne: Verlag Wissenschaft und Politik, January 1985), p. 444.

10 Ibid., p. 53.

11. German Democratic Republic, *Panorama DDR,* p. 54.

12. Ibid.

13. Ibid., p. 29.

14. Ibid.

15. Ibid., p. 61.

16. Ibid., p. 56.

17. Ibid., p. 55.

18. Ibid., p. 56.

19. German Democratic Republic, Ministry of Education, *Act on the Integrated Socialist Educational System of the German Democratic Republic* (Berlin: Staatsverlag der Deutschen Demokratischen Republik, 1972), p. 16.

20. Ibid., p. 10.

21. Ibid., p. 11.

22. German Democratic Republic, State Secretariat for Vocational Education, *Vocational Education* (Dresden: Verlag Zeit im Bild, 1974), p. 10.

23. Claudia Prinz, *Seminar: Frauen,* Heft 1, Gleichberechtigung, Frauen/Sozialisation (Bonn: Bundeszentrale fur Politische Bildung, 1984), p. 25.

24. German Democratic Republic, *Panorama DDR,* p. 39.

25. Friedrich-Ebert-Stiftung, *Frauen in der Deutschen Demokratischen Republic* (Bonn: Velag Neue Gesellschaft, 1981), p. 5.

26. Ibid.

27. G. E. Edwards, *GDR Society and Social Institutions* (London: Macmillan Press, 1985), p. 61.

28. Ibid., p. 60.

29. Dietmar Waterkamp, *Handbuch zum Bildungswesen der DDR* (Berlin: Verlag Arno Spitz, 1987), p. 12.

30. Edwards, *GDR Society,* p. 57.

31. Heinrich Huss, "Zu einigen Fragen der inhaltlichen Ausgentaltung der zehn-klassigne allgemeinbildenden polytechnischen Oberschule der DDR in der ersten Hälfte der siebzinger Jahre" (Ph.D. diss., Karl-Marx University, Leipizig, 1982), p. 44.

32. Ibid., p. 92.

33. Erich Honecker, in *GDR: Youth in the German Democratic Republic and the Tasks of Our Time* (Dresden: Verlag Zeit im Bild, 1972), p. 26.

34. Johannes Niermann, *Socialistische Pädagogik in der DDR* (Heidelberg: Quelle & Meyer, 1972, p. 49.

35. Heinrich Huss, "Zu einigen Fragen," p. 16.

36. Carola Rentzsch, "Zur Entwicklung der Wehrerziehung und des Wehrunterrichts in den allgemeinbildenden Schulen der DDR von 1945–1982" (*Diplomarbeit* thesis, Karl-Marx University, Leipzig, 1985), p. 4.

37. Ibid., p. 36.

38. Federal Republic of Germany, Bundesministerium fur innerdeutsche Beziehunger, *Zahlenspiegel, Bundersrepublik Deutschland/Deutsche Demokratische Republik—Ein Vergleich* (Bonn: Gesamtdeutsches Institut, 1982), p. 65.

39. Margot Honecker, "Die Schulpolitik der SED und die wachsenden Anforderungen an den Lehrer und die Lehrebildung," *Pädagogik* 41, no. 1 (1986): 11.

40. Ibid., p. 17.

41. Friedrich Kuebart, ed., *Halbjahresbericht zur Bildungspolitik und Pädagogischen Entwicklung in der DDR, der UdSSR, der VR Polen, der CSSR and der VR China,* 1st Half Year 1985 (Ruhr-University Bochum: Institut für Pädagogik, 1985), p. 18.

42. Eckhardt Schurig, Supervisor for Polytechnic Education, Kreis Döbeln, GDR; interview, April 28, 1987.

43. Glogowski, Humboldt Erweiterte Oberschule, Leipzig; interview, April 23, 1987.

44. Heinz Frankiewicz, "Stand und Entwicklungsprobleme der Verbindung von Schule und Betrieb in der polytechnischen Oberschule," *Jahrbuch der Akademie der Pädagogischen Wissenschaften der DDR* (1979): 66.

45. Ibid.

46. Edwards, *GDR Society*, p. 63.

47. Ibid., p. 61.

48. Ibid., p. 62.

49. Ibid., p. 62.

50. Ibid., p. 63.

51. German Democratic Republic, Staatliche Zentralverwaltung fur Statistik, *Statistisches Jahrbuch 1986 der Deutschen Demokratischen Republik* 31 (Berlin: Staatsverlag der Deutschen Demokratischen Republik, 1986), p. 297.

52. Edwards, *GDR Society,* p. 61.

53. Ibid., p. 65.

54. Ibid., p. 68.

55. Günther Filipiak, Acting Head of the Pedagogical Section, Karl-Marx University, Leipzig; interview, April 22, 1987.

56. Jürgen Henze, ed., *Halbjahresbericht zur Bildungspolitik und Pädagogischen Entwicklung in der DDR, der USSR, der VR Polen, der CSSR und der VR China,* 1st Half Year 1986 (Ruhr-university Bochum: Institut für Pädagogik, 1986), p. 5.

57. Friedrich-Ebert-Stiftung, *Freie Deutsche Jugend und Pionierorganisation Ernst Thälmann in der DDR* (Bonn: Verlag Neue Gesellschaft, 1984), p. 13.

58. Ibid.

59. Gottfried Uhlig, Karl-Marx University, Leipzig; interview, April 21, 1987.

60. Ibid., p. 13.

61. Ibid., p. 14.

62. Ibid., p. 15.

63. Edwards, *GDR Society*, p. 73.

64. German Democratic Republic, *Panorama DDR*, p. 15.

65. Zimmermann, *DDR Handbuch*, p. 335.

66. Ibid.

67. Friedrich-Ebert-Stiftung, *Frauen in der Deutschen Demokratischen Republik,* p. 23.

68. Gerhard Schreier, "Der XI. Parteitag der SED und die Bildungspolitik der DDR in den achtiger Jahren. Eine Skizze," *Pädagogik und Schule in Ost und West* 34 (Third Quarter, 1986): 41.

69. Ibid., p. 47.

70. Kurt Sontheimer and Wilhelm Bleek, *Die DDR Politik, Gesellschaft, Wirtschaft* 5th expanded ed. (Hamburg: Hoffmann & Campe, 1979), p. 157.

71. Federal Republic of Germany, Bundesministerium fur innerdeutsche Beziehungen; *Zahlenspiegel*, p. 40.

72. Ludwig Liegle, "Private oder offentliche Kleinkinderziehung? Politische Steuerung und gesellschaftliche Entwicklung im Systemvergleich (Bundesrepublic Deutschland, Sowjetunion, Deutsche Demokratische Republic)," in *Staatliche Steuerung und Eigendynamik im Bildungs—und Erziehungswesen osteuropaischer Staaten und der DDR,* ed. Oskar Anweiler (Berlin: Verlag Arno Spitz, 1986), p. 214.

73. Rita Süssmuth, "Mädchen und Frauen in beiden deutschen Staaten. Tatbestande geschlechtsspezifischer Sozialisations-forchung und ungeloste Probleme," in Bernhard Dilger, Friedrich Kuebart, and Hans-Peter Schäfer, eds., *Vergleichende bildungsforschung, DDR, Osteuropa und interkulturelle Perspektiven* (Berlin: Verlag Arno Spitz, 1986), p. 90.

74. Barbara Hille, "Familie in der DDR als Vermittlerin sozialistischer Normen und Werte?" *Lebensbedingungen in der DDR,* 17th Meeting on GDR Research in the Federal Republic of Germany, Cologne, June 12–15, 1984, p. 100.

75. Dietmar Waterkamp, "Erziehung in der DDR Zwischen Optimismus und Resignation," *Vergleichende Bildungsforschung,* p. 245.

76. Council of Europe, *Forum,* 1/86 (Strasbourg: Council of Europe, 1986), p. IV.

13
GREAT BRITAIN

Gage Blair

From the nineteenth century to the present day, educational opportunities for women in Great Britain have increased at a steady pace. Throughout this history, however, prevailing ideologies and social practices have made women's education different from that of men and different across class and ethnic lines. This chapter presents an overview of the education of British women over the last two centuries. The first part of the chapter briefly covers the period from Queen Victoria to the 1940s, describing how educational progress became possible for women in spite of profound ideological resistance. The second part of the chapter discusses contemporary aspects of women's education from the end of World War II to the present day. Although landmark legislation was passed during this period, inequalities persist.

While the discussion of women's education is relevant to England, Wales, and Scotland, general discussion of education in Britain often focuses on the single system of England and Wales. The educational system of Scotland, while broadly similar, has distinctive organizational features.[1]

VICTORIAN EDUCATION, IDEOLOGIES, AND CHALLENGES

The Victorian Age began in 1837 and ended just after the close of the nineteenth century. It was a period of economic, social, and intellectual changes brought about by vastly new industrial conditions that connected rural and urban life. Increasingly unable to make a living on the land and faced with the loss of cottage industries, rural dwellers left their villages for the towns in search of work.

These shifts in working conditions led to changes in working women's employment. With the loss of home businesses, many women entered wage labor, working as factory laborers or domestic servants. In sharp contrast to these working women was the "lady" of the early Victorian era, who had almost complete leisure. This ideal of the well-to-do lady filtered down to other classes, especially the rich country landowners. As families grew wealthier and could afford servants, women's household tasks grew less burdensome.[2] The feminine ideal, though hardly applicable to all British women, became all-pervasive in the era and many women aimed for an education suitable for those with many unhurried hours that would equip them with refined skills (such as sketching, drawing, and decorating) and allow them to be elegant wives and charming hostesses.

In the first half of the nineteenth century, middle- and upper-class males were educated in the public schools and in endowed and proprietary schools. Lower-class boys had only an inadequate elementary education available to them, which they shared with girls. Upper-class girls were educated separately from boys of their class but received only minimal instruction. In the Victorian era, men dominated the active, public sphere, whereas women were given responsibility for the private sphere, which was characterized by femininity, innocence, and efficiency. Women were therefore educated at home or in socially select private schools which imparted womanly skills that would qualify them for marriage.[3]

An educational revolution took place in Britain from 1846 to 1895 and forever changed the provision of education for middle- and upper-class girls. Several groups of reformers advocated an intellectual rather than a social education for women. One group, the feminists, such as Emily Davies,[4] sought to expand women's role in society in spite of the fierce opposition of medical professionals and religious groups.[5] A second group, academics and teachers, espoused the broadening of women's educational institutions. For their part, parents supported intellectual education for girls in public schools and women's colleges because it was socially and financially advantageous.[6] Although society did not expect all women to work, not all women married and, in order to avoid poverty, they needed professional jobs.[7] In order to obtain such jobs, a more thorough education than had hitherto been available became a necessity.

In the second part of the nineteenth century, 200 endowed and private schools were established, as were the earliest colleges for women in London, Cambridge, and Oxford.[8] The new schools differed from the earlier private schools in that they required entrance examinations, they admitted students from more varied social backgrounds, and they stressed educational achievement. The curriculum was broad, emphasizing "solid subjects" rather than "showy accomplishments."[9]

In 1870, universal primary education was instituted, and between 1870 and 1890 school attendance on average increased from 1.2 million to 4.5 million.[10]

The provision of secondary education for the lower classes, however, was still inadequate; only the brightest children were able to receive education beyond the primary level. Elementary and secondary schools would remain separate spheres, divided by social class, until the 1940s. Middle-class assumptions about gender added to class inequalities. For example, while it was assumed that all girls would take on the dual role of work and the family, the curriculum of working-class girls actually included "training" in domestic science that would prepare them for a career as household servants and housewives.[11]

1900 TO 1940: THE CURRICULUM DEBATE

Margaret Bryant has called the first half of the twentieth century a time that might have been one of feminist advance but was not.[12] This might surprise us when we think of the feminist movement led by the Suffragettes who kept women's issues at the forefront in the early 1900s and won women the vote in 1918. Her statement, however, must be seen in the context that during this period women were beleagured by assumptions about the proper female role, an assumption that lasted into the second half of the century.[13]

At the turn of the century, the eugenics movement made the curriculum a key issue.[14] Felicity Hunt has described how the debates of the 1920s and 1930s differed from those of the late nineteenth century: now the belief became current that women's education should not have a dual function but a divided function.[15] That is, secondary education had previously stressed the necessity of providing women with a liberal education that would fit them for life as professionals or as mothers. Now educators considered whether there should be, as there already was in elementary schools, a special curriculum consisting of practical skills to prepare women for life as wives and mothers.

Changes in educational organization helped to institute a differentiated curriculum. The 1902 Education Act gave England and Wales a secondary education system that was organized centrally through a Board of Education. This board promoted the idea that women had a proper role, as several regulations indicated. In 1905, training in housewifery was made mandatory for girls. In 1907, girls were allowed to substitute domestic science for natural and physical science and, later, to discontinue studying mathematics.[16] Most schools did institute domestic science, although many women administrators and teachers strongly questioned the change. In the 1920s and 1930s, the Board of Education justified a female curriculum. Girls, it was thought, needed a different education that would enable them to work in the home, as well as outside it, because once they married they would give up work and become homemakers.[17]

The post–World War I "back-to-the-home" movement seemed to reinforce these educational reforms. However, the 1921 census revealed that approximately one in three women was self-supporting.[18] Beginning in the early 1900s, more and more women had been entering the workforce owing to structural changes in industry. As the agricultural sector declined, the productive industrial sector (manufacturing, mining, and construction) grew, as did female employment in these areas. Approximately 50 percent of women workers at the turn of the century were employed in the service occupations; another 45 percent were employed in manufacturing.[19]

The 1914–1918 war period further increased women's work participation as women replaced male workers in large numbers and in many of the jobs they had been previously thought unqualified to perform.[20] By 1921, there were large increases in women's activities in extractive industries (i.e., mining), construction, commerce and finance, transport, and communications, whereas women's participation in the agriculture, manufacturing, and service sectors remained stable.[21] In 1931, the census revealed that 6.2 million women out of a total of 24 million were in paid employment. The largest number of these women workers were in industry and agriculture (2.4 million), followed by domestic servants and charwomen (1.6 million), clerks and typists (700,000), and professional workers (500,000; 206,000 of whom were teachers).[22]

During the period between the two wars, teaching became a predominantly female profession. As shown in Table 13.1, the number of female teachers in elementary schools had already overtaken males by 1900 (47 percent male, 53 percent female). From 1910 to 1919–1920, a period encompassing the Great War, the number of female teachers in elementary schools jumped from 56 to 65 percent, while the proportion of male teachers fell from 44 percent to 35 percent. In secondary schools, the number of male and female teachers was on a par during the first half of the century, except for the war period.

Despite these changes, female educators felt threatened by the 1902 Education Act, which gave local authorities the power to establish coeducational secondary schools.[23] The Association of Head Mistresses, for example, was widely concerned that in a coeducational school women would be deprived of their positions of authority.[24] The National Union of Women Teachers not only defended its own opportunities in schools, but also believed that girls received more attention and careful treatment when they were educated in a single-sex environment.[25]

Statistics for student enrollment in the early 1900s show progress for girls at the primary and secondary levels. Girls and boys attended coeducational public elementary and secondary schools equally during this period (see tables 13.1 and 13.2). In the elementary schools, the school-leaving age was 12 in 1899; it was raised to 14 in 1918, after which a student, with permission from the local education authority, could attend either a technical or trade school.[26] In 1929–1930 in England and Wales, of the 166,378 students who remained in school after the age of 14, 50 percent were boys and 50 percent girls.

In the largely middle-class secondary schools in England and Wales, the proportion of total males to total females attending school in 1905 was 54 percent to 46 percent. It remained about the same through 1930. Probably because of the war, the number of girls age sixteen and over who stayed in school was 60 percent, compared to 40 percent of boys. By 1930, the figures for this age group were more balanced (52 percent boys and 48 percent girls).

Table 13.1
Elementary School Enrollment, England and Wales, 1900–1930

Year	Students Aged 5–12 Years Boys N	%	Girls N	%	Students Aged 12 and Over Boys N	%	Girls N	%	Certified Full-Time Teachers Men N	%	Women N	%
1900	4,271,309				789,560				17,436	47	19,317	53
1902	4,342,963				927,799				18,389	48	20,263	52
1904	2,226,544	50	2,189,438	50	482,575	50	486,434	50	19,456	47	21,995	53
1906	2,229,588	50	2,198,059	50	536,558	50	533,565	50	20,476	46	24,074	54
1908	2,262,837	50	2,224,471	50	533,962	50	531,184	50	22,024	45	26,752	55
1910	2,300,785	50	2,262,372	50	546,937	50	541,855	50	23,381	44	29,950	56
1912	2,327,584	50	2,289,470	50	543,536	50	544,161	50	25,402	42	34,429	58

Statistics suspended during war

Year	Students Aged 5–14 Years N	%	Students Aged 14 and Over Boys N	%	Girls N	%	Certified Full-Time Teachers Men N	%	Women N	%
1919–20	2,839,517	50	58,151	49	60,476	51	26,420	35	50,107	65
1921–22	2,788,740	51	79,024	52	73,565	48	27,985	34	54,627	66
1923–24	2,642,750	51	86,407	51	83,323	49	29,907	35	55,539	65
1925–26	2,652,620	51	86,629	50	85,515	50	31,614	34	60,050	66
1927–28	2,656,130	51	86,990	50	86,860	50	32,868	34	62,900	66
1929–30	2,636,908	51	82,735	50	83,626	50	34,369	34	65,651	66

Source: Great Britain Central Statistical Office. Annual Abstract of Statistics. No. 61: 1899–1913, pp. 412–413 and No. 75: 1913 and 1917–1930, pp. 48–49. Reprinted by arrangement with Her Majesty's Stationery office, London, by Kraus Reprint Ltd. Nendeln, Liechtenstein, 1966.

Table 13.2
Secondary School Enrollment, England and Wales, 1905–1930

Year	Students Under 12 Years				Students Aged 12-16				Students Aged 16 & Over			
	Boys N	%	Girls N	%	Boys N	%	Girls N	%	Boys N	%	Girls N	%
1905	Information not available											
1910												
1914	24,311	55	19,562	45	69,089	54	58,041	46	6,597	40	10,047	60
1920	44,718	52	41,090	48	105,141	53	93,410	47	9,435	40	14,068	60
1925	44,572	51	43,114	49	126,635	54	107,898	46	17,283	46	20,119	54
1930	49,645	51	48,474	49	142,357	54	121,081	46	20,901	52	19,047	48

TOTAL

Year	Boys N	%	Girls N	%
1905	61,179	65	33,519	35
1910	84,273	54	71,993	46
1914	99,997	53	87,650	47
1920	159,294	52	148,568	48
1925	188,490	52	171,131	48
1930	212,903	53	188,602	47

Source: Great Britain Central Statistical Office. Annual Abstract of Statistics. No. 61: 1899-1913, p. 415 and No. 75: 1913 and 1917-1930, p. 52. Reprinted by arrangement with Her Majesty's Stationery Office, London, by Kraus Reprint Ltd. Nendeln, Liechtenstein, 1966.

The total percentage of female students at institutions of higher education (Table 13.3.) fluctuated between 20 and 30 percent from 1919 to 1939. Oxford University began granting degrees to women beginning in 1920, but Cambridge did not do so until 1948. Scottish universities, some northern English institutions, and the University of Wales had begun awarding women degrees long before the 1890s. Polytechnics were open to women from the time these schools were founded. Predictably, large numbers of women enrolled in "female" courses, such as the arts, but they barely reached half of the total student enrollment in this area.

The gains which women made in the nineteenth century were consolidated in the twentieth. Enrollment, particularly at the university level, continued to rise; the old debates continued over the purposes of coeducation, the educational needs of girls, and the curriculum. Some new debates also rose to the fore.

THE POST–WORLD WAR II PERIOD

The period of recovery after World War II and the restructuring and upsurge of the economy in the 1950s was followed by the period of Social Democracy, a period spanning the late 1950s to the end of the 1970s. With the economy doing well during this time, more money was spent to implement social policies for the benefit of those who were deprived. The general concern for equity extended to education.

After 1950, two important debates dominated education. First, in the 1950s and 1960s, as the welfare state grew, concern was voiced about widening the educational opportunity of diverse social classes. The Educational Act of 1944 provided all children with a free secondary education. A gradual "comprehensivization" of the school system took place in the 1960s. The division of secondary schools into academic and vocational types was abandoned, and comprehensive schools offered a broad range of subjects to students from different backgrounds. Second, educators began to be concerned about educational processes and how they discriminated against and affected the progress of children, undermining *de jure* social policies.

In order to place these debates in context, we will examine the postwar reforms which sought to democratize education. Then we will discuss the legislation which attempted to provide more educational opportunity for women. Finally, the outcomes of education in the workforce and the family will be reviewed. First, however, since race became an important part of the educational debates in this period, adding to class and gender considerations, we will briefly discuss black Britons.

The Changing Composition of the United Kingdom

Britain changed from a largely monocultural to a multiethnic society as the result of a large postwar entry of people from New Commonwealth countries.

Table 13.3
Courses Taken by Full-Time Students at Universities, etc., Great Britain, 1919–1939

Academic Year	Arts, incl. Theology, Fine Arts, Law, Music. Commerce, Economics, Education		Pure Science		Medicine & Dentistry		Technology, incl. Engineering. Applied Chemistry, Mining, Metallurgy, Architecture, etc.		Agriculture, incl. Forestry, Horticulture & Dairy Work	
	Men	Women	Men	Women	Men	Women	Men	Women	Men	Women
1919/20										
N	5,888	5,015	4,814	1,400	8,282	2,623	5,286	42	498	103
%	54	46	77	23	76	24	99	1	83	17
1925/26										
N	11,622	9,138	5,250	2,081	7,288	1,402	3,999	54	676	96
%	56	44	72	28	84	16	99	1	88	12
1929/30										
N	14,657	9,652	5,596	1,942	7,623	1,136	4,081	71	725	120
%	60	40	74	26	87	13	98	2	86	14
1938/39										
N	14,841	7,533	5,815	1,846	13,375	1,996	5,199	89	890	153
%	66	34	76	24	87	13	98	2	85	15

Source: Great Britain Central Statistical office, Annual Abstract of Statistics. No. 75: 1913 and 1917 – 1930, p. 45 Kraus Report Ltd. Nendeln, Liechtenstein, 1966. No. 88: 1938 – 1950, p. 104, reprinted by permission of the Controller of Her Britannic Majesty's Stationery Office, Kraus Reprint, a Division of Kraus-Thomson Organization Ltd. Nendeln, Liechtenstein, 1970.

These newcomers attracted a great deal more interest than fellow immigrants from Ireland, Europe, and the Old Commonwealth.[27]

Blacks started entering Britain in the postwar period partly because the 1948 British Nationality Act conferred British citizenship on all citizens of British colonies and Commonwealth countries. In addition, employment and material conditions in the colonies became restricted, Britain had a need for their labor, and legal entry to other countries was more difficult.[28]

In 1951, an estimated 1.6 million people who now resided in Britain had originated from outside the United Kingdom, 0.2 million of whom were from New Commonwealth countries. In 1971, the figures were, respectively, 3.0 million and 1.2 million.[29] The total British population at that point was about 55 million. By the end of the century, it is estimated that blacks will represent 6 percent of the entire British population.[30] The West Indians comprise the largest group of black immigrants, arriving largely before immigrants from the Indian subcontinent.[31] About half of the total black population in Britain was born there.

In many aspects, blacks have had a troubled relationship with British society because of racism. With regard to education, the government and the local education authorities made inadequate efforts to meet the needs of the children coming into the British schools in the postwar period or to understand their special problems, leading to a situation where black children are in a position of greater inequality educationally than white children at the same social and economic level.[32]

Blacks have been disadvantaged in regard to education in four basic areas.[33] One area is language. At first language training was provided only for Asian children. In recent years the language problems of West Indian children speaking dialects of English has been recognized and some attempts have been made to introduce patois into the schools, although it is not officially recognized as a formal language.

Secondly, there is the area of the curriculum. The fact that black children have entered schools has shown up the underrepresentation of their culture in the curriculum; moreover, when it does appear it is devalued. The implications of this are that the curriculum as it exists works to the educational disadvantage of white as well as black children and certainly contributes to the dissatisfaction of black children with the school system.

Third is the area of teachers. The majority of teachers in Britain are white. Many are ignorant of the background of their black students and have stereotypical views about how Asian and West Indian children behave in the classroom. Finally, while some research has shown that black youth perform better in school than their white counterparts and that West Indian girls do better academically than West Indian boys,[34] West Indian children are disproportionately represented in special schools. Black underachievement has led both the West Indian community and other concerned groups to call for transformation of the schools; the economic disadvantage of blacks also needs to be addressed.

In the next section we describe secondary school reform in Britain, which began just after the Second World War and attempted to do away with class and gender disadvantage in education.

The Comprehensive School Reform

The 1944 Education Act ushered in comprehensive schools. Through its law, all parts of the tertiary system of education became the responsibility of the Ministry of Education (which in 1964 became the Department of Education and Science). The Ministry's duty was to ensure that local education authorities in England and Wales "provided an efficient education . . . available to meet the needs of the population of their area."[35] The 1944 act emphasized the need to provide free secondary education for all children at age eleven. In the period after the act until the 1960s, three types of secondary schools were available for which children were selected by the so-called 11 + examination: grammar (for the academic), the "secondary modern" (for the not so academic), and "technical" schools.[36] In many ways, this system was not favorable to working-class children and girls, and it was hoped that comprehensive schools would remedy the inequalities of the three-tier secondary school system.[37]

Comprehensive schools, officially defined as schools which "take pupils without reference to ability or aptitude and provide a wide range of secondary education for all or most children of a district,"[38] developed slowly over the 1960s and 1970s. The Education Act of 1976 made comprehensives a national policy; 76 percent of English and Welsh students of secondary school age were in comprehensive schools in 1976.

Some grammar schools were retained, but secondary modern schools were phased out into the new nonselective secondary schools, which provided a broad range of subjects.[39]

"Comprehensivization" came to be viewed skeptically by a number of observers.[40] The equality of opportunity that comprehensive school reform claimed to provide proved to be something of a myth. Henry M. Levin discusses the issue in class terms, stating that although these educational reforms opened up education at the secondary level to vastly more students, inequalities still pervaded the educational system but at a higher level and in the workforce.[41] Other criticisms were also voiced about the effect of schools on gender-based differences. These criticisms are examined in the next section where the comprehensive school legislation that attempted to open up educational opportunity for women is discussed.

LEGISLATION COVERING EDUCATIONAL OPPORTUNITY

Coeducation

As a result of the comprehensive school reform, secondary schools were required to become coeducational. In 1975, 77 percent of all secondary schools maintained by the state were coeducational. Most independent schools (schools charging fees) remained single-sex. At the outset, coeducational schools were seen as benefiting girls in several ways.[42] As Madeleine Arnot notes, R. R. Dale, for instance, thought coeducation had social advantages; girls and boys could meet each other as they would in real life.[43] It was also thought that school reorganization would direct more girls to scientific and technical subjects and thus a place in the labor market. Today, however, women educators point to the detrimental effect of the coeducation system on women's education, just as they did in the early part of the twentieth century.[44] As Margaret Sutherland states,

One might expect that coeducation would reduce the differences between the sexes as they are taught by the same teachers and have access to the same facilities. . . . In fact, coeducation does not necessarily give equal opportunity or identical education. Nor does it reduce differences between the educational interests and achievements of boys and girls. In fact, girls are more likely to choose a science and boys a language in a single-sex school than they are in a mixed school. Differences in choice of subjects are, in some cases, *greater* in coeducation than in single-sex schools.[45]

Why is it that single-sex schools are less likely to force girls and boys to conform to certain subjects than coed schools? One factor is the organization of coed schools. While the variety of subject choice exists, girls may not choose science subjects either because the option was not made available or they are inhibited by their own awareness of gender difference. While coed schools have social advantages for boys, girls often find the general environment of the coed school hostile. Fascinating research has been done on how boys monopolize space physically and linguistically.[46] The school's hierarchical structure also explains how boys and girls experience school differently. Sutherland points out that many more men than women are heads of schools and in positions of authority[47] and that authority is bestowed differently on male and female leaders. Researchers have reported that girls in coed schools are more likely to believe men are the superior sex.[48]

Gender socialization in the family and at school begins early. Katherine Clarricoates's work on gender conformity in primary schools shows how it varies by class but is recognizable all the same.[49] Eileen Byrne observes that insignificant progress has been made in educating girls for leadership roles; there is a lack of women in community level politics in Britain, let alone the "top echelons of public service."[50] Complicating easy conclusions about the effects of socializing forces on girls, however, are the findings that girls (and boys) resist gender stereotyping.[51] But the very fact that girls need to resist seems to demonstrate that schools encourage competition rather than cooperation.[52] Pat Mahoney's research on the hidden curriculum of the coed classroom reveals many of the problems girls face:

Second-year girl: 'Some of them (the boys) are alright but when we're watching the video they make too much noise and we can't say anything to them. If you tell them to shut up they give you the fist and if it looks like we're interested in the programme they think we're trying to be it.'[53]

Should there be a return to single-sex schools as a way to enable girls to combat gender oppression? Madeleine Arnot raises some hard questions about this. What about the fact that boys seem to benefit from coed schools even if girls do not? Shouldn't we try to make coed schools work for girls? Also,

it is important to remember that the issue of coeducation involves the problem of selective and nonselective schools, of the private and public sector, of denominational and boarding schools; that the resources are unlikely to bring all single-sex schools up to the level of coed facilities; and that since most of the single-sex schools are private schools or were grammar schools, single-sex education is closely tied to social class divisions in education.[54]

Sexual inequality in education has been challenged both by those within the school system and those without it. "Second-wave feminism," as it has been called, began in the late 1960s.[55] Since that time, the women's movement in Great Britain has continously challenged sex discrimination in society at large and in education at all levels, in both the formal and hidden curriculum. It was in response to women's agitation and in recognition of the need to ameliorate women's position in society that a broad-sweeping law was passed in the 1970s which had the potential to affect the schooling process for girls.

Curriculum Reform

The Sex Discrimination Act of 1975 (coinciding with International Women's Year) was sponsored by a Labour government and provided legislation to deal with inequality in the areas of education and training, as well as employment. It was widely heralded, for it was believed that policy change together with practical school change would profoundly alter teaching practices and the school environment. Only five years later, however, many observers concluded that the act had failed to live up to its promise.[56]

Despite the difficulty of implementing change, debate over sex differentiation continues at the government, local, and school levels.[57] A plethora of research projects and programs emerged in the 1970s and 1980s, aimed at combatting discrimination in the schools and promoting girls' achievements. Women academics have outlined, for example, ways to make schools more "girl friendly," such as increasing opportunities for girls in science by making teachers more sensitive to issues of sexual equality, and by developing local education policy that will promote equal opportunities, as well as questioning whether a "girl-friendly" policy is good for all women.[58]

During the 1970s and 1980s, the educational disadvantages of minorities were questioned along similar lines as the underachievement of girls. It was believed that problems within the school could be remedied by "decolonizing" the curriculum, making teachers more aware of their attitudes, and again by effecting policy changes.[59]

Further attempts to achieve equalization have been quite successful. In recent years, nonformal learning experiences or "compensatory" education have increased for women.[60] "Compensatory" education comprises work with youth, work with adults, and alternative training. Such courses are usually part-time and are often scheduled in the evening or on weekends. Ranging from arts and crafts courses to remedial and technological courses, they are provided by local education authorities, residential colleges, extramural departments of universities, and voluntary organizations, or self-help initiatives.[61]

Another program which has filled an educational gap is the Open University (OU) which began in 1971. This part-time nonresidential university has no academic entrance qualifications and was established to provide degree-level education for "all those who, for any reasons, have been precluded from achieving their aim through an existing institution of higher education." [62] Large numbers of mature students, particularly women, attend. According to Moira Griffiths, from 1970 to 1977 women's applications to OU rose from 30 to 44 percent.[63] Most OU students are middle-class, and Griffiths argues that the institution is having a powerful effect on women, 38 percent of whom are housewives. As one of these women states, "It has meant that I have started to find myself as a person, and has opened up the world."[64]

We now turn to data which will illustrate the outcomes of attempts to achieve equal education at the secondary level. Positive results have been achieved in terms of enrollments and exam results; underlying these achievements, however, are some contradictions.

Outcomes in Terms of Enrollments

Since the post–World War II period, women's access to education has equaled that of men at the primary level, and it approaches equality at the secondary level. Table 13.4 examines statistics for boys' and girls' enrollment in secondary schools (for ages 14 to 18 only) for the years 1965, 1975, and 1984. For boys and girls, as a percentage of the age-group population, there is 100 percent attendance until around school-leaving age (14 until 1972, when it was raised to 16). After the school-leaving age, a declining proportion of the population age group stays on to complete the final years of school. In 1984, however, the rates of seventeen-year-old boys and seventeen-year-old girls in the second to last year of school were equal, 50 percent. The percentage of girls compared to boys staying on in school in the final year has increased since 1965, when it was 66 percent boys and 34 percent girls. Currently, 57 percent of eighteen-year-old boys are in school compared with 43 percent girls, which still represents

Table 13.4
Pupils in School, by Age and Sex, Great Britain, 1965, 1975, and 1984 (N in Thousands)

Students' Age in Years	1965	% of Population	1975	% of Population	1984	% of Population
14						
Boys						
N	395	99	452	100	457	101
%	52		51		51	
Girls						
N	378	100	430	102	435	101
%	48		49		49	
15						
Boys						
N	257	62	432	99	453	99
%	52		51		51	
Girls						
N	233	59	409	99	433	99
%	48		49		49	
16						
Boys						
N	121	27	219	50	145	31
%	54		51		49	
Girls						
N	104	25	210	50	152	34
%	46		49		51	

17						
Boys						
N	75	15	86	20	91	19
%	57		52		50	
Girls						
N	57	12	80	20	91	20
%	43		48		50	
18						
Boys						
N	29	6	31	7	16	3
%	66		57		57	
Girls						
N	15	4	23	6	12	3
%	34		43		43	

Source: Great Britain Central Statistical Office, Annual Abstract of Statistics, No. 105, p. 95 (London: Her Majesty's Stationery Office, 1968); No. 122, p. 90 (1986 Edition).

a significant difference. We can expect around 40 percent of girls to go on to higher education.

The major exams in England and Wales are the General Certificate of Education (GCE) Ordinary (''O'') level and the Certificate of Secondary Education (CSE), normally taken at age 16. After another 2 years of study the GCE Advanced (''A'') level is taken. In Scotland 16-year-old students take the Scottish Certificate of Education (SCE) Ordinary grade followed by the SCE Higher grade. Since the 1960s, girls have overtaken boys in the number of O'level and CSE (introduced in 1965) passes they achieve (Table 13.5). They are also more likely than boys to get at least one A'level. There is a marginal difference between the number of boys and girls leaving with two or more A'levels (the number required to enter university). In 1983 to 1984, 52 percent of boys received two or more A'levels compared to 48 percent of girls.

As impressive as the changes in secondary education are in terms of enrollment, they are dramatic at the tertiary level. From 1948–1949 to 1983–1984, the number of women taking courses at institutions of higher education increased more than five times (Table 13.6). In the 1980s, women represented 40 percent of all those taking ''post-school courses,'' a doubling since the 1940s when about 20 percent of all students in post-school courses were female. Starting in the 1960s, dramatic increases have occurred in courses taken by women in ''nontraditional'' subject areas: in science and technology, from 26 to 45 percent; in agriculture, from 16 to 36 percent (although it is still dominated by men). A dramatic example of this domination is the percentage of women in engineering and technology in 1983–1984: women accounted for 9 percent of all students in this area of study. In 1983–1984, as in all other academic years, more women studied arts and education than any other field. Over 50 percent of all women in higher education were in arts and education in 1984. Only in the last decade, however, have the arts become predominantly female. Table 13.7 illustrates the dominance of women over men in educational training courses since the 1960s.

A parallel development with the number of women entering university since the 1940s has been the dramatic increase in university degrees and diplomas obtained by women. The absolute number of women receiving degrees (Table 13.8) has increased eight times since 1948–1949. During the same period, the number of men receiving degrees increased only fourfold. In 1983, the proportion of women receiving diplomas was nearly on a par with the proportion of men (45 percent and 55 percent, respectively). Byrne has noted, however, that in the area of further education (post-school education outside universities often with greater emphasis on technical and vocational subjects) women predominated in lower, nonadvanced subjects.[65] In some regions (the north, for example), women's access to colleges of further education is not as easy as in other regions, because of a lack of easy transportation.

Although women make up about 40 percent of those entering higher education, only about 30 percent of them receive higher degrees. Women are not as likely as men to get a degree. In the teaching profession, at the primary and secondary

Table 13.5

Pupils Leaving School, by Sex and Highest Qualification Held, United Kingdom, 1966–1984 (N in Thousands)

		Academic Years			
	1966/67	1969/70	1974/75	1979/80	1983/84
Letters with GCE 'A' level/SCE 'H' grade passes					
2 or more 'A' 3 or more 'H'					
Boys					
N	50	52	57	64	68
%	60	56	55	54	52
Girls					
N	33	41	47	58	63
%	40	44	45	46	48
1 'A' 1 or 2 'H'					
Boys					
N	11	14	14	16	17
%	48	50	45	48	47
Girls					
N	12	14	17	17	19
%	52	50	55	52	53

Table 13.5 (continued)

		Academic Years			
	1966/67	1969/70	1974/75	1979/80	1983/84
Letters with GCE 'O' level/CSE/SCE 'O' grades alone					
5 or more A–C awards CSE grade 1					
Boys					
N	24	25	30	39	43
%	44	45	45	46	47
Girls					
N	30	31	37	45	49
%	56	55	55	54	53
1–4 A–C awards SCE grade 1					
Boys					
N	52	65	97	115	111
%	48	50	48	48	47
Girls					
N	56	64	104	127	126
%	52	50	52	52	53
No higher grades					
1 or more other grades					
Boys					
N	––	38	––	––	152
%		54			72

Girls				
N	—	—	33	—	60
%			46		28
No GCE/SCE or CSE				
Boys				
N	—	—	173	—	137
%			51		77
Girls				
N	—	—	165	—	42
%			49		23

Source: Great Britain Central Statistical Office. Annual Abstract of Statistics, 1980
Edition, ed. Ethel Lawrence. London: Her Majesty's Stationery Office, No. 116,
p. 125, and 1986 Edition, No. 122, p. 93.

Table 13.6
Courses Taken by Full-Time Students at Universities, etc., Great Britain, 1948–1984

		1948/49	1958/59	1968/69	1978/79	1983/84
Arts, incl. Theology, Fine Art, Law, Music, Commerce, Economics, Education						
Male	No.	25,028	27,909			
	%	67	65			
Female	No.	12,106	15,223			
	%	33	35			
Pure Science						
Male	No.	13,614	18,373			
	%	80	79			
Female	No.	3,303	5,029			
	%	20	21			
Medicine						
Male	No.	11,183	9,491			
	%	79	77			
Female	No.	2,964	2,897			
	%	21	23			
Dentistry						
Male	No.	2,430	2,384			
	%	89	81			
Female	No.	294	559			
	%	11	19			

		Col 1	Col 2	Col 3
Technology, incl. Engineering, Applied Chemistry, Mining, Architecture, Metallurgy				
Male	No.	10,709	14,788	
	%	98	98	
Female	No.	224	255	
	%	2	2	
Agriculture incl. Forestry, Dairy, Horticulture				
Male	No.	2,405	1,814	
	%	87	88	
Female	No.	368	24	
	%	13	12	
Veterinary Science				
Male	No.	621	1,120	
	%	92	91	
Female	No.	63	115	
	%	8	9	
Education				
Male	No.	4,197	5,713	5,274
	%	52	47	43
Female	No.	3,918	6,534	6,942
	%	48	53	57

305

Table 13.6 (continued)

		1948/49	1958/59	1968/69	1978/79	1983/84
Medicine, Dentistry, Health						
Male	No.			15,733	19,633	18,026
	%			74	62	55
Female	No.			5,477	11,954	14,885
	%			26	38	45
Engineering & Technology						
Male	No.			33,535	40,202	39,366
	%			98	94	91
Female	No.			527	2,457	3,940
	%			2	6	9
Agriculture, Forestry, Veterinary Science						
Male	No.			3,557	4,271	3,910
	%			84	70	64
Female	No.			690	1,858	2,154
	%			16	30	36
Science						
Male	No.			42,211	47,650	48,623
	%			77	72	68
Female	No.			12,420	18,973	22,464
	%			23	28	32

Social Administration and Business			
Male	No.	28,970	42,947	39,774
	%	68	62	57
Female	No.	13,412	26,295	30,503
	%	32	38	43

Architecture & Other Professional Vocational Subjects			
Male	No.	2,955	4,158	3,668
	%	81	70	64
Female	No.	698	1,777	2,068
	%	19	30	36

Language, Literature, and Area Studies			
Male	No.	11,738	12,804	11,567
	%	46	37	33
Female	No.	14,017	21,772	23,588
	%	54	63	67

Table 13.6 (continued)

	1947/49	1958/59	1968/69	1978/79	1983/84
Arts other than Language, Music, Drama, Visual Arts					
Male No.			9,900	13,280	11,475
%			57	49	48
Female No.			7,339	13,645	12,366
%			43	51	52
TOTAL					
Male No.	65,990	76,179	152,796	190,658	181,683
%	77	76	72	49	60
Female No.	19,322	24,325	58,498	196,885	118,910
%	23	24	28	51	40

Source: Great Britain Central Statistical Office. Annual Abstract of Statistics. No. 97, p. 101 (Kraus Reprint, 1970) and No. 108, p. 120 (Her Majesty's Stationery Office, 1971) and No. 122, p. 103 (London: Her Majesty's Stationery Office, 1986).

Table 13.7

Training of Teachers: Students Successfully Completing Courses of Initial Training, Great Britain, 1959–1975

Graduates		Academic Year		
One-year Courses	1959/60	1964/65	1969/70	1974/75
In University Departments of Education				
Male				
N	1,868	1,837	2,204	2,117
%	60	52	48	47
Female				
N	1,231	1,722	2,372	2,405
%	40	48	52	53
In Colleges of Education				
Male				
N	547	809	1,417	2,785
%	48	49	43	43
Female				
N	592	835	1,883	3,711
%	52	51	57	57

Table 13.7 (continued)

	Academic Year				
	1959/60	1964/65	1969/70	1974/75
Non-Graduates				
One-year general courses				
Male				
N	145	99	103	195
%	57	66	43	41
Female				
N	110	51	135	285
%	43	34	57	59
One-year specialist course				
Male				
N	737	1,422	1,345	1,565
%	60	63	49	52
Female				
N	493	841	1,395	1,461
%	40	37	51	48
Two-year courses				
Male				
N	3,211	354	555	232
%	27	42	31	33
Female				
N	8,603	499	1,250	471
%	73	58	69	67

Three-year courses

Male				
N	169	4,132	6,721	6,097
%	6	25	24	23
Female				
N	2,379	12,629	21,857	20,735
%	94	75	76	77

Four-year Courses

Male				
N	169	163	210	1,947
%	62	53	41	36
Female				
N	104	145	308	3,452
%	38	47	59	64

Source: Great Britain Central Statistical Office. Annual Abstract of Statistics. No. 108, p. 114 (London: Her Majesty's Stationery Office 1971) and No. 114, p. 139 (London: Her Majesty's Stationery Office 1977).

Table 13.8
University Degrees and Diplomas Obtained, United Kingdom, 1948–1984 (excluding Open University)

Academic Year	Total Degrees	1st Degree Honors	1st Degree Ordinary	Higher Degrees	Diplomas
1948/49					
Male					
N	14,626	8,363	5,476	2,000	4,903
%	77	79	76	88	69
Female					
N	4,364	2,282	1,700	266	2,242
%	23	21	24	12	31
1958/59					
Male					
N	17,402	9,920	4,693	2,789	5,465
%	76	74	73	58	70
Female					
N	5,528	3,459	1,770	299	2,345
%	24	26	27	42	30
1968/69					
Male					
N	41,592	25,101	7,264	9,227	8,647
%	73	70	69	89	64
Female					
N	15,064	10,529	3,348	1,187	4,798
%	27	30	31	11	36

1978					
Male					
N	55,307	33,095	7,631	14,581	7,238
%	67	64	66	79	58
Female					
N	26,822	19,004	3,927	3,891	5,290
%	33	36	34	21	42
1984					
Male					
N	59,564	36,940	7,031	15,593	6,613
%	62	59	62	72	54
Female					
N	35,806	25,577	4,293	5,936	5,587
%	38	41	38	28	46

Source: Great Britain Central Statistical Office. Annual Abstract of Statistics, No. 88: 1938-1950, p. 104 (Kraus Reprint, Nendeln, Liechtenstein, 1970); No. 108, p. 120 (London: Her Majesty's Stationery Office, 1971); No. 117, p. 142 (London: Her Majesty's Stationery Office, 1981); No. 123, p. 103 (London: Her Majesty's Stationery Office, 1987).

levels, a smaller proportion of women are graduates than men. While an equal proportion of women and men teaching at universities are graduates, only a very small number of women are hired as full-time staff at universities and higher education institutions. In 1983–1984 women were 10 percent of lecturers in the United Kingdom.

When we examine enrollments of the black population, using survey data collected by the Policy Studies Institute (PSI) on the age of completion of full-time education,[66] we find that half of all white men and women left school before age sixteen, compared to one-third of West Indian men and women. Broadly speaking, figures are the same for West Indians who left school aged seventeen and over, although it increases for whites. With regard to the Asian community, they are less likely to leave school than the whites and West Indians are.

In terms of qualifications, PSI notes that both ethnic and gender variation is noticeable. Although Asian men are generally as qualified academically (with GCE passes or degrees) as whites, they are not as qualified vocationally (i.e., practically skilled); West Indian men are less qualified than whites both vocationally and academically. West Indian and Asian women are less qualified academically than white women. However, although among the younger age groups surveyed (sixteen to twenty-four), fewer Asians have A' levels than whites, and the qualifications of West Indian women tend to be lower (O'level or CSE's), Asian women and black women are more likely to remain in full-time education beyond the school-leaving age of sixteen than whites. Black women are also more likely to study on a part-time basis compared with their Asian and white counterparts. Such data suggests that so-called black under-achievement must be analyzed carefully.

Education and Work

The economic situation of the 1980s means that most women can expect to work, if a job can be found. The kind of education men and women get, however, and where it will lead differ for a variety of reasons.

Educative processes, career advice, family life, and the separate spheres of school partly explain why male and female students have different expectations of the kind of work they will do after completing school. Groups of fifth-form girls interviewed from the north in the 1970s firmly declared that they accepted work as a normal pattern, but it was "female" work for the most part.[67] In industrial Birmingham, the transition of working-class girls from school to work is similar. The girls want work but tend to divide it into female and male jobs. Female jobs are shop work, hairdressing, office work, and factory work, whereas male jobs include engineering, for example. Race and ethnicity also affect the decisions a girl makes about education and training. Black girls are made twice subordinate by virtue of their race and gender, but Mary Fuller's study shows that West Indian girls use their exclusion in a positive way in one London comprehensive school.[68] They have a strong identity as black females and are determined to succeed because of their environment. Other researchers have suggested that the so-called overaspiration of Asian students is not a cultural norm but rather a response to the educational and occupation system.[69]

What girls do after school is closely tied to the kind of training they have, economic and demographic factors changing women's workforce participation, discrimination of employers, and women's dual role as worker and mother. In terms of training, girls are most likely to choose "soft" subjects, women are less likely to take day release courses and receive in-service training. On government training courses such as the Youth Training Scheme (YTS) started in 1983 women dominate in traditional female areas. The kind of training women get exacerbates rather than improves their position in the labor force. Although women's position in the labor market has changed over the twentieth century, women's eventual employment position remains similar.

The female labor force, 19 percent in 1900, now stands at 41 percent of the total economically active population.[70] The composition of the female labor force has also changed during this period of time. In the 1900s, most women in the workforce were single, and 75 percent were under 35 years of age. In the 1980s female employment rose at all age levels. Forty-five percent of working women are under 45, and 60 percent are married and likely to be in part-time employment.[71] Changes in women's participation in the workforce are due not only to demographic factors but also to economic growth and the demand for a more qualified workforce.

As a result of the economic boom of the 1960s, vast changes occurred in the distribution of industries (Table 13.9), which have affected the kinds of opportunities open to women. In 1951, the number of women in the industry and service sector was constant. By 1971, the productive sector had fallen, while the service sector had risen. (It remains a source of employment to the present day.) The number of females in the commercial and financial sector also increased to almost 40 percent of total female employment in 1971. At the turn of the century, women's involvement in agriculture was very low, about 2 percent of total female employment. This figure remained more or less stable over the century.[72]

In terms of an occupational shift, however, little has changed during the second half of the century. Women are still to be found in typically female jobs. From 1951 to 1961, clerical and personal service work (such as catering, cleaning, and hairdressing) accounted for the majority of female employment in Britain. As employers, managers, and administrators, only a marginal change has taken place in their significance as a source of employment for women. The professional class has grown, but only minimally; it can also be divided into lower and higher levels. More women are represented in the lower professional levels as nurses and teachers. Blacks tend to be concentrated in unskilled and semiskilled jobs, and today the unemployment rate among black young people is disproportionately

Table 13.9

Economically Active Population, by Major Industrial Groups, Great Britain, 1901–1971

	1901	1911	1921	1931	1951	1961	1971
Agriculture, Forestry, Fishing							
Male	1,390	1,489	1,261	1,181	1,025	777	643
Female	86	117	111	76	117	97	97
Extractive Industry							
Male	931	1,202	1,396	1,272	847	728	256
Female	6	8	14	9	14	21	5
Manufacturing							
Male	4,062	4,688	4,813	4,958	6,153	6,308	6,121
Female	2,123	2,430	2,187	2,355	2,654	2,666	1,505
Construction							
Male	1,216	1,140	783	1,108	1,390	1,597	1,476
Female	3	5	12	14	41	69	182
Commerce							
Male	597	739	1,702	2,314	1,838	2,066	2,391
Female	76	157	863	1,021	1,322	1,773	3,561
Transport, Communication							
Male	1,409	1,571	1,461	1,563	1,517	1,486	1,811
Female	27	38	109	110	217	230	453
Services							
Male	1,056	1,361	1,897	2,267	2,806	3,136	2,910
Female	2,358	2,560	2,331	2,644	2,560	2,861	3,128
Others							
Male	887	741	344	137	173	135	276
Female	75	98	75	44	36	64	375

Source: European Historical Statistics, 1750–1975, 2nd Rev. Ed. 1981, B. R. Mitchell, London: MacMillan Press Ltd. p. 171.

high. Fewer black females work part-time than white females; they therefore
tend to earn more although pay rates are lower.[73] Discriminatory employment
practices continue to undermine women's participation in the workforce.

Women's Position in the Workforce

The state has played a role in providing equal educational opportunity for
women. In the 1960s, the government began to realize that it needed to improve
both the attitude and behavior of industry in recognition of the growing number
of women in the workforce.

The Sex Discrimination Act of 1975, briefly discussed above in relation to
education, prohibits both direct and indirect discrimination against men and
women. The law focuses on employers and stipulates that no employer can refuse
to hire a person because of sex. The law may not be significant in practice since
it is open to interpretation and provisions for enforcing it are not very effective.[74]

The Equal Pay Act of 1970 deals with discrimination in the area of wages on
three levels: (1) women should be paid the same salary as men who do similar
work, (2) women should have equal employment conditions, and (3) equal pay
for women must not be affected by maternity leave. This act has also proven to
be disappointing. For one thing, discrimination by employers continues. Second,
when we look at the overall earnings of men and women, we see that the
"average" pay of a woman is always below that of a man. The hourly wage
for women in Britain in 1982 was 74.8 percent of men's earnings.[75]

One other issue should be mentioned regarding the state's attempt to aid women
in their working lives: daycare. Current forms of provision include day nurseries,
nursery schools, play groups, and childminders.[76] But the state is reluctant to
go beyond a limited provision of daycare. Daycare is provided only for those
in extreme cases who need it. The ordinary working woman, therefore, is at a
disadvantage in this area. Since black women are more likely to work than white
women, their children are more likely to be cared for by others, and they often
receive early child care in unsatisfactory conditions. The state has not attempted
to remove the role of caring from the mother, for it is still assumed that a
woman's work is mothering.[77] There may exist a surface equality between husband and wife, but not in women's "enduring role as housewives and as the
main rearers of children."[78]

CHANGES FOR THE FUTURE

The 1980s are Margaret Thatcher's era, a period when conservative ideology
has once again reared its head. Educational "reform" has taken place, with a
national curriculum proposed, the exam system reorganized, and tenure likely
to be abolished.[79] We do not yet know how these changes will affect the education
of women, but thus far they present little cause for optimism. Generally, the
times are not favorable to women in Britain. Unemployment is high, and, as

Rosemary Deem states, "The welfare provisions and expenditure on social policies are being cut back at the same time as the central importance of women's domestic and child caring role in the family is being re-emphasized."[80] Under such a state of affairs, without much hope for further policy measure that will remove some of the biases against women, the future for women in Britain is uncertain.

Women must therefore help themselves and find their own keys to equality in education and in society. As Nawal el Saadawi notes, women must develop political awareness and show their ability to fight.[81] Ten years ago, an American observer was critical of the weight of tradition in Britain, which she contended did not support political change.[82] Today, contemporary onlookers[83] see the woman's movement as representing many more groups of women than it did at that period—black women, for instance. It is involved in the most critical issues of our time, and, most important, it shows a strong affiliation with the government opposition parties, which, though in disarray, provide some hope of consolidating power and bringing change.

NOTES

1. *Britain 1983: An Official Handbook* (London: Her Majesty's Stationery Office, 1983), pp. 145–160. Great Britain comprises England, Wales, and Scotland. The Department of Education and Science (DES) holds responsibility for education in England and university support in England, Wales, and Scotland. The departments of education in Wales and Scotland supervise all educational institutions outside universities in those countries. Education in Great Britain is decentralized and locally provided by education authorities in England and Wales and councils in Scotland.

2. See G. M. Trevelyan, *English Social History: A Survey of Six Centuries, Chaucer to Queen Victoria* (Middlesex, England: Pelican, 1964), pp. 499–503.

3. Joan N. Burstyn, *Victorian Education and the Ideal of Womanhood* (Totowa, N.J.: Barnes & Noble Books, 1980), Chapter 2.

4. Susan Raven and Alison Weir, eds., *Women in History: Thirty-Five Centuries of Feminine Achievement* (London: Weidenfeld & Nicolson, 1981), pp. 65, 68. Emily Davies "pioneered" women's higher education. She was the first principal of Girton College, Cambridge, one of the first women's colleges in Britain, founded in 1873. Other well-known educators of the period were Frances Buss and Dorothy Beale, headmistresses of secondary schools for girls.

5. Burstyn, *Victorian Education*, Chapter 8. Religious arguments against higher education for girls were basically that women were not ordained by God to speak in public. The arguments of the scientific professions was that education would endanger the health of women.

6. Joyce Senders Pedersen, "The Reform of Women's Secondary and Higher Education: Institutional Change and Social Values in Mid and Late Victorian England," *History of Education Quarterly* (Spring 1979): 61–87, 72, 73.

7. Burstyn, *Victorian Education*.

8. Pedersen, "The Reform of Women's Secondary and Higher Education," p. 73.

9. Margaret Bryant, *The Unexpected Revolution: A Study in the History of the Ed-*

ucation of Women and Girls in the Nineteenth Century (London: University of London, Institute of Education, 1979), p. 94.

10. Trevelyan, *English Social History,* p. 594.

11. Carol Dyhouse, "Towards a 'Feminine' Curriculum for English Schoolgirls: The Demands of Ideology, 1870–1963," *Women's Studies International Quarterly* 1 (1978): 297–309, 300.

12. Bryant, *The Unexpected Revolution,* p. 121.

13. Ibid., p. 114. Bryant suggests that not only old attitudes hindered the women's movement, but also new ones, for example, the impact of scientific and technical advances.

14. Felicity Hunt, "Divided Aims: The Schooling of Girls and Women, 1850–1950," in Felicity Hunt, ed., *Lessons for Life,* (Oxford: Basil Blackwell Ltd., 1987), pp. 9–11. According to the eugenics movement of the late 1890s, woman's proper function was to be a mother, and training should prepare her for this role.

15. Ibid., p. 20.

16. Ibid., pp. 12–13.

17. Ibid., pp. 16–20.

18. Ibid., p. 18.

19. *European Historical Statistics, 1750–1975,* 2nd Revision, ed. B. R. Mitchell (London: Macmillan Press Ltd., 1981).

20. Dyhouse, "Towards a 'Feminine' Curriculum"; Trevor Lloyd, *Suffragettes International: The World-wide Campaign for Women's Rights* (New York: American Heritage Press, 1971); Gladys Cudderford, *Women and Society: From Victorian Times to the Present Day* (London: Hamish Hamilton, 1967).

21. *European Historical Statistics.*

22. Joan Beauchamp, *Women Who Work* (London: Lawrence & Wishart, 1937).

23. Bryant, *The Unexpected Revolution,* p. 107. In 1919, 224 of 1,080 secondary schools were coeducational.

24. Carol Dyhouse, "Miss Buss and Miss Beale: Gender and Authority in the History of Education," in Hunt, ed., *Lessons for Life,* p. 37.

25. Alison Opram, "Inequalities in the Teaching Profession: The Effect on Teachers and Pupils, 1910–1939," in Hunt, ed., *Lessons for Life.*

26. Hunt, ed., *Lessons for Life,* p. xvii.

27. *Britain's Black Population: The Runnymede Trust and the Radical Statistics Race Group* (London: Heinemann Educational Books, 1980); Gajendra Verman and Brandon Ashworth, "Educational and Occupational Aspirations of Young South Asians in Britain," in Megarry Jaquetta et al., eds., *World Yearbook of Education, 1981, Education of Minorities* (London: Kogan Page, 1981). New Commonwealth countries are Bangladesh, India, Pakistan, and countries in Africa, the Caribbean, and Southeast Asia. The term "black" has been used in Britain to describe people from all these areas. Old Commonwealth countries are Australia, Canada, and New Zealand.

28. *Britain's Black Population.*

29. Ibid.

30. Ibid.

31. Ibid. Black immigration reached a peak in the 1960s; immigration has been steadily cut as a result of the harsh immigration acts of 1962, 1968, and 1971. While those first entering the United Kingdom were primarily male, since the late 1960s this has changed.

32. Ibid, pp. 92–107.

33. Ibid.

34. G. Driver, cited in *Britain's Black Population*, p. 107; Richard Jenkins, "Intervening against 'Racial' Disadvantage: Educational Policy and Labor-Market Outcomes in the United Kingdom," *Comparative Education Review* 32 (February 1988): 1–19.

35. Edmund J. King, *Other Schools and Ours: Comparative Studies for Today*, 5th ed. (London: Holt, Rinehart & Winston, 1979).

36. Ibid.

37. Rosemary Deem, "State Policy and Ideology in the Education of Women, 1944–1980," *British Journal of Sociology of Education* 2, No. 2 (1981).

38. *Britain 1983*, p. 148.

39. King, *Other Schools and Ours*.

40. Henry M. Levin, "The Dilemma of Comprehensive Secondary School Reforms in Western Europe," in Philip Altbach et al., eds., *Comparative Education* (New York: Macmillan Publishing Co., 1982); Deem, "State Policy and Ideology."

41. Levin, "The Dilemma of Comprehensive Secondary School Reforms." Levin argues that capitalism cannot accommodate large numbers of trained members of society.

42. Eileen Byrne, *Women and Education* (London: Tavistock Publication Ltd., 1978), p. 134.

43. Madeleine Arnot, "State Educational Policy and Girls' Educational Experience," in Veronica Beechey and Elizabeth Whitelegg, eds., *Women in Britain Today* (Philadelphia: Open University Press, 1986). R. R. Dale wrote several books in the 1970s on coed and single-sex schools.

44. Byrne, *Women and Education;* Pat Mahoney, *Schools for the Boys? Coeducation Reassessed* (London: Hutchinson, 1985).

45. Margaret B. Sutherland, *Sex Bias in Education* (Oxford: Basil Blackwell, 1981).

46. Mahoney, *Schools for the Boys?*

47. Sutherland, *Sex Bias in Education*.

48. Ibid.

49. Katherine Clarricoates, "The Importance of Being Ernest . . . Emma . . . Tom . . . Jane: The Perception and Categorization of Gender Conformity and Gender Deviation in Primary Schools," in Rosemary Deem, ed., *Schooling for Women's Work* (London: Routledge & Kegan Paul, 1980) pp. 26–41.

50. Byrne, *Women and Education*, p. 171. See also Melville Currell, *Political Women* (London: Croom Helm, 1974).

51. Lynn Davies, "Gender, Resistance, and Power," in Stephen Walker and Len Barton, eds., *Gender, Class, and Education* (London: Falmer Press, 1983), pp. 39–52.

52. Lynn Davies, "Gender and Comprehensive Schooling," in Stephen J. Ball, ed., *Comprehensive Schooling: A Reader* (London: Falmer Press, 1984), pp. 47–65.

53. Mahoney, *Schools for the Boys?*, p. 40.

54. Arnot, "State Educational Policy," p. 164.

55. Vicki Randall, *Women and Politics: An International Perspective*, 2nd ed. (London: Macmillan Education Ltd., 1987).

56. Deem, "State Policy and Ideology"; Lynda Carr, "Legislation and Mediation: To What Extent Has the Sex Discrimination Act Changed Girls' Schooling?," in J. Whyte et al., eds., *Girl Friendly Schooling* (London: Methuen, 1985).

57. Patrick Orr, "Sex Bias in Schools: National Perspectives," in Whyte et al., eds., *Girl Friendly Schooling*.

58. Whyte et al., eds., *Girl Friendly Schooling*.

59. *Education of Minorities;* Amon S. Saakana and Adetokunbo Pearse, eds., *Towards the Decolonization of the British Education System* (London: Frontline Journal/Karnak House, 1986).

60. Pam Flynn et al., *You're Learning All the Time* (Nottingham: Spokesman, 1986). Flynn et al. describe three representative courses, one provided by the Southampton Women's Education Center offering a free second chance education to working-class women; the Leeds High Technology Training Centre providing courses in micro electronics and computing; and a Scottish community-based adult education project providing a "feminized educative process."

61. *Britain 1983.*

62. Moira Griffiths, "Women in Higher Education: A Case Study of the Open University," in Deem, ed., *Schooling for Women's Work,* p. 131. Quote from Report of the Planning Committee to the Secretary of State for Education and Science, 1969.

63. Ibid., p. 132.

64. Ibid., p. 141.

65. Byrne, *Women and Education.*

66. Colin Brown, *Black and White Britain: The Third PSI Survey, The Policy Studies Institute* (London: Heinemann, 1984), pp. 137–149.

67. Christine Griffin, *Typical Girls: Young Women from School to the Job Market* (London: Routledge & Kegan Paul, 1985).

68. Mary Fuller, "Black Girls in a London Comprehensive School," in Deem, ed., *Schooling for Women's Work,* pp. 52–65.

69. Verma and Ashworth, "Educational and Occupational Aspirations."

70. A. T. Mallier and M. J. Rosser, *Women and the Economy: A Comparative Study of Britain and the USA* (London: Macmillan Press Ltd., 1987); George Joseph, *Women at Work: The British Experience* (Oxford: Philip Allan, 1983).

71. Ibid.

72. *Abstract of British Historical Statistics,* B. R. Mitchell with Phyllis Deane (Cambridge: Cambridge University Press, 1962).

73. *Britain's Black Population,* p. 63; Mallier and Rosser, *Women and the Economy.*

74. Mary Ruggie, *The State and Working Women: A Comparative Study of Britain and Sweden* (Princeton, N.J.: Princeton University Press, 1984).

75. Mallier and Rosser, *Women and the Economy,* p. 118; Ruggie, *The State and Working Women.* In 1982, the European Court of Justice charged that Britain's definition of equal work was not broad enough and overturned the Equal Pay Act.

76. Ruggie, *The State and Working Women.*

77. Miriam David, "Women, Family, and Education," in S. Acker et al., eds., *World Yearbook of Education, 1984. Women and Education* (New York: Kogan Page, 1984), pp. 191–202.

78. Ann Oakley, *The Sociology of Housework* (Oxford: Martin Robertson, 1974), p. 165.

79. The Education Reform Act of 1988 applies to England and Wales and includes the Scottish universities. Some of its parts are a national curriculum and "opting out" : schools may leave the control of the local education authorities and become schools funded directly by the government.

80. Deem, "State Policy and Ideology," p. 141.

81. Nawal el Saadawi, "Women and Politics: United Kingdom," in *Women: A World Report* (New York: Oxford University Press, 1985).

82. Ruth Ross, "Tradition and the Role of Women in Great Britain," in Lynne B. Iglitzin and Ruth Ross, eds., *Women in the World: A Comparative Study* (Santa Barbara, Calif.: ABC-Clio Press, 1986), pp. 163, 174.

83. Randall, *Women and Politics;* Nawal el Saadawi, "Women and Politics."

14
POLAND

Renata Siemienska

This chapter analyzes women's education in Poland in relation to that country's political and social upheavals. It focuses on how changes in the political and economic system have affected attitudes toward women's roles and the kind of education women have received.

PRE-PARTITION POLAND

In medieval Poland most women were uneducated, although there were a few exceptions.[1] One example was Poland's only queen, Jadwiga Angevine, who ruled at the end of the fourteenth century and was well educated for those times. It was she who arrested the decline of the university, which had been created in Cracow in 1364. Over the next centuries the nobility, as well as the wealthy urban dwellers, educated their daughters, even though it is difficult to establish the level and scope of this education. In the sixteenth century the Reformation reached Poland, and the ability to read became necessary for religious purposes. At this time, girls from devoted nobility families were increasingly sent to elementary schools. In the seventeenth century, various monastic orders began to organize boarding schools, in which girls from both the nobility and rich urban families received an education which at the time was considered proper for women from these classes. The girls were taught reading and writing, home economics, music, and catechism, as well as French.

In the eighteenth century, the situation did not change much with regard to access to education of members of different social groups. The knowledge taught did widen, however. French cultural influences became very strong, with the Polish nobility versing their sons and sometimes their daughters in the French language and literature as well as emergent social trends. Girls in boarding schools were introduced to those aspects of French culture which narrowly defined women's roles. In the eighteenth century, Polish reformers like Adam Kazimierz Czartoryski and Grzegorz Piramowicz urged the country to introduce French-style reforms. At the time, the number of girls from the bourgeoisie and poor nobility increased slightly in parish schools.

THE PERIOD OF PARTITION (1772–1918)

From the close of the eighteenth century to the end of World War I, Poland was divided into three parts governed by Austria, Russia, and Prussia. The partition profoundly affected Poland's social structure. Specifically, the middle class arose more slowly than in the rest of Europe, and urbanization and industrialization proceeded at a snail's pace. The weak bourgeoisie was incapable of either imposing its system of values or creating an industrial labor market. The landed gentry retained its cultural, social, and economic influences for a longer period of time than in Western Europe, despite the economic and political difficulties which most of the nobility faced. Most of Polish society consisted of farming peasants. Permanent or periodical emigration abroad at the end of the nineteenth and beginning of the twentieth centuries became a mechanism whereby the peasantry finally achieved tolerable living conditions.

In the second half of the nineteenth century, the landed gentry experienced increasing bankruptcy. Many migrated to the cities and became the bases for the newly emergent intelligentsia. The intelligentsia, as in the rest of Central Europe, over time incorporated persons from outside nobility. Nonetheless, the intelligentsia retained the nobility's cultural models and system of values.[2] Even though its economic bases differed from those of the nobility, the intelligentsia's aspirations were close to those of the landed gentry. The vast gulf between those performing white-collar and professional work—worthy of the higher classes—and manual labor—carried out by peasants and workers—sharply divided Polish society.

The need for popular education, including women's education, became more pressing in the nineteenth century. This gave rise to debates as to what girls should be taught. Should woman deepen the knowledge needed only in performing their traditional roles, or should they be given a general education that would prepare them for professional work? Klementyna (Tanska) Hoffman, for example, advocated general education for women. In her popular book, *Remembrance of a Good Mother for the Young Pole* [Pamiatka po dobrej matce dla mlodej Polki], Hoffman stressed the need to widen women's education to include Polish literature and history as well as national customs and habits. She argued that women so educated could help keep national traditions and national awareness alive in a country deprived of its freedom. Women's role was defined as participating in the political socialization of the new generation to Polish national culture. Although people like Hoffman advocated women's education, they also stressed that girls should not be taught the same things as boys, since an equal education would threaten femininity. Despite these ideas, there was little agreement in Poland about the nature of education appropriate to women. Some argued that denying women the right to an education according to their abilities only for the reason that it might be considered "masculine" was unfair.

Nonetheless, the idea that women's education be distinct from men's remained dominant. The number of schools and boarding schools for girls expanded. In 1828, there were twenty-eight schools for girls in Warsaw, of which fifteen taught more than an elementary education.[3] The Warsaw Institute of Governesses, created in 1825 to train teachers, was the first school that prepared women for professional work. This school was modeled after similar institutes of learning in Russia and was meant for girls from the nobility. In the Russian-controlled part of Poland (the Polish Kingdom) in the 1850s, the Russian tsar called for the creation of government schools for women with the learning program similar to the one in schools for boys. These schools provided a shorter course of study, however, and women were not allowed to sit for final exams. In 1861, in the whole Polish kingdom ruled by Russia there were 7 state secondary schools with 1,400 female pupils, 45 elementary schools for girls, and 984 schools in which boys and girls studied in separate classes. Private schools also existed. They were chronically short of qualified teachers and were beset by regulations imposed by the Russian partition of Poland.

The debates about the future direction of women's education, which began in the 1820s, gained momentum thirty years later, especially after 1863 when a Polish uprising aimed at regaining independence failed. The economic situation of the nobility worsened as those who actively took part in the uprising lost their estates. The future of girls from noble families became even more uncertain than boys. Industry developed slowly. Nonetheless, urban migration accelerated, and the city became a place in which both women of noble families deprived of financial support, as well as girls from peasant families, whose small farms were unable to feed everyone, congregated. Contemporary discussions on the topic of women's education clearly differed from those at the beginning of the century. Emphasis was increasingly placed on supplying women with the kind of education that would give them qualifications to undertake professional work. Such views were articulated by, among others, Eleonora Ziemiecka in her monthly *The Pilgrim,* Julia Molinska-Woykowska working with the *Literary Weekly* in Poznan (later co-edited with her husband), as well as by Narcyza Zmichowska.

The movement to raise the educational level of women coincided with the development of positivism as a social and literary trend proclaiming the principle of organic work, "work at the roots" which accompanied it. Distinguished writers of the mid-nineteenth century pointed pointed to the urgent need for Poland's economic and social development which was hindered by the partitioners. Education was thought to contribute to this goal. Without Poland's own national institutions, the task of national development fell as a moral obligation on members of the upper classes. The idea of raising the educational level of the masses by extending all forms of education to as wide social groups as possible was conducive to providing more education to women. Polish nationalism was not the only impetus to extending women's education. Poles were also influenced by Western European struggles for women's rights.

In the nineteenth century, the part of Poland ruled by Russia was the major arena for the struggle for women's right to education on an equal footing with men.[4] In Prussian-ruled Poland, the struggle for women's education flared up particularly in the years 1840 to 1850, and again in the 1880s and 1890s. However, the leaders of the struggle moved relatively quickly to the part of Poland ruled by Russia. In Galicia, ruled by Austria, the debate on women's education became particularly heated in the 1870s and 1880s. Practical steps aimed at providing girls schooling were initiated by women who had arrived from the part of Poland Russians ruled. The reasons why women from the Russian-ruled part of Poland spearheaded the struggle for equal rights with men in the field of education have been explained as being the result of the breakdown, including economic, of the landed gentry and its subsequent urbanization, professionalization, and intellectualization. This process was most advanced in the Russian-ruled part of Poland where the "outline of the new capitalist society was most clearly seen to emerge in the 19th century."[5] In the Prussian-and Austrian-ruled parts of the country, the economic collapse of the landed gentry was much more gradual. The women from the landed gentry who suddenly found themselves in towns with no hope of going back later developed the Polish women's movement.

Before the 1890s, Polish women who wanted to enter a university went abroad to Switzerland, France, Belgium, or the United States, in many cases, sponsored by Polish women's organizations. First, Polish women graduates took their degrees from foreign universities. Twenty-five years later, Galician universities admitted numbers of female students, drawn from all other parts of Poland. This happened because in the second half of the 1890s, the Ministry of Education in Vienna allowed women to study at the philosophical and medical faculties in the Jagellonian and Lvov universities. At the time, philosophical faculties also encompassed physics and mathematics, traditionally believed to be masculine fields of study.

Studies abroad were basically accessible to youth from more affluent families, though women's organizations did arrange small scholarships for girls from poorer families. Their recollections and memoirs demonstrate the conditions under which they studied and the many sacrifices they had to make in order to complete their degrees. Most of these women were not motivated by hopes of becoming rich after finishing their education. Most considered education a value in itself. Some women treated their education as a social obligation that would allow them to actively participate in the work of various organizations aimed at raising the educational level of the country, the living standards of the masses, as well as furthering educational and professional opportunities for women.

During 1878–1918 about 200 women were educated in Russia in Petersburg in the special school for women (Higher Courses for Females). Some Polish women who graduated from universities at the turn of the twentieth century became exceptional scientists. Among them were Maria Sklodowska-Curie who received a Nobel Prize first in 1905 on her own and in 1911 with her husband, Jozefa Joteyko, who lectured in experimental psychology in Brussels and also in the Sorbonne in Paris; and Zofia Daszynska-Golinska who worked at the Humbolt Academy in Berlin. The list is much longer. Many of them participated in the creation and reconstruction of Polish institutes of higher learning when Poland became independent in 1918. Some of them were also active in various women's organizations. They won the right for women to enter universities largely with the support of a major part of the Polish intellectual elite.

State and private elementary and secondary schools, and foreign colleges and universities in the Austrian-ruled part of Poland constituted only part of the opportunities available to Polish youth to get an education. Underground schools which served youth from a range of social classes, sought to give the young generation knowledge of Polish history and literature, and generally to foster Polish national identity. Women also organized their own institutions of underground learning which they also used to raise women's consciousness of their social situation. Women's Circles of Popular Education in the Polish Kingdom were created in 1883, and beginning in 1894 underground courses led by Cecylia Sniegocka were conducted in all the Warsaw districts and in other towns. These schools used texts created especially for them. In 1886, Zofia Szczawinska established the so-called Flying University in Warsaw. This was an underground institution at which outstanding scholars lectured. Although the Flying University did not hand out any diplomas, it played a large role in the formation of Polish intellectual and scientific life. After 1905, in the short-lived period of liberalization in the tsarist policies, this university went above ground under the name of Higher Scientific Courses.

Underground learning was directed at both boys and girls. Conspirational teaching was to a large extent carried out by women. Nonetheless, the number of illiterates in Poland at the close of the nineteenth century was still high. According to the population census from 1897, illiteracy reached 75 percent in the countryside and 50 percent in the cities under Russian rule. In Galicia, ruled by Austria, the situation was similar. In 1880, the illiterates constituted about 77 percent of the population and in 1900 about 58 percent.[6]

In summary, the 150-year period of partitions was a period of struggle for a national education system. The Austrian authorities were more liberal in this respect than the Prussians and the Russians. Despite the fact that at the close of the nineteenth century women gained the right to study at universities, the education of girls was still a rarity. The number of women studying at universities was clearly smaller than men. There was also inequality in male and female secondary school attendance.[7]

INDEPENDENT POLAND (1918–1939)

After Poland achieved independence in 1918, women gained the right to vote and formal political and social equality with men. Nevertheless, women did not have the same educational or professional opportunities as men, nor was their participation in political life at a level similar to that of men.

The creation of an independent state after such a long period of partition placed a number of burdens on the new government in political, economic, and social life. The government focused on, among other things, creating a uniform educational system, upgrading teacher qualifications, and rapidly expanding education at all levels. The government inherited debts from the period of the partitions. At the time Poland regained independence, the worst situation presented itself in the old Russian partition. Poland was an economically backward country, with a low level of urbanization. In 1900, urban dwellers constituted 17.7 percent of the total population, in 1921, 24.6 percent, and in 1931, 27.2 percent. A significant part of the population could neither read nor write. In 1931, the percentage of illiterates reached 23.1 percent of all citizens, and it was higher among women (27.9 percent) than men (17.8 percent). The number of illiterates was more than double the rate in the countryside than in the cities, and it was much higher among women than men: in the cities it was 12.2 percent among men 8.9 percent and women 15 percent; in the countryside it was 27.6 percent, among men 21.3 percent and women 33.4 percent.

There were also large differences between provinces. The lowest percentage of illiterates was found in the western provinces of Silesia, Pznanian, and Pomerania, where it did not exceed several percent. It was highest in eastern provinces: in Polenian and Wolynian it reached almost 50 percent, and in Nowogrodzki and Stanislawowski—over 30 percent (the then capital of the Stanislawowski province—Stanislawow—is at present called Ivan Frankowskij because after World War II the eastern provinces were included in the Soviet Union). In the first two previously mentioned provinces, the percentage of women who could not read or write reached almost three-quarters of all the women in the countryside, and in the two following provinces, 50 percent. In the cities of these provinces, about one-fifth of the women were illiterate.[8]

The problems of education were complicated by the fact that in the interwar period Poland was a multiethnic and multinational state. A sizable proportion of the population spoke languages other than Polish. This factor, as well as the differences in religious beliefs, meant that a number of youth attended schools which only the members of their own ethnic group attended. In the 1938–1939 school year, 86 percent of children attending elementary schools were in Polish-language schools and 11.2 percent attended schools that offered education in Polish and other languages (Ukrainian, Byelorussian, German, Yiddish, Hebrew,

Lithuanian, Czech, Russian). An additional 2.8 percent went to schools where all classes were conducted in a language other than Polish.[9]

The new educational system created after independence met with a series of other difficulties. Central authorities were gradually taking over the management of the educational system in areas formerly ruled by Russia, Austria, and Prussia. The Silesian education system, which from 1920 was based on the Constitutional Act and which encompassed the organic statute of the Silesian voivodship, retained its autonomy.[10] On the basis of the decree, in 1919 elementary education became compulsory for all schoolage children, that is, from seven to fourteen inclusive, but this did not mean it was obligatory to study in a public elementary school. The lack of an educational infrastructure resulted in the predominance of one-class schools. In 1920, in the area of the late Polish kingdom they constituted 86 percent and in Galicia 53 percent of all the existing schools.

The educational system was therefore hampered by the lack of an infrastructure as well as the lack of financial means for its development. There was a chronic shortage of trained teachers. Large numbers of children did not attend school because their parents were too poor. Some families were unable to give their children appropriate clothing, in particular in winter. In many areas the children were expected to go out to work in order to be able to satisfy the basic needs of the family. For example, in the school year 1923–1924 around 1,124 million schoolage children did not attend school, in the school year 1928–1929 around 134,000, and in the school year 1937–1938 around 512,000.[11]

Most communities could not afford schools. The maintenance costs of schools were divided between the state treasury and the communities' councils. Neither the state nor the communities were able to cover the costs of maintaining and developing the educational system. The Education Act issued after Poland regained independence removed the dependency of the school authorities from political administration. Local control characterized the school system until 1932 when a new Education Act was promulgated. The schools were not uniform throughout Poland. In accordance with the political tendencies existing at the time, the Act of 1932 subordinated the educational system to the state and its interests. There were three kinds of elementary schools. In the first a four-grade program was offered; in the second type, there were six grades; and in the third seven grades. Secondary schools were based on six grades of elementary school. The seventh grade was a terminal year for those pupils who did not plan to enter secondary schooling. The 1932 Education Act provided for compulsory education for youth up to the age of eighteen. The act waived compulsory schooling for the children which the schools could not accommodate. In the 1936–1937 school year, vocational schools had room for only 97,600 pupils out of a total of 3 million youth aged fourteen to eighteen years. Secondary general schooling consisted of a four-year grammar school that had uniform programs and two-year secondary schools that had differentiated academic programs. A number of vocational schools offered different levels of training. The school system lacked uniformity before the 1932 Education Act, and the 1932 Education Act allowed the lack of uniformity to continue. A large majority of youth could not continue schooling beyond the four grades of elementary school. In the 1937–1938 school year, almost half of all rural children were educated in four-grade elementary schools.

The Education Act of 1932 provided for greater state control over private schools. Private schools could obtain public rights if they offered state school programs and ensured an appropriate level of education. The tendency to limit the independence of the education system from the state through the Act of 1932 was also reflected in the decisions regarding the self-management of higher schools. The earlier large independence was substituted by a decision that the minister of religious beliefs and public education would perform the "supreme state control over academic schools."

Despite compulsory school legislation, the proportion of girls in school was lower than that of boys even in primary schools.[12] In the 1938–1939 school year, girls constituted 48.1 percent of all pupils; in the countryside, their enrollment share was slightly less (47.9 percent) than that in the city. Female enrollment was lower in private than in public schools (42.8 percent of all those attending such schools). Parents were more likely to pay for the education of their sons rather than for the education of their daughters. Girls more often than boys ended their education upon completing primary school. In 1938–1939, girls represented 43.9 percent of the pupils in four-year secondary grammar schools and 40.5 percent in higher two-year secondary schools. In the 1937–1938 school year, the proportion of girls accepted in secondary grammar schools was higher for girls than for boys; 76.6 percent of girls compared to only 71.9 percent were accepted for grammar school. In the 1936–1937 school year, among the graduates of the general secondary schools of the old type (from before the reforms of the education system) the girls were in the majority, constituting 62.4 percent of all the graduates. Women were also in the majority among pupils and graduates of teacher education programs. This profession was not as feminized in the 1930s as it became after World War II. In teacher-training schools which were at semi-university level, at the time women formed the minority of graduates (37.6 percent), and they dominated in the secondary-level teacher-training schools (60.4 percent of the total number of graduates). In the schools that trained kindergarten and home economics teachers, there was not one man among the graduates.

Men were in the majority (52.2 percent) among the pupils of vocational schools and courses, and more often than women they chose vocational schools with a longer period of learning (two and more years), whereas women more often took courses or went to schools that lasted shorter periods of time.[13] Men more often than women chose such areas of study as farming (89 percent of all those studying in 1937–1938 were males), communication (men represented 98 percent of all students), or industrial and crafts areas (47 percent male), not to mention land-surveying where there were no girls at all. In turn, the areas of study chosen solely by girls had to do with the health service. They were in the majority in such areas as home economics and personal services (98 percent of all those studying), commerce, and administration (53 percent). Girls were also in the majority in lower degree artistic schools in such areas as music and artistic dance. The fine arts areas were dominated by men. In secondary schools, the number of girls studying there was rather high; the percentage of girls completing them was also high. The situation was significantly different as far as institutions of higher learning were concerned. Women constituted a lower percentage than men among the students, and the increase in the number of studying women was slow in the interwar period (Table 14.1).

Women represented 27.2 percent of all students in 1928–1929, and 28.3 percent in 1937–1938. A particularly large proportion of women studied pharmacy and dentistry. (Women were especially visible in dentistry.) Women also dominated among those studying philosophy but were not enrolled in technical studies or in theology. Although the 1930s did not bring about a clear increase in the number of women students enrolled in higher education, the pattern of female enrollment changed. There was an increase in their enrollment in law, the fine arts, and farming, and women began studying veterinary science and physical education, as well as the newly created field of journalism. Women's graduation roles were the same as men's. Although women's enrollment in higher education diversified, women still remained a very small minority in technical studies.

In the interwar period several educational and cultural associations arose which sought to raise the educational level through activity in extracurricular education, additional training courses for adults and young people, Sunday and popular universities, and preparatory farming courses. Because of lack of funds, however, their activities attracted only a small enrollment.

Women, burdened by a great number of duties in general, were less likely than men to find the time to take part in the training programs designed to upgrade their skills. For example, in the 1937–1938 school year, women accounted for 16.4 percent of the students in training courses for adults and young people.[14] The Central Organization of Country Women's Circles, with a membership of 53,000 in 1938, organized libraries and educational courses with the goal of providing women further training.[15] All the efforts undertaken at the time, even though they brought some improvement, did not produce a fundamental change in the educational level of Polish women.

Women had significantly less education than men, and as mentioned earlier, there were significantly more female than male illiterates. Women thus had greater difficulty than men in finding work. The countryside had a large number of unemployed and underemployed people, and farming could not begin to absorb the rural population. Industry did not develop rapidly enough to absorb the surplus labor supply. Women who were in general more poorly educated than men obtained jobs that did not require any qualifications and were paid less than men. Many were employed as servants, and some emigrated abroad. High unemployment made women accept marginal work; women were the first to be laid

Table 14.1
Women as Students and Graduates in Higher Education in the Interwar Period

	1928–29		1937–38		1936–37	
	Total Number Students in thousands	Percent Women	Total Number Students in thousands	Percent Women	Total Number Graduates in thousands	Percent Women
State schools	37.9	27.1	37.5	27.4	5333	27.4
Private schools	5.7	28.0	10.5	31.4	781	29.7
Theology & Canonic Law	1.0	—	1.0	—	—	—
Law and Political Science	11.0	10.9	13.2	18.1	2027	16.2
Medicine	3.8	18.4	3.9	20.5	520	19.2
Pharmacy	0.8	50.0	1.2	50.0	277	55.9
Veterinary Sciences	0.7	—	0.8	12.5	136	1.4
Dentistry	0.4	100.0	0.5	60.0	85	71.8
Philosophy	13.6	55.1	12.0	53.3	1301	56.6
Farming	1.8	16.6	2.4	25.0	361	23.0
Technical Sciences	6.3	4.7	7.6	6.5	667	4.0
Fine Arts	0.7	28.5	0.7	42.8	a	—
Trade & Commerce	3.4	26.4	4.3	32.5	448	27.2
Physical Education	0.1	—	0.2	50.0	—	—
Journalism	—	—	0.3	33.3	—	—

Judaic Studies	—	—	0.1	—	—	—
Doctor's Diplomas					233	10.3
Law					40	7.5
Philosophy					70	17.1
Foreign diplomas					89	6.7
Medicine					33	6.0
Dentistry					5	40.0
Technical Studies					29	—
Total	43.6	27.2	48.0	28.3	6114	27.7

[a]Author's calculations based on Small Statistical Yearbook 1939 (Warsaw: GUS, 1939), p. 332 and 334.

off work in the event of reductions in the numbers employed. Nevertheless, in the 1930s there was a slow increase in the number of women employed. In 1931, they constituted 22.4 percent of all those employed in heavy and medium industry, and in 1938, 23.5 percent. The most feminized industries were clothing (in 1938 women constituted 60.4 percent of all those employed) and textiles (with women accounting for 53.8 percent of the labor force). The foodstuffs industry was also predominantly female, as were the polygraphic, paper, and electrotechnical industries in which women made up one-third of the work team. The chemical and manufacturing industries were female dominated, even though they employed slightly fewer women. The smallest number of women was employed in the timber industry (1.3 percent). Not many more formed the workforce in mining and metallurgy.

Women received significantly lower pay than men. The average weekly wages of female workers were 48.1 percent lower than those received by men in 1935.[16] Women employed as housemaids were particularly poorly paid. The wages of men employed in the same type of work were almost twice as high. Similarly badly paid in comparison to men were women in mining and quarrying. The relatively smallest differences in pay between female and male workers were found in the foodstuffs industry, where women on the average received 89 percent of men's wages and in the timber industry were they received 76.3 percent. In the textile industry which employed an almost exclusively female labor force, women received 70.1 percent of the average men's wages.

The differences between female and male white-collar and professional workers employed in the main sectors of the economy were slightly smaller; the monthly wages of women were on the average 39 percent lower than men's wages. In some of the industries, women received only 55 percent of men's wages; those employed in transport and education received more—around 70 percent of men's wages.

The proportion of men and women employed in the education system is of special relevance here. This is almost entirely female today, but this was not the case in the 1930s. In the 1935–1936 school year, the teaching staff in kindergartens was almost exclusively female, but woman accounted for less than half the teachers in primary schools. Men dominated in higher level schools; in general secondary schools, they constituted 62.4 percent of all those teaching, in teacher-training schools 59.5 percent and in vocational schools 62 percent. In university-level schools, women formed a small percentage—only 11 percent.

Attention should be focused on one additional professional group, the composition of which underwent dramatic change after World War II—the doctors. In the interwar period, the number of doctors was low. Poland ranked fifteenth in Europe with 3.7 doctors per 10,000 inhabitants. There was an evident majority of men; women constituted only 15.7 percent of all doctors. They were found mainly in the large cities (over 100,000 inhabitants) where they made up one-fifth of all the doctors working there; in the small cities and the country, their percentage was two times less.

Women were almost totally absent from politics. In the lower chamber of the Polish Parliament, 2 percent were women, and in the upper chamber 5 percent.

WORLD WAR II

World War II destroyed the Polish economy. Six million Poles lost lives in the war at the hands of the Nazis who purposefully sought to annihilate the Jews and Poles. Most of Poland's highly educated elite died in the war. Many others were displaced and never returned to the country.

Nazi policies were aimed at the destruction of the Polish nation and its educated elite. Between 1939 and 1944, the Nazis pursued an educational policy that denied Polish culture. In the territories Germany annexed to the Reich, there were no Polish schools; in the territories over which the General Government had control, Polish youth could only study in primary and vocational schools under strict German supervision. Polish history and geography were not taught in elementary schools; the Polish language was not taught in vocational schools. The Nazis stipulated that Poles were to study only to enable them to become a skilled workforce integrated into the German economy.

Almost immediately after the outbreak of war, in October 1939, underground teaching was organized, and the Underground Teacher's Organization was formed. Almost a year later, the Department of Education and Culture of the Delegation of the Government of Poland, part of the Ministry of Education of the emigré Polish government in London, was created. Underground educational authorities for all levels of schooling were established to coordinate teaching in the underground elementary, secondary, and tertiary schools. The underground education authorities also prepared plans for the reconstruction of the educational system and cultural life after the war. Both boys and girls participated in these educational groups. Being discovered by the Germans carried the threat of death or a concentration camp. Despite such danger, these courses functioned throughout the war. They became one of the basic means by which Polish culture survived Nazism.

POSTWAR POLAND

With the end of World War II Poland not only regained independence, but also experienced territorial changes (Poland lost its eastern territories and gained new ones in the West) as well as economic and political changes.

The postwar era was a time of disruption and change with mass migrations resulting from changes in Poland's border and the communist revolution transforming the economy. In the postwar period, government policies were designed to bring about rapid industrialization and urbanization. The reconstruction of the education system began immediately. Politically, the Polish United Workers' Party (the new Communist Party) focused on creating a new intelligentsia of peasants and workers that would form the support for the new authorities. At first, the reconstruction of the school system was based on the 1932 act, with some modifications.[17] The new education system was to be (1) uniform so that education given in all types of schools led to further study; (2) universal; (3) public; (4) free of charge. Not only were school fees to be eliminated, but also the costs of education incurred by the parents were to be lowered through the development of a system of boarding schools, scholarships, and the like. The postwar education system is a state system, although the Catholic Church still runs a small number of elementary and secondary schools as well as one university.

The school system has been reformed several times since the 1950s. At the base of the system is an eight-year elementary school. Postprimary education is offered in a four-year general secondary school, a four- or five-year technical school, or a vocational secondary school. Two- or three-year vocational schools are also part of postprimary education. Upon completion of these schools, students can matriculate to technical or vocational secondary schools. Upon completion of secondary school, students can attend university. The university offers a four- to five-year course of study leading to a master's degree, a master's in engineering, or a doctor's degree. Youth from the countryside who do not wish to continue their studies but to work on parents' farms are obliged to finish preparatory farming courses. In the first few postwar years, a much larger proportion of schoolaged children enrolled in the schools than was the case in the interwar period. Ninety percent of primary schoolaged children attended school in 1937–1938. This proportion was reached again in 1946–1947. In 1949–1950, primary education became universal; in 1985–1986, 99.9 percent were enrolled. In 1937–1938, only 14 percent of the youth aged fourteen to seventeen were being educated, in 1946–1947, 28 percent, in 1965–1966, 73.2 percent,[18] and in 1985–1986, 82.1 percent.[19]

After World War II there was a rapid increase in school enrollment in comparison to the earlier period. This increase was marked in the case of girls (Table 14.2).

Differences in male and female educational patterns emerged in the 1960s. Girls more often than boys choose education routes that take longer. Girls choose a relatively high level of education. They dominate in schools that provide a full secondary education, particularly academic secondary schools, and in four-year vocational schools. Since the beginning of the 1980s, they have accounted for more than one-half of the students in university-level institutions. Boys, on the other hand, are a clear majority in three-year vocational secondary schools which enable them to become qualified workers in a relatively short period of time and get relatively well-paid jobs. Girls graduate from secondary schools in numbers comparable to boys. Because of the type of education they receive, they work in lower paying jobs. Comprehensive school leavers often become unskilled workers.

Rapid growth in the number of women students is partially due to the increased credentials required for people seeking jobs in a modernizing economy. A uni-

Table 14.2
Women as a Percentage of Elementary School Graduates Admitted to General Secondary Schools and Vocational Schools, 1960–1986

Type of School	1960/61[a]	1970/71[b]	1980/81[b]	1985/86[b]
Vocational (short education)	38.3	40.7	38.6	39.1
Secondary (total):		64.5	64.0	63.9
general	65.9	72.0	71.3	72.4
vocational (long education)	48.7	56.4	58.7	56.6

Author's calculations based on:

[a]Statistical Yearbook 1966, p. 408;
[b]Statistical Yearbook 1986, p. 461

versity diploma no longer opens the way for well-paid jobs. Thus, women take the place of men in the university. Aspirations to raise the level of education is strong among working women. They choose the same types of schools as non-working women (Table 14.3). Women continue to dominate general secondary, postsecondary, and tertiary education, whereas men remain in elementary and vocational schools which afford men with the opportunity to get better paid jobs. The increases in women's educational levels have not resulted in increases in their salaries.

In the last twenty-five years, the percentage of women being educated in vocational schools has increased, especially in areas which in the past were already particularly feminized. Examples are economics and education, where at present they constitute over 90 percent of all students. A particularly high percentage of women are in schools that train health workers, a sector that has been almost totally feminized for a long time. The percentage of women choosing technical schools and forestry schools remains relatively small (Table 14.4).

Therefore, an increased interest in attaining better education is not necessarily associated with a change in sex segregation in the workforce. Women are enrolled in secondary and postsecondary schools that are already predominantly female. A similar phenomenon has occurred to a lesser extent in university-level institutions (Table 14.5).

In some institutions, until 1985 a quota has been in effect as to the number of women to be admitted in medicine and agriculture, regardless of their number among the candidates. In Poland, women account for a considerably large percentage of law students; however, among Poland's executive cadres, legal studies do not constitute a particularly desirable line of study as in other countries. More often than not, such persons are graduates of schools of economics or technical universities or on the lower level of general and vocational secondary schools.[20] Although women constitute a large proportion of the faculties in economics and technical fields, they are rarely promoted to executive positions in the economy or politics.

Research has demonstrated that, in the case of girls and boys, different influences affect their decisions regarding further education.[21] The girls' selection of schools is more strongly modeled on sex-role expectations and on convictions about personal dispositions. Girls more often than boys aspire to professional status higher than that of their parents. The number of siblings also more strongly affects the educational plans of girls than boys; girls who are single children often wish to pursue university studies.

In Poland, the number of youths served by various forms of education reflects the state Planning Commission's projections of current and prospective workforce needs for skilled workers. The economy is centrally controlled by the state. Each year the number of people seeking university entrance exceeds the number of places planned for the various schools. On some university faculties (history, the arts, psychology, electronics), the number of candidates seeking admission and those undergoing examinations exceeds by many times the number of offered

Table 14.3

Women as a Percentage of Students, by Educational Level, 1985–1986

	Schools for Non-Employed		Schools for Employed	
	Total number of students in thousands	Percent Female[a]	Total number of students in thousands	Percent Female[a]
Women	3,339,703		164,741	
Schools:				
elementary	4,885,014	48.2	18,506	18.5
vocational (short education)	766,862	38.8	5,881	14.1
secondary:				
general	819,643	61.5	192,686	49.8
vocational (long education)	337,989	72.8	44,915	72.8
	481,654	53.5	147,771	42.8
post-secondary	64,974	73.5	29,971	79.7
university levels schools	262,767	50.1	73,321	55.5
Total	6,799,260		320,365	

[a]Author's calculations on the basis of Statistical Yearbook 1986, Warsaw, GUS, 1986.

Table 14.4

Women as a Percentage of Graduates of Vocational Schools, by Field, 1961–1985[a]

Field	1961-62[b]	1970-71[c]	1980-81[d]	1984-85[e]
Technical	23.7	27.9	27.1	26.7
Farming	48.9	68.2	57.1	54.7
Forestry		6.6	8.3	
Economic	79.0	90.7	90.4	90.3
Education	69.6	81.9	88.3	90.6
Health Service	96.5	96.5	96.7	94.1
Artistic	56.0	58.3	60.3	62.7
Other	17.5			
Total	43.1	48.0	47.2	46.7

[a]Graduates of secondary and post-secondary schools counted together

Author's calculations based on:

[b]Statistical Yearbook 1963, Warsaw, GUS, 1963, p. 470
[c]Statistical Yearbook 1972, Warsaw, GUS, 1972, p. 371
[d]Statistical Yearbook 1982, Warsaw, GUS, 1982, p. 408
[e]Statistical Yearbook 1986, Warsaw, GUS, 1986, p. 468.

places. In some faculties (i.e., mathematics, physics), often there are not enough applicants. Therefore, the educational processes do not always and do not completely follow the planners' assumptions, even though spontaneous processes in this case play a marginal role.

The school system is also planned on the basis of politics. The state ensures that youth from peasant and worker backgrounds account for a given percentage among university-level students. Attempts have been made to ensure peasant and worker enrollments by various methods. In the early postwar years, particularly in the 1950s, a system of preparatory courses was made available to enable workers and peasants to enter university in a short period of time. A system was also created in which the proportions of persons from different social backgrounds among new students were established. This system, which gave preferential treatment in admission to youth from certain social groups, was strongly criticized during the economic and political crisis of 1956 and discarded at that time.

Later, as a result of the clear underrepresentation of peasant and worker youth among students, a system of additional points for social origin was adopted. The aim was to equalize working-class youth's chances of university entry. This system also met with society's disapproval as it discriminated against the children of the majority of the intelligentsia. Critics of the system stressed that the differentiation of chances did not occur in accordance with the current formulated class definition of social origin. The system discriminated against youth from small towns and the country and gave the edge to children from large cities, among whom no great differences in level of knowledge were noted, despite their various social origins.

Results of studies also demonstrate that the underrepresentation of youth of peasant and worker origin among university students is a result of their small numbers among university applicants. Persons living in rural areas are three times less likely than urban dwellers to consider higher education. This, in turn, is the result of a culturally conditioned concept of a life's career in which many years of education culminate in a diploma and a relatively low-paid job—a not overly attractive prospect. Girls choose their career routes only after completing secondary school, but boys make their decision after they complete elementary school.[22] Social background on the first selection threshold, that is, when making the decision on the choice of secondary school, accounts for 33 percent of the differentiation of boys' school selection. On the second selection threshold, when making the decision after completing secondary school, social background accounts for only 11 percent. With regard to girls, the influence of social background is slightly smaller (29 percent) on the first threshold and greater on the second one (15 percent).

The crisis at the beginning of the 1980s brought a new wave of discussion on this topic and harsh criticism. As a result, the system of points was again discarded and substituted by a hierarchy of preferences based on the background of persons attaining equal results in the exams.

It is often opined that women who have both professional and household duties

Table 14.5
Women as a Percentage of University Students, by Field of Study, 1962–1986

	Total Number of Students in thousands	Percent Women in Total	Percent of Women by Field of Study				
			technical	farming	economic	law adm.	
Years							
1962–63[a]	141.6	38.3	14.2	31.3		41.3	
1971/72	221.1	47.5	25.2	42.8	63.6	50.0	
1985–86	340.7	50.9	19.8	45.2	56.6	45.7	
Type of Studies in 1985–86:							
day	265.8	49.6	19.2	46.6	57.0	46.0	
evening	4.9	22.4	10.8	—	25.0	—	
extra-mural	68.4	57.9	17.7	41.5	56.9	45.2	
external	1.6	50.0	33.3	33.3	—	—	

342

Table 14.5 (continued)

| | Percent of Women by Field of Study | | | | | |
	humanist	math. science	medic.	phys. ed.	artistic	teaching
Years						
1962–63[a]	63.8	58.5	59.6	--	45.2	--
1971/72	74.5	59.9	65.8	37.5	46.9	70.4
1985–86	75.5	61.5	62.3	35.8	51.3	--
Type of Studies in 1985–86:						
day	74.3	61.4	61.9	35.6	47.7	--
evening	--	100.0	--	--	71.4	--
extra-mural	78.8	61.0	100.0	38.2	75.0	--
external	57.1	--	--	0.0	--	--

[a]Author's calculations based on: Statistical Yearbook 1963, Warsaw, GUS, 1963, p. 380, Statistical Yearbook 1972, Warsaw, GUS, 1972, p. 478, Statistical Yearbook 1981, Warsaw, GUS, p. 533; Statistical Yearbook 1986, Warsaw, GUS, 1986, p. 471.

343

are less capable than men of finding the time and strength to continue studies in a later period of life. It is often thought that many of them do not care about continuing education, since they concentrate on the family. This opinion is not confirmed in fact. Women make up over one-half of the students in extramural and external studies. The exception here are evening studies, a relatively marginal form of completing education in Poland, where women account for only about one-quarter of all students. Evening studies, more than other forms of education, conflict with women's everyday chores, and most of their studies are usually conducted in areas that women seldom choose. Women constitute a significant percentage of those completing higher education. They are seldom students in postgraduate and doctoral studies. There has been a stable increase in the number of women in postgraduate programs. For example, the percentage of women enrolled in postgraduate studies was 24.6 percent in 1970 and 43.8 percent in 1985. In 1970, women accounted for 35.5 percent of doctoral students, and in 1985, 28.9 percent.[23]

In summing up the changes that have taken place in women's education since World War II, we must stress the increase in the number of women being educated. In the 1980s, the number of women exceeded the number of men enrolled in university-level studies. The increased participation of women in some faculties has led to the further feminization of professions which were believed to be female dominated. Men have relatively lower interest in university-level studies and long-term studies because, contrary to the prewar period, these forms of education do not guarantee well-paying jobs. Certain workers' professions or even setting up one's own profession, even the smallest enterprise, gives a chance of earning larger incomes. For women who avoid vocational careers and are unwilling to perform "dirty" and hard physical work, the white-collar work they can get with a secondary school or university-level education is attractive. Education has traditionally conferred social status, even though in the postwar period it has not been associated with increased incomes. The economic crisis of the early 1980s came as a shock to Poland. The ability to earn a living became more pressing, and the social attraction that education has traditionally held has been eclipsed.[24]

The feminization of certain areas of study has exacerbated trends in the sexual segregation of the workforce. Finance and insurance institutions, education, culture, and art and trade are female dominated. In 1985, women made up 71 to 84 percent of the workforce in each of these fields.

In traditionally male fields such as industry, construction, and farming, the increase in women's participation among all employees did not exceed 10 percent. The percentage of women employed in the health service and social welfare, already previously high, increased by a few percentage points, reaching 80 percent in each of the fields. The structure of women's employment became stabilized. There was a large difference in women's participation among those employed in the basic sectors of the socialized economy even between 1955 and the end of the 1970s. But there were practically no changes between 1979 and 1985.[25]

Despite the constitutionally guaranteed equality between the sexes in the economic, social, and cultural areas, women to this day earn less than men. Their wages are about 70 percent those of men (partly because of the effect of the "appreciation" manipulation of part of the wages by the superiors). An increase in women's education and their mass participation in the labor market (in 1986 they constituted 45.1 percent of all workers, and only 30.7 percent in 1950) were not associated with a significant change in their numbers in leadership positions. Women still remain underrepresented in management in the national economy, as well as in the country's administration and political life.[26]

Women account for 20.6 percent of all the council representatives. Their percentage in the Seym (Polish Parliament) is almost identical and from the beginning of the 1960s has not changed much. Women are most often members of such commissions as the internal market, social policy, national education, administration, environmental protection, complaints, and motions commissions. They are totally absent on commissions such as the national protection commission or foreign affairs.

Their presence in the highest authorities is symbolic (not more than one) both as far as the government and the authorities of the ruling Polish United Workers party are concerned. They more often appear on the lower levels but mainly in deputy positions.

In East European countries, where the economic and social order as well as the political system have undergone a radical change, the propaganda of the period directly following the changing of the political and economic system offered concepts of male and female roles that were entirely different from traditional concepts. Women and men were represented (part of the concept of a "new man") as citizens capable of participating in the construction of the economic foundation of the new system to the same extent and in the same manner. A policy of low wages, coupled with the development of a network of nurseries, kindergartens, and canteens "pushed" women into new, nontraditional roles. The gap between patterns promoted by the mass media and those widespread among society differed depending on social class. And so in intelligentsia circles, women relatively more often worked, considering their job as a way not only of supplementing the family incomes but also of gaining self-fulfillment. In other social groups, a woman's job was considered almost exclusively a financial necessity.

The Roman Catholic Church with its concept of the family, in which a woman has a traditionally defined role, has played an important role in shaping social relations in Poland. Its influence has been very powerful in as much as it is viewed not only as a religious, but also as a national institution, supporting the Polish nation's efforts to restore the Polish state.

Public opinion research in 1980 and 1984 shows that the equality of men and women is perceived as a secondary problem compared to housing construction, care of the elderly, education, and so on.[27]

The multidimensional crisis in Poland in the early 1980s, which apart from its economic dimension, had important political, social, and moral aspects, created demands to increase women's rights. Demands concerning women were contained in the Gdansk and Szczecin agreements signed by Interfactory Strike Committees and the authorities in late August and early September 1980. Among these demands was the introduction of three-year paid maternity leaves. The Interfactory Strike Committee also proposed the introduction of an allowance that would equal a woman's pay in the first year of the leave and half her previous wage in the second year, as well as ensure a sufficient number of places in nurseries and kindergartens for children of working women.

These agreements did not contain any specific provisions to increase women's participation in political decisions or to increase their say in the running of work enterprises. Few women were elected in 1981 to the newly created solidarity union's executive bodies. A similar tendency emerged in totally spontaneous elections of delegates to the Ninth Extraordinary Congress of the Polish United Workers' party in the same year.

More than forty years have passed since the beginning of the period in which women en masse entered the labor market and began to raise their educational qualifications. Nevertheless, in comparison to women from Western countries (like Italy or Canada), Polish women exhibit more traditional attitudes about the roles they should perform. The desire to remain at home, at least when bringing up small children, is observed in particular among young women, including women with secondary school or university education. Their choice is often justified by their unwillingness to repeat their mothers' attempts to cope with the excessive burdens of combining professional work with child care and house-keeping. They also point out that giving priority to professional work by sac-rificing traditional women's roles and the experienced frustrations do not at all guarantee promotions in professional work. Young women, in particular, rec-ognize their promotion ceiling, which is difficult, if not impossible, to overcome.

The recurring economic and political crises, strongly experienced by the whole of society regardless of sex, are the source of social and political tension. They involve a significant part of society in discussions regarding solutions, reform of the economic and political structure of the country, an increased participation of women in management and the decision-making process, and development of more democratic forms of political participation.

NOTES

1. K. Mrozowska, "Polish Women in Science and Education" [Kobiety polskie w nauce i oswiacie], in *Kobiety polskie* (Warsaw: Ksiazka i Wiedza, 1986), p. 236, f.

2. Jozef Chalasinski, *Past and Future of the Polish Intelligentsia* [Przeszłość i przy-szłość inteligencji polskiej], (Warsaw: Ludowa Spółdzielnia Wydawnicza, 1958).

3. Mrozowska, "Polish Women in Science and Education," p. 243–245.

4. Renata Siemienska, "Women and Social Movements in Poland," *Women and Politics* 6, No. 4 (Winter 1986): 13–14.

5. Jan Hulewicz, *The Struggle of Polish Women and Access to Universities* [Walka kobiet polskich o dostep na uniwersytety], (Warsaw: 1936), p. 4.

6. Mrozowska, "Polish Women in Science and Education," p. 258.

7. *Small Statistical Yearbook 1939* [Maly Rocznik Statystyczny 1939]. (Warsaw: GUS, 1939), p. 263.

8. Ibid., pp. 29–34.

9. Ibid.

10. Mieczyslaw Pecherski and Maciej Swiatek, *Organization of Education in Poland in 1917–1977.* [Organizacja oswiaty w Polsce w latach 1917–1977], 2nd ed. (Warsaw: Panstwowe Wydawnictwo Naukowe, 1978), pp. 25–26.

11. Ibid., pp. 30–44.

12. *Small Statistical Yearbook 1939,* p. 322–326.

13. Ibid., pp. 328–329.

14. Ibid., p. 337.

15. Ibid., p. 351.

16. Ibid., p. 270.

17. Pecherski and Swiatek, *Organization of Education in Poland,* p. 66.

18. *Statistical Yearbook 1966* [Rocznik statystyczny 1966], (Warsaw: Glowny Urzad Statystyczny, 1966), p. 408.

19. *Statstical Yearbook 1986* [Rocznik statystyczny 1986], Warsaw: Glowny Urzad Statystyczny, 1986), p. 460.

20. Aleksandra Jasinska, Renata Siemienska, and Joanna Sobolewska, "Who Are Leaders?" [Kim sa dzialacze?] in J. Wiats, ed., *Local Authorities on the Eve of the Crisis* [Wladza lokalna u progu kryzysu], (Warsaw: Institute of Sociology, University of Warsaw, 1983).

21. M. Stasinska, "Influence of Status and Psycho-social Factors on Educational Paths of Polish Youth" [Wplyw czynnikow statusowych i psychospolecznych na drogi edukacyjne mlodziezy polskiej], (Ph.D. diss., University of Warsaw, 1986).

22. Ibid.

23. *Statistical Yearbook 1986,* p. 473.

24. Aleksandra Jasinska and Renata Siemienska, "The Socialist Personality: A Case Study of Poland," *International Journal of Sociology* 13, No. 1 (Spring 1983).

25. Renata Siemienska, "Women, Work and Gender Equality in Poland: Reality and Its Social Perception," in Sharon L. Wolchik and Alfred G. Meyer, eds., *Women, State and Party in Eastern Europe.* (Durham, N.C.: Duke University Press, 1985), pp. 344–361.

26. Renata Siemienska, "Women's Political Participation and the 1980 Crisis in Poland," *International Political Science Review* 6, No. 3, 1985, pp. 332–346; Siemienska, "Women and Social Movements in Poland."

27. Ibid.

15
SWEDEN

Annika Andrae-Thelin
and Inga Elqvist-Saltzman

Side by side in classrooms and at work, side by side in the everyday tasks of housework and child care, side by side into political assemblies and administrative departments, equal in terms of power and influence—such are the objectives of sexual equality.[1]

This firm statement is found under the heading "Towards the Year 2000" in the Swedish government's latest report on equality between women and men. The minister responsible for sexual equality describes developments during the International Women's Decade as follows: "Compared with most other countries, Sweden has made considerable progress in the field of equal opportunities."[2] This chapter analyzes Swedish policies aimed at promoting gender equality in education. We ask how far Sweden has progressed in achieving equality for women in education and in society. The focus here is on educational reforms from the 1940s to the 1980s. During this period, education in Sweden has undergone radical transformation.

We will begin by discussing the context of Swedish education reforms, namely, the formation of a modern welfare state, and the policies the government has pursued to bring about equality. Next, we will describe reform policies for each level of education. The second part of the chapter presents a statistical overview of women's education. We will then look at how the objectives of sexual equality, verbalized in the quotation that began this chapter, have been fullfilled. We end by considering differences between ideology and practice and demand for policies as well as research that would further equality in education and society.

IDEOLOGY—EDUCATIONAL POLICY

Formation of the Modern Welfare State

Sweden has a long history of policies directed toward equalizing society. The government initiated wide-ranging services for children and parents beginning in the 1930s which gave Sweden a worldwide reputation as the prototypical welfare state. A somewhat later, but nonetheless comprehensive, reform program covering all levels of education has also attracted the interest of planners as well as researchers abroad.[3] The educational reforms have constituted major elements of the democratic reform of the whole of Swedish society. Waves of reforms have gone hand in hand with optimism and expansion and have triggered major organizational change in different social and economic spheres.

Security, equality, democracy, solidarity, and economic efficiency became key elements guiding Swedish government policy. They lent direction to a steadily increasing number of reforms. To encourage a rise in the birthrate in the 1930s and 1940s, the government pursued active labor market policies to eliminate unemployment, housing improvement programs, and family policies to ensure minimum standards of care for young children.

Modern Swedish reforms have been characterized by consensus, rational decision making, and sociopolitical values shared by most of the 8.5 million Swedes. During the reform era, the country benefited from being relatively homogeneous in language and race and from being secular. This situation has changed since World War II, when Sweden began to host great numbers of immigrants. By 1980, roughly one-fifth of the population in Sweden were immigrants holding permanent residence permits. The total number of immigrants would be considerably higher if all people who are in the country on shorter term permits were included.

Equal Opportunity Policy—Retrospect

In Sweden equality of opportunity between women and men is considered one of the most important elements of equality. The Swedes have a specific concept, *jämställdhet,* for equality between the sexes. To a higher degree than in any other Nordic country, Sweden has "institutionalized" this ideology through legislation. On different decision-making levels, there are councils and advisory bodies on equal opportunities. The Equal Opportunities Ombudsman (*JämO*) is an independent authority under the Ministry of Labor and has existed since the Act on Equality between Women and Men at Work (the Equal Opportunities Act) was enacted on July 1, 1980. The JämO's main task is to ensure compliance with the Equal Opportunities Act.

The idea of equal opportunity for women and men in Sweden means equal rights, obligations, and opportunities for women and men alike; to have a job that makes the individual financially independent; to care for children and the home; and to participate in political and social life.

Progress has extended over a period of many years. A short chronology of educational reforms and reforms in women's status since the mid-nineteenth century is presented below:

1842   Elementary education for girls as well as boys becomes compulsory for every municipality.

1859   Women become eligible for certain teaching appointments.

1873   Women become entitled to take academic degrees, with the exceptions of theology and higher law degrees.

1919   A governmental bill on women's suffrage is passed.

1921   Married women become legally competent at twenty-one. The new Marriage Code treats husband and wife as equals. (Unmarried women had acquired political rights at twenty-one in 1874.)

1923   Women become eligible for national government appointments.

1927   State grammar schools are opened to girls.

1935   Equality for women and men is declared under the national pension scheme.

1937   Maternity benefits are introduced.

1938   Contraception becomes legal.

1939   The state is forbidden to dismiss women on account of pregnancy, childbirth, or marriage.

1947   Equal pay for identical national government appointments is instituted.

1950   Both parents become legal custodians of their children.

1958   Women are admitted to the Lutheran priesthood.

1962   A nine-year comprehensive compulsory school for all citizens is declared.

1971   Individual taxation of the earned incomes of husband and wife is put into effect.

1971   Secondary education is reformed to integrate theoretical and vocational tracks within a new upper secondary school.

1974   Parental insurance is introduced, entitling parents to shared leaves of absence in connection with childbirth.

1975   Abortion legislation is passed entitling women to the right to decide to terminate pregnancy up to and including the eighteenth week without consulting others.

1977   Higher education is reformed, giving among other things university status to teacher and nursing preparation.

1979   Parents of infant children become entitled to a six-hour working day.

1980   Legislation is passed prohibiting sexual discrimination at work.

1982   Child care at home is regarded as qualifying for the national pension scheme.

1982   The display of pornographic material in public places is banned.

1983   All occupations are declared open to women, including the armed forces.

1984   The national government sector adopts an equal opportunity policy.

In sum, the major steps which the Swedish government has taken to ensure women the same rights as men, have been in providing employment opportunity and child care and in promoting shared responsibility between parents for home and children.

In 1968, Sweden became the first country in the world in which the government through a series of policies tried to achieve equality between the sexes by changing the role of men as well as that of women. In a statement to the United Nations, the Swedish government declared that "every individual, irrespective of sex, shall have the same practical opportunities, not only for education and employment, but also in principle the same responsibility for his or her own maintenance as well as shared responsibility for the upbringing of children and the upkeep of the home."[4]

Educational Policy

Sweden has long stressed literacy and schooling: it made public school education compulsory for all Swedish children as early as 1842. Compulsory education entailed not only the obligation of children to attend school, but also the obligation of communities to provide educational facilities.

Even before 1842, almost all citizens in Sweden were able to read, owing to training in the parish and the family. Reading was linked to the Lutheran religion and its strong belief in every woman's and man's duty and ability to understand the "Word" of God. The clergy undertook yearly examinations of households in each parish. Before getting a marriage license, both women and men had to prove their ability to read. In church women and men sat side by side but on different sides of the aisle, using the Hymnal. According to the Swedish literacy researcher E. Johansson, the hymns were a good test of reading ability.[5] The church's reading campaigns before the advent of modern schools meant Sweden had a very low illiteracy rate (one per million of the population over fifteen years of age according to the census of 1930).[6]

Despite Swedish patriarchy, which by law subordinated women to their husbands, women were entitled to learn to read on a basis of equality with men. There was, however, a difference where writing and counting were concerned. As in other countries, the Swedish school system was based on a sexually segregated ideology that was obvious in organization as well as in curriculum content.

The public debate in Parliament before the introduction of a compulsory public school in the 1840s revealed the doubts many had concerning the usefulness of girls receiving the same education as boys, and their capacity for doing so. "I believe that this minimum of knowledge is far too high, especially for women," stated one member of Parliament.[7]

Sex discrimination in secondary education was greater. The public grammar school provided males with access to employment and social status. Girls—mainly from the upper classes—were denied grammar school education. Instead, they were taught language, music, and the like in municipal sex-segregated schools and good behavior in the private and family sphere. Public grammar schools were not opened for girls until 1927. Girls' municipal schools started in the nineteenth century, but they did not give comparable education to boys' grammar schools until 1909. Linked to compulsory education, shorter courses in citizenship education were opened in the early twentieth century. In content, these were traditionally male or female oriented (housework for girls and economy for boys). Even within the same subject there were different courses for girls and boys, for example, in mathematics. Boys were supposed to take a more rigorous, longer course than girls. At the basis of this segregation was the profound belief that girls and boys were to be educated to perform different roles and have different positions in society. This belief was called in question during the reform era in education starting after World War II.

The Reform of Compulsory Education

After a twelve-year experimental period, which began in 1950, a nine-year comprehensive school for compulsory education was established by the Education Act of 1962. This reform defined the goal of formal schooling as "social upbringing." All students were to be provided with a general education to build a common foundation in cultural and political knowledge and values in light of their future roles in participatory democracy. Elitism in education could no longer be tolerated. Student-centered teaching methods were to be used in order to engage students actively in their own learning. Training in communicative skills and in collaborative work were based on similar "democratic" grounds. One school and the same education for every child between seven and sixteen years of age in Sweden was the password, and coeducation was the rule.

The new nationwide curriculum of 1962 was the first step in promoting new sex roles. In handicrafts, girls were taught woodwork and boys textile work for twenty hours at the intermediate level. Home economics became a compulsory subject for both girls and boys in Grade 7 and an optional subject in Grade 8. Child care was made a school subject in Grade 9.

In 1969, when the curriculum was revised, schools were given even more of a key function in transforming sex roles. The curriculum required all pupils, regardless of sex, to take instruction in subjects like home economics and child care which were central to changing the sex-role division of labor in the home. All pupils, regardless of sex, were to receive the same treatment and be met with the same expectations and demands. Traditional sex-role attitudes held by pupils were to be challenged, for example, in educational and vocational guidance. An equal opportunities program was formulated by the National Board of Education.

In the nationwide curriculum issued in 1980, gender equality remained unchanged as a goal, but less space was devoted to "ideological embroidery."[8] One important difference between the 1980 and earlier curricular revisions is that home and family are not mentioned as often in the 1980 curriculum. In the 1962 curriculum, the main focus was concentrated on questions of sex stereotypes in the home and family. In 1969, equal opportunities in society and in the labor market were added as the goals of reform. In the latest curricular revision, the main focus of interest is on providing girls equal opportunities in the labor market. The trend has been to pay less attention to the home/family/sphere and more to the labor market.[9]

Current Swedish policies to promote gender-based equality have been fundamentally concerned with the ability of each individual to achieve economic independence through gainful employment. This goal has also influenced the reform of secondary and higher education.

Reform of Upper Secondary Education

The reform process, which in 1971 resulted in the development of a new upper secondary school, aimed at reducing the difference in status between "practical" and academic programs of study. Academic continuation and vocational secondary schools were integrated under one roof.

In 1969, the Swedish Parliament accepted a proposal for an integrated secondary school featuring twenty-one lines of study. These fell under three broad categories:

—Three- and four-year academic programs

—Two-year academic programs

—Two-year vocational programs.

Common to all was the objective of acquainting students with working-life conditions. Any of these programs can lead to admission to higher education. In some instances, however, students are required to take additional courses in Swedish and in English.

In 1981, new proposals for the further reform of secondary education were issued by a Parliament-commissioned study. These reforms seek to further obliterate the differences between academic and vocational programs and to reinforce the linkages between school and work. The goal is to establish a common secondary school for everyone and to combat growing youth unemployment.

About 90 percent of the age cohorts continue their studies beyond the nine years of compulsory schooling and attend upper secondary school. Older students who ended their studies in the ninth grade can also apply for admission to upper secondary school at a later date. The proportion of male and female students is about the same in secondary school. There is, however, sex segregation by course of study. The Ministry of Education, concerned about the underrepresentation of girls in science and technology programs, has allocated a considerable sum of money to promote female entry into these programs.

Reforming Higher Education

About 25 percent of upper secondary school graduates go on to higher education. Higher education has undergone almost continuous reform since the mid-1940s. This reform activity reached a frenzied peak near the end of the 1960s. During the "student explosion" of the 1960s, reforms focused on bringing efficiency and rationalization to higher education. At a time of social and economic boom, the relation between higher education and the labor market became very important. Measures were taken to reduce the number of dropouts and to promote the flow of students through higher education. The instructional programs were reorganized into smaller subcourses and groups. A tighter organization of educational programs, rules for pass-rates, intake restrictions in certain programs, and a more rigid organization of university studies were introduced.

In Sweden as well as in other countries, universities in the 1970s became "involved in a thorough questioning and rethinking of the purposes and structures of higher education."[10] In 1968, the Swedish government appointed a commission to reconsider fundamental principles of higher education. One important concern was to bring higher education closer to society by reorienting its content. To impose a broad occupational orientation on graduate studies, courses were organized according to the following labor market sectors:

—Technical

—Medical and nursing

—Administrative, economic, and social work

—Teaching

—Cultural and information professions

A reform of higher education in 1977 gave a number of programs of study the status of higher education. These included teaching and nursing, which have been traditionally female dominated. A new admission system opened access to higher education to new groups of students, among whom were adults with work experience but with less formal schooling.

In this new and broader concept of higher education, three different subsectors were integrated:

—The traditional university sector

—Vocational institutions with fairly close university ties, for example, teacher-training colleges and schools for social work

—Vocational institutions with very weak, if any, connections to university education, for example, nursing schools and training colleges

To strengthen the chances of tertiary education being more socially relevant, the 1977 reform called for the inclusion of representatives from working life on curricular planning boards.

While efficiency had been stressed in the reforms during the 1960s, the focus of the 1977 reform was on the goals of societal relevance and on adjusting university training to the needs of the labor market. The same trend occurred in compulsory school, where labor market considerations occupied a more prominent position.

Adult and Preschool Education

Besides universities and colleges, there are other forms of adult education in which several million Swedes over the age of eighteen participate:

—Municipal adult education, conferring essentially the same qualifications as compulsory school and upper secondary school
—Folk high school
—Labor market training
—Study circles

Adult education is free of charge, as are other educational activities in Sweden.

Preschool education was reformed in 1975. All children aged six and over are eligible for preschool education. Although municipal authorities must provide preschools, children are not obligated to attend them.

Preschool education is the responsibility of the National Board of Health and Welfare, whereas the National Board of Education is the central authority responsible for compulsory schooling, upper secondary school, and adult education (below postsecondary level). Higher education falls under the authority of the National Board of Universities and Colleges.

All education in Sweden is free. In compulsory schooling, free books and school lunches are provided. A special system of study assistance is available to help Swedish students to meet the total cost of living during their studies. A small portion of this assistance comprises a grant that does not have to be paid back.

Equality Is the Goal

Equality has been the overriding goal in all educational reforms of the postwar era. Swedish educational policy has been concerned with underprivileged groups in society, first and foremost with students from working-class homes. It has also focused on adults who have not had the same schooling opportunities as their children and on women whose history of enrollment in higher education is much shorter than men's.[11]

Have the postwar reforms brought equality to women in education, in the labor market, and in decision making at all levels in Swedish society? Have the reforms made a difference in women's life patterns? The remainder of this chapter focuses on these questions. Much of the discussion that follows is based on material from Statistics Sweden (SCB) which recently established a unit for equal opportunity statistics.[12]

SIDE BY SIDE? A STATISTICAL PICTURE OF WOMEN AND MEN IN THE SWEDISH WELFARE STATE

" . . . side by side in classrooms . . . "

The reforms in Swedish education which have been outlined in this chapter have attempted to provide women with equality of education at the secondary level and in higher education. Emphasis, as was pointed out earlier, was placed at these levels, since they relate most to the workforce.

Although women's access to secondary education has increased as a result of reform, secondary education remains sex segregated, despite intensive efforts to encourage girls to enter nontraditional fields of study. Figure 15.1 illustrates the sex segregation in secondary education. It shows that only five of the twenty-eight programs of study in upper secondary school enroll nearly equal proportions of males and females, whereas eleven programs which emphasize nursing and secretarial work as well as the social sciences are predominantly female. Eleven programs of study which are technologically oriented are male dominated.

Girls who enter courses of study that have traditionally excluded them on the secondary level have a higher dropout rate than do girls who pursue study in traditional fields. Girls, on an average, have a greater tendency to drop out of school than do boys.

In higher education, the pattern of sex segregation also holds, but women's participation in higher education has expanded markedly. Since 1981 women have outnumbered men. Women's share is now 60 percent of all undergraduate students. There are differences in age distribution between women and men enrolled in higher education. Women are particularly well represented in the age groups eighteen to twenty and forty to fifty-five. An increasing number of mature women have entered higher education during the 1980s.

Much of the rise in female enrollment is due to the reorganization of higher education which has made teacher education and nursing part of higher education. Even so, more women are enrolling in postsecondary education. In the early 1970s in the age group twenty-four to thirty-four, 5 percent enrolled in post-secondary education compared to 27 percent in the 1980s. Today, women are awarded two-thirds of all first degrees as compared to 9 percent in 1910.

Figure 15.1
**Integrated Upper Secondary School Leavers Completing Courses in the 1986–
1987 School Year**

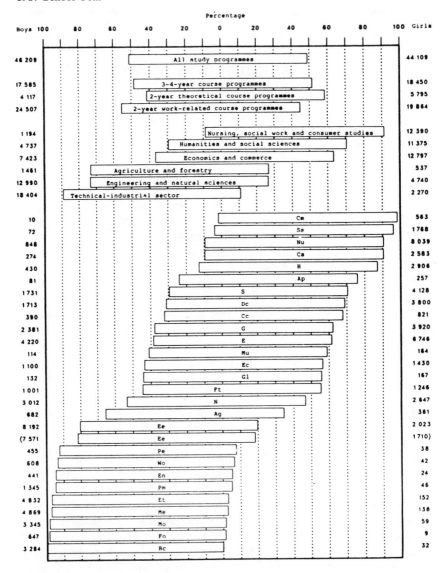

Table 15.1

Women's Share of New Undergraduate Enrollment in Higher Education, by Specialization, 1977–1978 to 1984–1985 (in Percentages)

Specialization	1977–78	1984–85
Technical professions	19	21
Administrative, Economic and Social Work	48	53
Health	81	85
Teaching	74	72
Information, Communication and Cultural Professions	54	63
Separate single subject courses (outside full degree programs)	54	58
Total	57	60

It is easy to fall into the trap of interpreting these data as meaning that the goal of equality between men and women has been reached. However, the picture changes if the analysis extends to consideration of graduate study and of fields of specialization. Women constitute only one-third of all graduate students. Women's share has increased, but progress has been slow. In 1974–1975, 23 percent of all graduate students were women, and in 1984, 31 percent.

In higher education, women are segregated from men in the fields of study they pursue. Table 15.1 describes their enrollment as undergraduates by field of study.

Women constitute 80 percent of students in health and only about 20 percent in technology. Each specialization in higher education consists of programs of varying length. Women tend to enroll in shorter term programs. In health women form a majority in all programs with the exception of those preparing medical doctors.

The sex segregation in higher education becomes clearer upon investigating the distribution of women in various courses within each specialization. In technical fields women cluster in "soft" courses like textile engineering, architecture, and chemistry, while the "hard" technology remains heavily male dominated. In times of growing economic restraint with investment reserved for new technology, the distribution of women in fields of specialization has broad implications for their pattern of distribution in the workforce and for their life-long earnings. In Sweden, as in other countries, there is a direct relation between women's entry into an occupation and the status of that occupation. The more women in an occupation, the lower its status and its economic rewards.[13]

Adult education, like secondary and higher education, also exhibits sexual asymmetry. Women make up 60 to 70 percent of all students in municipal adult education and study circle programs.

In sum, despite massive educational reform, equality in educational enrollment has remained elusive in Sweden. The pattern of inequality in schooling relates to women's pattern of participation in the workforce.

" . . . side by side at work . . . "

Women's participation in the labor force today is almost as high as that of men. In 1986, 83 percent of all women twenty to sixty-four years of age were in the workforce as compared to 90 percent of men in the same age group (Figure 15.2). By international standards, women in Sweden have a high employment rate. The pattern of women's workforce participation and the status of occupations women hold are, however, different from men's. About half of the women in the labor force work part time as compared to a small fraction of the men. Part-time employment is the kind of work that has increased most significantly for women during the last fifteen years. This has implications for average income. The average income in 1985 was SEK 62,000 for women and SEK 95,500 for men (Figure 15.3). Even for those with full-time employment, on an average men earned a higher income than women despite the fact that Sweden has had a long-standing policy of equal pay.

How can the apparent existence of one labor market for men and another for women be explained? When Swedish women entered the workforce in large numbers in the 1960s and 1970s, they were recruited for certain occupations and sectors. Women's occupations became an extension of the traditional role of women, that is, care and service occupations in both the private and public sectors.

The heavy growth of public sector employment opened up a large labor market for women and gave them a firm foothold in the workforce. The expansion of public service also made it possible for women to enter the workforce since the state provided childcare, care of the elderly, and public transport. The result was strict sexual segregation of the labor market. Relatively few women have been recruited for the manufacturing industry, transport and communications, or technical and economic private service. In the 1980s, a slower expansion of the public sector has coincided with increasing automation and computerization of working life. The sexual segregation of the labor market does have implications for women's continued workforce participation. In times of hard economic reality, new investments are mainly reserved for new technology. Many jobs currently held by women may disappear.

Women have a much narrower labor market than men. Women constitute over 60 percent of the workforce in forty-four occupations; men, on the other hand,

Figure 15.2
Population in the 20–64-Year-Old Group, by Occupational Status, 1970–1986 (in Percentages)

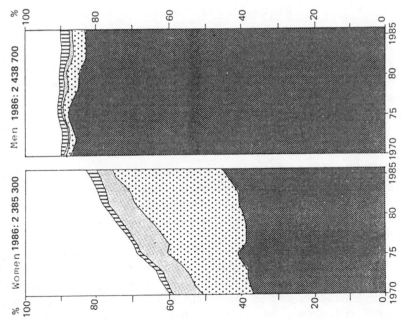

Source: AKU.

Figure 15.3

Total Income, 1985: Average Income at Different Ages

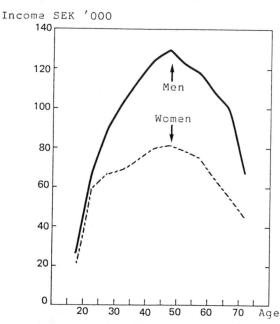

Income SEK '000

Source: Be 20 SM 8701. SCB.

are 60 percent of the workforce in 138 occupations. The ten most common occupations for women attract more than half of all working women, whereas the ten most common occupations for men attract 35 percent of male employees. These occupations are illustrated in Table 15.2.[14]

"... side by side in the everyday tasks of house-work and child care ..."

The labor and educational statistics have so far shown that women and men use their working time and school years differently. What about their spare time? A survey performed by Statistics Sweden in 1982–1983 on the amount of time spent on work, studies, housework, and repairs shows that in all age groups women have less spare time than men.

The above-mentioned survey also included some questions on housework performed by children. Girls and boys in younger age groups (five to ten) do roughly the same amount and type of work. In older age groups (eleven to eighteen), however, girls are more inclined than boys to perform traditional women's activities such as cooking, washing up, and cleaning, whereas boys are more likely to do gardening and run errands.

"... side by side into political assemblies and administrative departments ..."

Table 15.2
Sex Segregation in the Workforce

Occupations in which 55 percent of all women are employed:

Occupation	No. of Women	Percentage Employed
Secretaries/typists	244,220	88
Paramedical staff	170,200	94
Shop assistants	119,400	78
Cleaners	116,700	90
Childminders	74,600	97
Homehelps	57,000	98
Accountants/office cashiers	56,100	82
Nurses	52,600	95
Junior school teachers	50,000	78
Kitchen staff	44,600	92
Total	985,400	

Occupations in which 35 percent of all men are employed:

Occupation	No. of Men	Percentage Employed
Machine fitters/assemblers	110,700	92
Drivers	101,500	94
Agriculture, forestry and horticulture	87,400	68
Commercial travellers/buyers	84,900	82
Workshop mechanics	83,800	84
Mechanical engineering	75,800	98
Building joiners	59,100	99
Construction engineering	52,500	95
Electricians	52,100	94
Warehouse workers, storekeepers	50,300	81
Total	758,100	

Not only has equality been elusive in education, the work force, and the household, but women also seem to lack political power. Although women have a slightly higher rate of participation in national elections than do men, women's influence in legislative bodies at all levels is still low. Since 1921, when the first women entered the Parliament, the percentage of women in that body has risen to 31 percent (1985 figure). Around the same figure is to be found in county and municipal government. One-fourth to one-third of the members in government bodies and committees are women. Very few women hold senior executive positions in private industry or in the public sector. Sweden is in this respect far behind a few other European countries.[15]

"Equal in terms of power and influence" . . . ?

The statistics presented here point to differences between objectives and reality in different sectors of society. In the labor market, where women accounted for most of the growth in employment throughout the 1970s and the beginning of the 1980s, there is a woman's as distinct from a man's labor market. The women's labor market is much more narrow and generally has lower wages and lower status. In education, where there has been a considerable increase in the number of women attending school at all levels, segregation is pervasive despite great efforts on the part of educational planners to give females equal opportunities. As for everyday work at home sex differences remain. The government's goals of 1968 in regard to equalization of housework have not yet been met. Women and men are not equal in power and influence either. How can the disparity between government goals and reality be explained?

Laws and regulations have made it possible for women to enter into what was formerly considered a man's world. The state has arranged for child care, for health care, for the sick and the old. Educational reforms have provided all citizens with opportunities to take advantage of a wide range of study opportunities aiming at enabling everybody to participate in all aspects of community life according to their capabilities.

Why Swedish policies have yet to bring about sexual equality is the focus of current research. It is to that research—which focuses on educational process rather than access and which explores the complexity of achieving equality—that this chapter now turns.

Research Findings on Sexual Equality in School

In a review of research on sex differences and sex differentiation in Swedish schools, the Swedish researcher I. Wernersson has found that this body of research is very small, especially considering the government's stated policy of promoting sexual equality through the schools. Wernersson has noted that curricular changes have changed girls' performances on tests in traditionally male areas since the 1960s.[16] Nevertheless, the Swedish pattern of sex differences in school performance does not deviate from that demonstrated in other countries. Girls tend to receive higher marks and to perform better in languages, whereas boys perform better in science.[17]

Studies of teacher-pupil interactions show that teachers in Sweden also tend to direct more attention to boys. One study focusing on language shows that boys in elementary school tend to dominate the classroom.[18] In general, the few Swedish studies on interaction patterns in the classroom point in the same direction as British and American studies. Boys generally receive more attention from teachers, they talk more, and they dominate discussions and debates in school. In spite of efforts to give boys and girls the same education, the informal life in school remains highly differentiated by sex.[19] Policies that focus solely on access to schooling have yet to deal with day-to-day practices in the classrooms.

A second reason why government policies may not have been successful in attaining sexual equality relates to the assumptions underlying public policy. Sex and social class have been regarded as similar forms of social differentiation. Planners have assumed that strategies to end class-based inequalities will work in the case of sex-based inequalities. Thus, the government has stressed equal responsibilities as well as equal rights and opportunities. As Wernersson points out: "When translated into practical experiments the ideas tend to come out as a mixture of socialist ideas of changing the base of the social structure and liberal ideas of giving all individuals 'equality of opportunity' in the struggle for the top of the hierarchy."[20]

The strong belief in the ability of the schools to break up rigid notions of "male" and "female" and to widen individual options is manifest in the 1970 Sex Role Project of the National Board of Education. Among the no less than twenty-two different areas of action, the most detailed parts dealt with guidance and counseling. This is the part of the equality program that has been most elaborated since 1980. There has been an obvious concentration on efforts to assist girls' entry into traditionally nonfemale educational routes and occupations. A Parliament grant to the Ministry of Labor has been used to fund different projects aiming at stimulating girls' entry into science and technology. Government intervention has been channeled in only one direction—to change the patterns of career choice of girls and women. Wernersson considers it a problem "that the power of the labor market and its high visibility tend to turn the whole issue of fairness and equality between the sexes into a matter of educational choice."[21]

Some of the assumptions behind the government's sexual equality policies have increasingly come to be seriously questioned. One such assumption is the government's implicit notion that if boys and girls are treated alike, there are identical outcomes. Another is the strong belief in changing girls' educational and career choices by encouraging them to enter male-dominated fields. Researchers point to the complexities of the problem of career choice. Today planners at the National Board of Education recognize the need for further research into how traditional sex-role stereotypes develop and affect girls' learning and development, and how schools continue to perpetuate and elaborate these stereotypes by new approaches.[22] Only the means, not the goals, of equal opportunity are being questioned. The struggle for these goals in school has to be seen as a perpetual process with continuous adjustment to changing conditions.

A Closer Look at Women in Higher Education

The scarcity of women in science and technology and in postgraduate studies has been the object of some governmental reports.[23] In 1983, a report was published under the title "If Half of Them Were Women." Besides statistical facts and data, the report also included reflections from fifteen women researchers from different research fields on the question: "What would happen in your research field if half of the researchers were women?"

The report reflects a new awareness of the particularities of women's knowledge. Most research fields have been dominated by a male perspective and by the man's way of defining knowledge. Women's knowledge and perspectives have been overlooked.

During the last decade, some Women Studies Sections have been developed at Swedish universities, supported by the National Board of Universities and Colleges. In a number of fields research from a "women's perspective" or, as it tends to be called, from a "gender theoretical perspective" is growing. The appointment of six researchers in the field of gender equality at the State Research Councils is a sign of a new awareness of the fact that organizational measures have to be supported by research contributions from different perspectives.

Hitherto, the body of research on women in higher education has been scanty. Few educational researchers have been interested in further investigations concerning the skewed sex distribution within higher education.[24] Quite to the contrary, the increasing number of female students has led some researchers to wrong conclusions concerning the state of equality between the sexes.[25]

Some studies are now underway to investigate the equality issue by combining qualitative analyses of educational policy as well as of women's reality. In a Nordic joint project—HEKLA—fifteen researchers from various disciplines in the Nordic countries are cooperating in order to analyze how educational reforms have influenced women's lives and work. By using a life-perspective approach, some Swedish studies have highlighted the differences between the "plain sailing" (straight roads) anticipated by educational planners and women's winding roads. Women's life stories illustrate the differences in values in two different segments of the labor market, the paid and the unpaid, the productive versus the reproductive. Theories, passing behind behavioral patterns to deeper structures of thought, seem to be required in order to understand what happens in education and how women make use of their education.[26]

A study of women graduates from upper secondary school in the 1960s showed that they were deeply occupied with problems of combining a career with a family. The cleavage between the two worlds of job and home, discussed by A. Myrdal and V. Klein in their book *Women's Two Roles* (1956), still seems to be prevalent in spite of all reform work.[27] Have the reforms in higher education focused so strongly on adjusting the education to the productive work that other life roles have been overlooked? This is a question that has been raised in the Nordic joint research program. In order to understand the complexity of the issue of women and education, researchers have felt the necessity of a historical perspective. Even when investigating educational reform policy, there are lessons to learn from the past.

Looking Back

The reform process in Swedish society started with family policy, initiated by Alva and Gunnar Myrdal's call for attention to the decreasing birthrate in the

1930s.[28] Alva Myrdal, later one of the key figures in school reform, had a great belief in education's role in promoting equality. As a woman, she also realized that the problem confronting "the childbearing sex" was to combine the dual role of raising a family and an educational and vocational career. In 1940, she found that the "disharmony in the relation between marriage and gainful employment is at the bottom of many women's problems." She stressed that women as well as men had the right and the obligation to assume both roles, and she discussed the obligations of society to take women's problems seriously. In 1940, she concluded her book *Nation and Family*, where she had commented on the Swedish family program as follows: "The risk is great that society will proceed so slowly in solving these problems of women's existence that a new and even more desperate crisis may invade the whole field of women, family and population."[29]

Recently, a downward trend in the Swedish birthrate has caused new concerns about the fertility pattern. In the 1980s demographers started to investigate the interplay between education and fertility. A series of studies have been presented pointing to new life patterns. Swedish women tend to combine part-time work, education, and childcare. The educational level has been found to be of great importance for the work behavior of women.[30] According to the demographer E. Bernhardt, however, the tendency to abandon a "work career strategy" in favor of a "combination strategy" has been equally strong, regardless of the educational level of the women.

Swedish women's life stories, collected in one project within the Nordic HEKLA framework, give some information concerning this new strategy. According to the women, part-time work tends to be good for the family but not for the career of these women. One woman says: "I feel that since my children were born I am constantly cruising between the demands of working life on me as a professional woman and the responsibility for home and children." She concluded her life story as follows: "There is a constant risk that the life that could make you a whole human being making use of your full potential, can be reversed, so that the too many different demands make you a disharmonious, divided person."[31] This statement shows that women's participation pattern in education also has to be related to other life roles, as important to society but not given the same visibility.

The conflict between productive and reproductive work and women's dual roles in society were very much in focus in Alva Myrdal's work. Feminists in the 1960s were critical. "We ought to stop harping on the concept of 'women's two roles'," said Eva Moberg, a popular journalist and editor of the Fredrika Bremer Association's bimonthly *Herta*. "Both men and women have *one* principal role, that of being people."[32]

Changing the role of men in the direction of taking more responsibility for the everyday tasks at home and for the family is one important goal in the Swedish equality policy. Another has been to strengthen the position of women in the labor market.

In an ongoing debate concerning the effects of sexual equality policies, some researchers argue that the reforms have been more beneficial for men than for women. They plead for more balance between actions directed toward the labor market and the private sector.[33]

The issue of gender equality is complex. Wernersson found it difficult to describe the policy of gender equality as successful in Swedish classroom practice, but she left it undecided whether it was a failure. In a 1982 review of Swedish equality policy in general, the American journalist Hilda Scott found that great efforts seemed to have produced insignificant results, and she pointed out that it was hard to attain sex-role equality through a series of separate policies.[34] However, she was optimistic in her prediction of the future: "And, given Sweden's record of designing policies and measures to meet new social situations, there is every reason to believe that Swedish women will be pioneers in the next phase of the women's liberation struggle—the development of a blueprint for a non-sexist society."[35]

Looking Ahead

At the time of this writing, the Swedish government has presented a new bill to Parliament on equality between men and women in the 1990s.[36] This legislation contains a five-year plan for desegregating the labor market by gender. Proposals for education are also included. A long-range goal is even to bring about sex distribution in all programs of study in the integrated upper secondary school. The five-year plan in education contains quotas for all educational levels as well as teaching staffs and school administration in order to change sexual segregation in schools and universities.

The Swedish government's continuous concern about social justice and equal opportunities provides, by international standards, an extremely favorable framework. However, whether the objectives of women and men side by side in the classroom and at work will become a reality is dependent on a complex interaction between economic, social, and demographic factors. This interaction has to be taken more into consideration when the government bill now suggests increased research on proposed equality measures in education as well as more research on women.

Research on the equality issue from a woman's perspective might bring about less disparity between ideas and realities in educational policy and practice.

NOTES

1. *Side by Side. A Report on Equality Between Women and Men in Sweden 1985* (Stockholm: Ministry of Labor, 1985), 107.

2. Ibid., p. 2.

3. See D. Moynihan, Foreword to *Nation and Family* by A. Myrdal (Cambridge, Mass.: MIT Press 1941); see also A. J. Heidenheimar, *Major Reforms of the Swedish Education System,* World Staff Working Paper No. 290 (Washington D.C.: World Bank, 1978).

4. "The Status of Women in Sweden: Report to the United Nations 1968," in E. Dahlstrom, ed., *The Changing Roles of Men and Women* (Boston: Beacon Press, 1971), p. 215.

5. E. Johansson, "Literacy Campaigns in Sweden," in R. F. Arnove and H. J. Graff, eds., *National Literacy Campaigns* (New York and London: Plenum Press, 1987).

6. Sveriges Officiella Statistik. A: *Foldrakningen 1930*. Del V och VI. [The Census of 1930, Vols. V and VI.]

7. B. Onsell, *Morske man och menlosa mamseller. En bok om roller och kon* [Bold men and harmless women. A book on roles and sex], (Stockholm: LT:s forlag, 1978), p. 61.

8. I. Wernersson, *Gender Equality—Ideology and Reality*, Manuscript (Gothenburg: Department of Education and Educational Research, 1987), p. 3.

9. See A. Andrae-Thelin, *Equal Opportunities for Girls: The Role of the Primary School* (The Council of Europe), Paper read at the 36th European teachers' seminary in Donaueschigen, Federal Republic of Germany, June 22–27, 1987.

10. W. F. Connell, *A History of Education in the Twentieth Century World* (Canberra: Curriculum Development Center, 1980).

11. See I. Elqvist-Saltzman and S. Opper, *Equality and Internationalism: Two Concepts at the Forefront of Educational Transformation in Sweden?* Paper delivered at 25th Annual meeting of the Comparative-International Education Society in Tallahassee, Florida, March 1981. Revised ed. Uppsala Reports on Education 12 (Uppsala: Department of Education, October 1981).

12. See *Kvinno- och mansvarlden. Fakta om jamstalldheten i Sverige 1986* [Stockholm: Statistics Sweden, 1986]. See also *Women and Men in Sweden. Facts and Figures. Equal Opportunity* (Stockholm: Statistics Sweden, 1985).

13. Compare M. L. Ranour, G. L. Strasburg, and J. Lipman-Blumen, "Women in Higher Education," *Harvard Educational Review* 52, No. 2 (1982).

14. *Side by Side*, 17.

15. G. Asplund, *Karriarens villkor* [The conditions of career] (Stockholm: Trevi, 1984).

16. I. Emanuelsson and A. Svensson, *Does the Level of Intelligence Decrease? A Comparison Between Thirteen-Year-Olds Tested in 1961, 1966 and 1980*. Report 1985:2 (Gothenburg: Department of Education and Educational Research, 1985). See also Wernersson, *Gender Equality*.

17. See G. Balke-Aurel and T. Lindblad, *Lar de sig nagot?* [Do they learn anything? Word and grammar knowledge in English from grade 5 in the compulsory school to grade 3 in the upper secondary school], Rapport no. 99 (Gothenburg: Department of Educational Research, University of Gothenburg). See also L. Bergmlan, *Utveckling av konsskillnader i skolprestationer mellan 10 och 15 ars alder* [Development of sex differences in school achievement between 10 and 15 years of age], Rapport no. 24 (Stockholm: Department of Psychology, University of Stockholm); C. Baverholm and U. Nilsson, *Nagra larares syn pa jamstalldhet mellan konen* [Some teachers' view of gender equality] (Gothenburg: Department of Education, University of Gothenburg), mimeo; E. H. Ekstrand, *Sex Differences in Second Language Learning?* Sartryck och smatryck No. 344 (Malmo: Department of Education); I. Emanuelsson and S. Fischbein, "Vive la Difference? A Study of Sex and Schooling," *Scandinavian Journal of Educational Research* 30 (1986): 71–84; A. Kelly, *Girls and Science. An International Study of Sex Differences in School Science Achievement* (Stockholm: Almqvist and Wiksell International, 1978); A. Svens-

son, *Relative Achievement. School Performance in Relation to Intelligence, Sex and Home Environment* (Stockholm: Almqvist & Wiksell, 1971); and I. Wernersson, *Konsdifferentiering i grundskolan* [Sex differences in the compulsory school] (Gothenburg: Acta universitatis Gothoburgensis, 1977).

18. J. Einarsson and T. Hultman, *Godmorgon flickor och pojkar?* [Good morning girls and boys?] (Stockholm: Liber, 1985).

19. See I. Wernersson, R. Lander, and E. Ohrn, *Hur blev det med jamstalldheten? Utvardering av forsoket "Jamstalld skola"* [What became of gender equality? Evaluation of the programme "Equal School"] (Stockholm: Arbetsmarknadsdepartementet, Jamstalldhetssekretariatet, 1984).

20. Wernersson, *Gender Equality*, p. 4.

21. Ibid., p. 13.

22. See Andrae-Thelin, *Equal Opportunities for Girls*.

23. SOU 1983: 4 *Om halften vore kvinnor* [If half of them were women] (Stockholm: Jamstalldhetskommitten).

24. I. Elqvist-Saltzman, *Fler kvinnor i hogskolan—problem eller tillgang?* [More women in higher education—a problem or a challenge?] Fou Skrift series, No. 3 (Stockholm: UHA, 1987).

25. A. Svensson, *Hogskolestudier—attraktivare for kvinnor?* [Higher education—more attractive for women?] Fou Projektrapport, No. 1 (Stockholm: UHA, 1985).

26. I. Elqvist-Saltzman, *Swedish Educational Reform—Women's Life Stories—What Can They Tell About a Rational Reform Era?* Paper delivered at AERA annual meeting, April 1987, Washington D.C.: see also H. Ve, "Ideals of Equality in School System of the Welfare State," Paper presented at the 10th World Congress Research Groups 32: Women in Society, Mexico City.

27. A. Myrdal and V. Klein, *Women's Two Roles. Home and Work* (London: Routledge and Kegan Paul, 1956.)

28. A. Myrdal and G. Myrdal, *Kris i befolkningsfragan* [The population problem in crisis] (Stockholm: Bonniers, 1935).

29. A. Myrdal, *Nation and Family. The Swedish Experiment in Democratic Family and Population Policy* (Cambridge, Mass.: MIT Press, 1968), p. 426.

30. See SCB, *Kvinnor och barn. Intervjuer med kvinnor om familj och arbete.* Information i prognosfragor, No. 4 (Stockholm: SCB, 1982); see also E. Bernhardt, "Women's Home Attachment at First Birth: The Case of Sweden," *European Journal of Population* 2, No. 1 (1986); and E. Bernhardt, *The Choice of Part-time Work Among Swedish One-child Mothers*, Research Reports in Demography 40 (Stockholm).

31. Elqvist-Saltzman, *Swedish Educational Reform*, p. 1.

32. E. Moberg is quoted in Sheila B. Kamerman and Alfred J. Kahn, eds., *Family Policy; Government and Families in Fourteen Countries* (New York: Columbia University Press, 1978), p. 33; see also A. G. Leijon, *Swedish Women—Swedish Men.* (Stockholm: The Swedish Institute, 1968), p. 149.

33. M. Eduards, *"Kon stat och jamstalldhetspolitik"* [Gender, State and Equality Policy], i *Kvinnovetenskaplig Tidskrift*, No. 3 (Gothenburg: 1986).

34. H. Scott, *Sweden's "Right to Be Human." Sex-role Equality: The Goal and the Reality* (New York: M. E. Sharpe, 1982).

35. Ibid., p. 167.

36. Proposition 1987–1988, p. 105.

16
THE SOVIET UNION

David H. Kelly

Russia (and the Soviet Union) has long had a sense of itself as a great nation and a people of pride and forbearance, yet the country has sensed itself as not quite equal to its Western neighbors. In 1917, the nation underwent a great revolution which added the element of Marxism to the historic concern for the health and vigor of the national state. Some of its early leaders, like V. I. Lenin, were more interested in Marxism and revolution, and others like Joseph Stalin, were more committed to the strength of the state. But no leader has ever completely neglected either element. Fortunately for women, both elements historically have operated to increase women's roles in education and in society as a whole to the point that today the Soviet Union can be seen as the world leader in many aspects of equality for women.

The organization of the Russian state as a power began with Ivan the Terrible in the sixteenth century and was greatly enhanced by Peter the Great in the early eighteenth century. Only in the late eighteenth century did Catherine the Great introduce the idea that education could increase state power. Influenced by the Enlightenment, Catherine felt that the state needed an educated noble class to serve its interest. Peter had long before stressed such ideas for men, but Catherine recognized that ignorant and superstitious mothers and wives could not produce or sustain men who could form an intelligent ruling class.[1] Catherine's answer was to decree equal education in 1784 and later to create the Smolny Institute in St. Petersburg in 1794 as a boarding school for young noble women and Novodevichy Convent Institute in Moscow for daughters of the urban classes.

Even as she created the educational system, Catherine found that the ideas and interests of the educated began to diverge from the interest of the state. Those who were schooled looked for personal fulfillment; the state, on the other hand, strove to consolidate and extend its power. In the nineteenth century, this divergence became a schism. While preparing and instituting reform, the Tsarist government hesitated to push for complete change until the crisis engendered by the defeat of the Crimean War forced the issue. The reign of Alexander II brought the liberation of serfs, improvements in the legal system, the creation of local government (*Zemstvos*), and a modern conscripted army. The *zemstvo* provided a way to vastly increase education, and the new army demanded literate recruits. Both the state and the educated public supported educational expansion. The late nineteenth and early twentieth centuries saw a vast increase in education, and women were not excluded from this expansion. By 1914, eight million pupils attended primary school; about one-third, 2.7 million, were girls (20 percent of the age cohort). Increases in primary education called for a teaching corps. By 1911, the majority of primary teachers were women. By 1909, there was more secondary education for women than men, with 958 girls' schools and 756 boys' schools. (This amounted to about one place for every 300 girls versus one for every 400 boys.) Even the class basis of women's secondary education had shifted downward, with 20 percent of the girls coming from the gentry and 25 percent from the peasantry. In higher education, the government opened the university to women in 1861 only to close it two years later. By 1916, the universities had for a time opened their doors to women; 30,000 women were in attendance, constituting almost one-fourth the total.[2] Despite this solid beginning, in 1917 Russia was an empire of vast peasant ignorance; less than one-half the men and one-quarter of the women were literate,[3] a situation comparable to France in the 1840s.

The revolutions of 1917 which created the Soviet Union made Marxism the official ideology of the state. Marxism advocates complete equality and a productive role for every individual in society. Karl Marx and particularly his collaborator, Friederich Engels, recognized the special position of women in society—their ties to the family structure which limits their independence and leads to exploitation. The Marxist answer was economic independence for women through paid work in the larger economy, particularly in the modern and industrial sectors. This clearly required education, and hence Marxist ideology held great promise for women. From the onset of the Soviet era, the Communist party, under the leadership of Bolsheviks and feminists like Aleksandra Kollanti and Lenin's wife, Natalya Krupskaya, attempted to fulfill that promise. In the 1920s, numerous experiments with progressive and adult education took place. More critically, a women's section of the Communist party tried to stamp out the very idea of patriarchy.[4] (This was a difficult task since as late as 1906 the male head of a peasant family had complete legal control over his wife and daughters, as well as over his sons and their wives.)[5]

Despite such efforts, the revolution and civil war that followed created great chaos affecting education. Many who might have aided in building education did not support the new government; most teachers, for example, were anti-Soviet. However, by 1927 the school system had recovered, and women came close to equality in enrollments in urban areas. In that year, 9 percent of urban boys starting school remained for nine years, whereas almost 13 percent of girls achieved the same educational level. In rural areas, the reverse was true; only 62 of every 100 girls beginning primary education remained in the second year of school, whereas 80 percent of rural boys continued. The urban-rural differences meant that girls represented only 39 percent of primary school enrollment but nearly half of secondary school enrollment. (Secondary schools were urban.) In higher education women accounted for 28 percent of all students, which represented little improvement over prerevolutionary Russia.[6]

The rise of Joseph Stalin in the late 1920s and his slogan "socialism in one country" meant a turn from Marxist concerns to a greater emphasis on the development of state power. This swing in priorities, continuing through World War II and the recovery era of the 1940s, did not diminish the push toward greater educational opportunity for women. Soviet leaders saw women's labor and intelligence as critical ingredients of development. By 1940, most of the urban-rural differences (except for Central Asia) had been overcome, and universal primary education (Grades 1 to 4) was a reality. Junior secondary education reached 65 percent of the age cohort, and almost half of this enrollment was female.[7] These statistics indicate tremendous advances in rural education. This was in part impelled by the need for trained workers who were rural migrants to the cities attracted by jobs in the growing industrial sector of the economy.

Stalin's policies had a negative side, as far as women were concerned. Gone was the experimentation and the separate organization within the Communist party for women. Patriarchal values were reaffirmed in new family laws, and greater role distinctions were created in education by gender. In 1943, sex segregation was reinstituted in Soviet schools as a wartime measure.[8] These moves, diametrically opposed to the further liberation of women, were contradicted by World War II. The great conscriptions of males for military service in World War II and the loss of men in the war created greater need and opportunity for female employment. The need can be demonstrated by looking at the employed population of 1959: 2 million more women were employed than men for the age cohorts that entered the labor force in the late 1930s through 1950.[9]

THE SCHOOL SYSTEM AFTER STALIN'S INFLUENCE

By the 1950s, there was universal primary education—Grades 1 through 4. The secondary system consisted of Grades 5 to 7; later, Grade 8 was added. This junior secondary level was also rapidly becoming universal by 1940. At age fourteen (later, age fifteen; until very recently, children began school at age seven), the upper secondary level was divided between general secondary education which led to the university and special (vocational) education. The

Table 16.1
Women Enrolled in Upper Secondary Education, 1950 and 1980

	1950	1980
All Secondary Schools	54%	56%
Special Secondary Schools		
Manufacturing, construction, etc.	35%	43%
Agriculture	41%	37%
Economics, Law	73%	85%
Health	85%	90%
Education	77%	85%

Source: Ratliff, Patricia. "Women's Educational Attainment Levels
         in the Soviet Union: 1950-1980." Paper presented at the
         American Educational Research Association Annual Meeting.
         April 20-24, 1987. Washington, D.C. From: Norodnoe
         Khoziaistvo (1970) and Vestnik Statistiki volumes 1, 2, and
         6.

general secondary school retained about one-third the students. (Recent reforms plan to limit this to one-quarter.)[10] Special secondary school consisted of a varying number of years of education and led to precise occupations from machinists in the industrial schools to primary school teachers, nurses, and clerks in the education, health, and economics schools.

Table 16.1 shows the pattern and percentage of female enrollment in secondary schools. The pattern established in the Stalin period and shown in the 1950s figures in the Stalin period reflects both the need for women due to wartime shortages and the general patriarchal values. Comparison of 1950 to 1980 shows this pattern has not changed. The proportion of females enrolled in upper secondary school has remained the same; however, major reforms and expansion have made upper secondary education almost universal. The table does not show that girls are the majority of students in the general (or university) track of secondary school. They are, however, a minority in specialized secondary education in manufacturing, construction, and transportation. They have a far higher share of enrollment than in comparable Western schools. These specialized secondary schools lead directly to the best paid skilled worker jobs in the Soviet Union.[11] Similar gender segregation also occurs in general secondary education. While there is a core curriculum in schools that stresses science and mathematics,

Table 16.2
Distribution of Women's Enrollment in Higher Education, 1950 and 1980

	1950	1980
All types taken together	53%	52%
Manufacturing, Construction, Transportation, Power	30%	42%
Agriculture	39%	34%
Economics and Law	57%	67%
Health, Physical Culture, Sport	65%	58%
Education and Culture	71%	69%

Source: Ratliff, Patricia. "Women's Educational Attainment Levels
         in the Soviet Union: 1950-1980." p. 12. Paper presented
         at the American Educational Research Association Annual
         Meeting, April 20-24, 1987, Washington, D.C. From:
         Norodune Khoziaistvo (1970) and Vestnik Statistiki volumes
         1, 2 and 6.

there is some indication that girls are directed away from the hard sciences and
encouraged to study social science, literature, and languages. [12]

STALIN'S INFLUENCE AND HIGHER EDUCATION

Soviet higher education, as it developed through the 1930s and 1940s to the
present day, is a complex mixture of institutions. Some of these institutions
directly parallel European universities and research institutes; others are tied
more directly to functional activities and are administered by departments of the
state for various industries, the military and security branches, and so on. Industry
and other state needs expanded so rapidly under industrial plans in the 1930s
that the training of high-level personnel could only be accomplished by creating
narrow, functionally specialized higher education.

Table 16.2 illustrates that, as a whole, the pattern by women's enrollment for
training in these higher education institutions is very similar to the divisions in
secondary education. However, specialized secondary education is not the path
to any of them; entrance to specific institutions is by examinations administered
to students holding a general secondary education certificate.

Since Table 16.2 is a percentage table, it does not reflect the tremendous
growth in enrollment that took place between 1950 and 1960. Between 1970
and 1979 alone, the proportion of women receiving higher and specialized secondary education rose from 19.4 percent to 29 percent of all women workers.

Comparable figures for men were 17.1 percent and 24.5 percent.[13] In the 1980s more than 20 percent of the age cohort continues on to higher education.

The pattern of educational placement is similar to that of secondary education. Women dominate in the social sciences, health, and education, and are a minority in industrial and agricultural fields. Even where they are a majority, women's percentages of enrollment at this educational level is reduced—health, 90 percent of specialized education, 67 percent of higher education; education 85 percent of secondary, 69 percent of higher education. The differences between the statistics on education and on industrial pursuits clearly reflect a gender segmentation of higher education—one that has led some to speak of a "feminization" of higher education. To reduce such differences, discrimination has been instituted against women, and higher test scores, grades, and so on, have been demanded from women for entrance to university-level education.[14] When women do enter the predominantly male fields of industrial studies, there are indications that they are trained for work in the less prestigious light and consumer industries.[15]

If moving from secondary to higher education denotes a pattern of discrimination, the proportion of women with higher degrees and their ranks in working situations demonstrate this even more clearly. Table 16.3 presents, as an example, the graduate school training and subsequent ranks in their profession of scientific workers by gender. Whereas 52 percent of enrollment in higher education is female, only 28 percent and 14 percent of scientific workers are attaining higher degrees.

In the academic profession in science, women are lumped in the lower ranks in a pattern similar to that seen in Western nations. However, we should also note that the percentage of women with higher degrees has gone up while a great expansion has occurred—by three percentage points in terms of candidates and the proportion of doctorates has doubled from 7 percent to 14 percent. There have also been sharp improvements in the two highest ranks of academics. Women professors rose from 7.1 percent of the total number of professors in 1950 to 10.4 percent in 1976, whereas women associate professors rose from 14.7 percent of the total at the rank in 1950 to 22.9 percent of a much expanded number of associate professors in 1976.

EDUCATION OF MINORITY GROUPS

Thus far, this chapter has considered the Soviet Union as a whole. The country is actually composed of republics whose attitudes toward women and progress vary sharply. The Russian, Ukrainian, Belorussian, and Baltic Republics have similarly high education levels and are among the most populated areas. The smaller Central Asian Republics with a strong Muslim influence present a rather different picture. Table 16.4 compares the all Union figures with one such typical republic, Uzbek SSR.

Although the figures in Table 16.4 show clear improvement in women's education in the 1970s for both the entire Soviet Union and for the Uzbek SSR,

Table 16.3
Number, Rank, and Training of Scientific Workers, 1950 and 1976

	1950		1976	
	Number	% Female	Number	% Female
Degrees of Scientific Workers				
Candidate of Science*	45,000	25.0	345,400	28.1
Doctor of Science*	8,300	7.2	34,600	13.8
Rank of Scientific Workers				
Academician, Professor	8,900	7.1	24,000	10.4
Associate Professor	21,800	14.7	92,500	22.9
Senior Research Associate	11,400	30.7	56,300	23.9
Junior Research Associate or Assistant	19,600	48.0	44,300	48.7
Total	162,500	36.3	1,253,500	39.7

*A Candidate of Science is roughly equivalent to the American Ph.D.
Doctor of Science recognizes lifetime achievement.

Source: Gail Lapidus, Women in Social Society: Equality, Development and Social Change. Berkeley: University of California Press, 1983. p. 6–157.

Table 16.4
Educational Level of Employed Persons, 1970 and 1979 (in Percentages)

| | 1970 | | | | 1979 | | | |
| | All Union | | Uzbek | | All Union | | Uzbek | |
	Men	Women	Men	Women	Men	Women	Men	Women
Elementary	26.8	22.8	17.9	20.4	16.6	16.0	10.5	13.6
Incomplete Secondary	32.7	29.5	27.8	31.3	28.3	24.0	19.4	21.9
Secondary General	15.6	16.2	24.5	17.8	28.2	27.1	42.6	40.0
Higher or Special Secondary	17.1	19.4	17.4	13.4	24.5	29.0	25.1	20.6

Source: "The All-Union Population Census: Levels of Education of the Employed Population of the USSR and Union Republic by Social Group." Social Education (January–February–March 1982): p. 261, 267.

the usual pattern is reversed. Women in the Uzbek SSR had less rather than more secondary and higher education than men, and the whole Republic had a much lower level of educational attainment for both men and women than in the case of the Soviet Union as a whole. Although no one would accuse the leaders of the Soviet Union of trying to limit women's education in Central Asian areas like Uzbekistan, the figures above do not relate the full extent of the problem. Employed persons are those most likely to have been to school and include Russians and other nationalities who have come to work in the Republic. Statistics from 1955 showed that only 26 percent of rural girls (i.e., from traditional Muslim families) attended secondary schools.[16] Figures for higher education from 1977 show improvement, but they also reveal that the problem persists. Of 31,673 persons enrolled in different types of higher education institutes in Uzbekistan, almost 40 percent were women, but one-third of these were not native to Uzbekistan. (A total of 26.8 percent of the total were indigenous.)[17] Islamic traditions of strong, closed family life with women at home seem to account for these differences. Soviet leaders and planners have long pushed for greater education and a liberation of Central Asian women. They have been motivated by Marxism's traditional ambivalence about religion, desires to use the labor power of women, and fear of overpopulation in a harsh, limited environment, but change has been slow.

Starting from a position of clear inferiority, the Soviet Union has caught up to the industrialized nations in terms of education and women's role within it. Universal education exists through junior secondary education and is being approached at the senior secondary level. As in other European nations, a significant proportion, 20 percent of the age cohort, goes on to higher education. Also as in the West, women use secondary and higher education more than men, but there are gender distinctions in curriculum, with women predominately in education, medicine, and other white-collar areas. Far fewer women enter science and the engineering fields, although more women do so in the Soviet Union than in most Western nations. At the university level and particularly in graduate training, there appears to be discrimination against women. Finally, minority women, especially in Asiatic areas, do not use the education system to gain even a semblance of equality.

EDUCATION AND WORK

Education is only a prelude to a life of work and social relationships. The critical questions are whether educational attainments and equalities lead to better jobs and equal compensation across the economic spectrum and to deeper, more equal personal relations between men and women. Since the 1940s nearly half or more of the labor force has been composed of women workers (from a low of 46 percent in 1955 to the current 51.5 percent). In 1980, more than 85 percent of women from each age cohort (twenty to fifty) were in the paid labor force.[18] However, the market for women's labor is segmented. Women predominate in communications where they make up 68 percent of the workforce, in trade where they are 76 percent of all workers, in health 85 percent of the workforce, in education 73 percent and in banking, 85 percent of all workers. In all these areas except health and education, the proportion of women increased between 1940 and 1974. In transportation women represented 24 percent of all workers and in construction, 30 percent.[19] Even in areas where women's participation is equivalent to their participation in the workforce as a whole, women are generally found in the light industries (textiles, clothing, food preparation) that are devalued by Soviet planners.

When women work in key industries like machine building, they often hold white-collar jobs. Data from Leningrad in 1965 showed that 87 percent of skilled mental workers and 90 percent of semiskilled mental workers in machine building were women, but only 8 percent of skilled manual workers (for example, welders), 30 percent of skilled machine operators, and 34 percent of unskilled manual workers were women. In agriculture, another field where women's participation is proportional to their participation in the workforce as a whole, only 5 percent of workers with machinery were women, whereas over 90 percent of the swineherds, milking personnel, and poultry workers were women.[20]

Women's achievements in education, particularly in secondary school, have earned them positions in the service sector of the economy and in many levels of white-collar occupations. Without education, women generally fall into the lowest manual work categories.

White-collar positions have traditionally led to positions of management and authority. This is no longer the case in Western economies and is not the case in the Soviet Union. Looking again at the Leningrad machine building industry in 1965 where the white-collar workforce was almost 90 percent female, only 16 percent of management positions were held by women. In industry and agriculture as a whole, women hold from 13 percent to 24 percent of responsible positions and constitute 9 percent of the directors of industrial enterprises. In fields where women dominate the workforce, they have a far smaller share of management positions than one would expect. The limited percentage of women who climbed the academic ladder in higher education has already been noted. At lower levels of education where 73 percent of the workforce was female in the mid-1970s, only 29 percent of the directors of secondary schools and 33 percent of the directors of eight-year schools were women. Only at the deputy director level did women approach their share of management positions. (About 60 percent of these posts were held by women.) Women also dominated the directorships of primary schools.[21] In medicine, where 85 percent or more of the workers are female and 77 percent of the doctors are also women, only 61 percent of chief doctors or heads of medical institutions were female.[22]

The Soviet Union's workforce is gender segregated by occupation both vertically and horizontally. Given the promise of equality, this is embarrassing to Soviet officials who have often challenged the Western nations on their treatment of women. Soviet officials have acted to correct their own situation through propaganda and special programs,[23] but they have also tried to hide the problem. Michael Sacks compared the occupational censuses of 1959 and 1970 and demonstrated shifts and combinations of categories that would either mask the hierarchy (proofreaders lumped in with heads of publishing houses, for example) or combine categories that were formerly heavily male or female so that segregation was not as noticeable.[24]

The result of gender-based occupational segregation is less pay for women. This has historical roots in the Stalin period of development when heavy industry was given greatest priority. In that era of primitive socialist accumulation, all wages were very low, but skilled manual workers, because of both a need for their skills and ideology (the Soviet Union is the worker's state) received significantly more pay. Women were forced to work for the generally low wages. Because wives were often trapped into their marriages by a family policy that made divorce more difficult, that no longer recognized illegitimate children, and that abolished abortion, women were willing to support family income by taking jobs as simple manual workers or in the less urgent (lower paid) sectors of the economy. The ideological justifications have persisted; white-collar jobs, trade and communications positions, and service sector work like education all receive lower rates. The average monthly earning for women in 1975 was 146 rubles. Women in construction and transport (where they made up less than 30 percent of the workforce) earned more than 170 rubles a month. The monthly average wages in credit and insurance, education, trade, and health (each sector employing more than 70 percent women) were 134, 127, 109, and 102 rubles, respectively. In industry, women represented 49 percent of the workforce and earned an average 162 rubles a month. However, there is a major difference in pay between industries. Pay in male fields like coal production, iron and steel, and machinery is much higher than in the light or food industries dominated by women. The pay scales of equally skilled and trained engineers show this difference. In coal production, pay averages 380 rubles a month; in iron and steel, 270 to 320 rubles; in machinery, 260 to 310 rubles, and in the food industry, 180 to 200 rubles. Given both the horizontal and vertical occupational segregation, women in the Soviet Union, as in most Western nations, receive 65 to 70 percent of men's average wage.[25]

Wage differentials between occupations within the economy do change or can be changed. The growing sophistication of technology and the need for scientific research have created a growing number of scientific workers in the Soviet Union. Given women's educational advancement they have come to account for 50 percent of this new workforce. Ideological considerations about the value of manual work have fallen to the wayside, and these workers average a relatively high monthly salary of 155 rubles. Throughout the world demand for iron and steel has diminished, as it will in the Soviet Union, whereas demand for light industrial goods (electronics, for example) has risen. Changes in priorities will be reflected in wages. Already, the Soviet Union has been forced to raise payments for agricultural products after leaders promised a better diet. Promises and demands for consumer goods and better distribution of all products may have positive effects for women in the trade sector. These are some of the positive prospectives, but low paid female textile, clothing, and food workers are likely to remain in the Soviet Union just as they continue to exist throughout the world.

FAMILY ROLE AND OCCUPATIONAL OBSTACLES

Although occupational segregation as a cause of lower women's wages may shift, the problem of hierarchical obstacles is more critical. Why is it that women who enter many fields with some educational advantage achieve nowhere near their share of advancement to managerial ranks? Advancement depends on in-service training, correspondence, and night schooling, as well as willingness to take part in volunteer community activity often organized through the workplace. Women simply lack the time to do these things since general patriarchal values mean that women perform most of the childrearing and household tasks. Although Soviet husbands are no more sluggardly than American husbands—each puts in about the same number of hours—the complexity of household tasks is greater in the Soviet Union. There are fewer labor-saving gadgets (automatic washers and dryers for clothes, for example), food is less conveniently packaged, shopping takes a great deal more time, and so on. The greater complexity of tasks means that women put in more than twice the time than men on household chores; all Soviet planners refer to women's "double job." Changing family structures have recently increased this household burden for women. More families have a simple nuclear structure, and there are fewer females to share the burden. There is also an increased divorce rate and a great increase in female-headed households. Children, of course, add enormously to household work. Conflicting demands of the workforce and the family have led to a major decline in the birthrate in the developed areas of the Soviet Union.[26]

Childcare is one area in which the Soviet state has acted to relieve the burden of household work. Over 30 percent of the three- to six-year-old age cohort is in preschool (some 10 million in 1975), and over a million more infants are in creches. The system almost doubled between the mid-1960s and mid-1970s, and millions more places were planned.[27] The government of the city of Leningrad has promised a place for every child. The lag between demand and the provision of centers is greatest in the rural areas, but even here at least seasonal centers have been established.

The unequal burdens of household work and childrearing are the structural obstacles to women's greater achievement in careers. It also limits their political role. The Communist party is a route to power, and acceptance into the party and rise within it are dependent on volunteer community spirit and work. About 14 percent of all Soviet men, but less than 4 percent of Soviet women, belong to the party. Women make up 25 percent of the party membership. (Many fewer women in the non-European areas of the Soviet Union belong). Within the party, women tend to fill the lower specialist and clerical positions. Those who have leadership responsibilities tend to come from the parts of the economy where women predominate. (About 25 percent of the women come from education, 18 percent from the health or trade union sector, 17 percent from propaganda, and 11 percent from light industry.) Fourteen women were members or candidate members of the Central Committee in 1976. Of these, six were simply superior workers who were being temporarily honored. Women made up 3.3 percent of the leadership at that level. Only one woman has ever served on the true ruling body of the Communist party and the Soviet state, the Politburo.[28] Lack of entry at the start and perhaps less than enthusiastic acceptance means there is no Soviet Indira Gandhi, Golda Meir, or Margaret Thatcher waiting in the wings.

WOMEN, CHILDREN, AND THE STATE

Clearly, state policy in the Soviet Union requires women to work, but it also encourages them to have children. The Soviet Union is one of a few nations in the world with a pronatalist policy. This desire to increase fertility has historic roots in an economy developed by drawing the underemployed from rural areas into industrial production. To Soviet planners growth seems to depend on an abundant labor supply. As the economy became more complex, they overcame the need for highly trained people by narrowly specializing education in order to reduce its cost. With more rapid technological change, such specialization has proven less effective, but the historic pattern of linking abundant population with growth remains part of policy. There are limits to this policy, as noted before, in areas of limited resources with high population growth rates and a traditionalist bias against migration such as Central Asia. There the Soviet planners would like to see a reduction in family size.

Generally, education has been linked to fertility rates in the Soviet Union. As in many countries, some education enhances fertility. One study suggests that in the Soviet Union women with eight to eleven years of education have the highest fertility rates.[29] The author does not separate women in Central Asia who have this primary level of education and a high birthrate from the general population and may overstate the case.

In European areas with higher levels of women's education, fertility rates have become quite low; the one- and, at most, two-child family is the norm. Education also enhances the value of workforce participation, and being in the workforce also dramatically depresses fertility rates. Fertility is especially depressed since work must be full time; there is little part-time work available in the Soviet Union.[30] In addition Marxist ideology, with its emphasis on productive labor, seems to have created a work ethic among women. A study of Soviet women who immigrated to Israel showed them working somewhat less than their Soviet counterparts but at a much higher rate than their Israeli compatriots.[31]

Soviet demographic planners face several dilemmas: low education and high fertility exist where they do not wish it, and a fairly high level of women's education accompanied by high workforce participation undercuts fertility where they would like to see more children. Further more, high levels of education for women and their economic contribution support current production but may undercut future economic growth. Soviet demographers, economic planners, and political leaders have all proposed solutions to these dilemmas, but almost all favor the reproductive over the productive role. All of these solutions suggest the idea of "biology as destiny."[32] There are four broad proposals: (1) shortening the hours of work for women; (2) introducing part-time work (in four-hour shifts) for women; (3) extending maternity leave; and (4) providing state support of children through direct payment to families and the extension of daycare facilities. The last proposal has roughly been followed as a compromise. Under Leonid Brezhnev, state payments for the first several children were granted to those with low income. To escape the dilemma of high fertility in some areas, the payments drop after the third child.[33] While pronatalists approve this policy, they object, on the basis of cost, to the extension of daycare. They also argue, among other things, that poor quality daycare is common, that daycare spreads childhood illness, that attendants are poorly trained, and that psychological damage can occur in these centers. As some studies indicate, these sentiments are widely shared. However, 70 to 90 percent of those with children in centers rank them positively. Thus, prejudice against childcare seems to be prevalent mainly among those who have little direct contact with daycare centers.[34]

Pronatalists have argued for an extension of paid maternity leave for up to three years after birth. Soviet policy has long allowed 112 days of paid leave and an additional three months of unpaid leave with no loss of job rights or seniority. The pronatalists have emphasized that maternal care is superior to childcare provided in state institutions, that women would prefer this option, and that it would insure the future workforce. This proposal has not been funded because of its direct costs and the economic waste of the previous investment in women's education and training.[35]

Another pronatalist proposal has been to reduce women's working hours by an hour a day or a half day a week. To relieve the double burden, the proposal's advocates suggest that women could use the extra time for study and advancement of their skills. Such a worktime reduction would relieve family pressures and at the same time encourage women's advancement in the workplace. Trial implementation of this proposal and the shift from a six- to five-day workweek in 1967 demonstrated that men simply shifted more of the household burden to women. The proposal did not have the desired effect.[36]

Along similar lines was a plan to introduce more flexible hours for women, particularly by allowing for part-time work in the form of four-hour shifts. Again, the proposal stated that women would use the time provided for job training and advancement as well as family concerns. The plan was actually directed at managers' concerns about flexibility. In light industry, low-paid women workers are loyal workers with little absenteeism, a grumbling willingness to accept shift work, and so on, but their jobs are also the least skilled and easiest to do without given variations in output demands. They are also more efficient to schedule in four- rather than eight-hour shifts because of the monotony of their jobs. The economy could also use many more part-time workers in trade to speed delivery of service in peak time periods. Some argue that this plan is simply a way to introduce unemployment into the system as a disciplinary method, and more skilled workers and professional women see it as a potential threat to their career development.[37]

The critical problem with three of these proposals is that they treat women as tied to biological functions in a way that does not promote equality. With the exception of extending child care and child payments (the actual policy), all the proposals, but particularly extended maternity leave and part-time work, undercut women's attempts to advance in the workplace by using internal and correspondence training. They undermine the idea that women are workers and professionals on a par with men—just as concerned, just as ambitious—and stress the special role of "motherhood." The pronatalist proposals exacerbate the problem of the double work role rather than act to solve it in a way that would allow women to gain the full benefit of their education.

THE PAST AND ITS MEANING FOR THE FUTURE

Concern for the strength of the state, coupled with Marxist ideology and its thrust toward equality, has generally served women in the Soviet Union well. Access to education at all levels is clearly equal to that in Western nations, an accomplishment made all the more impressive in as much as the Soviets started far below them on any measure of development. As in the West, some inequality is apparent in the fields in which women are trained and the levels they attain in terms of graduate degrees. (The educational segmentation is probably less severe than that in the West, given that 30 to 40 percent of women are trained in fields that are all male elsewhere.) Soviet policy has opened all types of employment to women, and women's workforce participation rates are higher than those in the West. But occupational structures remain sex segregated, and there are obstacles to achieving positions of leadership. The Soviet pattern of women's workforce participation is similar to the West's, with women's payment for work averaging about two-thirds that of men's wages.

Undoubtedly, the most negative aspect of state planning for women is the current pronatalist policy which seems determined to define women's place by biological differences. Even here, however, actual policy has resulted in an infant care and full-time preschool network that is probably unequaled anywhere in the world. (More American children, measured by percentage of age cohort, attend preschool, but there are major questions about the length of time they spend in such care compared to their Soviet counterparts.)[38]

It is possible to blame Soviet state policy for some of the double burden placed on women. The Stalinist era undercut active criticism of patriarchy by Aleksandra Kollanti (the Revolutionary Reformer) and others, and the emphasis on heavy industry and armaments limited production of consumer goods, appliances, and services which might have made the double burden easier to handle. Generally, however, state planning and Marxism have produced a situation for women that is at least on a par with the West, in terms of educational levels and wage differentials, and perhaps in some areas, such as child care, superior to the West.

Today the Soviet Union is a state in the midst of change, a new era of reform. Mikhail Gorbachev has launched two new policies—*perestroika* and *glasnost*. The first has been defined as revolution and restructuring, an attempt to open the system of rigid planning to greater control by managers selected on a performance basis and operating in a system using greater reliance on concepts like the market and profit. To support this policy, Gorbachev has called for greater popular debate and a new level of criticism from outside the party.[39] This policy is referred to as openness or *glasnost*.

Will this new era of reform improve women's position in the Soviet Union? Doubts abound; Nikita Khrushchev made the last major attempt to shake up the tightening bureaucratic structure, and it had the opposite effect. Khrushchev attempted to democratize the system and invigorate Marxist ideals by using work or armed services experience as a prerequisite for continuing on, like all modern elites, to higher education. The Soviet elite of Moscow and Leningrad had proven adept at using the school system to perpetuate their status among their children. The reform attacked this practice but also favored the typical male route into Soviet middle and upper positions to the detriment of women with their slight but real educational advantage earned in continuous study. Elite, not feminist, opinion had the reform canceled.

What is the future of *perestroika?* Given the lack of a vocal feminist point of view, the prevalence of male-dominated managerial structures, and the stress on competition and performance in factory and other voluntary institutional structures like the communist party that help in the selection process, the likely result of this program will be "finding the right *man* for the job." While feminist arguments can be discerned within Soviet debates (for example, in regard to part-time work), there seems to be little general feminist consciousness and certainly no broad movement or organization making such demands. A recent survey of a dozen leading Soviet men and women in various fields—economics, demography, law, and philosophy—demonstrates a concern about women's questions and an admiration of Kollanti as a remarkable socialist woman. They also clearly reject her more radical ideas on the social changes necessary for a full human role for women.[40] This absence of a conscious feminist voice is perhaps the greatest difference between the Soviet Union and the West.

One could argue that *glasnost* will provide just such a movement, but that has yet to occur. *Glasnost* has resulted in major criticisms of policy in regard to environmental questions deriving from the impact of urbanization, the exploitation of Siberia, and, of course, Chernoble. Nationalistic protest against Soviet policy has occurred in the Caucasus and Central Asia where Soviet policy has supported Marxist feminist equality as part of the modernization process. *Glasnost* has led to protest of the very policy feminists would see as positive.

Given male domination and the nature of current protest under *glasnost*, these new reforms are likely to move against women's interests, at least in the short run. If *glasnost* continues over an extended period, then women are likely to organize their own voice (women workers have played a major role, for example, in the Solidarity movement in Poland) and give these reforms a positive dimension for the future of women in the Soviet Union.

NOTES

1. Marc Raeff, *Understanding Imperial Russia* (New York: Columbia University Press, 1984) pp. 57–87.

2. Gail Lapidus, *Women in Soviet Society: Equality, Development and Social Change* (Berkeley: University of California Press, 1983). pp. 30–31.

3. Patricia Ratliff, "Women's Educational Attainment Levels in the Soviet Union: 1955–1980," Paper presented at the annual meeting of the American Educational Research Association, April 20–24, 1987, Washington, D.C., p. 6.

4. Lapidus, *Women in Soviet Society*, pp. 80–81.

5. B. A. Engel, "The Women's Side: Male Out-Migration and Family Economy in Kostroma Province," *Slavic Review* 45 (Summer 1986): 232.

6. Lapidus, *Women in Soviet Society*, p. 139.

7. Ibid., pp. 140–141.

8. Ibid., p. 116.

9. Norton Dodge, *Women in the Soviet Economy* (Baltimore: Johns Hopkins University Press, 1966), p. 37.

10. Seymour Rosen, *Education and Modernization in the USSR* (Reading, Mass.: Addison-Wesley, 1971), pp. 68–74.

11. Lapidus, *Women in Soviet Society*, p. 185.

12. Ibid., p. 144.

13. "The All-Union Population Census," *Soviet Education* (January-February-March 1982): 261.

14. Lapidus, *Women in Soviet Society*, p. 151.

15. Ibid., p. 173.

16. Dodge, *Women in the Soviet Economy*, p. 107.

17. N. Lubin, "Women in Soviet Central Asia: Progress and Contradictions," *Soviet Studies* 33 (April 1981): 195–197.

18. Lapidus, *Women in Soviet Society*, pp. 166, 168.

19. Ibid., p. 172.

20. Ibid., pp. 173, 186.

21. Ibid, pp. 184–187.

22. M. P. Sacks, "Missing Female Occupational Categories in the Soviet Census," *Slavic Review* 40 (Summer 1981): 254.

23. M. Mollaeva, "Activity of Soviet Women in Society Is Increasing," *Soviet Review* 21 (Summer 1980): passim.

24. Sacks, "Missing Female Occupational Categories," pp. 254, 260–261.

25. Lapidus, *Women in Soviet Society*, pp. 190, 192, 194.

26. Ibid., pp. 251, 170–273.

27. Ibid., p. 131.

28. Ibid., pp. 214–222.

29. Joseph Berliner, "Education, Labor-Force Participation, and Fertility in the USSR," *Journal of Comparative Economics* 7 (1983): 145–146.

30. Anna Kuniansky, "Soviet Fertility, Labor-Force Participation, and Marital Instability," *Journal of Comparative Economics* 7 (1983): 122–123.

31. Gur Ofer, and Aaron Vinokur, "The Labor-Force Participation of Married Women in the Soviet Union," *Journal of Comparative Economics* 7 (1983): 175.

32. Mary Buckley, ed., *Soviet Social Scientists Speak* (London: Macmillan Press, 1986), passim.

33. Lapidus, *Women in Soviet Society*, pp. 305–308. Joel C. Moses, *The Politics of Women and Work in the Soviet Union and the United States* (Berkeley: Institute of International Studies, University of California, 1983). p. 52.

34. Lapidus, *Women in Soviet Society*, pp. 133, 311–312.

35. Ibid., pp. 306–309.

36. Ibid., pp. 276, 277.

37. Moses, *The Politics of Women and Work*, pp. 17, 41.

38. Lapidus, *Women in Soviet Society*, p. 131.

39. Mikhail Gorbachev, *Perestroika: New Thinking for Our Country and the World* (New York: Harper and Row, 1987), pp. 40–59.

40. Buckley, *Soviet Social Scientists Speak*, passim.

LATIN AMERICA

17

CHILE

Josefina Rossetti

This chapter focuses on women's education in Chile from a feminist perspective.[1] It begins with a historical overview of the recent changes in the political system and discusses the traditional roles of women. It then discusses women's school enrollment patterns and curriculum, textbooks, and educational practices which contribute to gender-based inequalities in the labor force and in the political system. In Chilean schools woman perform as well as, if not better than, men. Nonetheless, the school continues to maintain women's subordinate role in Chilean society. Education has been unable to close the gap between male and female income, and occupational segregation in the workforce remains.

HISTORICAL BACKGROUND

Since 1973, some important changes have taken place in Chile. The Pinochet military regime ended the democratic political system which characterized Chile since independence from Spain. Since 1983 the country has experienced consistent economic development under a succession of governments that have often been at odds with each other.[2] Pinochet has pursued economic policies that have reinforced the gap between social classes. Extreme poverty is a reality for much of the country.

Women's lives in Chile have been structured by patriarchy, which it inherited from Spanish culture and the Catholic Church. Since the end of the nineteenth century, women have struggled for emancipation. Chilean women, known for their staunch feminism, struggled for the same political rights as men and obtained them in 1949. The Christian Democrat government (1964–1970) sponsored and promoted a women's organization called the Mothers' Association. Through this group thousands of women throughout the country were for the first time encouraged to go outside the home, meet other women, earn a small income, and participate in politics. Salvador Allende's government extended the Mothers' Associations and created a ministry devoted exclusively to women's concerns, the Secretaria Nacional de la Mujer. This ministry continued Frei's policies of building kindergartens. It also initiated a system of distributing prepared food to poor working women and installing public laundries in poor neighborhoods. Allende's government was the most progressive the country had ever seen on women's issues, promoting the participation of women in paid work and in political life. The Allende government developed family planning programs and, in the days before the coup d'etat which brought Pinochet to power, had begun considering a liberalized divorce law.

Pinochet's regime reversed the trends Allende had set into motion. The government adopted conservative policies stressing anticommunist and women's roles as housewives and mothers. The Mothers' Associations remain, but they are exclusively government controlled. Pinochet has created a vast movement of middle- and upper class volunteer women, who are known by the color of the delantal they use ("ladies in red," "ladies in green"). These women direct the Mothers' Associations and work without pay in social institutions, thereby displacing women's paid labor. The Pinochet government has refused to promote any form of family planning other than the "natural way." Divorce laws remain stringent, and abortion is outlawed as part of the programs designed to bolster the family.

In the face of these repressive policies, since the end of the 1970s the women's movement in Chile has grown. A number of organizations share common objectives and have acted in concert on occasion, sometimes demonstrating together in opposition to government policies. While most of these feminist organizations are the preserve of middle-class women, their concerns focus on working-class and poor women.

In short, the education of women in Chile occurred within the context of remarkable progress from 1949 to the onset of the Pinochet regime in 1973. Today Chilean society is deeply divided along social class lines. The government's regressive policies have given rise to oppositional protest movements and have stimulated the growth of an independent women's movement.

SILENCE ON WOMEN AND EDUCATION

A full history of women's education in Chile remains to be written. Very little is actually known. Most of the current scholarship consists of chronologies focusing on women's access to the different levels and types of education. There is no information on women's fight for education and on the socioeconomic context in which that occurred. Nor is there information on women as educators and their participation in unions and educational reforms.

The first primary schools for women in Chile were created around 1810, during the fight for independence from Spain. The expansion of educational opportunities for women met with fierce conservative opposition, especially from the Catholic Church

which believed that advanced schooling and entry to the professions would detract from women's natural roles as wives and mothers. Indeed one official church journal predicted in the 1870's that state controlled secondary schools for women would "be nothing more than mere brothels financed by the taxpayers." Liberal Chilean intellectuals nonetheless continued to argue that women should receive the same education as men, and over time their views prevailed.[3]

Secondary schools for girls were created in 1895. In 1877, women were admitted to the university, thirty years after the first Chilean university, the University of Chile, was created. Women were admitted to secondary and post-secondary technical education beginning in 1925, but their attendance in such schools did not grow significantly until after 1965.

The first coeducational schools were experimental and created between 1930 and 1950. They expanded under the educational reform of 1965, during the Christian Democratic government, but neither the Frei nor the Allende government had specific policies toward women's schooling. Gender was invisible as an issue. As soon as women were admitted to all levels of education, the problem of gender inequity was considered over.

In recent years, under the military dictatorship of Pinochet, both male and female enrollments have declined in primary and higher education. Whereas higher education was free in the past, Pinochet has now imposed fees. The fees explain the decline in enrollment. The very poor cannot afford to send their children to primary school, in spite of the fact it is free. Not surprisingly, the quality of education under Pinochet has suffered.

At the secondary education level, enrollments have increased. In fact, secondary education has become a necessary prerequisite for jobs outside of agriculture. Most primary schools and a majority of secondary schools in Chile today are coeducational.

The educational policies of the military regime have not affected female students differentially. The rightist dictatorship has not initiated educational policies overtly designed to reinforce traditional sex roles in schools and in society. The military regime has prohibited the introduction of libertarian ideologies, thereby reinforcing traditional values.

EQUAL ACCESS FOR WOMEN AND MEN TO EDUCATION

The fight for equal access to all levels of education for women has ended.[5] The same proportion of female and male students is enrolled in primary schools and has been since 1975 (Table 17.1). A slightly higher proportion of women than men is in secondary education, a situation that has held since 1955 (Table 17.2). The difference in favor of women as of 1985 was 5 percentage points. One possible explanation is that male students, especially those from working-class and poor families, must leave school earlier to work. Another is that families prefer their male children to work because they can earn more than girls.

Women's access to the university level remains a problem: they make up only 40 percent of the total enrollment. Nevertheless, in other higher education institutions—technical training and professional institutes—the proportion of male and female students is equal (Tables 17.3 and 17.4).

Access to the different levels of education is segregated by social class for both sexes. Educational selection follows family income. Almost all women attend primary school, at least some years, until the age of fourteen. Only 55 percent of them attend secondary school, and only 10 percent attend higher education.

TRADITIONAL CHOICES

Inequality between the sexes in Chilean education is not due to lack of access to schools; rather, it is reflected in the subjects women study and the workforce ramifications of what they study. Despite equal enrollment in the schools, students' options are still the same as they were thirty years ago. Women tend to study the humanities and arts and men the sciences and technology.

At the end of primary education, 80 percent of all students, male and female, choose to enter the academically oriented *liceos* and only 20 percent go to vocational *liceos*. The *liceos* programs are the same for male and female students, but in vocational schools important gender differences arise. Commercial education is female dominated. Seventy percent of the students are women. Industrial education, on the other hand, is male dominated, and only 3 percent of the students enrolled in these programs are female. The student body enrolled in agricultural education is 20 percent female, whereas in technical education 90 percent of all students are women. (Technical education in Chile focuses on traditionally female subjects such as sewing, knitting, food preparation, and health.)

Higher education in Chile is segregated by sex along traditional gender lines. Women in universities concentrate in education (40 percent of female enrollment), in health professions (17 percent), and in social sciences (12 percent). Men are enrolled in programs linked to careers in technology (46 percent). Males also study education (16 percent) and the social sciences (14 percent). Today's trends are very similar to those of fifteen and thirty years ago.

A pattern of gender segregation in enrollment similar to that in universities is found in the professional institutes and in the technical training schools. In the professional institutes, 69 percent of female students follow courses in education, whereas men pursue training in business and commerce (43 percent). In the

Table 17.1
Primary Education Enrollment, by Sex, 1935–1985

	A	B	C	D	E	F	G	H	I	J	K
Year	Total Enrollment	Population 6-14 years	A.100/B %	Females Enrollment	D.100/A %	Females 6-14 years	D.100/F %	Males Enrollment	H.100/A %	Males 6-14 yrs.	H.100/J %
1985	2.062.344	2.153.894	95,7	1.003.671	48,7	1.061.029	94,6	.058.673	51,3	1.092.865	96,9
1984	2.045.893	2.135.632	95,8	995.317	48,6	1.051.944	94,6	1.050.576	51,4	1.083.688	96,9
1983	2.065.126	2.122.610	97,3	1.015.518	49,1	1.045.512	97,1	1.069.610	51,8	1.077.098	99,3
1982	2.092.597	2.114.530	99,0	1.016.101	48,6	1.041.580	97,6	1.076.496	51,4	1.072.950	100,3
1981	2.139.319	2.111.099	101,3	1.046.326	48,9	1.039.998	100,6	1.092.993	51,1	1.071.101	102,0
1980	2.185.459	2.112.013	103,5	1.069.048	48,9	1.040.609	102,4	1.116.411	51,0	1.071.404	104,2
1979	2.235.861	2.121.380	105,4	1.095.027	49,0	1.045.478	104,7	1.140.834	51,0	1.075.902	106,0
1978	2.232.990	2.139.396	104,4	1.096.700	49,1	1.054.706	104,0	1.136.200	50,9	1.084.690	104,7
1977	2.242.111	2.159.907	103,8	1.101.900	49,1	1.065.201	103,4	1.140.200	50,9	1.094.706	104,2
1976	2.243.274	2.176.758	103,1	1.104.100	49,2	1.073.865	102,8	1.139.000	50,8	1.102.893	103,3
1975	2.298.998	2.183.788	105,3	1.130.400	49,2	1.077.604	104,9	1.168.600	50,8	1.106.184	105,6
1970	2.039.185	2.112.712	96,5	1.009.000	49,5	1.043.055	96,7	1.031.000	50,6	1.069.657	93,4
1965	1.699.100	1.823.933	93,2	830.900	48,9	899.211	92,4	868.200	51,1	924.722	92,9
1960	1.284.900	1.602.695	80,2	631.000	49,1	793.450	79,5	653.900	50,9	809.245	80,8
1955	1.035.856	1.457.340	71,1	505.613	48,8	724.106	69,8	530.243	51,2	733.234	72,3
1950	831.843	1.260.398	66,0	403.156	48,5	624.982	64,5	428.687	51,5	635.416	67,5
1945	707.660	1.184.893	59,7	342.888	48,5	587.174	58,4	364.772	51,5	597.719	61,0
1940	674.910	1.113.911	60,6	334.945	49,6	551.652	60,7	339.965	50,4	562.259	60,5
1935	564.781	996.405	56,7	264.613	46,9	493.201	53,7	300.168	53,1	503.204	59,7

In 1970 and in 1975 the total enrollment does not match with the male and female enrollment because the source of the data a different.

Source: 1935–1981: Las transformaciones educacionales bajo el regimen militar. PIIE. Santiago, El Grafico, 1984, Vol. 2, pp. 551–552.
1982–1985: Matricula ninos ano escolar 1982, 1983, 1984, 1985. Ministerio de Educacion.

Table 17.2
Secondary Education Enrollment, by Sex, 1935–1985

	A	B	C	D	E	F	G	H	I	J	K
Year	Total Enrollment	Population 15-19 years	A.100 % B	Females Enrollment	D.100 % A	Females 15-19 yrs.	D.100 % F	Males Enrollment	H.100 % A	Males 15-19 yrs.	H.100 % J
1985	667.797	1.177.598	56,7	344.631	51,6	581.525	59,3	323.166	48,4	596.073	54,2
1984	637.092	1.187.368	53,7	327.960	51,5	586.540	55,9	309.132	48,5	600.828	51,5
1983	613.546	1.200.562	51,1	317.818	51,8	593.262	53,6	295.728	48,2	607.300	48,7
1982	565.745	1.213.195	46,6	293.910	52,0	599.703	49,0	271.835	48,1	613.492	44,3
1981	554.749	1.221.281	45,4	296.324	54,4	603.875	49,1	258.425	46,6	617.406	41,9
1980	541.639	1.220.838	44,4	287.710	53,1	603.793	47,7	253.929	46,9	617.045	41,2
1979	536.428	1.211.009	44,3	285.269	53,2	599.044	47,6	251.159	46,8	611.965	41,0
1978	510.471	1.194.452	42,7	268.215	52,5	590.954	45,4	242.256	47,5	603.498	40,1
1977	487.264	1.172.447	41,6	258.092	53,0	580.138	44,5	229.172	47,0	592.309	38,7
1976	465.935	1.146.280	40,6	250.951	53,9	567.215	43,1	215.984	46,1	579.065	37,1
1975	448.911	1.117.234	40,2	238.533	53,1	552.801	43,1	210.378	46,9	564.433	37,3
1970	302.100	920.257	32,8	160.300	53,1	454.256	35,3	141.800	46,9	466.001	30,4
1965	148.444	850.672	17,5	76.499	51,5	423.798	18,1	71.945	48,5	426.874	16,9
1960	108.819	757.637	14,4	56.031	51,5	376.823	14,9	52.788	48,5	380.814	13,9
1955	69.502	638.960	10,9	35.419	51,0	317.089	11,2	34.083	49,0	321.871	10,6
1950	49.343	571.299	8,6	24.265	49,2	283.022	8,6	25.078	50,8	288.277	8,7
1945	37.525	539.928	7,0	18.014	48,0	268.830	6,7	19.511	52,0	271.098	7,2
1940	25.729	510.280	5,1	12.018	46,6	255.337	4,7	13.774	53,4	254.943	5,4
1935	23.053	489.371	4,7	10.154	44,0	247.747	4,1	12.899	56,0	241.624	5,3

Source: 1935–1981: Las transformaciones educacionales bajo el regimen militar. PIIE. Sangiago, El Grafico, 1984, Vol. 2, pp. 571–572.

1982–1985: Matricula ninos ano escolar 1982, 1983, 1984, 1985. Ministerio de Educacion.

Table 17.3
University Enrollment, by Sex, 1935–1985

	A	B	C	D	E	F	G	H	I	J	K
Year	Total Enrollment	Population 20-24 years	A.100 B	Females Enrollment	D.100 A	Females 20-24 yrs.	D.100 F	Males Enrollment	H.100 A	Males 20-24 yrs.	H.100 J
1985	130.331	1.210.064	10,8	51.505	39,5	599.970	8,6	78.826	60,5	610.064	12,9
1984	128.568	1.200.133	10,7	51.449	40,0	595.178	8,6	77.120	60,0	604.955	12,7
1983	127.353	1.183.974	10,8	50.985	40,0	505.362	10,1	76.368	60,0	510.612	15,0
1982	118.150	1.161.541	10,2	42.692	38,7	576.247	7,9	72.458	61,3	505.362	14,3
1981	118.984	1.135.274	10,5	48.587*	40,5	563.273	8,⁵	70.397*	58,5	571.999	12,1
1980	118.978	1.105.957	10,8	49.357	41,5	548.743	9,0	69.621	58,5	557.214	12,5
1979	127.446	1.069.987	11,9	51.008	40,0	530.782	9,6	76.438	60,0	539.205	14,2
1978	130.208	1.026.567	12,7	55.016	42,3	509.003	10,8	75.192	57,7	517.564	14,5
1977	130.676	981.099	13,3	55.293	42,3	486.210	11,4	75.383	57,7	494.889	15,2
1976	134.149	938.983	14,3	56.996	42,5	465.206	12,3	77.153	57,5	473.777	16,3
1975	147.049	905.622	16,2	61.077	41,5	448.793	13,6	85.972	58,5	456.829	18,8
1970	76.979	834.121	9,2	29.511	38,3	416.919	7,1	47.468	61,7	417.202	11,4
1965	41.801	740.630	5,6	s/d	—	369.661	-,-	s/d	-,-	370.969	-,-
1960	24.703	625.128	4,0	8.859	35,9	311.272	2,9	15.844	64,1	313.856	5,1
1955	19.749	557.536	3,5	7.782	39,4	277.116	2,8	11.967	60,6	280.420	4,3
1950	14.917	551.600	2,	5.368	36,0	274.024	2,0	9.549	64,0	277.576	3,4
1945	8.893	499.769	1,8	2.369	26,6	254.744	0,9	6.524	73,4	245.052	2,7
1940	7.846	452.857	1,7	1.969	25,1	236.518	0,8	5.877	74,9	216.339	2,7
1935	6.283	434.483	1,4	s/d	-,-	223.603	-,-	s/d	-,-	210.880	-,-

*Estimate

Source: 1935-1981: Las transformaciones educacionales bajo el regimen militar. PIIE. Sangiago, El Grafico, 1984, Vol. 2, pp. 582-583.
1982-1985: Matricula ninos ano escolar 1982, 1983, 1984, 1985. Ministerio de Educacion. Proyecciones de poblacion 1970-2000. Instituto Nacional de Estadisticas.

Table 17.4
Enrollment in Higher Education, by Type, 1984–1986

Type of Higher Education	Percent Female	Percent Male
University	38.9	61.1
Professional Institutes	54.6	45.4
Technical Training Schools	50.1	49.9
Total	44.2	55.8

Source: Unidad de Estadisticas, Division de Educacion Superior. Ministerio de Educacion.

technical training schools, where students of both sexes prepare for clerical employment, only 1 percent of women enroll in industrial education in contrast to 23 percent of men. Women's participation in technological fields is very limited.

Cultural barriers affect vocational choice in young people of both sexes. The choice of a career is based not on individual interests and aptitudes but rather on sex-role stereotypes.

Traditional messages concerning future professions and occupations are transmitted throughout school life, from kindergarten on. Children learn not only mathematics and Spanish but also how to be women and men in accordance with preestablished sex roles. As a result, for more than two-thirds of the adult women population marriage is the principal destiny. Those who study further and enter the labor market choose professions and occupations that correspond to what tradition considers feminine options. These positions carry a lower level of responsibilities and pay. Very often traditional choices mean a life of poverty and little autonomy and self-confidence, especially if they are working-class or poor women.

Women Are Very Good Students

Women in Chile are excellent pupils (Table 17.5). At all school levels throughout the country, women achieve better than men, and they repeat and drop out less than men. The differences between females and males are not very important (usually 2 or 3 percent in favor of women). Their significance derives from the fact that they are constant: they occurred in all levels of education for the five consecutive years 1980, 1981, 1982, 1983, and 1984 and in the whole country.

The most important difference between male and female students concerns achievement.[6] In primary education, 2.84 percent more women than men pass

Table 17.5

Achievement, Repetition, and Dropping Out Rates, by Educational Level and Sex, 1980–1984 (in Average Percentages)[1]

Level of Education	Achievement (+ women)[2]	Repetition (+ men)[2]	Dropping Out (+men)[2]
Primary	2,84	2,54	0,32
Secondary	2,48	0.57	1,47
-Liceos cientifi co-humanistas*	2,62	0,56	1,68
-Technical/vocational schools	3,76	1,12	0,97
Average Differences	2,92	1,19	1,11

[1]These are average differences of the annual differences in 1980, 1981, 1982, 1983, 1984.

[2]The scores are higher in women or men, when the contrary is not indicated in the small cells.

*Academically oriented secondary education.

Source: Informes de los establecimientos educacionales remitidos por las Secretarias Ministeriales de Eduacion. Superintendencia de Eduacion.

all the courses in primary education; at the secondary level, 2.48 percent more girls than boys pass secondary courses. The biggest difference in achievement occurs in the secondary technical education course where 3.76 percent more girls than boys pass all courses. Nevertheless, on tests administered at the end of secondary school, women score significantly lower than men. Male students obtain 60 percent of the best scores and women only 40 percent.[7] Since female students sitting for university admission tests have higher scores than male students at the secondary education level, this decrease is due not to lack of intellectual ability but to poor motivation. Female students are not as interested as men in getting excellent marks because they do not need them for entry into the higher education programs in which they are interested.

Gender in Curriculum and Textbooks

The ways in which schools produce sexual inequality are hidden and subtle. There are no explicit gender differences in the education boys and girls receive in primary and secondary school. The one exception is physical education where boys and girls have different training. In manual training, it is the Ministry of Education policy not to segregate female and male students, although very often female pupils receive instruction in sewing. The changing pattern of gender relations in the Chilean society is mentioned in curriculum guides, and it is recommended that education contribute to that process. However, there are no concrete proposals suggesting how teachers should deal with the question in the classroom.

The curriculum assumes that students and teachers are gender neutral. However, the language used is masculine in word and content (in Spanish, teacher and pupil are masculine words). Women's role in history, literature, and the sciences is not noted. School texts are explicitly sexist. The pictures and stories they use relating to everyday life and to the society in which the students live reflect the sexism of the past. The texts deny changing social reality and ignore conditions of actual life.

Neither the formal curriculum nor school texts show women's role in history and education. Nor do they legitimize women's participation in work outside the home and in the political sphere. They especially avoid stimulating women's creativity, ambition, and courage. At the same time they do not propose new roles for men; specifically, they do not encourage them to share domestic chores or to express their feelings and emotions as do women.

Good Students, Poor Workers

The relationship between women's school attainment and their place in the labor market is mixed. If we compare women fifteen years of age and more, and women who work outside the home and those who do not, more education is clearly associated with higher participation in paid work (see Table 17.6). In

Table 17.6
Women's Level of Education and Participation in the Labor Force, 1960, 1970, and 1982

Level of Education	1960 Women 15 yrs. old and more (n)	1960 Women in the labor force (n)	1960 Women in the labor force (%)	1970 Women 15 yrs. old and more (n)	1970 Women in the labor force (n)	1970 Women in the labor force (%)	1982 Women 15 yrs. old and more (n)	1982 Women in the labor force (n)	1982 Women in the labor force (%)
None	467,078	64,870	13.88	296,930	35,134	11.83	293,943	34,152	11.61
Primary	1,605,907	295,615	18.40	1,934,634	321,559	16.62	2,084,164	398,804	19.13
Secondary	563,733	135,838	24.09	828,713	223,086	26.91	1,344,820	383,030	28.48
Higher Education	27,441	14,061	51.24	77,449	36,377	46.96	249,963	143,469	57.39
Other	25,611	15,403	60.14	—	—	—	—	—	—
Ignored	32,547	8,514	26.15	296	51	17.22	—	—	—
Total	2,722,337	534,301	19.62	3,138,022	616,207	14.63	3,972,889	959,455	24.15

Source: Censos de Poblacion y Vivienda. Instituto Nacional de Estadisticas (INE). 1960, 1970, 1982.

Table 17.7

Levels of Education, by Sex and Occupational Categories, 1960, 1970, and 1982

									OCCUPATIONAL CATEGORIES							
LEVEL OF EDUCATION	MANAGERS AND ADMINISTRATORS		PROFESSIONALS AND TECHNICIANS		CLERICAL EMPLOYEES		SALESMEN (WOMEN)		DOMESTIC SERVICE		DRIVERS		AGRI-CULTURAL WORKERS	
YEAR	W*	M**	W	M	W	M	W	M	W	M	W	M	W	M
NONE														
1960	0.7	0.4	0.6	0.1	0.4	0.4	5.3	2.5	67.6	2.6	0.0	1.1	13.9	69.6
1970	0.6	0.2	0.5	0.2	0.6	0.4	6.8	3.1	57.9	2.3	0.1	1.1	10.9	61.5
1982	1.0	0.5	1.0	0.3	1.5	1.2	8.0	4.3	56.9	3.5	0.1	1.6	6.4	52.7
PRIMARY														
1960	1.2	0.9	2.2	0.4	1.4	1.7	8.0	5.6	55.4	5.8	0.1	4.5	4.4	36.1
1970	1.0	0.7	1.7	0.3	1.2	1.4	8.8	5.6	50.1	5.1	0.1	4.8	3.8	31.7
1982	1.7	1.2	1.3	0.3	4.2	3.8	10.5	6.6	52.1	5.1	0.1	5.7	3.4	31.8
SECONDARY														
1960	2.4	5.7	17.9	4.3	30.9	21.6	12.7	12.8	11.5	5.8	0.1	5.9	0.7	7.1
1970	1.8	4.1	18.7	4.4	29.2	22.1	10.4	10.1	10.7	5.5	0.2	7.8	0.5	5.3
1982	2.4	4.2	15.1	3.9	29.4	18.4	13.2	11.0	18.9	5.0	0.2	7.0	0.6	7.0
HIGHER EDUCATION														
1960	1.1	7.7	82.7	62.2	11.1	12.3	1.5	5.8	0.7	0.9	0.1	0.7	0.2	5.5
1970	1.3	6.4	72.6	53.4	15.7	16.8	1.6	4.5	1.0	1.0	0.1	1.0	0.3	3.0
1982	1.8	9.0	59.2	44.5	23.7	19.2	4.6	7.3	2.6	1.0	0.1	2.0	0.1	2.1

*Women
**Men

Source: Censo de Poblacion y Vivienda. Instituto Nacional de Estadisticas. 1960, 1970, 1982.

402

Table 17.7 (continued)

LEVEL OF EDUCATION / YEAR	MINERS		CRAFTSMEN (WOMEN)		OTHER CRAFTSMEN (WOMEN)		INDUSTRIAL AND OTHERS MANUAL WORKERS		OTHER		TOTAL	
	W*	M**	W	M	W	M	W	M	W	M	W	M
NONE												
1960	0.1	3.6	5.3	7.1	1.8	2.9	1.3	5.4	3.0	4.3	100.0	100.0
1970	—	—	5.2	8.5	1.8	6.3	1.4	6.9	14.8	9.5	100.0	100.0
1982	—	—	4.3	5.2	1.3	5.2	10.0	13.6	9.5	5.6	100.0	100.0
PRIMARY												
1960	0.1	3.7	18.8	22.4	3.6	6.0	1.7	7.1	3.1	5.6	100.0	100.0
1970	—	—	15.0	19.9	2.7	7.6	3.0	10.1	12.6	12.6	100.0	100.0
1982	—	—	9.0	19.2	1.8	5.9	7.3	13.7	8.8	6.7	100.0	100.0
SECONDARY												
1960	0.0	0.9	15.6	19.3	2.0	3.2	0.7	2.4	5.4	10.9	100.0	100.0
1970	—	—	12.1	18.1	1.2	3.9	1.3	4.4	14.0	14.8	100.0	100.0
1982	—	—	5.6	16.7	1.0	4.5	3.5	8.2	10.1	14.1	100.0	100.0
HIGHER EDUCATION												
1960	0.0	0.1	0.5	1.4	0.1	0.2	0.0	0.1	1.9	3.1	100.0	100.0
1970	—	—	0.7	3.1	0.1	0.6	0.0	0.3	6.6	9.8	100.0	100.0
1982	—	—	0.7	5.2	0.2	1.0	0.6	1.1	6.4	7.5	100.0	100.0

OCCUPATIONAL CATEGORIES

*Women
**Men
Source: Censo de Poblacion y Vivienda. Instituto Nacional de Estadisticas. 1960, 1970, 1982.

1982, when the last Chilean census was conducted, 20 percent of women in the workforce had primary education, 30 percent secondary education, and 60 percent higher education. This relation does not hold with men; regardless of their educational level, men work.

According to the 1982 National Census, women represent only 24 percent of the economically active population, and less than a third of women fifteen years of age and over work outside home. These figures have changed very little in the last twenty years. The distribution of women workers among occupations depends on their class origin (see Table 17.7). Chilean women are consistently concentrated in service occupations. For the most part, they do not work in productive sectors of the economy. A very small proportion of women (5 percent) work as professionals. Most women who work are employed as domestic laborers (one-third of all working women are domestic servants) or in clerical jobs and commerce.

Women are also confined to a narrower range of occupations than are men. Women who have completed primary education tend to become employed as domestic servants (52 percent), saleswomen (11 percent), craftswomen (9 percent), and industrial workers (7 percent). Men with the same level of education are employed in more diverse occupations: 32 percent are agricultural workers, 19 percent craftsmen, 14 percent industrial workers, and 5 to 6 percent salesmen, domestic servants, and bus/truck drivers.

This pattern is repeated at all levels of education and is related to the social concept of what constitutes appropriately feminine and masculine occupations. These concepts are reinforced, or at least not questioned, by the schools. Men with similar class origin and educational attainment have better work conditions because they have access to a wider range of occupations and jobs that command higher responsibility and pay.

With the same level of education, women regularly earn 40 or 50 percent less than men. Acquiring better qualifications does not have the same consequences for women as for men. One year of training increases a male's earnings over 20 percent beyond that which a female worker with one year of training would obtain.[8] In a word, excellent female students end up as poor workers. Even professional women are not privileged; 45 percent of them are school teachers and earn very low salaries.

This inequality is fashioned by the schools. School, together with the family and other socialization agents, conveys values and norms that are internalized by students and accepted as a just sexual order.

NOTES

1. This chapter is part of an ongoing research project on teachers and traditional sex-role reproduction at school conducted by the author.

2. The most progressive periods were the radical Christian Democratic and Allende governments.

3. Ernesto Schiefelbein and Joseph Farrell, "Women, Schooling and Work: Evidence from a Longitudinal Study," *Comparative Education Review* 24 (1980): S160–S179.

4. Primary school in Chile lasts eight years; by law, all children must attend it. Pinochet's regime has transformed all public schools into two types of schools: one depends on the municipality, which is the government of a commune, and the second is private. The state keeps control over such schools because it finances them and also controls the technological aspects of education. This transformation has provoked opposition from teachers.

Secondary education lasts four years. At the beginning of the third year, students have to choose between the curriculum oriented to university entrance (*liceo cientifico-humanista*) or to technical and manual studies or jobs (*liceo tecnico-professional*).

Since 1981 (the military regime), the higher education system has become diversified. Students can enter the university or the professional institutes or the technical schools. The technical institutions have less prestige, their courses are of shorter duration, and they offer more limited occupational possibilities than those of the university.

All schools and higher education institutions are class segregated. Upper classes attend private and usually religious schools.

5. There is no comparative register of scores of higher education students.

6. Achievement is defined as the percentage of students who matriculate each year who are enrolled in a particular grade level.

7. Ricardo Rojas and Angelica Bochieri, *Caracteristicas de los Candidatos de Promociones Anteriores y su Incidencia en resultados de la P.A.A. 1982* (Santiago: University of Chile, Study Division, 1983, No. 17).

8. Ricardo Paredes, "Diferencias de ingreso entre hombres y mujeres en el Gran Santiago 1969 y 1981," *Estudio de Economia,* No. 18, Facultad de Ciencias Economicas y Administrativas, Departamento de Economia (Santiago: University of Chile, 1982).

18
PERU

Nelly P. Stromquist

Peru is a multiracial, multilingual, fragmented society in which economic and political power continues to be highly concentrated in the hands of a small number of whites and mestizos who have supported a dominant culture that disdains the Indian population. In this context, the formal education system has promoted the dominance of Spanish-speaking whites and mestizos and maintained the secondary status of women and Indians. In the case of women, the schools have imparted the skills and attributes considered desirable for performing traditional patriarchally defined roles as mothers and wives.

A brief review of the history of women's education in Peru shows that education has only modestly contributed to the improvement of women's conditions. Educational access for women has expanded, and more women today are able to attain higher education and, concomitantly, positions with better pay and status. However, the majority of women do not share these gains, and the current world economic crisis puts the life and education of low-income women in greater jeopardy than before.

EDUCATION DURING THE INCA PERIOD

A large number of Peruvians today see the pre-Spanish past as a source of national identity and as a time when a great society existed. Under the Inca Empire, Peru indeed knew moments of glory. But from the perspective of women, this time of history was characterized by a rigid sexual division of labor, in which women were explicitly assigned domestic roles that included cooking, weaving the family's clothing, raising the children, and other related duties. Through the chroniclers, particularly Garcilazo de la Vega, we know that the Incan authorities provided structured education to the children of their caste. Future male leaders were trained for four years in special schools under recognized teachers, called *amautas*. Noble women were taught in their own schools, the *acllahuasi* or house of chosen women, where they remained for about three years learning skills such as weaving, knitting, embroidery, lace making, food preparation, child delivery, and religious education.[1] Apparently, the education of these women was specialized because some prepared to serve the Inca himself, while others were trained to serve in some holy mountains or to perform religious duties in burial hills.[2] The ordinary people received only informal education in their communities and homes, an education that also reproduced gender divisions of labor. There is evidence that on the northern coastal region of Peru some form of female leadership existed, as wives of village chiefs could inherit their husband's authority. The existence of these women, called *capullanas* by the Spaniards, indicates that in some cases women held power under the Inca Empire, but by and large the "golden era" of Peru's history was characterized by the subordination of women.

EDUCATION IN COLONIAL TIMES

The Spanish *conquistadores* brought formal education with them. They also added to the class-based education of the Incas' racial distinctions and, for women, a stronger sexual bias in their education. The conquerors made it possible for children of the Incan nobles to attend chieftain schools (*escuelas de caciques*) in Lima and Cuzco. The purpose of these schools was to train noble children aged ten and above in Spanish customs and language, and to convey to them political and administrative knowledge so that they could represent Spanish authorities to Indian communities. The curriculum in the chieftain schools emphasized religious instruction, but it also covered math, music, and reading and writing in Spanish.[3] Basic education for the masses was seen as a labor of charity, advisable under Christian mores but to be extended cautiously. According to several ordinances by the viceroys, "for the welfare of the people and social tranquility no education whatsoever should be provided."[4] This led to the founding of private and religious schools, restricted to children or orphans of Spanish parents.

The role of education during colonial times was to create the minimal number of local elites needed to facilitate Spanish rule. Since women were not considered part of any power structure, the education they received was extremely limited. Crown regulations as early as 1594 forbade coeducation. Primary school teachers were told "not to accept girls into their schools to teach them how to read or pray, because it is not proper and certain inconveniences could follow."[5] The Spaniards' daughters were educated in convents, nunneries, and in a very small number of private schools (run by philanthropists) where the Catholic Church defended male-created dogmas about the indispensability of the woman's role in the family or in the service of God through the adoption of the veil and seclusion.

The Catholic religion introduced to education the notion of women as self-sacrificing mothers and the ideal of marriage as the earthly paradise. Very few women had access to education during colonial times. Most were daughters of rich Spanish families (who went into convents) or the parentless women of Spanish descent (who entered the less prestigious nunneries). In the handful of schools that existed catering to women (there were eighteen such institutions by the end of the eighteenth century), women learned their catechism and such skills as reading, writing, sewing, and knitting of all kinds.[6] Readings were limited to religious books, which were made available to them through the choice of their "spiritual leaders," usually the family or parish priest. Girls who entered the convents remained there "until their parents chose for them a suitable marriage partner or gave them permission to take the vows and remain in the convent for life."[7]

Various religious orders ran mission schools in the provinces. These schools emphasized the Catholic doctrine, the transmission of manual skills, and the development of agricultural fields and textile factories. Since these schools were run mostly by friars, they served men almost exclusively.[8]

THE PROMISE OF THE REPUBLIC

The joint action of church and state in guiding the education of women continued after Peru obtained its independence. Although the first constitution of the country, in 1823, stated that education was a right of "all peoples under the Republic," in practice it was not so because the provision of schooling was left in the hands of the municipalities, many of which were too poor or unprepared to cope with the task.

The Education Regulation of 1850 decreed education to be a public service. At the same time, these regulations prohibited coeducation. Article 20 addressed "feminine education," stating: "In the [primary] schools for girls they will be taught drawing, music, simple sewing, weaving, embroidery, and other tasks pertinent to their sex, morals, home economics, languages, history, personal hygiene, and religion."[9] To be sure, these educational prescriptions were in total harmony with the dominant belief of those days and were well expressed in the writings of a prominent Liberal party member in 1872:

No nation is possible without the family, and it cannot be conceived without the permanent existence of women. We consider women's participation in public affairs unnecessary, and their role in the setting of the home indispensable. We wish women to be surrounded by the greatest respect, purified by the devotion and silent love of her family.[10]

Access to Schooling

Women's access to primary education was extremely limited. In general, few schools existed, and, when they were available, most of them served male students. By 1849—after twenty-six years of independent rule—there were 260 schools for boys, enrolling 13,118 students, and only 33 schools for girls, enrolling 295 students.[11] In Lima, Peru's capital and the city with the best educational infrastructure, conditions for women were significantly better. Data for 1857 show that 34 percent of the women aged six to fourteen were enrolled in school compared to 46 percent of the men in the same age group.

Women's secondary schooling was possible under the 1850 educational law, but it was not until 1928 that the first public high school for females was created.[12] During most of the late 1800s, women's education reached only the "second level," the equivalent of today's third grade (primary school), and was characterized by a curriculum that covered poetry, world history, language, rhetoric, calligraphy, drawing, music, and handicrafts.[13]

During the period between the 1850s and 1880s, a number of feminist writers emerged in the Peruvian scene. Salient among those who realized the power of education for women were Mercedes Cabello de Carbonera, Elvira Garcia y Garcia, Teresa Gonzales de Fanning, and Maria Jesus Alvarado. Cabello de Carbonera criticized the "superfluous adornments" produced by the requirement that women (in the upper social classes, at least) learn to sing and play the piano, and advocated instead a scientific education for women. But, being a product of her time, Cabello de Carbonera wanted an education that "would not take [the woman] away from her domestic home, but on the contrary give her an additional attractive feature by surrounding her with the charm of knowledge, which will make her inaccessible to boredom."[14] Whereas Cabello de Carbonera defended the importance of women's education because it would improve women's performance in their families, Garcia y Garcia saw the need for women to work but considered that "women's work is justified only in terms of the needs for subsistence and thus it is valid only for women of popular sectors." Gonzales de Fanning shared this view. In contrast, Alvarado felt that "the struggle for survival, in other words, work, is a universal law and it is a moral duty that woman be subject to it the same as man."[15] Alvarado created a movement, Feminine Evolution, which demanded greater public support for women's education and the access of women to government jobs and liberal professions.

For the feminists of those times, the question of women's autonomy as individual human beings—independent of social expectations regarding marriage and motherhood—was still incipient. There is no evidence that their writings influenced educational policies in their time, although it is interesting to observe that the law making it possible for women to attend secondary school was passed in 1855 and that the law authorizing women's entry into the university was passed in 1908, periods in which the writings of the female authors cited above were in wide circulation. In any case, their writings are carefully studied today by Peruvian feminists and constitute important instances of women's rebellion against oppressive conditions.

By 1908, Peruvian girls and made significant gains. Among girls 67 percent of all six to four year olds went to school (as compared to 71 percent of boys). Some of these gains can be attributed to legislation in 1905 declaring primary education to be both free and compulsory. Since 1931, the gender differences for that age group have remained no more than 2 percentage points in favor of men. However, gender differences for the nation as a whole are much greater than those of Lima. In 1972, the enrollment rate in Lima was 92 percent for women and 94 percent for men; for the country in general, female enrollment was 75 percent compared to 82 percent for men.[16]

Access to school has always been easier for women of the upper social classes. This pattern is evident in the enrollment in urban areas compared to that in the countryside. Women in rural areas register very low levels of access. While not everyone in the urban areas is rich, the higher enrollment of women in the cities reflects not only the better educational offerings there, but also the participation of daughters from wealthy families.

If in terms of expansion women made progress, in terms of content matter education continued to be authoritarian, based on rote memorization and the scholastic approach, which meant that questions such as class and gender ine-qualities in society were never a subject of discussion in the school setting. Writers in the early twentieth century called attention to the plight of the Indians in Peruvian society and to the extreme poverty and discrimination they suffered. However, Indians were described exclusively as men. Female Indians, doubly and even triply oppressed as workers, mothers, and wives, were not discussed.

Although women have made progress in terms of access to the formal school system, there continues to be a large number of women who do not benefit from any schooling. According to the 1981 census, 9.2 percent of the male population over fifteen years of age are illiterate as compared with 23.3 percent of the female population.[17] Most illiterates reside in the countryside and tend to be monolingual in either Quechua or Aymara. The Indian population is particularly vulnerable to illiteracy because of the limited educational facilities in the rural areas and the persistent racial discrimination that is reflected in the absence of governmental policies to improve the conditions of the autochtonous Peruvians. For decades, the illiteracy rate has been considerably greater in rural than in urban areas, although the gap has been decreasing slightly. The 1981 census found that 70 percent of all illiterates resided in the countryside and that 73 percent of the rural illiterates were women.[18] Herman Fernandez estimates that a woman living in a rural area is fourteen times more likely to be illiterate than a man in the city.[19] This condition, however serious, has not led to any action on the part of the government to design and implement literacy programs for women.

Investigations of Peruvian peasant women have found that most commonly, women do not enroll in school at all or leave it after a few years because of economic hardships, the need for girls to work at home in agricultural or domestic

Table 18.1
Repetition, by Level of Education and Sex, 1970

Level of Education	Percentage of Men	Percentage of Women
Primary school	56	46
General secondary school	64	38
Technical secondary school	59	41
Teacher training school	46	54

Source: OSPE, Ministry of Education, cited in Gabliera Villalobos, _Diagnostics de la Situacion Economica y Social de la mujer Peruana_ (Lima: Centro de Estudios de Poblacion y Desarrollo, March 1975).

work, and parents' unwillingness to allow their daughters to study. In the case of dropping out, the exigencies of domestic work were cited most frequently, as girls were needed to take care of younger siblings, ill relatives, or widowed or single mothers. Two-thirds of the female children studied worked; in the area of Cuzco, the proportion of working girls was as high as 80 percent, of whom 31 percent has been engaged in domestic tasks from age seven. Many of these girls also entered school when they were eight years old or older, which put them at a psychological disadvantage vis-à-vis other students because, being older than the rest, they "felt ashamed" of their lack of knowledge.[20]

A U.S. observer of conditions in rural Peru, aided by her contrasting cultural experience, describes the education of women in this manner:

In the sierra (the highlands), if a young girl is permitted by her family to attend high school, which is unlikely because her work is highly valued at home, she will usually attend only up to the third grade. On weekends when young boys are not in school, they are likely to be playing or studying, while young girls who do go to school seldom have time to study or play. Schools offering courses beyond the primary grades are far away, and it is risky and costly to let daughters go on buses to school and return late at night. For those who live in the high altitudes where there are no teachers, attendance at school is impossible.

Once rural men have received some education and are fluent in Spanish, they generally refuse to carry loads on their back or do other chores they consider beneath their dignity. Even my companero, Raul, who was conscious of the inequality of women and men and was committed to struggle against it, found carrying water degrading. He thought that being seen carrying water would jeopardize the position of leadership he had been given as the community was about to form a cooperative on expropriated land.[21]

Once in school, women perform as well as men. Data on repetition rates across different types of education for 1970 indicate that girls tend to repeat less than men, except when they are enrolled in teacher-training colleges (Table 18.1). A similar pattern has been found in other countries. It is unclear whether this finding indicates a better academic performance by females, or a tendency by teachers to let females matriculate with lower levels of achievement. A recent investigation, based on a nationwide sample of young people of various social classes, reported that the most often cited reasons for difficulties in performing well in school were economic problems that prevented students from having books and materials, the need to help at home, and the need to work. Having no books and helping at home were mentioned more often by women than men, a pattern that was manifest across all four social classes sampled in the study.[22]

The Educational Reform of 1972

Although Peru has undergone several educational reforms during its republican life, none was as comprehensive and progressive as that attempted during the military government of General Velasco Alvarado in the late 1960s and early 1970s. The reform had multiple objectives, including the democratization of teaching, the decentralization of administration and decision making in education, and the incorporation of bilingual and work-oriented education. The main architect of the reform was a philosophy professor, Augusto Salazar Bondy. Bondy was acutely aware that "education transmits the world in its established order" and that "historically, the relations of power have been exercised by some men to the detriment of others. There have been dominated and dominating men and groups, oppressed and oppressive men and groups."[23] Thanks to his influence, Article 11 of the education reform law of 1972 (Law 19326), states: "Education will be oriented toward the revaluing of women, offering them the maximum opportunities for full and free personal development, which is the only authentic basis of their decisive function in the family and their creative participation in the process of transformation and improvement of Peruvian society."

Guidelines for the implementation of this article were enacted in February 1973 (Supreme Decree 16–72–ED). This document, *Regulations for the Revaluing of Women,* stated that all types and levels of education must orient their activities toward the "revaluation of women." It also mandated access to all training programs regardless of sex, and it advocated the civic and political participation of women, particularly through training in leadership programs. The guidelines also proposed a Permanent Committee for Educational Coordination, to be composed of representatives from the ministries of education, work, health, transport, and communications; the national commission for Unesco; and the revolutionary regime's mobilization agency, SINAMOS. Unfortunately, these ideas and discourse previously unheard of in Peru's history were not implemented because, shortly afterward, a more conservative military faction took power away from Velasco.

The 1972 educational reform also considered creating coeducational schools throughout the country. Although this proposal was not implemented, a democratically elected government took explicit steps to reject coeducation. Thus, in 1983 coeducation was introduced at the primary school level but was permitted in high schools only in cases where the schools could meet certain infrastructural standards.

As in many other countries, coeducation has been controversial. The only study in Peru on the effects of coeducation was conducted by Violeta Sara-Lafosse and associates in 1987. Using a sample of fifty-five coeducational and single-sex schools in Lima, they found that, contrary to widespread beliefs, the incidence of pregnancy was greater in girls' than in coeducational schools.[24] Male students attending coeducational schools were more willing to share domestic tasks with women than boys in single-sex schools.[25] The study also found that coeducation had polarizing effects on the participation of female students. Participation was defined in terms of three indicators: "expressing ideas in class," "engaging in protests against injustices," and "acting publicly, whether individually or collectively." In coeducational schools, a higher number of female students reported high levels of participation; however, coeducational schools also tended to have a greater proportion of female students who reported low levels of participation. The researchers concluded that the masculine presence both fostered and inhibited female participation.[26]

Two Peruvian writers, Jose Carlos Mariategui and Jose Antonio Encinas, both writing in the 1930s, currently shape much of the educational discourse in Peru. Their philosophy is humanist and seeks a new type of education to serve the needs of Peru's society. In their view, exploitation of the Indian and racial discrimination are major obstacles to social justice and progress. However, these writers—in part because of the times in which they produced their ideas—pay scant attention to women. Encinas, considered one of the most original and foremost Peruvian educators, is deeply aware of women's problems in education, but he deals with the question in the following manner. Toward the end of his book, *Un Ensayo de Escuela Nueva en el Peru* [An essay on the new school in Peru], he states: "It is not possible to consider in these pages, with the attention it deserves, the important problem of women's education, a problem that today has reached the highest concern, given the conditions under which it takes place."[27] Although, as will be seen later, feminism is making a significant contribution to the education of women in Peru, no major writings examining education from a women's perspective have appeared in the country.

Higher Education

Peru prides itself on having one of the oldest universities in Latin America—the University of San Marcos, which was created in 1551 and has been in continuous operation since 1577. Until recently, the university system discriminated on the basis of class, race, and gender. During colonial times and for many years after independence, only those who could prove their "legitimacy and purity of blood" could be admitted. Consequently, mixed breeds, Indians, and blacks were excluded. Women were not explicitly barred from the university, but there were no provisions for accepting them. The first woman able to attend

Table 18.2
Enrollment Rates, by Age and Sex, 1940–1981

	6-16 Age Group			15-19 Age Group		
	Men	Women	Total	Men	Women	Total
1940	34	26	30	23	11	17
1961	62	53	58	41	26	33
1972	82	75	78	57	41	49
1981	91	88	90	61	52	56

Source: Hernan Fernandez, "Aspectos sociales y economicos de la Educacion en el Peru," in Problemas poblacionales peruanos, Roger Guerra, ed., Vol. 2 (Lima: AMIDEP, 1986), based on census data.

university was Trinidad Maria Enriquez, a high school teacher who in 1875— more than 300 years after the founding of the Peruvian university—took exams during nine days to be admitted in the law faculty of the San Antonio Abad University in Cuzco. She conducted her studies successfully but did not receive a degree because she needed special permission from the government and at that moment, the war between Peru and Chile broke out, paralyzing civil life.[28] A law authorizing women's admissions to the university was not enacted until 1908.

A normal school for women existed since 1836, but for many years it imparted a very traditional education. According to Encinas, it was "mistakingly placed in the hands of a religious denomination, which, despite the impetus that new doctrines place on the primary school, continues to prepare teachers under a convent regime and with an exclusively sectarian purpose."[29]

CONTEMPORARY PERU

The last four decades of Peru's education have been characterized by rapid expansion. Total enrollment in primary school increased from 30 percent in 1940 to 90 percent in 1981, whereas enrollment in secondary schools increased from 17 percent during the same period. As Table 18.2 shows, access to school has been improving over time for both men and women.

A careful analysis of enrollment by place of residence, ethnicity, and gender shows that for some social groups in Peru access to school is "nil, or else exceedingly late and of short duration."[30] According to 1972 census data, the enrollment rates for those in the six to fourteen age group were much higher for Spanish-speaking individuals than for those who speak only Quechua (84 percent versus 25 percent). If we compare women in those two languages, the differences are even greater (81 percent versus 19 percent).[31] As Table 18.3 shows, school enrollment ratios are much higher for Lima than for the rural population as a whole. Again, if we observe gender inequalities within these settings, the dif-

Table 18.3
Enrollment Rates, by Place of Residence, Age Group, and Sex

	Age 6	Age 10	Age Group Age 15	Age 20	Age 25
Lima:					
Men	80.2	98.5	90.5	41.9	20.7
Women	80.3	97.6	82.4	27.7	10.0
Rural Areas:					
Men	29.7	81.3	58.6	7.6	0.7
Women	25.2	69.1	30.3	2.5	0.3

Source: Adapted from; Herman Fernandez and Carmen Montero, Designualdades
          en el Acceso la Escuela (Lima: INIDE, Ministerio de Educacion,
          1982) pp. 148-149.

ferentials are significant, with female enrollment in rural areas lagging between 15 and 57 percentage points behind those of men. These statistics show that gender differences are a persistent feature of Peru's education. They also show that gender differences are magnified by distinctions of ethnicity and residence. (In Peru, rural residence is almost a proxy for poverty.)

Although women acquire important skills and knowledge in school that prepare them to cope better with the immediate society, evidence from a number of studies shows that the messages women receive in primary schools contain negative gender stereotypes. The messages given to women in Peruvian schools have been very traditional. Their content is well illustrated in the following quote from a book on moral and civic education:

The father, by nature and by common agreement among men, exercises *patria potestas*, that is to say a strong and at the same time kind authority, and the mother represents the sweetness that coats everything, the solicitude that remedies everything, the patience that solves everything, and the abnegation that makes tolerable the saddest moments of life.[32]

As early as 1973, a study conducted by DESCO, a nongovernmental organization devoted to rural and urban research and development efforts, found that the image of women in textbooks was strongly associated with the concept of *marianismo*, the long-suffering, spiritually superior woman, usually limited to the role of mother.[33] A review of curricular programs for high school noted that the secondary schools sought to teach " subjects useful to the general functions of social life," and the "plan of studies for women was less extensive than that of men, focusing on training for family and practical matters."[34]

A recent study of primary school textbooks by Jeanine Anderson and Cristina Herencia, produced in response to a Unesco initiative, found that the number of female characters in both illustrations and text decreased as the grade of the textbook increased. Whereas women represented 27 percent of the characters during the first grade, they comprised only 11 percent by Grade 6.[35] The study also found that, whereas men were given psychological attributes that were both positive and negative (e.g., daring, just, proud, idealistic, selfish, grateful), women were characterized by a smaller number of traits. Three traits were ascribed exclusively to them: obedience and discretion (on the positive side), and lack of a sense of shame (on the negative side). In the various stories, men were found to "provide assistance" forty-one times, whereas women did so only twenty-seven times. More damaging to women's self-esteem was the finding that men "behaved intelligently" on thirty-eight occasions and women in only five.[36] The same study revealed that of 1,838 historical references in the primary school textbooks, 1,666 (91 percent) were to males. A more recent study of preschool textbooks also found marked sexual stereotypes in these textbooks. Male characters were depicted in outdoor activities, such as playing on the street and public activities, whereas female characters were almost exclusively engaged in domestic activities or taking care of children, either inside or outside the home.

Although the textbooks continue to advance a passive role for women, they merely reinforce socialization at home. A study of socialization practices (social class was not distinguished nor were parents' level of education in this particular research) found that both fathers and mothers expected their sons to have long professional careers (leading to the more prestigious occupations), while they expected their daughters to enter either short-term careers or technical fields.[38]

The Anderson and Herencia study also examined teacher-student interactions in Peruvian schools. Although their observations were based on a very small number of schools, no differences were found in the participation of girls and boys in the first grade. Grade 3 however, there were significant differences in seating arrangements, use of physical space during break times, and propensity to ask questions of the teacher. Girls in the third grade were found to sit together toward the front of the class, to occupy the corners and sides of the play yard, and more likely to answer than initiate questions. These observations also revealed that male students were much more likely to receive attention from teachers, particularly female teachers.

Despite the need to intervene seriously in the textbooks and in the training of teachers to improve the treatment of girls in the school system, educational authorities are doing little in this regard. At present, INIDE, the research center of the Ministry of Education, is carrying out yet another study of school stereotypes in textbooks, though it could be argued that the Anderson and Herencia study already provides enough evidence to warrant the implementation of textbook and teacher-training reforms. Through the United Nations Development Program (UNDP) funding and initiative, the Ministry of Education is engaged in a four-year effort to develop a population program at the primary level. This program, which will involve curriculum development, teacher training, and the production of teachers' and student guides, concentrates on knowledge about demographics, family planning, and biological differences between the sexes. Although Peru's current population policy reportedly aims at "revaluing the role of women and creating a conscience about the equality of rights among men and women," the guides produced so far pay only minimal attention to the questions of the social and economic discrimination of women, thus missing an excellent opportunity to make the educational system address the needs of women.

A more positive development in Peru's education was the appointment, for the first time in the nation's history, of a woman as minister of education. Mercedes Cabanillas, an Alianza Popular Revolucionaria Americana congresswoman, became the new minister in July 1987.

THE UNIVERSITY TODAY

When we examine current enrollments in the university, it is easy to assume that the condition of women is improving dramatically, as women now comprise 30 percent of the student body.[39] The actual progress is less substantial, given the segregation of women into a very few fields. In 1979 women comprised almost the entire enrollment in obstetrics (97 percent), social work (97 percent), and nursing (95 percent), and were heavily represented in psychology (64 percent) and education (55 percent). In contrast, they represented only 2 percent of mining engineering, 8 percent of civil engineering, and 10 percent of oil engineering students.[40]

The participation of women in the various fields has changed slightly over a nineteen-year period (see Table 18.4). Women are well represented in education but underrepresented in engineering, the humanities, the sciences, and medicine. The only field that registered a gain was medicine, in which women increased their presence from 14 percent in 1960 to 30 percent in 1968, though it decreased to 26 percent in 1979.

Women are also more likely than men to enroll in short-term postsecondary training courses. According to 1981 census data, women comprised 51 percent of those enrolled in nonuniversity postsecondary training, in contrast to 38 percent of those enrolled in universities.[41] Another characteristic of women's higher education is that, for some unknown reasons, women tend to have higher attrition rates than men between enrolling in the university and completing their studies. As Table 18.5 shows, they lose between 5 and 8 percentage points in their representation by the time they graduate. Women do seem to be doing slightly better than men in obtaining professional degrees (which requires either writing a thesis or passing special exams) after they finish their coursework.

As in most countries, a high proportion of the teaching force in Peru is female. According to 1986 Ministry of Education statistics, they comprise 98 percent of preschool, 60 percent of primary, and 46 percent of secondary teachers. This considerable presence of women in the formal school system has not yet been mobilized in favor of a fairer treatment of women in textbooks and classrooms.

Table 18.4
Women's Enrollment in the University, by Field, 1960–1979

	1960*	1965*	1968*	1970**	1979***
Sciences	1,223 (33)	1,121 (33)	1,452 (30)	(31)	———
Education	3,234 (51)	10,516 (44)	14,477 (45)	(46)	8,267 (56)
Humanities	2,680 (23)	5,076 (23)	9,048 (26)	(26)	———
Engineering and Architecture	250 (4)	429 (4)	864 (5)	(6)	———
Medicine	543 (14)	1,050 (24)	1,774 (30)	(30)	1,640 (26)

Source: *CONUP (National Council of the Peruvian University) statistics, 1966.
**CONUP statistics, 1971.
***Comision Nacional Interuniversitaria, December 1981.

Note: Figures in parentheses represent percentages.

Table 18.5

Women Enrolling, Graduating, and Receiving Professional Degrees, 1960–1983

Year	Enrolling	Graduating	Receiving Professional Degree
1960	25%	17%	26%
1965	28%	28%	27%
1970	30%	25%	34%
1975	33%	28%	33%
1979	34%	36%	33%
1983	35%	40%	37%

Source: Comision Nacional Interuniversitaria, Estadisticas No. 30 (Lima:
          Comision Nacional Interuniversitaria, April 1982) and Asamblea
          Nacional de Rectores, Estadisticas No. 46, (Lima: Asamblea Nacional
          de Rectores, July 1985).

Women constitute 70 percent of the members of SUTEP—the national federation of teachers. By 1985, only one woman was on SUTEP's National Executive Committee.

Women also teach at the university level, but, as is true in most of the world, they are grossly underrepresented at this level. In 1982, women comprised 15 percent of the permanent university professors and were distributed as follows: teaching assistants (a regular faculty rank in Peru), 21 percent; assistant professors, 36 percent; associate professors, 27 percent; and full professors, 16 percent. Women represent only 9 percent of all the full professors.[42] Peruvian universities do not offer programs in women's studies, though some courses, such as the sociology of women, given at the Catholic University of Lima since 1983, focus on women's issues. The number of dissertations on women is increasing, yet "it is unusual to find professors/researchers whose scientific interests address women's issues."[43]

Another factor that tends to discourage women's progress in higher education is the paucity of educational statistics by gender. Universities are not obligated to produce statistics indicating career choices made by men and women or indicating those who graduate or abandon their studies by gender. Basic data, such as what happens to the numerous men and women who apply for university admission but fail to obtain it, are not available. In 1983, there were 300,000 candidates for 50,000 vacancies. What happened to the 250,000 individuals who were not admitted? From 1960 and 1979 university statistics, we know that the gender proportion of those who apply is very similar to the proportion of those who are admitted, thus indicating that women perform as well as men in university entrance exams. But, we can ask, what happens to the women who fail in their attempt to enter university? Are their occupational chances similar to those of men? Observers agree that a large number of young people in Peru see limited educational and occupational opportunity for them, and that feelings of frustration and the desire for drastic social change are leading many of them to take an active part in the ever stronger "Shining Path" and "Tupac Amaru" guerrilla movements. The scanty information about these movements indicates not only that women are substantial participants, but also that many of them, usually university-trained, are guerrilla leaders.[44]

The Catholic University of Peru, which keeps the best available university statistics, gathers information covering forty-two variables. Yet, gender appears in only one table, showing enrollment by sex in each department.[45] With these kinds of data, policy decisions regarding the conditions of women in the university become difficult.

A recent law designed to improve the Peruvian university system (1983) provides guidelines for many important aspects of university planning and functioning, including university objectives and characteristics. But again, as in the case of primary and secondary education, the question of women is not considered one that Peruvian universities need to improve their performance. Recent university plans, at both the collective (involving all universities) and individual level (e.g., the plan for development and operations of the Catholic University), consider a number of important aspects of the university, such as the economic situation, the postgraduate programs, the need for research, and extension programs. They do not refer to the situation of women, thus defining it—by implication—as a nonproblem.

FEMINISM AND POPULAR EDUCATION

Today Peru is one of the most advanced Latin American countries in terms of feminist theory and mobilization. As many as 250 groups—operating in low-income communities, labor unions, and feminist action centers—have identified themselves as part of the feminist movement. In 1987, ninety-seven nongovernmental organizations that describe themselves as being run by women and pursuing a feminist agenda were identified by the national planning agency. Many of these groups are also linked to the popular education movement. This movement, inspired by the teachings of Paulo Freire and the ideas of Antonio Gramsci, seeks to instill political awareness in the educational programs addressed to the marginal and disadvantaged sectors of the population.

Through the feminist movement in Peru, education is playing a liberating role for women. Groups with nationwide outreach such as Peru-Mujer, Flora Tristan, and Manuela Ramos have developed programs for women that combine elements of gender conciousness-raising with the provision of income-generating skills, legal knowledge, and leadership and organizational skills. These programs have helped adult women in various walks of life—from factory workers to operators in the informal sector of the economy to housewives—to be more aware of their rights as women and citizens. According to Virginia Vargas, a well-known Peruvian feminist:

The various feminist centers and groups carry out extensive work in education, addressing it to the various expressions of the women's movement: slum dwellers, workers, peasants, homeworkers, promotors of urban and rural work, etc. Taking as the point of departure the women's daily struggle and their concrete needs, these groups aim at providing evidence and strengthening the women's consciousness regarding the structures that oppress them and their specific gender oppression, thus connecting this oppression to the other structures of domination in society.[46]

The educational labor of these feminist groups takes several forms: (1) workshops lasting six to ten sessions and emphasizing group discussion on a specific theme (usually selected by the participants themselves) related to the day-to-day life experiences of women; (2) courses lasting six to twelve sessions and combining lectures and group discussions; (3) *jornadas,* day-long sessions lasting one to two days, with lectures and debates on selected themes treated previously in workshops and courses; and (4) *encuentros,* usually nationwide meetings in which women from several organizations gather to develop a consensus about the various realities confronting women.[47]

No formal studies have been conducted assessing the impact of participation on these types of nonformal and informal education for women. However, judging from women's increased political participation in the established political parties, in current government efforts to produce a national plan of action for women, and in neighborhood mobilizations to demand basic needs, it is apparent that women have attained a level of political participation never seen in the country before.

The feminist groups have not developed a systematic pedagogical methodology. Yet, it is important to observe that they are aware of important parameters in their educational efforts. As Vargas notes:

We begin with practice itself, establishing democratic ties, not vertical, idealizing, or maternalistic ties. Experience has shown us that educators and educatees can integrate a vast amount of knowledge in an active, changing and mutually enriching relationship. The objective is not merely to convey information, rather, with it, the life experiences are rescued, revalued, and integrated to scientific knowledge, promoting in this manner a new enriched knowledge, capable of integrating the different shades of reality.[48]

A particular feature of Peru's feminism is its strength among popular sectors. According to one observer:

The growth of women's political consciousness in the cities can be understood primarily as a reaction to the ineffectiveness of male political leadership in addressing the problems of workplace and community felt most acutely by women. In the barriadas, or shantytowns, the double burden of home and work keeps women out of neighborhood organizing once the family has settled, but when confidence in male leadership is shattered, the latent organizing force of women emerges.[49]

The action by feminists in the popular sectors is related primarily to the satisfaction of basic needs, such as water, housing, and health services, but the women's experience in solidarity and organization and in exerting pressure on governmental authorities has generated a politicization process of great significance among women.[50] Feminists were active in the formulation of a national plan for the improvement and equality of women's conditions proposed by the United Left (Izquierda Unida), a major and influential coalition of leftist parties. This plan contains several educational policies; they address only the question of sexual education and prescribe that the content of this subject cover sexuality, family life, responsible parenthood, and family planning. It recommends that such knowledge be given to adolescents and to future teachers, psychologists, social workers, doctors, and nurses. The plan makes no reference to other types of educational intervention, such as revising and producing new textbooks, retraining teachers, and encouraging the participation of women in nontraditional career choices.[51] More recent feminist participation has occurred in the design of the national plan produced by the National Institute of Planning. This plan reportedly considers gender problems in curricular programs for adults, preschool and primary education, training of teachers at these levels regarding gender issues, and a mass-media project (involving radio, press, and television) to offer an alternative vision of the two genders and their roles in society.[52] It remains to be seen whether these objectives are translated into specific program guidelines and eventually implemented in the schools.

EDUCATION AND WORK

The process of modernization has created employment conditions that are beyond the ability of education to resolve. In Peru, women participate mainly in the tertiary sector of the economy and occupy many positions in the informal sector of the economy (about 36 percent in 1983), which, of course, does not operate on the basis of formal education credentials. The protracted economic crisis affecting most of the Third World has forced many low-income women to join the labor force. As a result, more women are employed than before. Yet, the evidence suggests that much of their incorporation in the labor force is at the lower levels of the occupational hierarchy and in jobs with low pay.

The average income in 1981 for the economically active population fifteen years of age or older is presented in Table 18.6. As can be observed, at any level of education women's salaries are lower than those of men. Surprisingly, the largest discrepancies between female and male salaries affect women in the educational extremes: those without formal education and those with university education.

It appears that as women increase their levels of education, they evince a higher rate of participation in the labor force. As Table 18.7 shows, although 97 percent of the men with university training are employed, a similar proportion of women in the same category—96 percent—also work. In contrast, whereas

Table 18.6

Average Income, by Sex and Level of Education (in 1981 Soles)

Education Level	Men's Income	Women's Income	Total Income	Women's Salary as % Men's Salary
Without education	53,000	30,000	41,000	57%
Primary education	58,000	35,000	52,000	60
Secondary education	75,000	58,000	71,000	77
Non-university higher education	107,000	76,000	94,000	71
University education	161,000	95,000	142,000	59

Source: Marfil Francke. Las Mujeres en el Peru (Lima: Centgro de la Mujer
         Peruana Flora Tristan, 1985) p. 20.

Table 18.7

Employed Population, by Sex and Professional Status, 1981

	Men	Women
With university education	188,338 (97)*	93,861 (96)
With tertiary education other than university	64,026 (97)	60,870 (94)
Without a profession	3,502,554 (97)	1,006,229 (90)

The figures in parentheses indicate the percentage of the population with a
given level of education that is employed as compared to the population that
is economically active.

Source: Peru. Censos Nacionales. VIII de Poblacion y III de Vivienda (Lima:
         Instituto Nacional de Estadistica, July 1984).

97 percent of men without a profession work, only 90 percent of the women in
this category do.

There are not many available studies linking levels of education to the occupational attainment of women. A notable exception is the investigation by
Alison Scott based on national census data for 1940, 1961, and 1972, and a
1974 employment survey centered on Lima.[53] Scott found that a significant
percentage of women with tertiary education find employment but that women
with secondary levels of education (who represent 46 percent of the labor force
with this level of education) had the lowest labor participation rates. Scott found
a strong relation between marital status and labor participation, as the rate of
women with either a legal or a common-law husband was almost half that of
unmarried women. But women with secondary education, even when single,

Table 18.8
Distribution of the Female Labor Force in Lima, by Economic Sector, 1940–1972

Economics Sector	1940	1961	1972
Manufacturing[a]	22.2	18.0	16.0
Construction	0.8	0.3	0.3
Transport	1.6	1.1	1.3
Commerce[b]	13.7	17.9	21.7
Services[c]	57.5	58.1	56.3
Unspecified	4.2	4.6	4.3
Total	100.0	100.0	99.9

[a]Includes gas, electricity and water to compare data to 1940 Census.

[b]Includes the categories of "financial and insurance enterprises" that appeared in the 1972 Census.

Source: Alison Scott. "Desarrollo dependiente y la segregacion ocupacional por sexo." Debates on Sociologia, no. 10 (1984) p. 26.

had very low levels of labor force participation. Scott attributed this fact to the existence of two separate labor markets—one for women and one for men, with the male market being larger than the female market. Therefore, women with secondary education, despite their knowledge, cannot find jobs.

Scott also found that women had an average monthly income half that of men. Again, she traced these differences to the existence of separate labor markets for women and men, with the "feminine" jobs placed in the lower occupational hierarchies. Thus, 37 percent of women were employed as unskilled workers and in service industries compared to 12 percent of the men. Differences in male and female salaries were found within each occupation, a difference that "was not related to their levels of education and, in some cases, the average level of education of women was higher than that of men."[54]

Longitudinal data for Lima (see Table 18.8) shows that the distribution of the feminine labor force across broad occupational categories has remained remarkably constant during a thirty-two-year period.

Scott's historical analysis, covering the period 1940–1972, showed that the incorporation of Peruvian women into the labor market had occurred through an expansion of the "feminine" occupations rather than through the integration of women into men's occupations. The labor force in Peru is polarized by gender, with four-fifths of the occupations strongly segregated by sex and two-thirds in jobs that are almost exclusively feminine or masculine (i.e., having a sex concentration of over 90 percent). Sixty-three percent of the women work in only 13 of 107 possible occupations.

The most gender-polarized occupations are those in the informal sector, where

Table 18.9
Number of Children per Woman, by Level of Education

Women's Level of Education	Number of Children
Illiterate	7.8
Able to read	6.8
Incomplete primary	6.6
Complete primary	5.3
High school or higher	3.8

Source: Marfil Francke. Las Mujeres en el Peru (Lima: Centro de
         la Mujer Peruana Flora Tristan, 1985) p. 22.

capital and on-the-job-training are more important than education. On this basis, Scott concluded that an increase in the educational level of women would lead to an occupational desegregation by gender only in a very few jobs and that it would not reduce the male-female salary gap. In her view, education could improve the occupational mobility of some women, but occupational mobility as a whole depended mainly on the expansion of feminine jobs demanding high skills. In her words, "until the politico-cultural aspects of gender segregation are integrated in the analysis of labor markets and the formulation of policies, gender inequalities will be neither understood nor eliminated."[55] She predicted that the combined expanded supply of educated women in the labor force and the weak demand for female labor force would produce a dissociation between education and income that would be greater among women than among men.

EFFECTS OF EDUCATION ON MOTHERS' BEHAVIORS

Practically no studies have explored the effects of women's education on behaviors and expectations toward family life, their expectations for life and occupational chances of their children, or decision making within the family. Statistics showing correlations between years of education and fertility indicate that women's education has a strong effect on the number of children they have and their knowledge of and willingness to use birth control measures. According to a fertility survey conducted by the National Office of Statistics during 1977–1978, women without education had 6.2 children compared to 2.7 children for women with higher education.[56] Similar associations were found in the 1981 census, as shown in Table 18.9.

These are, of course, gross statistics that might hide or confound influences that might be due to the role of poverty, cultural norms, and employment in family decisions. Nevertheless, the strong decline in the number of children as women acquire some high school education has led several researchers to hypothesize the existence of a threshold at the end of primary schooling.

EDUCATION AND POLITICAL POWER

The extent to which education may be correlated with political participation has not been systematically studied in Peru. It is rare to find women in high political positions who do not have high levels of education. On the other hand, very few women play important public political roles, despite the fact that an increasing number of them are attaining tertiary education.

We have evidence that many of the feminist leaders have university experience as students and even as teachers. They have substantial experience in political parties, in both the center and center left of the political spectrum.[57]

A study conducted in 1973—the period of the military "revolution" in Peru—examined the characteristics of women in high-level positions in ministries and universities. The author, who interviewed fifteen of the eighteen women who were identified as having "leading administrative positions," found that twelve had studied in private schools. Of the group, nine had studied in nonreligious schools and six in coeducational schools. From these findings the author inferred that it was important for women to avoid religious education and to experience coeducational schooling.[58] Her findings, however, also showed that the majority of these female leaders rejected feminism, considering it "imprudent, in bad taste, or felt that to endorse the movement was tantamount to a public acceptance of feminine limitations they said they had overcome long ago."[59]

CONCLUSIONS

The historical evidence suggests that, in Peru, formal education has not played a significant liberating role for women, and chances are that it will make only weak efforts to do so in the future. Although the access of women to primary and secondary education has almost reached parity vis-à-vis men, it hides two processes that continue to be detrimental to women. The first is that women in rural areas, especially Indian women, register limited or no access to primary school, with the result that they evince high levels of illiteracy. The second is that many women in universities follow "feminine" careers, and thus their increased level of education has not had the effect of weakening social stereotypes about women fulfilling secondary economic roles in society.

Nonformal education, to a large extent provided by grass-roots groups and feminist organizations, offers a great deal of potential for an alternative education for women, an education that makes them aware of exploitative conditions in society and at the same time trains them for political mobilization and economic independence. These efforts, though small in number, are nonetheless making a dent in the otherwise patriarchal Peruvian society. Furthermore, the participation of feminist groups in various governmental and independent initiatives to improve the conditions of women is likely to affect policies in the formal education system and to greatly expand the role of "popular education" in the transformation of women's conditions. The feminists' ability to press the state to accelerate its economic and social reforms, their willingness to create temporary alliances with established political parties, and their ability to struggle for demands made both by middle-class women and by low-income marginal women will shape further developments considerably. In the forthcoming process, education will have to be both a means and an end of feminist action.

NOTES

This study was made possible, in part, by a grant from the Andrew W. Mellon Foundation, administered by the Center for Latin American Studies of Stanford University.

1. Alfredo Hernandez, *Compendio de Sociologia Peruana* (Lima: Editora y Distribuidora Lima, S.A., 1986); Sara Beatriz Guardia, *Mujeres Peruanas: El otro lado de la Historia* (Lima: Empresa Editorial Humboldt, 1985).

2. Guardia, *Mujeres Peruanas.*

3. Hernandez, *Compendio de Sociologia Peruana*

4. Juan P. Castro Fernandini, *Legislacion Escolar del Peru* (Lima: Editorial Antena S.A., 1939).

5. Luis Martin and Jo Ann Guerin Petters, *Scholars and Schools in Colonial Peru* (Dallas: School of Continuing Education, Southern Methodist University, 1973).

6. Castro, *Legislacion Escolar;* Ricardo Mariategui Oliva, *Historia del Peru y America Virreynato, Independencia* (Lima: Talleres de Grafica Mundo, 1944); Carlos Daniel Valcarcel, *Breve Historia de la Educacion Peruana* (Lima: Editorial Educacion, 1975).

7. Martin and Petters, *Scholars and Schools,* p. 17.

8. Castro, *Legislacion Escolar.*

9. Quoted in ibid.

10. Juan Francisco Pazos, quoted in Maritza Villavicencio, "Las Raices del Movimiento de Mujeres en el Peru. Informe Final" (Lima: Centro de la Mujer Peruana Flora Tristan, July 1987, Mimeo).

11. Villavicencio, "Las Raices," p. 15.

12. Cited in Hernan Fernandez, "La situacion educativa de la mujer en el Peru" (Lima: INIDE, 1987, mimeo).

13. Villavicencio, "Las Raices," p. 23.

14. Cited in Ana Maria Portugal, *Maria Mercedes Cabello o el Riesgo de Ser Mujer* (Lima: Centro de Documentacion sobre la Mujer, 1987), p. 3.

15. Quoted in Villavicencio, "Las Raices."

16. Hernan Fernandez and Carmen Montero, *Desigualdades en el Acceso a la Escuela* (Lima: INIDE, Ministerio de Educacion, 1982), p. 27.

17. Carmen Montero, "Ser pobre y ser mujer," *Autoeducacion,* year III, No. 6, (April-June 1983): 34–39.

18. Instituto Nacional de Estadistica, *El analfabetismo en el Peru 1940–1981* (Lima: Instituto Nacional de Estadistica, 1986).

19. Fernandez, "La situacion educativa," 1987.

20. Violeta Sara-Lafosse, *Campesinas y Costureras* (Lima: Pontificia Universidad Catolica del Peru, Fondo Editorial, 1983); Carmen Chira, "Campesina de Huaro," *Allpanchis* year XV, 26, No. 25 (1985); Carmen Chira, "Campesinas de Santa Rosa de Ocopa," *Allpanchis,* year XV, 21, No. 25 (1985); Violeta Sara-Lafosse, "Campesinas de Characato," *Allpanchis,* 15, No. 25 (1985).

21. Carol Andreas, *When Women Rebel: The Rise of Popular Feminism in Peru* (Westport Conn.: Lawrence Hill & Co., 1985), pp. 63–64.

22. Fernandez, "La situacion educativa," 1987.

23. Augusto Salazar Bondy, *La Educacion del Hombre Nuevo* (Buenos Aires: Editorial Paidos, 1976), p. 21.

24. Violeta Sara-Lafosse, Blanca Fernandez, and Carmen Chira, *El Problema de la Coeducacion en los Colegios Secundarios Estatales de la Ciudad de Lima* (Lima: Pontificia Universidad Catolica del Peru, 1987), p. 53.

25. Ibid., p. 112.

26. Ibid., pp. 93–96.

27. Encinas, *Un Ensayo de Escuela Nueva en el Peru* (Lima: Imprenta Minerva, 1932), p. 240.

28. Maria Luz Crevoisier, "Trinidad Maria, la primera universitaria," *Viva* (November 1987).

29. Encinas, *Un Ensayo de Escuela Nueva,* p. 10.

30. Fernandez and Montero, *Desigualdades*.

31. Ibid., p. 79.

32. Luis C. Infante, *Educacion Moral y Civica* (Lima: Editorial Minerva, 1938), p. 19.

33. Susan C. Burke and Kay Barbara Warren, *Women of the Andes* (Ann Arbor: University of Michigan Press, 1981).

34. Valcarcel, *Breve Historia* p. 191.

35. Jéanine Anderson and Cristina Herencia, *L'image de la femme et de l'homme dans les livres scolaires peruviens* Paris: Unesco, August 1983), pp. 18–19.

36. Ibid., pp. 20–27.

37. Maria Eugenia Mancilla, "Aprendiendo a ser mujer. Estereotipos sexuales en los textos escolares," *Debates en Sociologia,* No. 9, 1983.

38. Violeta Sara-Lafosse, *La Familia, la Mujer y la Socializacion de los Hijos en Contextos Sociales Diferentes* (Lima: Pontificia Universidad Catolica del Peru, March 1983), pp. VIII–11.

39. Marfil Francke, *Las Mujeres en el Peru* (Lima: Centro de la Mujer Peruana Flora Tristan, March 1985), reporting on 1981 census data.

40. Ibid.

41. Ibid.

42. Comision Nacional Interuniversitaria, *Estadisticas No. 43* (Lima: Comision Nacional Interuniversitaria, September 1984).

43. Victoria Ponce del Castillo, "50 anos de tesis universitarias sobre la mujer en la Universidad Catolica," *Debates en Sociologia,* No. 10 (1984): 204.

44. Guardia, *Mujeres Peruanas,* 1985; Carlos Castillo, Carlos Alvarez, and Hernan Fernandez, "Un mundo complejo y poco conocido," *Autoeducacion,* No. 12 (January-March 1985).

45. *Censo de Alumnos,* 1982 (Lima: Direccion Universitaria de Planeamiento, Pontificia Universidad Catolica del Peru, 1982; *Censo de Alumnos, 1986* (Lima: Direccion Universitaria de Planeamiento, Pontificia Universidad Catolica del Peru, 1986).

46. Virgina Vargas Valente, "Reflexiones en torno a la educacion de las mujeres en el Peru," Paper presented at the conference on World Perspectives on the Education of Women at Mount Holyoke College (Lima: Centro de la Mujer Peruana Flora Tristan, 1987, mimeo), p. 12.

47. Ibid., p. 29.

48. Ibid., p. 13.

49. Andreas, *When Women Rebel,* p. 15.

50. Grupo de Accion Flora Tristan, ''Mesa Redonda, Feminismo y Movimiento Social de Mujeres'' (Lima: Centro Flora Trista, June 1987).

51. Izquierda Unida, *Programa Nacional de Reconocimento de la Igualdad y Dignidad de la Mujer. Plan de Gobierno de Izquierda Unida* (Lima: Women's Commission, Izquierda Unida, September 1985).

52. Vargas, ''Reflexiones en torno,'' 1987.

53. Alison Scott, ''Desarrollo dependiente y la segregacion ocupacional por sexo,'' *Debates en Sociologia,* No. 10 (1984).

54. Ibid., p. 14.

55. Ibid., p. 53.

56. Fernandez, ''La situacion education,'' 1987.

57. Guardia, *Mujeres Peruanas,* 1985; Vargas, ''Reflexiones en torno,'' 1987.

58. Gabriela Villalobos, *Diagnostico de la Situacion Economica y Social de la Mujer Peruana* (Lima: Centro de Estudios de Poblacion y Desarrollo, March 1975).

59. Ibid., pp. IV 26–IV 27.

THE MIDDLE EAST

19
EGYPT

Kathleen Howard-Merriam

"Education of women has probably been by far the most important factor in bringing about changes in their role and status all over the world in the last fifty years."[1] Does this statement apply to Egypt's women? In the following pages we will examine this question by putting into perspective the considerable educational achievements of many Egyptian women on the one hand, and the persistent high rate of female illiteracy on the other. Women's education in Egypt is a major factor in their considerable visibility in the professions over the last thirty years. Yet a high level of illiteracy among women remains.

This chapter first provides a historical overview, discussing the role of religion and ideology in the education of women in Egypt. Second, the effect of social class differentiation on women is examined. Third, the chapter discusses the post-1952 state educational policy and provides enrollment figures for the different educational levels. Next, the impact of educational achievement on women's labor force participation, on their decision-making roles, and on their political participation is investigated. The chapter concludes with a discussion of what lies ahead for women's education in Egypt.

HISTORICAL OVERVIEW

Women's education in Egypt is the story of the interplay among (1) forces of tradition, which worked against women in the centuries of patriarchy, (2) Islam and its interpretations after the death of the Prophet Muhammad, and (3) European influence beginning with Bonaparte's brief Egyptian campaign in 1798.

Egypt's rich ancient heritage included a prominent place for women in public life, with women learning to read and write and some becoming expert scribes. The level of education for both men and women declined considerably during the successive periods of foreign domination.[2] The most important and lasting of the foreign rulers were the Arabs who brought Islam to Egypt in the eighth century A.D. Today Egypt is 90 percent Muslim, and the remainder are Coptic Christian. Although the Prophet Muhammad preached equality between men and women and provided for women's rights, he did not do away with patriarchy: rather, he strengthened it. His followers and Islamic scholars over the centuries have interpreted Qur'anic messages (God's revelations to Muhammad) and his sayings to suit the social trends of the day.

Consequently, even though women were urged as co-believers with men to study religion, the other verses speaking of men's superiority in physical strength over, and therefore responsibility for, women came to be broadly interpreted, as were their superior mental ability and sole role in religious leadership and saintship. Moreover, as marriage and childbearing were encouraged as well as women's modesty, women's education suffered throughout these years, although examples existed of women scholars such as Shuhda in twelfth century Baghdad and Amat al Wahid, known as a brilliant judge.[3] These women, though few in number, became the historical role models of modern-day Muslim women, seeking liberation from the confined role they had been socialized to accept by an Islamic male leadership.

Not until the nineteenth century was the idea of educating women in public institutions for national or state purpose rather than simply individual satisfaction introduced in Egypt. Muhammad Ali, Egypt's first modernizer of the nineteenth century, saw the need for women to acquire skills in order to staff the new governmental institutions. In 1831–1832, he established the first government school for girls to train them as nurse-midwives for the new medical school. Encountering resistance from the middle and upper classes, he finally had to recruit Abyssinian and Sudanese slave girls bought in the Cairo markets to the school. Later, orphan girls were added.[4] This was the only school for girls until the foreign missionaries established primary schools for girls beginning in 1846. These were followed by a few Egyptian private schools. These private schools made a major contribution to women's education.[5]

The first government secular primary school for girls opened in 1873 under the sponsorship of Cheshmat Hanum, the third wife of Ismail, Khedive (Ottoman viceroy of Egypt). Again, white slaves (from the Caucasus) belonging to the Khedive's extended family and high government officials were the first students.[6] Most of the upper class still preferred to educate their daughters at home, often with European women tutors. But the number of these government schools remained limited owing to the strained financial conditions (high debts to European creditors) and the new de facto foreign ruler, the British high commissioner who acted for the British government.

By the last quarter of the nineteenth and the first half of the twentieth century, women's education was marked by contradictions. On the one hand, there were the conservative British policy considerations against state involvement in education; on the other, there was the limited interest of a growing Egyptian elite in promoting social change. For the British colonial ruler, public education for women was subsumed under the general principle of educating only those who were easily absorbed into a government of strained resources, though with due regard for indigenous cultural values. Lord Cromer, the British high commissioner from 1882 to 1906, pursued a policy that called for modernizing the traditional religious primary school, the *kuttab,* and he preferred that the private schools bear the burden of educating women.[7] With a meager 1 percent of the budget allocated to education during this period, Egyptians' access to education was limited to a small upper class willing to pay for it. Education could not therefore serve as a channel of upward mobility.[8]

Countering the British conservative approach was the spirit of Islamic reformism in the leadership of Muhammad Abduh and Qasim Amin. Muhammad Abduh (1849–1905) was a scholar of Islam who urged reform by applying modern education and scientific inquiry which had brought Europe to a predominant place in the world.[9]

Qasim Amin, a judge, was one of Muhammad Abduh's followers and applied his ideas to the issue of women's emancipation. He argued that since woman is the backbone of the family, the foundation of society, her "progress or backwardness in intellectual level is the first influence on the progress of backwardness of the nation."[10] Later, in another work, Amin forcefully argued that women's intellectual capacity was equal to that of men because God gave them equal legal obligations.[11]

In dramatic contrast, with a message that was to be revived in the Middle East some fifty or sixty years later in the Islamic revivalist movements, there were other disciples of Abduh who opposed Amin's views on women's emancipation. Tal'at Harb, the Egyptian nationalist financier, and Mustafa Kamil, the nationalist leader, tied women's emancipation to European imperialist designs to bring immorality and decadence to the east.[12] For many, national unity and independence preempted the questions of social reform, tainted as it was with Western influence.

The reform movement, in forming an essential component of the liberal nationalist leadership, guided Egypt's governing elite until the 1952 military coup d'etat. The feminists who emerged to press for women's public education found support among these male reformers, as well as from the foreign missionary schools established for girls. Women also participated in the debate on the need for women's education but envisioned a limited set of subjects for women appropriate to maternal and homemaking roles within the family.[13]

The gradual growth in the number of girls' primary schools established by the government, private groups, and these foreign missionary groups can be seen in Table 19.1. Indeed, it was the private and missionary efforts that carried the major burden of educating women until even the 1950s. This was hardly sur-

Table 19.1

Enrollment, Female Enrollment, and Number of Schools, by Type of School, 1913–1914 and 1944–1945

	1913–14			1944–45		
	N Sch.	Students	%F	N Sch.	Students	%F
Elementary						
Public	3,669	232,458	11	3,985	895,089	46
Private	3,577	91,916	5	737	111,325	28
Foreign	---	----		---	4,029	31
Total	7,246	324,374	9	4,722	1,010,443	44
Kindergarten & Primary						
Public	94	13,978	15	2·	59,939	19
Private	615	66,093	20.8	400	88,331	35
Foreign	302	41,511	48	---	46,305	27
Total	1,011	121,582	29	616	194,575	28
Secondary						
Public	6	2,532	0	53	36,654	9
Private	5	14	.6	74	14,406	6
Foreign	10	4,326	34	---	11,330	44
Total	21	6,872	16	127	62,390	14.8

Source: Roderic Matthews and Matta Akrawi, Education in the Arab Countries of the Near East, Washington, D.C. American Council on Education, 1949), p. 34.

prising, given the conflict among the elite over women's education, the fragmented character of the educational system divided as it was among private, religious (Islamic and Christian alike), and the secular government institutions; and finally, the fairly low priority accorded to education in general.[14] A concerted effort was made to improve women's education and continued after independence was granted in 1922.[15]

At the time of independence, the religious *kuttab* (mosque-based) schools were reformed as four-year elementary schools to expand the number of schools providing secular subjects along with religious education to tackle the low literacy problem. At independence a new constitutional provision for compulsory and free primary education for all children between six and twelve years of age was made, but the government sought to provide as little financial commitment as possible.[16]

The nationalist uprising of 1919 and the resulting politicization of the liberal nationalist women helped to broaden the concept of women's education. These liberal nationalist women, who belonged to the governing political-economic elite, converted their nationalist participation of demonstrations and provision of support services for the men into concrete demands for equal rights. When the male writers of the 1923 constitution granted "equality of rights before the law for Egyptian citizens," the women read this statement as including women. The nationalist Wafd leaders promised to work for the liberation of women. The first nationalist government of 1924, however, claimed that women were not ready for equality.[17]

The Egyptian Feminist Union was established thereafter, and it demanded that educational opportunities for women be expanded. In 1924, the first government secondary school for girls opened in Cairo.[18] By 1929, the first three women had been admitted to Cairo University.[19] A year later women's share of the general educational secondary school enrollment was 6 percent. Meanwhile, women had come to represent 36 percent of the total enrollment of teacher training institutions.

The first thirty years of Egypt's nominal political independence were marked by preoccupation with relations with Great Britain, and the struggle among the monarch and his conservative allies, and the nationalists, the Wafd. This situation, combined with the generally conservative social outlook of the medium-sized landowners and urban bourgeoisie who comprised the national elite, the world Depression, and the Second World War stalled educational expansion. By 1952, the female illiteracy rate was still 91.3 percent, the total primary enrollment ratio was 26 percent, the secondary enrollment ratio was 7 percent, and third-level student enrollment was 165 per 1,000 population. The female shares of these students were 36 percent, 19 percent, and 7 percent, respectively.[20]

POST-1952 STATE EDUCATION POLICY

The young military officers who seized power in 1952 were products of the military academy established under the 1936 treaty between Great Britain and the Wafdist government. These military academy graduates had experienced the limitations of the educational facilities of the 1920s and 1930s. Most came from peasant farmer families or minor officials' families who comprised the majority of the population. With educational and other social services heavily concentrated in the urban areas, these young officers had been sent to the city for secondary education to prepare for the civil service or university.[21] Experiencing the logistical difficulties in obtaining a secondary education away from their home, they were imbued with the need for social reform and modernization which meant further development and expansion of the educational system.

The regime's educational policy had four distinct phases which were characterized by uneven educational progress for women. During the first phase (1952–1956), the government universalized primary education; extended the compulsory education period from six to nine years; developed scientific, technical, and vocational education; reorganized private education; and upgraded educational facilities.[22] The entire educational system was further secularized and reorganized: a unified primary school of four years, a four-year preparatory school (later reduced to three years), and a three-year secondary school. The new regime retained the Wafd government's policy of no tuition fees for secondary schools but with the condition that students qualify by examination for admission.[23]

The second period (1956–1961) was marked by ideological development and state expansion of control. Social justice and equality were emphasized during this period that the foreign schools were nationalized in reaction to the Anglo-French-Israeli invasion of 1956. The third period (1961–1973) was the "socialist phase" devoted to expanding the school facilities throughout the country. During this period, the National Charter was issued (1962) proclaiming "the equality of women with men," an example of reform from above.

The state educational system consisted of primary, preparatory, secondary, and higher education. Primary education totals six years. The primary school examination serves as a gatepost to preparatory school of three years. Successful completion of the preparatory school examination admits students to secondary education, which is divided into general secondary, vocational, and teacher training. The general secondary track prepares students for university education; the vocational technical track prepares youth for the skilled labor force. Students in the technical track can qualify for university if they have a 75 percent average. Teacher-training schools prepare students to teach in the primary school system. Students in the teacher-training schools obtaining a 75 percent average or above may also enroll in the university.[24] Higher education consists of university or a specialized high institute education, and possibly graduate training.

The emphasis that the government has placed on education can be seen in its budgetary allocation for education which expanded from 10.8 percent in 1952–1953 to 26 percent in 1969–1970.[25] In terms of government expenditure as a percentage of the gross domestic product (GDP), the increase from 3 percent in

1952–1953 to 5 percent in 1976 is higher than that in the other countries of the developing world but lower than that in Europe and North America.[26]

The fourth phase, which extends from 1974 to the present, marks the "Open Door" policy of President Anwar Sadat which has continued under President Hosny Mubarak. The key feature of this policy is economic liberalization to attract foreign and domestic private investment in order to promote the country's economic growth. In education, the goal has been to harmonize the theory with the environment and to link the educational with the industrial establishments. This period has been one of considerable public debate over the quality of education to meet Egypt's pressing economic problems.[27]

The proportion of public expenditures on education decreased to 14.6 percent in 1970, increased to 17.6 percent in 1973, and then decreased to 10.6 percent in 1985.[28] Despite the fairly heavy investment in education, the state has not kept pace with the increasing costs of providing education to a rapidly expanding population and growing school enrollments. Most (81.9 percent) of the educational expenditures during this 1970–1979 period went to teacher's salaries and only 6.7 percent to new buildings.[29]

In view of the emphasis Sadat placed on the need for training technicians, 31 percent of the capital expenditures for the school went to secondary education, 37 percent of which was for industrial education. The largest proportion of recurrent expenditures was allocated to primary education (48 percent), whereas the proportion of the total of recurrent expenditure for secondary education was 26 percent, 24 percent of it devoted to industrial education.[30]

During this period, the number of primary schools grew from 8,415 in 1970 to 10,818 in 1977–1978, and the number of secondary schools increased from 604 to 1,388 during the same period.[31] The number enrolled during this period rose dramatically as the population had increased at an annual growth rate of 2.54. Primary schools had enrolled 75 percent of the six year olds in 1979, whereas they had enrolled only 46 percent in 1959.[32] By 1984, the percentage had increased to 84. Secondary school enrollment also increased from 34 percent in 1970 and reached 46 percent by 1984.[33]

At the same time, the number of students passing the primary examination more than doubled between 1967 and 1972.[34] By 1975–1976, the proportion of students passing both the preparatory examination and the secondary education was between 70 and 75 percent.[35] As the schools have become more and more crowded, the Ministry of Education has resorted to two or three shifts a day for some schools. In 1986, however, it decreed that there would be no more than two shifts per day, which in many cases led to more overcrowding. The size of one classroom, for example, increased from 75 to 150 pupils.[36]

University education also expanded with the 1952 military regime's commitment to reform and development of the nation's scientifically trained human resources. In fact, higher education expanded at a faster rate than secondary or elementary education in a society where until the 1950s the access to education was pretty much limited to those youth from urban middle- and upper class families. They represented a small portion of the population who could and did make the financial commitment for their children's education.[37] But in 1962 the Egyptian government made all public education free through the university level, and grants and fellowships were extended to poor students. Besides the upgraded and expanded Alexandria University, new universities were established in provincial centers to accommodate the rapid rise of secondary school graduates seeking admission. From an enrollment of 41,315 in 1952–1953, the university student enrollment increased to 97,927 in 1962–1963 and to 168,425 in 1971–1972. In 1984–1985, the figure reached 682,348.[38] In twenty years, the enrollment ratio of twenty to twenty-four years olds in higher education had gone from 7 percent to 21 percent.[39]

IMPACT OF EDUCATIONAL DEVELOPMENT ON EGYPTIAN WOMEN

The impact of these changes on women's education has been uneven. Women's access to education has been affected by environmental sociopolitical factors as well as by governmental policies. Women who have been able to complete primary education have benefited from educational reforms more than any other group.

The impact of the educational reforms on women must be put in the context of economic and political changes in Egypt in recent times. In the first decade of the military regime, the country experienced considerable demographic growth. This growth was accompanied by rural migration in search of employment. In the countryside, the government implemented a moderate land reform program. An activist foreign policy resulted in three wars. The disastrous 1967 war and the psychological victory of the 1973 war provided the greatest changes for the country. The country's economy became stagnant despite, and partly because of, the population explosion. Much of Egypt's population continues to live in poverty. Changes in women's education occurred at a time when the country's economy suffered greatly and underwent a number of changes.

The universalization of education, together with the industrialization program, contributed to changes in both women's educational pattern and social status. The number of women with a primary and intermediate (including secondary) education rose from 0.8 percent in 1947 to 2.2 percent in 1960, 11.6 percent in 1976, and 13.2 in 1986. The proportion of women with university-level degrees increased from 0.5 percent in 1947 to 0.3 percent in 1960, 1.2 percent in 1976, and 2.8 percent in 1986.[40] Illiteracy has decreased little, however. It declined from 88 percent in 1947 to 84.2 in 1975–1976, to 61.8 percent in 1986.[41]

The gap in educational level between urban and rural areas has not narrowed. The proportion of female literates in the urban areas grew from 25 percent in 1974 to 41 percent in 1986. In the same time period in the more rural areas of Upper Egypt, the proportion of literate women grew from 11 percent to 13.8

percent. (This contrasts with the generally more urbanized Delta where literacy increased from 15 percent to 18.9 percent between 1974 and 1986.) Women in urban areas are much more likely to hold postprimary diplomas than women in rural areas. A total of 27 percent of urban women held preparatory diplomas as opposed to 7 percent of rural women. As of 1986, 7 percent of urban versus 0.9 percent of rural women held diplomas from higher education.[42]

If we take the enrollment ratios as another measure of educational progress, we can see considerable expansion of educational opportunities. The primary education enrollment ratio for women rose from 52 percent in 1960 to 60 percent in 1965 and to 72 percent in 1984.[43] The female proportion of students enrolled in primary school went from 36 percent (1950) to 38 percent (1975) and to 39 percent in 1984–1985.[44] The enrollment of girls in general secondary education increased from 9 percent in 1960 to 15 percent in 1965 and to 46 percent by 1984. The female share of the secondary educational enrollment also increased from 19 percent in 1953 to 33 percent in 1971, to 37.5 in 1979–1980 but declined to 33.5 in 1984–1985.[45] Within the secondary level, the female proportion of the vocational/technical secondary levels increased dramatically from 2 percent in 1954 to 31 percent in 1971 to 38 percent in 1979, but returned to 30 percent in 1984–1985.[46]

Changes in women's education (including high institutes) may not seem impressive in terms of actual enrollment figures, but they are remarkable when compared with those of other countries in the Middle East and Africa. In 1960, the enrollment ratio was 1.68, and it rose to 4.27 ten years later. In 1974, the ratio jumped to 7.40 and by 1985 it was 11 percent. For the Middle East region generally, the ratio has risen from 1 to 7 percent.[47] When looking at the female share of university enrollments, the picture is even more favorable to women in comparison to other countries. In 1960, the female share of the student population was 17 percent and in 1971, 27 percent. By 1984–1985, the percentage was 32.8.

Considerable variation in women's share of the enrollment and the feminization of some of the scientific faculties exists. For instance, in the faculties of pharmacy the female share is 43.8 percent, a gain of 18 points from 1975. In the Faculty of Engineering, the female share is 13 percent, a drop of 16.2 percent from 1980. On the other hand, in the humanities faculties, women comprise 47 percent of the Faculties of Arts, a gain of 27 percent, and 56 percent of the Faculty of Economics, a drop of 16.6 over a five-year period.[48] The shifts in enrollment, understood in the context of the changing socioeconomic conditions brought about under the Nasser, Sadat, and Mubarak regimes, will be explored further below.

WOMEN'S EDUCATION AND EMPLOYMENT

The new social policies, including the redistribution of land, had a positive effect on women's educational opportunities. Land no longer was a means of

Table 19.2

Female Educational and Employment Status, by Educational Level, Industry, and Occupation, 1960–1986

	1.	2.	Education 3.	4.[a]				
1961								
% Female	7.8	1.3	11.3	10.1				
% of Females	82.2	5.2	9.9	2.5				
1976								
% Female	62.0	30.6	33.5	16.7				
% of Females	71.0	16.2	11.6	1.2				
1986								
% Female	61.7	34.2	38.0	30.0				
% of Females	61.8	18.0	17.4	2.8				
			Industry					
1961	1.	2.	3.	4.[b]				
% Female	4.8	2.0	5.3	14.3				
% of Females	43.0	3.4	10.0	40.2				
1976	1.	2.	3.	4.	5.	6.	7.	8. .@
% Female	3.0	1.0	7.0	18.0	6.0	4.0	17.	12.0
% of Females	22.2	1.0	.7	2.4	12.8	.2	47.0	9.3
1983								
% Female	17	2.0	7.0	24.0	15.0	5.9	33.0	21.6
% of Females	41.0	.7	.3	1.9	13.0	.09	28.9	10.2

Key: [a] = 1. = Illit. 2. Read & Write. 3. Less than Univ. 4. Univ. and higher;
[b] = Agriculture. 2. Industry 3. Trade & Transport. 4. Services;
1 = Agriculture, Forestry, Hunting & Fish; 2. Construction; 3. Electricity, Gas & Water; 4. Finance, Insurance and Business Services; 5. Manufacturing; 6. Mining & Quarrying; 7. Services (Community, personal and other); 8. Trade, Restaurants and Hotels and Transport, Storage, Communication)

Source: CAPMAS, <u>Al Ta'dad a; Aam li sukan al askan an munshaat 1986</u> (The Population and Housing Survey for 1986), (Cairo: CAPMAS, 1987), p. 51 and CAPMAS, <u>Statistical Yearbook 1952-1986</u> (Cairo: CAPMAS, 1986), p. 22.

Table 19.2 (continued)

1960	1.	2.	Occupation 3.	4.	5.	6.	7.	8.[d]
% Female	22	4.7	4	5.6	15	3	3	
% of Females	12	.9	2.8	7.7[e]	23.9	32	9	
1976								
% Female	25	11	19	5.0	7.0	2.0	2.0	24
% of Females	22	1.0	16	5.0	11	15	8.0	19
1983								
% Female	30	16	29.6	20	8.6	17	7.6	29.6
% of Females	17	1.0	13	6.9	3	36	9.0	10

[d]Key: 1. Professional and technical; 2. Administrative/executive; 3. Clerical; 4. Sales; 5. services; 6. Farmers, fishermen, loggers and related workers; 7. Craftsmen, Production workers; 8. laborers not elsewhere classified.

[e]Figure taken from 1961, data from CAPMAS, The Egyptian Woman in Two Decades, p. 48.

Sources: Data for 1960 from International Labor Organization, Yearbook of Labor Statistics, 1965 (Geneva: International Labor Office, 1965); for 1976 and 1983 respectively: CAPMAS, Statistical Yearbook, Arab Republic of Egypt, 1952-1986 (Cairo: CAPMAS, 1986) and CAPMAS, Bahth Al-amalat bil einat (Study of the Labor Force in the Arab Republic of Egypt according to the results of the May 1983 Round) in Arabic (Cairo: CAPMAS, 1985), p. 50; and CAPMAS, Statistical Yearbook 1952-1986, p. 24.

Source: CAPMAS, *Al Ta'dad a; Aam li sukan al askan an munshaat 1986* (The Population and Housing Survey for 1986), (Cairo: CAPMAS, 1987), p. 51; and CAPMAS, *Statistical Yearbook 1952–1986* (Cairo: CAPMAS, 1986), p. 22.

gaining status. Education has come to take its place as conferrer of social status: if one could get a free education through the university level and then obtain the coveted white-collar employment, or at least a government position that commanded higher status than a manual worker, then certainly this avenue was preferred.[49] These aspirations were particularly prevalent among the urban population.

For rural families, too, as the plots of land became smaller and smaller and the factories began attracting labor from the agricultural sector, rural women were encouraged to gain an education. White-collar positions or jobs in industry required a primary certificate.

The shift in the employment of women over the last forty years has been dramatic. In 1947, the proportion of women participating in the labor force was 2.3 percent. This figure went up slightly to 4.8 percent in 1960, but there was no increase in the following five years. This lack of change may be attributed to the increase in the number of females in school.[50] The participation rate has since risen to 9 percent in 1976 and reached 15 percent in 1983.[51] (See also Table 19.2.)

Several points are in order regarding participation rates for the female labor force. The labor force figures vastly underestimate the actual female labor participation in agriculture where women constitute unpaid (and therefore uncounted) labor. It has been estimated that women, in fact, contribute more than half of the agricultural workforce, despite the fact that they are considered "wives doing their housework."[52]

There is a dynamic between education and workforce participation. Although the female labor force rates have declined for ten to nineteen year olds, they have increased for twenty to thirty-four year olds. The labor participation rate is higher for women who have more education. Thus, while in 1976 the female illiteracy rate was 76 percent, the labor force participation of women was only 8 percent. Whereas those with secondary or less education accounted for only 5.8 percent of the population, their participation rate was 38.8 percent.[53] University graduates represented only 1 percent of the female population, but 13.7 percent of the female university graduates were in the labor force.[54]

The urban-rural differences are also striking. Although female activity rates in urban areas increased from 5.8 percent in 1960 to 8.1 percent in 1976, rural female activity rates went down from 4.3 percent to 3.5 percent during the same period.[55] According to 1983 statistics, 26 percent of urban females have a higher education degree (bachelor's or higher), whereas only 4 percent of rural working women have attained this level of education. Those urban working women with a preparatory degree comprise 38 percent of the total, whereas rural working women with the same educational level account for 21 percent of the rural female workforce. In contrast, 59.7 percent of rural working women are illiterate compared with only 10 percent of urban working women.[56]

The distribution of the female workforce by economic sector has shifted over the past twenty years: namely, there are higher participation rates for educated women, and a growing marginalization of women into agriculture. A shift has taken place in employment from agriculture to services and manufacturing and back to agriculture. The proportion of women working in agriculture declined from 43 percent (in absolute numbers, 180,200) in 1961 to 25.8 percent (147,500) in 1972. By 1983, their share had gone back up to 41 percent (or 803,200). The number of women in manufacturing, on the other hand, increased from 8,000 or 3.3 percent in 1961 to 67,000 or 11.7 percent in 1971 and then to 254,300 or 13 percent in 1983. Most women were employed in the service sector. They made up 40.2 percent (168,200) of the service workers in 1961, 45.7 (238,000) in 1971, and 28.9 percent (562,900) in 1983.[57] Earl Sullivan notes that the decline in women's participation in manufacturing has been matched by an increase in female employment in the banking and service sectors.[58] But while the banking or finance services had a higher share of employed women than employed men (2.4 percent and 0.8 percent, respectively) in 1976, these proportions were reversed in 1983 (1.9 and 2.4 percent, respectively), despite the increased female share of this sector from 18 to 24 percent.[59]

The greatest opportunities for women's employment have been in the sectors requiring higher levels of education, although the salaries are not commensurately higher. The professional and technical sector's proportion of the female work-force increased from 8.1 percent in 1961 to 25 percent in 1976. The sector then decreased to 17 percent in 1983. This sector comprises the largest share of working women second to craftspeople in the rural areas. When one compares the distribution of the economically active force with the labor force, one sees the advantage that even the intermediate certificate gives in employment. There is a greater gap between those available and those actually working than in the higher educated categories. Moreover, women with a university education had a better rate of employment (13.7 percent in 1976) than males (4.2 percent).[60]

Wages have increased in the chemical, food, and textile industries over the last twenty years and compete almost equally with agricultural wages. Public sector employees have become the underdog in comparison to agricultural work-ers.[61] For women, given equal pay provisions, public sector and government employment is more lucrative, despite the generally low fixed salary structure. Women's wages are generally two-thirds to three-fourths those of men.[62]

The state has been the largest single employer of women. In 1976, women made up 16.9 percent of employees in public enterprises. This figure represents a 6-percent increase since 1966. By 1983, the percentage had increased to 22 percent.[63] Most women in public employment are teachers or in health services. Women have gained access to public administration over the last twenty years, where they have grown from 3.6 to 9 percent of all employees.[64] The private sector employs most women who work in the rural area as family workers (51 percent), self-employed (17 percent), and employers (5 percent).[65]

Cultural and demographic changes account for the greater contribution to the professional group than the administrative and executive sector. Men still resist women's authority in executive positions. Women have succeeded in assuming top positions in the traditionally female field of education. Education was one of the early fields in which women could pursue a career. When the primary and secondary schools were established in greater numbers in the years following nominal independence in 1922, women comprised a third of the teacher-training students. The number has steadily increased since then: by 1983, women rep-resented over 50 percent of primary school teachers and one-third of university teachers.[66] Certainly, teaching has been a major avenue of upward social mobility for lower class rural girls.[67]

Where women have gained ground in the professional fields is in the mass media, a relatively new field not dominated by men. With the increase in the number of women graduates from the university in the 1960s and the development of the Egyptian mass media during this period, women were readily recruited. Significantly, the directors of the state-run television and radio authorities have been women.

Women have also gained in the professional sectors requiring a scientific education. With the revolutionary regime's emphasis on scientific development and the promise of employment opportunities in these fields, medicine and engineering gained prestige among upwardly mobile families. Parents began to favor their daughters studying in these nontraditional female fields to compensate for the parents' poverty and own lack of education. As one father put it: "I want my daughter to have a career; she will help make up for our poverty, and she is our hope in this world."[68]

Again, the extensive state role until the Sadat *Infitah* (Open Door or liberal economic policy emphasizing private enterprise) has helped women's employment in these nontraditional fields. An earlier study showed how 42 percent of women engineers, 31 percent of women medical doctors, and 50 percent of women in the other sciences have been employed by the government.[69]

THE OPEN DOOR POLICY AND MIGRATION: EFFECT ON WOMEN'S EDUCATIONAL AND EMPLOYMENT OPTIONS

The Infitah and the related labor migration fostered by the Sadat and Mubarak governments have had both a positive and negative effect on women's employment in the professions. The positive effect has been the opportunities afforded women teachers, physicians, and engineers to replace men who migrated to the oil-rich Arab Gulf states for higher salaries as well as to migrate themselves. The exodus of males to the oil-rich countries, spurred by the oil price boom in the late 1970s, created more opportunities for women to advance in the large public sector, particularly in such formerly male-dominated fields as engineering. Interviews with women electrical engineers in the Electricity Authority in the spring of 1987 revealed that they dominated midlevel technical positions.

University women graduates benefited to some extent from the new opportunities in banking and the tourist services established under the new Open Door policy. These positions offered considerably higher salaries than those in state employment. Women who graduated from foreign language schools (formerly foreign-operated private schools which came under state supervision in the late 1950s), drawn from the upper urban classes, moved into these jobs.[70]

Women also started to migrate to the oil-rich Gulf states in response to the demand for skilled labor in the sex-segregated educational and medical institutions of these states. It was estimated that more than one-third of the 1.5 to 2 million Egyptian migrants were female, and the majority were professional and subprofessional white-collar workers. Although most of the women were single, married women also started to migrate, accompanied by their husbands.[71]

Another effect of the migration has been the feminization of the farm family. With the migration of male farmers to the Arab Gulf states, women have been left to tend the farm. As a result, women have assumed new roles, becoming the major economic decision makers and managers of households, for some husbands send the money to their wives and not to their male relatives. Women have had to make contacts with social and economic community officials, including agricultural cooperative bureaucrats, bank officials, and teachers. These new roles have given women a sense of new competence and power which they will not readily relinquish.[72] Their new position, however, is contingent on their ability to establish households independent from those of their husband's family. Some of these women have also acquired new appreciation of the value of educating daughters and, accordingly, will provide private lessons to help them pass the state examinations for preparatory, secondary, and tertiary school admission. This new priority can be difficult to realize when the migrant husband returns, determined to pursue the traditional marriage avenue to economic and social security.[73]

The migration has also had negative effects on the education of children: the increased demand for agricultural labor in the absence of the adult male often pulls children out of school to perform the needed agricultural tasks. The migration of teachers and medical personnel abroad has left villages with a critical shortage of teachers. Unqualified teachers have been recruited which, in turn, places greater burdens on families to spend extra money for private tutoring.[74]

The migration has had negative effects nationally as well by exacerbating the shortage of teaching personnel throughout the educational ladder. Teachers migrated for temporary periods and, in its encouragement of migration, the government guaranteed the returning migrants their jobs in the skilled sectors. Hence, enormous dislocation has occurred, with an oversupply of teachers in some areas and a critical shortage in other areas and no replacements for them. Egyptian universities, struggling to cope with increased enrollments, are further disadvantaged by the secondment of professors abroad, where in four years they can earn twice as much as they could earn in thirty years at home.[75]

The educational system is therefore struggling to cope with drastic personnel and equipment shortages in an era of increasing privatization. Ambitious parents must spend increasing sums of money on private tutoring to compensate for the overcrowding of schools and shortages, compelling half-day school sessions. Because of the low salaries paid, the teachers secure second jobs as tutors during the remainder of the day or seek jobs abroad. Either way, the student is the loser.

WOMEN IN THE POLITICAL SYSTEM

The growing frustrations of facing a limited job market in the Open Door era of the Egyptian economy continue to foster a growing conservatism among all classes of men and women. The Islamic call is for the return of the woman to the home or at least the adoption of Islamic dress. There is also a growing sense of futility with the political system, as the governing party eliminated guarantees of women's political representation instituted in 1979.

The women's movement in the 1920s paved the way for the gradual increase in educational opportunities throughout the succeeding sixty years. Educated women had perhaps some impact on President Gamal Abdel Nasser's favoring the establishment of women's rights in suffrage, political office, and education.

Educated women, encouraged by the state's promotion of modernization and the expansion of the state apparatus for this role, have found employment in the bureaucracy and the professions. They have taken a leading role in trying to reform the Islamic marriage and divorce laws to improve their status. Educated women have also run for the parliamentary seats, encouraged by the grant of thirty reserved seats for women in the national Parliament. At the local level, women teachers and bureaucrats have been recruited for political representation, assured in the 1979 legislation. But environmental factors of the economy, the influence of the conservative Gulf States on attitudes toward women, and the recognition of the limited ability of the state to solve these problems have contributed to the increasing dichotomization of the women's movement with implications for education.

One path which the young educated woman is taking is a religious one: adopting Islamic dress and responding to the Islamic leaders' call for resumption of a motherhood role on a full-time basis. Whether this call will lead to an increase in the birthrate is debatable, given the economic pressures and new, higher levels of education, especially in urban areas. Another path is a non-political one: pursuing one's own career for the economic and personal ends of supporting a family. The majority of the women at the present time are taking this route.

Substantial numbers of women in the government bureaucracy and in the professions, especially the media, suggest that they have a stake in maintaining and protecting their rights and they will fight to retain them. An example of their successful effort in this regard occurred in March 1987 when the general director of the General Organization for Textile Industries issued a decree forbidding the employment of women in all Egyptian textile factories. This decree was addressed to all levels of employment at the textile factories, including medical doctors, engineers, and accountants. There was an immediate reaction from the women political activists, and the general director then denied having issued such a decree.[76]

CONCLUDING NOTE

In net terms, the education of Egyptian women has been a success story. More women of all social classes, from the countryside as well as the city, have been and are being educated. Given the obstacles of overcrowded classrooms, a curriculum heavily oriented to memorization, and the expenses of private tutoring, it is remarkable that as many women do succeed in advancing through to the university level and do well, even better in many cases than the men. Even if they return to their homes or remain in their homes, the quality of their lives and their families will be vastly improved. More and more women, present neo-Islamic trends notwithstanding, will head for the commercial workplace, some even at the urging of their husbands. One example of the impact of education is that family size decreases with advancement of education, as shown even in 1960: mothers with a university education had 1.86 children, those with a primary education had 3.66 children, and those women with no education had an average of 4.05 children. Education does make a difference.

The Egyptian political leadership, as expressed by President Mubarak, has recognized education to be a critical national issue in Egypt's struggle to continue development. As noted by Ahmed El Mahdi in *The Middle East Times,* the country suffers from a simultaneous glut and shortage, contributing to the obvious disorder in the economic and social structure.[77] This glut and shortage is exemplified in the annual graduation of 80,000 students from universities with insufficient preparation in the sciences and languages. Many people believe that the realization of free access to a university education leading to a white-collar job has, in the opinion of many, contributed to a dilution of quality in that the state has been unable to keep adequate pace with mass expectations. Technical education has also suffered. The government pledges reform in the form of administrative reorganization and budgetary allocation. It remains to be seen what will be implemented and accomplished.

What does the current situation mean for women's education? On the dark side, the growing limitation of employment opportunities in the private sector may have negative repercussions for women's future educational pursuits. On the positive side, in these years of economic hardship, women's presence in the workplace is a necessity. Despite conservative Islamic trends, therefore, women's enrollments may well continue and increase, preparing them for careers and jobs that will maintain, and hopefully increase, their standard of living.

NOTES

1. Barbara Ward, "Women and Technology in Developing Countries," *Impact of Science on Society* 20 (January-March 1970): 96.

2. Hind AbouSeoud Khattab and Syeda Greiss El Daeiff, "Female Education in Egypt: Changing Attitudes over a Span of 100 Years," in Freda Hussein, ed., *Muslim Women,* (New York: St. Martin's Press, 1984), p. 169.

3. Naila Minai, *Women in Islam* (New York: Seaview Books, 1981), p. 38.

4. J. Heyworth-Dunne, *An Introduction to the History of Education in Modern Egypt* (London: Frank Cass & Co., 1968), p. 132.

5. Joseph Szyliowicz, *Education and Modernization in the Middle East* (Ithaca, N.Y., and London: Cornell University Press, 1973), p. 130.

6. Heyworth-Dunne, *Introduction to the History of Education,* p. 375.

7. Earl of Cromer, *Modern Egypt* (London: Macmillan and Co., 1908), pp. 524–542 passim.

8. Szyliowicz, *Education and Modernization,* p. 122. See also Robert L. Tignor, *Modernization and British Colonial Rule in Egypt, 1882–1914,* (Princeton, N.J.: Princeton University Press, 1966), pp. 342–345.

9. See Nadav Safran, *Egypt in Search of Political Community* (Cambridge, Mass.: Harvard University Press, 1961), pp. 62–74.

10. Valerie J. Hoffman-Ladd, "Polemics on the Modesty and Segregation of Women," *International Journal of Middle East Studies* 19, No. 1 (February 1987), quoting from Qasim Amin, *Tahrir al mar'a,* in Imara, Qasim Amin, 2, pp. 37, 38.

11. Imara, *Qasim Amin,* p. 26.

12. Thomas Philipp, "Feminism and Nationalist Politics in Egypt," in Lois Beck and Nikki Keddie eds., *Women in the Muslim World* (Cambridge, Mass.: Harvard University Press, 1978), pp. 278–279.

13. Ibid., p. 283. Malak Hifni Nassif was a leading woman intellectual who wrote and spoke out on the need for women's emancipation within an upper and middle-class context and on confining her focus to education for social and maternal purposes, not political involvement.

14. See Judith Cochran, *Education in Egypt* (London: Croom Helm, 1986), pp. 22–36 for a discussion of the early nationalization of education efforts.

15. Christine Sproul, "The American College for Girls, Cairo, Egypt: Its History and Influence on Egyptian Women: A Study of Selected Graduates," Ph.D. diss., University of Utah Department of Educational Studies, June 1982. Sproul notes that in 1900 there were thirty-five girls' schools, and of the 14,181 students in the mission schools, 26 percent were girls. Quoting from Dr. Andrew Watson, United Presbyterian Mission Records, Cairo, Egypt, 1903 report. In 1914, according to Hekmat Abou-Zeid et al., *The Education of Women in the U.A.E. During the 19th and 20th Centuries* (Cairo: Cairo University Press, 1970), p. 12 as reproduced in Khattab and El Daeiff, "Female Education," p. 189, 67 percent of the 28,338 girls in Egyptian schools were in private institutions. Szyliowicz has a different set of figures for this year: 782 girls were enrolled in government schools, whereas 5,517 were in American institutions. Szyliowicz, *Education and Modernization,* p. 130.

16. Cochran, *Education in Egypt,* p. 35 quotes from Dr. Ed. Claparede's Report, 1930, p. 100 (Arabic) on the proportion of the budget devoted to education in Egypt: 7.3 percent.

17. Huda Shar'rawi, *Mudhakkirati,* pp. 257–258.

18. Huda Shar'rawi, *Harem Years: The Memoirs of an Egyptian Feminist,* translated by Margot Badran (London: Virago Press, 1986), p. 135.

19. Nineteen women were allowed to sit in on classes in 1909–1910 at Cairo University, then a private university, and in 1907 women were sent abroad for postgraduate studies. "Women in Higher Education," mimeographed paper, no date, in the Office of Women in Development, Agency for International Development, Washington, D.C.

20. Unesco, *Statistical Annual, 1964* (Paris: Unesco, 1964) for primary and secondary education figures, and Szyliowicz, *Education and Modernization,* Appendix 3 taken from Unesco, *Statistical Annual, 1969.*

21. P. T. Vatikiotis, *The Egyptian Army in Politics* (Bloomington: Indiana University Press, 1961), p. 46.

22. See Syliowicz, *Education and Modernization,* p. 264 for discussion of the educational policy in Nasser's Egypt.

23. Malcolm H. Kerr, "Egypt" in James S. Coleman, ed., *Education and Political Development* (Princeton, N.J.: Princeton University Press, 1965), p. 176.

24. Khattab and El Daeiff, "Female Education," pp. 172–173.

25. Georgie D. M. Hyde, *Education in Modern Egypt* (London: Routledge & Kegan

Paul, 1978), p. 74. She quotes Robert Mabro, *The Egyptian Economy 1952–72* (London: Oxford University Press, 1974) as indicating the LE 23 million budgeted in 1952–1953 was raised to about LE 126 million in 1969–1970, while public investment in education increased from LE 2.5 million to about LE 33.3 million.

26. Byron G. Massialas and Samir Ahmed Jarrar, *Education in the Arab World* (New York: Praeger Publishers, 1983), p. 48.

27. M. Hyde, *Education in Modern Egypt*, p. 21.

28. Massialas and Jarrar, *Education in the Arab World*, p. 49 quoting from Conference of Ministers of Education and Those Responsible for Economic Planning in the Arab States, *Recent Quantitative Trends and Projections Concerning Enrollment in Education in the Arab Countries* (Abu-Dhabi, November 7–16, 1977 (Paris: Unesco, Office of Statistics, Ed–77 MINEDARAB/Ref. 3, 1977), p. 43.

29. Massialas and Jarrar, *Education in the Arab World*, p. 53.

30. Ibid., p. 54.

31. Central Agency for Public Mobilization and Statistics (CAPMAS), *Statistical Year-book* (Cairo: CAPMAS) for the year 1979.

32. Amir Boktor, *The Development and Expansion of Education in the United Arab Republic* (Cairo: ARE Ministry of Education, 1979). See also Cochran, *Education in Egypt* p. 57.

33. Massialas and Jarrar, *Education in the Arab World*, p. 63 and the World Bank, *World Development Report 1987* (Washington, D.C.: World Bank, 1987).

34. Khalid Ikram, *Egypt: Economic Management in a Period of Transition* (Baltimore and London: Johns Hopkins University Press, 1980), p. 126.

35. Ibid., p. 127.

36. KR Kamphoefner, "Reshaping Literacy Programming to Fit Select Women's Lives: Considering Women's Role in the Household," Paper presented at the Annual Meeting of the Middle East Studies Association, November 15–17, 1987, Baltimore, Maryland, quoting Paul Attallah, Director of Literacy Programming, Caritas Catholic Charities, October 1986.

37. Even in 1964–1965 after the Arab Socialist property seizures and land-ownership reforms further limited the number of feddans (1 feddan = 1.038 acres) a family could own (reduced from 200 to 100 to 50 feddans from 1954 to 1964), the top 10 percent of the Egyptian households held 31.9 percent of the income as opposed to the lowest 20 percent which had only 4.6 percent. R. Hrair Dekmejian, *Islam in Revolution: Fundamentalism in the Arab World* (Syracuse, N.Y.: Syracuse University Press, 1985), p. 105.

38. Figures taken, respectively, from CAPMAS, *The Egyptian Woman in Two Decades (1952–1972)* (Cairo: CAPMAS, 1974), p. 209 for 1952–1953, 1962–1963, and 1971–1972 figures, and CAPMAS, *Statistical Yearbook 1952–1986 for Arab Republic of Egypt* (Cairo: CAPMAS, 1987) for 1984–1985 figures.

39. World Bank, *World Development Report*.

40. CAPMAS, *Al Ta'dad al' Aam li-sukan al-askan al munshaat 1986* (Population and Housing Survey for 1986) (Cairo: CAPMAS, 1987).

41. CAPMAS, *Statistical Yearbook 1952–1986*.

42. CAPMAS, *Al Ta'dad al 'Aam*.

43. Baha Abu-Laban and Sharon McIrvin Abu-Laban, "Education and Development in the Arab World," *Journal of Developing Areas* 10 (April 1974): 290 for the 1960 figure and *World Development Report 1987* for the 1965 and 1984 figures.

44. Massialas and Jarrar, *Education in the Arab World*, p. 230 for the 1960 figures

and CAPMAS *Statistical Yearbook 1952–1985* (Cairo: CAPMAS, June 1986) for the 1984–1985 year.

45. Abu-Laban, and Abu-Laban, "Education and Development," p. 293 for the 1953 figures and CAPMAS for the 1979–1980 and 1984–1985 years.

46. *World Survey of Education* II (Paris: Unesco, 1958), p. 343 for the 1954 figure and CAPMAS 1973, 1979, and 1986 for the later years.

47. Unesco, *Statistical Yearbook, 1976* (Paris: Unesco, 1976) for the years 1960 to 1974; Ruth Leger Sivard, *Women: A World Survey* (Washington, D.C.: World Priorities, 1985), p. 40, for the comparisons with other countries and the year 1985.

48. CAPMAS, *Statistical Yearbook 1952–1986*.

49. Khattab and El Daeiff, "Female Education," pp. 179–180.

50. Hoda Badran, "Arab Women in National Development," prepared for the Seminar on Arab Women in National Development, Cairo, September 24–30, 1972, sponsored by UNICEF in cooperation with the Arab League and Arab States Fund for Economic Cooperation (ASFEC).

51. Badran, "Arab Women," for 1960 figures; John Waterbury, *The Egypt of Nasser and Sadat,* (Princeton, N.J.: Princeton University Press, 1983), p. 44, for 1976 figure; and CAPMAS, *Bahth al amalat al 'ainat* (Labor Force Survey) (Cairo: CAPMAS, May 1983), p. 133 (in Arabic), for 1983 figure.

52. Ahmed a. Gouali, *Some Features of Agricultural Labour Employed in Egypt* (Cairo: 1980), mimeographed.

53. Bent Hansen and Samir Radwan, *Employment Opportunities and Equity in Egypt* (Deneva: International Labour Office, 1982), p. 68.

54. Ibid.

55. Ibid., p. 57.

56. CAPMAS, *Bahth al amalat al ainat*, p. 34, 133.

57. See Table 19.2 for figures and sources.

58. Earl Sullivan, "Women and Work in Egypt," *Cairo Papers in the Social Sciences* 4, Monograph 4 (December 1981), pp. 5–44.

59. CAPMAS, *Statistical Yearbook, Arab Republic of Egypt, 1952–1986* (Cairo: CAPMAS, 1986), p. 25 and *Bahth al Amalat*, 1985, p. 109.

60. Hansen and Radwan, *Employment Opportunities*, p. 68.

61. See ibid., pp. 70–77 for a comparison of wages and salaries among sectors, public and private.

62. Ibid. See also Sullivan, "Women and Work," pp. 125–149; for his discussion of women in business, particularly since the launching of the Open Door economic policy.

63. Hansen and Radwan, *Employment Opportunities*, p. 64 for the years 1966–1976; CAPMAS, *Labour Force Statistics for 1983*, p. 161.

64. The proportion of women in education and health services increased from 76.3 percent in 1966 to 80 percent in 1983. See CAPMAS, *The Egyptian Woman in Two Decades*, p. 65 for the 1966 figures and Robin Morgan, *Sisterhood Is Global* (Garden City, N.Y.: Anchor Books, 1984), p. 195.

65. *Bahth al amalat*, p. 42.

66. Interview with Dr. Shafika Nasser, Majlis as Shura member (the advisory upper house of the Egyptian Parliament), April 1987.

67. Nagat Al Sanabary, "Continuity and Change in Women's Education in the Arab States," in Elizabeth Warnock Fernea, ed., *Women and the Family in the Middle East,* (Austin: University of Texas Press, 1985), p. 101.

68. Khattab and El Daeiff, "Female Education," p. 180, quoting one of their respondents.

69. Kathleen Howard-Merriam, "Women, Education, and the Professions in Egypt," *Comparative Education Review* (June 1979) 266–267.

70. See Earl Sullivan, *Egyptian Women in Public Life* (Syracuse, N.Y.: Syracuse University Press, 1986) for a discussion of the new breed of woman business entrepreneur.

71. Saad ed Din Ibrahim, *The New Social Order: A Study of the Social Impact of Oil Wealth* (Boulder, Colo.: Westview Press, 1982), p. 46.

72. Fatma Khafagy, "One Village in Egypt" *MERIP Reports* 14, No. 5 (June 1984): 20–21.

73. Elizabeth Taylor, "Egyptian Migration and Peasant Wives," *MERIP Reports* 14, No. 5 (June 1984): 8–9. My findings in a study of Egyptian farm women in 1983 regarding their access to village bank services, provided by a U.S. AID agricultural project, confirm these findings.

74. Taylor, "Egyptian Migration," p. 6.

75. Massialas and Jarrar, *Education in the Arab World*, p. 160. See also Ibrahim, *The New Social Order*, pp. 88 and 69.

76. I was interviewing women political activists in Cairo at this time and experienced their anger and direct action to quell such an attempt.

77. *The Middle East Times*, January 11–17, 1987.

20
IRAN

Marzieh Goli Rezai-Rashti

Women, education, and Islam have for centuries been inextricably intertwined in the Iranian socioeconomic formation. The role of women in society and their corresponding educational opportunities have largely depended on the ebb and flow of power experienced by the nation's Muslim religion.

Only in the beginning of the twentieth century did state-sponsored and -organized schooling for Iranian women come into being. Traditional Islamic society in Iran had defined women's role as restricted to household chores, care of elders and children, and sexual reproduction. Accordingly, access to education had been limited to a very small segment of upper class females who obtained some literacy skills mostly through private tutoring or paternal instruction.

Facilitating some of the early improvement in the condition of women was Iran's increasing contact with the West. This interaction, which began through economic and diplomatic relations, made itself present at the ideological level as well. Acquaintance with Western institutions motivated some Iranians to express their strong desire for Western democratic ideals along with a commitment to national economic development. Education was perceived to be one of the most important means to attain such goals. At the turn of the twentieth century, a group of Iranian intellectuals organized the Learning Society which ultimately founded fifty-six secondary schools in Tehran and the country's first national library.

For these educated people, progress and education were closely related. As one of the society's members stated at the inauguration ceremony of a new school in Tehran:

It is education that separates humans from animals, useful citizens from useless igno-ramuses, civilized beings from savage barbarians. Education generates light in an envi-ronment of intellectual darkness. Education shows us how to build power plants, steam engines, factories, railways, and other essential prerequisites of modern civilization. Education has enabled Japan to transform itself in one generation from a backward weak nation into an advanced powerful nation. Education, likewise, will enable Iran not only to regain its ancient glory but also to create a new generation that will be conscious of individual equality, social justice, personal liberty, and human progress. Education, in short, is a social factory that produces not goods but responsible citizens and fully developed human beings.[1]

The longing among some Iranians for Western-style political, economic, and cultural modernization eventually materialized in the so-called Constitutional Revolution of 1906.[2]

Women played an important role in this revolution, owing largely to the encouragement they received from some "anti-despotic" *Ulama* (religious peo-ple). Although women also formed their own organizations and societies at this time, it was mostly through the work of male intellectuals that questions con-cerning the conditions of women in Iran initially gained relevance. These intel-lectuals—more likely influenced by their acquaintance with Western culture, and their perceptions of the status of women there—openly debated equality between men and women in Iran. Indirectly attacking Islamic teachings on the subject, the new intelligentsia called for the abrogation of the veil women were forced to wear. They also advocated women's improved access to educational institu-tions. Eshghi, one of Iran's most famous poets at the turn of the century, wrote a poem entitled "Women in Shrouds" in which he expressed his views on the status of women in Iran as well as those of his fellow poets Iraj Mirza and Bahar:

Why the fuss? Men are God's servants and women are too. What have women done wrong to feel shame before men? What are these unbecoming, uncouth, cloaks and veils? They wear winding sheets meant for the dead, not the living.

I say, "Death to the men who bury women alive in the name of religion." That is enough to say here.

If two or three poets add their voices to mine, the people will soon start gumming this song. Their hums will uncover the women's fair faces, the women will proudly throw off their vile masks, the people will then have some joy in their lives. But otherwise, what will become of Iran? With women in shrouds, half the nation is dead.[3]

The first school for girls in Iran was established by North American mission-aries in 1837. Missionaries opened two more schools for girls in 1875 and 1896, but admission was restricted to non-Muslim students. Until 1888, only Christian girls had been able to attend these schools, though later some Jewish and Zo-roastrian girls also enrolled. In 1906, missionaries founded another school in Rezai-ye which both Muslim and Jewish girls were permitted to attend. As a consequence of the 1906 Constitutional Revolution, other schools were opened and run by Iranian women, either individually or in the form of a collective. The new schools were concentrated in Tehran and other large cities. The well-known schools at this time were Namus, established in 1907 by Tuba Azmudeh, and Iffatiyeh, founded by Safiyeh Yazdi in the city of Isfahan. In 1908, a French Immersion School for girls, L'Ecole Franco-Persan, was created. This was followed by the establishment of Jandark, another French-sponsored school for girls, in Tehran in 1910.[4] In that year, according to the foreign correspondent of the *London Times*, there were fifty schools for girls in the capital city of Tehran.

Opening schools for girls was not without problems. Religious authorities routinely denounced them and accused the schools of being centers of corruption and prostitution.[5] Some *mullahs* used their Friday prayers to encourage people to attack teachers and students and to destroy school buildings. Given the clergy's strong influence in society, it is not a surprise to learn that the Education Act approving compulsory elementary education for boys and girls was never fully enforced by civilian authorities; the Constitutional Revolution had granted the Iranian clergy veto power over all educational legislation. Religious leaders were thus able to dominate educational affairs; they vocally opposed the opening of schools for Iranian girls. Nevertheless, new girls' schools continued to be opened. In 1918, the government was forced to establish the first state-run school for girls in Tehran.

Along with their concern for better access to education, women also fought a hard battle for the right to full citizenship. Symptomatic of the extent of male domination was the fact that the Constitutional Revolution which women had struggled for did not extend the franchise to them. As the *Majlis*, or Parliament, made clear, "those deprived of the right to vote shall consist of all females, minors and those under guardians; fraudulent bankrupts, beggars, and those who earn their living in a disreputable way."[6]

This exclusion from meaningful political participation was disappointing to many women. In 1911, women activists organized to agitate for improved educational programs for women, and, at the same time, they began to exert some pressure on Parliament to grant them the franchise. They met a sympathetic deputy, Hadji Vekil Roya, who in addressing the Speaker of the *Majlis* asked; "I beg leave to ask for what reason should women be deprived of the vote; are they not human beings? Are they not entitled to have the same rights as [men] have? I beg the *Ulama* for a reply." The Speaker, Sheik Assadollah, replied; "This question we must not discuss, for it is contrary to the etiquette of the Islamic parliament . . . the reason for excluding women is that God has not given them the capacity needed for taking part in politics and electing the representatives of the nation . . . [they] are the weakest sex, and have not the same power of judgment as men have . . . however, their rights must not be trampled upon, but must be safeguarded by men as ordained in the *Quran* by the God Almighty."[7] This attempt to gain political rights ended in dismal failure.

Down but not out, women continued to form their own autonomous organizations. They began publishing their own periodicals and magazines in which they furthered their demands for educational reform. Women activists during this period were either affiliated with "feminist" groups which took as their primary mandate the attainment of full emancipation or with nationalist groups which focused on national development and independence from foreign domination. All, however, viewed women's education as a driving force to achieve their objectives. Their concern with educational activities encompassing the nation's women did not go unnoticed. As the *London Times* reported in 1910:

It is stated that there are now more than fifty girls' schools in Tehran. Several older girls at the [North] American schools are training to become teachers, and a few of them are already teaching in Persian schools during part of the day. The [women's] movement is in its infancy, but the fact that in last April for the first time Persian women held a large meeting in Tehran to discuss problems of education seems to suggest that the education of women will play an important part in the evolution of Persia.[8]

Women activists of this era came mostly from the upper and middle classes and had been educated at home. Yet their standing on social and political issues of the time did not appear to have been colored by their social background. Their analyses of some important issues such as marriage and divorce laws, hygiene and disease, and child prostitution had a classless character.[9]

Publications by and for women began to appear in Iran as early as 1910. One of the first to be published that year was *Danish* (Knowledge); another was *Zaban Zanan* (Women's Voice) published by Sadighe Dowlatabadi, the daughter of one of the Ulamas of the city of Isfahan. Dowlatabadi was educated at home but later went to Paris where she studied psychology. On her return, she founded a school for girls in Isfahan, published *Zaban Zanan,* and in 1918 organized the Isfahan Women's Association. In her publication, she highlighted her deep commitment to the Constitutional Revolution and emphasized the role women had played in bringing it about. Her desire for a better education, which she saw as leading to the country's independence, is reflected in an editorial entitled "The Enemies Drew Their Guns." There she wrote:

It was love for Iran and the desire to see the constitutional government [succeed], as well as the thought of honoring and protecting the independence of Iran that brought (women) into the field of education. [Women] took up the pen to free Iran, to save our forsaken daughters and to help our nation. [Women] are not only unafraid to die but [women] consider it as an honor to make sacrifices for the good of the country and [women's] freedom. Long live Iran. Down with the dictatorship and the enemies of Iran.[10]

Dowlatabadi's activities provoked strong religious opposition, which soon materialized in the stoning and looting of her offices. Religious intolerance and harassment were so pervasive that she was forced to move to the capital city of Tehran.

In 1920, two other magazines began publication. One of them was *Nameh*

Banovan [Women's Letter] edited by Shahnaz Azad. It was outspoken in its condemnation of the veil, and critical in its coverage of national and international news. Another magazine was the *Alam Nesvan* [Women's Universe], published by the Association of American Schools of Tehran. Its main concerns were literacy programs for women, women's welfare, women's political rights, and the elimination of the veil as well as of family-arranged marriages.

Some social and/or political organizations led by women also sprang up during this period. The Anjoman Mokhadarat Vatan (National Ladies' Societies) was founded in 1910. An important organization was the Jamieh Nesvan Vatankhah Iran (Patriotic Women's League of Iran), formed in 1922 by a group of intellectual women. It published a magazine called *Patriotic Women*. Other organizations of the period were the Women's Freedom Society; and the Jamiet Paeyk Saadat Nesvan (Messenger of the Prosperity of Women) and the Majma-E-Enqelam Nesvan, both founded in 1927.[11]

In brief, at the turn of the century the social and political activities of Iranian women was led by a small group of upper and middle-class women, all of whom were highly educated for their time. Their activities did not find much popular support, for most of their organizations were forced to operate in secret. However, this early movement deserves credit as the best example of women's autonomous activity in Iranian history. The movement struggled without historical precedent or tradition of political action to guide their efforts.[12] The emphasis was on education as the means to emancipate women and society at large. Guity Nashat, one of these activists, wrote the following in the *Patriotic Women Magazine* in 1923:

Many of the women activists have reached this conclusion, realising that the greatest obstacle to removing the injustice from which women suffered was their ignorance, which caused them to be hostile to those who tried to improve their lot. The activists devoted their energies to enlightening Iranian women; they began their efforts by opening schools and hoped a good education would teach the younger generation of women to use their minds and not waste their intelligence in the pursuit of men.[13]

REZA SHAH'S REIGN AND THE STATUS OF IRANIAN WOMEN

Only when Reza Shah came to power (1925–1941) did administrative authorities begin to pay more attention to the education of Iranian women. Iran's integration into the world capitalist economic system required substantial infrastructural changes. Accordingly, Reza Shah moved decisively to implement a modernization program for the country. He was greatly influenced by the reforms accomplished by the Turkish leader Kamal Ataturk in the early 1930s which had given priority to education. Better access to education, reflected in the number of new schools and the opening of the University of Tehran to female students, remain part of the legacy of Reza Shah's reign.

Table 20.1
Girls' Education in Schools, 1910, 1929, and 1933

Year	Number of Schools	Enrollment
1910	41	2,167
1929	190	11,489
1933	870	50,000

Source: Woodsmall, Ruth Frances. Moslem Women Enter a New World. (George Allen & Unwin, London, 1936), p. 146.

In 1932, the government began to focus reform efforts on improving the status of women. In 1932, the Oriental Feminine Congress was held in Tehran. There, the education of women had been one of the major issues. The Congress passed a resolution calling for compulsory education for women, educational training for female teachers, their right to vote and to run for elections, and equal pay for equal work.[14] Reza Shah's regime heeded the advice of the Congress and improved girls' access to public schooling and modernized marriage and divorce laws. Reza Shah continuously stressed how important it was for the country to make public schooling more available to women. He also linked education to creating a supply of skilled labor. One of the major obstacles to educating women was the lack of women teachers. In 1934, the Majlis approved laws for the establishment of a number of teachers' training colleges.[15]

Table 20.1 indicates the extent of the educational expansion for women during Reza Shah's first years of rule.

Reza Shah also reformed civil law. Marriage was placed under the jurisdiction of civilian authorities. The age of marriage for Iranian women was increased from thirteen to fifteen years. A 1936 law made it illegal for women to wear the veil. This legislation was strictly enforced by police who had the authority to arrest women who persisted in wearing the traditional veil. Drivers of public transportation vehicles were ordered not to accept veiled women as passengers. The Ministry of Education also set regulations regarding the appearance of girls and women teachers in schools. Schoolgirls had to attend school unveiled wearing European dresses. Female teachers were ordered to wear blue uniforms and a small hat. Any woman who disobeyed these regulations was subject to dismissal.[16]

During Reza Shah's first years in power, women's independent publications and activities continued unhindered. However, once he had consolidated his political power and enhanced it by creating a strong professional army, he became an authoritarian ruler. By 1935, all women's activities were channeled into a single organization, the Kanoon Banovan (The Ladies Center), which was formed on direct orders from Reza Shah. The Kanoon Banovan was the first women's organization openly sponsored by the state. Its main objectives were to improve the conditions of women in regards to childrearing and housework and to help parentless children. The Center also organized lectures, adult classes, and sport clubs for women. Two of Reza Shah's daughters, Ashraf and Shams, were involved in the Center's activities.[17]

In brief, the reforms undertaken during Reza Shah's reign affected Iranian women's lives in three major aspects: improved schooling, abandonment of the traditional veil, and new marriage and divorce laws. These reforms did not affect women of all classes equally: the benefits of these reforms were limited to upper and middle-class urban women. For a large segment of the Iranian female population, especially those of a working-class background or those residing in rural areas, the benefits associated with the reforms were rather intangible. As Azar Tabari has written:

The professional women of the 1920s and 1930s were mostly from the upper middle classes . . . [they] largely accepted and adapted to the changes and secularization imposed by Reza Shah. [They] emerged . . . from social layers that identified with general notions of social progress and modernization associated with European civilization and endorsed by the modernists and reformers of the constitutional movement. This overall climate of opinions had modelled the integration of that early generation of women into social life.[18]

MOHAMMAD REZA SHAH AND THE STATUS OF IRANIAN WOMEN

The period 1941 to 1953 was reportedly an exceptional era for politics in Iran inasmuch as political democracy actually flourished. Despite the temporary occupation of the country by the Allied forces, freedom of the press was restored, political parties were legalized, and the new monarch, Mohammad Reza Shah (1941–1979), received a constitutional mandate to reign but not to rule. The Majlis, in turn, witnessed a revitalized pluralism as three main political forces competed for power: the conservatives and loyalists; the communists, represented by the Tudeh party; and the liberal nationalists led by progressive reformer Mossadegh. In 1949, Mossadegh succeeded in bringing about a coalition of several political groups which led to the formation of the national front. Mossadegh then became prime minister.

Women's activism had to adapt to the political changes occurring in the country. Several women's organizations formed at the time. Unlike their predecessors in the earlier part of the century, they lost some of their autonomy since they were closely linked to legal political parties. Women's demands more often than not were subordinated to the general political programs and strategies being pursued by the National Front. The Ladies Center, established during the Reza Shah's reign, continued its work while remaining staunchly pro-monarchy. In 1944, some of the center's members created a new organization with the name of Hezb Zanan (Women's Party). The previous year, the Tashkilat Zanan Iran (Organization of Iranian Women), one of the most radical associations of women

Table 20.2
Enrollment, by Kind of School and Sex, 1947–1948 and 1955–1956

Kind of School	ENROLLMENT Boys		ENROLLMENT Girls	
	1947–48	1955–56	1947–48	1955–56
Kindergarten		3,878		3,181
Elementary	290,379	501,329	95,887	309,200
Secondary	38,483	77,802	7,870	21,603

Source: Woodsmall, Ruth Frances. Women and the New East, 1960. The Middle East Institute, Washington, D.C., p. 84.

in Iranian history, had also been established. Their objectives were publicized in a magazine called *Bidar-Ye-Ma* (Our Awakening) and included the political, economic, and social liberation of Iranian women.[19]

Women's access to educational institutions continued its steady growth at all levels during this time. Table 20.2 shows that in the short span between 1949 to 1956, three times more girls were enrolled in primary and secondary schools than ever before.

As of 1956, there were 68,322 women employed in Iran. A rather slim majority of them—33,947—were involved in crafts, productive processes, and related occupations, whereas some 20,029 women were occupied in professional jobs or other activities requiring some technical capacity.[20]

To further improve the status of women, some reforms were introduced in the early 1960s. In 1962, accompanying the much-heralded White Revolution— the Shah's modernization attempts to set the conditions for the country's rapid capitalist development—came the right to vote. With the franchise now at their disposal, women felt further encouraged to participate in public life. Education became one of the most important channels for this participation to become meaningful. Within the year the effects of the franchise were felt: six women were elected to the Majlis and two to the Senate. In 1968, the first Iranian woman ever was appointed to the Cabinet.

The Family Protection Law of 1967 also improved the legal status of Iranian women. Up to that time, family laws were deeply rooted in the *Shiah* doctrines of Islam. Although the Shah's reforms concerning family matters did not substantially digress from the *shari-a*, they went far beyond any previous reforms in guaranteeing legal protection to the female population.[21] The new law contained twenty-three articles, the most significant pertaining to the curtailment of men's unilateral prerogatives in divorce and polygamy. The law had a threefold purpose: first, it established that a man could no longer divorce his wife readily or *in absentia,* nor could he remarry without the permission of the court; second, under specified conditions, a woman could petition for divorce; and, third, parents had to make arrangements for adequate care of their children before a divorce could be granted. The legislature was very cautious in not completely abolishing the *Ithna Ashari,* that part of Islamic doctrine which allows for temporary marriages and subsequent divorces. In 1977, abortion became legal for women. However, in 1978 as a concession to the religious leaders, abortion became illegal again.[22]

The combination of social, political, and legal reforms affecting women, accelerated industrialization, and rapid capitalist development helped improve the access of women to education. Prior to 1936, women had no access to higher education. In 1925, there were only six institutions of higher secular learning in the country with an enrollment of less than 600 male students.[23] Women were admitted for the first time to university during Reza Shah's rule. By 1941, 3,300 students were enrolled in the eleven colleges that were part of the University of Tehran which Reza Shah established. In the period 1943–1944, 38 percent of the students were women.[24] It was during Mohammad Reza Shah's rule that the number of higher educational institutions increased significantly. In 1960, new laws allowed for the opening of private universities and colleges. Women's enrollment in higher education jumped from 5,000 in 1966 to over 74,000 in 1977.[25] Higher education opened new opportunities for women in the labor market: in 1977, women constituted 28 percent of all civil servants, 30 percent of secondary school teachers, 54 percent of elementary school teachers, and nearly 100 percent of kindergarten teachers.[26] There were changes in the educational levels of women in the paid labor force. The percentage of employed women who were literate increased from 30 percent in 1966 to 65 percent in 1976. The number of women with a high school diploma rose from 73,000 to 198,000 in the same period; those with higher education increased from 17,000 to 181,000.[27] Literacy rates also grew during the period, especially among urban women (see Table 20.3).

The reforms aimed at making women socially, economically, politically, and culturally equal to their male counterparts, but the traditional attitudes regarding women's role remained. The attitudes of a conservative religious-dominated society, not a liberal, progressive one, were reinforced by sexist instructional material used in schools as well as Mohammad Reza Shah's negative views on women's rights. While being interviewed by Italian journalist Oriana Fallaci in 1975, Mohammad Reza Shah had this to say: "Nobody can influence me, nobody. Still less a woman. Women are important in a man's life only if they are beautiful and charming and keep their femininity . . . [Women] are equal in the eyes of the law but not, excuse my saying so, in ability . . . [Women] have never produced a Michelangelo or a Bach . . . [Women] have never produced a great chef. . . . [Women] have produced nothing great, nothing."[28]

Most educational materials used in Iranian schools emphasized highly differ-

Table 20.3
Literacy Rates, by Area and Sex, 1956, 1966, and 1971

Year	Urban		Rural		Total	
	Men	Women	Men	Women	Men	Women
1956	45.9%	22.4%	10.9%	1.2%	22.4%	8.0%
1966	61.9%	38.9%	25.4%	4.3%	40.1%	17.9%
1971	68.7%	48.1%	31.9%	8.3%	47.7%	25.5%

Source: Sabi, M. Literacy Projections of Iran's Population in School and the Active Age Group (Iran-UNDP-UNESCO, 1977).

entiated unequal roles for women and men. A study by the Iranian Women's Organization on primary school textbooks revealed that women were portrayed mostly as mothers, friends, teachers, and students, whereas men were represented as doctors, scientists, heroes, and military leaders. The texts portrayed men positively, while women were depicted either as mothers or as evil beings. Stories in the texts focused on women as superstitious while men were heroic. The texts promoted the image of woman as a feminine member of a household while men always assumed nondomestic, professional identities. Religious books recognized no place for women. In general, women were downplayed and presented as weak individuals whose main tasks were to take care of children, clean, and cook, and sometimes become primary school teachers.[29]

THE 1978 ISLAMIC REVOLUTION AND ITS IMPACT ON THE STATUS OF IRANIAN WOMEN

The Islamic Revolution of 1978, led by religious leader Ayatollah Ruhollah Khomeini, has dramatically affected the overall status of women in Iran. Changes have taken place since 1978 which are said to be based on a fundamentalist interpretation of traditional Islamic laws; the revolutionary regime has pursued a policy of re-islamization of Iranian society at large. To achieve this goal, the revolutionary regime has manipulated the mass media and the schools. All schools are now sex segregated, although it should be mentioned that secondary schools were sex segregated in the past. By the end of the 1979–1980 academic year, foreign and private schools also had to become sex segregated. In addition, the curricula of Iranian schools have been rewritten to reflect the social relevance of Islamic teachings, and access to some technical fields of higher education such as mining, agriculture, engineering, and geology is at present being denied to women as is a woman's right to be appointed as a judge. Greatly affected by these reforms are women from middle-class backgrounds who had been the main beneficiaries of the Shah's early modernization efforts. Their opportunities for higher education and professional jobs are now severely limited.

Shortly after the revolution and one day before International Women's Day, Khomeini denounced the celebration as a Western phenomenon, irrelevant for Iranian women. He then emphasized the importance of the *Hejab* ("Islamic cover") and initiated compulsory veiling for women. On International Women's Day, Iranian women organized a rally and protested. Marching women converged on the university, the office of the Prime Minister, Bazargan, and the Ministry of Justice. On March 9, 1979, the prime minister announced that wearing the veil would not be compulsory. However, after Khomeini consolidated his power the *Hejab* became law. On July 4, 1980, it was decreed that all women attending government offices or other public organizations observe Islamic dress and cover their hair.[30]

Iranian religious scholars, even before the revolution, had paid special attention to the social position allocated to women in Islamic teachings. Some interpreters did not oppose the efforts undertaken by previous secular governments to down-play some of the most sexist connotations of Islam. Modernization seemed to have meant that, even though polygamy was "technically" possible, most Iranian men did not exercise their right to have more than one wife. Even their "religious" right to divorce women unilaterally was restricted by secular law. However, some of the most reactionary elements within Khomeini's theocratic government narrowly interpret passages in the *Quran* which suggest women are not, and cannot be, equal to men. Yahya Nuri, an orthodox theologian considered to be one of Khomeini's mentors, is an example. In 1964, he wrote a book entitled *Women's Rights in Islam and the World* in which he discusses the different treatment which, because of biological differences, Islam is said to accord to the two sexes. He tried to demonstrate that women are basically emotional which results from their innate inability to reason. He concluded that woman's responsibility is to raise children who need the emotional support and affection that comes with motherhood. Men, on the contrary, can be part of broader activities outside the home because they possess physical strength and the ability to reason.[31]

This is the line of thought justified by the Islamic scholar, Morteza Motahari, a Tehran University professor assassinated by an extremist fundamentalist after the revolution. In defending the institution of polygamy, Motahari argued that it was justified on three counts: (1) economic necessity; (2) biological needs; and (3) surplus female population. The first two situations are justified only in special circumstances, whereas the third, unlike what most critics may say, is a right which women may exercise over society and which truly benefits females. Polygamy, rather than being a man's right, is a duty society imposes on males. Similarly, in defending the *Hejab,* Motahari argued that the veil's role is to establish a meaningful separation between the private and the public spheres of life insofar as it lessens the interaction between the sexes in society at large.

Accordingly, he recommended that women enter only those kinds of occupations such as teaching, nursing, tailoring, and the like which do not interfere with the wearing of the *Hejab*.[32]

A rather moderate position on the status of women has been suggested by Ali Shariati, an Islamic scholar who is popular among religious middle-class professionals and university students. While not directly questioning the *Quran* he has strongly criticized fundamentalist interpreters, describing as "unacceptable fanaticism" the conservative clergy's opposition to the "inevitable diffusion" of Western modernizing ideas in Iranian society. Progress cannot be arrested, in his view. He has suggested that religious leaders accept some Western ideas, while at the same time creating alternative values to "save" youth from the most negative and pernicious effects of the modernization process. Shariati has also criticized the so-called traditional Iranian society as "phony" because it uses religion to discriminate against women. According to him, women are forced to live a degrading life in their own society—restricted in their given role as mothers, daughters, and wives. He believes that women have a responsibility to become active in public life, mainly through their own efforts, and to fight the fundamentalists' preoccupation with regulating female sexuality. For him, the moderate use of the *Hejab* is justified as it may help women to escape the pressures generated by a consumer-oriented, sex-obsessed society like Iran.[33]

Events in postrevolutionary Iran clearly show that the fundamentalist, traditional sectors have gained the upper hand regarding the status of women. The present situation contrasts greatly with what spiritual leader Ayatollah Ruhollah Khomeini said before coming to power. Thus, in 1978 he said that:

Women are free in the realm of education as well as in the professions, just as men are. [Shiism] . . . not only does not exclude women from social life, but it elevates them to a platform where they belong . . . [Islam] raises the level of women in society so that they might regain their human dignity, not be objectified, and can assume responsibilities in the structure of the Islamic government . . . [Islam] has considered women's rights to be higher than men's. Women have the right to vote and this is a right which is higher than women's rights in the West. [Our] women have the right to vote and be elected. They are free in all aspects of their lives and they can freely choose most areas of employment. [We] promise you that in the Islamic government every person will be free and will achieve his/her rights.[34]

Since seizing power, he and his cohorts have done quite the opposite.

Although the Ayatollah Khomeini himself has not written specifically on women's issues, some of his thoughts are present in his book *A Clarification of Questions*. There, in the section "Precepts of the Permanent Contract," he writes that

A woman who has been contracted permanently must not leave the house without the husband's permission and must surrender herself for any pleasure that he wants and must not prevent him from having intercourse with her without a religious excuse. And if she

Table 20.4
Ratio of Male-Female Enrollment, by Level, 1975 and 1984

Year	Sex	First Level	Second Level	Third Level
1975	MF	93	45	4.9
	M	114	57	7.0
	F	71	33	2.8
1984	MF	107	43	4.4
	M	117	51	6.1
	F	95	35	2.6

Source: UNESCO Statistical Yearbook, 1986, pp. 111-47.

obeys the husband in these the provision of her food and clothing and dwelling and other appliances mentioned in books is obligatory for the husband and if he does not provide them he is indebted to the woman, whether or not he can afford them.

Conversely, "If the wife does not obey her husband in those actions mentioned in the previous problem, she is a sinner and has no right to food and clothing and shelter and sleeping [with the husband] but her dowry will not be lost."[35]

The spiritual leader's chauvinistic thinking is also reflected in his admonishment that "A Moslem woman cannot be contracted by an infidel nor can a Moslem man marry an infidel woman in a permanent fashion . . . however, there is no concern in concubinage with those women who are . . . Jews and Christians."[36]

Notwithstanding the bleak picture presented above, recent statistical information concerning women's access to all levels of education does not differ significantly from that of prerevolutionary Iran. On the contrary, there is even some improvement in the enrollment ratio for the first, second, and third levels (see Table 20.4) While this may disprove commonplace assumptions that education for women is severely restricted at all levels, a critical point also needs to be made at this stage. There are statistical data which show that enrollment has declined at a higher level, namely, women's access to certain university careers (see Table 20.5). The data indicate that women are being channeled into technical studies in higher education which prepare them for entry to careers acceptable to conservative Islamic clergy. Before the Islamic revolution, women could enter almost all fields of studies. Soon after the revolution, women's access to many technical and scientific fields became restricted. Fields such as mining, civil, chemical, industrial, mechanical, and material engineering are at present not open to women. Similarly, women are denied access to faculties preparing students in veterinarian sciences.[37] As Table 20.5 shows, women's enrollment in engineering was 3,063 in 1976; it declined to 1,451 by 1983. Although it has

Table 20.5
Distribution of Students, by Sex and Field of Study, 1976 and 1983

Year	1976		1983	
Sex	MF	F	MF	F
Total	154,215	46,019	151,333	45,418
Education and Teacher Training	5,342	2,765	43,110	11,555
Humanities and Theology	26,348	11,429	12,547	5,206
Fine & Applied Art	4,659	1,820	1,091	404
Law	2,973	676	2,509	560
Social Science	27,093	8,568	7,957	3,330
Commercial & Business Administration	-	-	8,336	2,351
Mass Communication & Documentation	-	-	465	253
Home Economics	-	-	646	470
Service Trades	-	-	126	65
Natural Science	27,317	6,885	11,878	4,339
Mathematics & Computer Science	-	-	6,198	1,518
Medical and Health Related Science	19,235	9,812	25,197	12,619
Engineering	34,411	3,063	22,839	1,451
Architecture & Town Planning	-	-	1,834	520
Trade, Craft & Industrial Programmes	-	-	237	47
Agriculture, Forestry & Fishing	6,837	1,001	5,159	354
Other & Not Specified	-	-	1,048	364

Source: UNESCO Statistical Yearbook, 1976, 1980, Pages 520, 296.

been argued that engineering should not be accessible to women since it involves tasks that prevent them from wearing the *Hejab,* the very fact that there are still 1,451 women enrolled in courses in this field raises some questions; the answers, unfortunately, are still unavailable. One might speculate that these 1,451 women were enrolled in engineering fields prior to the revolution and before government policies restricting the admission to these careers were enforced.

Women's employment rates in urban areas show no significant change when compared to their situation prior to the revolution. Earlier, women comprised 11.2 percent of the total urban labor force; by 1983, that percentage dropped to 11.1 percent. This decline is important considering the urban population increased during this period. In 1976, the total urban population ten years of age and over was 11,428,000; in 1982, it rose to 23,232,600. In 1976, there were 460,000 urban women wage-earners; in 1982, this figure rose to 558,000.[38] A greater number of working women after the revolution became government employees. An explanation for this increase is that the state took over many private enterprises. Added to that is the increase in urban population as a result of internal migration created by the war with Iraq. Employed urban women are encouraged to take jobs in the areas of teaching, nursing, and the like which are sex segregated. Considering the restriction to some technical fields of studies, women will more and more be channeled into traditional jobs.

The female unemployment rate increased to 18.1 percent in 1983 from 13.1 percent in 1976.[39] This increase can partly be attributed to the conservative clergy's opposition to women's activities outside of the private sphere. It also is an outgrowth of the high birthrate in the country as a whole—population growth has exceeded the growth of employment opportunities—and of internal migration which has swelled the cities. The unemployment of women is part of the general increase in unemployment in Iran as a whole. Unemployment has been recognized by the Majlis Speaker, Hashemi Rafsanjani. In a speech delivered in 1986, he promised women that once the Iran-Iraq War was over, the country's economy would need their labor in medicine and education.[40] Like many other apparently contradictory developments in Iran, the fact that the employment rate for women has not declined significantly in spite of the tremendous ideological pressure which the Islamic regime brought to bear on Iranian women after the revolution is, to say the least, a remarkable indication that not all has been lost. A brighter future may be waiting ahead.

In regard to future trends, one can feel little hope that government-sponsored policies of any kind will do anything to improve the situation of women. On the contrary, as the laws and regulations of the Islamic Republic of Iran adhere strongly to those most reactionary interpretations of Islamic law which reinforce the rights of men over women. Iranian women are at present living under such formidable ideological control which, even though they are allowed to work and study, marriage and motherhood are considered the best jobs available to them. Women are banned from certain professions and are encouraged to take only those jobs in which they do not have to have any contact with men. In spite of all these limitations, an increasing number of Iranian feminists are optimistic and speculate that Iranian women may for the first time in their recent history of social mobilization challenge their subordinate position and demand specific rights to improve their situation.

NOTES

1. Cited in Ervand Abrahamian, *Iran Between Two Revolutions* (Princeton, N.J.: Princeton University Press, 1982), p. 76.

2. On the Constitutional Revolution of 1906, see Fattaneh Mehrain, "Emergence of Capitalist Authoritarian State in Periphery Formations: A Case Study of Iran" (Ph.D. diss., University of Wisconsin, 1979).

3. Elizabeth Sanasarian, *The Women's Rights Movement in Iran: Mutiny, Appeasement, and Repression from 1900 to Khomeini* (New York: Praeger, 1981), p. 31.

4. Reza Arasteh, *Education and Social Awakening in Iran, 1850–1968* (Leiden: E. J. Brill, 1969), p. 177.

5. Guity Nashat, ed. *Women and Revolution in Iran* (Boulder, Colo.: Westview Press, 1983), p. 24.

6. Shahla Haeri, "Women, Law and Social Change in Iran," in Jane I. Smith, ed., *Contemporary Muslim Societies* (Lewisburg, Pa.: Bucknell University Press, 1980), p. 219.

7. Mangol Bayat-Philip. "Women and the Revolution in Iran, 1905–1911," in Lois Beck and Nikki Keddie, eds., *Muslim Women in the Middle East* (Cambridge, Mass.: Harvard University Press, 1978), p. 301.

8. Ibid., p. 300.

9. Sanasarian, *The Women's Rights Movement*, p. 46.

10. Arasteh, *Education and Social Awakening*, p. 180.

11. For a good description of women's publications, see Sanasarian, *The Women's Rights Movement*; Arasteh, *Education and Social Awakening*.

12. Bayat-Philip, "Women and the Revolution," p. 306.

13. Nashat, *Women and Revolution*, p. 23.

14. Arasteh, *Education and Social Awakening*, pp. 181–182.

15. Sanasarian, *The Women's Rights Movement*, p. 61.

16. Arasteh, *Education and Social Awakening*, p. 185.

17. Sanasarian, *The Women's Rights Movement*, p. 68.

18. Azar Tabari, "The Enigma of Veiled Iranian Women," *MERIP Report* (February 1982), p. 24.

19. For a good summary of women's publications and activities during this period, see Sanasarian, *The Women's Rights Movement*.

20. Arasteh, *Education and Social Awakening*, p. 187.

21. For a good summary of the changes in the legal situation during this period, see Gholam-Reza Vatandoust, "Iranian Women During the Pahlavi Regime," in Asghar Fathi, ed., *Women and Family in Iran* (Leiden: E. J. Brill, 1985). Also see Shahla Haeri, "Women, Law and Social Change in Iran," in *Women in Contemporary Muslim Societies* (Lewisburg, Pa.: Bucknell University Press, 1980). Also see Behnaz Pakizegi, "Legal and Social Position of Iranian Women," in *Muslim Women in the Middle East* (Cambridge, Mass.: Harvard University Press, 1978).

22. Azar Tabari, "The Women's Movement in Iran: A Hopeful Prognosis," *Feminist Studies* 12, No. 2 (Summer 1986): 350.

23. Abrahamian, *Iran Between Two Revolutions,* p. 145.

24. Ministry of Education, Bureau of Statistics, Educational Statistics, Iran, 1962.

25. Abrahamian, *Iran Between Two Revolutions,* p. 434.

26. Ibid.

27. Tabari, "The Enigma of Veiled Iranian Women," p. 23.

28. Oriana Fallaci, *Interview with History* (Boston: Houghton Mifflin, 1976), pp. 271–272.

29. Sanasarian, *The Women's Rights Movement,* p. 109.

30. Farah Azari, "The Post-Revolutionary Women's Movement in Iran," in Farah Azari, ed., *Women of Iran* (London: Ithaca Press, 1983), p. 206.

31. Nahid Yeganeh, "Women's Struggle in the Islamic Republic of Iran," in Azar Tabari and Nahid Yeganeh, eds., *In the Shadow of Islam: The Women's Movement in Iran* (London: Zed Press, 1982), p. 43.

32. Ibid., p. 45.

33. Ibid., p. 51.

34. Jessie Bernard, *The Female World from a Global Perspective* (Bloomington: Indiana University Press, 1987), p. 231.

35. Sayyed Ruhollah Khomeini, *A Clarification of Questions,* trans. J. Borujerdi (Boulder, Colorado: Westview Press, 1984), p. 318.

36. Ibid., p. 316.

37. Ministry of Culture and Higher Education, *Rahnemaye Entekhabe Reshtehhayeh Tahseelee, Baraye Daneshgaha va Moassesate Amoozeshe Aleye Keshvar, 1366–1367* [Guide for the Selection of Fields in Higher Education] (Educational Evaluation Organization, 1986).

38. Islamic Republic of Iran, Plan and Budget Organization, *Salnameye Amar 1363* [Statistical Yearbook] (Tehran: Statistical Center of Iran, 1984–1985), pp. 59, 61.; and also for 1976 statistics see Plan and Budget Organization, General Census of Population and Housing, 1976 (Tehran: Statistical Center of Iran, 1981).

39. Plan and Budget Organization, *Salnameye Amar,* p. 59, 61.

40. *Iran Times,* March 28, 1986, p. 5.

21
ISRAEL

Drora Kfir, Hanna Ayalon, and Rina Shapira

This chapter presents the current status and achievements in girls' education in Israel, with a view to both its historical and future dimensions. The focus is on different subpopulations within Israeli society, as well as developments for the entire population since the establishment of the state of Israel in 1948. Five main topics are surveyed: The educational processes in society as a whole, and processes in four subpopulations—the ultra-orthodox religious Jews; Jews of Asian-African origin; non-Jewish minorities; and the kibbutz population. Modern and traditional forces particular to each group are analyzed because they play an important role in the subsequent analysis.

A HISTORICAL PERSPECTIVE

Throughout modern history, Jews have lived as a minority group in their host countries. As such, their lifestyle in many ways have mirrored the dominant lifestyle of their adopted homelands. This pattern set women's place in Jewish society and, consequently, the methods of socializing young girls. Until the "Emancipation" in eighteenth century Central and Western Europe, which also affected Jewish society, a girl was educated by female members of her own family. Formal education for Jewish girls was introduced in Western Europe and later spreading to Eastern Europe and only last to Islamic countries of the Middle East. For some of the Jews immigrating to Israel after 1948 from Asia and Northern Africa, this change in female socialization postdated their arrival in Israel. From the beginning of the new Jewish settlement in Eretz-Yisrael

("Palestine" at that time), women were very active in building the modern Jewish state. Those pioneers, most of whom lived a secular lifestyle as socialists and Zionists, constituted a revolutionary force within Judaism, particularly in Palestine.

The pre-twentieth-century Jewish population in Palestine, whose ties to the land extended centuries back, kept to the old tradition which dictated that women belonged at home. This strict traditionalism diametrically opposed the pioneers and all of the social changes they tried to implement, including the subject of women's status and girls' education. Even today, these two groups continue to exert contradictory forces on Israeli society in general, especially in education and subsequent adult roles.

The Zionist leadership, controlled by secular socialists and liberals, supported total equality for women in line with their ideological goals of freedom, democracy, and social justice. Stringent orthodox groups viewed women's participation in public life as irreconcilable with the traditionally defined role in the family and sexual modesty.

Since the early twentieth century, the socialist pioneers had strongly influenced evolving Israeli society. Some of the pioneers worked as laborers in the cities and towns, and others established a community unique to Israel called the kibbutz. In the kibbutz there was ostensible equality between men and women, in terms of both obligations and rights. Women, after quite a struggle, were able to enter all occupations if only for a brief period.[1] This success manifested itself primarily in public affairs and political leadership. Israeli youth have grown up on the myth of "liberated" women pioneers.

Since the state of Israel does not have a constitution, its Declaration of Independence provides the main legal source for the principle of equal rights for all citizens, regardless of nationality, religion, race, or sex. Hence, "The legal status of women in Israel is determined at the same time by one of the most modern and one of the most ancient legal systems of the world . . . The latter—the Hebrew (religious) law—views the man and the woman as different and not equal."[2]

SEX DIFFERENCES IN EDUCATIONAL PROCESSES

The State Education Law of 1949 requires every boy and girl to attend school from age five to fourteen (today extended to age sixteen). This is one expression of the principle in that Declaration of Independence. The Education Law revolutionized girls' schooling for three groups: ultra-orthodox Jews, minority non-Jewish (mostly Arabs) citizens, and new Jewish immigrants from Islamic states (Middle Eastern and North African).

In addition to the Compulsory Education Law, the educational system underwent reforms aimed at extending the years of schooling for all students. In practice, this meant that even a student who came from an ethnic or family background with traditionally weak emphasis on education was likely to remain in school until the age of eighteen. The concept of equality, which today is not just a principle but a state law, affected both genders in the same way. The median level of education for the Jewish population was 11.6 and 11.4 years in 1985 for men and women, respectively. (All data in this chapter, unless otherwise noted, are taken from the yearly statistical reports of the Israeli Central Bureau of Statistics.) The small advantage for men is found only among those aged thirty-five years and older. Among younger age cohorts women have a small advantage. Equality in enrollment in Israeli schools represents significant progress for girls.

Educational policy is expressed in the memos of the general director of the Ministry of Education. These memos are the primary means for disseminating centralized policy from the Ministry to local educators and administrators. In those memos the subject of gender equality has been mentioned frequently over the last ten years. These directives are based on the need to allocate places for girls in technological secondary education (which originally was meant for boys only) and the need to consider an equal curriculum for boys and girls in areas of study traditionally offered to one sex only. Since 1980, those memos have contained clear instructions to raise the subject of women's status and gender equality in schools. For instance, the memo of November 1983 requires equal ways of relating to male and female images in children's books and school readings, and in 1986 the kindergarten teachers were instructed to avoid any comment that might bring pressure on boys for ''masculine'' and on girls for ''feminine'' behavior. One can therefore conclude that formally everything possible has been done in Israel to achieve equal education for males and females. (A process of writing a new curriculum ''to be a boy—to be a girl . . . '' for elementary schools is presently being conducted at Oranim College.)

Data concerning intelligence scores (WISC-R Hebrew version) seem to refute this equality. A. Leiblich found considerable advantage for boys aged six to sixteen in total IQ scores and in eight of twelve subscales. This gap appears at age nine and is significant from age thirteen on.[3] The idea of girls' inferiority is least evident among Jews of Asian-African origin and most apparent among the non-Jewish minority. Supporting the Lieblich data are M. Sepher-Mizrachi's findings concerning the gifted. She found that among children seven to nine years of age, of the top 10 percent in intelligence, as reflected by IQ scores, two-thirds were boys; and of those children seen as gifted by their teachers 70 percent were boys and only 30 percent girls.[4]

Despite findings which indicate sexual differentiation at an early age, analysis of major trends in women's education in Israel concentrates mainly on secondary and higher education. Being compulsory, uniform, and attended by almost everyone, primary education constitutes a relatively gender-neutral setting. This situation contrasts with secondary education.

Secondary Education

Secondary education in Israel is highly differentiated. Its main feature is curricular tracking. Students are channeled into either the academic or the vocational track at the beginning of high school. This differentiation has obvious implications for future social mobility since most of the vocational tracks do not prepare their students for the matriculation exams. Since the matriculation diploma is a necessary (albeit insufficient) "entrance ticket" to higher education, most of the vocational tracks serve as barriers to social mobility. The assignment of students to the different tracks is nonvoluntary and is based mainly on students' academic achievements.[5] Israel's secondary education is characterized by an exceptionally high proportion of students in the vocational tracks—more than 50 percent. In addition to the differentiation between the academic and the vocational tracks, there exists a further differentiation between courses of study that are distinguished by both domain and prestige.

Two obvious and consistent findings emerge in any analysis of women's secondary education in Israel over the last twenty years. Girls appear to have relatively higher school attendance rates. For example, in 1962, 486.3 per 1,000 girls in the respective age group attended high school, compared to 445.3 per 1,000 boys. (Thus, the girls-to-boys ratio is 1.09.) Twenty-three years later (in 1985), the respective rates were 767 and 645 (a ratio of 1.19). Other findings indicate that after controlling for family background and achievements in Grade 7, girls have more schooling than boys at age eighteen.[6] It appears that both males and females have improved their attendance rates (which is due partly to the substantial growth of the vocational system), but since girls' improvement is considerably higher, the gap has increased significantly. The second finding is that higher proportions of girls are geared to the academic track. Of every 1,000 girls of the respective age group, 268 were placed in the academic track in 1962, as compared to 174.1 of the boys, yielding a ratio of 1.54. The parallel ratio in 1985 was 1.57. It appears that during this twenty-three-year period the gender gap was constant. This finding, together with higher attendance, reveals that the secondary education system operates in favor of girls. This tendency can be traced from junior high school. Girls in junior high school, though their standardized academic achievement equals that of boys, get better evaluations from teachers and are classified in better ability grouping.[7]

Within each track, however, there is a good deal of gender differentiation. The various vocational fields of study are highly segregated. Some of them are almost totally "masculine" (e.g., electronics, mechanics), whereas others are clearly "feminine" (e.g., secretarial work, nursing, fashion design). The "feminine" courses of study in vocational education are less prestigious. The correlation between percentage of male students in the vocational programs and the prestige of the occupations studied in them is as high as 0.50.[8] The gender composition in the different vocational programs indicate that this section of secondary education reproduces the sex segregation in the labor market. Moreover, in the matriculation-oriented vocational track, the percentage of boys allowed to take the full number of exams is higher than the percentage of girls (in 1985, 72 percent versus 61 percent respectively). The percentage of students in the academic track who complete the full number of matriculation exams is

93 for boys and 89 for girls, with the girls' school grades falling below those of the boys. Furthermore, the matriculation diploma of female seniors in the academic track tends to be valued less than that of their male counterparts, owing to the greater tendency of girls to study the humanities and social sciences rather than mathematics, physical sciences, and biological sciences which provide more credit to university applicants. Psychometric entrance exams further enhance boys chances of acceptance to university. These tests, combined with the matriculation grades, constitute the universities' basis for student selection. It appears that boys maintain a constant advantage of 50 points above girls in these tests.[9] Of this 50-point gap, boys' scores exceed girls scores by 31 points in mathematics alone (one out of five subtests).

Attitudes and Motivations

As noted above, in the Israeli secondary educational system higher proportions of girls than boys are placed in the academic track. However, girls superiority in the process of tracking does not correlate with higher levels of educational and occupational aspirations. Owing to structural features of the Israeli educational system, high school students' aspirations are highly correlated with the track in which they are placed.[10] However, it appears that girls' tendency to base their aspirations on their location in the educational system is relatively weak. Girls constantly express lower levels of ambition, but the gender gap varies in accordance with the type of aspirations. The disparity between the sexes is relatively low as far as educational aspirations are concerned. The same is true for occupational prestige. However, when the occupations aspired to by youngsters are analyzed in terms of the monetary rewards attached to them, the inferiority of females' aspirations is apparent.[11] The occupations which girls aspire to are characterized by both lower economic rewards and reduced returns on education. It appears that high school girls tend to adhere to existing divisions in the labor market: the occupations aspired to are "feminine," namely, they contain a high proportion of female workers.

Postsecondary Education

As noted previously, the proportion of girls in the academic track exceeds that of boys. However, boys take more prestigious courses of study both in the vocational and academic tracks and score higher on IQ and psychometric tests. Hence, the relative advantage of girls in the process of tracking is not mirrored in their attendance rates in higher education, though the proportion of women among university students has improved substantially during the last twenty years. In 1964, women made up only 36 percent of the student population; twenty years later they were 47 percent. The proportion of women decreases as one progresses through the university system. Here, too, the change during the last twenty years is evident. In 1966, women constituted 43 percent of bachelor's

Table 21.1
Women University Students, by Subject Major

Subject	% Women
Language, literature and regional studies	80.0
Art, crafts and applied arts	79.4
Education and teacher training	79.4
General humanities	56.7
Biological sciences	63.5
Social sciences	50.9
Law	39.6
Medicine	33.4
Physical sciences	33.0
Mathematics, statistics and computer sciences	32.5
Business and administration	24.4
Engineering and architecture	13.3

students and 19 percent of the master's and doctoral students. In 1985, the respective values were 48 percent for B.A. students, 47 percent for M.A. students, and 40 percent for Ph.D. candidates.

Female students are highly differentiated from their male counterparts in their chosen subjects, as indicated by Table 21.1.[12] The table shows that traditionally female subjects—education and the humanities—contain the highest percentage of female students. Conversely, the technological subjects and the various fields of engineering contain the lowest.

Israeli female students are better represented in postsecondary nonacademic education where they constitute about 50 percent of the students. Even here women are highly concentrated in traditional "feminine" fields; they constitute 84 percent in the teacher-training programs and 93 percent in nurse-training programs. (Teaching and nursing programs are currently being upgraded academically leading to a bachelor's degree.) Women's percentage in the traditional "masculine" fields is much lower: 35 percent of the students of nonacademic programs of business administration and accounting are female. The respective value for technician-training programs is 20 percent.

The attempts to establish formal equality for women and equal access to education were partially successful. There are no differences in years of schooling, but girls still stick to traditionally "feminine" courses of study.

SEX DIFFERENCES IN SUBPOPULATIONS

This section addresses the concerns of special populations in Israel.

Religious and Ultra-Orthodox Jews

All the major religions have strict gender roles. The idea of woman's special place and duties begins in the Bible, which is the basis for many Jewish, Christian, and Islamic beliefs. The traditionalists of the three religions have more in common, as regards the role of women, than a secularist and a traditionalist of the same religion.[13] In Judaism, separating girls from boys and socializing them differently serves two purposes: (1) it prepares the girl for her unique role of homemaker, childbearer, caretaker, and wife; (2) it preserves the sexual innocence of males and females.

According to observant Jews, the woman's role befits her nature, and the fact that she is restricted to the home suits her most inner tendencies and ambitions. However, there is no contradiction between the perception of a woman's place and her gaining education. Quite the opposite: an educated girl will better socialize her own children, providing, of course, that she receives the "right" education. Higher learning and education for both sexes is in accordance with Jewish tradition and spirit.

This explains why a system of formal education for girls has developed in the Israeli religious sector, parallel to girls' entrance into the secular educational system. The religious sector can be divided into several groups. Among the moderates, girls study in state religious schools together with boys, at the same class or in different classes within the same school. Most of the courses are supervised by the state. In the ultra-orthodox community, separate institutions for girls are run by the community, with instructions in Yiddish, not Hebrew. Between those two extremes are the Beit-Yaakov schools, where girls are also educated separately.

In the state's religious school (in 1985, 18.5 percent of the total student population aged five to fifteen) even when boys and girls study together the curriculum is not exactly the same. The main difference is in religious studies: only boys study Talmud, and in Dinim (religious law) boys and girls study different subjects, reflecting different adult roles.

Beit-Yaakov institutions for girls (where 5.6 percent of all Jewish girls are educated) service the orthodox community which has not totally separated from Israeli society. Girls in Beit-Yaakov study many subjects of general education, but special attention is given to their preparation for adult roles. The girls are directed toward strict religious observance, against enlisting in the army (which is obligatory in Israel at age eighteen except for girls who request an exemption on religious grounds) and preferring a religious scholar for a husband. The encouragement of girls to acquire education beyond the high school level means continuation in Beit-Yaakov's own institutions for higher education.

Education is the foremost factor in preserving the isolation and segregation of the ultra-orthodox community.[14] The need to develop educational institutions for girls emerged when parents had no choice but to send their daughters to schools outside the community (mainly to Biet-Yaakov). In boys' institutions, where learning is restricted to religious subjects and texts, past traditions continue until today, with no change whatsoever. Girls' schools, on the other hand, undergo constant change, aiming at the same goals: keeping the stability and continuity of the community and its special lifestyle by maintaining girls' education within the community,[15] while at the same time bringing them up to be good wives and mothers.[16] The need to compete with girls' schools outside the community stimulates changes and development of girls' schools within the community.[17] From one small and badly equipped school in Jerusalem in 1948, today the community has a complete educational system. The girls study five days a week; there are six working and studying days a week in Israel. (On Friday they have duties at home, helping their mothers.) Their courses cover history, geography, mathematics, science, languages, art, gymnastics, music, and teacher training. This is much more than is available to the boys, who concentrate exclusively on religious studies.

The ultra-orthodox schools prepare the girls for two occupations only: teaching and sewing. The schools have responded to parental pressure and have included some religious subjects for girls, previously an exclusively male domain, as well as Hebrew and the secular courses, which boys do not study at all. Not surprisingly girls and women from the ultra-orthodox community read more newspapers, listen to the radio (television is prohibited), speak Hebrew better, and even participate more in elections. Overall, girls and women are more involved in Israeli society, and they are agents for change within their own community without rebelling against traditional authority. The general level of formal education for females in this community is ten to fourteen years of schooling.[18]

One can divide the religious Jewish population of Israel into two main groups. In more religious circles, a girl is more likely to accept the traditional woman's role.[19] One end is attached to past tradition, though exposing girls to innovations and education does not necessarily contradict that primary principle. The other group consciously tries to accept modern trends and changes in women's and girls' place in society. The moderate group searches for the golden path between keeping the traditional roles and adopting new ones.

Jews of Asian and African Origin

During 1949–1950, the population of the newly established state of Israel doubled. Most of the new immigrants were Jews, usually refugees, from Arab states. As a group, those immigrants differed significantly from earlier waves

Table 21.2
Educational Distribution of Jews Aged 15 and Older, by Birthplace and Sex, 1985 (in Percentages)

| | Number of Years of Schooling | | | |
	0–8	9–12	13 or more	Total
MEN				
Born in Israel	10.2	65.1	24.7	100.0
Born Abroad	36.2	40.0	23.3	100.0
Total	25.1	51.1	23.8	100.0
WOMEN				
Born in Israel	9.2	62.5	28.4	100.0
Born Abroad	44.1	37.5	18.4	100.0
Total	30.1	46.5	22.4	100.0

of Jewish immigration. Apart from being refugees, similar to the Holocaust survivors from Europe, they were usually religious, with no democratic tradition, and with limited education and almost no technological knowledge. Those deficiencies were even more common among women. For instance, in 1961 the median number of years of schooling among women from Asia and Northern Africa was 3.4 versus 8.8 among women from European and American origin. (The statistic among men is 6.9 and 9.6, respectively.)[20] The merging into Israeli society, and the law of compulsory education, brought the Asian-African girls and boys into the schools.

As shown in Table 21.2, in 1985 Israelis born in Israel had more schooling. This gap was even wider among women; women who were born in Israel were more educated than men, whereas among Israelis who were born abroad, men were more educated than women.

This discrepancy between men and women who were born abroad and the native-born is even more prominent if one distinguishes between Asian-African and European-American origins. For example, men and women from Asia-Africa fall mostly in the category of zero to eight years of schooling (45.2 percent and 58.5 percent respectively). Among the first generation, those who were born in Israel but whose fathers came from Asia or Africa, the category of zero to eight years of schooling diminishes to 15.2 percent of the men and 12.9 percent of the women. A second example is presented in Table 21.3.

The biggest change from 1964 to 1982 was among girls of Asian-African origin. The number of seventeen year olds in schools jumped from 15.6 percent to 73.4 percent in 1982. The highest school attendance rate was among girls of European-American origin at 80.2 percent. Within each ethnic group, more girls than boys remained in school until age seventeen. Moreover, about one-half of

Table 21.3
**Percentage of 17-Year-Olds Who Attend Secondary School, by Jewish Ethnic
Group and Sex, 1964 and 1982**

	Asia and Africa		Europe and America	
	1964	1982	1964	1982
Boys	16.0	52.4	41.2	67.1
Girls	15.6	73.4	58.4	80.2
TOTAL	15.8	62.6	44.7	73.4

the girls of Asian-African origin were placed in the academic track (compared to about one-third of the boys). Among Israeli girls and boys of European-American origin, the number was three-quarters and one-half respectively.[21]

In higher education, the participation of Jewish students of Asian-African origin changed dramatically between 1965 and 1985. In 1965, they constituted 11.6 percent of all students and in 1985, 24.1 percent. As presented in Tables 21.2 and 21.3, the girls in that group have come even further in gaining education in Israel.[22]

The Non-Jewish Sector: Girls' Education among Israeli Minorities

At the time of the establishment of the state of Israel, the mostly Arab minorities had the least education (especially since many of the more educated Arabs fled the country in 1948 during the War of Independence). These groups, which included Moslem and Christian Arabs, Druze, and various other small groups, provided the least, if any, formal education for females. An Arab woman's place is strictly defined by tradition and religion. The contact with Jewish society and the relevant state laws changed the status of minority women, but only marginally. (In addition to the law requiring a minimum educational standard, the state enacted laws guaranteeing equal rights for women and laws outlawing polygamy, preventing divorce without a wife's consent, and prohibiting marriages before the age seventeen.) The Israeli-Arab community defines female roles very conservatively. This may symbolize a different and separate national identity within Israeli society.[23] Within the minority populations, Christian women, more than Muslim women, enjoy freedom of movement and contact with modern society.

The educational level is lower in the non-Jewish than the Jewish sector. The median years of education for people over fourteen years of age in 1985 was

Table 21.4
School Enrollment among Minority Groups, by Sex, 1970 and 1985 (in Percentages)

	Age			
	6–13		14–17	
	1970	1985	1970	1985
Boys	93.2	96.0	38.4	65.6
Girls	80.6	93.5	20.0	58.1
TOTAL	87.1	94.7	29.4	62.1*

*By religion: Moslems - 59.0
Christians - 80.7
Druze - 62.0 (however, the Druze women are the least educated even among minority women)

11.5 among Jews and only 8.6 years among non-Jews. Among minorities, males have 9.3 years of schooling and females 7.7. This picture is constantly changing, and at a faster rate for girls, as shown in Table 21.4. The table depicts the growth in elementary and secondary education, in proportion to the total number of students, especially for girls, between 1970 and 1985. About 95 percent of Israeli minority youth completed at least eight years of schooling. At the secondary level (where the last two years are not compulsory), the percentage of boys attending school doubled within fifteen years, while that of girls tripled. Today, boys represent 50.2 percent of all Jewish students and 51.8 percent of non-Jews. In 1986, minority boys made up 52.3 percent of all minority high school students (whereas only 47.9 percent of Jewish students were boys).

As one climbs the education ladder, the number of minority girl students decreases. As stated above, the gap between Jewish males and females in attaining postsecondary and higher education is quite small. This is not so in the non-Jewish sector.

Men and women in the Jewish sector have nearly identical rates in obtaining high school and post-high school education, whereas men do have some advantage in higher education. In the non-Jewish sector men complete secondary and postsecondary education at 2.5 times the rate women do and three times the rate that women complete academic degrees (Table 21.5). One should remember that acquiring postsecondary and higher education requires leaving the family, moving away from home, and usually studying in Hebrew. This entails special difficulties for non-Jewish girls and their families.

Israeli Arabs, including the urban communities exposed to Israeli-Jewish society, have succeeded in keeping their daughters relatively segregated. They

Table 21.5
Jews and Non-Jews Holding Diplomas and Degrees, by Sex, 1985

	Jews		non-Jews	
	High School and Post-High School	Academic Degree	High School and Post-High School	Academic Degree
Males	50.9	10.3	24.6	4.1
Females	50.3	7.6	10.7	1.3
TOTAL	50.6	8.9	20.6	2.6

receive less formal education and maintain a stricter observance of the traditional gender roles.[24] However, even the partial exposure that was inevitable has brought change. For example, the younger generation plans to have smaller families. Girls and women are slowly moving toward integration into modern Israeli society and have begun accepting employment outside the home, albeit in traditional fields such as pink-collar office jobs and teaching.

Kibbutz

The kibbutz has provided the most promising social organization for equality, particularly gender equality, since the beginning of the twentieth century. Here, in a collective where production and services are owned and shared by all members, coupled with an ideology of total equality for all and a reduced role for the nuclear family, one can picture women entering any position without inhibitions based on traditional roles or gender-typed expectations.

Surely, the first generation in the kibbutz approached that goal but never fully applied the ideology. Nor did the reality coincide with the image of kibbutz life depicted for outsiders and members alike.[25] Women did work in all levels of production and took on public roles. However, since men did not correspondingly take up traditionally female duties, women had to gradually return to their traditional responsibilities as the needs for services grew, especially in childcare and education. In principle, a woman can have any position she chooses, but social pressure and the collective needs push her back to where she is needed the most: that is, childcare, education, and other services.[26]

From the very beginning, education in the kibbutz for boys and girls was totally equal, and it has been keep strictly so in all formal aspects. A sociologist, a kibbutz member himself, explains that the gender gap in school achievement and standardized tests (greater even than that outside of the kibbutz) is due to an unequal distribution of roles in adulthood.[27] The girls prepare themselves for the roles that exist in the community where they live.[28] These findings from the 1970s may not hold today. The feminist movement has since reached the kibbutz, and women have organized to demand changes.[29] The fourth kibbutz generation, undergoing socialization processes today, may grow up to be different from the second and third generations, perhaps resembling more the founding generation in terms of women's roles.[30]

Other studies on kibbutz and gender differences in childhood and adolescence, in such areas as interests, nonverbal thinking, and creativity,[31] confirm the conclusion that traditional gender stereotypes are quite strong in that "egalitarian" community.

WOMEN IN THE LABOR FORCE AND POLITICS

The participation of women in the labor force has increased steadily, though moderately, during the last thirty years. In 1955, 26 percent of women aged fourteen and over participated in the labor force. In 1975, participation rose to 32 percent.[32] In 1985, it stood at about 37.6 percent.[33]

Working women in Israel operate, to a considerable degree, in a "feminine" labor market. In other words, the Israeli labor market, like many others, is characterized by considerable occupational sex segregation. Women tend to concentrate in a few occupations in which they are highly overrepresented. For example, in 1985, 46 percent of employed women were found in public and community services (as compared to 20 percent of working men); the respective proportions for industry were 15 percent for women and 28 percent for men. In the Israeli labor market, there are almost four times as many "male" occupations as "female" occupations.[34] On average, the occupational prestige of the Israeli working women equals that of their male counterparts.[35] This equality stems mainly from women's tendency to concentrate at medium-level positions, whereas men are found in larger proportions at the extremes—in the most prestigious and the least prestigious occupations. However, this equality stems, at least partially, from the crude occupational groups usually used by both the Israeli central bureau of statistics and sociologists who analyze occupational prestige in Israel.[36]

A closer examination of women's jobs indicates that within the various occupational groups women tend to have positions characterized by limited opportunities for advancement and less authority.[37] One of the most "feminine" fields, education, demonstrates this point. In 1987–1988, 33 percent of the female staff in Israeli formal education were classified as regular teachers, 10 percent as kindergarten teachers, and about 4 percent had managerial positions. The respective values for the male staff were 84 percent, less than 1 percent and 13 percent. Women are clearly underrepresented in managerial positions. They constitute about 78 percent of those employed in primary and secondary education and only about 50 percent of the school headmasters. This situation cannot be attributed to lack of proper schooling: 44 percent of the women have at least a bachelor's degree compared to 33 percent of the men.

The gender gap within the broad occupational groups is repeated in higher education. In 1980, women constituted 32 percent of the academic staff in Israel. Inspection of the distribution by degree indicates that women comprise about 48 percent of the teaching and research assistants, 41 percent of the instructors, 30 percent of the lecturers, 17 percent of the senior lecturers, 8 percent of the associate professors, and only about 4 percent of the full professors.

Women and men in the Israeli labor market are highly differentiated in terms of income. Similar to other industrial societies, the average income of the Israeli working woman is much lower than that of her male counterpart. In the 1970s, the mean income of Jewish women twenty-five to sixty-four years of age employed full-time was about 73 percent of that of men with parallel characteristics.[38] This gap cannot be attributed to human capital resources. It appears that Israeli working women are recruited from higher socioeconomic groups, and are better educated, and, as already noted, their average occupational prestige does not fall beneath that of men. Hence, control for human capital resources has, in fact, no effect on the gender gap in income. In Israel, as in other industrial societies, this gender gap may stem mainly from differential rates of return, as women's assets bring fewer economic rewards.[39]

Israeli women are extremely underrepresented in politics. The percentage of women in the Israeli Parliament—the Knesset—stands consistently at under 10 percent. Moreover, it appears that women's participation in the Knesset reached its peak at 9.1 percent of all Knesset members in the first years of the state. After the 1959 elections, women's participation rate in the Knesset declined to 7.5 percent. Twenty-five years later, the proportion has not changed.

The rate of women in local municipalities is equal to their proportion in the Knesset—7.6 percent. However, the trend in local politics is somewhat different. During the last twenty years, there has been constant, albeit small, improvement from 3.6 percent in the 1969 elections to 7.6 percent in the 1983 elections.[40]

CONCLUSION

In this chapter we have examined Israeli society as an evolving entity historically, according to ideologies held by different groups as well as by the heterogeneity and complexity of its social fabric. We found many changes in Jewish and non-Jewish groups over the last forty years, some of which can be traced to the nineteenth century. Even before the establishment of the state of Israel, two contradictory and conflicting forces within the Jewish sector affected women's roles and prerequisite socialization and education for girls. On the one side, tradition and religion demanded that women stay at home, occupied by the traditional duties of homemaking and motherhood. On the other side, the principles of social equality and justice held by the socialists and liberals stated that woman was equal to man and therefore could and should participate in any position and role she chose.

Formally, the forces for equality prevailed, at least in education. Since its establishment, the state of Israel has enacted many laws to ensure equality for women in society, especially equality in education. However, Hebrew (religious) law creates contradictions and problems in achieving equality. The government's policies did achieve impressive results, most notably among Jewish girls from Asia and Africa. Although minority non-Jewish females advanced considerably, still they did not close the gap between themselves and the males in their group. In the ultra-orthodox Jewish sector, girls benefit from educational advancement but still do not have access to the same opportunities as boys.

Alongside the formal equality in all educational tracks for girls as for boys exist traditional expectations of different adult male and female roles. The disadvantage of girls in intelligence scores, in gaining matriculation diplomas, especially in "masculine" subjects, and in higher education can be traced back to different socialization processes based on gender.

The trend with regard to kibbutz, whereby females have returned to more traditional roles, parallels a trend in Israeli society as a whole. It is not enough that decisions about equality are made in principle and that educational tracks have opened up. Equal opportunities in employment and overall role patterns, as much as psychological readiness, will eventually determine equality in education and its effectiveness. The process seen in the history of the kibbutz, from more to less equality, symbolizes a potential pattern for Israeli society as a whole, if social positions do not move toward gender equality.

It seems that the main struggle for gender equality today has moved from formal reforms in the educational system toward fighting the sexual stereotypes, by which the young generation is socialized today. What is needed is direct education through examples of women entering traditionally male adult roles.

NOTES

We thank Ms. Dafna Kariv who shared our efforts in the data collection for this chapter.

1. D. Bernstein, *The Struggle for Equality: Urban Women Workers in Prestate Israeli Society* (New York: Praeger, 1987).

2. D. Izraeli, "Status of Women in Israel," *Encyclopedia Judaica Yearbook 1986–1987* (Jerusalem: Keter s.r., 1987), p. 37.

3. A. Lieblich, "Intelligence Level and Structure Among Ethnic Groups and Minorities in Israel," in M. Nisan and U. Last, eds., *Between Education and Psychology* (Jerusalem: Magness, 1983), pp. 335–358 (Hebrew).

4. M. Sepher-Mizrachi, "Intelligence Levels Among Boys and Girls in Israel and Elsewhere," *Maamad Haisha* 11 (1986): 10–14 (Hebrew).

5. A. Yogev, "Determinants of Early Educational Career in Israel: Further Evidence for the Sponsorship Thesis," *Sociology of Education* 54 (1981): 191–194.

6. D. Kfir, "Achievements and Aspirations Among Boys and Girls in High-School:

A Comparison of Two Israeli Ethnic Groups," *American Educational Research Journal,* in press.

7. Ibid.

8. A. Yogev and H. Ayalon, "Vocational Education and Social Reproduction: Students' Allocation to Curricular Programs in Israeli Vocational High Schools," Tel Aviv: The Pinhas Sapir Center for Development, Tel Aviv University, Discussion Paper No. 14–86, 1986.

9. B. Nevo, "Sex Differences in Universities' Entry Tests," *Maamad Haisha* 11 (1986): 15–22 (Hebrew).

10. A. Yogev and H. Ayalon, "Sex and Ethnic Variations in Educational Plans: A Cross Cultural Perspective," *International Review of Modern Sociology* 12 (1982): 1–19.

11. H. Ayalon, "Economic Aspects of Boys' and Girls' Occupational Aspirations," *Megamot* 31 (1988, in press) (Hebrew).

12. R. Shapira, E. Etzioni-Halevy, and S. Tibon, "Occupational Choice Among Israeli Academicians," *Journal of Comparative Family Studies* 9 (1978): 69–81.

13. J. Wilson, *Religion in American Society* (Englewood Cliffs, N.J.: Prentice-Hall, 1978).

14. R. J. Simon, *Continuity and Change: A Study of Two Ethnic Communities in Israel* (Cambridge, Mass.: Cambridge University Press, 1978), p. 51.

15. R. Schneller, "Continuity and Change in Ultra-Orthodox Education," *Jewish Journal of Sociology* 22 (1980): 35–46.

16. Simon, *Continuity and Change,* p. 62.

17. Schneller, "Continuity and Change."

18. Simon, *Continuity and Change,* p. 95.

19. J. Shuval, "Professional Interest and Sex Roles," *Megamot* 12 (1963): 244–251 (Hebrew); R. Bar-Yoseph, *Sex Role Perceptions Among 17 Year Old Girls* (Jerusalem: Hebrew University of Jerusalem, Work and Welfare Research Institute, 1976), (Hebrew).

20. Y. Peres, *Ethnic Relations in Israel* (Tel-Aviv: Hapoalim, 1976) (Hebrew).

21. Israel Ministry of Education, *School System in Numbers,* 1987, Table 3.

22. Kfir, "Achievements and Aspirations."

23. A. Shtandall, "The Status of Arab Women in Israel," *Betahon Socially* 9–10 (1975): 137–143 (Hebrew).

24. Simon, *Continuity and Change.*

25. Bernstein, *The Struggle for Equality.*

26. E. Ben-Rafael and S. Weitzman, "The Reconstitution of the Family in the Kibbutz," *European Journal of Sociology* 25 (1984): 1–27.

27. Y. Dar, *Sex Differences in Scholastic Achievement Among Kibbutz Adolescents,* Kiryat-Tivon: Seminar Oraniml, The Ichud Hakvutzot Vehakibbutzim's Institution for Social Research, 1974 (Hebrew).

28. "Sex Equality in the Kibbutz," *Hakibbutz* 3–4 (1976).

29. V. Silver, ed., *Male and Female Created He Them: The Problem of Sexual Equality on Kibbutz* (Yad-Tabenkin, 1984), (Hebrew).

30. A. Lieblich, *Kibbutz Makom* (Jerusalem: Shoken, 1984), (Hebrew).

31. Silver, *Male and Female,* pp. 100–108.

32. D. N. Izraeli. "Sex Structure of Occupations: The Israeli Experience," *Sociology of Work and Occupations* 6 (1979): 404–429.

33. Izraeli, "Status of Women in Israel."

34. Izraeli, "Sex Structures of Occupations."

35. M. Semyonov and V. Kraus, "Gender, Ethnicity and Income Inequality: The Israeli Experience," *International Journal of Comparative Sociology* 26 (1983): 252–272.

36. M. Hartman, "Prestige Grading of Occupations with Sociologists as Judges," *Quality and Quantity* 13 (1979): 1–19; V. Kraus, O. E. Schild, and W. Hodge, "Occupational Prestige in the Collective Conscience," *Social Forces* 56 (1978): 900–918.

37. Izraeli, "Sex Structures of Occupations."

38. Semyonov and Kraus, "Gender, Ethnicity and Income."

39. Y. Haberfeld and Y. Shenhav, "Gender-Based Wage Discrimination, or Level of Analysis? Aggregated vs. Organizational Data?" in F. Hoy, ed., Academy of Management Best Paper Proceedings, New Orleans, 1987, pp. 364–368.

40. Izraeli, "Status of Women in Israel." H. Herzog, Women in Local Politics, Research Report Submitted to Keren Mifal Hapais, Tel Aviv, 1987 (Hebrew).

NORTH AMERICA

22
CANADA

Jane Gaskell

The revitalized women's movement has placed women's concerns back on the Canadian educational policy agenda over the past twenty years, and has pointed to the ways in which women's continued economic and social inequality affects their educational chances. In this period, women in Canada have argued for a wide variety of educational changes, and some change has occurred. Women have increased their participation in higher education, especially in programs leading to higher paying professional fields. The curriculum has been critically examined for its portrayals of women and its male biases, and new materials have been introduced. Women have accumulated a wealth of experience with educational change, much of it at the local level and little publicized. The process of political change put into motion by the women's movement has led to a great deal of new research and political activity around education. The changes that women want ultimately involve reorganizing the educational system in ways that affect both men and women, inside the classroom and outside it, at all levels of education.

This chapter begins by briefly outlining the position of women in Canadian society, looking at both their legal equality and their continuing economic and social inequality. It then turns to education and examines levels of achievement, types of enrollment, and curriculum issues that have been of concern to women.

One caveat is important. Education in Canada is not centrally controlled by the federal government. It comes under provincial jurisdiction, and there are ten provinces with rather different political agendas and economic conditions. Within each province, there are school boards that have a good deal of input into educational practice. This makes national surveys difficult, and of necessity limited, even while they are important. It also makes comprehensive solutions to persistent problems unlikely, while local initiatives and variations in practice abound.

THE POSITION OF WOMEN IN CANADIAN SOCIETY

Women in Canada achieved the right to vote in federal elections in 1918. They have gradually fought to remove restrictions by sex on their participation in all areas of life. In 1984, women succeeded in getting a provision for equal treatment included in the new constitutional accord. The Canadian human rights commission is charged with monitoring the equality of men and women, and most educational institutions endorse policies explicitly providing equal opportunities for all.

But legal theory is not the same as social practice. Women and men perform different, and not equally valued, kinds of work in Canadian society. Myths about women's inferior abilities and stereotyped interests persist in the face of economic and social change. Women in Canada do not have equal social, political, and economic power.

The family is one site of continuing inequality. Women continue to perform most of the work in the family, caring for children and doing housework. Even though women's rate of participation in the paid labor force has increased dramatically, their share of the domestic labor has barely decreased.[1] Women have a double workday, half in the home and half outside it. Images of women in the media and in everyday discourse are fully bound up with their family and sexual roles.

Domestic living arrangements in Canada are changing rapidly. There has been a substantial increase in single-parent families, most of them headed by women and many of them poor. Almost one in every ten Canadian families is headed by a lone female parent. For the 60 percent of adult women who are either married or living in common law arrangements, life is also changing. Since 1970, divorce rates have increased, fertility rates have decreased (from 71 to 56 per 1,000 women aged fifteen to forty-nine), and families are becoming, on average, smaller (from 1.7 to 1.3 children).[2]

The participation rate of women in the paid labor force has increased dramatically, and it continues to increase. Fifty-four percent of women over the age of fifteen are part of the paid labor force compared to 77 percent of men. This compares to a 16 percent rate for women in 1901 and a 34 percent rate in 1970. Today, 54 percent of married women, 54 percent of women with preschool-aged children and 64 percent of women with children from six to fifteen are in the labor force. Participation rates increase with education—77 percent of university-educated women, 58 percent of secondary school graduates, and 26 percent of women with elementary school education are in the labor force.[3]

But increased economic participation has not meant increased economic equality. Women earn, on average, sixty cents for each dollar men earn. Much of the difference can be accounted for by the fact that women work in jobs that are different from men's jobs. Women are concentrated in clerical jobs, in service jobs, and in the traditionally female professions—nursing, teaching, and social work. These jobs do not give women a great deal of economic power, and, considering the educational background they require, they are underpaid.

Thus, women in Canada enjoy equal rights within a social structure that continues to locate them primarily in the family and to pay them less than men. This has profound implications for women's participation in education, for education reflects the values and behavior patterns of the society, at the same time as it formally offers an equal chance for each student. What becomes clear is that formal equal opportunity is not enough to equalize the educational chances of girls. The educational system must take into account the different positions which male and female students have and anticipate, in order to provide an equal education for both. Providing an equal education for women and girls ultimately means bringing about social and economic equality throughout the society.

ENROLLMENT PATTERNS: EQUALITY OF ACCESS AND ACHIEVEMENT

Equal access to education was not granted to women in Canada without a fight. Before the turn of the century, feminists struggled to ensure equality of opportunity in its most basic form: the right to attend all educational institutions. Although most public schools had been coeducational since their inception, in 1865 the Ontario provincial government tried to tighten up its requirements by stopping local school boards from admitting girls to grammar schools and to the study of Latin. George Paxton Young, the grammar school inspector, argued that

There is a very considerable diversity between the mind of a girl and that of a boy; and it would be rash to conclude that, as a matter of course, the appliances which are best adapted for bringing the faculties of reflection and taste to their perfection in one must be the best also in the case of the other . . . they are not studying Latin with any definite object. They have taken it up under pressure . . . there is a danger of grown up girls suffering as respects the formation of their moral character, from attending school along with grown up boys.[4]

George Paxton Young's arguments did not prevail over the economic interest of local school boards in enrolling girls in their schools. Recruiting more girls meant more money for the grammar schools. So coeducation prevailed, not primarily because of a belief in sexual equality, but because of the need for financial stability, especially in rural schools.

The admission of women to higher education and professional training took more time and struggle. Even admission to teacher training in the Toronto normal school was not granted without a fight. Universities were considered "a male sphere, a place of serious learning that fitted men for positions in the public world. Women's entrance into the university was considered unnatural, both for the institution and for women. Higher education was considered at best irrelevant, and more likely detrimental, to women's future roles as wives and mothers."[5] Women who finally won admittance to universities on an equal basis with men challenged the stereotypes of women and began an assault on male educational power.

To win the right to attend educational programs does not ensure that women will attend on an equal basis with men. To understand women's participation in education today, two kinds of statistical patterns are important. One concerns levels of achievement; the other concerns types of enrollments. There are differences between men and women in both, but it is the statistics on types of enrollment that most clearly reveal the patterned inequalities between men and women.

Female students have succeeded well in Canadian schools, if levels of achievements are what is counted. Canadian women are more likely than Canadian men to have completed a Grade 9 level of education, and thus to be officially designated as literate. In 1983, 20.4 percent of women aged fifteen and over had less than a Grade 9 education, compared to 21.3 percent of men.[6] Moreover, women's superior attainment in the early school grades is not a recent phenomenon. Women have been overrepresented among elementary students since the mid-nineteenth century, when systematic educational statistics were first gathered in Canada. The gap in illiteracy rates has narrowed over time as overall levels of education have increased.

A similar picture emerges in relation to high school. Women are more likely to attend and graduate than men, and this has been true since the mid-1800s. The gap has narrowed recently as the educational levels of the population have increased, but it is still true that more women than men have completed high school. In 1983, 51.7 percent of Canadian women over fifteen years of age had attended high school compared to 48.5 percent of men.[7] The disparity was much greater before the turn of the century when few attended secondary school. For example, statistics from one province, British Columbia, show that in 1900, 63 percent of secondary school students were female.[8] Only in 1950, with the postwar expansion of postsecondary enrollments, did the participation rate of boys aged fifteen to nineteen equal the participation rate of girls in the same age group.[9]

The reasons for women's persistence in school (despite beliefs like those held by George Paxton Young) can be traced to a variety of factors. Girls seem to do better in school, getting higher grades and failing less often, which would help explain why they stay on. Alternatives to school may have been less appealing for girls, who would be confined to domestic duties or a narrow range of paid jobs, than for boys with a greater range of options. Job opportunities in heavily female fields like teaching and clerical work have been closely tied to educational credentials, whereas male jobs offer more opportunities for those without formal credentials and provide more on-the-job training.

Even at the level of postsecondary certificates and diplomas, women have attained and continue to attain more than men. Women constituted 51 percent of full-time community college enrollment in 1985.[10] In 1983, 11.9 percent of women over fifteen and 9.9 percent of men had some sort of postsecondary certificate. In 1971, the percentage was 7.1 for females and 5.0 for men.[11]

Only at the level of university education have women historically fallen behind men in their educational achievement. Today, however, women and men are equally represented among university students. The percentage of women undergraduates has grown from 15 percent in 1920 to just over 20 percent in 1950 to 52 percent today.[12] Women earned 52 percent of the bachelor's and first professional degrees granted in Canada in 1985.[13] But population statistics still show a gap. In 1983, 7.7 percent of women and 11.3 percent of men in Canada had a university degree.[14]

Women continue to lag behind men in doctoral and master's degrees, but here again women have made major advances recently. Women were awarded 22 percent of all master's degrees in 1970 and 42 percent in 1985; 9.3 percent of doctoral degrees in 1970 and 26.4 percent in 1985.[15] A very small percentage of the population attains such high levels of education. The significance of these statistics lies in women's resulting lack of access to high-level positions in the educational system and to their consequent lack of ability to affect the production and transmission of knowledge.

School achievement rates for women are patterned unequally across the country, by class, by ethnic group, and by geographic area. Success in school is closely related to social class background for girls, as it is for boys. Students from less wealthy backgrounds are less likely to complete high school and less likely to attend university. As schools struggle with reduced resources and as female-headed households with low incomes increase, children's experiences in school suffer. It is often women, as mothers and as teachers, who are called on to put in extra time to help children, but these women rarely control the resources.[16]

Native students, who make up between 3 and 4 percent of the population and experience the worst socioeconomic conditions of any group, are much less likely to complete high school than are nonnative students. In 1981, 7.7 percent of native men and 8.7 percent of native women had a high school diploma. Only 1.1 percent of native men, and 1.6 percent of native women had a university education.[17]

One in ten Canadians is a member of a visible minority group. Recent immigrants and visible minorities have relatively high average rates of educational achievement, partly because Canada's immigration policy favors those with more educational credentials. The 1981 census reported that 11.6 percent of Canadians of Chinese background, 18.2 percent of those with Indo-Pakistani background, 13.2 percent of those with Japanese background, and 6.7 percent of blacks had attained a university education. The comparable statistic for those of British background was 6.2 percent. Chinese, Indo-Pakistani, and Japanese males are much more likely to have a university degree than women of the same background. Only among blacks were levels of participation in higher education equal for men and women.[18]

Although education increases women's salaries, the increase is much smaller for women than it is for men, and the salary that each level of education buys is much lower. In 1983, the average woman with a university degree who was working full time in Canada earned $20,107; a man with similar education earned $33,841. A woman with a high school degree earned, on average, $9,960; a man with a high school diploma earned $18,686. The average woman with a university degree earns barely more than the average man with a high school diploma. Differences persist at every level of education.[19] The difficulty of turning education into income is particularly acute for women who do not speak fluent English, who have educational credentials from other countries, and who face discrimination as visible minorities. Recent immigrants and visible minorites tend to be overrepresented among professional women, owing to their educational backgrounds, but they are also overrepresented among those with the lowest paying jobs in the service sector.[20]

Clearly, the cause of women's lower salaries is not their lack of educational attainment. The kind of schooling, rather than the amount of schooling, women obtain is related to their lack of earning power. The kinds of programs women enroll in are different from the kinds of programs men enroll in, and lead to lower paying jobs. This difference begins to emerge in the high school, where males and females enroll in different courses and prepare themselves for different jobs, even though they all obtain similar high school diplomas. Canadian high schools are organized on a "credit" system, where students must accumulate enough credits to graduate but can do so in a variety of subject areas.

The result is that students develop a wide variety of different kinds of programs in their high school years, and girls systematically take different courses from boys. Girls are more likely to avoid mathematics, technology, and the physical sciences; they are more likely to take courses in home economics, commerce, and languages. The statistics that would summarize the magnitude of this difference are not easily available, because the structure of high school courses is so complex and so variable from school to school and province to province. But an example illustrates the problem. In 1980 in Ontario, Ministry of Education statistics showed that girls made up 1 percent of the students enrolled in senior courses in welding in high school, 9 percent of those in construction courses, and 22 percent of those in senior-level physics, but 98 percent of those in business procedures courses, 97 percent of those in family studies, and 72 percent of those in senior French courses.

At the level of postsecondary education, comprehensive figures are easier to obtain. Table 22.1 shows the enrollment of women in a variety of programs at the community college in 1976 (when comprehensive statistics became available) and in 1982.[21] Women are overrepresented in secretarial education, in nursing, in education, and in social services. They are underrepresented in engineering, in technologies, and in natural resource programs. Women are slowly increasing their representation in male-dominated areas, but men are not entering traditionally female fields. Only nursing shows any increase at all in male participation in the heavily female areas.

Job training programs are subject to the same segmentation as formal educational programs. In 1985, women constituted 93 percent of trainees in clerical fields, 88 percent in social science-related fields, but 2 percent in mining and 5 percent in construction and transportation.[22] Although women are more likely to participate in adult education courses than men, women are less likely to enroll in job training courses and more likely to enroll in personal interest courses.[23]

University enrollments are also heavily segregated, but they are changing rapidly.[24] Table 22.2 shows the patterns of enrollment from 1971 to 1985. Women are overrepresented in nursing, education, arts, and humanities. They are underrepresented in engineering, mathematics, dentistry, medicine, and law. Women have increased their participation in the university across the board. The only field in which women have not become more numerous is nursing, where the numbers were already so high there was little room for an increase. There is no evidence that men are moving into female fields. Where the greatest gains have been made depends on how one calculates it. The largest absolute gains are in the social sciences, particularly law, commerce, and economics. As a percentage increase on the starting figure, however, engineering and the applied sciences do very well.

These differences in enrollment patterns are linked to the labor market and take their importance from this fact. The fields in which men predominate are higher paying than the fields in which women predominate. For example, in a study of 1982 graduates from postsecondary institutions across Canada, researchers found that among trades and vocational graduates, those from engineering technologies and applied sciences earned the most and arts graduates the least. At the bachelor's level, engineering and applied science graduates were the highest paid, whereas fine and applied arts graduates earned the least.[25]

THE CURRICULUM AND SCHOOL PROCESSES

Equal access has been only part of the political agenda that the Canadian women's movement set for schooling in Canada. Equally important has been the question of what women are gaining access to, the question of curriculum, in its broadest sense. The women's movement has raised the question of what knowledge is important and what students learn about women and their contributions to Canadian life. Even more importantly, the women's movement has pointed out how our knowledge is distorted by the biases of male scholarship, and it has begun to call for changes in what is taught to everyone.

Table 22.1

Community College Graduates, by Sex and Field of Study, 1976 and 1982

Field of Study	Total Graduates 1976 Women No.	1976 Men No.	1976 Women as a Percent of Total	1982 Women No.	1982 Men No.	1982 Women as a % of Total	Percentage Distribution 1976 Women %	1976 Men %	1982 Women %	1982 Men %
Arts	1,768	1,338	56.9	3,321	1,883	63.8	7.7	8.8	11.5	8.9
Business	5,182	3,502	59.7	10,113	5,321	65.5	22.5	23.0	35.0	25.2
Secretarial	2,820	30	98.9	3,596	10	99.7	12.2	0.2	12.4	0.0
Community and social services	4,018	1,418	73.9	5,065	1,626	75.7	17.4	9.3	17.5	7.7
Education	130	30	81.2	82	19	81.2	0.6	0.2	0.3	0.1
Engineering	179	3,249	5.2	518	5,085	9.2	0.8	21.3	1.8	24.1
Medical sciences	10,847	895	92.4	8,409	1,105	88.4	47.0	5.9	29.1	5.2
Nursing	8,323	276	96.8	6,150	335	94.8	36.1	1.8	21.3	1.6
Natural resources	382	1,636	18.9	870	2,161	28.7	1.7	10.7	3.0	10.2
Technologies	226	2,327	8.9	362	3,264	10.0	1.0	15.3	1.3	15.5

Transport	5	248	2.0	7	272	2.5	0.0	1.6	0.0	1.3
Other	123	270	31.3	149	293	33.7	0.5	1.8	0.5	1.4
Total[1]	23,082	15,252	61.3	28,909	21,091	57.9	100.0	100.0	100.0	100.0

[1]Includes "Not reported."

Sources: Enrolment in Community Colleges, Statistics Canada Catalogue 81-222.
Education, Culture and Tourism Division, Statistics Canada, unpublished data.

Table 22.2

Bachelor's and First Professional Degrees Granted, by Sex and Field of Study, 1971 and 1982

Field of Study	Total Graduates						Percentage Distribution			
	1971			1982			1971		1982	
	Women	Men	Women as a Percent of Total	Women	Men	Women as a % of Total	Women	Men	Women	Men
	No.	No.		No.	No.		%	%	%	%
Education	8,129	7,277	52.8	11,309	4,855	70.0	31.9	17.5	25.5	11.4
Fine and applied arts	639	526	54.8	1,770	993	64.1	2.5	1.3	4.0	2.3
Humanities	4,137	4,658	47.0	5,339	3,342	61.5	16.3	11.2	12.0	7.8
Social sciences	4,238	12,081	26.0	13,099	15,679	45.5	16.7	29.1	29.5	36.7
Commerce	215	3,229	6.2	3,534	6,810	34.2	0.8	7.8	8.0	15.9
Economics	131	1,620	7.5	808	2,035	28.4	0.5	3.9	1.8	4.8
Law	183	1,775	9.3	1,166	1,937	37.6	0.5	4.3	2.6	4.5
Agriculture and biological sciences	1,214	1,886	39.2	2,614	2,366	52.5	4.8	4.5	5.9	5.5
Engineering and applied sciences	51	4,375	1.2	666	6,522	9.3	0.2	10.5	1.5	15.3
Medical and health professions	1,842	1,945	48.6	3,784	2,269	62.5	7.2	4.7	8.5	5.3
Dentistry	16	353	4.3	95	385	19.8	0.1	0.9	0.2	0.9
Medicine	145	991	12.8	691	1,219	36.2	0.6	2.4	1.6	2.9
Nursing	1,221	37	97.1	1,573	47	97.1	4.8	0.1	3.5	0.1

Mathematics and physical sciences	751	3,119	19.4	1,387	3,485	28.5	3.0	7.5	3.1	8.2
Computer	76	284	21.1	423	1,177	26.4	0.3	0.7	1.0	2.8
No specialization	4,449	5,634	44.1	4,429	3,266	57.6	17.5	13.6	10.0	7.6
Total	25,450	41,501	38.0	44,397	42,777	50.9	100.0	100.0	100.0	100.0

Source: Education, Culture and Tourism Division, Statistics Canada, special updated tabulations.

Women have tried to have an impact on the curriculum in many ways. One of the first attempts which organized women's groups in Canada made to change the curriculum involved incorporating home economics, a subject totally identified with women, into the elementary and secondary schools. As the Local Council of Women told the Royal Commission on Industrial Training and Technical Education in 1913, "The Local Council of Women would like to see service in the home lifted to the same plane as the profession of nursing. The Council does not believe the home should continue to be the only place for which special training is not regarded as necessary."[26] They wanted women's work to be publicly recognized as worthy of study; they wanted its scientific knowledge base acknowledged. They accepted as natural the division between men's and women's spheres, and they wanted recognition for women's.

There were a few dissenting ("equal rights") feminists who challenged the notion of separate spheres for men and women, arguing that the inclusion of home economics would channel women away from industrial and technical studies and confirm their position in the domestic sphere. But when home economics was eventually introduced, it was seen as a victory for women because it represented their experience and their interests in the curriculum.[27] Today, on the other hand, home economics often gets criticized as a "ghetto" for women, echoing the concerns of earlier dissenters. What is taken to be in the interest of women changes as the economic and social context changes.

The renewed women's movement in the 1960s led the government to appoint a Royal Commission on the Status of Women, headed by Florence Bird. The commission held hearings across the country, commissioned research studies, and wrote a report reflecting the concerns of the women's movement, urging far-reaching changes in the way women were treated in every sector. The report still has not been fully implemented, but even over the past ten years it has served as a rallying point for women who want change.

The 1970 Royal Commission called for changes in the curriculum, stating that "Changes in education could bring dramatic improvements in the social and economic position of women in an astonishingly short time."[28] The commission focused on stereotyping in curriculum materials. After examining the sex-role imagery in the textbooks used to teach reading, social studies, science, mathematics, and guidance courses in Canadian schools, their report concluded that "a woman's creative and intellectual potential is either underplayed or ignored in the education of children from their earliest years. The sex roles described in these textbooks provide few challenging models for young girls, and they fail to create a sense of community between men and women as fellow human beings."

The many studies that were done over the next ten years by teachers' federations, community groups, and women academics confirmed their verdict.[29] These studies revealed that women and girls were underrepresented in schoolbooks and that when they were represented, they were stereotyped. Boys were equally stereotyped in more powerful and active roles. Little girls in elementary texts played with dolls while their brothers played baseball; mothers wore aprons and baked cookies, while fathers drove off to work; adult women were princesses and witches, while men were doctors and farmers.

The research, in combination with political lobbying, had an effect on the schools. Under pressure from women's groups, publishers and ministries of education across the country appointed advisory groups on sexism and began to issue new guidelines for nonsexist materials. In the province of British Columbia in 1974, for example, the Ministry of Education, which had appointed a provincial advisory committee and a special advisor on sex discrimination, issued "On the Equal Treatment of the Sexes: Guidelines for Educational Materials." The guidelines were "to make educators aware of the ways in which males and females have been stereotyped" and "to assist educators and others who seek to provide equal treatment of the sexes in textbooks. The same year, the Ontario Status of Women Council published "About Face: Towards a Positive Image of Women in Textbooks," and in 1976, the Quebec government published "L'Ecole Sexiste, C'est Quoi?"

Alternative materials were developed and published. The British Columbia Teachers Federation published "Breaking the Mould: Non Sexist Curricula Materials for B.C. Elementary Schools" in 1975. In 1977 the British Columbia ministry issued a Resource Guide for Teachers in Women's Studies and an annotated bibliography of materials that might be used in courses. In 1976, the Ontario Ministry of Education published a resource guide entitled, *Sex-Role Stereotyping and Women's Studies* "to assist educators in the on-going task of developing a learning environment that is free from sex role stereotyping of males and females and a curriculum that accurately depicts the roles of women."

By the early 1980s, there had been a dramatic change in the primary readers that were being issued. Equal numbers of males and females were represented. The stereotypes began to disappear. The new readers had boys playing with girls, and represented adult women as police officers and doctors. The old books continue to be used in schools because of the costs of replacing materials as well as the preferences of teachers; the implementation of nonsexist guidelines is more difficult than their promulgation.[30] But significant victories were won, and progress was made.

Another area that has been of great concern to women is the persistence of sexual stereotyping in guidance materials. A 1986 study on the aspirations of Canadian elementary schoolchildren aged six to fourteen concludes that, even among the youngest of the research subjects, boys and girls differed in their responses to questions about the attractiveness of activities that involved responsibility, mechanical skills, and advanced education.[31] Girls preferred "to look after small children," to "type letters for someone," and to "bake a cake." Boys preferred to "tell other workers what to do," to "fix a car," and to "design rocket ships." Clearly, sex-role stereotypes persist among young children. A 1985 study of adolescent girls concluded that they are romantic and unrealistic in their future plans. Girls tend to restrict their choices of jobs to a narrower

range than boys do, and "both sexes seem to be bound by the traditional stereotypes about gender and work. However, women seem to be breaking out of
the pattern more than men are."[32]

In a 1987 report on educational activities in relation to women's issues,[33] all
ten provinces reported that they had instituted some kind of action to "promote
realistic career planning for female students." Their initiatives vary, but they
include elimination of sex bias in guidance materials, pairing of career women
with students, special meetings and conferences, and educational materials for
guidance counselors. Programs have been mounted to give more counseling to
women, to encourage them to be assertive, and to provide them with more
information about the labor market.

To get rid of stereotyping, however, is to tackle only part of the problem of
sexism in education. More far-reaching changes in the provision of educational
programs are necessary if women are to achieve equality with men. In 1985,
another Royal Commission report, written by Judge Rosalie Abella, who had
long been active in the women's movement, argued that "to treat everyone the
same may be to offend the notion of equality. . . . it is not fair to use the differences between people as an excuse to exclude them arbitrarily from equal
participation . . . ignoring differences and refusing to accommodate them is a
denial of equal access and opportunity."[34] Abella proposed an attack on "sys-
temic" discrimination, arguing that institutions must adapt to women's needs
and produce equal results for women, as well as for other disadvantaged groups.
She proposed that all institutions should monitor women's performance, in order
that problem areas be identified and attacked. Educational institutions, she maintained, should then be held responsible for producing equity in whatever ways
it could be accomplished.

This very active concept of equal educational opportunity means that schools
should be responsible for analyzing the participation of males and females in
every program and changing the program until both male and female students
can participate equally. It means tailoring the curriculum to the needs and interests
of women so that they do well. For, as the New Brunswick advisory committee
on the status of women argues, "if equality of results is not occurring, then,
quite simply, the system is failing."[35] Accountability rests with educators; they
must find ways to educate everyone equally.

Getting more women into science and mathematics is one of the issues that
might be treated this way. A major study conducted in 1982 by the Science
Council of Canada concluded that many more girls needed to be encouraged to
study science.[36] There have been a few responses across the country. Special
classes in mathematics and science, which give girls experience with tools and
mathematical problems and seek to allay "math anxiety," have been started in
some areas. Special opportunities for girls to participate in a variety of scientific
endeavors have been developed in order to encourage them to seek out scientific
careers.

But the statistics remain discouraging. If Abella's criteria for equity were applied, all science and math classrooms would need to change in order to become more "girl-friendly." Girls are more attracted to science classrooms where teachers intervene to ensure equal participation and where the social issues associated with scientific discoveries are discussed. They avoid classrooms where males "hog" the equipment and teachers ignore girls' responses. There is also some evidence that all female classes encourage girls to participate in nontraditional areas.[37] These kinds of initiatives might begin to include girls on an equal basis with boys.

A variety of other program changes have been advocated by women's groups in order to select women's needs in the curriculum and equalize opportunities for girls and women. The development of new "bridging" curricula, for example, job entry programs for women returning to the workplace after a period at home, or computer skills programs for clerical workers who want to move into management, have been emphasized by the Canadian Congress on Learning Opportunities for Women. This important women's pressure group is concerned with women's educational opportunities. The introduction of less segmented programs has also been advocated. Instead of separating all the clerical students (female) from all the management students (male) in a community college program, more attempts should be made to introduce both groups of students to theories of information processing in the office and to courses on the organization of business.

Criteria for admission and patterns of recruitment can also have an impact on girls' enrollment. Some federal job training programs have set aside places that can only be filled by women in training programs in nontraditional areas. When educational requirement, and requirements for prior experience or full-time study eliminate women from eligibility for some programs, the requirements can be changed. For example, a medical program at one Canadian university cut down on the number of science courses it required, became more lenient in its age requirements, and encouraged applicants who had a broad background and experience working with people. The number of women who applied and were admitted to the program shot up.

Central to the agenda of the women's movement in Canada has been a demand to include female experience in the curriculum. The most straightforward index of women's omission from the curriculum is a count of various indices—the number of female characters in elementary school readers, the number of female authors on the reading list, the number of women mentioned in a history text, and the number of women in tenured university positions responsible for creating scholarship. The omission of women is clear.

But to include women's experience also means reexamining the content of what is taught in more thoroughgoing ways. It means diversifying the curriculum so that native women, children from single-parent homes, businesswomen, and Chinese-Canadian women see that what they are taught has some relevance for their lives. Women have developed new materials for language training programs, for literacy programs, for native-controlled schools, and for inner city classrooms, so that the diversity of women's experience in Canada is represented in instructional settings.[38]

To include women means reexamining the rules used for inclusion in the first place and often changing the way the subject is conceptualized. If the people mentioned in history texts are those who have played an important role in governing the country, clearly women cannot be equally represented. The process of adding women involves changing ideas about what students should learn in history classes and why they should study history in the first place. It means learning about the ways ordinary people lived their lives so children can understand the history of people like themselves. It means including more social history, more studies of how families were organized and work was distributed in other historical periods. It means understanding the ways gender has shaped the organization of Canadian society.

The omission of women is not just a question of oversight. Our very conception of education, of what is worth knowing, and of the disciplines is challenged by the process of including women. This kind of analysis has meant a reworking of knowledge so that it includes women's experience. "Malestream" thought, as Mary O'Brien has dubbed traditional scholarship,[39] is revealed as partial, based in male experience, and therefore inadequate. Seemingly objective and value-free inquiry is revealed to be based on male assumptions.

One of the most influential Canadian documents to address the way feminism must transform all knowledge was published in 1985 by the Social Sciences and Humanities Research Council. M. Eichler and J. Lapointe point out that scholarship that does not take adequate account of women is simply bad scholarship.

As long as women were de facto excluded from intellectual work and higher education, sex related bias in research was not widely recognized as a problem for the social sciences and humanities. Culture and our way of thinking were shaped by a male perspective which applied even when the life, identity and thought of women were considered. There was little or no awareness that such an androcentric perspective generates serious intellectual problems. Central concepts were seldom examined with respect to their applicability to both sexes, and sexist language was usually uncritically accepted, in spite of its inexactness.[40]

The pamphlet goes on to give specific examples of how male bias operates and what can be done about it. Eichler and Lapointe discuss how research has transformed statistical differences into innate differences (as in psychological scales of masculinity and femininity), overgeneralized concepts that apply to males ("universal" suffrage was granted before women got the vote) and failed to consider the way assumptions about gender affect data gathering ("Do you think women doctors are as good as men doctors?" does not allow the response that women are better doctors).

This has meant the development of feminist scholarship which has been having an impact on academic work in every discipline and field of study, although the progress remains slow and far from even.

Since the early 1970s, there has been an explosion of knowledge about women's experience in Canada. Where women were invisible in academic texts, they are beginning to have a presence. Where questions about women were never asked, they are now being pursued. The enormous gaps in our knowledge about how women live, think, and feel are providing opportunities for new research and innovative scholarship.

The concern about putting women's experience in the curriculum has meant the emergence of Canadian journals devoted to the study of women, the appearance of women's studies programs in Canadian schools and universities, and an increase in the number of women academics who brought their own experiences and questions to their research. In 1972, a journal now called *Resources for Feminist Research* was founded in order to provide reviews, bibliographies, and a comprehensive periodical and resources guide to materials being published on women. *Atlantis,* a journal of women's studies, was founded in 1976 in Atlantic Canada. University women's studies courses appeared at Concordia in 1971, at the University of Toronto in 1972, at the University of British Columbia in 1973, and Simon Fraser in 1975.[41]

The Social Sciences and Humanities Research Council initiated a program of funding research on "Women and Work" broadly construed to "foster and encourage research and scholarship which is non-sexist in language and methodology and which will contribute to an integrated understanding of women's paid and unpaid work." The Canadian Research Institute for the Advancement of Women was begun in 1976, and the Canadian Women's Studies Association was founded in 1982. Five regional chairs in women's studies were funded by the secretary of state from 1983 to 1985.

All this activity has had an effect on education, from the university down to the preschool. Hamilton, for example, is optimistic about the extent to which an oppositional current has been established by feminist politics and scholarship within academic disciplines.

(F)eminists have indeed carried their protest into the university . . . (T)hey have challenged not only the structure of the university, and the limited place of women within it, but also the very parameters of what constitutes knowledge, and many of the assumptions underlying the traditional academic disciplines. In simplest terms, the feminist slogan, borrowed from the New Left, that "the personal is political" not only legitimated new areas of research, but also probed their links with broader political, economic and social relations.[42]

But the impact is not as great as many would like. With cutbacks to educational expenditures and a wavering commitment to women's issues on the part of politicians and educators, progress is slow. The struggle continues.

CONCLUSIONS

Florence Bird's Royal Commission Report in 1970 and Rosalie Abella's Royal Commission report in 1984 mark two recent and important points in the development of women's educational equality in Canada. Both reports dealt with issues much broader than education. Both saw education as an important indicator of and contributor to women's equality. It is significant that the 1970 report was a good deal more optimistic about the prospects for change and the importance of education than the 1984 report, despite the progress that had been made in the meantime. As women's concerns get more prominence, the obstacles become clearer, and the agenda develops and changes. There is plenty of evidence to support the contention of Abella that educational change is "glacially slow" :

Education has been the classic crutch upon which we lean in the hopes of coaxing change in prejudicial attitudes. But education is an unreliable agent, glacially slow in movement and impact, and often completely ineffective in the face of intractable views. It promises no immediate relief despite the immediacy of the injustice.[43]

Continued progress depends on continued representation of women's concerns, both through grass-roots organizations and the highest policy-making bodies. A variety of federal and provincial institutions represent women at the level of government, and their development over the past twenty years has been enormously important in having women's concerns heard. The Canadian Advisory Council on the Status of Women, established in 1973, monitors trends, conducts research, consults with women's groups, and informs and advises government committees, task forces, and officials on issues of concern to women. The Women's Program in the Secretary of State was established in the same year and is the principal means by which the federal government funds women's voluntary organizations designed to improve the status of women. Since 1971, a minister has been responsible for the status of women; in 1976, Status of Women Canada was instituted to coordinate government activities in relation to women. At the provincial level, there are a variety of institutions, from the Women's Secretariats that exist in some ministries and provide local groups with discretionary grants, to Human Rights Commissions which receive complaints alleging sexual harassment and are responsible for monitoring equal pay for work of equal value.

The development of such institutions has been enormously helpful in putting women's concerns in front of policy makers and in front of the public at large. But their impact on education is intermittent and indirect. The strength of the women's movement in relation to education, and the responses of educational institutions, depend largely on what is happening in communities across the country, on the state of the economy, the structure of the family, the provision of social services, and the status of women in other spheres of life. The organization of employment, the family, the media, poverty, racism, and health care, to name only some of the most important areas, affect the provision of education and the uses women make of the education that is available. It is important to keep in mind the social embeddedness of education as an antidote to calls for reform that place the entire onus for change on teachers and students. The provision of equal pay for work of equal value, the provision of child care services for preschool children and after-school hours, the extension of opportunities for native women, and an increase in the resources available to the poor would all increase women's chances for an equal education.

What the future holds will depend on the commitment to equality that is generated in every community across the country. There are many reasons to be optimistic, because awareness of women's inequality has been heightened over the past twenty years, and attention to women's concerns has been institutionalized in a variety of laws, in administrative mechanisms, and in the increased representation of women in positions of authority. However, with cutbacks in educational expenditures, an uncertain economic climate, and the emergence of a small but vocal right-wing opposition to the women's movement, every step is uncertain. A constitutional change designed to enshrine women's equality in the constitution, for example, has been used mainly by those who want to attack programs designed especially for women. Women's studies programs are always being questioned and have declined in some areas of the country. We have no assurance that the women's movement will march onward and upward, bringing further changes that will enhance women's opportunities. The prospects for the 1990s include more struggles about women's educational opportunities.

NOTES

1. M. Meissner, E. W. Humphries, S. M. Meiss, and W. J. Scheu, "No Exit for Wives: Sexual Division of Labour and the Cumulation of Household Demands," *Canadian Review of Sociology and Anthropology* 12 (1975): 424–439; S. Clark and A. Harvey, "The Sexual Division of Labour: The Use of Time." *Atlantis* 2 No. 1 (1976): 46–66.

2. Statistics Canada, *Women in Canada: A Statistical Report* (Ottawa: Minister of Supply and Services, 1985), pp. 1–5.

3. Ibid., p. 27.

4. Quoted in A. Prentice and S. Houston, *Family, School and Society in 19th Century Canada* (Toronto: Oxford University Press, 1975), pp. 253–255.

5. S. Marks and C. Gaffield, "Women at Queen's University: 1895–1905. A Little Sphere All Their Own," *Ontario History* 78, No. 4 (1986): 331–346.

6. *Women in Canada*, p. 36.

7. Ibid., p. 36.

8. *British Columbia Public School Report, 1900* (Victoria, B.C.: Government Printers, 1900).

9. A. L. Robb and B. G. Spencer, "Education: Enrollment and Attainment," in G. Cook, ed., *Opportunities for Choice* (Ottawa: Information Canada, 1976), pp. 53–92.

10. Women's Bureau, Labour Canada, *Women in the Labour Force* (1986–1987 Edition) (Ottawa: Minister of Supply and Services, 1987), p. 78

11. *Women in Canada*, p. 36.

12. Royal Commission on the Status of Women, *Final Report* (Ottawa: Information Canada, 1970), p. 168.

13. Women's Bureau, *Women in the Labour Force,* p. 70.

14. Ibid., p. 28.

15. Ibid., pp. 74 and 76.

16. See N. Jackson, *Between Home and School: The Crisis in Educational Resources* (Ottawa: Canadian Teachers Federation, 1982); A. Griffith and D. Smith, "Constructing Cultural Knowledge: Mothering as Discourse," in J. Gaskell and A. McLaren, eds., *Women and Education: A Canadian Perspective* (Calgary: Detselig, 1987), pp. 87–104.

17. S. Sharzer, "Native People: Some Issues," in R. Abella, ed., *Equality in Employment,* Vol. 2. *Research Studies,* pp. 547–588.

18. Abella, *Equality in Employment,* Vol. 1, pp. 143–144.

19. M. S. Devereaux and E. Rechnitzer, *Higher Education—Hired? Sex Differences in Employment Characteristics of 1976-Post Secondary Graduates* (Ottawa: Minister of Supply and Services, 1980).

20. K. Seydegart and G. Spears, *Beyond Dialogue: Immigrant Women in Canada 1985–1990* (Ottawa: Erin Research, 1985).

21. *Women in Canada,* p. 35.

22. Employment and Immigration Canada, *Annual Statistical Bulletin, 1984–85* (Ottawa: Minister of Supply and Services, 1985), p. 72.

23. M. S. Devereaux, *One in Every Five: A Survey of Adult Education in Canada* (Ottawa: Minister of Supply and Services, 1985).

24. *Women in Canada,* p. 31, Table 2.

25. Secretary of State, *The Class of 82: Summary Report on the Findings of the 1984 National Survey of the Graduates of 1982* (Ottawa: Minister of Supply and Services, 1986), p. 52.

26. *Royal Commission on Industrial Training and Technical Education* (Ottawa: Queens Printer, 1913), p. 51.

27. For a discussion of home economics in Canada, see R. M. Stamp, "Teaching Girls Their God Given Place in Life," *Atlantis* 2, No. 2 (1977): 18–34; M. Danylewcyz, N. Fahmy-Eid, and N. Thiverge, "L'Enseignement Menager et les 'Home Economics' au Quebec et en Ontario au Debut du 20e Siecle: Une Analyze Comparee," in J. D. Wilson, ed., *An Imperfect Past: Education and Society in Canadian History* (Vancouver: Centre for Curriculum and Instruction, 1985); N. Sheehan, "National Issues and Curricula Issues: Women and Educational Reform, 1900–1930," in Gaskel and McLaren, eds. *Women and Education.*

28. *Royal Commission Report on the Status of Women in Canada. Information Canada* (Ottawa: Queens Printer, 1970), p. 161.

29. S. Pyke, "Children's Literature: Conceptions of Sex Roles," in E. Zureik and R. Pike, eds, *Socialization and Values in Canadian Society* (Toronto: McClelland & Stewart, 1975); J. Gaskell, "Stereotyping and Discrimination in the Curriculum," in J. D. Wilson and H. Stevenson, eds., *Precepts, Policy and Process: Perspectives on Contemporary Education* (Calgary: Detselig, 1977); L. Fisher and J. A. Cheyne, *Sex Roles: Biological and Cultural Interactions as Found in Social Science Research and Ontario Educational Media* (Toronto: Ontario Ministry of Education, 1977); Women in Teaching, "Text Book Study" (Vancouver: British Columbia Teachers Federation, 1975); C. Pascoe, "Sex Stereotyping Study," Halifax, mimeo, 1975; L. Cullin, "A Study into Sex Stereotyping in Alberta Elementary Textbooks" (Edmonton, Alberta, 1972), mimeo.

30. P. Galloway, *What's Wrong with High School English? It's Sexist—UnCanadian—Outdated* (Toronto: OISE Press, 1980); National Film Board, *Report of the National*

Board/Educators' Forum on Women's Studies in Secondary School (Ottawa, 1986).

31. *When I Grow Up—Career Expectations and Aspirations of Canadian Schoolchildren* (Ottawa: Government of Canada, Minister of Labor, 1986).

32. M. Baker, *What Will Tomorrow Bring? A Study of the Aspirations of Adolescent Women* (Ottawa: Canadian Advisory Council on the Status of Women, 1985), p. 160.

33. Council of Ministers of Education, *Women's Issues in Education in Canada* (Toronto, 1987).

34. R. Abella, *Report of the Royal Commission on Equality in Employment* (Ottawa, 1985).

35. New Brunswick Advisory Council on the Status of Women, *Plan of Action on the Status of Women in Education* (New Brunswick, 1984.)

36. Science Council of Canada, *Who Turns the Wheel? Proceedings of a Workshop on the Science Education of Women in Canada* (Ottawa, 1982).

37. Ibid.; J. Whyte, *Girls into Science and Technology* (London: Routledge & Kegan Paul, 1986); B. Collis, "Adolescent Females and Computers: Real and Perceived Barriers," in Gaskel and McLaren, eds., *Women and Education.*

38. See, for example, Committee to Advance the Status of Housework, "All in a Day's Work: An ESL Kit of the Value of Housework" (Toronto, 1981); Barb Thomas, "Multiculturalism at Work: A Guide to Organized Change" (Toronto: YWCA, 1987); A. Prentice, *Canada and the International Women's Movement: A Teaching Unit for Intermediate History* (Toronto: OISE, 1977).

39. M. O'Brien, *The Politics of Reproduction* (London: Routledge & Kegan Paul, 1981).

40. M. Eichler and J. Lapointe "On the Treatment of the Sexes in Research" (Ottawa: Social Sciences and Humanities Research Council, 1985), p. 5.

41. V. Strong Boag. "Mapping Women's Studies in Canada: Some Signposts," *Journal of Educational Thought* 17 No. 2 (1983): 94–111; S. Brodribb, "Canadian Universities: A Learning Environment for Women?" *Resources for Feminist Research* 12, No. 3 (1983): 70–71.

42. R. Hamilton, "Feminists in the Academy: Intellectuals or Political Subversives?" *Queen's Quarterly* 92 No. 1 (1985): 13.

43. R. S. Abella, *Report of the Commission on Equality in Employment* (Ottawa: Minister of Supply and Services, 1984), p. 8.

23
THE UNITED STATES

Maxine S. Seller

Women's education in the United States has been shaped both by ideologies about women's innate nature and proper "place," and by the social and economic roles women have actually played. Because these ideologies and roles usually relegated women to a separate and inferior sphere in a male-dominated society, women's education has generally been different from and inferior to that of men. Yet women have struggled to widen their access to education and to shape it to their needs and purposes. This chapter will describe the institutions American women attended, what they studied, and the uses they made of their education. It will also describe the factors that led to change. "Progress" will be assessed not only by increases in educational attainment over time, but also by the narrowing of the educational gap between women and men and by the extent to which education helps women control their lives.

COLONIAL BEGINNINGS

Influenced by the Biblical view that woman had brought sin into the world and by a long classical and European tradition of mysogyny, colonial Americans viewed women as the "weaker vessel," morally, intellectually, and physically inferior to men.[1] Women's work in homemaking and domestic manufacture, in childrearing, and in the fields and shops was essential to the survival and growth of the colonies. Yet women had no political rights and, except in special circumstances, no control over their property or their children. Free women were subordinated to their fathers or husbands, and indentured servants and black slaves were ruled by their masters.

Despite women's inferior social and legal status, frontier conditions dictated that their education in the early years was similar in many respects to that of their brothers. In the seventeenth century, the education of both took place primarily in the home and focused on the acquisition of survival skills, although the skills were gender specific. Children were sometimes put out as apprentices, boys more often than girls, but most boys learned farming or crafts from their fathers and most girls learned the preservation and preparation of food, the manufacture of clothing, the use of medicinal herbs, and other aspects of house-wifery from their mothers. The household was the center of work, education, and family life for men and women.

In the seventeenth century, few Americans, female or male, had the resources, leisure, or need for much formal education. Children learned to read from their parents or minister if they learned to read at all. Since literacy was useful mainly for the reading of the Bible, an activity appropriate for both sexes in the staunchly Protestant colonies, a child's chance of being literate depended mostly on parental literacy or proximity to a village. Nevertheless, even in the seventeenth century there was a gap between male and female attainment; about a third of white women could read compared to about half of the men.[2]

By the mid-eighteenth century, the "starving times" were over, and subsistence farming gave way to exchange. As contractual relationships replaced the older face-to-face negotiations and life became more complex, the need for formal education increased. Well-to-do families hired tutors for their children; churches and charitable societies opened schools for the poor (including, in some cases, American Indians and slaves); New England towns opened quasi-public district schools; and private schools sprang up in the growing towns. On the eve of the American Revolution, nine colleges offered a classical education, including Latin, Greek, and mathematics, to prepare young men for professions and political leadership.

The expansion of schooling at all levels in the eighteenth century was linked to commerce and politics, from which women were excluded, rather than to religion. Education was still an expensive and relatively scarce commodity; therefore, it was available to women only on a limited and attenuated basis. Girls in wealthy homes might benefit from the family tutor or their father's library, but they could not attend secondary schools, colleges, or even the New England district schools. Upwardly mobile young men could study mathematics, geography, navigation, and bookkeeping as well as the college preparatory classical curriculum in private academies, a curriculum that prepared them for commerce, politics, and professions. Private schools offered young women of upwardly mobile families dancing, music, and fancy needlework, pious treatises on deferential female behavior, and watered down academic texts such as *The Lady's Geography* and *Newton's Ladies Philosophy*. This curriculum prepared women for marriage and—unrealistically—the indolent life of an upper class

English "lady," a life even well-to-do American women were rarely able to lead. Less affluent girls might learn to read and to count in "dame schools" taught by needy women in their homes, but few learned to write. Writing was taught separately from reading in colonial America, often in a special "writing school." As a skill associated with business and other areas of public life, it was seen as more appropriate for boys than for girls.[3]

As a result of differential access, the expansion of schooling in eighteenth-century America widened the educational gap between women and men. Men in New England advanced to near universal literacy on the eve of the Revolution (1775), while more than half of the women remained illiterate.[4] Eighteenth-century men's literacy was strongly linked to social class, whereas women's was a function of gender. In Boston, for example, all women shared a literacy rate similar to that of the poorest men.[5] Handicapped by lack of formal education, many women felt—and were—less prepared than men to cope with the complexities of an increasingly commercial society and, after 1775, with political revolution, war, and nation building.[6]

NINETEENTH-CENTURY PROGRESS

Between 1800 and 1920, the United States grew from a string of preindustrial states on the Atlantic coast to an urban, industrial giant with colonies of its own. As the country underwent first a commercial and then an industrial revolution, men left the household for the shop, the factory, or the office. Poverty forced lower class, black, and immigrant women to leave home also, to enter the paid workforce as domestics or factory hands. Most native-born white women remained at home, which was now defined, indeed virtually sanctified, as the only proper sphere for the "true" woman. Here they were expected to exemplify the piety, sexual purity, submissiveness, and domesticity of "true womanhood," to rear children with minimal assistance from men preoccupied with making money, and to provide emotional and logistical support for their husbands' entry into the competitive capitalist economy.[7] Women's education reflected the ideology of "separate spheres" that dominated nineteenth- and early twentieth-century thought and behavior. Changes in women's education reflected women's effort to redefine and enlarge their sphere and, in some cases, to break out of it altogether.

Despite the ideology of separate spheres and, indeed, in some ways because of it, women's education made enormous strides in the nineteenth century, both in absolute numbers and relative to the education of men. In the early nineteenth century, many formerly all-male academies opened their doors to women, as did the district schools of New England. Academies for women were opened, often by women with funding and support from other women, including Emma Willard's Troy Female Seminary (1823), Catherine Beecher's Hartford Female Seminary (1828), and Mary Lyons' Mt. Holyoke Seminary (1837). Academies provided secondary, even collegiate education and a first taste of living away from home for thousands of women. Many of the women who attended academies later established schools of their own or became teachers in the new public schools.[8]

While academies served relatively privileged women, the creation of public elementary schools in the antebellum North, Midwest and, a few decades later, in the South as well, provided education for many more. By midcentury, 90 percent of all American schoolchildren, boys and girls, were enrolled in the new state-supported common, or public, schools.[9] The common schools were co-educational from their inception because they were not meant to teach vocations or prepare students for college. Rather, they were created to provide a shared civic culture, to Americanize immigrants, to discipline people for the work routines of the commercial and industrial society, and to teach morals and basic skills, goals applicable to children of both sexes. Because sex differentiation was taken for granted virtually everywhere else, separate public schools for girls were viewed as an unnecessary expense.

Public secondary as well as elementary schools became available in the nineteenth century, gradually replacing most private academies. Worcester, Massachusetts, opened the first public high school for girls in 1824, and by 1890 there were 2,526 public high schools in the nation, some single sex but most coeducational.[10] Although a relatively small percentage of all children, perhaps 5 percent, finished high school in the late nineteenth century, two-thirds of those who did were girls. Indeed, because of the preponderance of girls in the high schools, women had a higher mean educational attainment than men in the late nineteenth and early twentieth centuries.[11] Unless they aspired to college and a profession, middle-class males left school for work, where they could advance through on-the-job training. Middle-class women of the same age were thought to need protection and supervision; thus, parents sent daughters to high school to keep them safe and busy in the years between childhood and marriage.

By the end of the century, some parents were sending daughters to high school because secondary school education trained them for employment as teachers and office workers. Teacher training was also available by midcentury in a new, predominantly female institution, the normal school. The first normal school opened in Massachusetts in 1838, and by 1892 there were 178 such schools nationwide, many of which became teachers' colleges in the twentieth century.[12]

Collegiate and professional as well as secondary education became available in antebellum America. Oberlin College admitted women in 1837, the first of many small, religious-sponsored western colleges to do so. By the closing decades of the century, women were also attending elite women's colleges such as Vasssar (1865), Wellesley and Smith (1875), and Bryn Mawr (1884). Many more, however, (over 70 percent) attended coeducational colleges and universities, especially the inexpensive state land grant institutions (see Table 23.1). By 1890, women constituted 35.9 percent of all undergraduates and 13.3 percent of all graduate students, including 5.5 percent of medical, 2 percent of dental, and 2.1 percent of pharmacy students.[13] Seventeen female medical colleges

Table 23.1
Women Enrolled in Institutions of Higher Education, 1870–1980

Year	Number of Women enrolled (thousands)	Percentage of all students enrolled	College women as % of 18–21-year-old women	College Women as % of 18–24-year-old women
1870	11	21.0	0.7	—
1880	40	33.4	1.9	—
1890	56	35.9	2.2	—
1900	85	36.8	2.8	—
1910	140	39.6	3.8	—
1920	283	47.3	7.6	—
1930	481	43.7	10.5	5.7
1940	601	40.2	12.2	7.1
1950	806	30.2	17.9	9.9
1960	1,223	37.9	—	15.4
1970	2,884	41.9	—	23.5
1975	3,847	45.4	—	27.7
1980	5,694	51.8	—	37.9

Sources: Mabel Newcomer, A Century of Higher Education for American Women (New York, 1959), p. 46. U.S. Bureau of the Census, National center for Education Statistics, Digest of Education Statistics (Washington, d.C., 1962, 1971, 1976, 1980, 1982, 1983. Barbara Miller Solomon, In The Company of Educated Women: A History of Women and Higher Education in America, New Haven: Yale University Press, 1985, pp. 63, 64.

opened between 1848 and 1895, most of which closed when women were finally admitted to coeducational medical colleges at the turn of the century.[14] Law was even more resistant than medicine, but in 1910 fifty-two women were graduated from the nation's law schools.[15]

Educational progress took place in informal as well as school settings. Middle-class white women established physiological, literary, and other self-improvement societies; women's clubs, missionary and charitable associations; and societies for abolitionism, temperance, suffrage, and other reforms. These organizations provided training in research, writing, public speaking, and administrative skills as well as imparting information to members and others. Separate black and ethnic women's organizations carried out similar educational activities. Minority women's societies also provided social and advocacy services for their communities, and, unlike their mainstream counterparts, included working-class as well as middle-class members.[16]

Although the "natural rights" ideology and rationalism of the Enlightenment were sometimes invoked, women's educational progress in the nineteenth century was usually justified by appeals to the separate spheres ideology. Better education would make women more efficient homemakers, more useful and agreeable companions for their husbands, and better mothers. The dramatic educational progress of the antebellum years was based on two new ideologies, "Republican motherhood" and "Christian nurture." Women were to insure the survival of the Republic by instilling virtue and patriotism in their sons and to insure the salvation of their children (and errant husbands and brothers as well) by religious instruction and example. They needed education, it was argued, in order to fulfill these awesome responsibilities.[17]

Better education was justified as enabling women to teach other people's children as well as their own. The employment of young, unmarried women as elementary school teachers in the new public schools was a logical extension of "Republican motherhood" and "Christian nurture," and a response to economic and social needs. As the men who had formerly dominated teaching found more lucrative occupations in the expanding capitalist economy, the cheap labor of women (who had few occupational alternatives) in the expanding schools was seen as essential. Educators such as Catherine Beecher prepared women for teaching, which they saw as an opportunity for women to serve others, improve society, and be self-supporting in a respectable profession of their own.

Economic and social change as well as ideology contributed to educational improvement. As the production of clothing and food moved from home to factory, families could spare more time for daughters' schooling. Later marriages also left more time for higher education, which some women could now finance by factory work or teaching. Moreover, as men moved west leaving large numbers of women unmarried, and as recurring economic crises reduced even married women to sudden poverty, women pursued education as insurance against dependency.

Finally, advances in nineteenth-century women's education were linked to the growth of the women's rights movement. Officially launched at Seneca Falls, New York, in 1848, "first wave" feminism was fueled at least in part by the anger of educated middle-class women at being excluded from the political enfranchisement recently extended even to uneducated white males. The Seneca Falls Declaration of Sentiments demanded not only suffrage and property rights for women, but also access to higher and professional education. Most women did not yet support the egalitarian political and economic demands of the Seneca Falls Declaration, but virtually all women, and many men as well, supported its stand on education.

The relationship between feminism and the expansion of women's education was symbiotic. Educated women, often former teachers or physicians, fought for expanded rights for women, winning first property rights and then suffrage, and feminists fought for, and won, expanded educational opportunity. Feminists lobbied, petitioned, and propagandized in speeches and in the press, and when all else failed, even bought their way into male educational institutions—Johns Hopkins Medical College, for example, in 1889.[18] A broad-based coalition of physiological societies, missionary societies, women's clubs, and other women's organizations endowed women's academies, built women's medical schools and hospitals, and provided scholarships and moral support to women seeking higher and professional education.[19]

Although the nineteenth-century movement for women's education was broadly based, the gains were not evenly distributed. By midcentury, the literacy gap between men and women was virtually eliminated in the North and Midwest, but illiteracy remained high among white southern women, both in absolute terms and relative to southern men. Frontier women, too, were at an educational disadvantage, as the hardships and isolation of initial settlement moved westward.

Immigrant women—Irish, Germans, and Scandinavians in the antebellum years and Southern and Eastern Europeans at the close of the century—were often kept out of school to care for younger siblings, to work, or, especially in the case of Mediterranean or Latino immigrants, to protect their reputations and prepare for marriage. Foreign-born Catholic girls attended parochial schools or, in extreme cases, no schools at all, because their parents disapproved of the Protestant or secular tone of the public school or, in the early twentieth century, its strident Americanization. Foreign-born East European Jewish girls usually left school early to help finance the education of brothers or of younger siblings, including younger sisters. Accustomed to moving more freely outside the family setting than women of many other ethnic groups, Jewish women were especially likely to take advantage of the education offered by night schools, settlement houses, and labor unions.[20]

Educational opportunities for black women in the antebellum years were meager in both the South and the North. Fearful of slave revolts, southern states outlawed the education of slaves. Northern states excluded their small communities of free blacks from the public schools or segregated them in inferior "African" schools. Fortunate black women in the North were educated in private schools established by abolitionists, or, more often, the black community itself. A few attended abolitionist-oriented colleges such as Oberlin or Wilberforce.[21]

Education for blacks in the North improved in the closing decades of the century, as public schools in many cities became integrated. Most nineteenth-century blacks continued to live in the rural South, however, where separate and dismally unequal public elementary schools provided a meager curriculum in basic skills to blacks able to get to them. Public high schools were not available until well into the twentieth century. Only a few southern black women attended quality black institutions such as Fisk University in Nashville, Tennessee, or Howard University in Washington, D.C. Most who went beyond the elementary level attended missionary colleges, industrial schools like Hampton Institute or Tuskegee, or public black land grant colleges. Industrial and land grant institutions offered normal school training, mostly at the secondary level or even below. Influenced by Booker T. Washington's advocacy of industrial training for blacks and by the views of northern philanthropists as well as by financial need, their programs for women students increasingly emphasized washing, ironing, cooking, and sewing, "uplift" through domesticity.[22] Government- and church-sponsored schools for American Indians also emphasized domestic skills for women as a means of "civilizing" native populations. Indian women were not uncommonly placed in white homes as maids as part of their education.[23]

By teaching black and Indian women housework, the lowest paid and lowest status occupation, schools were reinforcing hierarchies of race and social class as well as gender. Nineteenth-century education reinforced traditional sex roles for more privileged women as well. Most women at Oberlin College in the antebellum years studied a less demanding "ladies course," and all were required to wash and mend clothes for the male students—good training for the future wives of struggling ministers and missionaries.[24] After the 1880s, women at coeducational colleges were confined to special dormitories and carefully "protected" from contact with men. Promoting upper class sex roles, Smith College hired a "director of social culture" to "preserve and increase those graces of manners and of social life which we justly esteem so highly."[25]

If many aspects of women's school experience in the nineteenth century reinforced female separateness and inferiority, other aspects subtly undermined it. Schools responded not only to the separate spheres ideology, but also to considerations of convenience and institutional tradition. Since convenience dictated that public elementary schools teach both sexes together, girls had the same chance as boys to win a spelling bee or read a prize-winning essay to an assembly of parents and neighbors. Because women's academies were modeled after male academies, women academy students demonstrated their academic achievements at public examinations at a time when it was not considered proper for women to speak in public. Thus, in both public and private schools many women participated in institutional cultures that rewarded "unwomanly" competitiveness and achievement. Moreover, women teachers and professors in the classroom (even under the authority of a male principal, school board, or college president) provided models of female independence and intellectuality.

Academic content as well as academic culture undermined traditional ideas. Since academic work was seen as mental discipline rather than preparation for vocation, boys and girls studied an identical curriculum in the public elementary schools. Although women's academies were often criticized for shallowness and for teaching frivolous subjects, many academies and colleges offered the same "English" (as opposed to classical) curriculum as men's schools at the same academic level and often from the same texts. Women's higher education paid less attention to ancient languages and more attention to modern languages and science, but by the end of the century men's education, too, had moved away from the classics.[26] Improvements in women's education did not eliminate negative stereotypes and discrimination, but with women studying the same subjects as men and often outperforming them, proponents of women's mental inferiority were increasingly on the defensive.[27]

Better education did not produce political and economic equality in the nineteenth century, but it did enhance women's control over their lives in many ways. By writing letters to family and friends, educated women in a mobile society were able to maintain networks that provided invaluable support in the event of illness or financial or marital crisis.[28] Women reduced the number of children they bore from an average of six at the beginning of the century to fewer than three at the century's close, a reduction social historians have attributed to education as well as, and independently of, urbanization and social mobility.[29] Education promoted choice in marriage as well as childbearing, allowing women to postpone marriage or, especially for the first generation of college women, forego it altogether. At the end of the nineteenth century, fewer than half of all college women married.[30]

Education helped women enlarge their allotted sphere, extending "feminine" concerns for morality and social welfare from the home to the community and ultimately to the nation. Schooling gave women the self-confidence and the speaking, writing, and organizing skills to become involved in church, charitable, and reform activities, including abolition, temperance, peace, the common school movement, the labor movement, and, as already noted, women's rights. Some schools provided not only skills, but also motivation and opportunity. Oberlin College, for example, and the antebellum Quaker boarding schools in the Delaware Valley actively promoted abolitionism and other moral reform activity among their students.[31]

Linkages between schooling and labor force participation in the nineteenth century were not strong. Although women's share of the paid labor force increased gradually throughout the century, in 1890 it was only 17 percent. Most nineteenth-century working women were blacks or immigrants, and they usually worked as domestic servants, laundresses, farm workers, or factory operatives, occupations requiring little, if any, formal education.[32] Middle-class educated

women had few respectable opportunities for paid employment. Economic realities as well as ideology dictated that they remain at home, where many used
their education to help husbands who were missionaries, ministers, lawyers,
professors, or businessmen.[33]

Gradually, new job opportunities for educated women emerged. The earliest
and most popular was teaching. During most of the century and in most parts
of the country, elementary school teaching was open to women who had completed only a few years of normal or secondary schooling, if that. By midcentury,
one in every four women in Massachusetts was or had been a teacher, and by
1900 over half a million women were staffing the nation's still rapidly expanding
schools.[34] By midcentury, too, the spread of literacy enabled significant numbers
to earn their living as writers and editors of novels, magazines, and newspapers,
especially publications directed at women and children. Urbanization created
jobs for women with good basic skills as shopkeepers and, by the end of the
century, department store clerks.

In the closing decades of the century, new technologies—the telephone, the
telegraph, and, most important, the typewriter—opened a new category of "respectable" work for women with some high school training, office or clerical
work, which would become the fastest growing field for women's employment
in the years ahead.[35] The Civil War opened nursing to women, and by the end
of the century it had become a profession with its own training programs and
schools. Jane Adams, Sophonisba Breckinridge, Edith and Grace Abbott, and
other college-trained women extended women's accepted roles as caretakers of
the poor into a new occupation, social work, which would soon require a college
degree. As the century drew to a close, a small but conspicuous group of educated
women were entering traditional male professions, becoming pharmacists, den-
tists, lawyers, and college professors. In 1900, there were 7,000 women physicians.[36] Nineteenth-century women had not achieved equality, but they had
narrowed the educational gap between themselves and men, and a small but
growing number had found uses for education within their "separate sphere"
and outside of it as well.

MALE "BACKLASH" : 1890–1920

The opening decades of the twentieth century seemed to promise even more
rapid advances. High school attendance became the norm rather than the exception. Girls continued to outnumber boys as both students and graduates (except
among immigrants), a reflection of the fact that men could find employment
without education, whereas girls needed high school to qualify for "good"
women's jobs in teaching and office work.[37] Between 1890 and 1920, the percentage of women aged eighteen to twenty-one in college rose from 2.2 to 7.6
percent, and the proportion of women among all undergraduates rose from 35.9
to 47.3 percent. During the same three decades, the number of women gainfully

employed doubled and the number of professional women tripled.[38] By 1920, a quarter of all women were in the labor force. Moreover, 11.9 percent of them were classified by the census as "professionals" compared to 3.4 percent of employed men.[39]

Minority as well as mainstream women appeared to gain. Good women's colleges opened for blacks, Spelman (formerly a secondary school) in 1924 and Bennett (formerly coeducational) in 1926. The number of Catholic colleges for women grew from three in 1900 to seventy-five in 1930. Jewish women surpassed the general population in educational attainment; by the 1930s, a remarkable 21 percent of New York City's college-age Jewish population, the daughters of East European Jewish immigrants, were enrolled in Brooklyn College or Hunter College.[40]

The three decades between 1890 and 1920 saw increasing numbers of women entering high school and college and increasing numbers of women participating in the workforce. However, the same three decades also saw a virulent and effective male "backlash" against these developments. Although the backlash did not halt the rise in women's educational attainment, by the mid-1920s it had checked women's progress in higher education in relation to men's. Equally important, it had channeled women's educational and occupational aspirations into areas that did not threaten male dominance. The opening decades of the twentieth century, the era of "progressive" reform for American education in general, were retrogressive for women.

Progress in women's education had never gone unopposed. In the Revolutionary Era, the educated woman was portrayed as pedantic, masculine, and "disgustingly slovenly in her person, indecent in her habits, imperious to her husband, and negligent of her children."[41] In the nineteenth century, opponents of higher and professional education for women argued, first, that women lacked the intelligence for such education; second, that it would ruin their morals and "unsex" them; and finally, that their health, sanity, and reproductive powers could not survive it.[42] Despite rebuttal by women educators and physicians and despite empirical evidence to the contrary, these arguments survived into the twentieth century. More important, the twentieth century introduced a new set of arguments. Reflecting male insecurity in the increasingly urban industrial society, these arguments were grounded in the new biological and social sciences.

As the frontier closed and physical work gave way to machines, American men were losing their traditional symbols of masculinity. Watching token numbers of women move into formerly male occupations and larger numbers of women, including perhaps their own wives and daughters, demand the vote, many worried about a blurring of sex roles.[43] They blamed the schools for feminizing males and luring females away from domesticity and urged educators to correct these mistakes. Equally important, critics blamed the educated, emancipated woman for a rising divorce rate, a falling birthrate (among native-born whites), juvenile delinquency, and other real or imagined evils of the new urban, industrial society. Schools could help solve social problems, they argued, by teaching the "new" woman to attend better to her traditional domestic and maternal duties.

Social Darwinists argued that women were lower on the biological hierarchy than men, less rational, less ethical, and had a mentality close to that of children. They also argued that civilization could progress only through sex-role specialization, with men active in public life and women passive and focused on the home. Prominent educators agreed, especially the pioneers of the new discipline of educational psychology, who dressed old prejudices against women in new, scientific garb. G. Stanley Hall, an early disciple of Sigmund Freud and author of the important treatise *Adolescence,* pronounced inherent sex differences to be so basic that schools should segregate women after puberty and educate them only for marriage and motherhood. Edward Thorndike, expert in the new field of educational testing and "individual differences," proclaimed that women were instinctively nurturing and submissive and unlikely to do creative intellectual work.[44] Research by academic women such as Helen Thompson and Leta Hollingworth refuted these views and stressed the emotional and intellectual similarities between the sexes, but this work attracted little attention.[45]

Between 1890 and 1920, the views of conservative critics and social scientists found expression in the schools and colleges in an increasingly sex-differentiated curriculum. This growing sex differentiation was a response not only to male fears and conservative ideology, but also to new pedagogical ideas and new economic needs. The emergence of the "comprehensive" multitract high schools and junior high school, the introduction of vocational and physical education, and the "progressive" idea that schools should prepare children for "life" rather than for college facilitated the introduction of sex-specific curricula. Equally instrumental was the demand for educated but inexpensive female labor in the growing clerical and service sectors of the maturing industrial economy.

New vocational curricula reflected the new ideologies and the new economic demands. As women's participation in low-paid but "respectable" office work grew, high school courses in typing and shorthand became so heavily female that they constituted a woman's curriculum. Although women as well as men held industrial jobs, young women were shut out of the new industrial arts programs in the schools and enrolled instead in supposedly parallel home economics courses, which did not usually provide saleable skills. Home economics fit well with the new emphasis on vocationalism because most educators thought homemaking was, or should be, women's true vocation. It also fit with efforts to Americanize immigrants and with the interests of businessmen in educating the middle-class housewife for a career of consumerism. Although commercial courses grew faster, by 1928 one of every three girls in public high schools was enrolled in a home economics class.[46]

Extracurricular activities, increasingly important in the new, comprehensive high schools and on the college campuses, also separated the sexes and reinforced traditional roles. In the late nineteenth and early twentieth centuries, girls were recruited into Little Mothers' Leagues in the high schools and into cultural activities in the colleges, whereas competitive team sports became a male preserve in both. Women at large universities such as Cornell and Berkeley were shut out of clubs and student government and ridiculed in the male-controlled student press. Women responded by building a social and cultural life of their own, including sororities and women's sports. This met the needs of many individuals and often preserved alternative female values; for example, women's athletics stressed participation rather than competition. However, women's campus culture lacked the status, legitimacy, and institutional support of its male counterpart.[47]

In higher and professional education, the opening decades of the twentieth century saw the strengthening and institutionalization of long-standing patterns of discrimination. Concerned that women, who already outnumbered men at some midwestern campuses, would "feminize" collegiate education and lower the prestige of their institutions, the new research universities limited the admission of women or segregated them in separate or coordinate women's colleges. Coeducational institutions segregated women by program, establishing teacher-training programs, which were overwhelmingly female, and home economics departments, which became ghettos for women faculty in the sciences and social sciences. By the 1920s, it was clear that the more prestigious the institution, the fewer and more isolated were the women on its campus, as students or as faculty.

Another turn-of-the-century development with negative consequences for women's education was the professionalization of many increasingly desirable occupations. Entry into these occupations came under the control of centralized, male-dominated professional associations that used their new power to exclude women. To protect the growing prestige and economic rewards of their profession from the dangers of "feminization," coeducational medical schools placed quotas of 5 percent on women students, and hospitals refused to provide internships and other postgraduate education even for this small number.[48] Universities denied women entry into training programs for lucrative and prestigious new "male" professions such as engineering, architecture, and business. Instead, they educated women for socially valuable but low-status, low-paid "semi-professions," including teaching, social work, nursing, librarianship, and laboratory technology. In these and other "women's" fields, the female practitioner was usually supervised by male authorities.

YEARS OF COMPROMISE: 1920–1960

Between 1890 and 1920, educational institutions helped to institutionalize an unstated compromise on the "woman question," a compromise that governed women's education and employment, with modifications, from the 1920s to the 1960s. Women's occupational roles were expanded but kept subordinate to those of men. Women would continue to increase their educational attainment, but they would be educated for homemaking or for work that was compatible with (or, like the formerly male occupation of clerical work, could be redefined as compatible with) traditional sex roles and gender hierarchies.[49] Most women accepted the compromise because clerical work and women's professions opened to them by high school and college education were more desirable than factory or domestic work, because psychologists and peers assured them that "women's" occupations were appropriate to their nature, and because discrimination in education and employment blocked their access to predominantly male occupations.

Educated women also accepted the lower status, lower paid jobs offered to them because they expected to leave the workforce for marriage in a few years, and from the 1920s through the 1950s, most did so. Although Charlotte Perkins Gilman and other late nineteenth- and early-twentieth-century feminists had called for kitchenless apartments and the collectivization of child care, societal supports for combining a career with marriage had not materialized, nor had men assumed domestic responsibilities. Thus, educated women in the opening decades of the century—indeed, until the post-World War II period—usually felt compelled to choose between marriage and a career, and most chose marriage. Moreover, after 1920 college attendance was no longer unusual among middle-class women. Therefore, most no longer felt the sense of "specialness" that had enabled many of their nineteenth-century predecessors to resist societal expectations. Finally, women's opportunities in the decades after 1920 suffered from the fact that organized feminism declined after the passage of women's suffrage in 1919. Although some feminist activity survived, the broad-based women's movement that had supported women's entry into higher education and into male-dominated occupations in the nineteenth century was no longer operative.

The ideological backlash and institutional changes that began between 1890 and 1920 had a dampening effect in the decades that followed both on the educational progress of women compared to men and on women's uses of education. Women had always been less likely than men to attend college, but after 1920 the gap in collegiate education, which had been narrowing, began to widen. Women's share of the total college enrollment declined from a high of 47.3 percent in 1920 to 30.2 percent in 1950.[50] Women's inroads into male professions, always modest, lost momentum after 1930 and, in some cases, were actually reversed. The percentage of women with doctorates decreased from 18 percent in 1930 to 10 percent in 1950, and women's share of positions as college presidents and faculty fell from 32 to 23 percent.[51] (See Table 23.2.) The proportion of women physicians declined between 1920 and 1930, and a woman architect, accountant, or engineer was a rarity.[52] The number of women lawyers increased, but many found employment only as law clerks or legal secretaries. Impressive figures about increasing numbers of women professionals (both before and after 1920) were misleading. Three-quarters of all women professionals were teachers or nurses, "semiprofessionals" with low status, low pay, and, in the

Table 23.2
Trends in Academic Degrees and Faculty Employment, 1870–1980

Year	Percentage of women as undergraduates	Percentage of women with bachelor's or first professional degree	Percentage of women with doctorates	Percentage of women as faculty
1870	21	15	0	12
1880	32	19	6	36
1890	35	17	1	20
1900	35	19	6	20
1910	39	25	11	20
1920	47	34	15	26
1930	43	40	18	27
1940	40	41	13	28
1950	31	24	10	25
1960	36	35	10	22
1970	41	41	13	25
1971	42	42	14	22
1972	42	42	16	22
1973	43	42	18	23
1974	45	42	19	24
1975	45	43	21	24
1976	45	44	23	24
1977	48	44	24	25
1978	49	45	26	—
1979	—	46	28	26
1980	51	47	30	26

Sources: Patricia A. Graham, "Expansion and Exclusion: A History of Women in American Higher Education," Signs: Journal of Women in Culture and Society 3 (Summer 1978); U.S. Department of Health, Education and Welfare, National Center for Education Statistics, Digest of Education Statistics 1980, 1982. Mabel Newcomer, A Century of Higher Education for American Women (New York, 1959), p. 46. Solomon, In The Company of Educated Women, p. 133.

increasingly bureaucratic, male-controlled world of large schools and hospitals, little power or autonomy.[53] (See Table 23.3.)

In the first half of the twentieth century, as in the nineteenth, linkages between education and the labor market were not strong. Despite increasing levels of educational attainment and the expansion of clerical work and the "semiprofessions," the proportion of all women employed increased by only half of 1 percent between 1910 and 1940. There was a sudden spurt in women's employment between 1890 and 1910, but it reflected not the entry of educated women into the labor market, but an influx of uneducated Southern and Eastern European immigrants. As late as 1930, 57 percent of all women workers were still, as in the nineteenth century, blacks or immigrants.[54] Women's second-class status in the labor force compared to men was reflected in low wages, the result of occupational segregation by sex and the undervaluing of jobs usually held by women. In 1920, women's wages were 63 percent of those earned by men. This figure declined to a low of 57 percent in 1974.

The Great Depression of the 1930s and the aftermath of World War II compounded the negative impact of ideology and institutional change. The preponderance of women in the high schools ended during the Depression, when unemployment forced men back into the schools. Black women retained their proportional advantage over black men (but were still far behind whites) in high schools and colleges only because the need for black teachers gave them an advantage over black men in a racist job market.[55] Since men were still seen as the primary breadwinners, popular disapproval of the working woman became stronger than ever during the Depression, and women lost jobs to men even in the traditionally female-dominated semiprofessions of teaching, library science, and social work. In some cases, the employment losses continued beyond the Depression years; for example, the percentage of women among elementary school principals fell from 55 percent in 1928 to 22 percent in 1968.[56]

Although women filled men's places in the factories during the labor shortage of World War II, most were forced out of the better paid jobs (though often not out of the labor force altogether) when the war ended. Educational and job benefits for veterans, 97 percent of whom were men, weakened women's educational and employment position relative to that of men in the postwar period. In the decade after World War II, the U.S. government paid for the education of 2,232,000 veterans, only 64,728 of whom were women, and admonished employers to "hire a vet."[57] In the conservative postwar decade, social scientists, the media, and the government urged women to seek fulfillment in marriage, motherhood, and self-abnegation rather than in "selfish," masculine careerism.

FEMINISM AND CHANGE: THE 1960s–1980s

In the 1950s, most women acted on the advice given them by the government, the psychologists, and the media, marrying earlier and in larger numbers than at any time in the past hundred years and producing the bumper crop of offspring

Table 23.3
Women in Selected Professional Occupations, as a Percentage of All Workers in Those Fields, 1910–1982

Occupation	1910	1920	1930	1940	1950	1960	1970	1980
Lawyers	1.0	1.4	2.1	2.4	3.5	3.5	4.7	14.0
Physicians	6.0	5.0	4.0	4.6	6.1	6.8	8.9	14.3
Nurses	93.0	96.0	98.0	98.0	98.0	97.0	97.4	95.6
Social Workers	52.0	62.0	68.0	67.0	66.0	57.0	62.8	66.4
Librarians	79.0	88.0	91.0	89.0	89.0	85.0	82.0	83.4

Sources: Nancy Woloch, Women and the American Experience (New York, 1984), p. 546. Woloch cites as her sources: Cynthia Fuchs Epstein, Woman's Place: Options and Limits in Professional Careers (Berkeley, 1970). Employment and Earnings, Bureau of Labor Statistics, U.S. Department of Labor, January 1983. The Female-Male Earnings Gap: A Review of Employment and Earnings Issues report 673, Bureau of Labor Statistics, U.S. Department of Labor, September 1982. 1970 Census of Population: Detailed Characteristics, United States Summary, Bureau of the Census, U.S. Department of Commerce. Solomon, In the Company of Educated Women, p. 127.

known as the "baby boom." By the late 1950s, however, a countertrend had begun. Increasing numbers of older women, so-called nontraditional students, were returning to the campus as undergraduate and graduate students to complete educations interrupted earlier. Even while women had been losing ground relative to men in higher education, the number of women in colleges and universities had continued to grow. Therefore, by the end of the 1950s, an unprecedented and growing "critical mass" of college-educated women had emerged. A similar trend was taking shape in employment. Responding to the demands of a consumer-oriented society, increasing numbers of women—including white, native-born, married women and mothers—began to enter the workforce, where they joined women who had taken jobs during World War II and refused to retire when the war was over.

The changes of the 1950s were so gradual as to be almost unnoticed, but this was not the case in the decades that followed. In just two decades—the mid-1960s to the mid-1980s—the negative trends in women's education and employment that had characterized the first half of the century were dramatically reversed, and the "compromise" that had institutionalized women's secondary position was no longer accepted. In the 1970s, the number of women undergraduates grew four times as rapidly as did the number of men. By the early 1980s, women were earning more than half of all undergraduate and master's degrees, over 30 percent of all doctorates, a quarter of all medical degrees, and more than a third of all law degrees.[58] The majority of a new, growing population of "nontraditional" older students returning to school were women. Women were still concentrated in the less prestigious institutions and programs, including the rapidly proliferating two-year, or community, colleges. But once again, as in the nineteenth century, they were making educational progress both in absolute terms and in relation to men.

The rise in the number and proportion of women in the paid workforce during the same period was even more dramatic. Women's labor force participation rose from 30 percent in 1940 to 42 percent in 1960, 50 percent in 1970, and 64 percent in 1986, including 62 percent of all mothers with children under eighteen.[59] The rise reflected both increased need and increased opportunity. Women of all ages and family situations went to work because inflation, divorce, and male unemployment and underemployment made it economically necessary and because the expansion of "women's jobs" in the clerical and service sectors made it possible.

In the latter half of the twentieth century, education and employment were closely linked, a situation unlike that of the nineteenth or even the early twentieth century. The same economic uncertainties that sent women into the job market in recent decades sent them into trade schools, colleges, and universities to obtain the credentials to improve their earning power. For the first time in American history, paid employment for women was positively rather than negatively correlated with education.[60]

As in the nineteenth century, educational progress in recent decades has been both a cause and an effect of organized feminism. An increase in the number of women completing both undergraduate and graduate school in the 1950s provided educated leaders for the women who came together in the 1960s to create a new women's movement, "third wave" feminism. ("First wave" feminism had written the Seneca Falls Declaration. "Second wave" feminism had culminated in suffrage.) In 1963, professional women in the Women's Bureau and the National Women's party (remnants of "second wave" feminism) used President John F. Kennedy's Commission on the Status of Women to launch a public discussion of discrimination in employment and education. In the same year Betty Friedan's best seller, *The Feminine Mystique,* expressed the educated housewife's dissatisfaction with mindless domesticity and consumerism, adding a second constituency. A third constituency, student activists from the civil rights and peace movements of the 1960s, shaped the movement's ideology by applying their hard-won insights about race and class oppression to the situation of women. Working women and the elderly added support, bringing in their concerns about job and wage discrimination, lack of child care, and poor health care. By the late 1960s, a loose coalition of professional and businesswomen, homemakers, students, and working women of all ages had formed a new feminist movement that would change many areas of American life, including education.

Led by a growing body of academics, feminists launched an unprecedented critique of education. Although nineteenth-century feminists had concentrated on getting women into schools, their late-twentieth-century counterparts investigated what schools did to women once they got there. Their studies showed that readers portrayed women as silly, helpless, and housebound, that arithmetic texts showed women cooking and sewing, but not earning money, and that history texts omitted women altogether. Studies of in-school behavior showed that teachers interacted more with boys than girls, reinforcing creativity in boys and conformity in girls; that teachers and counselors discouraged girls from taking the advanced science and mathematics courses necessary for well-paid occupations; and that vocational education, physical education, and extracurricular activities reinforced traditional sex roles. They also documented discrimination in school administration and on school boards.[61]

Extending the critique to higher education, feminists demonstrated that "coeds" were taken less seriously than male students, especially at the graduate level, that women had less access than men to scholarships and grants, and that women faculty were concentrated in traditionally female fields, low academic ranks, and less prestigious institutions. They noted, too, that minority women were doubly disadvantaged; in 1973, only 14 percent of black women were in college compared to 19 percent of black men and 25 percent of white men.[62]

Moving beyond the critique of male-dominated education, women developed alternative models. Feminist scholars recovered knowledge by and about women which had been excluded from their respective disciplines and began to reexamine the premises as well as the content of those disciplines.[63] A new, interdisciplinary field, women's studies, emerged. As the academic arm of political feminism, women's studies programs were centers for research about women, advocates for women, and testing grounds for nonhierarchical, participatory instruction and governance.[64]

Although an equal rights amendment to the constitution was defeated, feminists made important legislative and judicial gains in the 1960s and early 1970s, including the outlawing of sexual discrimination in employment and the legalization of abortion.[65] Women benefited from a range of educational reforms enacted during these years of social activism, including desegregation, bilingual education, compensatory and head start programs, the "education for all handicapped" act, federal aid to higher education, grant and loan programs for college students, and literacy and job training for adults. The most important educational reform specifically for women, however, was Title IX of the Educational Amendments of 1972. Title IX outlawed sex discrimination in admissions, in access to academic and extracurricular programs, including athletics, and in employment at any educational institution receiving federal funds (which included most institutions).[66] In addition, educational institutions receiving federal funds were required under the controversial affirmative action policy to seek out women and minorities for faculty and administrative positions.

Educational progress for women was supported in the 1960s and early 1970s by a political climate favorable to the pursuit of racial and gender equity through educational reform. Economic prosperity also facilitated change during these years by making it possible for many fields to absorb women without displacing men. Moreover, with many young men in the armed forces in Vietnam, opposition to the admission of women to universities and professional schools was muted. Despite the protests of disgruntled alumni, elite institutions such as Princeton, Yale, and Columbia finally admitted women, and by 1981 only 3 percent of all colleges were exclusively male.[67]

By the mid- and late 1970s, however, the social and political climate was less favorable to change. An economic recession in the mid-1970s led to retrenchment in education and employment and therefore to increased opposition to women in formerly male preserves. Politically, the nation moved toward the right—a move fueled by the dislocations of "deindustrialization," by a revival of religious fundamentalism, by nostalgia for "traditional values," and by a backlash against the social changes of the 1960s, including feminism. After the election of President Ronald Reagan in 1980, the federal government made no secret of its opposition to affirmative action. Never vigorously enforced, Title IX was effectively gutted by the *Grove City College v. Bell* decision of 1984, as were laws dealing with discriminataion on the basis of race, age, and disability.[68] Ideological as well as political reaction threatened women's gains. "Sociobiologists" argued, once again, that women's reproductive functions shaped their social roles, and psychologists found women's brains wrongly organized for mathematics or, indeed, abstract thought of any kind.[69]

By the late 1980s, sex discrimination in American education had been reduced but not eliminated.[70] Home economics and industrial arts classes were opened to both sexes, but in vocational high schools and community colleges girls studied cosmetology and secretarial and health-related fields, while boys studied auto mechanics, computers, and other technical fields.[71] Title IX created more opportunities for women to compete in high school and college athletics and made athletic scholarships available to women, but institutions continued to spend more money on male than on female athletics and the "integration" of male and female sports programs cost many women coaches their jobs.[72] Feminist scholarship flourished, but "by and large male-biased disciplinary frameworks remain firmly entrenched."[73]

Although women continued to make better grades than men in high school, their scores on the Scholastic Aptitude Tests were lower in both verbal and mathematical skills and they received only 35 percent of the scholarships based on these scores.[74] Although women's educational attainment equaled or exceeded men's at the bachelor's and master's levels, women, especially blacks, Hispanics, and Asians, were disproportionately concentrated in the less prestigious community colleges and state teachers colleges and relatively scarce in the prestigious research universities and technical institutes.[75] Moreover, despite affirmative action and a larger pool of qualified women, in the mid-1980s women held only 27 percent of faculty positions, about the same as in 1964. Black women held only 2 percent, Hispanic women 0.4 percent, Asian women 0.4 percent, and American Indian women less than 0.1 percent. Women faculty were disproportionately part time and untenured and earned about 20 percent less than comparably qualified male faculty.[76]

Although women made inroads into traditionally male occupations, they did not achieve parity with men (see Table 23.4). For example, between 1971 and 1981, women's share of master's degrees in business rose from 3.9 to 25 percent, in architecture from 14.1 to 29.1 percent, and in computer science from 10.3 to 23 percent.[77] Despite such gains, in the late 1980s women remained underrepresented in these and other scientific and technical fields close to the power centers of American life. Most women continued to receive their terminal degrees in education, allied health professions, library science, fine arts, and foreign languages, low prestige fields that remained 75 to 95 percent female.[78] Moreover, even in medicine and law, women were concentrated in the less prestigious, less lucrative areas, in pediatrics rather than surgical specialties, in family rather than corporate law.[79]

Not only was parity not reached, but also many special populations did not share equally in the gains. In the mid-1980s, the high school dropout rate of Hispanic women was more than double that of whites or blacks. Nor were disabled women getting the education they needed. Only a third of all children receiving "special education" for mental or physical disabilities were girls, and they were older and further behind in their schoolwork than comparable boys when they were identified. In 1982, the mean earnings for disabled women were $5,935, compared to $13,363 for disabled men, and the percentage of disabled women in the workforce was 7.4 percent compared to 22 percent of disabled

Table 23.4
Workers in Major Occupational Groups, by Sex, 1972 and 1985

Occupational Group	1972					1985				
	Thousands of Employed Wkrs.		Percent Women	Percent Distribution Among Occupations		Employed Wkrs.		Percent Women	Percent Distribution Among Occupations	
	Men	Women		Men	Women	Men	Women		Men	Women
Managerial and Professional Specialty	10,795	5,314	33	21	17	15,151	11,104	42	25	23
Executive, Administrative, Managerial	5,846	1,433	20	11	5	7,988	4,353	35	13	9
Professional Specialty	4,948	3,881	44	10	12	7,163	6,751	49	12	14
Technical, sales, and admin. support	9,561	14,958	60	19	45	11,715	21,715	65	19	46
Technicians & related support	1,188	740	38	2	2	1,780	1,584	47	3	3
Sales Occupations	5,093	3,473	41	10	11	6,554	6,095	48	11	13
Administrative support, incl. clerical	3,280	9,845	75	6	31	3,381	14,036	81	6	30
Service occupations	4,216	6,614	61	8	21	5,673	8,614	60	9	18
Private household	35	1,405	98	*	4	41	925	96	*	2
Protective service	1,122	78	7	2	*	1,480	233	14	2	0
Service, other	3,059	5,131	63	6	16	4,152	7,456	64	7	16

Precision, pro- duction, craft, repair	9,853	493	5	19	2	12,169	1,202	9	20	3
Operators, fab- ricators, and Laborers	13,201	4,183	24	26	13	12,697	4,256	25	21	9
Machine operators assemblers, inspectors	5,278	3,322	39	10	11	4,697	3,076	40	8	6
Transportation & material moving occs.	3,996	146	4	8	*	4,211	358	8	7	1
Helpers, laborers, others	3,926	715	15	8	2	3,789	822	18	6	2
Farming, forestry, fishing	3,250	593	15	6	2	2,992	579	16	5	1
Total	50,876	31,255	38	100	100	60,397	47,470	44	100	100

*Less than 0.5 percent.

Source: Barbara R. Bergmann, The Economic Emergence of Women, New York: Basic Books, Inc., Publishers, 1986, p. 70.

men.[80] The high dropout rate of teenage mothers suggested that the needs of many women for sex education, self-esteem, and emotional and logistical support were not being met.[81]

Equal educational attainment has not led to economic equality. Although women in traditionally male professions have gained, a sex-segregated job market still relegates most women to undervalued "pink-collar" clerical, retail sales, and service jobs. Only 3 percent of employed women are in the relatively well-paid skilled crafts as opposed to 20 percent of men.[82] In 1984, women college graduates earned 63 percent of what male college graduates earned and $2,427 a year less than male high school graduates. Moreover, two-thirds of the discrepancy represents discrimination, not inferior credentials or experience.[83] In 1984, one of every three female householders was designated as poor compared with one of eleven male householders.[84]

In recent decades, as in the nineteenth century, education has enhanced women's control over their lives. It has enabled them to use contraception more effectively, it has increased their participation in politics, and it has widened their employment options.[85] Education has not equalized the economic status of men and women, but it has mitigated the effects of discrimination; women college graduates earn 40 percent more than women with only a high school diploma, and their jobs are likely to be more interesting and of higher status.[86]

Unlike nineteenth- and early-twentieth-century women, most late-twentieth-century women refuse to choose between marriage and career, determined to "have it all." Like their earlier counterparts, however, most still do so with minimal support from husbands and outside agencies. The trend toward more labor force participation for women, including more inroads into traditionally male occupations, seems likely to continue. The future of the recent trend toward greater educational and economic equity, however, remains uncertain, depending in large measure on the general political climate and on the fate of "third wave" feminism.

Throughout American history, schools have transmitted traditional ideas about female inferiority and women's biologically determined sphere. At the same time, schools have given some women the skills and confidence to reject these ideas. The history of women's education in the United States suggests that education can widen the economic and status gap between the sexes or narrow it, and that women's efforts to influence education, especially through organized feminism, have been instrumental in determining which it will do. The history of women's education in the United States also suggests that, although educational change can mitigate gender inequality, it cannot eliminate it without radical supporting changes in the home, in the workplace, and in political and social ideologies.

NOTES

1. For background on colonial ideologies about women, see Mary Sumner Benson, *Women in Eighteenth-Century America: A Study of Opinion and Social Usage* (New York: Columbia University Press, 1935).

2. Kenneth A. Lockbridge, *Literacy in Colonial New England: An Enquiry into the Social Context of Literacy in the Early Modern West* (New York: W. W Norton, 1974), pp. 38–42; Julia Cherry Spruill, *Women's Life and Work in the Southern Colonies* (New York: W. W. Norton 1938, 1972), p. 187.

3. Spruill, *Women's Life and Work*, pp. 185–231. See also Thomas Woody, *A History of Women's Education in the United States*, 2 vols. (New York and Lancaster, Pa.: Science Press, 1929), vol. 1, pp. 124–268.

4. Lockbridge, *Literacy in Colonial New England*, p. 97.

5. Ibid., p. 42.

6. Historian Mary Beth Norton found the diaries of women fortunate enough to be able to write filled with laments about their helplessness, failings, and "imbecility." Nancy Woloch, *Women and the American Experience* (New York: Alfred A. Knopf, 1984), p. 73.

7. Barbara Welter, "The Cult of True Womanhood, 1820–1860," *American Quarterly* 18 (Summer 1966): 151–175; Nancy F. Cott, *The Bonds of Womanhood: Women's Sphere in New England, 1780–1833* (New Haven, Conn.: Yale University Press, 1977).

8. Anne Firor Scott, "The Ever Widening Circle: The Diffusion of Feminist Values from Troy Female Seminary 1822–1872," *History of Education Quarterly* 19 (Spring 1979); Joan N. Burstyn, "Catherine Beecher and the Education of American Women," in Esther Katz and Anita Rapone, eds., *Women's Experience in America: A Historical Anthology* (New York: Transaction Books, 1980), pp. 219–234.

9. Maris Vinovskis and Richard M. Bernard, "Beyond Catherine Beecher: Female Education in the Antebellum Period," *Signs* 3, No. 4 (Summer 1978): 856–869.

10. Barbara J. Harris, *Beyond Her Sphere: Women and the Professions in American History* (Westport, Conn.: Greenwood Press, 1978), p. 79.

11. James P. Smith and Michael P. Ward, *Women's Wages and Work in the Twentieth Century* (Santa Monica, Calif.: Rand, Prepared for the National Institute of Child Health and Human Development), October 1984, p. 35.

12. Woody, *A History of Women's Education*, pp. 545–546, 471, 482.

13. Mabel Newcomer, *A Century of Higher Education for American Women* (New York: Harper, 1959), pp. 37, 46, 49.

14. Mary Roth Walsh, *Doctors Wanted, No Women Need Apply; Sexual Barriers in the Medical Profession, 1835–1975* (New Haven, Conn.: Yale University Press, 1977), pp. 179–180.

15. Frederick J. Allen, *The Law as a Vocation* (Boston: Vocation Bureau of Boston, 1913).

16. Karen Blair, *The Clubwoman as Feminist: True Womanhood Redefined, 1868–1914* (New York: Holmes & Meier, 1980), passim; Dorothy Sterling, ed., *We Are Your Sisters: Black Women in the Nineteenth Century* (New York: W W. Norton 1984), passim; Gerda Lerner, *Black Women in White America: A Documentary History* (New York: Vintage Books, 1973), pp. 435–477; and Maxine S. Seller, ed., *Immigrant Women* (Philadelphia: Temple University Press, 1981), pp. 157–165, 174–188.

17. Linda K. Kerber, "The Republican Mother," in Linda K. Kerber and Jane De Hart-Mathews, eds., *Women's America: Refocusing the Past*, 2d ed. (New York: Oxford University Press, 1987), pp. 83–91; Donald M. Scott and Bernard Wishy, eds., *America's Families: A Documentary History* (New York: Harper & Row, 1982), pp. 271–276.

18. Walsh, *Doctors Wanted*, pp. 176–177.

19. Ibid., pp. 76–89.

20. Seller, *Immigrant Women,* pp. 197–204; Charlotte Baum, Paula Hyman, and Sonya Michel, *The Jewish Woman in America* (New York, 1975), p. 129.

21. Meyer Weinberg, *A Chance to Learn: A History of Race and Education in the United States* (Cambridge, Mass.: Cambridge University Press, 1977), pp. 11–39; Sterling, *We Are Your Sisters,* pp. 180–213.

22. Weinberg, *A Chance to Learn,* pp. 55–85; Earle H. West, eds., *The Black American and Education* (Columbus, Ohio: Charles E. Merrill Publishing Co., 1972) pp. 59–64, 101–103, 113–115, 134–135.

23. Mary E. Young, "Women, Civilization, and the Indian Question," in Kerber and De Hart Mathews, eds., *Women's America,* 1982, pp. 149–155; Frederick J. Stefon, "Richard Henry Pratt and His Indians," *Journal of Ethnic Studies,* 15, No. 2 (Summer 1987): 102.

24. Barbara Miller Solomon, *In the Company of Educated Women: A History of Women and Higher Education in America* (New Haven, Conn.: Yale University Press, 1985), pp. 24–28.

25. Helen Leftkowitz Horowitz, *Alma Mater; Design and Experience in the Women's Colleges from Their Nineteenth Century Beginnings to the 1930s* (Boston: Beacon Press, 1984), p. 78.

26. A minority of women's colleges, however, such as Mary Sharp College in Winchester, Tennessee (founded in 1853), and Bryn Mawr College stressed Latin, Greek, and higher mathematics, modeling their curricula on those of the most conservative and prestigious male institutions. They did so both from the conviction that classical training developed the mind best and from the desire to demonstrate that women could master even the most difficult "masculine" subjects. Solomon, *In the Company of Educated Women,* p. 24; Horowitz, *Alma Mater,* pp. 118–119.

27. Mary Roth Walsh and Francis R. Walsh, "Integrating Men's Colleges at the Turn of the Century," *Historical Journal of Massachusetts* 10 (June 1982): 9–11. At Tufts in 1905, for example, all five seniors elected to Phi Beta Kappa were women.

28. Marilyn Ferris Motz, *True Sisterhood: Michigan Women and Their Kin, 1820–1920* (Albany: State University of New York Press, 1983).

29. Maris A. Vinovskis, "Socioeconomic Determinants of Interstate Fertility Differentials in the United States in 1850 and 1860," *Journal of Interdisciplinary History* 6, no. 3 (1976): 375–396.

30. Solomon, *In the Company of Educated Women,* pp. 117–119.

31. Ibid., p. 40; Joan M. Jensen, *Loosening the Bonds: Mid-Atlantic Farm Women, 1750–1850* (New Haven, Conn.: Yale University Press, 1986), p. 178.

32. W. Elliot Brownlee and Mary M. Brownlee, eds., *Women in the American Economy: A Documentary History, 1675–1929* (New Haven, Conn.: Yale University Press, 1976), pp. 3, 20, 24–25.

33. Solomon, *In the Company of Women,* p. 38.

34. Barbara Meyer Werthheimer, *We Were There: The Story of Working Women in America* (New York: Pantheon Books, 1977), pp. 243–244. Teaching was widely accessible because the demand for teachers was great, and, since marriage meant dismissal, the turnover was high. Teaching was also accessible because qualifications were low; Indiana in 1907 was the first state to insist that licensed teachers be high school graduates.

35. Werthheimer, *We Were There,* p. 233. The number of women holding office jobs increased from 19,000 in 1870 to 503,000 in 1900. In 1870, women held 4.5 percent of all stenographers and typists jobs; by 1900, their share had increased to 76.7 percent.

36. Walsh, *Doctors Wanted*, p. xvi.

37. Less than 25 percent of women born between 1866 and 1870 could expect to complete high school, but for the cohort born between 1916 and 1920 the figure had increased to 60 percent. James P. Smith and Michael P. Ward, *Women's Wages and Work in the Twentieth Century* (Santa Monica, Calif.: Rand, 1984), p. 39. See also B. Carter and Mark Prus, "The Labor Market and the American High School Girl 1890–1928," *Journal of American History* 42 (March 1982): 163–171.

38. Solomon, *In the Company of Educated Women*, pp. 63–64; Woody, *A History of Women's Education*, p. 381.

39. William H. Chafe, *The American Woman: Her Changing Social, Economic, and Political Roles, 1920–1970* (New York: Oxford University Press, 1972), p. 56; Harris, *Beyond Her Sphere*, p. 124.

40. Beverly Guy-Sheftall, "Black Women and Higher Education: Spellman and Bennett Colleges Revisited," *Journal of Negro Education* 5, no. 3 (Summer 1982): 278–287; Mother Grace Dammann, RSCJ, "The American Catholic College for Women," in Roy U. Deferrari, ed., *Essays on Catholic Education in the United States* (Washington, D.C.: Catholic University of America Press, 1942), pp. 173, 179–80, 184–185; Nettie Pauline McGill, "Some Characteristics of Jewish Youth in New York," *The Jewish Social Service Quarterly* 24 (December 1937): 257.

41. Linda K. Kerber, "Daughters of Columbia: Educating Women for the Republic 1787–1805," in Kerber and De Hart Mathews, eds., *Women's America*, p. 88.

42. See, for example, Edward H. Clarke, M.D., *Sex in Education; or, A Fair Chance for the Girls* (Boston: James R. Osgood & Co., 1873). Educated women such as Julia Ward Howe, Virginia Dall, and Dr. Mary Putnam Jacobi refuted these views. See Julia Ward Howe, ed., *Sex and Education: A Reply to E. H. Clarke's "Sex in Education"* (Boston: Roberts Brothers, 1874).

43. Suzanne Hildebrand, "Ambiguous Authority and Aborted Ambition: Gender, Professionalism, and the Rise and Fall of the Welfare State," *Library Trends* (Fall 1985): 189. See also Peter Filene, *Him/Her/Self: Sex Roles in Modern America* (New York: Harcourt, Brace, & Jovanovich, 1974), p. 77.

44. Maxine S. Seller, G. Stanley Hall, and Edward Thorndike, "On the Education of Women: Theory and Policy in the Progressive Era," *Educational Studies* 11 (Winter 1981): 365–374.

45. Ibid., p. 373; Rosalind Rosenberg, *Beyond Separate Spheres: Intellectual Roots of Modern Feminism* (New Haven, Conn.: Yale University Press, 1982), passim.

46. John L. Rury, "Vocationalism for Home and Work: Women's Education in the United States 1880–1930," *History of Education Quarterly* 24, no. 1 (Spring 1984): 27.

47. Lynn D. Gordon, "Co-education on Two Campuses: Berkeley and Chicago, 1890–1912," in Mary Kelley, ed., *Women's Being, Women's Place: Female Identity and Vocation in American History* (Boston: C. K. Hall & Co., 1979), pp. 180–189. See also Carlotte W. Conable, *Women at Cornell: The Myth of Equal Education* (Ithaca, N.Y.: Cornell University Press, 1977) and Dorothy G. McGuigan, *A Dangerous Experiment: One Hundred Years of Women at the University of Michigan* (Ann Arbor: University of Michigan Press, 1970). On early-twentieth-century women's sports, see Nancy Theriot, "Toward a New Sporting Ideal: The Women's Division of the National Amateur Athletic Federation," *Frontiers: A Journal of Women Studies* 3, no. 1 (Spring 1978): 3–7.

48. Walsh, *Doctors Wanted*, pp. 219–224.

49. Rosenberg, *Beyond Separate Spheres*, pp. 48–51.

50. Solomon, *In the Company of Educated Women,* p. 63.

51. Ibid., p. 133; Cynthia Fuchs Epstein, *Women's Place: Options and Limits in Professional Careers* (Berkeley: University of California Press, 1971), p. 7.

52. Epstein, *Women's Place,* p. 7.

53. Barbara Melosh, *The Physician's Hand: Nurses and Nursing in the Twentieth Century* (Philadelphia: Temple University Press, 1982); Michael Apple, "Teaching and Women's Work," in Edgar B. Gumbert, ed. *Expressions of Power in Education: Studies of Class, Gender, and Race* (Atlanta: Center for Cross Cultural Education, College of Education, Georgia State University, 1984).

54. Chafe, *The American Woman,* pp. 55, 57.

55. Ibid., p. 145.

56. Ibid., p. 60. See also Lois Scharf, *To Work and to Wed: Female Employment, Feminism, and the Great Depression* (Westport, Conn.: Greenwood Press, 1980), passim.

57. Solomon, *In the Company of Educated Women,* p. 190.

58. No author, *Girls and Women in Education: A Cross-National Study of Sex Inequalities in Upbringing and in Schools and Colleges* (Paris: Organization for Economic Co-operation and Development, 1986), pp. 180–183; Angela Simeone, *Academic Women: Working Toward Equality* (South Hadley, Mass.: Bergin & Garvey Publishers, 1987), pp. 7–8.

59. Barbara R. Bergmann, *The Economic Emergence of Women* (New York: Basic Books, 1986), pp. 21–24.

60. Ibid., pp. 41–54.

61. For representative collections of this extensive material, see Judith Stacey, Susan Bereaud, and Joan Daniels, *And Jill Came Tumbling After: Sexism in American Education* (New York: Dell Publishing Co., 1974) and Elizabeth Steiner Maccia, *Women and Education* (Bloomington, Ind.: Charles C. Thomas, 1975). See also Nancy Frazier and Myra Sadker, *Sexism in School and Society* (New York: Harper & Row, 1973); *Signs* (Winter 1975): 363–386; and Myra Pollack Sadker and David Miller Sadker, "Sexism in Teacher-Education Texts," *Harvard Educational Review* 50, no. 1 (February 1980): 36–46.

62. Ester Westervelt, *Barriers to Women's Participation in Post Secondary Education: A Review of Research and Commentary as of 1973/74* (Washington, D.C.: Government Printing Office, 1975); Roberta M. Hall, "The Classroom Climate: A Chilly One for Women?" (Washington, D.C.: Project on the Status and Education of Women and the Association of American Colleges, 1982); Association of American Colleges, "Minority Women and Higher Education," Eric Doc. ED 098 852, 1974.

63. Elizabeth Langland and Walter Grove, eds., *A Feminist Perspective in the Academy: The Difference It Makes* (Chicago: University of Chicago Press, 1982; Ellen Carol Dubois, G. P. Kelly, E. L. Kennedy, C. W. Korsmeyer, and L. S. Robinson, *Feminist Scholarship: Kindling in the Groves of Academe* (Urbana: University of Illinois Press, 1985).

64. Florence Howe, ed., *Women and the Power to Change* (New York: McGraw-Hill, 1975); Marilyn J. Boxer, "For and About Women: The Theory and Practice of Women's Studies in the United States," *Signs* 7 (1982): 661–695.

65. Sex discrimination in employment was prohibited by the Civil Rights Act of 1964. Abortion was legalized in *Wade v. Roe* (1973).

66. Margaret C. Dunkle and Bernice Sandler, *Sex Discrimination Against Students: Implications of Title IX of the Educational Amendments of 1972* (Washington, D.C.: Association of American Colleges, 1975).

67. Solomon, *In the Company of Educated Women,* pp. 44, 203.

68. Sally Berman, "Justice Denied: Civil Rights Enforcement Since Grove City," *Civil Liberties,* no. 356 (Winter 1986): 4. The Grove City College decision stated that Title IX regulations against sex discrimination were applicable only to the specific program within an educational institution that received federal funds, not to the institution as a whole. Other laws affected by the Grove decision were Title VI of the Civil Rights Act of 1964, Section 504 of the Rehabilitation Act of 1973, and the Age Discrimination Act of 1975. The Grove decision was reversed by Congress with the passage of the Civil Rights Restoration Act in 1988.

69. Naomi Weisstein, "Tired of Arguing about Biological Inferiority," *Ms Magazine,* November 1983, pp. 41–46; C. P. Benbow and J. C. Stanley, "Sex Differences in Mathematical Ability: Fact or Artifact?" *Science* 210 (1980): 1262–1264; P. L. Peterson and E. Fennema, "Effective Teaching, Student Engagement in Classroom Activities, and Sex Related Differences in Learning Mathematics," *American Educational Research Journal* 22 (1985): 309–335.

70. For a recent many-faceted evaluation of the status of women in education, see Susan S. Klein, ed., *Handbook for Achieving Sex Equity in Education* (Baltimore: Johns Hopkins University Press, 1985).

71. Corinne H. Rieder, "Work, Women, and Vocational Education," *American Education* 13, no. 5 (June 1977): 27–38; Arthur Cohen and Florence Brawer, *The American Community College* (San Francisco: Jossey-Bass, Publishers, 1982), pp. 40–41. Cohen and Brawer found only 3 percent of vocational community college students in curricula not fitting traditional sex stereotyping.

72. Susan True, *Data on Percentages of Girls' High School Athletic Teams Coached by Women* (Kansas City: National Federation of State High Schools, 1983) and P. L. Geadelmann, "Sex Equity in Physical Education and Athletics," in Klein, ed., *Handbook for Achieving Sex Equity.*

73. Dubois, Kelly, Kennedy, Korsmeyer, and Robinson, *Feminist Scholarship,* p. 181.

74. Lynn Olson, " 'Biased' Tests Said Hurting Women's Chances for Aid," *Education Week,* April 29, 1987, p. 8. See also Phyllis Rossner, *Sex Bias in College Admissions Tests: Why Women Lose Out* (Cambridge, Mass.: FairTest, National Center for Fair and Open Testing, 1987).

75. Michael A. Olivas, *The Dilemma of Access: Minorities in Two Year Colleges* (Washington, D.C.: Howard University Press, 1979), pp. 25–27, 207–208.

76. Angela Simeone, *Academic Women: Working Toward Equality* (South Hadley, Mass.: Bergin & Garvey Publishers, 1987), pp. 29–33. See also William B. Harvey and Diane Scott-Jones, "We Can't Find Any: The Elusiveness of Black Faculty Members in American Higher Education," *Issues in Education* 3, no. 1 (Summer 1985): 68–76.

77. *Girls and Women in Education,* pp. 180–181.

78. Ibid., p. 180.

79. Rieder, "Work, Women, and Vocational Education," p. 28.

80. M. K. Gregory, "Sex Bias in School Referrals," *Journal of School Psychology* 15, no. 3 (1977); Frank Bowe, *Disabled Women in America* and *Disabled Adults in America,* Statistical portraits drawn from Census Bureau Data, President's Committee on Employment of the Handicapped (Washington, D.C.: U.S. Government Printing Office, 1983).

81. For figures on teenage pregnancy and information on relevant school programs,

see Asta M. Kenney, "Teen Pregnancy: An Issue for the Schools," and James Buie, "Teen Pregnancy: It's Time for the Schools to Tackle the Problem," *Phi Delta Kappan* (June 1987): 728–736, 737–739.

82. Bergmann, *Economic Emergence of Women,* p. 680.

83. Ibid., p. 68.

84. Barbara C. Gelpi, Nancy C. M. Hartsock, Clare C. Novak, and Myra H. Strober, *Women and Poverty* (Chicago: University of Chicago Press).

85. Bergmann, *Economic Emergence of Women,* pp. 50–51; Gelpi et al., *Women and Poverty,* pp. 211, 216.

86. Bergmann, *Economic Emergence of Women,* p. 50.

WORLDWIDE TRENDS

24
ACHIEVING EQUALITY IN EDUCATION—PROSPECTS AND REALITIES

Gail P. Kelly

Over the past twenty years, educational access for women has widened dramatically. In 1960, it would have been a truism to state that everywhere women were undereducated relative to men—fewer females than males entered school and female attrition rates were much higher than those of males. Worldwide, gender was the single greatest predictor of educational access. Today, this is not necessarily the case. The number of females in school in the 1980s is higher than in any period in history. The proportion of girls in primary, secondary, and higher education has risen in almost every country in the world. In most nations, particularly in the Third World, the pattern of gender-based inequality in education persists, although the gaps between male and female enrollments have narrowed appreciably. In a minority of countries, male and female school enrollments have equalized; in a handful of nations, women actually form a higher proportion of those attending school than do men. There is no question, as the chapters in this handbook have documented, that major changes have taken place in female education in the past decades.

What do the changes in women's education mean? Has increasing educational provision served to eradicate gender-based inequalities in the distribution of power and authority in society? Does equalization of education mean equalization of men and women in the workforce, in the political system, and in income? Is education an enabling condition of gender equality? This chapter explores these questions. It begins by charting worldwide trends in female schooling and then explores what such trends mean in terms of changing gender relations in society.

ENROLLMENT TRENDS

Without question, since 1960 there has been unprecedented expansion of women's access to schooling all over the world. Table 24.1 reports the percentage of the age cohort of females versus males enrolled in primary school in most nations of the world. The table also compares 1960 figures with 1981 figures. It shows that in most of the world women's representation in primary school is approaching that of men. In 1960, the proportion of schoolaged females attending primary school ranged from 12 percent in some of the Middle Eastern countries to 100 percent in industrialized nations like Japan and the United States. By 1981, the proportion ranged from 58 to 100 percent.

Table 24.2 presents the changes in the proportion of schoolaged boys versus girls attending primary school between 1960 and 1981 by level of economic development of individual nations. It compares low-income countries where the gross national product (GNP) per capita is under $410 with high-income oil-exporting countries and with countries that are industrial market economies. As the table shows, the gains in female enrollment are impressive. In high-income oil-exporting nations, the proportion of schoolaged girls in primary school rose from 12 percent to 73 percent in the two decades; in the poorest countries, the proportion went from 25 to 58 percent.

The gains in the proportion of girls receiving primary school education, charted in the chapters in this handbook and in Tables 24.1 and 24.2, are real. However, there are twenty-one low-income and lower middle-income nations that still enroll less than 50 percent of girls of primary school age (see Table 24.3). Of these, eight enroll less than 20 percent. Some, like the Arab Republic of Yemen and Upper Volta, enroll less than 15 percent of schoolaged girls, while they provide schooling to nearly 80 percent of schoolaged boys.

Much of the world has approached equality between the sexes in the provision of primary education. Rich countries in which universal primary education is a reality provide girls with primary schooling. As a rule, however, countries that have not attained universal primary education for males do not provide primary schooling equally to males and females. Girls lag behind with few exceptions (see Table 24.1). Only after universal primary schooling is given boys do girls begin to obtain education in proportions approximating boys'. Primary education becomes universal for males before it does for females, despite the fact that the gains for females since 1960 in primary school enrollment have been far greater. In countries like Pakistan, 13 percent of primary schoolage girls were in school in 1960, and 31 percent by 1981. In Niger, 3 percent of primary schoolage girls attended school in 1960; the figure rose to 17 percent in 1981.

The proportion of schoolaged girls in school exceeds the proportion of boys in Israel, Lesotho, Trinidad and Tobago, Denmark, Czechoslovakia, and the German Democratic Republic. But the gap is only about 1 percent. When the proportion of the male age cohort enrolled in primary schools exceeds that of females, the spread ranges from 1 to 2 percentage points to 30 percent or more

Table 24.1

Percentage of the Age Cohort Enrolled in Primary School, 1960 and 1981

	1960		1981	
Country	Male	Female	Male	Female
AFRICA				
Angola	28	13	n.a.	n.a.
Benin	38	15	88	42
Burundi	27	9	40	25
Cameroon	87	43	117	97
Central African Republic	53	12	89	49
Chad	51	25	84	58
Congo, Peoples' Republic	103	53	163	148
Ethiopia	11	3	60	33
Ghana	52	25	77	60
Guinea	44	16	44	22
Ivory Coast	68	24	92	60
Kenya	64	30	114	101
Lesotho	63	102	84	123
Liberia	45	18	82	50
Madagascar	58	45	n.a.	n.a.
Mali	14	6	35	20
Mauritania	13	3	43	23
Mozambique	60	36	102	78
Niger	7	3	29	17
Nigeria	46	27	94	70
Rwanda	68	30	75	69
Senegal	36	17	58	38
Sierra Leone	30	15	45	30
Somalia	13	5	38	21
Sudan	35	14	61	43
Tanzania	33	18	107	98
Togo	63	24	135	87
Uganda	65	62	32	46
Upper Volta	12	5	26	15
Zaire	n.a.	n.a.	73	51
Zambia	51	34	102	90
Zimbabwe	107	86	130	121
ASIA				
Bangladesh	66	26	76	47
Burma	61	52	87	81
China	n.a.	n.a.	130	106
Hong Kong	93	79	108	104
India	80	40	93	64
Indonesia	86	58	106	94

Table 24.1 (continued)

Country	1960		1981	
	Male	Female	Male	Female
LATIN AND CENTRAL AMERICA				
Argentina	98	99	120	119
Brazil	97	93	93	93
Chile	111	107	115	114
Colombia	77	77	129	132
Costa Rica	97	95	109	107
Cuba	109	109	110	104
Dominican Republic	99	95	109	107
Ecuador	87	79	109	105
El Salvador	82	77	61	61
Guatemala	50	39	74	63
Haiti	50	42	74	64
Honduras	68	67	96	95
Jamaica	92	93	99	100
Nicaragua	65	66	101	107
Panama	98	94	113	108
Peru	95	71	116	108
Trinidad and Tobago	89	87	93	95
Uruguay	111	111	124	120
Venezuela	100	100	105	104
MIDDLE EAST				
Algeria	55	37	106	81
Egypt	80	52	89	63
Iran, Islamic Republic	56	27	111	78
Iraq	94	36	117	109
Israel	99	97	94	96
Jordan	94	59	105	100
Kuwait	131	102	96	93
Lebanon	105	99	123	114
Libya	92	24	128	119
Morocco	67	27	97	60
Oman	n.a.	n.a.	90	57
Saudi Arabia	22	2	77	51
Syrian Arab Republic	89	39	112	89
Tunisia	43	12	92	30
Turkey	90	58	110	95
Yemen Arab Republic	14		82	12
Yemen People's Democratic Republic	20	5	94	34

Table 24.1 (continued)

Country	1960		1981	
	Male	Female	Male	Female
NORTH AMERICA AND AUSTRALIA				
Australia	103	103	110	110
Canada	108	105	106	104
United States	100	100	n.a.	n.a.

Source: World Development Report, 1984, p. 266-267.

Table 24.2
Percentage of the Age Cohort Enrolled in Primary School, by Type of Economy and Level of Economic Development, 1960 and 1981

Type of Economy	1960		1981	
	Male	Female	Male	Female
Industrial Market Economies (includes Western Europe, Japan, U.S.)	107	112	103	103
Non-Market Economies of Eastern Europe	101	99	101	99
High Income Oil Exporters (includes Oman, Libya, Saudi Arabia)	44	12	93	73
Upper-Middle Income Countries (includes Jordan, Malaysia, Korea, Chile, Greece, etc.)	93	107	83	101
Lower Middle Income Countries (includes Nigeria, Jamaica, Ecuador)	76	56	106	91
Low Income Countries (includes Bangladesh, Zaire, Vietnam, Burma)	51	25	84	58

Source: World Development Report, 1984, pp. 266-267.

in thirteen countries (Chad, Ethiopia, Nepal, Benin, Central African Republic, Pakistan, Afghanistan, People's Republic of Yemen, Liberia, Yemen Arab Republic, Morocco, Ivory Coast, and Oman) and between 20 and 29 percentage points in another thirteen countries (Bangladesh, Malawi, Uganda, India, Bu-

Table 24.3
Countries with Less than 50 Percent of School-Aged Girls Attending Primary School, 1981

Country	Percent of School-Aged Girls in Primary School
Yemen Arab Republic	12
Afghanistan	13
Upper Volta	15
Bhutan	17
Niger	17
Chad	19
Mali	20
Somalia	21
Guinea	22
Mauritania	23
Burundi	25
Sierra Leone	30
Pakistan	31
Ethiopia	33
Yemen, People's Democratic Republic	34
Senegal	38
Benin	42
Sudan	43
Uganda	46
Bangladesh	47
Central African Republic	49

rundi, Guinea, Mauritania, Senegal, Egypt, Nigeria, Guatemala, Iran, and Saudi Arabia). Equality in enrollment in primary school characterizes more or less Eastern Europe, the industrial market economies of Western Europe, North America, and Japan. It has also been attained in some very poor countries: Vietnam, China, Sri Lanka, and Kenya. Several lower middle-income countries like Honduras, El Salvador, the Philippines, Zimbabwe, Nicaragua, the People's Republic of the Congo, Costa Rica, Peru, Ecuador, Colombia, Paraguay, Cuba, North Korea, Lebanon, and Mongolia have also achieved parity in access to primary school. Likewise, there are a number of upper middle-income countries, including Jordan, South Korea, Panama, Chile, Brazil, Mexico, Argentina, Uruguay, Venezuela, Greece, Hong Kong, and Iraq, that have managed to provide equal opportunity to girls to attend primary school. There are also a number of upper middle-income countries that have not.

Secondary Education

Although the gap between male and female enrollment in primary school has declined worldwide to the point that in many countries it no longer exists, the same cannot be said for secondary education. Not all countries that have equalized primary enrollment have equalized secondary school enrollment. Worldwide in 1980, 46.4 percent of females twelve to seventeen years of age were in school versus 54.8 percent of males.[1] The gaps were greatest in Africa and Asia. In Africa, in 1980, 30 percent of girls of secondary school age attended school versus 44.1 percent of boys. In Asia, 29.7 percent of girls versus 43.0 percent of boys age twelve to seventeen were in school. In Europe and North America, however, female secondary school enrollments were overall slightly higher than those of males: 82 percent of all twelve to seventeen-year-old girls attended secondary school versus 78.7 percent of boys in Europe. In North America, the figures tend to be equal—at about 90.3 percent of all twelve to seventeen year olds. In Latin America, enrollments in secondary education approach gender equality, with 65.4 percent of twelve- to seventeen-year-old males and 62.7 percent of twelve- to seventeen-year-old females in some form of postprimary education.

Secondary school enrollment patterns show a trend toward increasing access of girls. This is apparent when considering postprimary enrollment trends in the decade 1970 to 1980. In 1970, in Africa 18.2 percent of twelve- to seventeen-year-old girls were in school; by 1975, 24.5 percent of secondary schoolaged girls were enrolled, and by 1980 the figure had risen to 30 percent.[2] Similarly, in Asia in 1970, 23.9 percent of twelve- to seventeen-year-old girls were in postprimary school; by 1975, the proportion had risen to 26.8 percent and by 1980 to 29.7 percent. In Europe, the corresponding increase was from 75.3 percent in 1970 to 82 percent in 1980.

The increases in secondary school enrollment for girls, however, have been accompanied everywhere by as dramatic a set of increases for males. This is particularly the case in Asia, Africa, and Latin America. Only in Europe and North America have female gains been more dramatic for women than for men; they are, for the most part, directly attributable to the universalization of some postprimary education for males. By 1970, postprimary education in North America and Europe had become universal for boys; in the 1980s, postprimary schooling became compulsory in Europe, and as a result girls gained equality of access.[3] In Africa, the gap between males and females in postprimary schooling declined only 0.9 percent in the decade 1970 to 1980; in Asia, it narrowed from 15.8 percentage points to 13.3 in 1980 (or 2.5 percentage points). In Latin America, the gap declined from 4.5 percentage points to 2.7. Male/female differentials in postprimary enrollments remain in the Third World. The gaps are narrowing but only slowly.[4]

There are differences among nations in postprimary educational access for females versus males, just as there are at the primary level. For example, in Africa in 1975 only 15.9 percent of girls twelve to seventeen were in secondary school. However, in southern Africa 70.4 percent of girls aged twelve to seventeen years attended secondary school versus 23 percent in North Africa and 19.8 percent in East Africa.[5] The differences among African nations with regard to secondary as well as primary enrollments are underscored in this handbook.

Female enrollment figures are less depressed in Nigeria than they are in Senegal or Zaire. In Botswana, more girls than boys are enrolled in secondary school.

In Asia, as in Africa, there is also great variation in female postprimary enrollment among countries. In Japan, 94.7 percent of all girls twelve to seventeen years of age went to secondary school in 1980; in the rest of East Asia the corresponding figure was 58.1 percent, and in parts of South Asia it fell to as low as 17.4 percent.

Despite the persistence of inequalities, opportunities to enroll in postprimary school have opened somewhat worldwide for girls. However, the number of girls dropping out of school has also grown except in Europe, Japan, and North America. Girls' relative chance of staying in school to complete secondary schooling is about equal to that of boys in North America and Europe. It is about half that of boys in Africa as a whole and a third that of boys in Asia.[6] In the Congo in 1975, for example, 4.8 percent of girls dropped out in the first year of secondary school; another 9.3 percent left in the second year, whereas an additional 5.1 percent dropped out in the third year and 31.7 percent stopped going to school in the fourth year. In the upper three years of the secondary school course, female attrition rates were 7.5 percent in the first year, 23.8 percent in the second year, and 60.3 percent in the third.[7] These kinds of attrition rates characterize most of Africa and Asia, with the exception of highly industrialized Japan where secondary education is compulsory and in countries where females continue to outnumber males in the secondary schools as in Botswana. In Botswana, as discussed in this handbook, males leave the country to work as migrant laborers in South Africa while girls stay at home and in school.

In some countries, male/female attrition rates are the same in postprimary education. This is the case in Venezuela and Chile as well as in the United States. In some countries—most of Western Europe, particularly France, and Eastern Europe, particularly East Germany and Poland—girls actually have a lower attrition rate than boys. This phenomenon is not limited to Europe. It also characterizes Kuwait where fewer girls than boys go to secondary school, but those who go tend to stay there to the completion of the secondary program.

While access to secondary school may have opened, despite high attrition rates in some countries, more females are obtaining more years of postprimary education than was the case in 1960. However, it is not clear whether girls obtain the same quality and kind of education as do boys. A look at several countries in which gender equality in secondary education enrollments has been attained is instructive. In France and the Soviet Union where girls' enrollments equal, if not exceed, boys' enrollments in academic tracks, as this handbook shows, girls do not study the same subjects. They dominate in arts and humanities and constitute a minority of students in science and mathematics programs. In countries where curricular diversification within academic tracks occurs on the secondary level—Poland, China, Israel, Germany, and Sweden, to name a few—similar patterns of sex segregation exist. In countries where academic secondary education is less diversified, like the United States and Great Britain, girls take fewer science and mathematics courses than do boys.[8]

Not only is there sex segregation within academic secondary education, but also sex segregation is even more pronounced in vocational and technical programs. Girls tend to be excluded from technical and vocational courses in most countries. Vocational and technical education, even if it has lower status than academic education, tends to be male dominated. Girls are shunted off to secretarial or commercial studies in vocational schools, and in countries where teacher and nursing training occurs at secondary schools, girls are concentrated in these programs.[9] In socialist as well as capitalist industrialized nations of Europe and North America as well as in Third World countries, girls rarely study the vocational subjects their male peers do. This is amply documented in the chapters in this handbook on countries as diverse as Israel, Zaire, Nigeria, Peru, Iran, India, the German Democratic Republic, and the USSR.

Higher Education

In most countries, inequality in female access to higher education persists, although, again, there are exceptions. In most Third World nations, women's chances of obtaining higher education are slim. In Africa, only 4.9 percent of females aged eighteen to twenty-three attended some form of higher education in 1980 versus 11 percent of males. In Asia, 6.5 percent of university-aged women attended colleges and universities versus 13.9 percent of men. In Latin America, the gap between male and female higher education enrollment ratios is lower: 20.8 percent of eighteen- to twenty-three-year-old females were in postsecondary studies versus 23.8 percent of similarly aged males. Europe's pattern in 1980 replicated Latin America's: 26.5 percent of females, aged eighteen to twenty-three years, versus 28.3 percent of similarly aged males enrolled in institutions of higher education. Only in North America was gender parity in access to higher education more or less achieved: 50.4 percent of all eighteen- to twenty-three-year-old women versus 50.7 percent of eighteen- to twenty-three-year-old men were in colleges and universities.[10]

The inequality of access by sex which characterizes higher education has deepened over the past decade in most of Asia and Africa while it has narrowed in Latin America, Europe, and North America. The expansion of higher education in Africa has benefited men more than women. In 1970, 6.3 percent of eighteen- to twenty-three-year-old men were studying at the tertiary level in Africa versus 2.1 percent of eighteen- to twenty-three-year-old women. By 1980, 11 percent of eighteen to twenty-three-year-old men and 4.9 percent of eighteen- to twenty-three-year-old women were in higher education. In Asia, the gap between males and females in higher education was always greater than that in Africa, and it continued to grow between 1970 and 1980. In 1970, 10.6 percent of males aged eighteen to twenty-three years went on to higher education versus 4.2 percent of females. By 1980, 13.9 percent of the male age cohort attended institutions of higher education versus 6.5 percent of females.[11]

While the gap in male/female access to higher education has narrowed in North America and Europe, some of that narrowing comes as a result of changes in what is considered higher education. Nowhere is this clearer than in Sweden and in the United States where teacher education and nursing—both traditionally and predominantly female fields of study—are part of higher education. In the United States, these fields have long been college and university subjects; in Sweden, as this Handbook points out, sexual equality was achieved suddenly in higher education when the reforms of the 1970s integrated teacher and nursing education into the universities. However, in many African and Asian countries, while teacher and nursing preparatory programs draw predominantly female clientele, much of that training is on the secondary level and is not part of higher education.[12]

Access to higher education for women varies greatly within as well as between regions. The gender-based equality that Europe as a whole appears to be approaching is not characteristic of every European country. The gap between male and female enrollment in higher education in Southern Europe—in countries like Greece, Italy, Spain, and Portugal—are greater than that in Eastern Europe.[13] In 1975, for example, 23.3 percent of women versus 34.5 percent of men aged eighteen to twenty-three were in some form of higher education in Europe as a whole. In Eastern European socialist nations, more females than males were in higher education: 17 percent of males aged eighteen to twenty-three were enrolled in tertiary institutions. In the Soviet Union, the figure was 22.8 percent of males and 25.2 percent of females.[14] Sweden had achieved parity in higher education, whereas the gap between male and female enrollments in the United Kingdom was reminiscent of the gap between the sexes in African universities.

Variations in female access to higher education and gender-based inequalities in the tertiary sector are underscored in this handbook. In Botswana, the difference between male and female enrollments in higher education is not the same as that of the rest of Africa. The gaps are greater in Senegal, Zaire, and Kenya. Similarly, in the Middle East women are more likely to go on to higher education in Egypt where they make up nearly a third of all enrollments, than they are in Tunisia, Morocco, Algeria, Libya, Syria, or Israel.

Within higher education, sex segregation by field of study is the norm, regardless of whether a country enrolls more female than male students in higher education (like Canada and Poland) or enrolls mostly men (as in Korea where women represent 24.8 percent of students or Mexico where they make up 31.7 percent of enrollments). As Table 24.4 shows, women tend to study in fields in which there are a lot of other women studying. In communist Poland where women account for 56 percent of all students in higher education, they represent 80.7 percent of all those studying education; in capitalist Canada where women make up a little over 50 percent of all higher education students, they represent 70.3 percent of students studying education. Women are also disproportionately

Table 24.4
Sex Segregation in Higher Education in Poland, Canada, Egypt, Mexico, and Korea, by Field of Study, 1981

Field of Study	Percent of Students Who are Female				
	Poland	Canada	Egypt	Mexico	Korea
Education	80.7	70.3	41.8	70.2	54.0
Humanities	72.5	52.2	45.1	55.3	33.6
Arts	50.3	63.1	39.7	50.0	71.5
Communications	81.7	58.5	50.4	43.5	54.5
Math/Computers	68.3	35.5	25.7	34.2	29.2
Engineering	24.6	8.5	14.5	10.5	2.9
Agriculture	47.7	31.6	27.0	10.3	10.7
Health Sciences	76.5	71.5	34.8	44.4	45.4
Architecture/Planning	48.9	21.0	0	18.4	1.7
Law	46.8	40.1	22.1	39.9	3.5
Social Sciences	61.9	58.6	38.0	52.7	8.8
Proportion of Students in Higher Education who are Female (1981)	55.8	50.5	31.9	31.7	24.8

Source: Susan McCrae Vander Voet, "The United Nations Decade for Women: The Search for Women's Equality in Education and Employment," in The Decade for Women: Special Report. Edited by Aisla Thomson (Toronto: Canadian Congress for Learning Opportunities for Women, 1985) p. 82.

overenrolled in education in Mexico where they represent 31.7 percent of all students in higher education and 70.2 percent of education majors. In Korea and Egypt, the pattern of overrepresentation of women in education remains, although it is less exaggerated in Egypt than elsewhere. Women worldwide are heavily concentrated in the humanities and arts as well, and, with the exception of Poland and Mexico, their enrollment in mathematics and computer sciences is disproportionately low. Everywhere few women study engineering, although the extent of their representation varies—in Korea women make up 2.9 percent of engineering students and in Canada 8.5 percent. In Poland, if sexual segregation were not occurring, women would constitute 55.8 percent, rather than 24.6 percent, of engineering students.[15]

National variations exist in the precise fields where women are clustered or excluded. These variations are not easily explained. Sex segregation does not diminish as more women are admitted to higher education. Rather, the gender-based segregation of fields of study either remains or intensifies. This is true not only of the five countries listed in Table 24.4, but also in countries as diverse as Vietnam, Nigeria, Peru, Chile, Israel, Japan, Sweden, the United States, and East Germany as this handbook demonstrates. There is very little variation between socialist and nonsocialist, industrialized high-income and low-income economies, and between continents. Sex segregation is the rule rather than the exception in higher education.

ENROLLMENT PATTERNS AND ECONOMIC DEVELOPMENT: IS THERE A RELATION?

Much of the research on education has led us to believe that equality in enrollment between males and females is related to national economic development.[16] Does cross-national analysis of gender-based inequalities in enrollments show this to be the case?

Table 24.2, presented earlier, shows primary school enrollments by level of economic development. It distinguishes between the industrial market economies of Western Europe, Japan, and North America, the nonmarket industrial countries of Eastern European, high-income oil-exploring countries, upper middle-income countries and low-income countries. The data on a gross level seem to indicate that as countries get richer, access to education tends to open up, and once provision is made for males, it follows for females.

Although economic development worldwide seems to accompany female access to primary education, increasing educational provision for females and equality in enrollments can occur and has occurred in the poorest countries in the world. By 1981, Kenya, Sri Lanka, and China (with annual per capita income of $380, $320, and $290, respectively), as well as Vietnam, provided greater equality of access to primary education for girls than did high-income oil-exporting countries of the Middle East like Saudi Arabia or Oman with a per capita income of $16,000 and $6,090 per year respectively. In short, although equal access to education seems to occur with economic development, economic development is not a precondition of equal education for women on the primary level. Nor does the fact of economic development and a high per capita income guarantee that girls have equal access to primary education, not to mention secondary and higher education.

Many of the countries where economic development and sex equality in primary school enrollments do not coincide are Middle Eastern Islamic nations. Although it might be tempting to relate Islam rather than economic development to sex inequality in primary school enrollments, any relationship that might be drawn in this manner is tenuous. In some instances, poor Islamic countries can and do provide greater equality in education on the primary level between boys and girls than do rich Islamic countries. Tunisia, with a GNP per capita of $1,390 in 1982, provided primary schooling to 92 percent of all school aged girls, whereas Saudi Arabia with a GNP per capita of over $16,000 per year accommodated only 51 percent of schoolaged girls. Similarly, Iraq with a GNP per capita of under $7,000 per year provided primary schooling to all schoolaged girls. Syria provided equality of access to both sexes despite its per capita income of $1,680. In addition, many non-Islamic countries have lower school enrollment ratios for girls than do Islamic countries. In short, economic development and Islam have tenuous relations to equality between the sexes in access to primary school.

Countries that have experienced socialist revolutions tend to provide gender equality in access to primary school, but this is only a tendency. Eastern European countries have achieved gender parity in primary school attendance similar to that achieved in richer Western Europe and North America. Among the thirty-four nations with a GNP per capita of under $410 in 1982, only four provided universal primary education. Of these four, two experienced socialist revolutions in the post–World War II era: China and Vietnam. Tanzania, an African socialist country, came close to providing gender-based equality. However, a number of poor and not so poor socialist nations have come no where close to providing girls with equal access to primary school: Laos, the People's Republic of Yemen, and Yugoslavia. More socialist nations provide parity to girls in entering primary schools than do not, but a socialist revolution is not a guarantee that girls will have the same access to primary education as do boys, any more than is the case with economic development.

Although cross-national comparison shows us that economic development, religion, and revolution may relate somewhat tenuously to equality for girls in the primary school, it also shows us that equality of access for girls is possible for poor as well as rich countries, for Islamic as well as non-Islamic nations, and for revolutionary socialist societies as well as capitalist societies. Provision of equal educational opportunity at the primary level is not a question of "evolution" as much as it is a question of educational and social policies that have clear-cut commitments to providing girls with education. Countries as diverse as Vietnam, Sri Lanka, New Zealand, Colombia, the Philippines, Singapore, Switzerland, and Jordan have managed to approach gender-based equality in primary education.

Although gender-based equality in access to primary education seems unrelated to the level of a nation's economic development, the provision of secondary education appears to be another matter. Countries like Vietnam and Kenya which have managed to provide girls access to primary school equal to boys have not done so at the secondary level. Indeed, as the chapters on these two countries point out, the gap between males and females becomes great and approximates that found in countries characterized by inequality of access to primary education like Egypt or Nigeria. Providing equality in primary school enrollment is not seemingly a guarantee of equality of access to secondary school.

Some countries provide equality of access to females in secondary education, and in several countries more girls than boys attend secondary schools. Except for Botswana and several countries in southern Africa which provide male laborers to the Republic of South Africa, countries that have more girls than boys in secondary school are without exception industrialized, relatively rich nations like Canada, the USSR, and other countries of Western Europe.

Few countries provide women with equality of access to higher education. Those that do—the United States, Canada, the Soviet Union, Poland, and East Germany—are without exception industrialized societies. However, the gap between male and female access to higher education does not appear to follow any definable pattern. The percentage of women in higher education is about the same in low-income countries like Vietnam and China, as it is in many middle-income countries. In a number of countries, women outnumber men in higher education. However, as we will see in the pages that follow, it makes very little difference whether women outnumber men, are equal to, or are a minority in higher education—in secondary or primary education, for that matter—in terms of the outcomes of education in the workforce, in income, and in the political system. The remainder of this chapter focuses on these outcomes and explores why, despite changes in education, there have been few changes in the workforce and political outcomes of education for women relative to those of men.

DOES EDUCATION CHANGE WOMEN'S ACCESS TO AND POWER IN PUBLIC LIFE?

Paradoxically, although countries vary substantially in the provision of education for women—how many women go to school for how long—there is less variation in women's workforce participation patterns and almost none in women's income relative to men's and their access to political power in society. This handbook, as well as the cross-national and individual country research listed in the Bibliography that ends this volume, shows that differences in the proportion of women educated and the amount of education they receive have resulted in few changes in their rate of entry into the workforce for a wage, the degree of gender segregation in the workforce, women's income relative to men's (although education does appear to relate to women's income relative to other women),[17] and women's access to political power.

The Workforce

Women's workforce participation rates worldwide have stagnated since 1960, despite the gains in education. In 1960, 47 percent of women over the age of eighteen were working for a wage; in 1980, that figure was 46 percent.[18] (The decline in women's paid workforce participation was matched by an even greater decline in men's. In 1960, 90 percent of men aged eighteen to sixty years worked for a wage; in 1980, that figure fell to 85 percent.) Although women's workforce participation for a wage stagnated worldwide, there are differences in industrialized versus Third World countries. In twenty-eight industrial economies (including the United States, Canada, France, Great Britain, the USSR, and Poland), women's workforce participation rates increased from 52 percent in 1960 to 57 percent in 1980. However, in the Third World where increases in women's access to education at all levels were probably the most dramatic, the rates of women entering the paid labor force declined from 45 percent to 42 percent. The declines were most dramatic in Oceania (a drop of 6 percent) and Asia (a drop of 5 percent).[19] The Indian case, reported in this handbook, is more typical than we would like to think. In short, education has expanded for women, but women's entry into the salaried workforce has not improved; it has eroded in much of the world. That erosion is chronicled in the case studies on Kenya, Iran, Nigeria, Zaire, Peru, Chile, and India presented in this work, and it has been documented in the research literature on countries like Mexico and Bangladesh.[20]

Individual countries differ in women's paid workforce participation rates. In general, rates are higher in the socialist countries of Eastern Europe than in Western Europe and Canada. The rates in Vietnam and China, when compared to those in other Third World countries like India or Bangladesh, are high. Socialist governments have sought to put women into the wage-earning workforce whether or not women are educated. Changes in education may have less to do with women's entry into paid labor than with economic policies aimed at exploiting women's labor in countries like China and the Soviet Union.

Although the rates of women's participation in salaried labor may have remained relatively stagnant, the jobs women hold have changed as a result of changes in their education. In developing nations as well as industrialized countries, the employment structure has changed, and as this structure has changed, so too have the educational levels of those who can successfully obtain employment in the industrial and service sectors of the economy.[21] In industrialized countries like Sweden, France, the United States, the Soviet Union, East Germany, Canada, and Great Britain, women have increasingly moved into occupations that require a secondary education or better. Many of these occupations, like primary and secondary school teaching and nursing, have been traditionally female occupations. But increasingly, women have entered lower level white-collar work, technical employment, and health-related professions as well as social services. Undoubtedly, without education many women would be unemployed. In some of these countries, women are staying in school longer to qualify for such work as jobs requiring low-skill levels that have been traditionally female have ceased expanding or even begun to decline.[22] As a number of studies have pointed out, in some Third World nations women have started to stay in school longer than men because the only paid employment open to them is employment that requires a secondary or better education.[23]

In part, the trend in industrialized countries for females to receive more education than males in order to compete in the wage labor market is a function of the sex-segmented occupational structure that exists worldwide. Most women work in occupations that are predominantly female, so much so that it has been estimated that in countries as diverse as Canada and the Soviet Union three-fourths of the workforce would need to change jobs in order to provide equal representation of males and females in all occupations.[24] The sex segregation in the workforce by occupation does parallel the segregation of women in specific tracks in secondary school and in fields of study in postsecondary education.

In Third World countries, the pattern of women's employment has also changed but somewhat differently. The labor force in these countries is segmented by sex in the context of a dual economy, one of which is traditional and involves subsistence farming and petty trade; the other is an urban industrial economy. In these countries, women's labor force participation has been traditionally high. Women, however, have been heavily concentrated in nonwage work in the traditional sector. In the process of modernization, such work has increasingly been taken over by mechanization and by the extension of corporate retailing.[25] In many countries, women's labor has been displaced in the traditional sector, and entry into the modern, urban, paid labor force is greatly contingent on education. The decline in women's employment is largely a function of women's undereducation and the decline of the parts of the economy which in the past had gainfully employed women. The relation between women's education and employment for a wage in many of these countries tends to be J-shaped.[26] Poor uneducated women enter the paid workforce out of necessity and work in low-wage jobs as domestic servants and in trade. The largest single wage employment of women in Latin America and Southeast Asia is in domestic labor. Women with primary education tend to withdraw from the paid workforce, and women with secondary education and above tend to enter wage employment in the modern sector in clerical, semiprofessional, and professional work. In some countries, like Turkey and Egypt, this has meant the increasing participation of women in the professions while the overall workforce participation rates of women have stagnated or declined.[27]

Secondary education has increasingly become a prerequisite for women's entry into paid labor. The increases in primary education, charted earlier in this chapter, have little meaning in terms of women's entry into the paid workforce, and there is evidence in some nations that, in the context of changing structures of the labor market, primary education may even depress women's rates of entry into paid labor.[28]

Although the outcomes of increasing women's educational levels on entry into the paid workforce are not always positive, increasing educational levels does seem to affect how long women stay in the workforce. A number of studies conducted in Canada, the United States, Argentina, and Paraguay, for example, suggest that increasing women's schooling means that women's workforce participation is sustained through marriage, childbearing, and childrearing.[29] The more education a woman receives, the less likely she is to leave the workforce during the childbearing and childrearing years than her less educated sisters. The number of years of education that yield this effect vary: in Paraguay, primary education has such an impact; in Canada, secondary education and university education have a similar influence. Whether it is education or social class which changes the length of time a woman remains in the workforce and the continuity of her participation in it is not known.

Increasing women's educational levels may have affected the jobs women work at and the continuity and length of their wage labor lives, but it has had little effect on the wages women earn.[30] Despite the changes in women's employment, women still earn about 75 percent of men's wages worldwide.[31] There are, of course, variations. In Japan, in 1980 working women earned 53.8 percent of the wages of working men; in Canada, they earned 58 percent of male wages, whereas in the Netherlands in 1982 women's wages were 76.7 percent of men's. In some Third World countries where women's workforce participation rates are on the wane, there is less inequality in wages for those in the paid labor force than is the case in highly industrialized societies. In Egypt, in 1980, for example, women working for a wage earned 93.7 percent of workingmen's wages; in Venezuela, in 1983 women earned 79.1 percent, and in Sri Lanka, the figure in 1981 was 93.3 percent.[32] Wage equality tends to occur in those nations where women's participation in wage labor is low—less than 25 percent of all women between fifteen and sixty years of age. The wage disparities appear greatest in countries where women's educational levels overall are higher, as is their participation in the salaried workforce.

Although it appears that income disparities between men and women in the paid workforce decline in nations with fewer educated women, in these countries the disparities are probably higher than they seem because of the large number of women who work without wages in farming and petty trade. In Egypt, for example, where women in the paid labor force earn 93.7 percent of men's wages, most women are wageless agricultural laborers. Male/female income disparities are enormous, but they are not apparent in considering those who work for wages. Women remain outside the wage-earning sectors of the economy. In Egypt, only 5.7 percent of the women were in the paid workforce in 1981. The disparities seem greatest when women earn wages in large numbers, as in Canada, Japan, the United States, and Vietnam. In these countries over 30 percent of women over age fifteen are in the paid labor force. These disparities have increased rather than decreased over time. In Japan, in 1975 women in the paid labor force earned 55.8 percent of men's wages; in 1980, they earned 53.8 percent. In the Netherlands, in 1971 female wage-earners brought home 79 percent of the salary of male wage-earners; in 1982, their income fell to 76.7 percent of males'. In South Korea, women wage-earners' income was 47.2 percent of men's; in 1983 it was 46.6 percent.[33]

These data, though fragmentary and possibly inaccurate, do suggest that increasing education for women has not necessarily brought about equality in the workforce. In fact, increasing women's educational levels appears to have little effect on entry into the workforce, whereas it strongly affects the work highly educated women do. Despite the changes in women's work, that work, particularly in highly industrialized countries, remains as underpaid, relative to men, as work women performed twenty years ago which required lower levels of skill and education. In short, education may sometimes serve to put women into wage labor and sustain them there through childrearing and childbearing, but it does not provide income equality even in countries like the Soviet Union, Poland, and France where women remain longer in school than do men.

Political Power

If the workforce outcomes of women's education provides little cause to be optimistic, even more disheartening is the relation of changing and equalizing access to education to providing women with access to power in the political system. As this handbook shows, research on this topic is even more fragmentary than is that on the workforce. This situation is borne out in the Bibliography. In part, the reason for the lack of research may be that the answer to the question—does education enhance women's political roles and access to power—is so self-evident. Nowhere have women obtained access to political power and full representation in national political decision-making bodies, Indira Gandhi, Golda Meir and Margaret Thatcher notwithstanding. As all the chapters in this work demonstrate, in most countries women's participation in politics and their roles in governing society have changed very little. In many countries, notably, Vietnam, China, Poland, Algeria, and Iran, increasing women's education appears to be associated with progressive political disenfranchisement.

The reasons for the seeming regression are complex, and research has been very spotty. Work such as Margery Wolf's, Phyllis Andors' and Elizabeth Croll's on China, Gail Lapidus' on the Soviet Union, and recently, Peter Knauss', Catherine Delcroix's, and Helene Vandevelde-Dailliere's studies on Algeria, suggest that, although women may be very active in politics during times of revolution, patriarchy reasserts itself in postrevolutionary society.[34] Often this occurs because production becomes the government's overriding concern in the context of underdevelopment. In China, the USSR, and Vietnam—as well as elsewhere—the government sought to bring women into the workforce, often via education. It thus brought the control of women's labor out of the family and placed it under the control of the state. Although women entered the workforce in unprecedented numbers, little was done to change women's work within the family and household. As a result, women have become saddled with two jobs—one paid, the other unpaid. As a number of time-budget studies have shown, [35] women have no time for politics. In countries like China and the Soviet Union, women, once actively involved in politics, have become less visible in both national and local government and in the Communist party. In Algeria and Iran, women who were prominent and active in revolutionary politics decades ago have become progressively less so. The anticolonial movements of which they were a part have adopted ideologies and policies that have reinterpreted Islamic traditions in such a way as to reinstate women's separate and unequal sphere.[36]

In sum, whereas education may relate to women's entry into paid labor, the very process of women's integration into paid work appears to have limited women's roles in the political system. However, in some countries the rise in women's education has paralleled the reemergence of the women's movement. This has particularly been the case in the United States, Australia, Canada, Great Britain, India, France, and the Scandinavian countries. In these countries increased education has not led to political power, but it has had the effect of changing women's consciousness of oppression and has provided the means for women to organize as women to put women's issues on national political agendas. Such developments are a cause for optimism. In the long run, education may serve to empower women to struggle for their rights and for control over their lives. The role of education in this struggle, however, is not very clear.

EDUCATION: A ROUTE TO GENDER EQUALITY?

The case studies in this handbook, the cross-national trends described in the preceding pages, and the research studies listed in the bibliography which concludes this volume are at once optimistic and pessimistic about achieving gender equality in school and society. Clearly it is possible for women to gain equal access to education at all levels. Over the past twenty years there has been a world-wide trend toward the equalization of primary school enrollments. As national economies get richer, the trend toward equalization extends to secondary education. In much of Europe and North America not only have higher education enrollments equalized, but women form the majority of students.

Although equality in access to schools is attainable, even in very poor countries, that equality does not carry over into life after school. The expansion of education has sometimes increased women's participation in the paid labor force, but it is not evident, particularly in the Third World, that this change signifies an increased participation of women in productive labor or how much women are compensated for their work relative to men. Over the past twenty years, while educational opportunities opened more dramatically for women than for men, their participation in salaried labor has stagnated at best, and in much of the world it has actually declined. The increasing levels of female education have meant in some countries changes in the work women do, but not the remuneration for that work. Women's income relative to men's has declined nonetheless. If women's unpaid labor in Third World countries were included, the income declines of women versus men would probably be dramatic. Equality in education, when it is obtained, has had little influence on the workforce outcomes of women's schooling relative to men's. More depressing than the labor force outcomes of educational expansion are the effects of increasing women's education on the political system. Women have never had access to political power in much of the world, and in those countries where they have made gains through their organized presence in revolutionary movements, they have progressively lost what little power they had. Socialist revolutions put women into the workforce and instituted the double shift: one job in the family and one for wages in the labor market. As noted earlier, women have no time for politics.

Why, despite increasing levels of schooling, have women failed to achieve equality in the public spheres of work and politics? The answer is complex. First, equality in access to education may be only part of the issue. As this handbook shows, few countries have even begun to deal with educational processes—more specifically, what schools teach to whom and with what effect. For the most part, women have been provided with access to some, but not all, male knowledge. Texts in countries as diverse as France, Togo, Chile, the United States, and India still ignore women or portray them primarily as wives and mothers. The history presented is still the history of men.[37] Sex segregation remains in secondary and higher education throughout the world. Teaching, nursing, social services, secretarial studies, literature, and the arts remain worldwide fields of study which are "women's." Engineering, the "hard sciences," and technical subjects are male domains into which women have made few inroads in nations as disparate as Vietnam, Iran, Sweden, Nigeria, England, Israel, Peru, Japan, and Senegal. Equality of access to education at all levels has meant access to gendered subjects. Increasing the number of women in schooling does little to change what women are educated to do. The chapters on Sweden, Canada, India, France, Great Britain, the United States, and Chile, for example, make this point eloquently and underscore how women's studies has arisen to challenge the male-centered educational processes. An exclusive focus on access may have guaranteed inequality in educational outcomes simply because educational processes have been left relatively untouched. However, gender-based inequalities in education—access and process—are not the only reason why gender-based inequalities have persisted and in some cases widened in the workforce, in income, and in the political system in most countries.

The whole conception of education as an enabling condition of equality is premised on the belief that gender-based inequality in society was somehow rational, stemming from women's lack of qualifications equivalent to those possessed by men. Women were also presumed to have little power or authority because they were not engaged, as were men, in earning a wage and therefore being productive. With earnings came power, authority, and autonomy. Ignored were the effect of marriage, childbearing, and childrearing on women. Education was seen as integrating women into male-dominated social structures on male terms. The sex-role division of labor in the family was deemed irrelevant. Thus, education was seen as a means of enabling women to work like men at a job for a wage and, unlike men, at home bearing and rearing children. Few efforts have been made to change expectations of women's roles in the household, the structure of occupations, workforce segregation, discrimination against women in employment and in remuneration, and the lack of opportunities for women to advance in the workplace and in the political structure. Education can only provide knowledge, skills, and credentials, but the extent to which these translate into equality in society depends on whether the structures that keep women subservient to men are changed. This extends not only to the workforce, but also to the sex-role division of labor in the family.

As long as the domestic sphere remains woman's domain, women are unlikely, unless in poverty, to work at jobs, no matter how educated they are, that do not allow them to combine their double shift of work at home and work outside of the home. Employers will continue to discriminate against women whom they consider "bad" workers because their work is divided between wage-earning employment and the family and because, as in the USSR, Vietnam, China, and Sweden, profits decline when employers are mandated to provide maternity benefits. Under the double shift, women will continue to be outside positions of power and authority in political life because they lack the time to be active in politics. Achieving equality in educational access is not elusive; it can be done. However, it takes more than opening schools to women.

NOTES

1. See Susan McCrae Vander Voet, "The United Nations Decade for Women: The Search for Women's Equality in Education and Employment," in Aisla Thomson, ed., *Decade for Women: Special Report* (Toronto: Canadian Congress for Learning Opportunities, 1985), pp. 78–79.

2. Ibid.

3. See Isabelle Deble, *The School Education of Girls: An International Comparative Study on School Wastage Among Girls and Boys at the First and Second Levels of Education* (Paris: Unesco, 1980).

4. Vander Voet, "The United Nations Decade," pp. 78–79.

5. Deble, *The School Education of Girls,* pp. 36–37.

6. Ibid., pp. 62–69; Vander Voet, "The United Nations Decade," p. 80.

7. Deble, *The School Education of Girls,* p. 66.

8. See especially Beatrice Dupont, *Unequal Education: A Study of Sex Differences in Secondary School Curricula* (Paris: Unesco, 1981).

9. See Dupont, *Unequal Education*; see also Lucita Lazo, *Work and Training Opportunities for Women in Asia and the Pacific* (Islamabad: International Labour Office, Asian and Pacific Skill Development Programme, Monograph 4, 1984).

10. Vander Voet, "The United Nations Decade," pp. 78–79.

11. Ibid.

12. Lazo, *Work and Training;* Dupont, *Unequal Education.*

13. Deble, *The School Education of Girls,* p. 34.

14. Ibid.

15. Vander Voet, "The United Nations Decade," p. 82.

16. See, for example, Noreen Clark, *Education for Development and the Rural Women.* Vol. 1. *A Review of Theory and Principles* (New York: World Education, 1979); Ester Boserup, *Women's Role in Economic Development* (New York: St. Martin's Press, 1970); Mayra Buvinic, *Women and Development: Indicators of Their Changing Role* (Paris: Unesco, 1981); C. Arnold Anderson and Mary Jean Bowman, "The Participation of Women in Education in the Third World," *Comparative Education Review* 24 (Part 2, June 1980): S13–S32.

17. See, for example, Maureen Woodhall, "The Economic Returns to Investment in Women's Education," *Higher Education* 2 (1973): 275–299; Albert W. J. Niemi, "Sexist Differences in Returns to Educational Investment," *Quarterly Review of Economics and Business* 15 (1975): 17–26.

18. E. A. Cebotarev, "Women, Work and Employment: Some Attainments of the International Women's Decade," in Thompson, ed., *The Decade for Women*, p. 70.

19. Ibid.

20. See, for example, Audrey Chapman Smock. *Women's Education in Developing Countries: Opportunities and Outcomes* (New York: Praeger, 1981); Rounaq Jahan and Hanna Papanek, eds., *Women and Development: Perspectives from South and Southeast Asia* (Dacca: Institute of Law and International Affairs, 1979).

21. See especially Gavin W. Jones, "Economic Growth and Changing Female Employment Structure in the Cities of Southeast and East Asia," in Gavin W. Jones, ed., *Women in the Urban and Industrial Workforce: Southeast and East Asia* (Canberra: Australian National University, Development Studies Centre Monograph No. 33, 1984), pp. 17–60; Chantel Bernard et al., eds., *La Politique de l'Emploi-Formation au Maghreb (1970–1980)* (Paris: Editions du Centre National de la Recherche Scientifique, 1982); Cynthia B. Lloyd, ed., *Sex Discrimination and the Division of Labor* (New York: Columbia University Press, 1975).

22. Jones, *Women in the Urban and Industrial Workforce*.

23. Ibid. See also E. Schiefelbein and J. P. Farrell, "Women, Schooling and Work in Chile: Evidence from a Longitudinal Study," *Comparative Education Review* 24 (Part 2, June 1980): S160–S179; see chapter on Botswana in this handbook.

24. Gail Lapidus, *Women in Soviet Society* (Berkeley: University of California Press, 1980); Elizabeth M. Almquist. "Women in the Labor Force," *Signs* 2 (1977): 843–855; Francine D. Blau and Carol L. Jusenius, "Economic Approaches to Sex Segregation in the Labor Market: An Appraisal," *Signs* 1 (1976): 181–199; Audrey Smock, *Women's Education in Developing Countries* (New York: Praeger, 1981).

25. Smock, *Women's Education;* Boserup, *Women's Role;* Claire Robertson, *Sharing the Same Bowl: A Socioeconomic History of Women and Class in Accra, Ghana* (Bloomington: Indiana University Press, 1984).

26. Jones, *Women in the Urban and Industrial Workforce*.

27. See chapter on Egypt in this handbook (Chapter 19). See also Earl L. Sullivan. "Women and Work in Egypt," in Earl L. Sullivan and Korima Korayen, eds. (Cairo Papers in Social Science, Monograph 4, December 1981), pp. 1–44; Nermin Abadan-Unat, *Women in the Developing World: Evidence from Turkey* (Denver: University of Denver School of International Studies, Monograph Series in World Affairs No. 22, 1986); Nermin Abadan-Unat, ed., *Women in Turkish Society* (Leiden: E. J. Brill, 1981).

28. Jones, *Women in the Urban and Industrial Workforce*.

29. Catalina Wainerman, "Impact of Education on the Female Labor Force in Argentina and Paraguay," *Comparative Education Review* 24 (1980): S180–S195; Liba Paukert, "Personal Preference, Social Change or Economic Necessity: Why Women Work," *Labour and Society* 7 (1982): 311–331.

30. Vander Voet, "The United Nations Decade," p. 84.

31. Ceberatov, "Women, Work and Employment."

32. Ibid.; Vander Voet, "The United Nations Decade," p. 85.

33. Vander Voet, "The United Nations Decade," p. 85.

34. Helene Vandevelde-Dailliere, *Femmes Algeriennes a Travers la Condition dans*

le Constantinois Depuis l'Independence (Alger: Office des Publications Universitaires, 1980); Catherine Delcroix, *Espoirs et Realities de la Femme Arabe: Algerie-Egypte* (Paris: Editions l'Harmattan, 1986); Gail Lapidus, *Women in Soviet Society;* Peter R. Knauss, *The Persistence of Patriarchy: Class, Gender and Ideology in Twentieth Century Algeria* (New York and Westport Conn.: Praeger, 1987); Margery Wolf, *Revolution Postponed: Women in Contemporary China* (San Francisco: Stanford University Press, 1985); Phyllis Andors, *The Unfinished Liberation of Chinese Women, 1949–1980* (Bloomington: Indiana University Press, 1983); Elizabeth Croll, *Chinese Women Since Mao* (London: Zed Books, 1983).

35. See Lapidus, *Women in Soviet Society;* Brenda G. McSweeney and Marion Freedom, "Lack of Time as an Obstacle to Women's Education: The Case of Upper Volta," *Comparative Education Review* 24 (1980): S124–S139.

36. See the chapter on Iran (Chapter 20) in this volume. See also Knauss, *The Persistence of Patriarchy*.

37. See, for example, Jatie Whyld, ed., *Sexism in Secondary Curriculum* (London: Harper & Row, 1983); M. Kalantzis and B. Cope, "Cultural Differences, Gender Differences: Social Literacy and Inclusive Curriculum," *Curriculum Perspectives* 7 (1987): 64–69; Shiam Sharma and Roland Meighan, "Schooling and Sex Roles: The Case of GCE 'O' Level Mathematics," *British Journal of Sociology of Education* 1 (1980): 193–206; Jeanine Anderson and Cristina Herencia, *L'Image de la Femme et de l'homme dans les livres scolaires peruviens* (Paris: Unesco, 1983); Linda Clark, *Schooling the Daughters of Marianne: Textbooks and the Socialization of Girls in Modern French Primary Schools* (Albany, N.Y.: SUNY Press, 1984).

BIBLIOGRAPHY

David H. Kelly
and Gail P. Kelly

The education of women is a relatively new research focus. Until 1970, research in education made a pretense of gender neutrality. Research often assumed that the male stood for female experiences and outcomes; other times males were deemed the only significant research subject. In education our research was on "students," "teachers," and "administrators"—without any consideration that many of the students and most of the teachers were female and almost all of the administrators were male. We did have a "sex difference" literature—but that literature charted, for the most part, what was presumed natured rather than nurtured. As a result, in most countries there were almost no studies of women's education—and the few we had described individual institutions or charted, in fragmentary fashion, enrollment patterns.

After 1970, with the rebirth of the women's movement in the United States and parts of Europe and with the United Nations International Decade for Women, scholarship on women became an important and growing part of educational research. In 1970, if one had wished to compile a bibliography of works on women's education in Europe, Africa, Asia, the Middle East, Australia, Latin America, and North America, selectivity would not have been a problem—the problem would have been finding enough studies to fill a bibliography. In 1988, it would take tomes to accommodate a comprehensive bibliography on the subject. The scholarship, begun tentatively as a critique of sexist assumptions undergirding educational research and as a charting of enrollment patterns, has grown dramatically in the number of serious research studies on women's education, in the facets of women's education investigated, and in the diversity of theoretical perspectives guiding study.[1] By 1980, when we put together a bibliography on women's education in the Third World for the International Bureau of Education, we were hardpressed to locate 500 items, both published and unpublished.[2] In 1988, when we compiled the bibliography that follows, we found it almost impossible to limit the bibliography to less than 1,000 published books, book chapters, and journal articles. In short, in 1970, few studied women; since that time, scholarship on women and on women's education has flourished—so much so that a bibliography such as this one is faced with the prospects of excluding a number of excellent studies.

This bibliography is on women's education. It focuses on research on a range of questions that place women and their education at the center of investigation. Such research may ask about the methodology of study and the theoretical assumptions about women and their schooling as well as about the context of women's education and its history. School provision for women as well as educational processes and the cognitive and attitudinal outcomes of education form a part of the research literature we have included here. An important facet of scholarship is the study of the outcomes of women's education in the public spheres of the workforce and the political system and the private sphere of the family. Such scholarship is part of this bibliography, as are studies that focus on strategies for change that result from education in social structures, in the distribution of power and wealth in society, in the family, and in the knowledge infrastructure.

Our mission is to focus on women's *education* seriously. There is a vast literature on women—their status, patriarchal structures that oppress women, women's networks and active agency, women's history, the women's movement, sexuality, and the like. We understand that this literature is critical to understanding the context of women's education and that much of this literature views education as both part of the structures that oppress women as well as an institution that can be made to aid in liberating women. The vast majority of such studies, however, are not on women's education directly, and we have not listed them in this bibliography for that reason. This bibliography's contribution lies in presenting the research on women's education. We cannot hope to do justice to the rich and important literature on all aspects of women's lives, their oppression and their struggle for liberation.

While there is a rich research literature of women which we did not include because its major focus was not on education, there is an extensive education literature which also does not appear in this bibliography because it does not place women at the center of inquiry. Research on social inequality, for example, acknowledges gender as a basis for inequality. We have included such studies only if they focus on gender. We have not listed research in which gender is a background variable treated in much the same way as class, ethnicity, or urban/rural residence. Studies of women's education is what this bibliography is about; it is not about inequality in general.

In this bibliography, we have also limited the number of studies on sex differences in education. A long tradition of this kind of research in education charts differences between males and females on a range of cognitive and psychological dimensions. We have listed some of this scholarship if the major focus is on explaining why such differences exist and/or the role of the schools in generating them. We have avoided filling this bibliography with the hundreds of studies that do little other than chart sex differences.

There is a difference between research on women and research on individuals who happen to be women, and we make this distinction in the bibliography. Our focus is women and studies on the significance of gender in education, and we recognize the fact that women are women and not men. Therefore, in developing this bibliography, we have been careful to include studies that are concerned with women. For example, there is a vast literature on teachers and teaching which ignores the fact that teachers in primary schools throughout most of the world (and for the most part in secondary schools as well) are women and that teaching is gendered labor. This bibliography makes a point of including research on women as teachers, on teaching as a feminized profession, and on teaching as gendered labor. We have avoided studies of the teaching profession which deny or ignore the gendered nature of the profession. Similarly, we have listed works on the home economics curriculum only insofar as such studies relate that curriculum to the social construction of gender. Although there is a vast literature on education and fertility in Third World nations, we have limited this bibliography to studies that examine the relation between women's education and fertility, and we have excluded those that simply use education as one variable related to fertility.

The bibliography lists key works on the education of women and is limited to published articles, books, and book chapters that are readily accessible. Since the 1970s, many dissertations have been written on the subject, and they are not included here. A guide to that literature is yet to be compiled, although Franklin Parker and Betty Jane Parker and Kay S. Wilkins[3] have listed dissertations in their bibliographies which were published in the 1970s. The dissertation literature is rich, particularly in the United States, Great Britain, India, and the Scandinavian countries. It is too vast to be listed in a bibliography as short as this one.

Also excluded from the bibliography are the many government reports and unpublished conference papers on the topic. We recognize this literature is important, but it is beyond the capabilities of this bibliography and the space allotted to it.

Not only have we limited the bibliography to published research, but we have also chosen to include substantial studies only. For reason of space, we selected articles and book chapters that were at least five printed pages in length. This eliminated most short research reports from the bibliography as well as interviews and think pieces. The choice was arbitrary and was made primarily in the interests of space. In a few rare instances we have included short articles. This has been the case when the short article was the only research published on women's education in a particular country.

The studies listed in the pages that follow are in five languages: English, French, German, Portuguese, and Spanish. We are aware that developing a bibliography on women's education in these five European languages greatly constricts research coverage. There is a lively literature on women's education in the Scandinavian languages and in Dutch which we were unable to include. Equally important are the works in Japanese, Korean, Italian, Arabic, and the Slavic languages which are also not listed in this bibliography. It is a sign of vitality of the scholarship on women and their education that research in these languages is flourishing. We regret we lacked the capacity to survey it.

This bibliography was compiled, as most are, through a search of the literature, bibliographies, and standard indexes. We were aided in our selection of materials by the authors of the chapters appearing in this handbook. Each provided us with a preliminary bibliography of the most important works on women's education in the country of her or his expertise. The published research they named formed one basis for the bibliography. We went beyond this preliminary listing to include works on the many countries that are not the subject of chapters in the handbook.

The bibliography is a selective one, but it is more selective in the case of some countries than in others. The literature on women's education in the United States, for example, could fill a volume on its own; so also we suspect could the literature from Great Britain and India—to name a few countries where the published research on the topic is vast. For these countries, we were highly selective because we did not want to develop a bibliography of education in the United States, Great Britain, and India. However, in the case of other countries, like Senegal, Tunisia, Malaysia, Kenya, and Colombia, we were less selective simply because there was a smaller volume of research in the languages in which we searched. For some countries, like Belize, Belgium, Mongolia, and Albania, there is no research on the education of women.

Despite our attempts to list research on all countries, the bibliography is not balanced geographically. We were able to locate far more studies of women's education in the United States, Great Britain, Australia, Canada, India, and Bangladesh than of women's education in Iran, Iraq, Greece, Burma, Vietnam, or Czechoslovakia. In part, this is a function of the languages covered in the bibliography, and in part of where scholarship on the subject is generated and the interests of individual scholars.

Despite its limitations, this bibliography does provide a guide to research studies on the full range of issues relating to women's education. We have taken care to include research on factors affecting access to education; on women's enrollment patterns and school processes; on women as teachers; on the curriculum and classroom interaction studies; and on sex-role stereotyping in the schools. Also listed in the bibliography are psychological studies; studies of girls' career, marriage, and educational aspirations; of nonformal education; of women and development; of women and the workforce; of women and the professions; of education and fertility; and of women's lives in the family. The bibliography is comprehensive in the topics covered; it is selective in terms of the research studies included.

The bibliography is organized topically and within each topic by region. We have chosen the topical organization because we believe that such an organization is more useful to the scholar or student. Much of the research focuses on more than one country and/or region, and there is considerable unevenness in the types of studies conducted for each country or region. For example, the research on nonformal and adult education for women is a literature generated on Third World nations of Latin America, Africa, Asia, and the Middle East. It is not particularly a North American or European literature. On the other hand, studies of women reentering higher education originate predominantly in the United States, as do "fear of success" and "mathematics anxiety" studies. Many of the studies of women as teachers are grounded in North America and Europe, as are studies of classroom processes, curriculum, and educational achievement. The literature on educational access, however, is conducted predominantly in Third World settings where education is not universal and the gaps between male and female enrollments are wide beginning in the primary school. We believe that a topical organization of the bibliography highlights the range of studies across region on women's education. Although there are many differences among nations, regions, and cultures in women's education, research on a given topic, such as the expansion of education and women's access to political power, has vast implications for all nations, regardless of the geographic area in which a particular study is grounded. A bibliography that is topically organized tells much about the state of the scholarship and illuminates areas in need of further study.

The topics used to organize the research are not always discrete. Many of the collections, which begin the bibliography, contain research on many topics, including women's enrollment patterns, the factors affecting those patterns, and the impact of education on marriage and the family and on the workforce. Many of the topics overlap. For example, the literature on women and the professions overlaps that of women in the workforce. Similarly, research on adult and nonformal education is often research on education and development, whereas much of the labor force participation studies conducted in Third World settings are studies that implicitly are on development. Many of the research reports on women in the Middle East are studies in part of the impact of a particular religion, Islam, on women's education. In many cases, it is impossible to provide discretion between topics; we have tried as best we could to avoid overlap. However, scholars writing about women's education often do not confine themselves to a single, discrete topic.

This bibliography focuses on works published since 1975. We have attempted to be less selective with works published in the past thirteen years. Some studies included here—like Ester Boserup's *Women's Role in Economic Development,* are earlier.[4] We have included such works either because they are the classic studies in the field or because they are the only works on a given country. A major contribution of this bibliography is that it is current. Other bibliographies—including one we compiled for the International Bureau of Education in 1980—cover an earlier literature, particularly on Third World nations.

This bibliography is not intended as a definitive listing. Our intent has been to bring together research studies on the full range of questions which scholars have addressed worldwide in five languages. We hope that such a listing will be useful to those who wish to extend their knowledge about the complex research issues in the current scholarship on women's education throughout the world today.

NOTES

1. See Ellen DuBois et al., *Feminist Scholarship: Kindling in the Groves of Academe* (Champaign: University of Illinois Press, 1985).

2. David H. Kelly and Gail P. Kelly, "Education of Women in Developing Countries," *Educational Documentation and Information: Bulletin of the International Bureau of Education* 56, No. 222 (1982).

3. Franklin Parker and Betty Jane Parker, *Women's Education—A World View: Annotated Bibliography of Doctoral Dissertations* (Westport, Conn.: Greenwood Press, 1979); Kay S. Wilkins, *Women's Education in the United States: A Guide to Information Sources* (Detroit: Gale Research, 1979).

4. Ester Boserup, *Women's Role in Economic Development* (New York: St. Martin's Press, 1969).

COLLECTIONS

Acker, Sandra, et al. *World Yearbook of Education: 1984 Women and Education*. London: Kogan Page; New York: Nicholas Publishing Co., 1984.

Baldock, C. V., and B. Cass, eds. *Women, Social Welfare and the State*. Sydney: Allen & Unwin, 1983.

Burns, R., and B. Sheehan, eds. *Women and Education. Proceedings of the Twelfth Annual Conference of the Australian and New Zealand Comparative and International Education Society*. Bundoora: La Trobe University, 1984.

Chabaud, Jacqueline, ed. *Education and Advancement of Women*. Paris: Unesco, 1970.

Covarrubias, Paz, and R. Franco, eds. *Chile: mujer y sociedad*. Santiago: Alfebeta Imp., 1979.

Deem, Rosemary, ed. *Schooling for Women's Work*. London: Routledge & Kegan Paul, 1980.

de Souza, Alfred, ed. *Women in Contemporary India and South Asia*. 2nd ed. New Delhi: Manohar, 1980.

Fennema, Elizabeth, and M. Jane Ayer, eds. *Women and Education*. Berkeley, Calif: McCutchan, 1984.

Flynn, Pam, ed. *You're Learning All the Time*. Nottingham: Atlantic Highlands, 1986.

Gaskell, Jane S., and Arlene T. McLaren, eds. *Women and Education: A Canadian Perspective*. Calgary: Detselig Enterprises, 1987.

Gumbert, Edgar B., ed. *Expressions of Power in Education: Studies of Class, Gender and Race*. Atlanta: Center for Cross Cultural Education, Georgia State University, 1984.

Hunt, Felicity, ed. *Lessons for Life: The Schooling of Girls and Women, 1850–1950*. New York: Blackwell, 1987.

Jancar, B. W., eds. *Women Under Communism*. Baltimore: Johns Hopkins University Press, 1981.

Kelly, Gail P., and Carolyn M. Elliott, eds. *Women's Education in the Third World: Comparative Perspectives*. Albany, N.Y.: SUNY Press, 1982.

Kuhrig, Herta von, and Wulfram Speigner, eds. *Die emanzipiert sind die Frauen in der DDR: Beruf, Bildung, Familie*. Koln: Pahl-Rugenstein, 1979.

Lapidus, Gail W., ed. *Women, Work and Family in the Soviet Union*. Armonk, N.Y.: M. E. Sharpe, 1982.

Lindsay, Beverly, ed. *Comparative Perspectives of Third World Women. The Impact of Race, Sex and Class*. New York: Praeger, 1980.

Maccia, Elizabeth Steiner, ed. *Women and Education*. Bloomington, Ind.: Charles C. Thomas, 1975.

O'Donnell, Carol, ed. *The Basis of the Bargain*. Sydney: Allen & Unwin, 1984.

Romao, Isabel, ed. *Situacão das mulheres Portuguesas perante a educacão*. Lisboa: Comissão da condicão Feminina, 1978.

Stacey, Judith, Susan Bereaud, and Joan Daniels, eds. *And Jill Came Tumbling After: Sexism in American Education*. New York: Dell Publishing Co., 1974.

Stein, Edith, *Essays on Women. The Collected Works of Edith Stein*, Vol. 2. Washington, D.C.: ICS Publications, 1985.

Thomson, Aisla, ed. *The Decade for Women*. Toronto: Canadian Congress for Learning Opportunities for Women, 1986.

Walker, Stephen, and Len Barton, eds. *Gender, Class and Education*. London: Falmer Press, 1983.

Weiner, Gaby, ed. *Just a Bunch of Girls*. Milton Keyner and Philadelphia: Open University Press, 1985.

Weis, Lois, ed. *Race, Class and Gender in American Schools*. Albany, N.Y.: SUNY Press, 1988.

Unesco. *Women, Education, Equality: A Decade of Experiment*. Paris: Unesco, 1975.

SPECIAL ISSUES

Berger, G., ed. "Changing Roles of Women." (Symposium.) *Journal of Research and Development in Education* 10 (Summer 1977): 1–76.

Brickley, L. T., et al., eds. "Women and Education: Symposium." *Harvard Educational Review* 49 (November 1979): 413–526 and 50 (February 1980): 1–69.

Collier-Thomas, B., ed. "Impact of Black Women in Education." (Symposium.) *Journal of Negro Education* 51 (Summer 1982): 173–357.

"Continuing Education for Women." (Symposium.) *Journal of the National Association for Women Deans, Administrators and Counselors* 46 (Summer 1983): 3–42.

"Education and the Process of Emancipation of Western European Women." (Symposium.) *Western European Education* 19 (Fall 1987): 3–103.

"Education of Women." (Symposium.) *Trends in Education* (Winter 1978): 3–35.

Evans, N. J., ed. "Facilitating the Development of Women." (Symposium.) *New Directions for Student Services*, No. 29 (1985): 1–110.

Ihle, E. L., ed. "Status of Women in Education." (Symposium.) *Educational Horizons* 60 (Fall 1981): 3–56.

Jayaweera, S., ed. "Women and Education." (Symposium.) *International Review of Education* 33, No. 4 (1987): 415–435.

Johnson, M., ed. "Special Issue: Teaching Psychology of Women." *Psychology of Women Quarterly* 7 (Fall 1982): 3–104.

Sutherland, M. B., ed. "Sex Differences in Education." (Symposium.) *Comparative Education* 23, No. 1 (1987): 5–102.

"Women and Higher Education." *Higher Education* 16, No. 7 (1988): entire issue.

"Women and Minorities in Education." (Symposium.) *Action in Teacher Education* 5 (Fall 1983): 1–57.

"Women's Development and Education." (Symposium.) *Journal of Education* 167, No. 3 (1985): 9–111.

"Women's Experience and Education." (Symposium.) *Harvard Educational Review* (1985). (Reprint of Special Issue, Fall 1979, Part 1, Winter 1980, Part 2.)

Wool, L. C., ed. "Women and Education." (Symposium.) *High School Journal* 64 (May 1981): 317–342.

GENERAL STUDIES

Books

Girls and Women in Education: A Cross-National Study of Sex Inequalities in Upbringing and in Schools and Colleges. Paris: OECD, 1986.

Smock, Audrey. *Women's Education in Developing Countries: Opportunities and Outcomes.* New York: Praeger, 1981.

Articles

Byrne, Eileen. "Gender in Education: Educational Policy in Australia and Europe, 1975–1985." *Comparative Education* 23, No. 1 (1987): 11–22.

Finn, Jeremy D. "Sex Differences in Educational Outcomes: A Cross-national Study." *Sex Roles* 6 (February 1980): 9–26.

MacDonald, M. "Schooling and the Reproduction of Class and Gender Relations." In *Education and the State: Politics, Patriarchy and Practice,* Volume 2. Edited by Roger Dale, et al. London: Falmer Press, 1981.

Madden, J. F. "Economic Rationale for Sex Differences in Education." *Southern Economics Journal* 44 (April 1978): 778–797.

Mbilinyi, M. F. "Women in Education." In *The International Encyclopedia of Education.* Edited by Torsten Husen and T. N. Postlethwaite. Oxford: Pergamon Press, 1985.

Sutherland, Margaret B. "Sex Differences in Education: An Overview." *Comparative Education* 23 (1987): 5–9.

Tomes, Hilary. "Women and Education." In *The Invisible Decade: UK Women and the UN Decade 1976–1985.* Edited by G. Ashworth and L. Bonnerjea. Aldershot, England: Gower, 1985.

Youssef, Nadia, and Shirley Hartley. "Demographic Indicators of the Status of Women in Various Societies." In *Sex Roles and Social Policy.* Edited by Jean Lipman-Blumen and Jessie Bernard. Beverly Hills, Calif.: Sage Publications, 1979.

AFRICA

Books

Hall, Marjorie, and Bakhita Amin Ismail. *Sisters Under the Sun: The Story of Sudanese Women*. New York: Longmans, 1981.

Pellow, Deborah. *Women in Accra: Options for Autonomy*. Algonac, Mich.: Reference Publications, 1977.

Robertson, Claire C. *Sharing the Same Bowl: A Socioeconomic History of Women and Class in Accra, Ghana*. Bloomington: Indiana University Press, 1984.

Articles

Callaway, Barbara J., and Enid Schildkraut. "Law, Education and Social Change: Implications on Hausa Muslim Women in Nigeria." In *Women in the World, 1975–1985: The Women's Decade*. Edited by Lynne B. Iglitzin and Ruth Ross. Santa Barbara, Calif.: ABC-Clio, 1986.

Greenstreet, Miranda. "Social Change and Ghanaian Women." *Canadian Journal of African Studies* 6 (1972): 351–355.

Steyn, Anna F., and J. M. Uys. "The Changing Position of Black Women in South Africa." In *Changing Position of Women in Family and Society*. Edited by Eugene Lupri. Leiden: E. J. Brill, 1983.

ASIA

Books

Andors, Phyllis. *The Unfinished Liberation of Chinese Women, 1949–1980*. Bloomington: Indiana University Press, 1983.

Cheng, Siok Hwa. *Women in Singapore: Legal, Educational and Economic Aspects*. Singapore: Institute of Humanities and Social Sciences, College of Graduate Studies, Nanyang University, 1976. (Institute of Humanities and Social Science Occasional Paper, No. 22.)

Condon, Jane. *A Half Step Behind: Japanese Women of the '80s*. New York: Dodd, Mead & Co., 1985.

Croll, Elizabeth. *Chinese Women Since Mao*. London: Zed Books, 1983.

Desai, Meera, and Maitreyi Krishnaraj. *Women and Society in India*. Delhi: Ajanta Publications, 1987.

Islam, S. *Women's Education in Bangladesh: Needs and Issues*. Dacca: Foundation for Research on Educational Planning and Development, 1977.

Khiang, Mi Mi. *The World of Burmese Women*. London: Zed Books, 1984.

Lebra, Takie S. *Japanese Women: Constraint and Fulfillment*. Honolulu: University of Hawaii Press, 1984.

Liddle, Joanna, and Rama Joshi. *Daughters of Independence: Gender, Caste and Class in India*. London: Zed Books, 1986.

Mazumdar, Vina. *Challenge of Education: Studies on Issues in Women's Education*. Bombay: Allied, 1985.

Patel, Tara. *Development of Education Among Tribal Women*. Delhi: Mittal Publishers, 1984.

Strange, Heather. *Rural Malay Women in Tradition and Transition*. New York: Praeger, 1981.

Tapa, Krishna B. *Women and Social Change in Nepal, 1951–1960*. Kathmandu: Ambikathapia, 1985.

Tu, Mai Thi, and Le Thi Nham Tuyet. *La Femme au Vietnam*. 2nd ed. Hanoi: Editions en Langues Etrangères, 1978.

Whyte, Robert Orr, and Pauline Whyte. *The Women of Rural Asia*. Boulder, Colo.: Westview Press, 1982.

Wolf, Margery. *Revolution Postponed: Women in Contemporary China*. Stanford, Calif.: Stanford University Press, 1985.

Articles

Chan, Itty. "Women of China from the Three Obediances to Half the Sky." *Journal of Research and Development in Education* 10 (Summer 1977): 38–52.

Cheng, Siak-Hwa. "Singapore Women: Legal Status, Educational Attainment, and Employment Patterns." *Asian Survey* 7 (April 1977): 358–374.

Don, Fatimah Hamid. "The Status, Roles and Achievements of Women in Malaysia." In *The Role of Women in Development: Seminar Papers and Statements*. Edited by Leonardo Z. Legaspi. Manila: University of Santo Tomas Press, 1976.

Ghosh, Ratna. "Women's Education in the Land of the Goddess Saraswati." *Canadian and International Education* 15 (1986): 25–44.

Joshi, Vibha, and Geeta Menon. "Research on Women's Education in India: A Review." *Perspectives in Education* 2 (April 1986): 77–98.

Jusuf, Maftuchah. "The Education of Women in Developing Countries: Focus on Indonesia." In *The Educational Dilemma of Women in Asia*. Edited by Alma de Jesus-Viardo. Manila: Philippine Women's University, 1969.

Lee Huyo-Chae, and Mim Chu-Suk. "The Status of Korean Women Today." In *Virtues in Conflict: Tradition and the Korean Women Today*. Edited by Sandra Mattielli. Seoul: Royal Asiatic Society, 1977.

Narumiya, C. "Opportunities for Girls and Women in Japanese Education." *Comparative Education* 22, No. 1 (1986): 47–52.

Sugisaki, Kazuko. "From the Moon to the Sun: Women's Liberation in Japan." In *Women in the World, 1975–1985: The Women's Decade*. Edited by Lynne B. Iglitzin and Ruth Ross. Santa Barbara, Calif.: ABC-Clio, 1986.

AUSTRALIA AND NEW ZEALAND

Books

Australia Schools Commission. *Girls, School and Society*. Canberra: Schools Commission, 1975.

Branson, J., and D. B. Miller. *Class, Sex and Education in Capitalist Society: Culture, Ideology and the Reproduction of Inequality in Australia*. Melbourne: Sorrett, 1979.

Foster, Victoria. *Changing Choices*. Sidney: Hale & Ire Monger, 1984.

Fry, Ruth. *It's Different for Daughters*. Wellington: New Zealand Council for Education Research, 1985.

Kyle, N. *Her Natural Destiny: The Education of Women in New South Wales*. Kensington, NSW: University of New South Wales Press, 1986.

MacKinnon, A. *One Foot on the Ladder: Origins and Outcomes of Girls' Secondary Schooling in South Australia*. St. Lucia: University of Queensland Press, 1984.

Porter, P. *Gender and Education*. Deakin: Deakin University Press, 1986.

Articles

Blackburn, Jean. "Schooling and Injustice for Girls." In *Unfinished Business: Social Justice for Women in Australia*. Edited by Dorothy Broom. Sydney: George Allen & Unwin, Australia, 1984.

McDonald, Geraldine. "Education and the Improvement Toward Equality." In *Women in New Zealand Society*. Edited by P. Bunkle and B. Hughes. Sydney: George Allen & Unwin, Australia, 1980.

Taylor, Sandra. "Teenage Girls and Economic Recession in Australia: Some Cultural and Educational Implications." *British Journal of Sociology of Education* 7 (1986): 379–396.

EUROPE

Books

Arnot, Madelein, ed. *Race and Gender: Equal Opportunities Policies in Education*. London: Pergamon, 1985.

Becker-Cantarino, Barbara. *Der Lang Weg zur Mundigkeit*. Stuttgart: F. B. Metzler, 1987.

Berg-Eldering, Lotty van den. *Colloquia on Women and Migration: Cultural and Economic Aspects*. Strasbourg: Council for Cultural Cooperation, 1986.

Borsch, Sabine. *Fremsprachen studium, Frauenstadium*. Tubingen: Stauffenberg, 1982.

Condition economique et sociale des femmes dans la communauté. Luxembourg: Office des publications officielles des Communautés européennes, 1981.

Deem, Rosemary. *Women and Schooling*. London: Routledge & Kegan Paul, 1978.

Diekershoff, Sibylle. *Empfehlungen zur Gestaltung von Bildungsangeboten für Frauen*. Stuttgart: W. Kuhlhammer, 1982.

Economic and Social Position of Women in the Community. Luxembourg: Office des publications officielles des communautés europeènes, 1981.

Elqvist-Saltzman, Inga, and Susan Opper. *Equality and Internationalism: Two Concepts at the Forefront of Educational Transformation in Sweden?* Uppsala: Department of Education, University of Uppsala, 1981.

Eskola, Katarina. *The Role of Women in Creative Cultural Work*. Helsinki: Department of Sociology, University of Helsinki, 1984.

Frauen in der Schweiz. Zug: Klett und Balmer, 1983.

Friedrich-Ebert-Stiftung. *Frauen in der Deutschen Demokratischen Republik*. Bonn: Verlag Neue Gesellschaft, 1981.

German Democratic Republic. *Panorama DDR: Equal Rights in Practice: Women in the GDR*. Dresden: Verlag Zeit im Bild, 1986.

Kuhn, Annette and Gerda Tornieporth. *Frauenbildung und Geschlechtsrolle: historische und erziehungswissenschaftliche Studien zum Wandel der Frauenrolle in Familie*. Gielnhausen: Burckhardthaus-Laetare-Verlag, 1980.

Lapidus, Gail W. *Women in Soviet Society: Equality, Development and Social Change.* Berkeley: University of California Press, 1983.

Levy, Marie-Francoise. *De mères en filles.* Paris: Calmann-Levy, 1984.

Loddenkemper, Hermann. *Kritische Perspektiven zur Frauenbilding.* Frankfurt am Main: R. G. Fischer, 1978.

McBride, Dorothy S. *Women's Rights in France.* Westport, Conn.: Greenwood Press, 1987.

Perkin, Joan. *It's Never Too Late.* London: Impact Books, 1984.

Puhlmann, Angelika. *Mädchenerziehung in der bürgerlichen Gesellschaft: Klassen Spezif.* Köln: Pahl-Rugenstein, 1979.

Schirmer, Jennifer. *The Limits of Reform: Women, Capital and Welfare.* Cambridge, Mass.: Schenkman Publishing Co., 1982.

Scott, Hilda. *Sweden's Right to Be Human. Sex Role Equality: The Goal and Reality.* London: Allison & Busby, 1982.

Shaffer, Harry G. *Women in the Two Germanies: A Comparative Study of a Socialist and Non-Socialist Society.* New York: Pergamon, 1981.

Spender, Dale. *The Education Papers: Women's Quest for Equality in Great Britain.* New York: Routledge & Kegan Paul, 1987.

Spender, Dale. *Invisible Women.* London: Writers and Readers Publishing Cooperative Society, 1982.

Articles

Deem, Rosemary. "State Policy and Ideology in the Education of Women, 1944–1980." *British Journal of Sociology of Education* 2, No. 2 (1981): 131–143.

Goldthorpe, J. H., and C. Payne. "On the Class Mobility of Women: Results from Different Approaches to the Analysis of Recent British Data." *Sociology* 20 (November 1986): 531–555.

Juillard, Joelle R. "Policy Impacts and Women's Roles in France." In *Women in the World, 1975–1985: The Women's Decade.* Edited by Lynne B. Iglitzin and Ruth Ross. Santa Barbara, Calif.: ABC-Clio, 1986.

Lapidus, Gail. "Changing Women's Roles in the USSR." In *Women in the World, 1975–1985. The Women's Decade.* Edited by Lynne B. Iglitzin and Ruth Ross. Santa Barbara, Calif.: ABC-Clio, 1976.

Means, Ingunn N. "Scandinavian Women." In *Women in the World, 1975–1985: The Women's Decade.* Edited by Lynne B. Iglitzin and Ruth Ross. Santa Barbara, Calif.: ABC-Clio, 1975.

Merkl, Peter. "West German Women: A Long Way from Kinder, Kuche, Kirche." In *Women in the World, 1975–1985: The Women's Decade.* Edited by Lynne B. Iglitzin and Ruth Ross. Santa Barbara, Calif.: ABC-Clio, 1986.

Polydopides, G. "Women's Participation in the Greek Education System." *Comparative Education* 21, No. 3 (1985): 229–240.

Robinson, R. V., and M. A. Garnier. "Class Reproduction Among Men and Women in France: Reproduction Theory on Its Home Ground." *American Journal of Sociology* 91 (September 1985): 250–280.

Siemienska, Renata. "Women, Work and Gender Equality in Poland: Reality and Its Social Perception." In *Women, State, and Party in Eastern Europe.* Edited by Sharon L. Wolchik and Alfred G. Meyer. Durham, N.C.: Duke University Press, 1985.

Szechy, E. "The Problems of Female Education in Hungary." *Comparative Education* 23, No. 1 (1987): 69–74.

Vicinus, M. "Distance and Desire: English Boarding-School Friendships." *Signs* 9 (Summer 1984): 600–622.

Woodward, Susan. "The Rights of Women: Ideology, Policy and Social Change in Yugoslavia." In *Women, State, and Party in Eastern Europe*. Edited by Sharon L. Wolchik and Alfred G. Meyer. Durham, N.C.: Duke University Press, 1985.

LATIN AMERICA

Books

Acosta-Belen, Edna, ed. *The Puerto Rican Woman*. New York: Holt, Rinehart & Winston, 1979.

Perez, Liria, et al. *La educadora de primaria*. Medellín: Universidad de Antioquia, Facultad de Educación, 1984.

Articles

Browner, C. H. "Gender Roles and Social Change: A Mexican Case Study." *Ethnology* 26 (April 1986): 89–106.

Cole, Johnnetta. "Women in Cuba: The Revolution Within the Revolution." In *Comparative Perspectives of Third World Women*. Edited by Beverly Lindsay. New York: Praeger, 1980.

Franco, Zoila. "Women in the Transformation of Cuban Education." *Prospects* 5, No. 3 (1975): 387–390.

González Salazar, Gloria. "La mujer: Condiciones estructurales y educación." In *Reforma educativa y "Apertura democratica."* Edited by Fernando Carmona, et al. Mexico City: Ed. Nuestro Tiemo, 1972.

Hamilton, Marlene, and Elsa Leo-Rhynie. "Sex Roles and Secondary Education in Jamaica." *World Yearbook 1984, Women's Education*. Edited by Sandra Acker et al. London: Kogan Page; New York: Nicholas Publishing, 1984.

McKensie, Hermione. "The Educational Experiences of Caribbean Women." *Social and Economic Studies* 35, No. 3 (1986): 65–105.

Perez-Venero, Mirna M. "Education of Women on the Isthmus of Panama." *Journal of the West* 12 (1973): 325–334.

Pico de Hernandez, Isabel. "The Quest for Race, Sex and Ethnic Equality in Puerto Rico." *Caribbean Studies* 14 (1975): 127–141.

Preston, Rosemary. "Gender, Ideology and Education: Implications at the Ecuadorian Periphery." *Compare* 15 (1985): 29–40.

Schmidt, Steffen W. "Women in Colombia." In *Women in the World, 1975–1985: The Women's Decade*. Edited by Lynne B. Iglitzin and Ruth Ross. Santa Barbara, Calif.: ABC-Clio, 1986.

Sutton, Constance, and Susan Makiesky-Barrow. "Social Inequality and Sexual Status in Barbados." In *The Black Woman Culturally*. Edited by Filomina Chioma Steady. Cambridge, Mass.: Schenkman Publishing Co., 1981.

MIDDLE EAST

Books

Abadan-Unat, Nermin, ed. *Women in Turkish Society*. Leiden: E. J. Brill, 1981.
Altorki, Soraya. *Women in Saudi Arabia: Ideology and Behavior Among the Elite*. New York: Columbia University Press, 1986.
Ingrams, Doreen. *The Awakened: Women in Iraq*. London: Third World Centre for Research and Publishing, 1983.
Knauss, Peter R. *The Persistence of Patriarchy: Class, Gender and Ideology in Twentieth Century Algeria*. New York and Westport, Conn.: Praeger, 1987.
Maher, Vanessa. *Women and Property in Morocco: Their Changing Relation to the Process of Social Stratification in the Middle Atlas*. Cambridge: Cambridge University Press, 1974.
Molyneux, Maxine. *State Policies and the Position of Women Workers in the Democratic Republic of Yemen, 1967–77*. Geneva: International Labour Office, 1982.
Rashedi, Khorram. *Les Femmes en Iran, avant et après la revolution*. Paris: Nouvelle Editions Rupture, 1983.
Soffan, Linda Usra. *The Women of the United Arab Emirates*. London: Croom Helm, 1980.

Articles

Abou Seoud Khattab, Hind, and Syada Greiss El Daeif. "Female Education in Egypt: Changing Attitudes over a Span of 100 Years." In *Muslim Women*. Edited by Freda Hussein. New York: St. Martin's Press, 1984.
Boneparth, Ellen. "In the Land of the Patriarchs: Public Policy on Women in Israel." In *Women in the World, 1975–1985: The Women's Decade*. Edited by Lynne B. Iglitzin and Ruth Ross. Santa Barbara, Calif.: ABC-Clio, 1986.
Cornell, M. Louise. "The Development of Education for Women in Kuwait." *Canadian and International Education/Education Canadienne et internationale* 5 (December 1976): 73–83.
El Guindi, Fadwa. "The Egyptian Woman: Trends Today, Alternatives Tomorrow." In *Women in the World, 1975–1985: The Women's Decade*. Edited by Lynne B. Iglitzin and Ruth Ross. Santa Barbara, Calif.: ABC-Clio, 1986.
El-Mahairy, Theresa. "Status and Education of Women: A Perspective on Egypt." In *Women's Worlds*. Edited by Marilyn Safir, et al. New York: Praeger, 1985.
Erkut, Sumru. "Dualism in Values Toward Education of Turkish Women." In *Sex Roles, Family and Community in Turkey*. Edited by Cigdem Kagitcibasi and Diane Sunar. Bloomington: Indiana University, Turkish Studies 3, 1982.
Es-Said, Nimra Tannous. "The Changing Role of Women in Jordan: A Threat or an Asset?" In *Sex Roles and Social Policy*. Edited by Jean Lipman-Blumen and Jessie Bernard. Beverly Hills, Calif.: Sage Publications, 1979.
Maher, Vanessa. "Women and Social Change in Morocco." In *Women in the Muslim World*. Edited by L. Beck and N. Keddie. Cambridge, Mass.: Harvard University Press, 1978.
Mujahid, Ghazy. "Education for Girls in Saudi Arabia." *Muslim Education Quarterly* 4, No. 3 (1987): 45–71.

Mustaffa-Kedah, O. "The Education of Women in the Arab States." *Literary Discussion* 6 (Winter 1975–1976): 119–139.

Ozbay, Ferhunde. "The Impact of Education on Women in Rural and Urban Turkey." In *Women in Turkish Society*. Edited by Nermin Abadan-Unat. Leiden: E. J. Brill, 1981.

NORTH AMERICA

Books

Fenema, Elizabeth, and M. Jane Ayer. *Women and Education: Equity or Equality?* Berkeley, Calif.: McCutchan, 1984.

Frazier, Nancy, and Myra Sadker. *Sexism in School and Society*. New York: Harper & Row, 1973.

Gaskell, Jane S. and Arlene T. McLaren, eds. *Women and Education: A Canadian Perspective*. Calgary: Detselig, 1987.

Giele, Janet Z. *Women and the Future: Changing Sex Roles in Modern America*. New York: Free Press, 1978.

Hayes, Christine. *Findings and Forecasts*. Washington, D.C.: Wider Opportunities for Women, 1985.

Sexton, Patricia. *Women in Education*. Bloomington, Ind.: Phi Delta Kappan, 1976.

Articles

Kelly, Gail P., and Ann Nihlen. "Schooling and the Reproduction of Patriarchy: Unequal Workloads, Unequal Rewards." In *Cultural and Economic Reproduction in Education*. Edited by Michael Apple. London: Routledge & Kegan Paul, 1982.

Schwager, Sally. "Educating Women in America." *Signs* 12 (1987): 333–372.

THEORETICAL AND RESEARCH ORIENTATIONS

Books

Langland, Elizabeth, and Walter Grove, eds. *A Feminist Perspective in the Academy: The Difference It Makes*. Chicago: University of Chicago Press, 1981.

Tobak, Fanny, ed. *A mulher como objecto de estudio*. Rio de Janeiro: Pontificia Universidad Catolica do Rio de Janeiro, Divisão de Intercambio e edicões, 1982.

Articles

Acker, Sandra. "Feminist Theory and the Study of Gender and Education." *International Review of Education* 33 (1987): 419–435.

Acker, S. "No-Woman's-land: British Sociology of Education 1960–1979." *Sociological Review* 29 (1981): 77–104.

Acker, Sandra. "Sociology, Gender and Education." In *World Yearbook of Education 1984. Women and Education*. Edited by S. Acker et al. New York: Kogan Page, 1984.

Arnot, Madeline. "Culture and Political Economy: Dual Perspectives in the Sociology of Women's Education." *Educational Analysis* 3 (1981): 97–116.

Davies, Lynn. "Gender, Resistance and Power." In *Gender, Class and Education*. Edited by S. Walker and L. Barton. London: Falmer Press, 1982.

Elliott, Carolyn, and Gail P. Kelly. "Perspectives in the Education of Women in Third World Nations." *Comparative Education Review* 24 (June 1980): S1–S12.

Henricksen, H. V. "Class and Gender: Role Model Considerations and Liberations in Advanced Capitalism" *Interchange* 12, No. 2–3 (1981): 151–164.

Kelly, Gail P. "Failures of Androcentric Studies of Women's Education in the Third World." In *For Alma Mater: Theory and Practice in Feminist Scholarship*. Edited by Paula A. Treichler, Cheris Kramarea, and Beth Stafford. Champaign: University of Illinois Press, 1985.

Lockheed, Marlaine, and Sandra Stein. "The Status of Women's Research in Educational Publications." *Educational Researcher* 9 (February 1980): 11–15.

Martin, Jane Roland. "Excluding Women from the Educational Realm." *Harvard Educational Review* 52 (1982): 133–148.

Martin, Jane Roland. "Philosophy, Gender and Education." In *World Yearbook of Education 1984. Women and Education*. Edited by Sandra Acker et al. London and New York: Kogan Page, 1984.

Martin, Jane Roland. "Re-defining the Educated Person: Rethinking the Significance by Gender." *Educational Researcher* 15 (June/July 1986): 6–10.

Megary, Jacquetta. "Introduction: Sex, Gender and Education." In *World Yearbook of Education 1984. Women and Education*. Edited by Sandra Acker et al. London and New York: Kogan Page, 1984.

Rendel, M. "Panorama mondial de la recherche et de l'enseignement sur la femme." *Cultures* 8, No. 3 (1982): 105–125.

Rockhill, Kathleen. "Gender, Language and the Politics of Literacy." *British Journal of Sociology of Education* 8, No. 2 (1987): 153–168.

Spender, Dale. "Education: The Patriarchical Paradigm and the Response to Feminism." In *Men's Studies Modified*. Edited by Dale Spender. Oxford: Pergamon Press, 1981.

Westkott, Marcia. "Feminist Criticism of the Social Sciences." *Harvard Educational Review* 49 (1974): 422–430.

HISTORIES

AFRICA

Books

Callaway, Helen. *Gender, Culture and Empire: European Women in Colonial Nigeria*. London: Macmillan, 1987.

Strobel, Margaret. *Muslim Women in Mombasa 1890–1975*. New Haven, Conn. and London: Yale University Press, 1979.

Articles

Barthel, D. L. "Rise of a Female Professional Elite: The Case of Senegal." *African Studies Review* 18 (December 1975): 1–17.

Barthel, Diane. "Women's Education Under Colonialism: Toward a Diachronic Model."
    Signs 11 (1985): 137–154.
Lamba, Isaac C. "African Women's Education in Malawi, 1875–1952." *Journal of
    Educational Administration and History* 14 (1982): 46–54.
Mann, Kristin. "The Dangers of Dependence: Christian Marriage Among Elite Women
    in Lagos Colony, 1880–1915." *Journal of African History* 24 (1983): 37–56.
Tibenderana, P. K. "The Beginnings of Girls' Education in the Native Administration
    School in Northern Nigeria." *Journal of African History* 26 (1985): 93–109.
Whitehead, Clive. "The Education of Women and Girls: An Aspect of British Colonial
    Policy." *Journal of Educational Administration and History* 16 (1984): 24–34.
Yates, Barbara. "Church, State and Education in Belgian Africa: Implications for Con-
    temporary Third World Women." In *Women's Education in the Third World:
    Comparative Perspectives*. Edited by Gail P. Kelly and Carolyn M. Elliott. Al-
    bany, N.Y.: SUNY Press, 1982.
Yates, Barbara. "Colonialism, Education and Work: Sex Differentiation in Colonial
    Zaire." In *Women and Work in Africa*. Edited by Edna Bay. Boulder, Colo.:
    Westview Press, 1982.

ASIA

Books

Ahmad, Karuna. *The Social Context of Women's Education in India, 1921–1981*. New
    Delhi: Nehru Memorial Museum and Library, 1983.
Borthwick, Meredith.*The Changing Role of Women in Bengal, 1849–1905*. Princeton,
    N.J.: Princeton University Press, 1984.
Misra, L. *Education of Women in India, 1921–1966*. Bombay: Macmillan Co., 1966.

Articles

Bradshaw, Sue. "Catholic Sisters in China: An Effort to Raise the Status of Women."
    In *Women in China: Current Directions in Historical Scholarship*. Edited by
    Richard W. Guisso and Stanley Johannesen. Youngstown, N.Y.: Philo Press,
    1981.
Bryson, Hugh. "The Education of Girls in the 19th Century." *Malaysia* (London) (1970):
    11–14.
Jahan Mehraj. "Women's Education in a Man's World: A Comparison Between Japan
    and Bengal in the 19th Century." In *Women, Development, Devotionalism, and
    Nationalism: Bengal Studies 1985*. Edited by John Thorp. East Lansing: Michigan
    State University South Asia Series, Occasional Paper No. 36, 1985.
Manderson, Leonore. "The Development and Direction of Female Education in Penin-
    sular Malaysia" *Journal of the Malaysian Branch of the Royal Asiatic Society*
    51, No. 2 (1978): 100–122.
Marr, David. "The 1920s Women's Rights Debates in Vietnam." *Journal of Asian Studies*
    35 (1976): 371–390.
Maskiell, M. "Social Change and Social Control: College-Educated Punjabi Women
    1913 to 1960." *Modern Asian Studies* 19 (1985): 55–83.
Molla, M. K. U. "Women's Education in Early Twentieth Century Eastern Bengal." In
    Women, Development, Devotionalism and Nationalism: Bengal Studies 1985.

Edited by John Thorp. East Lansing: Michigan State University South Asia Series, Occasional Paper No. 36 (1985): 41–48.

Spade, Beatrice. "The Education of Women in China During the Southern Dynasty." *Journal of Asian History* 13 (1979): 15–41.

Taylor, Jean. "Education, Colonialism and Feminism: An Indonesian Case Study" In *Education and the Colonial Experience*. Edited by Philip G. Altbach and Gail P. Kelly. New Brunswick, N.J.: Transaction Books, 1984.

AUSTRALIA AND NEW ZEALAND

Books

Connell, R. W., et al. *Making the Difference: Schools, Families and Social Divisions*. Sydney: George Allen & Unwin, 1982.

Jones, H. *Nothing Seemed Impossible: Women's Education and Social Change in South Australia, 1875–1915*. St. Lucia: University of Queensland Press, 1985.

Kyle, Noeline. *Her Natural Destiny*. Kensington, Australia: New South Wales, University Press, 1986.

Mackinon, Alison. *One Foot on the Ladder*. St. Lucia: University of Queensland Press, 1984.

Articles

Brian-Thompson, G. "The Sex Differential of Selective Promotion in New Zealand Primary Schools: 1929–1981." *New Zealand Journal of Educational Studies* 18, No. 1 (1983): 76–79.

Cumming, A. "Education of New Zealand Girls Toward the End of the Nineteenth Century." *Paedagogica Historica* 21, No. 1 (1981): 49–68.

Lingard, Bob, M. Henry, and S. Taylor. "A Girl in a Militant Pose: A Chronology of Struggle in Girl's Education in Queensland." *British Journal of Sociology of Education* 8, No. 2 (1987): 135–152.

Oram, A. M. "'Sex Antagonism' in the Teaching Profession: The Equal Pay Issue 1914–1929." *History of Education Review* 28 (1984): 309–318.

Williamson, N. "The Feminization of Teaching in NSW: A Historical Perspective." *Australian Journal of Education* 27 (1983): 33–44.

Wimhurst, K. "Control and Resistance: Reformatory School Girls in Late Nineteenth Century South Australia." *Journal of Social History* 18 (Winter 1984): 273–287.

EUROPE

Books

Blade, Melinda. *Education of Italian Renaissance Women*. Mesquite, Texas: Ide House, 1983.

Bogerts, Hildegard. *Bildung und berufliches selbstverständnis lehrender Frauen in der Zeit von 1885 bis 1920*. Frankfurt am Main: Lang, 1977.

Bourgade, Germaine. *Contribution à l'étude d'une histoire de l'education feminine à Toulouse: de 1830 à 1914*. Toulouse: Association des publications de l'Université de Toulouse—Le Mirail, 1980.

Bryant, Margaret E. *The Unexpected Revolution*. London: University of London, 1979.

Burstyn, Joan. *Victorian Education and the Ideal of Womanhood*. New Brunswick, N.J.: Rutgers University Press, 1984.

Cannon, Mary A. *The Education of Women During the Renaissance*. Westport, Conn.: Hyperion Press, 1981.

Capel Martinez, Rosa Maria. *El trabajo y la educación de la mujer en España (1900–1930)*. Madrid: Minsterio de Cultura, 1982.

Fletcher, Sheila. *Feminists and Bureaucrats: A Study of the Development of Girls' Education in the Nineteenth Century*. Cambridge: Cambridge University Press, 1980.

Gorham, Deborah. *The Victorian Girl and the Feminine Ideal*. London: Croom Helm, 1982.

Heinze, Thomas, et al., eds. *Interpretationen einer Bildungsgeschichte: Uberlegunjen zur sozialwissenschuftl*. Bensheim: Pad-extra-Buchverlag, 1980.

Jyanga Pendi, Augusto C. *La educación de la mujer en la historia*. Valencia: NAU Libre, 1984.

Julia, Dominique. *Les Trois couleurs du tableau noir*. Paris: Belin, 1981.

Labalme, Patricia, ed. *Beyond Their Sex: Learned Women of the European Past*. New York: New York University Press, 1980.

Ladj-Teichmann, Dagmar. *Erziehung zur Weiblichkeit durch Textilarbeiten*. Weinhrim: Beltz, 1983.

Mayeur, Françoise. *L'Education des filles en France au XIXe siecle*. Paris: Hachette, 1979.

Mayeur, Francoise. *L'Enseignement secondaire des jeunes filles sous la Troisième Republique*. Paris: Presses de la Fondation nationale des scienses politique, 1977.

Meiners, Karin. *Der besondere Weg ein Weib zu werden*. Frankfurt am Main: Lang, 1982.

Pedersen, Joyce Senders. *The Reform of Girls' Secondary and Higher Education in Victorian England*. New York: Garland, 1987.

Prelinger, Catherine. *Charity, Challenge and Change: Religious Dimensions of the Mid-Nineteenth Century Women's Movement in Germany*. Westport, Conn.: Greenwood Press, 1987.

Randt, Ursula. *Carolinenstrasse 35*. Hamburg: Selbs verlag Verein für Hamburgische Geschichte, 1984.

Risse-Stumbries, Susanne. *Erziehung und Bildung der Frau in der zweiten Hälfte des 18 Jahrhunderts*. Frankfurt am Main: R. G. Fischer, 1980.

Rousselot, Paul. *Histoire de l'education des femmes en France*. New York: Lenox Hill, 1971.

Rudolph, Maria. *Die Frauenbildung in Frankfurt am Main*. Frankfurt am Main: Lang, 1978.

Soury-Lavergne, Françoise. *Chemin d'education*. Chambray: C.I.P., 1985.

Stephenson, Jill. *Women in Nazi Society*. New York: Barnes & Noble, 1975.

Strumingher, Laura S. *What Were Little Girls and Boys Made of? Primary Education in Rural France, 1830–1880*. Albany, N.Y.: SUNY Press, 1983.

Warnicke, Retha. *Women of the English Renaissance and Reformation*. Westport, Conn.: Greenwood Press, 1983.

Wiede-Behrendt, Ingrid. *Lehrerin des Schönen, Wahren, Guten*. Frankfurt am Main: P. Lang, 1987.

Zulueta, Carmen de. *Misioneras, feministas educadoras*. Zurbano: Editorial Castalia, 1984.

Articles

Albisetti, James. "Women and the Professions in Imperial Germany." In *German Women in the Eighteenth and Nineteenth Centuries*. Edited by Ruth-Ellen B. Joeres and Mary Jo Maynes. Bloomington: Indiana University Press, 1986.

Arnot, M. "Male Hegemony, Social Class and Women's Education." *Journal of Education* 164 (Winter 1982): 64–89.

Bernstein, G., and L. Bernstein. "The Curriculum for German Girls' Schools, 1870–1914." *Paedagogica Historica* 18, No. 2 (1978): 237–256.

Dyhouse, Carolyn. "Toward a 'Feminine' Curriculum for English School Girls: The Demands of Ideology, 1870–1963." *Women's Studies* 1 (1978): 297–312.

"Education des filles. Enseignement des femmes." *Penelope, Pour l'histoire des femmes*, No. 2 (1980): 1–106.

Freeze, Karen J. "Medical Education for Women in Austria: A Study in the Politics of the Czech Women's Movement in the 1890's. In *Women, State, and Party in Eastern Europe*. Edited by Sharon L. Wolchik and Alfred G. Meyer. Durham, N.C.: Duke University Press, 1985.

Fumat, Y. "La Socialisation des filles en XIXe siecle." *Revue Française de Pedagagie*, No. 52 (1980): 36–46.

Green, L. "The Education of Women in the Reformation." *History of Education Quarterly* 19, No. 1 (1979): 93–116.

Jacobs, E. "Diderot and the Education of Girls." In *Women and Society in Eighteenth Century France*. Edited by E. Jacobs et al. London: Athlone Press, 1979.

Moore, L. "Invisible Scholars: Girls Learning Latin and Mathematics in the Elementary Public Schools of Scotland before 1972." *History of Education* 13, No. 2 (1984): 121–137.

Purvis, J. "Working Class Women and Adult Education in Nineteenth Century Britain." *History of Education* 9, No. 3 (1980): 193–212.

Schneider, Joanne. "Enlightened Reforms and Bavarian Girls' Education." In *German Women in the Nineteenth Century: A Social History*. Edited by John C. Fout. London: Holmes & Meier, 1984.

Secondy, L. "L'Education des filles en milieu catholique au XIXe siecle." *Cahiers d'Histoire* 26, No. 4 (1981): 337–352.

Senders Pederson, J. "The Reform of Women's Secondary and Higher Education: Institutional Change and Social Values in Mid and Late Victorian England." *History of Education Quarterly* 19, No. 1 (1979): 61–91.

Shank, Michael H. "A Female University Student in Late Medieval Krakow." *Signs* 12 (1987): 373–380.

Watts, R. E. "The Unitarian Contribution to the Development of Female Education 1790–1850." *History of Education* 9, No. 4 (1980): 273–286.

Wynants, P. "L'Ecole des femmes. Les Catholiques belges et l'enseignement primaire feminin (1842–1860)." *Revue Nouvelle* 77, No. 1 (1983): 69–76.

LATIN AMERICA AND THE CARIBBEAN

Books

Martin, Louis. *Daughters of the Conquistadores: Women of the Viceroyalty of Peru*. Albuquerque: University of New Mexico Press, 1983.

Stolara, Juan Antonio. *La educacion de la mujer panameña en el siglo XIX*. Panama: Ministerio de Educación, Dirección Nacional de Cultura, 1966.

Articles

Cole, Joyce. "Official Ideology and the Education of Women in the English-Speaking Caribbean, 1835–1945 with Special Reference to Barbados." In *Women and Education. Women in the Caribbean Project,* Volume 5. Edited by Joycelin Massiah. Cave Hill, Barbados: Institute of Social and Economic Research, University of the West Indies, 1982.

daSilva, Maria Beatriz Nizza. Educacão feminina e educacão masculina no Brasil colonial. *Revista de Historia* 55 (1977): 149–154.

Little, Cynthia Jeffress. "Education, Philanthropy and Feminism: Components of Argentine Womanhood, 1860–1926." In *Latin American Women: Historical Perspectives*. Edited by Asuncion Lavrin. Westport, Conn.: Greenwood Press, 1978.

Vaughan, Mary K. "Women, Class and Education in Mexico, 1880–1928." *Latin American Perspectives* 4, No. 1/2 (1977): 135–152.

Vazquez, Josefina Z. "La educación de la mujer en Mexico en los siglos XVIII y XIX." *Dialogs* (Mexico) 17 (March-April 1981): 10–16.

Yaeger, Gertrude M. "Women's Roles in Nineteenth Century Chile: Public Education Records, 1843–1883." *Latin American Research Review* 18, No. 3 (1983): 149–156.

MIDDLE EAST

Books

Davis, Fanny. *The Ottoman Lady: A Social History from 1718 to 1918*. Westport, Conn.: Greenwood Press, 1986.

Kader, Soha Abdel. *Egyptian Women in a Changing Society, 1899–1987*. Boulder, Colo. and London: Lynne Rienner Publishers, 1987.

NORTH AMERICA

Books

Brewer, Eileen M. *Nuns and the Education of American Catholic Women 1860–1920*. Chicago: Loyola University Press, 1987.

Malouin, Marie-Paule. *Ma soeur, a quelle école allez-vous?* Montreal: Fides 1, 1985.

Woody, Thomas. *A History of Women's Education in the United States*. 2 vols. New York and Lancaster, Pa.: Science Press, 1929.

Articles

Burstyn, Joan N. "Catherine Beecher and the Education of American Women." In *Women's Experience in America: A Historical Anthology.* Edited by Esther Katz and Anita Rayone. New Brunswick, N.J.: Transaction Books, 1980.

Carter, S. B., and M. Prus. "Labor Market and the American High School Girl 1890–1928." *Journal of Economic History* 42 (March 1982): 163–171, 187–189.

Gillett, M. "Leacock and the Ladies of R.V.C." *McGill Journal of Education* 16 (Spring 1981): 121–129.

Green, N. "Female Education and School Competition: 1820–1850." *History of Education Quarterly* 18, No. 2 (1978): 129–142.

Griffin, G. B. "Emancipated Spirits: Women's Education and the American Midwest." *Change* 16 (January/February 1984): 32–40.

Hohnor, R. A. "Southern Education in Transition." William Waugh Smith, The Carnegie Foundation, and the Methodist Church." *History of Education Quarterly* 27 (Summer 1987): 181–203.

Perkins, L. M. "The Impact of the 'Cult of True Womanhood' on the Education of Black Women." *Journal of Social History* 39 (Fall 1983): 17–28.

Rossiter, M. W. "Doctorates for American Women 1868–1907." *History of Education Quarterly* 22 (Summer 1982): 159–183.

Rury, J. L. "Vocationalism for Home and Work: Women's Education in the United States, 1880–1930." *History of Education Quarterly* 24 (Spring 1984): 21–44.

Vinovskis, Maris, and Richard M. Bernard. "Beyond Catherine Beecher: Female Education in the Antebellum Period." *Signs* 3 (1978): 856–869.

Weiss, J. "Education for Clerical Work: The Nineteenth-Century Private Commercial School." *Journal of Social History* 14 (Spring 1981): 417–423.

RELIGION AND WOMEN'S SCHOOLING

Books

Minai, Naila. *Women in Islam: Tradition and Transition in the Middle East.* New York: Seaview Books, 1981.

Timm, K., and Schahnus Aalami. *Die Muslimische Frau zwischen Tradition und Fortschritt: Frauenfrage und Familienentwicklung in Ägypten und Iran.* Berlin: Akademie Verlag, 1976.

Articles

Al-Haini, Rafeda. "Islam's Point of View on Women's Education in Saudi Arabia." *Comparative Education* 23 (1987): 51–57.

Csapo, M. "Religious, Social and Economic Factors Hindering the Education of Girls in Northern Nigeria." *Comparative Education* 17 (1981): 311–319.

King, Ursula. "World Religions, Women and Education." *Comparative Education* 23, No. 1 (1987): 35–49.

Kleinman, S. "Women in Seminary: Dilemmas of Professional Socialization." *Sociology of Education* 57, No. 4 (1984): 210–219.

Menon, M. Indu. "Education of Muslim Women: Tradition Versus Modernity." In *Women in the Family and the Economy: An International Comparative Survey.* Edited by George Kurian and Ratna Ghosh. Westport, Conn.: Greenwood Press, 1981.

Nelson, Cynthia. "Islamic Tradition and Women's Education in Egypt." In *World Year-book of Education 1984. Women in Education*. Edited by Sandra Acker et al. London: Kogan Page, 1984.

Oduyoye, M. A. "Standing on Both Feet: Education of Women in the Methodist Church, Nigeria." *Ecumenical Review* 33 (January 1981): 60–71.

Siann, Gerda, and Rohi Khalid. "Muslim Traditions and Attitudes to Female Education." *Journal of Adolescence* 7 (June 1984): 191–200.

ENROLLMENT PATTERNS AND STATISTICS

WORLDWIDE

Books

Deble, Isabelle. *The School Education of Girls. An International Comparative Study on School Wastage Among Girls and Boys at the First and Second Levels of Education*. Paris: Unesco, 1980.

Articles

Barber, Elinor G. "Some International Perspectives on Sex Differences in Education." *Syns* 4 (Spring 1979): 584–592.

Eliou, Marie. "Equality of the Sexes in Education: And Now What?" *Comparative Education* 23 (1987): 59–67.

Finn, J. D., Loretta Dulberg, and Janet Reis. "Sex Differences in Educational Attainment: A Cross-National Perspective." *Harvard Educational Review* 49 (November 1979): 477–503.

Finn, J. D., Janet Reis, and Loretta Dulberg. "Sex Differences in Educational Attainment: The Process." *Comparative Education Review* 24 (June 1980): S33–S52.

Gergusson, D. M. "The Utilization of Preschool Health and Education Services." *Social Science and Medicine* 19, No. 11 (1984): 1173–80.

Kelly, Gail P. "Setting State Policy on Women's Education in the Third World: Perspectives from Comparative Research." *Comparative Education* 23 (1987): 95–102.

Kelly, Gail P. "Women's Access to Education in the Third World." In *World Yearbook of Education, 1984. Women and Education*. Edited by Sandra Acker et al. London: Kegan Paul, 1984.

Klein, S. S. "The Role of Public Policy in the Education of Girls and Women." *Educational Evaluation and Policy Analysis* 9 (Fall 1987): 219–230.

Kotwal, Marilyn. "Inequalities in the Distribution of Education Between Countries, Sexes, Generations and Individuals." In *Education, Inequality and Life Chances*. Edited by Organization for Economic Cooperation and Development. Paris: OECD, 1975.

Kutner, Nancy G., and D. Brogan. "Sources of Sex Discrimination in Educational Systems: A Conceptual Model." *Psychology of Women Quarterly* 1, No. 1 (1976): 50–69.

Timur, Serim. "Demographic Correlates of Women's Education." In *International Pop-

ulation Conference, Volume 3. Edited by International Union for the Scientific Study of Population. Liege: The Union, 1977.

Vander Voet, Susan McCrae. "The United Nations Decade for Women: The Search for Women's Equality in Education and Employment." In *The Decade for Women.* Edited by Aisla Thomson. Toronto: Canadian Congress for Learning Opportunities for Women, 1986.

Weiss, Y., et al. "Effect of Price and Income on Investment in Schooling." *Journal of Human Resources* 15 (Fall 1980): 611–640.

AFRICA

Books

Bruchhaus, Eva-Maria. *Frauen in Obervolta.* Freiburg im Breisgau: Arnold-Bergstraesser Institut, 1979.

Mbilinyi, Marjorie. *The Education of Girls in Tanzania.* Dar-es-Salaam: University of Dar-es-Salaam, 1969.

Articles

Adams, Milton, and Susan Kruppenbach. "Gender and Access in the African School." *International Review of Education* 33 (1987): 437–453.

Cooksey, Brian. "Education and Sexual Inequality in the Cameroun." *Journal of Modern African Studies* 20 (March 1982): 167–177.

Eliou, Marie. "The Education and Advancement of Women in Africa (Ivory Coast, Upper Volta, Senegal)." *International Review of Education* 19, No. 1 (1973): 30–46.

Grisay, Alette. "Analyse des ineqalités de rendement liées au sexe de l'élève dans l'enseignement primaire Ivoirien." *International Review of Education* 30, No. 1 (1984): 25–40.

Kinyanjiu, Kabiru. "Education and Formal Employment Opportunities for Women in Kenya: Some Preliminary Data." *Kenya Education Review* (December 1975): 6–25.

Mblinyi, Marjorie J. "Education, Stratification and Sexism in Tanzania: Policy Implications." *African Review* 3, No. 2 (1973): 327–340.

Robertson, Claire C. "The Nature and Effect of Differential Access to Education in Ga Society." *Africa* 47 (1977): 208–219.

Stichter, Sharon. "Appendix: Some Selected Statistics on African Women." In *African Women South of the Sahara.* Edited by Margaret Jane Hay and Sharon Stichter. New York: Longman, 1984.

Weis, Lois. "Women and Education in Ghana: Some Problems of Assessing Change." *International Journal of Women's Studies* 3 (1980): 431–453.

ASIA

Books

Desai, Chitra. *Girls' School Education and Social Change.* Bombay: A. R. Smith, 1976.

Khawaja, Sarfaraz. *Promotion of Girls' Education in the Context of Universalization of*

Primary Education. Islamabad: Academy of Educational Planning and Management, 1985. (AEPAM Research Study No. 29.)

Mahmud, Siraj-ul-Hag. *Statistical Profile of Females of Pakistan*. Islamabad: Health, Demography and Social Welfare Section, Planning and Development Division, Government of Pakistan, 1980.

Mitra, Asok. *Status of Women: Literacy and Employment*. Bombay: Allied Publishers, 1979.

Nepal. Siksha Anusandhana, Pravartana, Tatha Vikasa Kendra. *Equal Access of Women to Education Programme in Nepal: An Evaluation Study*. Kathmandu: National Education Committee, Centre for Educational Research, Innovation, and Development, 1978.

Articles

Ashby, A. Jacqueline. "Equity and Discrimination Among Children: Schooling Decisions in Rural Nepal." *Comparative Education Review* 29, No. 1 (1985): 68–79.

Ghosh, Ratna. "Sexism in Indian Education." *Dalhousie Review* 65 (Fall 1985): 437–455.

Hamid, Don Fatimah. "Educational Opportunities for Girls in Malaysian Secondary Schools." In *World Yearbook of Education 1984. Women and Education*. Edited by Sandra Acker et al. London: Kogan Page; New York: Nicholas Publishing, 1984.

Harve, F. "Education for Women: The Personal and Social Damage of Anachronistic Policy." *Japan Quarterly* 29 (July/September 1982): 301–310.

Hirschman, C. "Political Independence and Educational Opportunity in Peninsula Malaysia." *Sociology of Education* 52 (April 1979): 67–83.

Jayaweera, Swarna. "Gender and Access to Education in Asia." *International Review of Education* 33 (1987): 455–466.

Narumiya, C. "Opportunities for Girls and Women in Japanese Education." *Comparative Education* 22, No. 1 (1986): 47–52.

Smith, Peter C., and Paul P. L. Cheung. "Social Origins and Sex Differential Schooling in the Philippines." In *Women's Education in the Third World: Comparative Perspectives*. Edited by Gail P. Kelly and Carolyn M. Elliott. Albany, N.Y.: SUNY Press, 1982.

Wang, Bee-lan Chan. "Sex and Ethnic Differences in Educational Investment in Malaysia: The Effect of Reward Structures." *Comparative Education Review* 24 (June 1980): S140–S159.

Wickramasinghe, Shanti, and D. Radcliffe. "Women and Education in South Asia." *Canadian and International Education/Education canadienne et internationale* 8 (1979): 117–125.

EUROPE

Articles

Davies, L. "The View from the Girls." *Educational Review* 30, No. 2 (1978): 103–109.

Lublin, N. "Women in Soviet Central Asia: Progress and Contradiction." *Soviet Studies* 33 (April 1981): 182–203.

Polydorides, G. "Women's Participation in the Greek Educational System." *Comparative Education* 21 (1985): 229–240.
Wiederkehr-Benz, K. "Frauen un der Hochschule." *Bildungsforschung und Bildungspraxis* 3, No. 1 (1981): 77–90.

LATIN AMERICA AND THE CARIBBEAN

Books

Braslausky, Cecilia. *Mujer y educación*. Santiago de Chile: Oficina Regional de educación de la UNESCO para América Latina y el Caribe, 1984.
Jerez Alvarez, Rafael. *La educación de la mujer en Honduras*. Tequcigalpa: Ministerio de Educación Pública, 1975.
Perez, Magaly. *Estadísticas sobre la mujer Cubana*. La Habana: Editorial Letras Cubanas, 1985.
Rama, Gierman, ed. *Educación y socieded en América Latina y el Caribe: Proyecto desarrollo y educación en América Latina y el Caribe*. NP: UNICEF, 1980.
Rosenberg, Fulvia. *A educacão da mulher no Brasil*. São Paulo: Global Editora, 1982.

Articles

Drayton, Kathleen. "Introduction: Women and Education." In *Women and Education. Women in the Caribbean Project,* Volume 5. Edited by Joycelin Massiah. Cave Hill, Barbados: Institute of Social and Economic Research, University of the West Indies, 1982.
Ferretti, C. J. "A mulher e a escola vocacional." *Cadernos de pesquisa* No. 16 (March 1976): 20–40.
Mohammed, Patricia. "Educational Attainment of Women in Trinidad-Tobago 1946–1980." In *Women and Education. Women in the Caribbean Project,* Volume 5. Edited by Joycelin Massiah. Cave Hill, Barbados: Institute of Social and Economic Research, University of the West Indies, 1982.
Schiefelbein, E. "La mujer en la educación primaria y media." In *Chile: Mujer y Sociedad*. Edited by Paz Covarrubias and R. Franco. Santiago: Alfebta Imp., 1978.

MIDDLE EAST

Articles

El-Sanabary, Nagat. "Continuing Change in Women's Education in the Arab States." In *Women and the Family in the Middle East*. Edited by Elizabeth Warnock Fernea. Austin: University of Texas Press, 1985.
Jones, Marie T. "Education of Girls in Tunisia: Policy Implications of the Drive for Universal Enrollment." *Comparative Education Review* 24 (June 1980): S106–S123.
O'Shaughnessey, T. J. "Growth of Educational Opportunity for Muslim Women, 1950 to 1973." *Anthropos* 73, Nos. 5–6 (1978): 887–901.
Ozbay, Ferhunde. "Women's Education in Rural Turkey." In *Sex Roles, Family and*

Community in Turkey. Edited by Cigdem Kagitcibasi and Diane Sunar. Bloomington: Indiana University Turkish Studies, 1982.

NORTH AMERICA

Articles

Alexander, Karl, and B. Eckland. "Sex Differences in the Educational Attainment Process." *American Sociological Review* 39 (1974): 668–682.

Alexander, K. L., and T. W. Reilly. "Estimating the Effects of Marriage Timing on Educational Attainment: Some Procedural Issues and Substantial Clarifications." *American Journal of Sociology* 87 (July 1981): 143–156.

Heath, K. G. "Educational Equity: How Long Must Women Wait?" *Educational Studies* 12 (Spring 1981): 1–21.

Klein, S. S., and K. Bogart. "Achieving Sex Equity in Education: A Comparison at Pre and Post-Secondary Levels." *Equity and Excellence* 22 (Spring 1987): 114–122.

Roeder, A. L., and R. D. Conger. "Differential Mother and Father Influences in the Educational Attainment of Black and White Women." *Sociological Quarterly* 25 (Spring 1984): 239–250.

Robb, A. Leslie, and Byron G. Spencer. "Education: Enrollment and Attainment." In *Opportunity for Choice: A Goal for Women in Canada*. Edited by Gail Cook. Ottawa: Information Canada (1976): 53–92.

Timberlake, C. H. "Demographic Factors and Personal Resources That Black Female Students Identified as Being Supportive in Attaining Their High School Diplomas." *Adolescence* 17, No. 65 (1982): 107–115.

WOMEN IN PRIMARY AND SECONDARY SCHOOL ADMINISTRATION

Articles

Atkinson, J. A. "Women in School Administration: A Review of the Research." *Review of Educational Research* 51, No. 3 (1981): 311–343.

Bottomley, M., and S. Sampson. "The Case of the Female Principal: Sex Role Attitudes and Perceptions of Sex Differences in Ability." *Australian and New Zealand Journal of Sociology* 13 (1977): 137–145.

Bowker, J. E. et al. "Do Women Aspire to the Same Administrative Positions as Men?" *Educational Administrative Quarterly* 19 (Spring 1983): 64–81.

Casanova, Ursula. "Between Principals and Secretaries: Gender Roles in the School Office." *Educational Foundations* 2 (Spring 1988): 94–117.

Davies, Lynn. "Research Dilemmas Concerning Gender and the Management of Education in Third World Countries." *Comparative Education* 23 (1987): 85–94.

Davies, Lynn. "Women, Educational Management and the Third World: A Comparative Framework for Analysis." *International Journal of Educational Development* 6 (1986): 61–75.

Ejiogu, Aloy M. "Sex Differences in the Leader Behavior of Nigerian College Principles." *Journal of Educational Administration and History* 14 (1982): 123–131.

Elberts, R. W., and J. A. Stone. "Male-Female Differences in Promotions: EEO in Public Education." *Journal of Human Resources* 20 (Fall 1985): 504–521.

Estler, Susan. "Women as Leaders in Public Education." *Signs* 1 (1975): 363–385.

Maienza, J. G. "The Superintendency: Characteristics of Access for Men and Women." *Educational Administration Quarterly* 22 (Fall 1986): 59–79.

Scribbins, K. "Women in Education: Some Points of Discussion." *Journal of Further and Higher Education* 1, No. 3 (1977): 17–39.

Shafer, Susanne. "Factors Affecting the Utilization of Women in Professional and Managerial Roles." *Comparative Education* 10, No. 1 (1974): 1–12.

Strober, M. H., and D. Tyack. "Why Do Women Teach and Men Manage?" *Signs* 5 (1980): 494–503.

Tyack, D., and M. H. Strober. "Jobs and Gender: A History of the Structuring of Educational Employment by Sex." In *Educational Policy and Management: Sex Differentials*. Edited by P. Schmuck and W. W. Charles. San Diego: Academic Press, 1981.

WOMEN TEACHERS IN PRIMARY AND SECONDARY SCHOOL

Books

Delhome, D., N. Gault, and J. Gonthier. *Les premières institutrices laïques.* Paris: Mercure de France, 1980.

Fahmy-Eid, N., and M. Dumont, eds. *Maitresses de maison, maitresses d'école: Femmes, famille et education dans l'histoire du Quebec.* Montreal: Boreal Express, 1983.

Hoffman, Nancy. *Woman's "True" Profession: Voices from the History of Teaching.* Old Westbury, N.Y.: Feminist Press, 1981.

Prevot, J., and P. Desanti. *La Première institutrice de France: Madame de Maintenon.* Paris: Belin, 1981.

Articles

Biklen, Sari Knopp. "Can Elementary School Teaching Be a Career?: A Search for New Ways of Understanding Women's Work." *Issues in Education* 3 (Winter 1985): 215–231.

Danylewycz, Marta, and Alison Prentice. "Lessons from the Past: The Experiences of Women Teachers in Quebec and Ontario." In *World Yearbook of Education 1984. Women and Education*. Edited by Sandra Acker et al. London: Kogan Page, 1984.

Dunkin, M. J. "Teacher Sex and Instruction." In *The International Encyclopedia of Education*. Edited by Tursten Husen and T. N. Postlethwaite. Oxford: Pergamon Press, 1985.

Eichler, M. "Sex-Role Attitudes of Male and Female Teachers in Toronto." *Interchange* 10, No. 2 (1979–1980): 2–14.

Evans, T. D. "Being and Becoming: Teachers' Perceptions of Sex Roles and Actions Towards Their Male and Female Pupils." *British Journal of Sociology of Education* 3 (1982): 127–144.

Gaskell, Jane. "The Changing Organization of Business Education in the High School: Teachers Respond to School and Work." *Curriculum Inquiry* 16 (Winter 1986): 417–437.

Goddard-Spear, M. "Sex Bias in Science Teachers' Ratings of Work and Pupil Characteristics." *European Journal of Science Education* 6, No. 4 (1984): 369–377.

Grumet, M. "Pedagogy for Patriarchy: The Feminization of Teaching." *Interchange* 12, Nos. 2–3 (1981): 165–184.

Julia, D. et al. "La Femme educatrice." *Histoire de l'education,* No. 9 (1980): 41–60.

Kelly, A. et al. "Traditionalists and Trendies: Teachers' Attitudes to Educational Issues." *British Educational Research Journal* 11, No. 2 (1985): 91–104.

Lebowitz, R. "Women Elementary-School Teachers and the Feminist Movement." *Elementary School Journal* 28 (1979): 369–375.

Maher, F. A., and C. H. Rathbone. "Teacher Education and Feminist Theory: Some Implications for Practice." *American Journal of Education* 94 (February 1986): 214–235.

Middleton, Sue. "Schooling and Radicalization: Life Histories of New Zealand Feminist Teachers." *British Journal of Sociology of Education* 8, No. 2 (1987): 169–190.

Mitrano, B. S. "Teaching on a Women's Occupation: A Feminist Critique." *Journal of Education* 160, No. 4 (1978): 50–63.

Mover, E. K. "Women in Teaching." In *Women in Changing Japan.* Edited by Joyce Lebra, Joy Paulson, and Elizabeth Powers. Boulder, Colo.: Westview Press, 1976.

Patrick, Al, Robert L. Griswold, and Courtney Ann Vaughn-Roberson. "Domestic Ideology and the Teaching Profession: A Case Study from Oklahoma, 1930–1983." *Issues in Education* 3 (Fall 1985): 139–157.

Prats, Pilar Dominquez. "La mujer en la enseñanza de la historia." In *Nuevas perspectivas sobre la mujer.* Edited by Seminario de Estudios de la Mujer. Madrid: Universidad Autonoma de Madrid, 1982.

Prentice, Alison. "The Feminization of Teaching." In *The Neglected Majority: Essays in Canadian Women's History.* Edited by Susan Mann Trofimenkoff and Alison Prentice. Toronto: McClelland & Stewart, 1977, pp. 49–65.

Prentice, Alison. "The Feminization of Teaching in British North America, 1845–1875." *Social History* 8 (1975): 5–20.

Roden, D. "From 'Old Miss' to New Professional: A Portrait of Women Educators under the American Occupation of Japan, 1945–1952." *History of Education Quarterly* 23 (Winter 1983): 469–489.

Stake, J. E., and J. F. Katz. "Teacher Pupil Relationship in the Elementary School Classroom: Teacher-Gender and Pupil Gender Differences." *American Educational Research Journal* 19, No. 3 (1982): 465–471.

Strober, Myra H., and Audri Gordon Lanford. "The Feminization of Public School Teaching: Cross-Sectional Analysis, 1850–1880." *Signs* 11 (1986): 212–235.

Tabakin, G., and K. Densmore. "Teacher Professionization and Gender Analysis." *Teachers' College Record* 88 (Winter 1986): 257–279.

Tan-Willman, C. "Prospective Teachers' Attitudes Toward the Rights and Roles of Contemporary Women in Two Cultures." *Psychological Reports* 45 (December 1979): 741–742.

Trotman, J. "Jobs for Girls: Family Ideology and the Employment of Women in Education." *Australian Journal of Education* 28, No. 2 (1984): 132–144.

Worrall, N., and H. Tsarna. "Teachers' Reported Practices Towards Girls and Boys in Science and Languages." *British Journal of Educational Psychology* 57 (November 1987): 300–312.

COEDUCATION

Books

Deem, Rosemary, ed. *Coeducation Reconsidered*. Milton Keynes and Philadelphia: Open University Press, 1984.

Grandpre, Marcel de. *La Coeducation dans les écoles de 45 pays*. Quebec: Editions Paulines, 1973.

Hepting, Roland. *Mädchenbildung versus Koedukation*. Stuttgart: Hochshulverlag, 1978.

Howe, Florence. *Myths of Coeducation: Selected Essays 1964–1983*. Bloomington: Indiana University Press, 1984.

Mahoney, Pat. *Schools for the Boys?* London: Hutchinson, 1985.

Martin, Jane Roland. *Reclaiming a Conversation: The Ideal of the Educated Woman*. New Haven, Conn.: Yale University Press, 1985.

Articles

Albisetti, J. C. "Could Separate Be Equal? Helene Lange and Women's Education in Imperial German." *History of Education Quarterly* 22 (Fall 1982): 301–317.

Benoit, A., et al. "Themanummer' coeductie en gemengd onderwifs." (Special Issue.) *Impuls* 14, No. 1 (1983–1984): 1–52.

Carpenter, P. G., and M. Hayden. "Girls' Academic Achievements: Single-Sex Versus Coeducational Schools in Australia." *Sociology of Education* 60 (July 1987): 156–167.

Hamilton, Marlene A. "Performance Levels in Science and Other Subjects for Jamaican Adolescents Attending Single-Sex and Coeducational High Schools." *Science Education* 69 (1985): 535–547.

Oates, M. J., and S. Williamson. "Women's Colleges and Women Achievers." *Signs* 3, No. 4 (1978): 795–806.

Schneider, F. W., and L. M. Coutts. "The High School Environment: A Comparison of Coeducational and Single Sex Schools." *Journal of Educational Psychology* 74, No. 6 (1982): 898–906.

Sutherland, M. B. "Whatever Happened About Coeducation?" *British Journal of Sociology* 33 (June 1985): 155–163.

SEX-ROLE STEREOTYPING IN SCHOOLS (GENERAL)

Books

Belotti, Elena G. *What Are Little Girls Made Of? The Roots of Feminine Stereotypes*. New York: Schocken Books, 1976.

Byrne, E. *Women and Education*. London: Tavistock, 1978.

Delamount, S. *Sex Roles and the School*. London: McThiren, 1980.

Harntnett, O., G. Boden, and M. Fuller, eds. *Sex-Role Stereotyping*. London: Tavistock, 1979.

Murray, Barbara. *Sex Differences in Education*. New York: P. Lang, 1985.

Pottker, G., and A. Fishel, eds. *Sex Bias in the Schools*. Teaneck, N.J.: Fairleigh Dickinson University Press, 1977.

Sexism in der Schule. Weinheim: Beltz, 1982.

Spender, Dale. *Invisible Women: The Schooling Scandal.* London: Writers and Readers, 1982.

Spender, D. and E. Sarah, eds. *Learning to Lose: Sexism and Education.* London: Women's Press, 1980.

Sutherland, Margaret. *Sex Bias in Education.* Oxford: Basel Blackwell, 1981.

Articles

Buswell, C. "Sexism in School Routines and Classroom Practices." *Durham and Newcastle Research Review* 9 (1981): 195–200.

Buswell, Carol. "Sponsoring and Stereotyping in a Working-Class English Secondary School." In *World Yearbook of Education 1984. Women and Education.* Edited by Sandra Acker et al. London: Kogan Page, 1984.

Clark, L. L. "Socialization of Girls in the Primary Schools of the Third Republic." *Journal of Social History* 15 (Summer 1982): 685–697.

Davies, Lynn. "Deadlier Than Male? Girls' Conformity and Deviance in School." In *Schools, Pupils and Deviance.* Edited by L. Barton and R. Meighan. Driffield: Nafferton Books, 1979.

Delamont, S. "Sex Roles and Schooling on 'See Janet Suffer, See John Suffer too.'" *Journal of Adolescence* 7 (December 1984): 329–335.

Hartley, David. "Sex Differences in the Infant School: Definitions and 'Theories'." *British Journal of Sociology of Education* 1 (1980): 93–106.

Mahony, Pat. "Silence Is a Woman's Glory: The Sexist Content of Education." *Women's Studies International Forum* 5, No. 5 (1982): 463–471.

Namo de Mello, Guiomar. "Os estereotipos sexuais na escola." *Cadernos de Pesquisa,* No. 15 (December 1975): 141–144.

Rosenberg, Fulvia. "A escola e as diferencas sexuais." *Cadernos de Pesquisa* (December, 1975): 78–85.

Sampson, Shirley. "The Role of the School in Sex-role Stereotyping." In *Australian Women: Feminist Perspectives.* Edited by Norma Grieve and Patricia Grimshaw. Melbourne: Oxford University Press, 1981.

Shafer, Susanne. "The Socialization of Girls in the Secondary Schools of England and the Two Germanies." *International Review of Education* 22, No. 1 (1976): 5–24.

Ward, Colleen. "Sex Trait Stereotypes in Malaysia Children." *Sex Roles* 12, No. 1–2 (January 1985): 35–45.

Wolleat, P. L. "Sex Roles and Gender in Counseling." In *The International Encyclopedia of Education.* Edited by Torsten Husen and T. N. Postlethwaite. Oxford: Pergamon Press, 1985.

Yoger, S. "Sexism in Education." In *The International Encyclopedia of Education.* Edited by Torsten Husen and T. N. Postlethwaite. Oxford: Pergamon Press, 1985.

TEXTBOOKS

Books

Anderson, Jeanine, and Cristina Herencia. *L'image de la femme et de l'homme dans les livres scolaires peruviens.* Paris: Unesco, 1983.

Children's Rights Workshop. *Sexism in Children's Books: Facts, Figures and Guidelines.* London: Writers and Readers Publishing Cooperative, 1976.

Clark, Linda. *Schooling the Daughters of Marianne: Textbooks and the Socialization of Girls in Modern French Primary Schools.* Albany, N.Y.: SUNY Press, 1984.

Decroux-Masson, Annie. *Papa lit, Maman coud, les manuels scolaires en bleu et rose.* Paris: Denoel Gonthier, 1979.

Kalia, N. N. *Sexism in Indian Education: The Lies We Tell Our Children.* New Delhi: Vikas, 1979.

Michel, Andree. *Non aux stereotypes: Vaincre le sexisme dans les livres pour les enfants et les manuels scolaires.* Paris: Unesco, 1986.

Organizations Françaises membres de la Federation internationale syndicate de l'enseignement (F.I.S.E.). *Etudes sur l'image que donnent des femmes et des hommes les manuels scolaires et les livres pour enfants en France.* Paris: Unesco, 1983.

Articles

Alrabaa, Sami. "Sex Division of Labour in Syrian School Textbooks." *International Review of Education* 31 (1985): 335–348.

Healy, P., and P. Ryan. "Sex Stereotyping in Children's Books." In *The Other Half: Women in Australian Society.* Edited by J. Mercer. Ringwood, Victoria: Penguin, 1975.

Hellinger, Marlis. "'For Men Must Work, and Women Must Weep': Sexism in English Language Textbooks Used in German Schools." *Women's Studies: An International Quarterly* 3 (1980): 267–276.

Jay, W. T., and C. W. Schminke. "Sex Stereotyping in Elementary School Mathematics Texts." *Arithmetic Teacher* 22 (1975): 242–246.

Kalia, N. N. "Images of Men and Women in Indian Textbooks." *Comparative Education Review* 24 (June 1980): S209–S223.

Mancilla, Maria Eugenia. "Aprendiendo a ser mujer. Estereotipos sexuales en los textos escolares." *Debates en Sociologia,* No. 9 (1983).

Nischol, K. "The Invisible Women: Images of Women and Girls in School Textbooks." *Social Action* 26 (July-September 1976): 267–281.

CURRICULUM

Books

Dupont, Beatrice. *Fille ou garçon: La méme education? Etude sur les programmes scolaires dans le secondaire.* Paris: Unesco, 1980.

Dupont, Beatrice. *Unequal Education: A Study of Sex Differences in Secondary School Curricula.* Paris: Unesco, 1981.

Evans, David R., and Gordon Schummel. *The Impact of a Diversified Educational Programme on Career Girls: Tororo Girls in the Context of Girls' Education in Uganda.* Amherst: University of Massachusetts, 1970.

Ssenkoloto, G. M. *Towards Realistic Curricla for African Women in the Process of Development.* Douala: International Association, Pan African Institute for Development, 1980.

Whyld, Janie, ed. *Sexism in Secondary Curriculum.* London: Harper & Row, 1983.

Articles

Bessant, B. "Domestic Science Schools and Women's Place." *Australian Journal of Education* 20 (1976): 1–9.

Bramwell, J. "Pupils'Attitudes Towards Geography in the Lower School: An Investigation into Gender Differences." *Geography* 72 (January 1987): 36–48.

Christian-Smith, Linda K. "Gender, Popular Culture, and Curriculum: Adolescent Romance Novels as Gender Text." *Curriculum Inquiry* 17 (Winter 1987): 365–406.

Clarricoates, K. "Dinosaurs in the Classroom—A Reexamination of Some Aspects of the Hidden Curriculum in Primary Schools." *Women's Studies International Quarterly* 1 (1978): 353–364.

Hout, M., and M. A. Garnier. "Curriculum and Educational Stratification in France." *Sociology of Education* 52 (July 1979): 146–156.

Kalantzis, M., and B. Cope. "Cultural Differences, Gender Differences: Social Literacy and Inclusive Curriculum." *Curriculum Perspectives* 7 (1987): 64–69.

Masemann, Vandra. "The Hidden Curriculum of a West African Girls' Boarding School." *Canadian Journal of African Studies* 8 (1974): 470–494.

Pinar, William F. "Gender, Sexuality and Curriculum Studies: The Beginning of the Debate." *McGill Journal of Education* 16 (Fall 1981): 305–316.

Russell, Susan. "The Hidden Curriculum of School: Reproducing Gender and Class Hierarchies." In *The Politics of Diversity*. Edited by Roberta Hamilton and Michele Barpet. Montreal: Brok Center, 1987.

Schusten, M., and S. Van Dyne. "Placing Women in the Liberal Arts: Stages of Curriculum Transformation." *Harvard Educational Review* 54, No. 4 (1984): 413–428.

Sharma, Shiam, and Roland Meighan. "Schooling and Sex Roles: The Case of GCE 'O' Level Mathematics." *British Journal of Sociology of Education* 1 (1980): 193–206.

Sherman, J. "Girls' and Boys' Enrollments in Theoretical Math Courses: A Longitudinal Study." *Psychology of Women Quarterly* 5, No. 5 (supplement, 1981): 681–689.

GIRLS IN SCIENCE COURSES IN PRIMARY AND SECONDARY SCHOOL

Book

Kelly, Alison, ed. *The Missing Half: Girls and Science Education*. Manchester: Manchester University Press, 1981.

Articles

Duxbury, J. "Girls and Physics—The Role of a Head of Physics." *School Science Review* 65 (1984): 648–654.

Harding, J. "Girls and Women in Secondary and Higher Education: Science for Only a Few." *Prospects* 15, No. 4 (1985): 553–564.

Harlen, Wynne. "Girls and Primary-School Science Education: Sexism, Stereotypes and Remedies." *Prospects* 15, No. 4 (1985): 541–552.

Kelly, Alison. "The Construction of Masculine Science." *British Journal of Sociology of Education* 6 (1985): 133–154.

Kelly, Alison. "Girls and Science and Technology." *International Review of Education* 33 (1987): 501–503.

McDade, Laurie. "Knowing the 'Right Stuff': Attrition, Gender, and Scientific Literacy." *Anthropology and Education Quarterly* 19 (June 1988): 93–114.

Price, F., and B. Talbot. "Girls and Physical Science at Ellis Guilford School." *School Science Review* 66, No. 234 (1984): 7–11.

CLASSROOM PROCESSES

Book

Best, Raphaela. *We've All Got Scars: What Boys and Girls Learn in Elementary School.* Bloomington: Indiana University Press, 1983.

Articles

Anyon, Jane. "Intersections of Gender and Class: Accommodation and Resistance by Working Class and Affluent Females to Contradictory Sex Role Ideologies." In *Gender, Class and Education.* Edited by Stephen Walker and Len Barton. Sussex: Falmer Press, 1983.

Biraimah, Karen Coffyn. "Different Knowledge for Different Folks: Knowledge Distribution in Togolese Secondary School." In *Comparative Education.* Edited by P. G. Altbach, R. Arnove, and G. P. Kelly. New York: Macmillan, 1982.

Davies, Lynn. "Gender and Comprehensive Schooling." In *Comprehensive Schooling: A Reader.* Edited by Stephen Ball. Philadelphia: Falmer, 1984.

Evans, Terry. "Gender Differentiation and Interaction in Australian Primary Schools." In *World Yearbook of Education 1984. Women and Education.* Edited by Sandra Acker et al. London: Kogan Page, 1984.

French, F., and P. French. "Gender Imbalances in the Primary Classroom: An Interactional Account." *Educational Research* 26 (June 1984): 127–136.

Hartley, D. "Sex and Social Class: A Case Study on an Infant School." *British Educational Research Journal* 4 (1978): 75–81.

Junge, Barbara, and Shashi M. Shrestha. "Another Barrier Broken: Teaching Village Girls to Read in Nepal." *The Reading Teacher* 37 (May 1984): 846–852.

McCormack. "The Sexual Harassment of Students by Teachers: The Case of Students in Science." *Sex Roles* 13 (July 1985): 21–32.

McRobbie, Angela. "Working Class Girls and the Culture of Femininity." In *Women Take Issue.* Edited by Women's Studies Group, Centre for Contemporary Culture Studies. London: Hutchinson, 1978.

Naik, Chitra. "Educating Rural Girls: A Review of an Acting Research Project." *International Review of Education* 33 (1987): 495–501.

Rushton, A. "Group Work with Adolescent Girls' Comprehensive School." *Journal of Adolescence* 5 (September 1982): 267–284.

COUNTERSEXIST STRATEGIES

Books

Kalia, Navendra Nath. *From Sexism to Equality: A Handbook on How to Eliminate Sexist Bias from Our Textbooks and Other Writings.* New Delhi: New Indian Publications, 1986.

Klein, Susan S., ed. *Handbook for Achieving Sex Equity in Education*. Baltimore: Johns Hopkins University Press, 1985.

Tobias, Sheila. *Overcoming Math Anxiety*. New York: W. W. Norton, 1978.

Articles

Agre, G. P., and B. Finkelstein. "Feminism and School Reform: The Last Fifteen Years." *Teachers College Record* 80 (December 1978): 307–315.

Bornstein, R. "Ambiguity as Opportunity and Constraint: Evolution of a Federal Sex Equity Education Program." *Educational Evaluation and Policy Analysis* 7 (Summer 1987): 99–114.

Chisholm, Lynne A., and Janet Holland. "Girls and Occupational Choice: Anti-Sexism in Action in a Curriculum Development Project." *British Journal of Sociology of Education* 7 (1986): 353–367.

Corkery, Mary. "Subversion: Chilean Women Learning for Changes." In *The Decade for Women*. Edited by Aisla Thomson. Toronto: Canadian Congress for Learning Opportunities for Women, 1986.

Grieve, Norma. "Beyond Sexual Stereotypes. Androgyny: A Model or an Ideal." In *Australian Women: Feminist Perspectives*. Edited by Norma Grieve and Patricia Grimshaw. Melbourne: Oxford University Press, 1981.

Harlen, Wynne. "Girls and Primary School Science Education: Sexism, Stereotypes and Remedies." *Prospects* 15 (1985): 541–552.

Loeb, F. W., M. A. Ferber, and H. M. Lowry. "The Effectiveness of Affirmative Action for Women." *Journal of Higher Education* 49, No. 3 (1978): 218–230.

Martin, J. R. "Sex Equality and Education: A Case Study." In *"Femininity," "Masculinity" and Androgyny*. Edited by M. Vetterling-Braggin. Totowa, N.J.: Littlefield, Adams, 1982.

Molyneux, Maxine. "Strategies for the Emancipation of Women in Third World Socialist Societies." In *World Yearbook of Education 1984. Women and Education*. Edited by Sandra Acker et al. London: Kogan Page, 1984.

Peterson, P. L., and Elizabeth Fennema. "Effective Teaching, Student Engagement in Classroom Activities and Sex Related Differences in Learning Mathematics." *American Educational Research Journal* 22 (1985): 309–335.

Scott, Hilda. "Sweden's Efforts to Achieve Sex Role Equality." *In World Yearbook of Education 1984. Women and Education*. Edited by Sandra Acker et al. London: Kogan Page, 1984.

Verma, Margaret. "Building Young Children's Self-Concepts Through a Nonsexist Approach to Early Childhood Education Curriculum Materials." *Indian Educational Review* 20 (October 1985): 20–33.

Yates, Lyn. "Counter-Sexist Strategies in Australian Schools." *In World Yearbook of Education 1984. Women and Education*. Edited by Sandra Acker et al. London: Kogan Page, 1984.

TECHNICAL/VOCATIONAL EDUCATION

Books

Gaudart, Dorothea. *Zugang von Mädchen und Frauen zu technischen Berufen: Beitrag Österreichs zu einer auf internationales ebene gestellten Frage*. Wein: Österr. Bundesverl., 1975.

Griechen-Hepp, Karin. *Emanzipatorische Frauenbildungsarbeit als Aufgabengebiet der Volkshochschule*. Bad Honef: Beck und Herchen, 1979.
Rosenberg-Gutschow, Sibylle. *Die Lebensperspektiven von Realschülerinnen unter den Bedingungen von Lehrstellenmangel und Fugendarbeitslosigkeit*. Hamburg: Ludke, 1980.
Schmid-Forg, I., C. Krebsbach, and S. Hubner. *Bildungschansen für Mädchen und Frauen in internationalen Vergleich. Regelungen zur Absicherung gleicher Chancen für Mädchen und Frauen in Buildungs- und Berufbildungsbereich*. Munchen: R. Oldenbourg, 1981.

Articles

Blunden, Gillian. "Vocational Education for Women's Work in England and Wales." In *World Yearbook of Education 1984. Women and Education*. Edited by Sandra Acker et al. London: Kogan Page, 1984.
Caniou, J. "L'Enseignement agricole feminin et son histoire." *Education Permanente*, No. 77 (1985): 87–95.
Caniou, J. "Les Fonctions sociales de l'enseignement agricole feminin." *Etudes Rurales*, No. 92 (1983): 41–56.
Gaskell, Jane. "Conceptions of Skill and the Work of Women: Some Historical and Political Issues." In *The Politics of Diversity*. Edited by Roberta Hamilton and Michele Barret. Montreal: Book Center, 1987.
Gaskell, Jane. "Gender and Skill." In *Critical Pedagogy and Cultural Power*. Edited by David W. Livingston. South Hadley, Mass.: Bergin & Garvey, 1987.
Harvois, Y. "La Place des jeunes filles dans l'enseignement agricole." *Pour*, No. 97 (1984): 16–26.
Jackson, N. S., and J. S. Gaskell. "White Collar Vocationalism: The Rise of Commercial Education in Ontario and British Columbia 1870–1920." *Curriculum Inquiry* 17 (Summer 1987): 177–201.

EDUCATIONAL ACHIEVEMENT

Books

Kelly, Alison. *Girls and Science: An International Study of Sex Differences in School Science Achievement*. Stockholm: Almqvist & Wiksell, 1978.
Mednick, Martha, Sandra Tangri, and Lois Hoffman, eds. *Women and Achievement: Social and Motivational Analyses*. Washington, D.C.: Halsted Press, 1975.

Articles

Boothroyd, Roger A., and David W. Chapman. "Gender Differences and Achievement in Liberian Primary School Children." *International Journal of Educational Development* 7 (1987): 99–105.
Eccles, Jacqueline S. "Gender-Roles and Women's Achievement." *Educational Researcher* 15 (June/July 1986): 15–20.
Engle, Patricia L., Charles Yarbrough, and Robert E. Klein. "Sex Differences in the Effects of Nutrition and Social Environment on Mental Development in Rural Guatemala." In *Women and Poverty in the Third World*. Edited by Mayra Buvinic,

Margaret A. Lycette, and William Paul McGreevey. Baltimore: Johns Hopkins University Press, 1983.

Hamilton, Marlene A. "Sex Differences in the Qualitative Performance of Jamaican Adolescents on the Circles Test of Creativity." *Caribbean Journal of Education* 9 (1982): 124–134.

Harnisch, Delwyn, et al. "Cross-National Differences in Mathematics Attitude and Achievement Among Seventeen-Year-Olds." *International Journal of Educational Development* 6, No. 4 (1986): 233–242.

Keeves, J. "Differences Between the Sexes in Mathematics and Science Courses." *International Review of Education* 19 (1973): 47–74.

Keeves, J. P. "Differences Between the Sexes in Mathematics and Science Courses." In *Sociology of Australian Education: A Book of Readings*. Edited by D. Edgar. Sydney: McGraw-Hill, 1975.

Keeves, J. P. "Sex Differences in Ability and Achievement." In *The International Encyclopedia of Education*. Edited by Torsten Husen and T. N. Postlethwaite. Oxford: Pergamon Press, 1985.

Lieblich, Amia. "Sex Differences in Intelligence Tests Performance of Jewish and Arab School Children in Israel." In *Women's Worlds*. Edited by Marilyn Safir et al. New York: Praeger, 1985.

Simmons, J., and L. Alexander. "The Determinants of School Achievement in Developing Countries: A Review of Research." *Economic Development and Cultural Change* 26 (January 1978): 341–357.

Treas, Judith. "Differential Achievement: Race, Sex, and Jobs." *Sociology and Social Research* 62 (1978): 387–400.

Walford, Geoffrey. "Girls in Boys' Public Schools: A Prelude to Further Research." *British Journal of Sociology of Education* 4 (1983): 39–54.

Wilken, Margaret. "Educational Opportunity and Achievement." In *Sex Differences in Britain*. Edited by Ivan Reid and Eileen Wofmald. London: Grant McIntyre, 1982.

Youngblood, R. L. "Female Dominance and Adolescent Filipino Attitude Orientations and School Achievement." *Journal of Asian and African Studies* 13, Nos. 1–2 (1978): 65–80.

STUDENT ASPIRATIONS

Book

Park, Eirlys. *Careers for Nigerian Boys and Girls*. Cambridge: Cambridge University Press, 1965.

Articles

Bach, R., et al. "Mothers' Influences on Daughters' Orientations Towards Education: An Egyptian Case Study." *Comparative Education Review* 29 (1985): 375–384.

Biraimah, Karen C. "The Impact of Western Schools on Girls' Expectations: A Togolese Case." *Comparative Education Review* 24 (June 1980): S196–S208.

Evans, D. R. "Image and Reality: Career Goals of Educated Ugandan Women." *Canadian Journal of African Studies* 6, No. 1 (1972): 213–232.

Furlong, Andy. "Schools and the Structure of Female Occupational Aspirations." *British Journal of Sociology of Education* 7 (1986): 367–378.

Gaskell, Jane. "The Reproduction of Family Life: Perspectives of Male and Female Adolescents." *British Journal of Sociology of Education* 4 (1983): 19–38.

Hariani, Kamala. "Educational and Vocational Aspirations and Planning by High School Girls (Haryana)." *Journal of Education and Psychology* 28, No. 3 (1970): 122–128.

Kande, Bolante E. "Rural-Urban Comparison of Female Educational Aspirations in South-Western Nigeria." *Comparative Education* 23, No. 10 (1987): 75–83.

Kelly, A., et al. "Gender Roles at Home and School." *British Journal of Sociology of Education* 3 (1982): 281–296.

Lindsay, Beverly. "Career Aspirations of Kenyan Women." *Journal of Negro Education* 49 (Fall 1980): 423–440.

Malta, Campos Maria M., and Yara Lucia Esposito. "Relacão entre sexo de criança e aspiracões educacionais e occupacionais das mães." *Cuadernos de Pesquisa*, No. 15 (December 1975): 37–46.

Maxwell, M. P. and J. P. Maxwell. "Women and the Elite: Educational and Occupational Aspirations of Private School Females 1966/76." *Canadian Review of Sociology and Anthropology* 21 (November 1984): 371–394.

Mehryar, A. H., and G. A. Tashakkori. "Sex and Parental Education as Determinants of Marital Aspirations and Attitudes of a Group of Iranian Youth." *Journal of Marriage and the Family* 40 (1978): 629–637.

Miles, Sheila. "Asian Girls and the Transition from School To . . . ?" In *Comprehensive Schooling: A Reader*. Edited by Stephen Ball. Philadelphia: Falmer Press, 1984.

Oey, Mayling. "Rising Expectations But Limited Opportunities for Women in Indonesia." In *Women and Development: Perspectives from South and Southeast Asia*. Edited by Rounaq Jahan and Hanna Papanek. Dacca: Bangladesh Institute of Law and International Affairs, 1979.

Saha, L. J. "Gender, School Attainment and Occupational Plans: Determinants of Aspirations and Expectations Among Australian Urban School Leavers." *Australian Journal of Education* 26 (1982): 247–265.

Sutherland, S. L. "The Unambitious Female: Women's Low Professional Aspirations." *Signs* 3, No. 4 (1978): 774–794.

Yogev, A., and M. Ayalon. "Sex and Ethnic Variations in Educational Plans: A Cross Cultural Perspective." *International Review of Modern Sociology* 12 (1982): 1–19.

WOMEN AS ACADEMICS AND PROFESSORS

Books

Abramson, J. *The Invisible Woman: Discrimination in the Academic Profession*. San Francisco: Jossey Bass, 1975.

Bramley, Gwenda M., and Marion Ward. *The Role of Women in the Australian National University*. Canberra: Australian National University, 1976.

Cass, Bettena, et al. *Why So Few? Women Academics in Australian Universities*. Sydney: Sydney University Press, 1983.

Simeone, Angela. *Academic Women: Working Toward Equality*. South Hadley, Mass.: Bergin & Garvey, 1987.

Wilson, Brian G., and Eileen M. Byrne, eds. *Women in the University: A Policy Report*. St. Lucia: University of Queensland Press, 1987.

Articles

Abel, E. "Collective Protest and the Meritocracy: Faculty Women and Sex Discrimination Law Suits." *Feminist Studies* 7 (Fall 1981): 505–538.

Acker, Sandra. "Women: The Other Academics." *British Journal of Sociology of Education* 1 (1980): 81–91.

"Actitudes y opiniones de alumnos y profesores frente a la sexualidad." *Educación Hoy* (Bogotá) 8 (September/December 1978): 83–144.

Blackstone, Tessa, and Oliver Fulton. "Sex Discrimination Among University Teachers: A British-American Comparison." *British Journal of Sociology* 26 (1975): 261–275.

Carter, S. B. "Academic Women Revisited: An Empirical Study of Changing Patterns in Women's Employment as College and University Faculty, 1890–1963." *Journal of Social History* 14 (Summer 1981): 675–699.

Emmons, C. A. "Longitudinal Study of the Careers of a Cohort of Assistant Professors in Psychology." *American Psychologist* 37 (November 1982): 1228–1238.

Erkut, S., and J. R. Mokros. "Professors as Models and Mentors for College Students." *American Educational Research Journal* 21, No. 2 (1984): 399–417.

Ervin, I., et al. "Sex Discrimination and Rewards in a Public Comprehensive University." *Human Relations* 37 (December 1984): 1005–1028.

Exum, W. H., et al. "Making It at the Top: Women and Minority Faculty in the Academic Labor Market." *American Behavioral Scientist* 27 (January/February 1984): 301–324.

Fapohunda, Eleanor. "Male and Female Career Ladders in Nigerian Academe." In *Women's Worlds*. Edited by Marilyn Safir et al. New York: Praeger, 1985.

Harvey, William B., and Diane Scott Jones. "We Can't Find Any: The Elusiveness of Black Faculty Members in American Higher Education." *Issues in Education* 3 (1985): 68–75.

Hoffman, F. L. "Sexual Harassment in Academics: Feminist Theory and Institutional Practice." *Harvard Educational Review* 56 (May 1986): 105–121.

Horning, L. S. "Untenured and Tenuous: The Status of Women Faculty." *American Academy of Political and Social Science Annals* 448 (March 1980): 115–125.

Hyer, P. B. "Affirmative Action for Women Faculty: Case Studies of Three Successful Institutions." *Journal of Higher Education* 56 (May/June 1983): 282–299.

Hyer, P. B. "Assessing Progress in the Status of Women Faculty." *Research in Higher Education* 22, No. 2 (1985): 169–184.

Jones, J. M., and E. H. Lovejoy. "Discrimination Against Women Academics in Australian Universities." *Signs* 5, No. 3 (1980): 518–526.

Kahn, E. D., and L. Robbins, eds. "Sex Discrimination in Academe." *Journal of Social Issues* 41 (Winter 1985): 1–154.

Keller, E. F., and H. Moglen. "Competition and Feminism: Conflicts for Academic Women." *Signs* 12 (Spring 1987): 493–511.

Koch, J. V., and J. F. Chizman, Jr. "Sex Discrimination and Affirmative Action in Faculty Salaries." *Economic Inquiry* 14 (March 1976): 16–24.

Lodge, Juliet. "New Zealand Women Academics: Some Observations on Their Status,

Aspirations and Professional Achievements.'' *Political Science* 28 (1976): 23–40.

Over, R. ''Women Academics in Australian Universities.'' *Australian Journal of Education* 25, No. 2 (1981): 166–176.

Reilly, Shalini. ''Gender Divisions in the Academic Workplace.'' *Compare* 15, No. 1 (1985): 41–52.

Schrank, W. E. ''Sex Discrimination in Faculty Salaries: A Case Study.'' *Canadian Journal of Economics* 10 (August 1977): 11–33.

Shapira, Rina, Eva Etzioni-Halevy, and Shira Chopp-Tibon. ''Occupational Choice Among Female Academicians—The Israeli Case.'' In *Women in the Family and Economy: An International Comparative Survey.* Edited by George Kurian and Ratna Ghosh. Westport, Conn.: Greenwood Press, 1981.

Sutherland, M. B. ''The Situation of Women Who Teach in Universities: Contrasts and Common Ground.'' *Comparative Education* 21, No. 1 (1985): 21–28.

Szreter, R. ''Opportunities for Women as University Teachers in England Since the Robbins Report of 1963.'' *Studies in Higher Education* 8, No. 2 (1983): 139–150.

Tinsley, A., et al., eds. ''Women in Higher Education Administration.'' (Symposium.) *New Directions for Higher Education,* No. 45 (1984): 1–91.

WOMEN AS STUDENTS IN HIGHER EDUCATION

Articles

Baker, T. L. ''Class, Family, Education, and the Process of Status Attainment: A Comparison of American and British Women College Graduates.'' *Sociological Quarterly* 23 (Winter 1982): 17–31.

Monk-Turner, E., and Y. Baba. ''Gender and College Opportunities: Changes over Time in the United States and Japan.'' *Sociological Inquiry* 57 (Summer 1987): 292–303.

Moore, Kathryn. ''Women's Access and Opportunity in Higher Education: Toward the Twenty-First Century.'' *Comparative Education* 23, No. 1 (1987): 23–34.

Selowsky, Marcelo. ''Women's Access to Schooling and the Value Added of the Educational System: An Application to Higher Education.'' In *Women and Poverty in the Third World.* Edited by Mayra Buvinic, Margaret A. Lycette, and William Paul McGreevey. Baltimore: Johns Hopkins University Press, 1983.

Woodhall, Maureen. ''The Economic Returns to Investment in Women's Education.'' *Higher Education* 2, No. 3 (1973): 275–299.

AFRICA

Books

Agheyisi, Rachel Uwa. ''The Labour Market Implications of the Access of Women to Higher Education in Nigeria.'' In *Women in Nigeria Today.* London: Zed Books, 1985.

Biraimah, Karen L. ''Class, Gender and Life Chances: A Nigerian Case Study.'' *Comparative Education Review* 31 (1987): 570–582.

ASIA

Books

Gorwaney, Naintara. *Self-Image and Social Change: A Study of Female Students*. New Delhi: Sterling Publications, 1977.

Maskiell, Michelle. *Women Between Cultures*. Syracuse, N.Y.: Maxwell School of Citizenship and Public Affairs, Syracuse University, 1984. (Foreign and Comparative Studies, South Asia Series, No. 9.)

Navawongs, Tippan. *Career Plans and Fertility Expectations of College Women in Bangkok, Thailand*. Singapore: Southeast Asia Population Research Awards Program, 1980. (Research Report, No. 7.)

Articles

Fujimura-Fanselow, K. "Women's Participation in Higher Education in Japan." *Comparative Education Review* 29 (November 1985): 471–489.

Korson, J. Henry. "Career Constraints Among Women Graduate Students in a Developing Society: West Pakistan—A Study in the Changing Status of Women." In *Women in the Family and the Economy: An International Comparative Survey*. Edited by George Kurian and Ratna Ghosh. Westport, Conn.: Greenwood Press, 1981.

Krishnaraj, Maithreyi. "Employment Pattern of University-Educated Women and Its Implications." *Journal of Higher Education* 2 (Spring 1977): 317–327.

Palmier, L. "Degree and Gender Distinctions Among Indonesian Graduate Officials." *Higher Education* 15, No. 5 (1986): 459–473.

AUSTRALIA AND NEW ZEALAND

Books

Powles, M. *Women's Participation in Tertiary Education: A Review of Recent Australian Research*. 2nd ed. Melbourne: University of Melbourne Centre for the Study of Higher Education, 1987.

Wilson, Brian G., and Eileen M. Byrne. *Women in the University: A Policy Report*. St. Lucia: University of Queensland Press, 1987.

Article

Craney, J., and C. O'Donnell. "Women in Advanced Education: Advancement for Whom?" *Higher Education Research and Development* 2 (1983): 129–146.

EUROPE

Book

Association Française des femmes diplomées des universités. *Etude sur l'accès, en France, des femmes à l'enseignement et à la formation scientifiques et aux carrières correspondentes*. Paris: Unesco, 1980.

Articles

Casjens, R., and H. Flessner. "Frauen auf dem zweiten Bildungsweg. Zur Lage von studentinnen, die über den zweiten Bildungsweg ün die Hochschulen kommen." *Deutsche Schule* 72, No. 1 (1980): 23–31.

Chiplin, B. "Alternative Approach to the Measurement of Sex Discrimination: An Illustration from University Entrance." *Economic Journal* 9 (December 1981): 988–997.

Connelly, Joan. "La enseñanza superior de la mujer an España." In *Nuevas perspectivas sobre la mujer*. Edited by Seminario de Estudios de La Mujer. Madrid: Universidad Antonoma de Madrid, 1982.

Cunningham, Shirley. "Women's Access to Higher Education in Scotland." In *World Yearbook of Education 1984. Women and Education*. Edited by Sandra Acker et al. London: Kogan Page, 1984.

Dach, Z. "Women's Participation in Higher Education in Poland, 1970–1984." *Higher Education* 17, No. 1 (1988): 27–39.

Lamoure, J. "Enseignement universitaire: orientation et scolarisation des étudiants." *Education et Formations*, No. 2 (1983): 57–64.

Luukkonen-Gronow, T. "University Career Opportunities for Women in Finland in the 1980's." *Acta Sociologica* 30, No. 2 (1987): 193–206.

Schmarsow, C. "Women in Higher Education—Some Information on the Situation in the Federal Republic of Germany." *Western European Education* 16 (Fall 1984): 68–74.

"Sex Stereotyping and Higher Education of Women." (Symposium.) *Western European Education* 14 (Spring/Summer 1982): 4–183.

Thagaard, T. "Academic Values and Intellectual Attitudes: Sex Differentiation or Similarity." *Acta Sociologica* 18, Nos. 2–3 (1975): 142–268.

Vicinus, M. "One Life to Stand Beside Me: Emotional Conflict in First-Generation College Women in England." *Feminist Studies* 8 (Fall 1982): 603–628.

LATIN AMERICA

Books

Barrera Pena, Maria Louisa. *Sociologia de la mujer en la universidad*. Santiago: Universidad de Santiago de Compostela, 1983.

Labadie, Gaston J. *La mujer universitaria uruguaya*. Montevideo: Direccion General de Extension universitaria, Division Publicaciones y Ediciones, 1980.

Articles

Aragones, Maria. "La mujer y los estudios universitarios en Chile 1957–1974." In *Chile: Mujer y sociedad*. Edited by Paz Covarrubias and R. Franco. Santiago: Alfebeta Imp., 1978.

Fernandes Berdaguer, M. L. "Educación universitaria y desempeño profesional: el caso de las mujeres estudiantes de ciencias economicas de la Universidad de Buenos Aires." *Revista Paraquay de Sociologia* 20 (January-April 1983): 75–97.

MIDDLE EAST

Articles

Al-Bassam, Ibtissam A. "Institutions of Higher Education for Women in Saudi Arabia." *International Journal of Educational Development* 14 (1984): 255–258.

Tomeh, Aida K. "Birth Order and Alienation among College Women in Lebanon." In *Women in the Family and the Economy: An International Comparative Survey.* Edited by George Kurian and Ratna Ghosh. Westport, Conn.: Greenwood Press, 1981.

Torki, M. A. "Achievement Motivation in College Women in an Arab Culture." *Psychological Reports* 56 (1985): 267–271.

NORTH AMERICA

Books

Fitzpatrick, Blanche. *Women's Inferior Education: An Economic Analysis.* New York: Praeger, 1976.

Horowitz, Helen Lefkowitz. *Alma Mater: Design and Experience in the Women's Colleges from Their Nineteenth Century Beginnings to the 1930s.* Boston: Beacon Press, 1984.

Solomon, Barbara Miller. *In the Company of Educated Women: A History of Women and Higher Education in America.* New Haven, Conn.: Yale University Press, 1985.

Westervelt, Ester. *Barriers to Women's Participation in Post Secondary Education: A Review of Research and Commentary as of 1973/74.* Washington, D.C.: U.S. Government Printing Office, 1975.

Articles

Blackman, S. "The Masculinity-Femininity of Women Who Study College Mathematics." *Sex Roles* 15 (July 1986): 33–41.

Bridges, J. S. "College Female's Perception of Adult Roles and Occupational Fields for Women." *Sex Roles* 16 (June 1987): 591–604.

Bridges, J. S., and M. S. Bower. "The Effects of Perceived Job Availability for Women on College Women's Attitudes toward Prestigious Male-Dominated Occupations." *Psychology of Women Quarterly* 9 (June 1985): 265–276.

Eaton, J. S., ed. "Women in Community Colleges." (Symposium.) *New Directions for Community Colleges,* No. 34 (1981): 1–90.

Ellis, R. A., and M. S. Herman. "Understanding Career Goals of College Women: Intradimensional Variation in Sex-typed Occupational Choice." *Sociology and Social Research* 68 (October 1983): 41–58.

Ferber, M. A., and W. W. McMahon. "Women's Expected Earnings and Their Investment in Higher Education." *Journal of Human Resources* 14 (Summer 1979): 405–419.

Fleming, J. "Black Women in Black and White College Environment: The Making of a Matriarch." *Journal of Social Issues* 39 (Fall 1983): 41–54.

Graham, Patricia. "Expansion and Exclusion: A History of Women in American Higher Education." *Signs* 3 (1978): 759–773.

Heilbrun, A. B., Jr., and C. M. Mulqueen. "The Second Androgyny: A Proposed Revision in Adaptive Priorities for College Women." *Sex Roles* 17 (August 1987): 187–207.

Holland, Dorothy, and Margaret Eisenhart. "Moments of Discontent: University Women and the Gender Status Quo." *Anthropology and Educational Quarterly* 19 (June 1988): 115–138.

Houseknecht, S. K., and G. B. Spanier. "Marital Disruption and Higher Education Among Women in the United States." *Sociological Quarterly* 21 (Summer 1980): 375–389.

Howe, F., ed. "Toward a History of Women's Higher Education." *Journal of Education* 159, No. 3 (1977): 1–64.

Komarovsky, M. "Female Freshmen View Their Future: Career Salience and Its Correlates." *Sex Roles* 8 (March 1982): 299–314.

Leduc, C. "Les Orientations des femmes a l'Université de Montréal en 1949–1950 et en 1974–1975." *Canadian and International Education* 7 (June 1978): 51–58.

Lindsay, Beverly. "Pursuing the Baccalaureate Degree in the United States: The Case of African American Women." In *World Yearbook of Education 1984. Women and Education.* Edited by Sandra Acker et al. London: Kogan Page, 1984.

Lyson, T. A. "Factors Associated with the Choice of a Typical or Atypical Curriculum Among College Women." *Sociology and Social Research* 64 (July 1980): 559–571.

Peng, S. S., and J. Jaffe. "Women Who Enter Male-Dominated Fields of Study in Higher Education." *American Educational Research Journal* 16, No. 3 (1979): 285–293.

Randour, Mary Lou, Georgia L. Strasburg, and Jean Lipman-Blumen. "Women in Higher Education: Trends in Enrollment and Degrees Earned." *Harvard Educational Review* 52, No. 2 (1982): 189–202.

Rice, Joy K., and Annette Hemmings. "Women's Colleges and Women Achievers: An Update." *Signs* 13 (1988): 546–559.

Roemer, R. E. "Changing Patterns of Degree Selection Among Women." *Research in Higher Education* 18, No. 4 (1983): 435–454.

Schneider, B. E. "Graduate Women, Sexual Harassment and University Policy." *Journal of Higher Education* 58 (January/February 1987): 46–65.

Schwager, S. "Educating Women in America." *Signs* 12 (Winter 1987): 333–372.

Spaeth, J. L. "Differences in the Occupational Achievement Process Between Male and Female College Graduates." *Sociology of Education* 50 (July 1977): 206–217.

Thomas, G. E. "Race and Sex Group Equity in Higher Education: Institutional and Major Field Enrollment Statistics." *American Educational Research Journal* 17, No. 2 (1980): 171–181.

Thomas, G. E., and S. L. Hargett. "Socialization Effects and Black College Women: Educational and Occupational Orientations." *Journal of Social Behavioral Sciences* 27 (1981): 65–72.

Tidball, M. E. "Women's Colleges and Women Achievers Revisited." *Signs* 5, No. 3 (1980): 504–517.

Vance, S. M. "Sexual Harassment of Women Students." *New Directions in Higher Education,* No. 33 (1981): 29–40.

Weeks, M. O., and D. R. Betkin. "A Longitudinal Study of the Marriage Role Expectations of College Women: 1961–1984." *Sex Roles* 17 (July 1987): 49–58.

REENTRY WOMEN

Book

Churgin, Jonah R. *The New Women and the Old Academe: Sexism and Higher Education.* Roslyn Heights, N.Y.: Libra Publishers, 1978.

Articles

Ballmer, H., and P. C. Cozby. "Family Environments of Women Who Return to College." *Sex Roles* 7 (October 1981): 1019–1026.

Berman, M. R., et al. "Efficacy of Supportive Learning Environments for Returning Women: An Empirical Evaluation." *Journal of Counseling Psychology* 24 (July 1977): 324–331.

Burwood, L. R. V., and C. A. Brady. "Married Women Students in Further Education: The Meaning of Coming to College." *Journal of Further and Higher Education* 4, No. 2 (1980): 21–33.

Kelly, S. "Changing Parent-Child Relationships: An Outcome of Mother Returning to College." *Family Relations* 31 (April 1982): 287–294.

Pitman, Mary Anne. "Developmental Stages and Institutional Structure: The Case of Continuing Education for Women." *Anthropology and Education Quarterly* 19 (June 1988): 139–154.

Tittle, C. K., and E. R. Denker. "Re-entry Women: A Selective Review of the Educational Process, Career Choice and Interest Measurement." *Review of Educational Research* 47 (1977): 531–584.

WOMEN, SCIENCE, AND TECHNOLOGY

Books

Aldrich, Michele. *Programs in Science, Mathematics and Engineering for Women in the United States 1968–1978.* Washington D.C.: Office of Opportunities in Science, American Association for Advancement in Science, 1980.

Jain, S. D., ed. *Women and Technology.* Jaipur: Rawat Publications, 1985.

Wright, Barbara Drygulski, et al., eds. *Women, Work and Technology Transformations.* Ann Arbor: University of Michigan Press, 1987.

Articles

Berner, Boel. "New Technology and Women's Education in Sweden." In *World Yearbook of Education 1984. Women and Education.* Edited by Sandra Acker et al. London: Kogan Page, 1984.

Biolchini, M., et al. "Formation des femmes et nouvelles technologies." *Actualité de formation permanente,* No. 68 (1984): 17–32.

Blackstone, T., and M. Weinreich-Haste. "Why Are There So Few Women Scientists and Engineers?" *New Society* 21 (1980): 383–385.

Bradford, J. "Pourquoi trouve-t-on si peu de femmes dans le domaine scientifique en Nouvelle-Zélande?" *Impact: Science and Society* 30, No. 1 (1980): 43–49.

Bruce, M., and G. Kirkup. "Post Experience Courses in Technology for Women." *Adult Education* 58, No. 1 (1985): 40–50.

Krishnaraj, Maithreyi. "The Status of Women in Science in India." *Journal of Higher Education* 5 (Spring 1980): 381–393.

Mya Mya Thein. "Women Scientists and Engineers in Burma." *Impact of Science on Society* 30 (January–March 1980): 15–22.

Pfafflin, Sheila. "Some Reflections on Women in Science and Technology after UNCSTD." In *Scientific-Technological Change and the Role of Women in Development.* Edited by Pamela D'Onofrio-Flores and Sheila M. Pfafflin. Boulder, Colo.: Westview Press, 1982.

Presvelou, Clio. "La Technologie et la science sont-elles au service des femmes rurales?" In *Femmes et Multinationales.* Edited by Andrée Michele, Helene Agbessi-Dos Santos and Agnes Fatoumata Diarra. Paris: Editions Karthala, 1981.

Reskin, B. F. "Sex Differences in Status Attainment in Science: The Case of the Post-doctoral Fellowship." *American Sociological Review* 41 (August 1976): 597–612.

"Some Ideas from Women Technicians in Small Countries." *Impact of Science on Society* 30 (January–March 1980): 3–66.

Srinivasan, Mangalam. "The Impact of Science and Technology and the Role of Women in Science in Mexico." In *Scientific-Technological Change and the Role of Women in Development.* Edited by Pamela D'Onofrio-Flores and Sheila M. Pfafflin. Boulder, Colo.: Westview Press, 1982.

Tadesse, Zenebeworke. "Women and Technology in Peripheral Countries: An Overview." In *Scientific-Technological Change and the Role of Women in Development.* Edited by Pamela D'Onofrio-Flores and Sheila M. Pfafflin. Boulder, Colo.: Westview Press, 1982.

Turi, Z. F. "Situation des femmes titulaires de diplomes scientifiques en Hongrie." *Impact: Science and Society* 30, No. 1 (1980): 27–38.

Ware, N. C., et al. "Undergraduate Women: Who Chooses a Science Major?" *Journal of Higher Education* 56 (January/February 1985): 73–84.

PSYCHOLOGICAL STUDIES

Books

Gilligan, Carol. *In a Different Voice: Psychological Theory and Women's Development.* Cambridge, Mass.: Harvard University Press, 1982.

Maccoby, E. E., and C. N. Jacklin. *The Psychology of Sex Differences.* Stanford, Calif.: Stanford University Press, 1974.

Tresmer, D. *Fear of Success.* New York: Plenum Publishers, 1977.

Articles

Baggio, Angela M. B. "Achievement Motivation of Brazilian Students." *International Journal of Intercultural Relations* 2 (1978): 186–196.

Brooks, V. R. "Sex Differences in Student Dominance Behavior in Female and Male Professors' Classrooms." *Sex Roles* 8 (July 1982): 683–690.

Calabrese, R. L., and C. A. Seldin. "Adolescent Alienation: An Analysis of the Female

Response to the Secondary School Environment." *High School Journal* 69 (December/January 1985–1986): 120–125.

Doherty, D. D. V., and S. E. Bielby. "Sex Characteristics and Roles." In *The International Encyclopedia of Education*. Edited by Torsten Husen and T. N. Postlethwaite. Oxford: Pergamon Press, 1985.

Fine, M. "Sexuality, Schooling and Adolescent Females: The Missing Discourse of Desire." *Harvard Educational Review* 58 (February 1988): 29–53.

Foon, A. E. "The Relationship Between School Type and Adolescent Self-esteem: Attribution Styles, and Affiliation Needs: Implications for Educational Outcomes." *British Journal of Educational Psychology* 58 (February 1988): 44–54.

Lomax, P. "The Attitudes of Girls with Varying Degrees of School Adjustment to Different Aspects of Their School Experience." *Educational Review* 30, No. 2 (1978): 117–123.

Meyer, B. "The Development of Girls' Sex-Role Attitudes." *Child Development* 51, No. 2 (1980): 508–514.

Onibokun, Yemi. "Achievement Motivation: Disparity Between Boys and Girls in a Nigerian Setting." *West African Journal of Education* 11 (June 1980): 108–112.

Rousseau, Ida Faye. "African Women: Identity Crisis? Some Observations on Education and the Changing Role of Women in Sierra Leone and Zaire." In *Women Cross-Culturally: Change and Challenge*. Edited by Ruby Rohrlick-Leavitt. The Hague: Mouton, 1975.

Salili, Farideh. "Determinants of Achievement Motivation for Women in Developing Countries." *Journal of Vocational Behavior* 14 (June 1979): 297–305.

Sassen, Georgia. "Success Anxiety in Women: A Constructivist Interpretation of Its Source and Significance." *Harvard Educational Review* 50 (1980): 13–24.

Shumener, B. "Educational Policy: Sex Roles and Biological Differences." *Philosophy of Education* (1981–1982): 175–186.

Sichel, Betty A. "Moral Development and Education: Men's Language of Rights and Women's Language of Responsibility." In *Women, Culture and Morality*. Edited by Joseph DeVitis. New York: Peter Long, 1987.

Tittle, C. K. "Gender Research and Education." *American Psychologist* 41 (October 1986): 1161–1168.

Tobias, Sheila, and Carol Weissbrod. "Anxiety and Mathematics: An Update." *Harvard Educational Review* 50 (1980): 63–70.

WOMEN'S STUDIES

Books

Balbo, Laura, and Ergas Yasmine. *Women's Studies in Italy*. Old Westbury, N.Y.: Feminist Press, 1982.

Bonder, Gloria, Cristina Zurutuza, and Seminario Regional Latinoamericano y de Caribe, Unesco. *Desarrollo de Curricula y de Enseñanza en Estudios de la Mujer para la Educación Superior en América Latina y el Caribe*. Buenos Aires: Universidad de Buenos Aires, Centro de Estudios de la Mujer, 1986.

Cambridge Women's Studies Group. *Women in Society*. London: Virago, 1981.

Culley, Margo, and Catherine Portuges, eds. *Gendered Subjects: The Dynamics of Feminist Teaching*. Boston: Routledge & Kegan Paul, 1985.

DuBois, Ellen Carol, et al. *Feminist Scholarship: Kindling in the Groves of Academe*. Champaign: University of Illinois Press, 1985.

Helling, R. *The Politics of Women's Studies*. Adelaide: Flinders University, 1981.

Minnich, Elizabeth, Jean F. O'Barr, and Rachel A. Rosenfeld. *Reconstructing the Academy: Women's Education and Women's Studies*. Chicago: University of Chicago Press, 1988.

Rendel, Margherita. *Women's Studies—The Study of Women*. Paris: Unesco, 1982.

Sei-wha, Chung, ed. *Challenges for Women: Women's Studies in Korea*. Seoul: Ewha Women's University Press, 1986.

Sievent, Maria Teresa. *La mujer y el proyecto principal de educación en América Latina y el Caribe*. Santiago: Unesco, Oficina Regional de Educación de la Unesco para América Latina y el Caribe, 1983.

Articles

Aiken, S. H. et al. "Trying Transformations: Curriculum Integration and the Problem of Resistance." *Signs* 12 (Winter 1987): 255–275.

Andersen, M. L. "Changing the Curriculum in Higher Education." *Signs* 12 (Winter 1987): 222–254.

Battel, Roisin, et al., eds. "So Far, So Good—So What: Women's Studies in the UK." (Special Issue.) *Women's Studies: International Forum* 6 (1983).

Biklen, S. K., and C. Dwyer, eds. "The New Scholarship on Women and Education." (Symposium.) *Educational Researcher* 15 (July 1986): 6–23.

Boxer, Marilyn J. "For and About Women: The Theory and Practice of Women's Studies in the United States." *Signs* 7 (1982): 661–695.

Faulkner, Constance. "Women's Studies in the Muslim Middle East." *Journal of Ethnic Studies* 8 (1980): 67–76.

Gannik, D., and K. Sjrup, eds. "Special Issue on Women's Studies." *Acta Sociologica* 30, No. 2 (1987): 133–232.

Hancock, M. A. "An Analysis of Women's Studies Courses for Adults in New Zealand, 1977–1987." *New Zealand Journal of Educational Studies* 15, No. 1 (1980): 54–68.

Howe, F. "Feminism and the Education of Women." *Journal of Education* 159 (August 1977): 11–24.

Johnson, M. "Women's Studies." In *The International Encyclopedia of Education*. Edited by Torsten Husen and T. N. Postlethwaite. Oxford: Pergamon Press, 1985.

Kashif-Badri, Hagga. "The History, Development, Organization and Position of Women's Studies in the Sudan." In *Social Science Research and Women in the Arab World*. Edited by Unesco. London and Dover, N.H.: Frances Pinter, 1984.

Klein, Renate Duelli. "Women's Studies: The Challenge to Man-Made Education." In *World Yearbook of Education 1984. Women and Education*. Edited by Sandra Acker et al. London: Kogan Page, 1984.

Levin, Tobe. "Women's Studies in West Germany: Community vs. Academy." *Women's Studies Newsletter* 7 (1979): 20–22.

Tabak, Fanny. "UN Decade and Women's Studies in Latin America." *Women's Studies International Forum* 8 (1985): 103–106.

"Teaching About Women and the Visual Arts." (Symposium.) *Women's Studies Quarterly* 15 (Spring/Summer 1987): 2–66.

"Teaching About Women, Race and Culture." (Symposium.) *Women's Studies Quarterly* 14 (Spring/Summer 1986): 2–57.

Weiner, Gaby. "Feminist Education and Equal Opportunities: Unity or Discord?" *British Journal of Sociology of Education* 7 (1986): 265–275.

Whelchel, M. "Transforming the Canon with Nontraditional Literature by Women." *College English* 46 (October 1984): 587–597.

Zuckerman, D. M. "Women's Studies, Self-esteem and College Women's Plans for the Future." *Sex Roles* 9 (May 1983): 633–642.

ADULT AND NONFORMAL EDUCATION

Book

Nimer, Kamal K. *The Role of Women's Organizations in Eradicating Illiteracy in Jordan.* Washington, D.C.: Abbe Publishers Association, 1986.

Articles

Antrobus, Peggy. "Reading Beyond University Walls." *Development,* No. 4 (1984): 45–49.

Bangun, Masliana. "The Advantages of Functional Education and Credit Facilities for Japanese Rural Women." In *The Endless Day: Some Case Material on Asian Rural Women.* Edited by T. Scarlett Epstein and Rosemary A. Watts. New York: Pergamon Press, 1981.

Cebotarev, E. A. "Non-oppressive Framework for Adult Education Programs for Rural Women in Latin America." *Convergence* 13, Nos. 1–2 (1980): 34–49.

Davis, D. "Australian Women in a Changing Society: Perspectives Through Continuing Education." *Convergence* 13, Nos. 1–2 (1980): 99–109.

Ellis, P. "Women, Adult Education, and Literacy: A Caribbean Perspective. *Convergence* 17, No. 4 (1984): 44–53.

Gayfer, Margaret. "Women Speaking and Learning for Ourselves." *Convergence* 13, Nos. 1–2 (1980): 1–12.

George Igoche, Martha H. "Integrating Conscientization into a Program for Illiterate Urban Women in Nigeria." *Convergence* 13, Nos. 1–2 (1980): 110–116.

Gerver, Elizabeth. "Women, Computers and Adult Education: Liberation or Oppression?" *Convergence* 17, No. 4 (1984): 5–16.

Haukaa, Runa. "Competence-building Adult Education for Women." *Convergence* 8 (1975): 68–81.

Highet, G. "Gender and Education: A Study of the Ideology and Practice of Community Based Women's Education as Observed in Three Groups Operating Within the City of Glasgow." *Studies in the Education of Adults* 18 (October 1986): 118–129.

Hootsman, H. M. "Educational and Employment Opportunities for Women: Main Issues in Adult Education." *Convergence* 13, Nos. 1–2 (1980): 79–90.

Islam, Shamima. "Strengthening Nonformal Education for Women in Bangladesh." In *Women and Development: Perspectives from South and Southeast Asia.* Edited by Rounaq Jahan and Hanna Papanek. Dacca: Bangladesh Institute of Law and International Affairs, 1979.

Jayaweera, S. "Programme of Non-Formal Education for Women." *Indian Journal of Adult Education* 40, No. 12 (1979): 33–45.

Jiagge, J. A. "The Role of Non-governmental Organizations in the Education of Women in African States." *Convergence* 2, No. 2 (1969): 73–78.

Kindervatter, S. "How Thai Village Women Become Adult Educators." *Convergence* 18, Nos. 3–4 (1985): 116–119.

Mahmud, Satnam. "Thoughts on Non-Formal Education for Women." In *Women and Development: Perspectives from South and Southeast Asia.* Edited by Rounaq Jahan and Hanna Papanek. Dacca: Bangladesh Institute of Law and International Affairs, 1979.

Mair, Lucille. "Adult Learning, Women and Development." *Prospects* 8, No. 2 (1977): 238–243.

Mathur, A., et al. "Participatory Training for Illiterate Women Trainees." *Convergence* 19, No. 1 (1986): 20–23.

McCall, C. "Women and Literacy: The Cuban Experience." *Journal of Reading* 30 (January 1987): 318–324.

McLaren, A. T. "Ambition and Accounts: A Study of Working-class Women in Adult Education." *Psychiatry* 45 (August 1982): 235–246.

McSweeney, Brenda G., and Marion Freedman. "Lack of Time as an Obstacle to Women's Education: The Case of Upper Volta." *Comparative Education Review* 24 (June 1980): S124–S139.

Meghji, Zakia. "Women and Cooperatives: Some Realities Affecting Development in Tanzania." *Community Development Journal* 20 (1985): 185–188.

Nxumalo, S. "Income-generating Project Develops Skills of Swazi Women." *Convergence* 15, No. 3 (1982): 48–55.

Oglesby, K. L., A. Krajnc, and M. Mbilinyi. "Adult Education for Women." In *The International Encyclopedia of Education.* Edited by Torsten Husen and T. N. Postlethwaite. Oxford: Pergamon Press, 1985.

Robertson, C. "Formal or Nonformal Education? Entrepreneurial Women in Ghana." *Comparative Education Review* 28 (1984): 639–658.

WOMEN AND THE PROFESSIONS

AFRICA

Book

Wessels, Dina Maria. *Career Orientation and Work Commitment of University Educated Women.* Pretoria: Human Sciences Research Council, 1981.

Articles

Gould, T. F. "A New Class of Professional Zairian Women." *African Review* 7, Nos. 3–4 (1977): 92–105.

Gould, Terri F. "Value Conflict and Development: The Struggle of Professional Zairian Women." *Journal of Modern African Studies* 16 (March 1978): 133–139.

ASIA

Books

Blumberg, Rhoda Lois, and Leela Dwaraki. *India's Educated Women: Options and Constraints*. Delhi: Hindustan Publishing Corp., 1980.

Chaturvedi, Geeta. *Women Administrators in India*. Jaipur: RBSA Publishers, 1985.

Meis, Maria. *Indian Women and Patriarchy: Conflicts and Dilemmas of Students and Working Women*. Delhi: Concept Publishing, 1973.

Articles

Cho, Haejong. "Korean Women in the Professions." In *Korean Women in Transition*. Edited by Eui-Young Yu and Earl Phillips. Los Angeles: Center for Korean American and Korean Studies, California State University at Los Angeles, 1987.

Dilatush, Lois. "Women in the Professions." In *Women in Changing Japan*. Edited by Joyce Lebra, Joy Paulson, and Elizabeth Powers. Boulder, Colo.: Westview Press, 1976.

Lebra, T. S. "Japanese Women in Male Dominant Careers: Cultural Barriers and Accommodations for Sex-Role Transcendence." *Ethnology* 20 (October 1981): 219–306.

O'Brien, Leslie Nola. "Sex, Ethnicity and the Professions in West Malaysia: Some Preliminary Considerations." *Akademika*, No. 14 (January 1979): 31–42.

Raj Krishna, Maithreyi. "Research on Women and Career: Issues of Methodology." *Economic and Political Weekly* 21 (October 25, 1986): 67–74.

AUSTRALIA AND NEW ZEALAND

Book

Hughes, Beryl. "Women and the Professions in New Zealand." In *Women in New Zealand Society*. Edited by P. Bunkle and B. Hughes. Sydney: George Allen & Unwin, Australia, 1980.

EUROPE

Book

Buckley, Mary, ed. *Soviet Social Scientists Talking*. London: Macmillan, 1986.

Articles

Balbo, L. "Women's Access to Intellectual Work: The Case of Italy." *Signs* 6 (Summer 1981): 763–770.

Bolli, M., et al. "Femmes et formation." *Cahiers de la Section des sciences de l'education: Pratiques et Theorie*, No. 38 (1985): 1–57.

Crompton, R. "Gender, Status and Professionalism." *Sociology* 21 (August 1987): 413–428.

Crompton, R., and K. Sanderson. "Credentials and Careers: Some Implications of the

Increase in Professional Qualifications Amongst Women." *Sociology* 20 (February 1986): 25–42.
Eskola, I., and E. Haavio-Mannila. "Careers of Professional Women and Men in Finland." *Acta Sociologica* 18, Nos. 2–3 (1975): 174–201.

LATIN AMERICA

Book

Borges, Wanda Rose. *A professionalizacāo feminina: una experiencia no ensino publico.* São Paulo: Edicões Loyola, 1980.

Article

Kinzer, Nora Scott. "Sociocultural Factors Mitigating Role Conflict of Buenos Aires Professional Women." In *Women Cross-Culturally: Change and Challenge.* Edited by Ruby Rohrlich-Leavitt. The Hague: Mouton, 1975.

MIDDLE EAST

Articles

Blitz, Rudolph C. "An International Comparison of Women's Participation in the Professions." *Journal of Developing Areas* 9 (1975): 499–510.
Howard-Merriam, Kathleen. "Women, Education and the Professors in Egypt." *Comparative Education Review* 23 (1979): 250–270.
Oncu, Ayse. "Turkish Women in the Professions: Why So Many?" In *Women in Turkish Society.* Edited by Nermin Abadan-Unat. Leiden: E. J. Brill, 1981.

NORTH AMERICA

Book

Walsh, Mary Ruth. *Doctors Wanted, No Women Need Apply: Sexual Barriers in the Medical Profession, 1835–1975.* New Haven, Conn.: Yale University Press, 1977.

Articles

Cancian, F. M. "Rapid Social Change: Women Students in Business Schools." *Sociology and Social Research* 66 (January 1982): 169–183.
Cole, S. "Sex Discrimination and Admission to Medical School, 1929–1984." *American Journal of Sociology* 92 (November 1986): 549–567.
Bielby, D. D. "Career Sex-Atypicality and Career Involvement of College Educated Women: Baseline Evidence from the 1960's." *Sociology of Education* 51, No. 1 (1978): 7–28.
Statham, A., et al. "The Professional Involvement of Highly Educated Women: Impact on the Family." *Sociological Quarterly* 28 (Spring 1987): 119–133.

WORKFORCE

Book

Youssef, Nadia H. *Women and Work in Developing Societies*. Berkeley: University of California, Institute of International Studies, 1974. (Population Monograph Series no. 15.)

Articles

"Equality of Opportunity and Treatment." *Social and Labor Bulletin* No. 3 (September 1980): 349–352.

MacDonald, J. S., and L. MacDonald. "Women at Work in Britain and the Third World." *New Community* 5 (Summer 1976): 76–84.

Mincer, J., and S. Polachek. "Women's Earnings Re-examined." *Journal of Human Resources* 13 (Winter 1978): 103–134.

Nelson, Cynthia. "Women, Education, and Labor Force Participation: Introduction." *Signs* 3 (Autumn 1977): 241–243.

Niemi, Albert W., Jr. "Sexist Differences in Returns to Educational Investment." *Quarterly Review of Economics and Business* 15 (Spring 1975): 17–26.

Ram, R. "Sex Differences in the Labor Market Outcomes of Education." *Comparative Education Review* 24 (June 1980): S53–S57.

Shields, N. G. "Female Labor Force Participation and Education: Developing Countries." In *The International Encyclopedia of Education*. Edited by Torsten Husen and T. N. Postlethwaite. Oxford: Pergamon Press, 1985.

Silver, P. "Sex Earnings Differentials." In *The International Encyclopedia of Education*. Edited by Torsten Husen and T. N. Postlethwaite. Oxford: Pergamon Press, 1985.

Smock, Audrey Chapman. "Sex Differences in Educational Opportunities and Labor Force Participation in Six Countries." In *Comparative Education*. Edited by P. G. Altbach, R. Arnove, and G. P. Kelly. New York: Macmillan Co., 1982.

Standing, G. "Education and Female Participation in the Labour Force." *International Labour Review* 114 (November-December 1976): 281–297.

AFRICA

Book

Schuster, Ilsa M. Glazer. *Female White Collar Workers*. East Lansing: Michigan State University, 1983. (Working Papers/Women in International Development, No. 29).

Article

Awosika, Keziah. "Women's Education and Participation in the Labour Force: The Case of Nigeria." In *Women, Power and Political Systems*. Edited by Margherita Rendel with the assistance of Georgina Ashworth. London: Croom Helm, 1981.

ASIA

Books

Lebra, Joyce, Joy Paulson, and Jana Everett, eds. *Women and Work in India*. New Delhi: Promilla, 1984.
Mitra, Asok, Lalit P. Pathak, and Shekhar Mukherji. *The Status of Women: Shifts in Occupational Participation, 1961–71*. New Delhi: Abhinav Publications, 1980.
Rani, Kala. *Role Conflict in Working Women*. New Delhi: Chetana Publications, 1976.

Articles

Chapman, Bruce J., and J. Ross Harding. "Sex Differences in Earnings: An Analysis of Malaysian Wage Data." *Journal of Development Studies* 21 (1985): 362–376.
Cho, Hyoung. "Labour Force Participation of Women in Korea." In *Challenges for Women: Women's Studies in Korea*. Edited by Chung Sei-wha. Seoul: Ewha Women's University Press, 1986.
Hirschman, C., and A. Aghajanian. "Women's Labour Force Participation and Socio-economic Development: The Case of Peninsular Malaysia, 1957–1970. *Journal of South East Asian Studies* 11 (March 1980): 30–49.
Papaneck, Hanna. "Purdah in Pakistan: Seclusion and Modern Occupations for Women." In *Separate Worlds*. Edited by H. Papanek and G. Minault. New Delhi: Chanakya Publications, 1982.

AUSTRALIA AND NEW ZEALAND

Books

Foster, V. *Changing Choices: Girls, School and Work*. Sydney: Hale & Ironmonger, 1984.
O'Donnell, C. *The Basis of the Bargain: Gender, Schooling and Jobs*. Sydney: Allen & Unwin, 1984.

Articles

Currie, J. "The Sex Factor in Occupational Choice." *Australian and New Zealand Journal of Sociology* 18 (1982): 180–195.
Earley, P. D. "Girls, School and Work: Technological Change and Female Entry into Non-Traditional Work Areas." *Australian Journal of Education* 25 (1981): 269–287.

EUROPE

Books

Bednarz-Braun, I. *Arbeiterinnen in der Elektroindustrie*. München: D J I Deutsches Jungendinstitut., 1983.
Dodge, Norton. *Women in the Soviet Economy*. Baltimore: Johns Hopkins University Press, 1966.

Articles

Flora, Cornelia Butler. "Incorporating Women into International Development Programs: The Political Phenomenology of a Private Foundation." In *Women in Developing Countries: A Policy Focus*. New York: Haworth Press, 1983.

"Women, Literacy and Development." *Literacy Discussion* 6 (Winter 1975–1976): 1–172.

Woodhall, Maureen. "Investment in Women: A Reappraisal of the Concept of Human Capital." *International Review of Education* 19 (1973): 9–29.

AFRICA

Articles

Due, Jean M., and Rebecca Summary. "Constraints to Women and Development in Africa." *Journal of Modern African Studies* 20 (March 1982): 155–166.

Lewis, Shelby F. "Education, Women, and Development in Africa." In *Patriarchy, Party, Population and Pedagogy*. Edited by Edgar B. Gumbert. Atlanta: Georgia State University, Center for Cross-Cultural Education, 1986.

Lindsay, Beverly. "An Examination of Education, Social Change and National Development Policy: The Case of Kenyan Women." In *Women and Politics in 20th Century Africa and Asia*. Edited by Sandra McGee. (Studies in Third World Societies, Publication No. 16.) 1981.

Niara Sudarkasa. "Sex Roles, Education and Development in Africa." *Anthropology and Education Quarterly* 13 (Fall 1982): 279–289.

United Nations. Economic Commission for Africa. African Training and Research Center for Women. "Women and National Development in African Countries: Some Profound Contradictions." *African Studies Review* 18 (December 1975): 47–70.

Van Allen, Judith. "African Women, 'Modernization' and National Liberation." In *Women in the World: A Comparative Study*. Edited by Lynne B. Iglitzin and Ruth Ross. Santa Barbara, Calif.: ABC-Clio Press, 1976.

ASIA

Books

Jahan, Rounaq, and Hanna Papanek, eds. *Women and Development: Perspectives from South and Southeast Asia*. Dacca: Bangladesh Institute of Law and International Affairs, 1979.

Gallin, Rita. *The Impact of Development on Women's Work and Status*. East Lansing: Michigan State University, 1982. (Working Paper. Women and International Development, No. 9.)

Sethi, Rajmohini. *Modernization of Working Women in Developing Societies*. New Delhi: National Publishing House, 1976.

Usha Rau, N. J. *Women in a Developing Society*. New Delhi: Ashish, 1983.

Articles

Chen, E. K. Y. "The Role of Women in Economic Development: An Analysis with Special Reference to Hong Kong." In *The Role of Women in Development: Seminar Papers and Statements*. Edited by Leonardo Z. Legaspi. Manila: University of Santa Tomas Press, 1976.

Elliott, Carolyn M. "Women's Education and Development in India." In *World Yearbook of Education 1984. Women and Education*. Edited by Sandra Acker et al. London: Kogan Page, 1984.

Hooper, Beverly. "China's Modernization: Are Young Women Going to Lose Out?" *Modern China* 10 (1984): 317–343.

Khatun, Sharifa. "Women's Education in a Rural Community in Bangladesh." In *Women and Development: Perspectives from South and Southeast Asia*. Edited by Rounaq Jahan and Hanna Papanek. Dacca: Bangladesh Institute of Law and International Affairs, 1979.

Mazumdar, Vina. "Education, Development and Women's Liberation: Contemporary Debates in India." In *Education and the Process of Change*. Edited by Ratna Ghosh and Matthew Zachariah. New Delhi: Sage Publications, 1987.

Nalla, Tan. "The Impact of Modernization on Women." In *Modernization in Singapore: Impact on the Individual*. Edited by Tham Seong Chee. Singapore: University Education Press, 1972.

Papanek, Hanna. "Implications of Development for Women in Indonesia: Research and Policy Issues." In *Women in Developing Countries: A Policy Focus*. New York: Haworth Press, 1983.

Ravindran, Dundar. "Confronting Gender, Poverty and Powerlessness: An Orientation Program for and by Rural Change Agents." *Community Development Journal* 20 (1985): 213–221.

Wang, Bee-Lan Chan. "Chinese Women: The Relative Influence of Ideological Revolution, Economic Growth, and Cultural Change." In *Comparative Perspectives of Third World Women*. Edited by Beverly Lindsay. New York: Praeger, 1980.

LATIN AMERICA

Books

Aragoneses, Josefina, et al. "El desarrollo de la educación Parvalaria en Chile y su influencia en desarrollo de la mujer." In *Chile: mujer y sociedad*. Edited by Paz Covarrubas and R. Franco. Santiago: Alfebeta Imp., 1978.

Chaney, Else M., and Marianne Schmink. "Women and Modernization: Access to Tools." In *Sex and Class in Latin America*. Edited by June Nash and Helen Icken Safa. New York: Praeger, 1976.

Verghese, Valso, Maria Teresa Chadwick, and Ximena Charnes. "Education and Communication." In *Women in Development: A Resource Guide for Organization and Action*. Edited by ISIS Women's International Information and Communication Service. Philadelphia: New Society Publishers, 1984.

MIDDLE EAST

Book

Al Sabah, S. M. *Development Planning in an Oil Economy and the Role of Women.* London: Eastlords Publishers, 1983.

Articles

Abadan-Unat, Nermin. "The Modernization of Turkish Women." *Middle East Journal* 32 (1978): 291–306.

Belhachmi, Zakia. "The Unfinished Assignment: Educating Moroccan Women for Development." *International Review of Education* 33 (1987): 485–494.

Klineberg, Stephen L. "Parents, Schooling and Modernity: An Exploratory Investigation of Sex Differences in the Attitudinal Development of Tunisian Adolescents." *International Journal of Comparative Sociology* 14 (1976): 221–244.

Meleis, Afaf J., Nagat El-Sanabary, and Diana Beeson. "Women, Modernization, and Education in Kuwait." *Comparative Education Review* 23 (February 1979): 115–124.

Youssef, N. H. "Education and Female Modernization in the Muslim World." *Journal of International Affairs* 30 (Fall-Winter 1976–1977): 191–209.

INTERNATIONAL AGENCIES

Book

Rogers, Barbara. *The Domestication of Women: Discrimination in Developing Societies.* London: Tavistock, 1981.

Articles

Cohn, S., et al. "U.S. Aid and Third World Women: The Impact of Peace Corps Programs." *Economic Development and Cultural Change* 29 (July 1981): 795–811.

Herbert, Suzanne, and Virginia Dichie. "Women in Decision-making and Leadership Positions in International Development Agencies." In *The Decade for Women.* Edited by Aisla Thomson. Toronto: Canadian Congress for Learning Opportunities for Women, 1986.

Karl, Marilee. "Women and Multinationals." In *Women in Development: A Resource Guide for Organization and Action.* Edited by ISIS Women's International Information and Communication Services. Philadelphia: New Society Publishers, 1984.

Thom, Betsy. "Women in International Organizations: Room at the Top: The Situation in Some United Nations Organizations." In *Access to Power: Cross National Studies of Women and Elites.* Edited by Cynthia F. Epstein and Rose Laub Coser. London: George Allen & Unwin, 1981.

WOMEN'S EDUCATION AND POLITICS

Books

Agnew, Vijay. *Elite Women in Indian Politics*. New Delhi: Vikas Publishing House, 1979.

Norris, Pippa. *Politics and Sexual Equality: The Comparative Position of Women in Western Democracies*. Boulder, Colo.: Rienner, 1987.

Vandevelde-Dailliere, Helene. *Femmes Algeriennes: À travers la condition feminine dans le Constantinois depuis l'independance*. Alger: Office des Publications Universitaires, 1980.

Articles

Bers, T. H. "Local Political Elites: Men and Women on Boards of Education." *Western Political Quarterly* 31 (September 1978): 381–391.

Camp, Roderic Ai. "Women and Political Leadership in Mexico: A Comparative Study of Female and Male Political Elites." *Journal of Politics* 41 (1979): 417–441.

Elu de Lenero, Maria del Carmen. "Educación y participación de la mujer en la P.E.A. de Mexico." *Revista del Centro de Estudios Educativos* 7, No. 1 (1977): 71–83.

Hahner, June Edith. "Women's Place in Politics and Economics in Brazil Since 1964." *Luso-Brazilian Review* 19 (Summer 1982): 83–91.

Maher, Janet. "The Social Composition of Women Deputies in Soviet Elective Politics: A Preliminary Analysis of Official Biographies." In *Women in Eastern Europe and the Soviet Union*. Edited by Tova Yedlin. New York: Praeger, 1980.

Miller, Linda. "Patrons, Politics and Schools: An Arena for Brazilian Women." *Studies in Third World Societies* 15 (1981): 67–89.

O'Brien, Mary. "Feminism and the Politics of Education." *Interchange* 17, No. 2 (1986): 91–112.

Tabak, Fanny. "Women's Role in the Formulation of Public Policies in Brazil." In *Women, Power and Political Systems*. Edited by Margherita Rendel with the assistance of Georgina Ashworth. London: Croom Helm, 1981.

WOMEN'S EDUCATION AND FERTILITY

Books

Cochrane, Susan H. *Fertility and Education: What Do We Really Know?* Baltimore: Johns Hopkins University Press, 1979.

Safilios-Rothschield, Constantina. *The Status of Women and Fertility in the Third World in the 1970–1980 Decade*. New York: Population Council, 1985. (Working Papers/ Center for Policy Studies, No. 118.)

Articles

Berliner, Joseph S. "Education Labor-Force Participation, and Fertility in the USSR." *Journal of Comparative Economics* 7 (1983): 131–157.

Cochrane, Susan. Effects of Education and Urbanization on Fertility." In *Determinants of Fertility in Developing Countries*, Volume 2. *Fertility Regulation and Insti-*

tutional Influences. Edited by Rodolfo A. Bulato and Ronald D. Lee with Paula E. Hollerbach and John Bongaarts. New York: Academic Press, 1983.

Dixon, Ruth B. "Education and Employment: Keys to Smaller Families." *Journal of Family Welfare* 22 (December 1975): 38–49.

Fernando, D. F. S. "Female Educational Attainment and Fertility." *Journal of Biosocial Science* 9 (July 1977): 339–351.

Hoffman, Lois. "The Employment of Women, Education and Fertility." *Merrill-Palmer Quarterly* 20, No. 2 (1974): 99–120.

Jain, Anrudh K. "The Effect of Female Education on Fertility: A Simple Explanation." *Demography* 18 (1981): 577–595.

Kuniansky, Anna. "Soviet Fertility, Labor-Force Participation, and Marital Instability." *Journal of Comparative Economics* 7 (1983): 114–130.

Wolfe, B. L., and J. R. Behrman. "Child Quantity and Quality in a Developing Country: Family Background, Endogenous Tastes, and Biological Supply Factors." *Economic Development and Cultural Change* 34 (July 1986): 703–720.

AFRICA

Articles

Caldwell, J. C. "Education as a Factor in Mortality Decline: An Examination of Nigerian Data." *Population Studies* 33 (November 1979): 395–413.

Ketkar, S. L. "Female Education and Fertility: Some Evidence from Sierra Leone." *Journal of Developing Areas* 13 (October 1978): 23–34.

Koenig, Dolores. "Education and Fertility Among Cameroonian Working Women." In *Education and Modernization of the Family in West Africa.* Edited by Helen Ware. Canberra: Department of Demography, Australian National University, 1981. (Changing African Family Project Series Monograph, No. 7.)

Lewis, Barbara. "Fertility and Employment: An Assessment of Role Incompatibility Among African Urban Women." In *Women and Work in Africa.* Edited by Edna G. Bay. Boulder, Colo.: Westview Press, 1982.

ASIA

Books

Goldstein, Sidney, Alice Goldstein, and Penporn Tirasawat. *The Influence of Labor Force Participation and Education on Fertility in Thailand.* Bangkok: Institute of Population Studies, Chulalongkorn University, 1972.

Prabowo. *An Empirical Analysis of the Effects of Income and Education on Fertility in Indonesia.* Quezon City, Philippines: Council for Asia Manpower Studies, 1982. (Discussion Paper Seven 82–12.)

Articles

Chaudhury, R. H. "Female Status and Fertility Behavior in a Metropolitan Urban Area of Bangladesh." *Population Studies* 32 (July 1978): 261–273.

Goldstein, S. "The Influence of Labor Force Participation and Education on Fertility in Thailand." *Population Studies* 26 (1972): 419–435.

Hermalin, I. Albert, et al. "Transitions in the Effects of Family Size on Female Educational Attainment: The Case of Taiwan." *Comparative Education Review* 26 (June 1982): 254–285.

Jain, Anrudh K., and Moni Nag. "Importance of Female Primary Education for Fertility Reduction in India." *Economic and Political Weekly* 21 (1986): 1602–1608.

Rosenzweig, M. R., and Robert E. Evenson. "Fertility, Schooling and the Economic Contribution of Children in Rural India: An Econometric Analysis." *Econometrica* 45 (July 1977): 1065–1079.

Teel, J. H., and R. K. Ragade. "Simulation Modeling Perspectives of the Bangladesh Family Planning and Female Education System." *Behavioral Science* 29 (1984): 145–161.

LATIN AMERICA

Articles

Bouvier, Leon F., and John J. Maceso, Jr. "Education and Husband and Wife Fertility in Puerto Rico." *Social and Economic Studies* 17, No. 1 (1968): 49–59.

Brady, Eugene B. *Sex, Contraception, and Motherhood in Jamaica*. Cambridge, Mass.: Harvard University Press, 1981.

Tienda, Marta. "Community Characteristics, Women's Education, and Fertility in Peru." *Studies in Family Planning* 15 (July-August 1984): 162–169.

MIDDLE EAST

Articles

Aghajanian, Akbar. "Fertility and Family Economy in the Iranian Rural Communities." In *Women in the Family and Economy: An International Comparative Survey*. Edited by George Kurian and Ratna Ghosh. Westport, Conn.: Greenwood Press, 1981.

Al-Kadht, Ann Bragdon. "Women's Education and the Relation to Fertility: Report from Bagdad." In *Women and the Family in the Middle East*. Edited by Elizabeth Warnack Fernen. Austin: University of Texas Press, 1985.

Kohli, K. L. "Regional Variations of Fertility in Iraq and Factors Affecting It." *Journal of Biosocial Science* 9 (April 1977): 175–182.

Suchindran, C. M., and A. L. Adlakha. "Effect of Infant Mortality on Subsequent Fertility of Women in Jordan: A Life Table Analysis." *Journal of Biosocial Science* 16 (1984): 219–229.

Youssef, Nadia H. "The Status and Fertility Patterns of Muslim Women." In *Women in the Muslim World*. Edited by Lois Beck and Nikki Keddie. Cambridge, Mass.: Harvard University Press, 1978.

WOMEN'S EDUCATION AND THE FAMILY

Book

Fernea, Elizabeth Warnock, ed. *Women and the Family in the Middle East: New Voices of Change*. Austin: University of Texas Press, 1985.

Articles

Baude, Annika. "Public Policy and Changing Family Patterns in Sweden 1930–1977." In *Sex Roles and Social Policy*. Edited by Jean Lipman-Blumen and Jessie Bernard. Beverly Hills, Calif.: Sage Publications, 1979.

Behrman, J. R., and B. L. Wolfe. "How Does Mother's Schooling Affect Family Health, Nutrition, Medical Care Usage and Household Sanitation." *Journal of Econometrics* 36 (September/October 1987): 185–204.

Behrman, J. R., and B. L. Wolfe. "More Evidence on Nutrition Demand: Income Seems Overrated and Women's Schooling Underemphasized." *Journal of Development Economics* 4 (January/February 1984): 105–128.

Conklin, George H. "Cultural Determinants of Power for Women Within the Family: A Neglected Aspect of Family Research." In *Women in the Family and the Economy: An International Comparative Survey*. Edited by George Kurian and Ratna Ghosh. Westport, Conn.: Greenwood Press, 1981.

Farkas, G. "Education, Wage Rates, and the Division of Labor Between Husband and Wife." *Journal of Marriage and the Family* 38 (August 1976): 473–483.

Grindstaff, C. F. "Educational Attainment for Females: The Long Term Consequences of Differential Timing in Marriage and the Onset of Childbearing." *Guidance and Counseling* 2 (November 1986): 21–31.

Kim, S. Y., and W. F. Stinner. "Social Origins, Educational Attainment and the Timing of Marriage and First Birth Among Korean Women." *Journal of Marriage and the Family* 42 (August 1980): 671–679.

LeVine, R. A. "Influences of Women's Schooling on Maternal Behavior in the Third World." *Comparative Education Review* 24 (June 1980): S78–S105.

Marini, M. M. "Women's Educational Attainment and the Timing of Entry into Parenthood." *American Sociological Review* 49 (August 1984): 491–511.

Ofer, Gur, and Aaron Vinokur. "The Labour-Force Participation of Married Women in the Soviet Union." *Journal of Comparative Economics* 7 (1983): 158–176.

Rolmos, Elssy Bonella de. "Women, Family and the Educational System of Colombia." *Two Thirds* 1, No. 3 (Winter 1978–1979): 19–23.

Taylor, P. A., and N. D. Glenn. "Utility of Education and Attractiveness for Females' Status Attainment Through Marriage." *American Journal of Sociology* 41 (June 1976): 484–498.

ASIA

Book

Tomeh, Aida K. *Familial Sex Role Attitudes Among College Students in Korea*. East Lansing: Office of Women in Development, Michigan State University, 1982. (Working Paper, No. 12.)

Articles

Diamond, Norma. "The Middle Class Family Model in Taiwan: Women's Place Is in the Home." *Asian Survey* 13 (September 1973): 853–872.

Gopaldas, Tara, Rama Raghavan, and Shubhada Kanan. "Nutrition Impact of Anti-

Parasite Drugs, Prophylactic Vitamin A and Iron-Folic Acid on Underprivileged School Girls in India.'' *Nutrition Research* 3 (1983): 831–844.

Kim, Soung-Yee, and W. F. Stinner. ''Social Origins, Educational Attainment and the Timing of Marriage and First Birth Among Korean Women.'' *Journal of Marriage and the Family* 42 (August 1980): 671–679.

Minturn, L., D. Boyd, and S. Kapoor. ''Increased Maternal Power Status, Changes in Socialization in a Restudy of Rajput Mothers of Khalapur, India.'' *Journal of Cross-Cultural Psychology* 9 (December 1978): 483–498.

Robinson, Jean C. ''Of Women and Washing Machines: Employment, Housework and the Reproduction of Motherhood in Socialist China.'' *China Quarterly,* No. 101 (March 1985): 32–57.

AFRICA

Book

Ware, Helen, ed. *Women, Education, and Modernization of the Family in West Africa.* Canberra: Department of Demography, Australia National University, 1981.

Article

Oppong, Christine. ''Women's Roles and Conjugal Family Systems in Ghana.'' In *Changing Position of Women in Family and Society*. Edited by Eugene Lupri. Leiden: E. J. Brill, 1983.

INDEX

ABOUT THE EDITOR AND CONTRIBUTORS

ANNIKA ANDRAE-THELIN, principal administrative officer at the Swedish National Board of Education, has a Ph.D. in education. Her dissertation focused on rural education in Sweden. She currently is involved in a project on women teachers in Zimbabwe.

HANNA AYALON, a lecturer at the School of Education and the Department of Sociology and Anthropology at Tel-Aviv University, received her Ph.D. in Sociology from that university. Her recent research focuses on gender differences in educational and occupational aspirations and second-chance education. She has also studied ethnicity in Israeli education.

DIANE BARTHEL, associate professor of sociology at SUNY Stony Brook, received her B.A. from Duke University and her M.A. and Ph.D. from Harvard. Her teaching and research interests revolve around problems of modernity, culture, and gender. She has published several articles on West African women, and her book on gender and advertising, *Putting on Appearances,* appeared Fall 1988. She has also taught at Boston College and has been visiting lecturer at the University of Essex and visiting research fellow at Cambridge University.

GAGE BLAIR is completing her doctorate in Comparative Education at the State University of New York at Buffalo. Born in New York, she was raised in Africa and attended school in England. She received her bachelor's degree from Aberdeen University in Scotland and her master's degree from Teachers' College,

Columbia University. Her dissertation focuses on role conflict among professional women.

SUMA B. CHITNIS is director of the Tata Institute of Social Sciences in Bombay. She is author of numerous books on women's education in India and on caste and class-like inequalities in that country. She has also written extensively on higher education.

WENDY A. DUNCAN, affiliated with the Institute for International Education at the University of Stockholm, is completing her dissertation on women and education in Botswana. She has spent considerable time in Botswana working on projects designed to improve the participation of girls in mathematics and science.

INGA ELQVIST-SALTZMAN is research fellow in equality between women and men, a position funded by the Swedish Research Council on Humanities and Social Sciences. She received her doctorate at Uppsala University in 1976 and served as chief administrator of the University of Umea in Sweden. Her current research focuses on the impact of educational reform on women's life patterns.

GEORGE S. ESHIWANI received his Ph.D. from Stanford University and holds advanced degrees from the University of East Africa in Nairobi. His extensive experience in the field of education includes teaching at secondary, undergraduate, and postgraduate levels at the University of Nairobi and Kenyatta University. In addition, he has held a number of consultant and administrative posts and has contributed articles to educational journals and conferences. Professor Eshiwani has been actively involved in research related to equity and internal efficiency in education. For the last ten years he has been the director of the Bureau of Educational Research at Kenyatta University.

KUMIKO FUJIMURA-FANSELOW received her Ph.D. in comparative education from Columbia University and is currently a teacher with the New York City Board of Education and an instructor at Teachers College, Columbia University. In spring 1989, she will be an assistant professor of education at Toyo Eiwa Women's University in Tokyo.

JANE GASKELL, professor and head of the Department of Social and Educational Studies at the University of British Columbia, has published a variety of articles and policy papers on women and education, and on education and work. In 1987, she and Arlene McLaren edited a book called *Women and Education: A Canadian Perspective*.

KATHLEEN HOWARD-MERRIAM was born and raised in Cairo, Egypt. She received her M.A. and Ph.D. in political science and Middle Eastern studies from Indiana University. She taught at the American University in Cairo 1964–1967, and has been teaching political science and women's studies at Bowling Green State University since 1967.

DAVID H. KELLY, associate professor in the Department of History at D'Youville College, received his Ph.D. in History from Indiana University and taught at the Rochester Institute of Technology. He has coauthored *The International Bibliography of Comparative Education* as well as several other bibliographic works, including a monograph for the International Bureau of Education on Women's Education in the Third World.

GAIL P. KELLY is professor and chair of the Department of Educational Organization, Administration, and Policy at the State University of New York at Buffalo. She has written extensively on education in colonial Vietnam, with articles appearing in the *British Journal of Sociology of Education, Comparative Education Review, Comparative Education,* and *Comparative Studies in Society and History.* She has also written on women and is the coauthor with Carolyn Elliott of *Women's Education in the Third World: Comparative Perspectives* (SUNY Press, 1982) and with Ellen Dubois, Elizabeth Kennedy, Carolyn Korsmeyer, and Lillian Robinson coauthored *Feminist Scholarship: Kindling in the Groves of Academe* (University of Illinois Press, 1984). She is the author of a number of books on comparative education as well. Gail Kelly is former president of the Comparative and International Education Society of the United States and former associate editor of the *Comparative Education Review.* She is currently editor of *Educational Policy.* In January 1988, she was part of an American delegation of scholars who traveled to Vietnam under the auspices of the Indochina Reconciliation Project.

DRORA KFIR received her Ph.D. in the sociology of education from Tel-Aviv University and is currently a lecturer in the School of Education at Tel-Aviv University and at Beit-Berl College. Her research interests include gender differences in education and school desegregation.

GRACE C. L. MAK is a Ph.D. candidate in comparative education at the State University of New York at Buffalo. She served for several years as assistant editor of the *Comparative Education Review.* In 1988, she was a visiting scholar at Beijing Teachers' College. During her tenure there, she conducted extensive interviews with women, focusing on education and their life histories. She is currently conducting similar research in Hong Kong.

EUNICE A. C. OKEKE received her B.S. from the University of Nigeria, Nsukka, and her M.S. and Ph.D. in science education from the University of Leeds. She is currently senior lecturer in the Faculty of Education at the University of Nigeria and is coordinator of the Science Education Program. Her research interests are in science education, and she served as national treasurer of the Science Teachers Association of Nigeria.

CATHERINE RAISSIGUIER is a doctoral student in comparative education at SUNY, Buffalo. She completed a master's degree in English and American Studies at the University of Aix-Marseille in France and a master's degree in Women's Studies at SUNY, Buffalo. She has been teaching French and Women's Studies at the University of Michigan and SUNY, Buffalo, and is currently working on a doctoral thesis on gender and racial cultural formation among working-class female students of Algerian and French descent in the French school system.

MARZIEH GOLI REZAI-RASHTI, an Iranian educator living in Canada, holds a Ph.D. in the sociology of education from the University of Toronto. She is an educational consultant (lead instructor) for the Toronto Board of Education. She is engaged in research on education and multiculturalism, adult literacy programs, and the development of curricula for the Persian Heritage Program in Canada.

JOSEFINA ROSSETTI received her Ph.D. at the University of Paris VII in sociology. She is currently residing in Santiago where she conducts research on teachers and sex role socialization under the auspices of the Centro de Investigacion y Desarrollo de la Educación. She worked at the Women's Ministry under the Allende government. In 1983, she coordinated the Women's Studies Center in Santiago.

MARY ELLEN SEAVER-TAYLOR received her doctorate in comparative education from the University of Illinois at Urbana-Champaign, where she was a foreign language and area studies fellow in the Center for African Studies. Previously, she served with the Peace Corps in the Ivory Coast.

MAXINE S. SELLER, professor of the history of education at the State University of New York at Buffalo, has published extensively in the area of American ethnic history and the history of education, particularly that of women. Her books include *To Seek America* and *Immigrant Women*. She is currently writing a history of women's education in the United States.

SUSANNE M. SHAFER, a professor of comparative education and policy studies at Arizona State University, has published widely on political education, bilingual/multicultural education, the education of women, and development education. A specialist on German education, she recently had a Fulbright grant to West Germany and extended her research at the Karl Marx University of Leipzig in the German Democratic Republic.

RINA SHAPIRA is professor of the sociology of education and chair of the Unit of Education and Community at Tel-Aviv University where she has served as dean of the School of Education. She received her Ph.D. in the sociology of education from Columbia University in New York. She has written three books on Israeli youth and politics and numerous articles on education and social stratification and issues relating to gender-based inequalities in Israeli society.

RENATA SIEMIENSKA, associate professor at the Institute of Sociology, University of Warsaw, completed her doctorate at the Jagiellonian University in Cracow, and her post-doctoral degree (habilitation) at the University of Warsaw. Professor Siemienska has participated in a number of major sociological research projects in Poland as well as in international projects on comparative themes (e.g., on political values, local government, and determinants of women's public participation). Among her books are *New Life in a New Town, Power of Tradition and Power of Interests, About Sources of the White Ethnic Movement in the United States, Studies, Profession, Work, About Students and Graduates of the Higher Agricultural Schools,* and *Personality Patterns of Socialism.* She has also published a number of papers on the situation of women in Poland and has also edited a volume entitled *Women in Politics.*

NELLY P. STROMQUIST is associate professor of education at the University of Southern California in the area of international development education. Previously, she taught at Stanford University and served as a senior program officer for the International Development Research Centre in Canada. She has written and taught on women's education, educational innovations, and the role of international development agencies in the improvement of women's education.

BARBARA A. YATES is professor emeritus of comparative education at the University of Illinois, Urbana-Champaign. She received her doctorate from Columbia University and is past president of the Comparative and International Education Society. Most recently, she was a guest lecturer at the University of California at Los Angeles. She has written extensively about women and education in Zaire.

LYN YATES is senior lecturer in education at La Trobe University, Australia. She has a particular interest in curriculum theory and nonsexist education (the subject of her Ph.D. thesis) and has written extensively on school policy and practice in Australia and on issues of educational inequality. She has frequently served as a consultant to teachers, schools, and government bodies on these areas.